The Writing Center Director's Resource Book

The Writing Center Director's Resource Book

Edited by

Christina Murphy
Byron L. Stay

Routledge
Taylor & Francis Group

NEW YORK AND LONDON

First published by
Lawrence Erlbaum Associates, Inc., Publishers

This edition published 2012 by Routledge
711 Third Avenue, New York, NY 10017
2 Park Square, Milton Park, Abingdon, Oxfordshire OX14 4RN

Cover design by Kathryn Houghtaling Lacey

Library of Congress Cataloging-in-Publication Data

The writing center director's resource book / edited by Christina Murphy, Byron L. Stay.
    p. cm.
Includes bibliographical references and index.
ISBN 0-8058-5607-2 (cloth : alk. paper)
ISBN 0-8058-5608-0 (pbk. : alk. paper)
1. English language—Rhetoric—Study and teaching—Handbooks, manuals, etc. 2. Report
    writing—Study and teaching (Higher)—Handbooks, manuals, etc. 3. Writing centers—
    Administration—Handbooks, manuals, etc. I. Murphy, Christina, 1947– II. Stay, Byron
    L., 1947–
PE1404.W694442005
808'.042'071—dc22   2005047317
                                                                              CIP

Contents

v

Part II: Writing Centers and Praxis

1. Ethics in the Writing Center

2. Tutor Training in the Writing Center

Preface

A resource book of this scope represents the work of many hands and minds, and we wish to express our appreciation to our authors for their acumen and talent in creating such broad insights into the many facets of writing center work and experience. Their voices, their lived experiences, and their knowledge are the core of this book and its best achievement. We thank our editor at Lawrence Erlbaum Associates, Linda Bathgate, for her help with the design of this book and for her support and confidence in us as we completed this project. Linda's knowledge of writing centers was invaluable to us as we progressed, and her awareness of the relationship of texts to informed practice was a special gift of great value to us.

In creating this book, we have attempted to answer the most important question the writing center community continues to pose: What knowledge do writing center professionals need to have in order to do their best work? Through our authors, we feel we have responded well to the challenge of answering that question in meaningful ways that embrace the historical, philosophical, theoretical, and practical and that provide interpretative frames for understanding these dimensions in institutional settings.

We owe a great debt to the writing center community as a whole, not only for the ways in which our interactions with people who work in writing centers and define its theory and practice have shaped our lives and careers personally, but for holding us to the highest standard in creating a book that will serve as a true resource for them in responding to their challenges and opportunities. We want to thank, too, people who are important in our own lives. Christina Murphy thanks, especially, Joe Law for seventeen years of a very special friendship and Byron Stay for the idea of this book and his tenacity and spirit in helping see it through to its conclusion. Byron Stay thanks Christina for being a wonderful friend and collaborator and, especially, his friend and colleague, Carl Glover, for his support, friendship, music, and sense of humor.

—*Christina Murphy*
—*Byron L. Stay*

Introduction

The *Writing Center Director's Resource Book* is intended to serve as a guide to writing center professionals in carrying out their various roles, duties, and responsibilities. It is a resource for those whose jobs not only encompass a range of tasks but also require a broad knowledge of multiple issues.

We have structured this book to provide information on the most significant areas of writing center work that writing center professionals—both new and seasoned—are likely to encounter. We envision writing center professionals as enacting multiple complex roles in being teachers, administrators, scholars, budget officers, technology coordinators, tutor trainers, mentors, and academic colleagues. We understand that writing center professionals enact their roles in varied academic structures from high schools to community colleges, small colleges, and universities. This diversity of institutional settings is one of the main challenges writing center professionals face in seeking a unified approach to such issues as setup, development, management, budget, and assessment. Thus, this book is structured to respond to diverse institutional settings by providing both current knowledge and case studies that illuminate this knowledge in specific settings representing the types of challenges and the possible outcomes writing center professionals may experience. We believe this blend of theory with actual practice provides a multidimensional view of writing center work.

We have provided a historical context for viewing the emergence of writing center work. Essentially, the history of the field is a framework for understanding the intellectual heritage of the writing center and for appreciating the past as a framework for responding to present challenges in determining future directions. Neal Lerner examines the various historical representations of the writing center and reveals a much longer, broader, and more diverse history than most practitioners and theorists realize. Carl Glover examines the ancient concept of *kairos* to explore the ways in which writing center directors can interpret and respond to opportune moments of insight in discovering new directions for writing center work. Susan DeRosa and Stephen Ferruci consider the issue of writing center sustainability by investigating the theoretical, practical, and institutional challenges new or experienced writing center directors might face in developing and advancing their writing centers. Ray Wallace and Susan Lewis Wallace look at the opportunities for writing center directors to advance professionally in their institutions.

The nature of institutional settings is a major component of the perspectives this book offers on the writing center's role within academics. Thus, several chapters provide insights on negotiating one's way through academic structures. Seeing the writing center in relation to institutional settings and structures is an essential component of good management, and so the chapter by Joan Mullin, Peter Carino, Jane Nelson, and Kathy Evertz discusses the politics and practices of location, whereas chapters by Jeanne Simpson and by Bruce W. Speck discuss communicating with central administration and managing for administrative success. Managing the writing center in institutional contexts also requires a broad knowledge of funding issues, as discussed by Evelyn Schreiber, and of assessment strategies, as Joan Hawthorne reveals. Clinton Gardner and Tiffany Rousculp consider community college writing centers, Byron L. Stay discusses the writing center in small college settings, and Helen Snively, Cheryl Prentice, and Traci Freeman discuss writing centers within graduate programs. Dennis Paoli examines writing centers in the context of remedial/developmental learning, and Amy Ward Martin discusses writing centers in multicampus settings. Albert C. DeCiccio explores the relationship of writing center work to the requirements and philosophical contours of core curricula that function to provide general education to students. Paula Gillespie, Brad Hughes, Neal Lerner, and Anne Ellen Geller discuss the benefits of the annual Summer Institute sponsored in part by the International Writing Centers Association for new and experienced writing center professionals. In addition to mentoring and fellowship, the weeklong Summer Institute offers intensive sessions with established leaders in the field and individualized attention for participants in special interest groups.

The writing center professional must map out management styles that will meet institutional needs/demands and that will enable success. In separate chapters, Pamela B. Childers and Kelly Lowe consider the impact of strategic planning on achieving the writing center's goals, and Brad Peters emphasizes the importance of documentation to assessment strategies. Margaret Weaver addresses managing for diversity in the writing center, Mike Mattison examines the role of the writing center director as a coach in managing and evaluating staff members, and Denise Stephenson and Lauren Fitzgerald encourage seeing the big picture as a manager when interpreting the writing center's many-centered relationships within an institution. Clearly, one of the most significant and least often explored managerial relationships is the one between the writing center director and the assistant director. Kevin Dvorak and Ben Rafoth explore this dynamic and consider ways in which this mentoring relationship can be beneficial to the individuals involved and to realizing the vision for the writing center itself.

The history of writing center practice reveals an intense and extensive examination of ethics in relation to writing center goals and outcomes. Michael Pemberton discusses the historical record and the issues that have surrounded writing center ethics in such areas as tutoring and tutor training, and Christina Murphy examines the current ethical issues writing centers face in responding to contemporary sociopolitical theories like postmodernism and communitarianism. David Bringhurst offers a criterion-based approach to determining and evaluating the ethical responsibilities the writing center faces in responding to all of its constituencies. Rebecca Moore Howard and Tracy Hamler Carrick examine the complex of issues surrounding plagiarism and authorship and consider the ways in which the writing center can play a leadership role in structuring academic and institutional responses and objectives.

Without question, the most extensive, visible, and immediate segment of writing center practice involves tutoring and tutor training. Writing center professionals need to know the range of options and the rationales for the broad range of approaches to preparing tutors to carry out their roles. Thus, Steven Strang considers the value of staffing the writing center with professional tutors, whereas Bonnie Devet examines the purpose and merit of certifying a tutoring program through a national agency, the College Reading and Learning Association. Muriel Harris discusses what principles best undergird our practice in tutorials, including the capacity to encourage flexibility, innovation, and discovery within the contours of knowledge in application. Paula Gillespie and Harvey Kail argue that peer tutoring can be the central program around which to organize, develop, and advance a writing center, and Carol Peterson Haviland and Marcy Trianosky explore peer tutoring from the vantage point of what peer-tutors need and want from writing center directors.

The future of writing centers will definitely contain—if not be defined by—technology, and so our authors consider the impact of electronic instruction on the design, goals, outcomes, and importance of the writing center in the twenty-first century. David M. Sheridan explores the valve of electronic technology in transforming the writing center into a multiliteracy center that is responsive to students' individual needs and backgrounds. Lisa Eastmond Bell questions whether the personal nature and the rhetorical function of the writing center can be retained in online tutoring and offers valuable insights for responding to this challenge when a conventional writing center goes electronic. Ben Click and Sarah Magruder review the considerations necessary for implementing electronic portfolios within a center. They also contend that writing centers are an ideal nexus for implementing institutional use of electronic portfolios for a variety of pedagogically sound purposes that include tutor training, writing classes, senior capstone projects, course development, and institutional assessment of writing. Lory Hawkes discusses the ways in which educational institutions and writing centers must comply with the legal requirements of Americans with Disabilities Act (ADA)-based accommodations and examines the value of the Internet in providing "fair and equivalent" access to writing help for students with disabilities.

We conclude this book with case studies that examine writing centers in the contexts of their institutional settings and in terms of the particular challenges, opportunities, and accomplishments these centers experienced. The focus of this section includes writing centers in secondary schools, colleges, and universities, and addresses a range of common issues from start-up, to assessment and justification, to funding, to working with faculty consultants. These case studies provide a window into the real-world, day-to-day activities of writing centers and give voice to the many individuals working in those centers and the aspirations and achievements they exemplify.

Our philosophy for this book has given rise to its structure. The historical legacy of the writing center and its contributions to academics begins the journey and creates the framework of interpretation that other chapters enact. The various writing centers that exist today and that have existed in the past exemplify visions of what writing centers can achieve and of what goals they often pursue. We have incorporated that sense of goal-directed visions into the design of this book by emphasizing strategic planning and assessment as the primary modes of vision and enactment. Moving from concept to reality often involves struggle, and so a number of the chapters in this book examine institutional settings, requirements, and demands and the ways in which writing centers can respond successfully to these challenges. Central to all writing center struggles is the requirement to survive, and chapters on funding, budget, management, documentation, and data-provision explore strategies for maintaining and expanding writing center operations. As academic components of complex institutions, writing centers often reveal a recurring problem in the evolution of modern social systems—the relationship between distributed and centralized responsibility and control. As a result, writing center professionals need to know how to achieve power and status within academic institutions in order to achieve a strong measure of autonomy and stability. Chapters on responding to and interacting with central administration offer insights into the complexities of this process, and chapters exploring the writing center's relationship to other academic structures like home departments programs, writing across the curriculum (WAC) programs, instructional technology and distance delivery programs, enrollment management, service learning programs, and a host of others examine the wisdom and practicality of various approaches to the myriad of institutional challenges the writing center will encounter and must navigate. To do so requires an ethical awareness of conflicting ideologies and sociopolitical philosophies that define writing instruction, literacy education, and writing center work, and so several chapters discuss the ethical landscape of modern and contemporary times on the assumption that writing center professionals will need to know and to master the arguments they will encounter both for and against maintaining the status quo or potentially crossing recognized borders when defining writing center work. And, of course, writing center work is primarily tutoring in all of its various forms, and so many chapters in this book consider how best we can conduct tutoring sessions and also conduct peer-tutor training.

In considering a metaphor for the structure and design of this book, we hope that both a hub and a tapestry have served us well. The hub of this book from which the many ideas emerge to form a cohesive vision is our plan to offer information to writing center professionals on the numerous situations and contexts they will encounter, the management skills they will need to carry out their duties and enact their varied roles, the philosophical contexts that undergird writing center work or, in many instances, critique and question its value, and the types of future challenges that writing centers are likely to experience in this new century. We hope the cohesive vision of this book is also a tapestry in which numerous themes move through the chapters, no matter what section they may be in, because no true isolation of ideas or concepts can occur in envisioning or in understanding writing center work. The history, the identity, the ethos, and the legacy of the writing center militate against any easy categorization of ideas—as all of the case studies in this book attest. Instead, we encounter the dramatic and vibrant interplay of ideas that interlace the many themes of the chapters and reveal that writing center history, work, institutional instantiation, and attainment are far more complex than many people realize. It is, indeed, a tapestry of rich achievement.

In the end, we hope this book serves as a resource and a guide to future directions for the writing center, which will, no doubt, be called on to evolve in response to a myriad of new challenges that will lie ahead. We have confidence that the writing center will continue to evolve as a more organic organization that adaptively serves the essential function of ensuring that the writing center, as a local entity, respects and serves the interdependent and collective needs and values of the academy and of the culture as a whole. Ultimately, we hope that the structure of this book reinforces our belief that although each writing center is an independent entity it is not an isolated entity because we are all of us, as writing center professionals, engaged in collective endeavors. Our history, our future, and our day-to-day realities confirm this experience for us and validate the significance of writing center work in modern, postmodern, and contemporary times.

—*Christina Murphy*
Byron L. Stay

Part I

Writing Centers
and Institutional Change

1

Time Warp: Historical Representations of Writing Center Directors

Neal Lerner
Massachusetts Institute of Technology

I have long been interested in the question of where writing center directors come from. Now, I don't mean a story of the birds and the bees or an analysis of writing center geography or even a tale about graduate school training. What I mean is, where did this all start? Who was the first writing center director? And what can an understanding of our roots offer a new or established writing center director?

That last question is the tricky one. It is difficult to answer because to many in our field, writing centers have come of age relatively recently or, most likely, their particular writing center is relatively young. In her 2001 survey of 107 writing center directors, Rachel Perkes found that 96% reported origins in the 1970s, and just two reported origins going back to the 1940s or 1950s. I have found, however, that our roots stretch much deeper, that writing centers, clinics, or laboratories have long been offered to help students learn to write. And the role and requirements of the person who directs those efforts have also been discussed for sometime. Overall, the professional qualities and attributes of a writing center director have been part of larger issues of the financial and time constraints that influence teaching and learning, particularly in the contested space that writing centers continue to occupy.

My intent in this chapter is to provide historical grounding in these long-standing issues and concerns for our field. In particular, the focus is on two relative heydays for writing centers: the late 1920s/early 1930s, when the "laboratory approach" to teaching writing achieved widespread support, and the early 1950s, when the free-standing writing center as we now know it came into its own. My premise is that although forming strong relationships with other writing center directors is essential to success, understanding one's relationship to those who have come before provides a strong measure of continuity and connectedness and indicates what work still needs to be done.

THE LABORATORY AS A COUNTER TO MASS INSTRUCTION

Although the discussion first focuses on the representation of writing center directors in the late 1920s and early 1930s, it is important to note that the roots of writing centers reach still further back. Starting in the 1890s, writers and teachers began to decry the "mass instruction" that had dominated American schooling at all levels. In what educator Frederic Burk described as "the smug impertinence of an ancient, persistent, and preposterous pedantry" (1), students largely learned by lecture, memorization, and recitation, and little attempt was made to individualize instruction. This system was accepted in an era when higher education was populated by a relatively small, homogenous elite, but an increase in enrollments from 52,000 students in 1869 to 238,000 in 1899 (National Center for Education Statistics) sent college and university administrators scrambling for alternatives. One solution was the use of "laboratory methods," particularly for increasingly common required composition classes.

In 1894, *The Dial* magazine ran a series on the practices of English departments at twenty institutions, and several writers invoked the idea of a laboratory to describe their approach. John Franklin Genung of Amherst College summed up his college's attempts to solve the "problem" of poor student writing by noting that "[t]he best term, perhaps, by which to characterize the way in which the teachers of English at Amherst have met these problems is *laboratory work*" (112). Fred Newton Scott agreed when he described the practices at the University of Michigan, "As Professor Genung has well said, the teaching of composition is properly *laboratory work*" (122). By 1904, high school teacher Philo Buck offered before the National Education Association, an account of his use of "laboratory methods in English composition," and the seemingly contemporary idea of teaching writing as a process of drafting, feedback, and revision was widely hailed. Brander Matthews of Columbia described a remarkably contemporary approach in his contribution to *The Dial* series:

> As the best way to teach students to write is to have them write freely and frequently, they are called upon to express themselves on topics in which they are interested, and often of their own choice…. These essays are criticized by the instructors in private talks with every individual student. The general tendency of the instruction is affirmative rather than negative. In other words, instead of telling the student what he must not do, and of dwelling on the faults he should avoid, the aim of the instructors is to show him how to express himself easily and vigorously. (40–41)

By the late 1920s, laboratory methods in the teaching of writing had achieved relative acceptance (Carino, "Early Writing Centers"). One mark of that acceptance is that such methods became the dissertation topic for E. F. Lindquist of the University of Iowa. Lindquist's intent was to offer his institution a means of handling large numbers of students who populated freshman English. Lindquist described his plan as follows:

> [T]he student will learn to write, primarily, by writing, and he will do his writing—*all* of it—under the eye of a person trained to detect errors and to aid the pupil in overcoming individual difficul-

ties. This writing will be done in a large "laboratory"—a specially equipped room with a capacity sufficient to handle a large fraction of the entire freshman class. All of the time which the student devotes to English composition, in addition to the one hour a week of attendance at the general lectures, will be spent in this laboratory. (31–32)

Lindquist was particularly concerned with the teacher or supervisor of this operation, and his descriptions serve as the basis for both the possibilities and limitations of the contemporary writing center director. Lindquist called for instructors in his method to be more highly skilled than the contingent and part-time faculty who generally staffed freshman English during this era (Connors):

> While the position of laboratory supervisor will be one that is highly technical, it should never become merely mechanical. In the interest of continued progress, it is essential that the methods used in the writing laboratory be always considered as experimental methods…. [I]t should be one of the most important functions of the laboratory supervisor to engage in the research and study that will effect such improvements. This research function will necessitate the services of people of just as high, or higher calibre than those at present engaged in the teaching of Freshman English, and will furnish the appeal needed to attract high-calibre people to the work. (38)

While anticipating the teacher research movement by some seventy years or so, Lindquist was also describing an ideal that most institutions would be hard-pressed to meet given limited resources and uneasy relationships with those hired to teach students most in need of intensive writing instruction. Lindquist's description of the laboratory supervisor still remains a challenge to fulfill:

> The position of the laboratory supervisor will be, then, a position quite different from that now found in a university faculty. Because of the specialized and technical nature of the position, its attainment will be considered as an end in itself, rather than as a "stepping stone" to other positions. With it will go a professional spirit, a dignity and respectability, a permanence of tenure, and a financial remuneration that will raise its attractiveness far above that of the present position of instructor in Freshman English. (38)

In my more speculative moments, I wonder what might have occurred had Lindquist's recommendations been accepted, triumphed, and duplicated. The idea of our field with an eighty-year head start on securing its professional status, on providing sound writing instruction to all students, is compelling. But one dissertation does not change the course of history (or at least Lindquist's did not). The structural impediments to Lindquist's ideal and the reliance on less expensive solutions would dominate for a very long time. That's not to say that laboratory methods were abandoned; instead, writing instruction as practice under the supervision of an instructor was well accepted by the 1930s. However, the working conditions for those instructors and their status vis-à-vis the English department and the larger institution would be contested for years to come.

Another example of the possibilities and limitations in this era comes from the University of Minnesota General College, which in 1932 instituted an approach similar to Lindquist's ideal. At Minnesota, Dean Malcolm MacLean and his staff created an institution dedicated to serve students who thought they were not "college material" or who had tried but dropped out of the regular course of study. An essential component of this approach was the Writing Laboratory, a substitute for freshman composition, and an elective course in which students would find "a room … equipped with desks and chairs designed for convenience in writing" (Appel, "A Writing Laboratory" 74). Although students received course credit for enrolling in the Writing Laboratory, the approach was remarkably similar to a contemporary writing center. As described by its director, Francis Appel, a student's "instructor in the laboratory merely conspires with him to achieve clear expression and never assigns him a theme" ("A Writing Laboratory" 71). In this setting, students wrote letters, assignments from their other courses, or any meaningful text while Appel and his assistant, Lorraine Kranhold, circulated and conferenced over the work in progress. Malcolm MacLean described the setup:

> In a quiet skylight room we provide chairs and slanting tables for ease in writing. There the students write all or parts of their papers; the instructor and his assistant criticize and help when called upon by the student during the progress and at the completion of each paper. We believe that habits of clear writing can be built only upon an interest in and sense of need for writing; therefore, at the outset we give no instruction in the so-called essentials of composition. The student is urged to write only on subjects which interest him or on which he is required to write for other courses, or, by home compulsions, to correspond. (244)

Francis Appel directed this operation on a three-quarter time appointment, but Lorraine Kranhold was assigned full time to the Writing Laboratory. Given this level of staffing, the two faced considerable challenges in meeting the needs of all students. In one of his accounts of the laboratory, Appel described some of those challenges: "The limitations of staff and classrooms forced us to accept 35 students in each section, but when by accident we have had only 25 students we have found that they made greater progress and had greater satisfaction in the course, and that there was much less strain on the instructors" ("Writing Laboratory" 296).

By spring 1935, Appel reported that although nearly three hundred students had enrolled in the Writing Laboratory for two-hour weekly sessions ("A Writing Laboratory" 77), staffing remained the same, and he and Kranhold continued "to handle the laboratory, as well as to teach or assist in several other courses" ("A Writing Laboratory" 77). No surprise, then, that Appel, in the same article, ended with a caution for any institution adopting a writing laboratory: "It is not, however, a method to be forced upon a staff, for the laboratory method requires enthusiastic and not mere perfunctory teaching by the instructors. They, too, must break down the walls which have been built around the study of composition" ("A Writing Laboratory" 77).

Certainly, walls are difficult to break without the money for demolition equipment. For Appel and Kranhold, the work must have been overwhelming at times. For students, the promise of constant feedback from an eager instructor instead became a relatively brief conference once every two weeks. As Appel described, "During the laboratory periods the instructor has conferences with about half the students in a section and answers general questions for the others" ("Writing Laboratory" 295). Although this level of contact seems far better than might occur in a large composition class, it does not quite fulfill Appel's promise. In his 1936 description of the lab, he noted that "[m]ore than half the achievement of the writing laboratory, I am sure, can be attributed to the fact that conferences with the student take place when the student is writing" ("A Writing Laboratory" 75). That leads one to wonder what students were doing in the much more frequent times when they were not conferencing. Francis Appel, in his work at Minnesota, might have been the kind of high-caliber writing laboratory director that

E. F. Lindquist envisioned in 1927; however, the demands on his time surely challenged that ideal, just as they would the contemporary writing center director.

One other graduate student helps to shed light on the status and conditions of writing center directors in this era. In 1938, Beulah Stebno Thornton conducted for her University of Oregon master's thesis "A Limited Survey of the Laboratory Method in Teaching English Composition." Covering nine institutions, Thornton's thesis offers a snapshot of writing laboratory practices consistent with the "laboratory-as-classroom" approach that had been around since the turn of the century. One exception was at Syracuse University, where "laboratory work is handled through personal, scheduled conferences by one of the assistant professors in his office. Attendance is optional to fit the students' time and need. The work is done with single individuals, and the length of the scheduled period is from twenty minutes to an hour" (34). The contemporary aspects of this approach—staffing by faculty members rather than by lab instructors, individually scheduled conferences rather than an assigned time for an entire group—would have to wait quite awhile longer before they became more widely accepted.

In terms of administration, the supervisors of the writing labs that Thornton studied were far from Lindquist's ideal. According to Thornton,

> Apparently no special method of selecting teachers for the Writing Laboratory is used in any of the schools investigated, and no school reported that any particular kind of academic training was necessary to qualify for this work.... All of the laboratory directors agreed, however, that personality factors are important elements in the services of a laboratory instructor or supervisor. (48)

We later find that such personality attributes as "tactfulness, cheerfulness, and ease of manner" (51) were key to the successful writing lab director. Any contemporary writing center director would likely agree with these needs, but the reduction of the writing lab director to merely these qualities is an indication of the struggle for status at this point. It is difficult to imagine the characterization of a dean, department chair, or even a rank-and-file faculty member solely along the lines of a "winning smile," but such a quality seemed sufficient in the writing laboratory of the late 1930s. It would not be until the next era in the evolution of writing centers that "specialized training" would be valued and writing laboratories began to look as they do today.

THE WRITING LABORATORY COMES OF AGE

By the early 1950s, the idea of a writing laboratory seemed tightly woven into the fabric of higher education. Workshops titled "The Organization and Use of the Writing Laboratory" were held during the first three Conference on College Composition and Communication (CCCC) meetings, 1949 to 1951, and by 1953 Claude F. Shouse, a graduate student at the University of Southern California and the director of the writing laboratory at San Diego State College (now University), focused on this growing movement for his dissertation research. Shouse's survey of sixty institutions nationwide reported instructional places that were essentially free-standing writing centers. The move from *laboratory method* in the composition classroom to the *writing laboratory* as an essential component of instructional support (or the shift from "method" to "site," as Elizabeth H. Boquet described it) was complete. One way of marking this shift was to label the free-standing unit a *writing clinic* in order to differentiate it from the classroom-based *writing laboratory*. Nevertheless, the two labels were used somewhat interchangeably ("Organization and Use of a Writing Laboratory" 17). The directors of these writing laboratories were similar to the directors of today's writing centers in at least two ways, according to Shouse's findings:

- 76% of those surveyed directed a "writing laboratory available, for the most part, to all students on a college-wide basis" (71).
- 43% of the one hundred faculty writing lab staff members held the rank of assistant, associate, or full professor, and 48% designated themselves as "instructor" (123).

One significant difference between Shouse's time and today was that over one third of the sixty laboratories that Shouse described were staffed by only one faculty member or instructor (119). In addition to that skeletal staffing, the vast majority of the "regular faculty" who ran writing laboratories in Shouse's time performed that duty as part of their "regular salary," whereas twelve faculty reported receiving "no financial compensation" (125). This situation is perhaps best characterized by the origins of a writing laboratory at Montclair State Teacher's College in New Jersey:

> [D]uring the school year 1950–51, Miss Annie Dix was allotted time on her schedule for the Composition Clinic, but there was no cooperation on the part of the faculty in referring students. During 1951–52, however, the Dean of Instruction gave his support and cooperation. The registrar in assigning rooms has left Miss Dix's regular classroom vacant as often as possible so that Miss Dix may see students in the room. At other times, she sees them on a bench in the hall. (95)

Such descriptions make one feel reasonably gratified for windowless but dedicated space and a small staff of peer-tutors. These constraints led Shouse to conclude that "[i]t is patent that teachers in general and English teachers in particular spend much time on their own in helping individual students, but a formal laboratory setup may fail if not given released time and space" (118). The familiarity of this struggle for resources—coupled with an assurance of the value of a writing laboratory—is testament to the writing center as a long-standing site of struggle. Few have ever doubted the value of one-to-one instruction in writing, and many instructors in Shouse's time were willing to provide that instruction under conditions that were challenging at best and ultimately defeating at worst. Writing laboratories and their directors seemed to pick at the conscience of higher education as in the following recommendations from the 1950 CCCC workshop:

> The [writing laboratory] director should be given as much assistance as he needs, and work by instructors in the laboratory should be credited hour for hour toward the teaching load of the instructor. No instructor should be assigned to the laboratory; only those genuinely interested and trained should do this work. Teaching or attending the laboratory should not be considered a penalty or a second-class activity. (17)

As we all know, such admonitions carried little power at most places. Instead, the phenomenon of the writing laboratory continued to exist largely because of its relatively low cost and flexibility in staffing. After all, the bulk of composition teaching was done by part-time instructors, adjunct faculty, and graduate students at this time (Connors)—as is true today (Laurence)—so it was quite easy for a department head or dean to divert one of those staff to the writing laboratory. This staffing pattern was coupled with a thinly veiled hostility toward students most likely to need the services of a writing laboratory. As described by Leonard Clark of Hillyer College in 1958, "Another scheme is for the English department to maintain a clinic to which perpetrators of badly written papers and murderers of the spoken tongue may be sent for help" (42). This attitude, too, is likely familiar to the contemporary writing center director and is an unfortunate legacy of higher education's unease with students least prepared for its challenges.

Still, all was not so dark and gloomy for writing laboratories in the early 1950s. The description of the Florida State Writing Clinic, offered in a 1951 *College English* article, demonstrates the enduring power of the writing center way:

> During the first year of the system one member of the English department gave weekly to the clinic what was supposed to be a few hours' time. The illusion as to the scope of the task ahead was quickly and painfully dispelled, only to be followed by another, that any instructor with an odd hour or two free could take part in this specialized work. By the time the group had built up to seven members with assorted hours and interests the need was established for a permanent staff. The present members apply themselves with something like missionary zeal to their students.... They have been welded into a homogenous group by frequent staff meetings, where department policies are formed, where friendly criticism is common, where a graduate assistant feels free steadfastly to present his point of view against that of a senior professor. (Stevenson 36)

Thus, more than twenty years before writing centers would be reborn as a result of the Open Admissions movement (Boquet; Carino, "Open Admissions"), the challenges and possibilities for most writing center directors were set. By 1960, Harold Madsen prefaced his study of a Brigham Young University writing lab "experiment" by noting that "even though the writing laboratory has only of late achieved widespread recognition, it has a surprisingly long history" (52). Such surprise possibly continues for today's writing center directors, but several events shortly following Madsen's statement put the kibosh on the writing lab movement. One was the rise of the two-year college system and the rerouting of underprepared students into those more local and less expensive options. Another was the subsequent tightening of admission standards at most four-year institutions and a general rise in the writing abilities of incoming students. Writing laboratories had been increasingly linked to remediation, particularly in terms of funding and staffing, so once institutions saw little need for remedial English classes, the need for writing laboratories and clinics evaporated as well. As described by Albert Kitzhaber in his 1962 study of composition practices nationwide, "At schools where the increase in quality of students has been marked, the writing clinics and laboratories are being abandoned, since students are seldom so poorly prepared as to require special remedial services of this sort" (477). The promise shown by writing laboratories since the late 1920s was seemingly depleted—or at least dormant until the early 1970s.

THE FUTURE FOR WRITING CENTER DIRECTORS

An essential component of the current wave of support for writing centers is a recognition of the highly specialized talents needed to direct such entities. Whether it is the National (now

International) Writing Center Association's 1985 "Position Statement on Professional Concerns" (Simpson) or the growing prevalence of directors with tenure track appointments, we have seemingly come far closer to reaching E. F. Lindquist's 1927 ideal than ever before. Not all is so rosy, however. I have argued elsewhere (Lerner) that the terrain of our field seems separated into two types of directors: an active, enfranchised group with faculty or secure status and a part-time, contingent—and largely silent—group doing the best they can under very difficult conditions. It is remarkable how little some of these conditions have changed in the hundred years since laboratory methods in writing were offered.

This history of writing center directors is marked by both limits and possibilities. Our progress on dealing with the limits might seem to move at a glacial pace at times, but the possibilities have long been clear. Consider, for example, the following comment from Albert Tillman, a staff member and graduate student in the Department of Rhetoric and the director of the Writing Clinic at the University of Illinois, in his 1951–52 annual report: "There is real pleasure in being in charge of the English Writing Clinic. This pleasure is derived from working with interested and appreciative students and with understanding and cooperative faculty and staff members in many departments of the university" (2). Two years later, Tillman's tone was both more personal and more resigned as he experienced the limits and possibilities of writing center work:

> The Writing Clinic is an ideal teaching situation—one teacher and one student sitting down informally to talk about writing, or a place of writing because both see a need for improvement. Therefore, it should not be surprising (although it is pleasantly so) that students rather frequently comment that they have learned more in a few visits to the Clinic than they have in a whole semester of Rhetoric. Such expressions, true or not, are warm compensation for long hours at the Clinic desk. ("Report of the English Writing Clinic, 1953–54" 1)

For Tillman and for many of us, such *pleasures* and *warm compensation* either brought us to writing center work in the first place or ensured its hold on us once we found ourselves in those basement locales. The ambivalence toward first-year composition is long-standing; an ambivalence toward laboratory methods of teaching writing, whether in the classroom or in the writing center, is uncommon. It is a story of the tangible power of the work we do, and the ways that this power emerges even under the most difficult working conditions. The directors of writing centers during the two eras described herein discovered this reality fairly quickly. Their struggle to overcome the limits of staffing, funding, and attitude was made even more urgent because they knew the tremendous possibilities for their work. That, to me, is a familiar story, a déjà vu moment for any contemporary writing center director. It is also a connection with those who have come before us, a connection that provides both a measure of comfort and an indication of the challenges that remain.

WORKS CITED

Appel, Francis S. "A Writing Laboratory." *Journal of Higher Education* 7 (1936): 71–77.

___. "Writing Laboratory." *Building a Curriculum for General Education: A Description of the General College Program.* Ed. Ivol Spafford. Minneapolis: U of Minnesota Press, 1943. 293–97.

Boquet, Elizabeth H. "'Our Little Secret': A History of Writing Centers, Pre- to Post-Open Admissions." *College Composition and Communication* 50 (Feb. 1999): 463–82.

Buck, Philo Melvyn. "Laboratory Method in English Composition." *Journal of the Proceedings and Addresses of the 43rd Annual Meeting of the National Educational Association.* Chicago: University of Chicago Press, 1904. 506–10.

Burk, Frederic. *Monograph C: In Re Everychild, a Minor Vs. Lockstep Schooling: A Suite in Equity.* San Francisco: San Francisco State Normal School, 1915.

Carino, Peter. "Early Writing Centers: Toward a History." *The Writing Center Journal* 15 (Spring 1995): 103–15.

___. "Open Admissions and the Construction of Writing Center History: A Tale of Three Models." *The Writing Center Journal* 17 (Fall 1996): 30–48.

Clark, Leonard H. "These Semi-Literate College Freshman." *Journal of Teacher Education* 9 (March 1958): 40–44.

Connors, Robert J. "Rhetoric in the Modern University: The Creation of an Underclass." *The Politics of Writing Instruction: Postsecondary.* Ed. Richard Bullock and John Trimbur. Portsmouth, NH: Heinemann-Boynton/ Cook, 1991. 55–84.

Genung, John Franklin. "English at Amherst College." Payne. 110–15.

Kitzhaber, Albert R. "Freshman English: A Prognosis." *College English* 23 (March 1962): 476–83.

Laurence, David. "The 1999 MLA Survey of Staffing in English and Foreign Language Departments." *Profession 2001*: 211–24.

Lerner, Neal. "Confessions of a First-Time Writing Center Director." *The Writing Center Journal* 21 (Fall/ Winter 2000): 29–48.

Lindquist, Everet Franklin. "The Laboratory Method in Freshman English." Diss. State University of Iowa, 1927.

MacLean, Malcolm S. "A College of 1934." *Journal of Higher Education* 5 (1934): 240–46.

Madsen, Harold Stanley. "Laboratory Versus Traditional Methods of Teaching Remedial English: An Analysis and Experiment." Thesis. University of Utah, 1960.

Matthews, Brander. "English at Columbia College." Payne. 40–43.

National Center for Education Statistics. "Table 3. Enrollment in Educational Institutions, by Level and Control of Institution: 1869–70 to Fall 2012." *Digest of Education Statistics, 2002.* US Department of Education. 19 Feb. 2004 <http://nces.ed.gov/programs/digest/d02/tables/dt003.asp>.

"Organization and Use of a Writing Laboratory: The Report of Workshop No. 9." *College Composition and Communication* 2 (1951): 17–18.

Payne, William Morton, ed. *English in American Universities.* Boston: D.C. Heath, 1895.

Perkes, Rachel. "How Old Is Your Writing Center?" *Writing Lab Newsletter* 26.4 (Dec. 2001): 15.

Scott, Fred Newton. "English at the University of Michigan." Payne. 116–23.

Shouse, Claude Fiero. "The Writing Laboratory in Colleges and Universities." Diss. University of Southern California, 1953.

Simpson, Jeanne H. "What Lies Ahead for Writing Centers: Position Statement on Professional Concerns." *The Writing Center Journal* 5.2/6.1 (1985): 35–39.

Stevenson, Hazel Allison. "Facing the Problem in Upperclass English." *College English* 13 (Oct. 1951): 32–37.

Thornton, Beulah Sterno. "A Limited Survey of the Laboratory Method in Teaching English Composition." Thesis. University of Oregon, 1938.

Tillman, Albert C. "Report of the English Writing Clinic, 1951–52." University of Illinois Archives, Senate Committee on Student English, Record Series 4/2/23, Urbana-Champaign.

___. "Report of the English Writing Clinic, 1953–54." University of Illinois Archives, Senate Committee on Student English, Record Series 4/2/23, Urbana-Champaign.

ᴇ**2**ᴋᴇ

Kairos and the Writing Center:
Modern Perspectives
on an Ancient Idea

Carl Glover
Mount St. Mary's University

Kairos, the ancient rhetorical concept of "timeliness" or "the opportune moment," has important implications for the work of tutors and directors in the modern writing center. This chapter begins with a brief historical survey of this concept, followed by a discussion of its applications to writing center work. Although the primary emphasis is on the more obvious uses of *kairos*, related to timeliness and the opportune moment, the chapter also explores the more mystical ways in which *kairos* is treated as a concept of time itself, independent from the normal flow of time.

In the ancient Greek language, according to the Liddell and Scott *Greek-English Lexicon*, *kairos* has several basic definitions. The most useful ones for our study include: "exact or critical time, season, or opportunity" and "due measure, proportion, fitness" (859–860). In his analysis of *kairos*, Richard Onians suggested that the term is not a mere abstraction but is derived from archery. *Kairos* is the shaft or opening through which the archer must shoot the arrow to accurately hit the target. The archer must exercise "due measure and proportion" in aiming the arrow and drawing the bow string; he must hit a "vital part of the body" to fell his prey; he must release the arrow at the "exact or critical time" to strike a moving target (343–45).

The concept of *kairos* was an ideal valued highly by the ancient Greeks, so it is not surprising that Kairos was considered a Greek god. According to Posidippus, a third century BC epigrammatist, a statue crafted by the sculptor Lysippus depicts Kairos as a young man, standing on tiptoe with winged feet, and with a strikingly long lock of hair in front yet bald at the back of his head. This unique hairstyle, in Posidippus's view, gave Kairos the character of decision, because the lock of hair was a "symbol that one must take the favorable opportunity by the forelock" (Delling 457). Once Kairos has raced by on his winged feet, he cannot be grasped by the hair from behind. When the opportune moment has passed, it can no longer be seized.

The earliest written record of the word *kairos* is attributed to Hesiod in his *Works and Days*, dating from around 800 BC (*Oxford Classical Dictionary* 421–22). In a passage devoted to navigational advice, Hesiod cautioned, "Observe [due] measures. Timeliness [kairos] is best in all matters" (694). Of the Seven Sages, four of whom lived in the latter half of the seventh to the early sixth centuries BC, four wrote about *kairos*.

Solon advised "Seal your words with silence, and your silence with kairos" (Diels and Krantz 63 16). Bias held that "[b]y kairos you will have eulabeian [discretion, circumspection]: a good hold of things" (Diels and Krantz 65 11). De Vogel added this paraphrase: "By acting at the right moment you will act prudently" (115 note 3). The apothegm "Know your time" is attributed to Pittacus (Diels and Krantz 64 12). Chilon was credited with the maxim "All good things belong to kairos" (Diels and Krantz 61 13).

References to *kairos* abound in Pindar. Some have the character of sage advice, as in *Olympian* 13. 47: "Yet measure due [kairos] is meet in all things, and the fitting moment is the best aim of knowledge." Other references to *kairos*, however, point to a fundamental, self-conscious attempt by the poet to ground his composition in a rhetorical *kairos*. In describing this new method of composition, Pindar wrote, "If thy utterance hitteth the critical moment, twining together in brief space the cords of many themes, less blame followeth from mankind; for tiresome satiety blunteth lively expectation" (*Pythian* 1. 81). For Pindar, *kairos* combines both the "critical moment" of a story and the "due measure" the poet must use to avoid saturating the audience with too much information. The poet's first task is to attain knowledge of *kairos*, the opportune moment, "the instant in which the intimate connection between things is realized" (Untersteiner 111). A knowledge of *kairos* then allows the poet to arrange things "in accordance with their significance" (Gundert qtd in Untersteiner 111).

Although Pythagoras left no writings, accounts of his work are attested to by many writers in the ancient world. In his ethically based cosmological system, *kairos* functions as the force that joins opposites together in harmony. According to this Pythagorean system, *kairos* is a generative element, because all matter in the universe springs from this harmony of opposing forces. The same *kairos* that brings harmony to opposing elements in the generation of the universe also unites individuals in harmony and justice. In his *Life of Pythagoras*, Imblichus highlighted Pythagoras's notion of the link between *kairos* and human relations: "[Pythagoras] taught about the relations towards parents and benefactors. He said that the use of the opportune time [kairos] was various. For those of us who are angry or enraged, some are so seasonably, and some unseasonably.... He further observed that to a certain extent opportuneness [kairos] is to be taught" (Guthrie *Sourcebook* 102). This passage calls attention to a fundamental problem in rhetorical pedagogy addressed later by Isocrates and of concern to writing center directors today. To what extent can *kairos* be taught? Can a Pythagorean *kairos*, firmly anchored in universal ethical principle, be "various" enough to address all situations? The previous passage seems to admit the possibility of teaching *kairos*, perhaps even reducing it to exercises in a handbook for writing center tutors, but all the while maintaining a sense of the limitations of such efforts. Life's contingencies are simply too numerous, complex, and unpredictable to reduce to a series of previously rehearsed "opportune" responses. Perhaps Pythagoras's notion can be taken to suggest a pedagogy based on a "*kairos*-consciousness," a readiness to respond appropriately to the opportunities created in the tutor–client relationship.

The *kairos* that brings harmony to opposing forces in the Pythagorean system is similar to Empedocles's notion of *kairos*, which synthesizes antithetical elements, such as love and strife. The difference between the two is that in the Pythagorean system *kairos* functions within an established framework of an ethically grounded cosmological system, whereas for Empedocles antithesis becomes the foundation for a relativistic epistemology predicated on *kairos*, the "situational context." According to Richard Enos, the harmony of antithetical elements brought about by *kairos* is best translated as "balance" (44). In Empedocles's view, all knowledge is probable because it is attained only through the senses, which are unreliable. No two people experience the same event in the same way. *Kairos*, based on this relativistic epistemology, maintains a balance among sense perceptions necessary for evaluating probable knowledge.

For the sophists, lifestyle factors such as travel over rugged terrain, agonistic speech performances before live audiences, and the ever-present exchange of ideas with student traveling companions fostered a "*kairos* consciousness." Responding appropriately to moments of opportunity was a mode of living necessary for the sophists' survival. *Kairos*, for the sophist Gorgias, is an irrational or nonrational force that resolves the antitheses in a relativistic world, but when used rhetorically *kairos* becomes the principle by which the rhetor determines the greater or lesser degree of probable truth. In addition, for Gorgias, *kairos* also becomes a prompting toward speaking, a moment of crisis or urgency to fill the void created by conflicting ideas, a seizing of an opportunity to speak in a moment of decision.

Despite fundamental differences between the sophistic emphasis on relativism and situational context and Plato's ideal rhetoric based on a priori principles, Plato's system, like that of the sophists, becomes functional through *kairos*. The use of *kairos* is clearly described in the *Phaedrus*, when Socrates outlined an ideal rhetoric: "It is only when he has … grasped the concept of the propriety of time [kairos]—when to speak and when to hold his tongue.… It is only then, and not until then that the finishing and perfecting touches will have been given to his science" (271d–72b).

Isocrates provided a middle ground between the practical orientation of the sophists and the philosophical position of Plato. In *Against the Sophists*, Isocrates disdained those who reduce the rules of rhetoric to handbooks, failing to take into consideration the doctrine of *kairos*. In his view, *kairos* is the first principle of rhetoric and cannot be reduced to rule-governed procedures. According to Isocrates, "Oratory is good only if it has the qualities of fitness for the occasion [kairos], propriety of style, and originality of treatment" (12–13).

Despite this seemingly rich history of *kairos*, I hasten to point out that during the first century BC, Dionysius of Halicarnassus wrote, "No orator or philosopher has up to this time defined the art of the 'timely' [kairos], not even Gorgias of Leontini, who first tried to write about it, nor did he write anything worth mentioning" (Sprague 63). Dionysisus' words notwithstanding, the evidence from ancient Greece indicates that *kairos* was an important concept in the development of Greek rhetoric and epistemology.

KAIROS AND THE MODERN WRITING CENTER

All of the ideas from ancient Greece surveyed thus far (timeliness, the opportune or critical moment, due measure, discretion, appropriateness, moments of insight or connection, harmonizing of opposites, a tool for selecting among alternatives, knowing when to speak and when to be silent) are relevant to a critical consciousness essential for writing center work.

The discussion of *kairos* in the writing center begins by exploring applications of this concept to the work of tutors. All of the ideas raised apply to directors as well, but because directors must assume additional responsibilities, their concerns are addressed separately.

Tutors must make an immediate judgment concerning how best to help their clients. In a sense, they must find the *kairos* point of the tutoring session, which requires a kind of double vision that looks for a balance between the abilities of the client and the demands of the paper. The tutor must take the following questions into consideration in those moments of decision early on in the tutoring session:

Time constraints: What are realistic goals for the tutor and client to reach given the time allotted? Is the appointment for thirty minutes, one hour, or in rare cases, is it open-ended?

The needs of the client: Has this client visited the writing center before? For this paper? Has the client worked with the same tutor on this or other papers? Has the client worked with another tutor on a previous draft of this paper? What strengths and weaknesses are immediately obvious to the tutor? How can the tutor help to build confidence in the writer using the strengths apparent in the paper? What opportunities for tutoring or growth do the writer's weaknesses present?

The demands of the assignment: What does the assignment ask the writer to do? What writing and thinking skills are called for? Is the writer asked to analyze, synthesize, summarize, paraphrase? Does the assignment suggest an organizational pattern? Must the paper be obviously thesis driven? Is the writer required to make a formal argument?

The kairos *of the paper itself:* Does the paper contain a point of resonance for the writer to build on? Does it suggest a new focus or direction for revision? Does it offer a new way of interpreting the assignment?

SETTING THE STAGE FOR MOMENTS OF KAIROS

Perhaps the best way to frame this discussion is in the Platonic sense of *kairos:* knowing when to speak and when to be silent and knowing how much to say or how little to say. This is the *kairos* of due measure. Establishing the proper atmosphere certainly helps make moments of *kairos* possible in writing center appointments. Opening the session with a warm greeting and small talk helps set the tone for a relaxed and attentive atmosphere. It is essential for the client to realize early in the appointment that the tutor has an open mind, open to possibilities for revision. The direction the appointment takes should not be controlled entirely by the tutor, but it is an open-ended process of continuing negotiation between tutor and client.

After breaking the ice with informal talk, the tutor might begin by asking two simple questions: "What can I help you with today?" and "Can you tell me the assignment in your own words?" Moments of *kairos* may develop merely through the process of talking the paper out.

There are several approaches to addressing the paper itself. Some tutors begin by quickly skimming the paper to get an overall sense of it before beginning the conversation with the client. Others have the client read the paper aloud or the tutor reads the paper aloud to the client. Clearly, this oral treatment of the paper allows both client and tutor to "hear" the paper, to be attentive to its strengths and weaknesses, and to look for opportunities for revision. I do not recommend that tutors read papers silently, pausing to point out grammatical errors or other problems. This approach limits the possibility for meaningful interaction to occur, disabling the flow of *kairos*.

During an appointment, an attentive tutor might recognize a moment of *kairos* when the "light bulb" goes off, either for the client or for the tutor or for both. This might occur, for example, when a connection between ideas is realized, or when a new direction for the paper is discovered. Tutors must learn to recognize these moments, to be attentive to the cues inherent in moments of insight. During these moments, the client may grow more inquisitive or animated in discussion. Or perhaps the client's body language might signal some form of intellectual breakthrough. This may be the right time to ask leading questions. In some cases, the identification of a weakness in the paper or a problem with surface error might become an opportunity, a moment of *kairos*, when learning takes place.

Not only must tutors know when to speak and how much to say, they also need to learn how to make the best use of silence. This is possibly the most difficult aspect of a *kairos* consciousness, because our natural tendency is to feel uncomfortable with moments of awkward silence and fill the void with our own words. By allowing moments of silence to occur in a writing center appointment, the tutor lets the client know that the tutor will not provide all the "answers," but that the client holds the primary responsibility for the progress of the paper.

KAIROS AND WRITING CENTER DIRECTORS

Because writing center directors either currently serve or have served as writing center tutors, the aforementioned discussion of *kairos* applies to their work as well. In addition, directors must also develop a sense of *kairos* to effectively carry out their leadership responsibilities in writing centers.

A *Kairos* of Tutor Selection

First of all, when selecting tutors, writing center directors must choose the best tutors in keeping with their centers' particular mission statements and goals. To be sure, the process of tutor selection varies among writing centers. Some prospective tutors must complete a training course, often for academic credit, before assuming their roles as tutors. Others might require a minimum grade point average or even a master's degree for professional tutors. Whatever selection procedure directors follow, the moment of *kairos* for many of them comes in the interviewing process.

While interviewing potential tutors, the director should look for certain traits indicative of a *kairos* consciousness: attitude, energy level, ability to focus, personality. Whereas tutors' writing and editing skills are essential, these other factors may contribute more to their ability to recognize moments of *kairos* in a writing center appointment.

The *Kairos* of Tutor Training

Tutor training programs vary from full-blown courses—complete with session observation, practice tutoring, and taped tutorials—to a few workshops and on-the-job training. Whatever the training program involves, directors should develop a program that is most specifically appropriate to the strengths and weaknesses of the individual tutor. A one-size-fits-all training program might seem to be the most cost-effective and time-efficient approach to training tutors, especially at larger schools, but a training program with *kairos* in mind will better serve the clients and the institution as a whole.

Clearly, a training program centered on the needs of the individual tutor is more time consuming and labor intensive, but the results are worthy of the extra effort.

The key to a *kairos*-based training program is careful observation of the tutors, both during training itself and during live tutoring sessions. New tutors at larger writing centers should be paired with mentors, or experienced tutors, for exchanging feedback, for assessing strengths and weaknesses, and for planning ways to grow and improve. The tutor–mentor relationship will set the stage for the opportune moment for growth and discovery in the training process.

A *KAIROS* OF WRITING CENTER PRACTICE

Directors must take care in formulating writing center policies and procedures to avoid interfering with moments of *kairos*. Without a doubt, the nondirective approach favored by many writing centers has great merit. This "client-centered" approach, influenced by the theories of psychotherapist Carl Rogers, allows writers to discover for themselves, through response to questions, the direction their papers ought to take. This method of tutoring allows the students to maintain ownership of their own texts. When carried too far, however, this approach can be counterproductive. For example, I know of a few writing centers who mandate a rather extreme hands-off approach to tutoring, forbidding tutors to hold pencils or pens in their hands, thus avoiding the temptation to mark on the clients' texts. Unfortunately, the *kairos* of the moment might demand a well-placed word or two, a mark of punctuation, or a circle and arrow connecting ideas on the paper. It is impossible to make such a mark, to respond to this opportune moment, without a writing implement in hand. The policy should not be whether or not to make marks on papers (and this should be done only with the client's permission), but *when* is it appropriate to write on a paper, and *what* and *how much* should be written. Tutors with a sense of *kairos* will learn the right time and the right way to intervene in a paper. Directors should not handcuff their tutors, but should develop writing center practice with *kairos* in mind.

Writing center directors fill a variety of roles within academic institutions, and the administrative challenges vary from institution to institution. Whatever the nature of this role, be it tenured or tenure track academic professional or administrative staff, the director must develop a sense of *kairos* in terms of the overall structure of the institution. The director must know when to either support or challenge the status quo in regard to the dictates of the institutional situation.

KAIROS AS A CONCEPT OF TIME

The reemergence of *kairos* as a philosophical concept in the twentieth century results in part from the influence of theologian Paul Tillich, who introduced the term in his writings in connection with the religious socialist movement in Germany after World War I. For Tillich, as for the writers of the Old and New Testaments, time is an empty form, an abstract, objective reflection that can receive any kind of content (*Protestant Era* 33). The quantitative measure of time is *chronos* and the qualitative measure of time is *kairos*. The relationship between *chronos* and *kairos* becomes dynamic when *kairos*, "an outstanding moment in the temporal process," breaks into *chronos*, the temporal dimension, "shaking and transforming it and creating a crisis in the depth of human existence" (45). According to Tillich, moments of *kairos* are the turning points when "the eternal judges and transforms the temporal" (47).

Awareness of *kairos* for Tillich is a matter of vision. Although psychological and sociological observation and analysis "serve to objectify the experience and to clarify and enrich the vision," they cannot create the experience of kairos ("Kairos" 370–71). To capture this vision, this *kairos* consciousness, one must be actively engaged in "involved experience" (370):

> The consciousness of the kairos is dependent on one's being inwardly grasped by the fate and destiny of the time. It can be found in the passionate longing of the masses; it can become clarified and take form in small circles of conscious intellectual and spiritual concern; it can gain power in the prophetic word; but it cannot be demonstrated and forced; it is deed and freedom, as it is fate and grace. (*Protestant Era* 48)

In Tillich's view, *kairos* also has the character of decision. These moments of decision are not abstract, metaphysical notions, but are concrete decisions "possible only in a concrete, material world" (142).

In the Old Testament, time is measured in terms of its content. For example, in the familiar "Catalogue of the Seasons" in Ecclesiastes 3:1-9, time is defined by its content:

1. For everything these is a season, and a time for every matter under heaven:
2. a time to be born, and a time to die; a time to plant and a time to pluck up what is planted;
3. a time to kill, and a time to heal; a time to break down, and a time to build up; etc.

The Hebrew word for time in the previous passage is *'eth*, which is translated in the Septuagint, the Greek version of the Old Testament, as *kairos*. What is the character of *kairos* in this passage? Following Tillich, these verses present *kairos* as "a moment," a "point of time," and a "time of crisis and decision." At first glance, this notion of *kairos* seems to apply, especially to crisis situations involving death, killing, and war. On the other hand, most of the other pairs mentioned are clearly not critical or decisive times: "to weep," "to laugh," "to mourn," "to dance," "to embrace," "to refrain from embracing," "to seek," "to lose," "to rend," "to sew." These occasions are the normal human emotions and reactions that make up everyday life. In addition, few of these experiences or events occur within a "moment" or a "point of time." Certainly war and peace extend beyond a moment's duration.

It can be concluded, then, that *kairos* as an interruption in the normal flow of time, can be either brief or last for an extended period. It can include both life-changing events and brief moments of insight, those "aha" moments, mentioned previously, that spring forth during our daily routines. All of us have experienced from time to time those moments when *kairos* breaks into our normal experience of the passage of time. For example, when I meet an old friend whom I have not seen for a long time, we spend some time together, perhaps consuming a few of our favorite beverages, and share our thoughts about old times and what is going on in our lives today. It seems that only a few minutes have passed, but in fact we have been together for maybe two or three hours. We have lost track of time, not because of inattentiveness, but because the normal flow of time as we experience it has been broken into by a moment of *kairos*. I would hope that occasionally a writing center conference would produce this type of moment of *kairos* for our tutors and clients.

What about those moments of crisis, or those life-changing experiences, or those profound extended moments of *kairos* that Tillich wrote about? Those are rare in writing center work, but they can happen. I offer an example from my own experience. When Greg first came to our writing center as a sophomore, he was a wayward youth in search of a direction. He had little interest in academics and seemed to be merely going through the motions. Although he had good ideas, he had a great deal of difficulty expressing himself in writing. He came to see me, the director of our writing center, because he was required to; as a freshman, he had failed the college's writing proficiency requirement. I assigned him to work with Deb, one of our professional tutors. Over the course of the next three years, Greg was transformed both as a writer and as a person. His thirst for knowledge was kindled and he became a strong writer. He also developed a sense of direction for his life. It was almost as if in the *kairos* of the present, he made sense of his past and envisioned a promising future. Although I realize that a number of factors might have contributed to Greg's transformation, he told me on more than one occasion that working with Deb in our writing center changed his life.

These life-altering extended moments of *kairos* are rare in writing center work, but they do occur, perhaps without our ever knowing it. But when tutors and directors discover these cases, they are richly rewarded, knowing that their work has borne fruit.

WORKS CITED

Delling, Gerhard. "Kairos." *Theological Dictionary of the New Testament*. Ed. Gerhard Kittel. Trans. and Ed. Geoffrey W. Bromley. Grand Rapids: Eerdmans, 1975.

DeVogel, C. J. *Pythagoras and Early Pythagoreanism*. The Hague: Royal VanGorcum, 1959.

Diels, Hermann, and Walter Kranz. *Die Fragmente der Vorsokratiker*. Berlin: Weidmannsche, 1956.

Enos, Richard Leo. "The Epistemology of Gorgias Rhetoric: A Re-examination." Southern Speech Communication Journal 42 (1976): 35–51.

Guthrie, Kenneth Sylvan. *The Pythagorean Sourcebook*. Ed. David R. Fideler. Grand Rapids: Phanes, 1987.

Hesiod. *Works and Days*. Trans. Hugh G. Evelyn-White. New York: Loeb Classical Library-Putnam's, 1920.

Holy Bible. Revised Standard Version. Camden, NJ: Thomas Nelson, 1959.

Isocrates. *Isocrates II*. Trans. George Norlin. Cambridge, MA: Harvard UP, Loeb Classical Library, 1968.

Liddell, Henry George, and Robert Scott, ed. *A Greek-English Lexicon*. Revised by Sir Henry Stuart Jones and Robert McKenzie. Oxford: Clarendon, 1968.

Onians, R. B. *The Origins of European Thought*. Cambridge: Cambridge UP, 1951.

Pindar. *The Odes of Pindar*. Trans. John Sandys. Cambridge: Loeb Classical Library-Harvard UP, 1961.

Plato. *Phaedrus*. Trans. W. C. Helmbold and W. G. Rabinowitz. Indianapolis: Bobbs-Merrill, 1956.

Sprague, Rosamund Kent, ed. *The Older Sophists: A Complete Translation by Many Hands of the Fragments in Die Fragmente der Vorsokratiker*. Columbia, SC: South Carolina UP, 1972.

Tillich, Paul. "Kairos and Kairoi." *Systematic Theology*. Chicago: U of Chicago P, 1948.

___. The *Protestant Era*. Trans. James Luther Adams. Chicago: U of Chicago P, 1948.

Untersteiner, Mario. *The Sophists*. Trans. Kathleen Freeman. New York: Philosophical Library, 1954.

3

Writing a Sustainable History: Mapping Writing Center Ethos

Stephen Ferruci and Susan DeRosa
Eastern Connecticut State University

Developing a writing center and/or maintaining an existing writing center is fraught with roadblocks, from finding start-up monies to perennial budget battles, from countering perceptions of our work as "remedial" to fending off efforts to incorporate the writing center into larger skills centers (although we recognize that for some writing center scholars such a move is not necessarily a bad one). We encounter these barriers especially as public universities face enormous budget cuts from state and federal governments, and as national leaders threaten to take us back to a time of skills and drills instruction and pre- and posttesting writing assessment policies under the guise of "progress." Facing tough economic times and pedagogical reasoning that undermines the progress of decades of composition research, mapping our sustainable histories in our writing programs and writing centers seems critical. How do we develop and maintain sustainability in our writing centers, while moving forward with pedagogically and theoretically sound, progressive writing programs?

In part, we realize that our writing center must reflect our ethos, which is rooted in our field's history and the lessons we've learned from critically reflecting on it. Yet, we know a writing center must be flexible enough to adapt to local changes in our institution's and students' needs, and be responsive to developments in the field—all while meeting the challenges presented by attitudes about literacy and public education on a national level. As Karen Bishop reminded us in "On the Road to (Documentary) Reality," writing program administrators (WPA) often suffer from their inability to translate the work they do into a form understandable to those unfamiliar with the work of WPAs. Carefully constructing the "text" of our writing center to reflect and subtly shape our audience's needs (administrators, faculty, and students without our specialized knowledge) may ensure its sustainability if the ethos reflected

21

in that text is malleable and responsive to change. Constructing such a sustainable history would counter Bishop's concern that "our work remains invisible because we lack effective means of making it comprehensible to those within and outside the field" (45). Writing our sustainable histories is critical to the survival of our centers—sustainability equals survivability for writing centers and their directors.

Our purpose here is to problematize for writing center directors some of the pedagogical and theoretical concerns that writing center directors may face as they map their sustainable histories. A sustainable history, one that is documented and flexible, is important not only because it enables us to work with faculty, administrators, and students, but also because "such documentary strategies allow us to expose areas in which we are lacking in order to make adjustments" (Bishop 46). A sustainable history, then, would be useful as a means of translating what we do for a larger, perhaps nonspecialized audience, and it would become a useful method for maintaining the responsiveness to audience and cultural climate we claim a writing center needs. To this end, our research has been two pronged: a local investigation of our university community and its needs for a writing center and an exploration into particular areas of concern for writing centers that may face some of the challenges already mentioned. This chapter raises questions about "standards" for operating writing centers. It also asks how these "ideals" are challenged when writing centers are influenced by the input of students, tutors, and others in the campus community—all of whom create the "face" of a center.

One key question is obvious: What would mapping a sustainable history involve or look like? To create such a history would suggest that rather than follow a hierarchical model, one reflective of corporate structures, writing center histories should be created democratically and allow participants' voices to effect changes in the writing center's structure and programs, as Ellen Mohr argued in "The Writing Center: An Opportunity in Democracy." For instance, because tutors spend the most time in the center, they know the ways that space and pedagogy work together to best help writers. Similarly, input from students and faculty allows center directors to chart perceptions of the writing center. And, a history created based on the needs, goals, and perceptions of people who use a writing center will, of course, change as students, faculty, and tutors leave and arrive at the university. Finally, the changing culture of the university itself calls for a writing center with a history that adapts to these shifts in the university community. For us, and probably for many other writing centers, sustainability and adaptability equal survivability. One concern for writing center directors may be how our local conditions suggest broader implications for writing sustainable writing center histories and creating adaptable environments.

The term *sustainability* indicates a growing need and imperative to plan for future generations and to live with minimal impact on our local environments. In *Composition and Sustainability*, Derek Owens provided a list of distinctive kinds of sustainability, from "weak sustainability," where it is "a modifier of [economic] growth" (21) to strong sustainability that mixes "personal and spiritual growth" with an awareness of the larger ecosystems (22–23). Whereas his discussion of sustainability is important for all educators as they develop their own pedagogies, it is his reliance on W. Edward Stead and Jean Garner Stead that is most important to us. He cited their six values of sustainability: "wholeness, posterity, smallness, community, quality, and spiritual fulfillment" (Owens 27), and then called for a pedagogy of sustainability and listed six tenets that would guide such a pedagogy, including the need for "sustainable conscious curricula," an awareness of the "social traps of unsustainability," and the need for the "daily operations of the college campus" to "reflect the ethics of sustainability" (27–33). In some ways, writing centers throughout the field's history have addressed these tenets pedagogically and/or theoretically. Especially interesting to our discussion are Owens's concerns for conscious curricula as it reflects local needs while simultaneously addressing global ones in the field. Planning consciously for the future, then, will allow writing centers to avoid social and political and ethical traps that could affect the sustainability of the center. Avoiding such pitfalls might mean developing/directing a center that serves current university curricular needs and goals locally while at the same considering the broader ethical and theoretical developments within the field of writing center scholarship.

In his introduction, Owens also purported that "thinking sustainably requires that we envision ourselves less as autonomous individuals than as collaborators who are not only dependent on but also literally connected to our local environments in complex ways" (1). For Owens, "sustainability" meant "meeting today's needs without jeopardizing the well-being of future generations" (1). Working loosely within the framework of Owens's concept of sustainability, we consider as we go forward in our work (a) the importance of collaboration, as a guiding developmental principle (e.g., who gets to envision, plan, and create the writing center?), as a pedagogical concept, and for governance; and (b) the significance of attention to local environment, space, and culture, and concerns for immediate and future conditions that inform writing programs and writing centers. Because we have no writing center *yet*, Owens's call for sustainability translates for us into particular concerns: How do we map a history of a writing center that does not yet exist? How do we make that writing center sustainable in a way that meets our particular goals and professional needs?

To begin to map a sustainable history, we surveyed sixty-five writing centers at a variety of institutions in the northeast in summer 2003. Our survey examined four primary areas of concern: Space and Design, Theory and Pedagogy, Resources and Technology, Governance. We also surveyed students and tutors and invited ideas from faculty and committees through workshops. From these conversations, we've begun to change the landscape of our writing and tutoring programs and to incorporate those changes into the development of a writing center. We have "tak[en] control of our documentary realities," as Bishop suggested, in order to "effect the best possible outcomes for our students, colleagues, programs and institutions" (52).

Similar to Nancy Maloney Grimm's analogy for writing center theorists as "quilt makers" in the introduction to *Good Intentions*, our process for putting together writing center research to initiate a center has been piecework. We've gathered scraps of ideas from training tutors and ideas from writing center scholarship. We've woven information from surveys and interviews we conducted of current writing center directors' experiences into the text of our writing center ethos. With our tutors, faculty, and administrators, we've workshopped and discussed our ideas in order to come face to face with those who make up our university's community. To better understand the "faces" of other writing centers, we've looked outward to the writing center community at their models and methods. We've done all of this dialoguing in hope of creating a writing center that will accommodate the needs of our local community while simultaneously reflecting current writing center theory and pedagogy. To guide us, we have developed parameters for the work we do. A sustainable writing center would need to be grounded in the needs of our students and faculty, but whose "footprint" on the community is minimized (with respect to Owens's concept of sustainability, development should concern itself with limiting disposable technology, reducing paper use, retrofitting preexiting space, and so on); reflective of current (and changing) composition and writing center theory; flexible enough to adapt to the inevitable changes within any institution; and professionally and personally sustaining. These four criteria have helped to guide us as we developed our plans for a new writing center.

Proceeding with our eyes on this concept of sustainability has led us to three key concerns to the creation and continued development of a sustainable writing center. Writing center directors need to consider the following: (a) What are the assumptions students have about literacy and the role of a writing center? How do students perceive the roles of the writing tutor? And how do we address their needs even as we work to understand their assumptions? (b) How do we negotiate space in order to encourage pedagogical practices that reflect current writing theory? And, how do we do this while also meeting the particular curricular demands of our institution? Finally, (c) how do we create professional and personal sustainability? That is, how do we create a writing center that is seen as an academic program and a site for creative and scholarly activity by administrators and faculty who influence our budgets, teaching loads, and tenure? Because our concern with a sustainable history must be in part rooted in a local context, we turn now to consider how ours has shaped our particular needs and the (future) shape of our writing center.

OUR LOCAL CONTEXT

At ECSU, incoming first-year students write short placement essays in which they argue either for placement in English 100, a genre-based first-year writing course, or for placement in English 100Plus, essentially the same course as 100, but with a two-credit "lab," which they attend twice a week.[1] In the lab, students apply what they learned in class while they get support and feedback from their instructor, their peers, or the writing tutors assigned to the course.

The first-year writing program is part of a well-supported WAC program run by a tenured teaching faculty member. The University Writing Program Director receives a six Faculty Load Credits (FLC) reduction in her course load each semester for her administrative work (see Malenczyk). The WAC requirement that every student must complete consists of three tiers. The first tier is the English 100/100P course required of all first-year students. The second tier requirement can be completed in three different ways, depending on the needs of the students and their major. Students can complete a 200 level writing intensive (WI) course, submit a writing portfolio consisting of all graded papers written after completion of Eng 100/100P, or take a timed writing exam. The third tier is the completion of a 300 or 400 level WI course in the student's major. Our faculty see writing as crucial to the intellectual development of our students; consequently, there are twenty to thirty WI courses offered (enrollment in WI courses are limited to twenty-five students and ECSU has an enrollment of five thousand students).

---

[1] Faculty teaching Eng 100Plus courses receive 4.5 FLCs; at Eastern the course load is a 4/4, so teaching two sections of Eng 100P each semester reduces the load to a 3/3. Furthermore, student enrollment in Eng 100P is capped at 18 students, while enrollment in Eng 100 is capped at 20.

As part of our writing programs, we have a Writing Associates Program (WAP) that supports our first-year writing program. Tutors are drawn from all majors, as we recruit in our writing intensive courses. Currently, WAP has eighteen tutors (spring 2004), and recruitment takes place each spring semester. Writing Associates work with writers in English 100/100P exclusively. Currently, two credit-bearing courses, English 371: Composition Theory and Pedagogy (three credits) and English 275: Tutor Training (one credit), provide academic training for students interested in tutoring and teaching writing. Tutors are required to enroll in one of these courses as part of their training. In pairs, tutors work in the lab section and hold "office hours" outside the class for approximately six hours each week. Yet, except for the "on the job" training, there is no opportunity for tutors to stay current with composition and writing center theory, and no opportunity to work with diverse groups of writers beyond 100 and 100P. The WAC program could be further enhanced by the writing center's existence: workshops with faculty and tutors, increased interaction with writers from across disciplines, and recruitment of tutors from a pool of WAC courses based on faculty's recommendations.

FACING THE CHALLENGES

Given this situation, we realized we and our students had the opportunity to write a "sustainable history" of the writing center—that is, a history that accounts for current conditions and needs but does not ignore the needs of future students, faculty, tutors, or for that matter, the needs of the larger community of which our university is a part. To make it truly a participatory site, we looked for assistance from all of those groups. And although there are many aspects to consider, for the purposes of this chapter, we focus on three: Negotiating Space and Pedagogy: Re-imagining a Writing Center; Discovering Assumptions About Literacy and Writing Centers; Creating Professional Sustainability: Writing Center as Teaching and Research Site. These areas of concern are based on our surveys of writing center professionals, writers, and tutors at our own institution, as well as our own experience and expertise. We imagine these are areas of concern for many writing centers as they continue to map their writing centers' histories.

Negotiating Space and Pedagogy: Re-imaging a Writing Center

One challenge we face as we discover and map our sustainable history is the space/pedagogy dynamic. We believe it is critical to the sustainability of the writing center for directors, tutors, and others involved in its spatial needs to consider a space that encourages a collaborative pedagogy that is so much a part of our writing center history and scholarship. In our survey of sixty-five writing centers in the northeast, we asked, among other things, what the single biggest road block has been in the development and ongoing operations of writing centers. The most common answer was "space." In particular, two fundamental concerns of writing centers at universities and colleges nationwide are spatial design and the ways it affects writing center pedagogy. For example, Elizabeth H. Boquet, of Fairfield University, replied simply "Space." She continued, "[I]t's not just more space—it's space appropriate to a variety of tasks." Sue Dinitz of University of Vermont advised that we "get a central location." And Phyllis Benay of Keene State College wrote simply that "space is critical to your success." Space isn't simply a practical matter as writing center scholarship reveals; Tim Peeples asked us to think about space as something more than location and size; space should also be understood rhetorically and discursively (121). "We must," he concluded, "acknowledge and understand the spaces of which we are subjects" (125). For anyone who has taught in a cavernous lecture hall and tried to stimulate discussion, the idea that space affects us in powerful ways will come as no great insight. Yet, all too often, this issue never gets directly confronted; the space crunch at universities across the nation is no new phenomenon, and most academic and co-curricular programs literally take whatever space they can get.

Yet an appropriate location, Boquet argued in *Noise from the Writing Center*, is crucial to the pedagogical work of writing centers. In her center, noise from tutoring and tutor training overflowing to faculty office space and hallways created a conflict between "neighbors" for obvious reasons—neither faculty nor tutors could do their work (xiii–xv). She suggested this encounter caused her to contemplate "a different way of imagining the work of writing centers and the relationship of the work that goes on in them to students, to faculty, to … me" (3–4). Boquet's example allows us to consider the challenges of establishing a writing center when faculty, tutors, and students do not understand the kinds of work writing centers do and the ways that writing requires noise: conversation, dialogue, and debate. If the writing center is to serve the entire campus community, then faculty and students must be aware that pedagogies intrinsic to writing center work require spaces that can accommodate collaborative and participatory pedagogical approaches.

In *The Center Will Hold*, Leslie Hadfield et al. drew on the work of architectural behaviorist philosophers and composition theorists who argued that space impacts creativity and learning, and participatory designs, which include input from all space users, ensure contentment and productivity. Hadfield et al. contended that it is critical for those developing writing centers to "arrive at a design that architecturally enhances and functionally contributes to the mission of a writing center.… Our goal is to create a nonthreatening environment that generates— rather than inhibits—conversation … and inviting learning space" (171). Further, Hadfield et al. made the need for a negotiated space clear: "According to architectural theorists, space and design decisions should result in a space where people enjoy spending time, where they are happy, productive, creative, and social. Those are certainly worthy goals for a writing center" (170). We emphasize that the workers, the tutors, must be part of this participatory design as well, because they enact the pedagogies that are intrinsically woven into the space.

Whereas professional and theoretical discussions of space and design are important ways to argue for and imagine space, we also want to stress the importance of local conditions and concerns derived from our own students and tutors. Students' perceptions of writing centers give us insights into how they perceive not only space needs for writers, but also how they perceive themselves as writers. How does their input help us to write a sustainable history of our centers? How do writers influence writing center programs and structures to effect changes in writing center work?

STUDENTS' ASSUMPTIONS ABOUT LITERACY AND WRITING CENTERS

Given our discussion and concern with sustainability, we thought it was important to examine how students understand the importance of space in terms of the work of writing centers. In fall 2003, we sent out surveys to all students (first-year through senior) enrolled in writing intensive courses, asking them three questions:

1. Please describe what you think of when you hear the term *writing center?*
2. If we had a writing center what would you want it to look like?
3. If Eastern had a writing center, would you use it?

Students' perceptions of writing centers space/design and writing centers functions provide us with important insights.

We asked students to draw what they thought the writing center should look like, and although we cannot reproduce them here, we do want to note what we found in those drawings. Our students generally revealed the need for a particular arrangement of space to facilitate their writing process. Some chose to draw rather fanciful spaces—most notably a bowling alley and Yankee stadium—but many students drew fairly traditional academic spaces. These spaces were arranged in ways one might expect to see in a computer lab or library: pod-ish, overrun with computers, "tech kiosks," with minimal, if any, attention to environment. But, surprisingly, many students imagined spaces that might come out of the writing center director's wish-book: open floor plans with tables for group work, rooms for privacy, shelves of reference books, carpets, lounges, and even background "mood music." Thus, students can draw what they do not articulate in writing; we hope this reveals a nascent understanding of what a writing center—and liberatory teaching/education—might mean than their textual responses actually reveal.

Although the drawings revealed that students have a sense of the importance of physical space on learning and they understood writing as a more complicated, recursive process than "getting it done," what they actually wrote in their responses revealed a much more ambiguous relationship with writing and with the imagined writing center. They have begun to imagine a writing center that both resists current models and reinscribes dominant myths about writing and especially conceptions of writing centers. We organized the responses into four general categories (we recognize there is slippage among them): the Fix-It Shop, the Computer Classroom, the Garrett, and the Utility Shed. What is interesting is how easily traditional conceptions about the learning and writing processes bubble to the surface. Our students' responses also reveal assumptions about the roles tutors play and their own roles as writers.

The Fix-It Shop

By far the most common response to the question about the writing center located the center between the history of writing remediation and the overbearing presence of the grammarian. Students seemed unambiguously direct about the role of the writing center: It was a place to get help, yes, but it was a place that would actually "fix" what was wrong with their writing—a place, as one student put it, "where people go when they're lousy at writing and need HELP." Among the many responses we got to the question that asked students to "describe what you think of when you hear the term *writing center*," the following comments were typical of most: "I think about a building with computers, and workstations. The primary element would be writing assistants and tutors that could proofread and answer writing questions as they come up." And, "I believe it is a place that I can go to for extra help on a paper that I am writing. My experience was good. An advisor proofread my paper and made corrections for me before I handed in my final draft." And, finally, it would be simply "[a] place to learn to write the proper way." Perhaps in the twenty-first century, and in the minds of students, a fix-it shop now means a place to bring your writing "to get work done" with the assistance of new tools: computers and workstations. In the process of imaging what might happen in the writing center, these writers also imagine certain roles for the people in this space. They see tutors as experts with specialized knowledge—often understood under the catch-all term of "grammarians"—who will correct mistakes in the paper. They, in turn, see themselves in the role of novice writers. One writer expressed it thus: "I never know if I've done something horribly wrong or not and I would like to have someone qualified review my paper with me before I turn it in."

The Computer Classroom

Whereas the conception of the center as a fix-it shop taps into a rather pervasive and long-standing myth about the nature of literacy and literacy instruction, we found that increasingly a new myth is redefining the writing center as a computer classroom. One student wrote, "A writing center is a computer lab with available resources for writing papers or assistance with proofreading." Perhaps in imagining the center as a computer lab, they indicate a dependency on computers to get any real writing done. The culture of our university links academic success to technology. Students reinscribed this idea. In doing so, they provide us with insight about their belief that technology will help them as writers, not human interaction or their own critical inquiry. "When I hear 'writing center,'" one student wrote, "I think of a little room where people go to write and ask questions to someone who has no idea how to write, but they know about computers." In other words, human interaction is secondary to the power of technology. Other students revealed no less a faith in technology; when asked if they would go to the writing center, one student wrote, "Probably not. I am comfortable enough with my writing skills to not need help. I also have my own computer and printer so I can do everything in my dorm room." As in the previous category, the tutor gets defined in the process of defining the space; here, the tutor transforms into the technician, who may not have any expertise in writing. And where the tutor is not identified, as in the first quote, the role of the tutor is implied: Who will take care of all that technology? And who will be there when it (inevitably) refuses to work properly?

The Garrett

Not surprisingly, perhaps, given their descriptions of writing centers as both fix-it shops and computer classrooms, privacy, solitude, and quiet are key features in their responses. As one student explained, A "writing center to me would be a place where you could write peacefully without interruption." Interestingly enough, although students are multimodal learners—media in background, instant messaging, cell phones, and other types of noise—they somehow reinscribe the myth that writing is a solitary act done in isolation; one student put it: "Depending on how it was structured and if there was some place I can have to myself that is quiet." Whereas the act of studying may imply silence and aloneness, this isn't the case for students.

On the other hand, while writing requires an audience to write to, and students see writing as something to be completed in private, a silent mode of learning or communicating. Somewhat dishearteningly, the tutor is all but effaced in this model of the writing center: If a writer sees writing as solitary, and if that writer is otherwise engaged with the computer, then there is little need for a tutor or any other kind of nonteacher writing specialist (we speculate that this scenario opens possibilities for online tutoring, the tutorial equivalent of an instant message).

The Utility Shed

The final model is the Utility Shed, which is a place where answers to questions are easily, immediately supplied. Clearly, this can be seen as a predictable outcome of the three preceding models; if the writing center is a solitudinous computerized fix-it shop, then its only purpose can be that of utility: "just give me what I need to get a good grade." This was a rather pervasive response. One student indicated that he doesn't care what the writing center looks like "as long as it served its purpose and the students who utilize it are happy." Others saw it as a sometime resource: "Yes I think I would use it, probably not very often but if I had a big paper and I was in a bind it might be helpful to get a new perspective." More disturbingly, one student saw the writing center as his personal advocate: "Yes [I would go to the writing center], I need 'official' help for classes that can pretty much be undisputed in a course, maybe to question a grade." These were, as is probably obvious, among the more troubling responses, for they reveal a dislike for this thing we called the "writing center," and perhaps a distrust of the writing instructor. Or, it signals that students see the writing center as an arbiter in disputes over grades between faculty and students. Knowing this attitude exists would be helpful to those trying to start or further develop a writing center for it sets up a situation where the tutor could be pitted against the instructor. And the tutors themselves occupy an odd position within the writing center—a tool—appropriate we suppose, in a conception of the writing center as a tool shed.

However, not all of the students who responded recreated traditional myths about literacy and writing centers. Instead, some responses were more in line with the way composition scholars understand literacy and the writing process. Drawing from the same survey of students in writing intensive courses, we found that they are imagining the center as a place for reflection, a place that is part of their writing processes, and a place to collaborate on their writing. Writers seek a place of refuge from a different type of noise, that is, the "white noise" of computers humming, printers clicking, and cell phones ringing. Similar to Hadfield et al.'s claim that "[t]he environment where interaction between and among people occurs is crucial as it affects the way people feel and, therefore, the way people interact" (175), one student wrote that it should be "a nice quiet place to write. This is a lovely place to collect your thoughts and emotions and express them through words on paper." Other students saw the center as a place they can go to at any point: "I would want it to have multiple aids so that you don't have to make an appointment. Problems arise and you never know in advance." Finally, according to one student, "I think it's where people go to collaborate on writing papers." Students' responses remind us of Hadfield et al.'s argument that "a well designed writing center has an identity that speaks implicitly to its patrons.... It is ... the collaboration of experts ... who come together in a participatory, iterative process to plan and structure an environment for learning" (175).

THE POWER OF OUR ESTABLISHMENT:
TUTORS WRITING WHAT WE KNOW

Despite more than forty years of composition and writing center theory, students hold fast to particular assumptions about learning and writing. But tutors enrolled in our tutor training class picked up pretty quickly on the "established ideas" of writing centers even when asked to imagine a writing center that does not yet exist. Tutors fed back the central tenets of writing center theory gleaned from our conversations and readings instead of reimagining the writing center. In many ways, their statements would be great public relations for our writing center—if we had one. We don't necessarily think their responses are problematic; after all, the theory of writing center design is sound, but we do find it cautionary: If we want students to help us rethink the writing center, we need to find ways to ensure that they imagine from where they are, not from where we are. Two tutors' responses invoke a number of the central tenets of writing center theory, in particular, the writing center as a safe space, "hush harbor" (Nunley), comfort zone. One tutor wrote that "the comfortable area [of the writing center] should be a 'cool' space … a place where students go to hang out. The writing center … can also be a place where students can have intellectual conversations; a place they can feel at home." Another tutor imagined the writing center as a psychological refuge for writers: "If a student comes to the writing center feeling flustered and nervous, upon his/her arrival he/she should almost immediately feel calmed by the comfort and style of the writing center."

Theories of space and our students' conceptions of a writing center, which reflect their particular needs, knowingly or not, help us to write our history by troubleshooting in some cases what roadblocks we anticipate in the form of attitudes about writing. They help us also to incorporate into our history building some creative strategies that foster connections and build sustainability between the writing center and the community it serves. After all, a writing center is only sustainable, in some sense, by the writers who are part of it.

CREATING PROFESSIONAL SUSTAINABILITY:
WRITING CENTER AS TEACHING AND RESEARCH SITE

In a program that is full of possibilities we face crucial choices that will affect the sustainability and overall progress of the tutoring program and the development of a writing center at Eastern. The map of our writing program is undergoing significant change in curriculum and in theoretical approaches. With this, the design of our tutoring program has experienced similar shifts, some producing progress and others unanticipated roadblocks: working with limited resources, facing administrative resistance to change, challenging writer's preconceptions about writing centers, and designing a democratic space for writers who use the center as well as tutors in the center.

So we return to our original question: How do we create sustainable histories to educate faculty and administrators about the kinds of work we do beyond "service" and in such a way that allows us both professional and personal sustainability? Nancy Grimm suggested in "In the Spirit of Service" that an "ideological model of literacy" should reframe the pedagogical role and the types of research that get done in writing centers. Based on theories of New Literacy Studies, Grimm explained:

An ideological model of literacy requires a fundamental renegotiation of writing center purpose. It asks us to serve students better by achieving a better understanding of how literacy works as social practice. It suggests a discovery approach to research rather than a prove-it approach.... An ideological model of literacy changes our understanding of what counts as data and how one interprets data. It encourages us to look at relationships, identities, cultural misunderstandings, and more. It includes data stories, interviews, case studies, and ethnographic observations. (46)

Reimagining the creative activity we do as writing center scholars in this way would help us avoid cringing at the thought of the "assessment behemoth" and, as Grimm pointed out, open up new avenues of research potential yet untapped. Instead, our work would involve more than responding to calls from administrators for retention statistics or statistical breakdown of grade improvements. Rather, it would involve research based on human interaction drawing from our students and tutors in the center and from their experiences with writing and literacy.

If we agree that part of sustainability means tapping into our students' ideas about writing and ideologies about education, we think we have begun to create a history of such a model by drawing from their local experiences as writers in our research practices. Grimm's call for a new vision of research in the writing center makes us realize how such efforts might yield a better understanding on the parts of our administrators of the purpose of a writing center. Beyond "service," the kinds of work we do in the writing center would be better understood by administrators and faculty at large as research in our discipline. Presenting this face of the writing center (where research, sometimes done collaboratively with the students and tutors who use the center, into issues of literacy informs our work) may help administrators and faculty who have a say in our tenure, promotion, and renewal to better understand the ethos of the writing center as a site for research and teaching. "Sharing what writing centers learn from students is clearly a kind of research that is not only an appropriate focus for the new millennium but also necessary for survival" (44), Grimm explained. In this way, the "texts" of writing centers would present our research/teaching ethos and make explicit our work as "history making." Rather than being perceived as a "service first" model by some administrators and faculty, the center would be perceived as a research/teaching site. Reimagining a center in this way would help make explicit the practices of writing center scholars and workers who are researchers and teachers— and perhaps be a move crucial for our survival and the sustainability of our writing centers.

Writing a sustainable history, part of which encompasses writing center ethos, is critical in these times especially. It is crucial to map, in writing, our histories for archives when we are gone, for administrators and for assessment agencies, some of whom control our budgets, some of whom will inevitably desire to see us incorporated (back) into a larger, more efficient "support" program. The history we create now will enable us efficiently to navigate the changing and fragmented landscapes of which our centers are a part. Thus, from this work that we have done, from our surveys of students and tutors, our work with administrators, we have devised a basic mantra: Sustainability is Survivability. Within that mantra, we put forth the following three tenets: (a) A writing center is an academic program—to consider it in terms other than as a "course" or co-curricular program is to invite a skills model, is to invite a constant struggle against "incorporation" into a skills center. (b) A writing center is a site for teaching and research: it is not solely, and perhaps only minimally, a site for administration. Because it is an academic program, it follows that what "happens" in the writing center is primarily pedagogical in nature, even when it seems not to be. What's the difference between a syllabus and a request for funding? Between a year-end report and a teaching journal? (c) The primary purpose of a writing center's documents must be to promulgate its mission as an academic program—a site for teaching, research, learning, and writing. As we create our histories with our students and tutors, we must ask ourselves, "What legacy will we leave? How will their input be part of our histories?" Their transitory presence is necessary, and so we are looking at history as always fluctuating. Mapping, and perhaps remapping, will be part of the job of those who work in writing centers—perhaps historical revision is a goal to be reached for.

WORKS CITED

Benay, Phyllis. Writing Center Directors' Issues. Eastern Connecticut State University, 2002. Unpublished survey.

Bishop, Karen. "On the Road to (Documentary) Reality: Capturing the Intellectual and Political Process of Writing Program Administration." *The Writing Program Administrator as Theorist: Making Knowledge Work.* Ed. Shirley K. Rose and Irwin Weiser. Portsmouth, NH: Heinemann-Boynton/Cook, 2002. 42–53.

Boquet, Elizabeth H. *Noise from the Writing Center.* Logan: Utah State UP, 2002.

Dinitz, Sue. Writing Center Directors' Issues. Eastern Connecticut State University, 2002. Unpublished survey.

Grimm, Nancy Maloney. *Good Intentions: Writing Center Work for Postmodern Times.* Portsmouth, NH: Heinemann-Boynton/Cook, 1999.

___. "In the Spirit of Service: Making Writing Center Research a 'Featured Character.'" *The Center Will Hold: Critical Perspectives on Writing Center Scholarship.* Ed. Michael A. Pemberton and Joyce Kinkead. Logan: Utah State UP, 2002. 41–57.

Hadfield, Leslie, Joyce Kinkead, Tom Peterson, Stephanie H. Ray, and Sarah S. Preston. "An Ideal Writing Center: Re-imagining Space and Design." *The Center Will Hold: Critical Perspectives on Writing Center Scholarship.* Ed. Michael A. Pemberton and Joyce Kinkead. Logan: Utah State UP, 2002. 166–76.

Malenczyk, Rita. "Productive Change in a Turbulent Atmosphere: Pipe Dream or Possibility." *Administrative Problem-Solving for Writing Programs and Writing Centers.* Ed. Linda Myers-Breslin. Urbana, IL: NCTE, 1999. 146–64.

Mohr, Ellen. "The Writing Center: An Opportunity for Democracy." *Teaching Developmental Writing.* Ed. Susan Naomi Bernstein. Boston: Bedford/St. Martin's, 2001. 344–53.

Nunley, Vorris. "Wade into Safety: Writing Centers as Hush Harbors." Writing Back. IWCA/NCPTW Conference. Hershey PA. 24 Oct. 2003.

Owens, Derek. *Composition and Sustainability: Teaching for a Threatened Generation.* Urbana, IL: NCTE, 2001.

Peeples, Tim. "Program Administrators as/and Postmodern Planners: Frameworks for Making Tomorrow's Writing Space." *The Writing Program Administrator as Theorist: Making Knowledge Work.* Ed. Shirley K. Rose and Irwin Weiser. Portsmouth, NH: Heinemann-Boynton/Cook, 2002. 116–28.

4

The Writing Center Summer Institute: Backgrounds, Development, Vision

Paula Gillespie
Marquette University

Brad Hughes
University of Wisconsin-Madison

Neal Lerner
Massachusetts Institute of Technology

Anne Ellen Geller
Clark University

The Writing Center Summer Institute provides new professionals, in the company of other more seasoned professionals who attend, a weeklong experience of mentoring and fellowship, of carefully planned sessions with established leaders and co-chairs. It also provides ample opportunities both for one-to-one time with leaders and other participants and for special interest groups. Because there are so many questions about the specifics of previous institutes, the four leaders of the first two institutes in 2003 and 2004 have decided to present an account of their antecedents, write a brief history of the twenty-first century institutes, explain their goals and philosophies, and include a description of their major events. Such an account necessarily leaves out the laughter, the running gags, the extended metaphors, and the collegial fun that have made these two events delightful, but we hope this account will be helpful as you attempt to convince your administrators that sending you would be valuable to your institution and well worth your time.

HISTORICAL CONTEXT FOR THE SUMMER INSTITUTE

For the writing center field, the 2003 Summer Institute was truly the first of its kind—the first to conceive of itself as an annual event, the first to have been established and funded in part by the International Writing Centers Association (IWCA), the first to incorporate a plan for future institutes. However, occasions for bringing together individuals with interests in writing centers have a long history. Whereas they do not provide exactly the Summer Institute's experience of a group of established leaders mentoring forty or so people relatively new to the field discussing a broad array of writing center issues over the course of a week, several events form the historical foundation for the Summer Institute. The link between the Summer Institute and these previous events demonstrates the long-standing need for writing center professionals to share and learn from each other and to create a sense of professional identity.

Among the many antecedents for the 2003 IWCA institute were the Conference on College Composition and Communication (CCCC) workshops on writing labs during the late 1940s and 1950s. The account of the 1949 CCCC workshop on "The Organization and Use of the Writing Laboratory" appeared amidst thirteen other workshop reports in the May 1950 issue of *College Composition and Communication* (CCC). According to this account, the participants spent the bulk of their time simply describing the work of the writing laboratory and listing its advantages, including "[i]mmediate attention can be given to individual writing difficulties, a significant advantage according to the laws of learning" (31), and "the existence of the laboratory can have a bracing effect in maintaining good English standards throughout the college" (32). Still, these professionals acknowledged the relative youth of their field and ended their account with the hope that "more materials on the organization and use of the writing laboratory would be published in the future" (32).

By the next year's workshop account (appearing in the December 1951, CCC), the need for professional organization was quickly becoming clear. Although offering a range of descriptions for physical setup and instruction in the writing lab, the participants also noted that "no instructor should be assigned to the laboratory; only those genuinely interested and trained should do this work. Teaching or attending the laboratory should not be considered a penalty or a second-class activity" (17). Not surprising, then, the politics of writing center work had become as important as choosing appropriate space or tutoring methods. It was more than twenty-five years before the start of the *Writing Lab Newsletter*, almost thirty years before the group would come together and form a national organization, and more than fifty years before the first Summer Institute. However, these writing center professionals were gathering at the annual conference and finding common challenges.

Workshops at CCCC continued for several more years, with accounts appearing in 1952 ("The Writing Laboratory"), 1953 ("Clinical Aids"), 1955 ("Writing Clinics"), and 1956 ("Skills Laboratories"). However, the talk of collective action that appeared in the early accounts had disappeared by 1956. By that point, the workshop title was "Skills Laboratories for Any Student," and writing center work seemed relegated to little more than "an attempt to salvage students in the lower third [of the class], or as a method for draining off the poorer students who would inevitably drag down the level of regular class instruction" (143). No wonder, then, the perception of early writing centers as holding tanks for punishing the underprepared.

Conferences and workshops specifically for writing center professionals would have to wait until the resurgence of our field in the 1970s and 1980s. However, for composition scholars more generally, including many who would go on to direct writing centers and contribute significant scholarship, the NEH summer seminars of the 1970s and 1980s contributed greatly to the development of the field and offered a model for the potential impact of the Summer Institute.

According to Maureen Daly Goggin, the importance of the National Endowment for the Humanities (NEH)-seminars "in the development of rhetoric and composition cannot be overstated" (113). For Ross Winterowd and Vincent Gillespie, the NEH seminars and related activities resulted in the "the development of other such programs, the growth of regional cooperation, the [development] of major, germinal texts, and of countless curriculum materials and publications, [and] the involvement of other disciplines in composition and rhetoric teaching" (xi).

In the early 1980s, the interest in collaborative learning in the classroom led to a more organized use of peer tutors in writing centers. Harvey Kail, who attended the specialized Brooklyn College Summer Institute in Training Peer Writing Tutors, still uses the methods espoused by Kenneth Bruffee. Harvey explained the series of institutes:

> Sponsored by the Fund for the Improvement of Post-secondary Education and directed by [Ken] Bruffee, the Institute brought thirty writing instructors from around the country to New York City in the summers of 1980 and 1981 for five-week seminars in training peer writing tutors. In order to be selected to participate in the Institute, faculty had to secure an agreement from their home institutions to designate a credit course for the training of peer writing tutors. This agreement insured that peer tutoring in writing would become a part of the curriculum rather than a non-credit extra-curricular activity. The Brooklyn College Summer Institute in Training Peer Tutors established peer tutor training as a rigorous, intellectually respectable course in universities, colleges, and community colleges across the country.

The institute ran for two years and then in the third year, participants were invited to return to Brooklyn to rework and refine their programs. The plan was to have this core group of participants publish and promulgate these methods and inspire others to incorporate peer tutoring programs.

And it turns out that the 2003 institute was not the first such event to be held in Madison. In 1981, Joyce Steward, the founder of the writing lab at the University of Wisconsin-Madison, and Mary Croft, the founder of the writing lab at the University of Wisconsin-Stevens Point, organized and led "The Writing Laboratory: A Workshop-Conference for Administrators and Teachers" on the Madison campus. Participants came from proposed and established labs around the country for this two-week workshop, which featured sessions on the philosophy and operation of writing labs, staff selection and training, facilities, publicity, and evaluation. This collaboration by Steward and Croft led to their pioneering 1982 book, *The Writing Laboratory: Organization, Management, and Methods*.

Pre- and postconference National Council of Teachers of English (NCTE), CCCC, and regional writing centers association workshops have targeted new writing center directors with sessions tailored to them. In April 2002, Jo Tarvers organized a postconvention workshop for new directors after the Savannah IWCA conference at the Savannah College of Art and Design. This workshop met for one afternoon with four leaders and sessions on administration, negotiating, tutor training, assessment, and research.

The process of creating an academic field with a base of knowledge, opportunities for growth, and a shared sense of mission and goals, is by no means straightforward. Writing center work in one form or another has a long history (see Boquet; Carino; Lerner), but the profession of writing center work, the idea of a writing center professional, is a much more contemporary phenomenon. These early events were small steps toward that professionalism, and the NEH seminars contributed greatly. Our hope, of course, is that the Summer Institutes will build on the foundation these events have constructed and learn from them.

CONCEIVING THE 2003 INSTITUTE

The current Writing Center Summer Institute got its start after Paula Gillespie, then vice president of the International Writing Centers Association, came home from the Writing Program Administration (WPA) Summer Workshop in 2001. She had found it wonderfully helpful, because she had gone to support the comp director who was just taking over at Marquette. She felt strongly that writing center directors should attend it for the excellent way it equips WPAs of all sorts to function well in their institutions. But it also had gaps. She felt that the few writing center directors who attended along with her could have used an entire extra week of work together; the idea began to grow that we needed our own.

We need this institute the way WPA needs a workshop, because research shows that there is often a quick turnover of writing center directors, every three years or so (Balester and McDonald). Often new directors are promoted internally and have no formal training as directors. Often they must step into fully formed programs they want to change; often they must establish new programs with little guidance on how to do so. Often they are drawn from composition and rhetoric programs but might never have worked in a writing center. Often they are alone on their campuses with no colleagues they can consult. Often they just need mentoring. And Paula felt that a summer program of our own would focus, as writing centers do, immediately and consciously on students, on student growth into their various stages of learning, and on student writing.

After floating the idea past some good friends, as the new IWCA president, Paula put the development of some kind of summer help for new directors on a high priority. The IWCA board was quite affirming about the idea. Muriel Harris wrote to Paula privately, saying that Brad Hughes, director of the Writing Center at of the University of Wisconsin-Madison was quite interested in starting up an institute as well. Her contact with Brad revealed that he was not only interested in helping plan it, but was willing to host it.

Brad had extensive experience, dating back to the 1980s, as a presenter and mentor about writing centers in regional and national institutes for learning center directors, and he was eager to help create this kind of experience specifically for the writing center profession. The learning center community has, in fact, a long tradition of holding outstanding annual institutes, first at Berkeley, led by Martha Maxwell, one of the leading scholars of and practitioners in learning centers. Frank Christ has subsequently led these institutes at Cal State-Long Beach and then at the University of Arizona (Christ, "History").

From this experience, Brad knew firsthand the power that institutes can have as learning and professional development experiences, different in critical ways from conferences, publications, listservs, and pre- or postconference workshops. This difference stems largely from the sustained nature of a carefully planned, coherent, weeklong residential institute, during which participants and leaders come to form a community, learning interdependently, with and from each other both formally and informally. Brad's approach to planning the writing center institute was strongly influenced by the philosophy that Frank Christ had developed for the learning center institutes. A student of cognitive psychology and an expert on learning theories and research, Christ created a roadmap that Brad thinks anyone planning an institute would want to follow. Frank Christ insisted not only that institutes feature recognized leaders who present "current research, methods, and technology" in carefully planned and interactive sessions, but also that institutes be thoughtfully structured to foster collegiality and to provide sustained opportunities for networking, mentoring, and discussions; that they tap the "collective intelligence" of all involved, participants as well as leaders; that they revolve around "in-depth common learning experiences" for a limited group of participants; and that they offer participants "structure with freedom" (Christ, "Philosophy").

A committee was formed, comprised of IWCA board members Jon Olson, Neal Lerner, Jill Pennington, James Inman, and Pam Childers, along with Brad Hughes, who is not an IWCA board member. The committee asked Brad to be chair because he had so many good ideas and was willing to host, and he asked to have Paula as co-chair. So the co-chairs and the committee drafted, revised, edited, and tweaked the plans until they had an agreed-on one-week, five-day, work intensive summer institute. They agreed there were to be two chairs and six leaders, they would work to keep costs to participants as low as possible, and those two priorities meant hosting it at a school, not at a resort, and it meant paying the leaders a stipend of only $500 plus housing, some meals, and a $400 allotment for travel. No leader would do this for the money; their commitment would be to the writing center community and to their fellow professionals.

The planning committee agreed that the chairs would select the leaders. These individuals would have depth of experience, knowledge, and success with writing centers; outgoing personalities that allow them to relate well with others; and the ability to work well on committees and with leaders. They hoped that, in addition to outstanding writing center expertise, they could find at least one leader who would have technological savvy, who would represent community colleges, a secondary school person, and other leaders from different-sized schools. The co-chairs considered many names, but chose the members of the committee to be leaders of the first institute, not because of their work on the committee, but because of their excellent qualifications. They did not disappoint. They worked tirelessly to make that first institute exceed expectations. They were delighted that Muriel Harris backed the idea enthusiastically and agreed to be a leader.

Guided by the vision of an institute, by their varied experiences of leading and taking part in workshops, and by the writing center community's commitment to collaboration, Paula and Brad planned an intensive week of activities that would both support newcomers and challenge and reinvigorate veterans. To ensure that participants had a say in the institute's structure, Paula, Brad, and the leaders developed an extensive questionnaire for participants, asking about their experience, their writing centers, and their interests and goals for the institute. After combing through this information, the co-chairs chose preliminary topics and invited leaders to collaborate on planning particular sessions. Each leader and each co-chair then collaboratively led some four sessions, and all leaders were present to participate in all sessions throughout the week. We wanted to plan a somewhat flexible institute that belonged to the participants, that they could have a hand in shaping. We said to them from the first day, "This is *your* Institute."[1]

The institute opened on a Sunday afternoon with an optional session, "Writing Centers 101," to welcome newcomers to the field, allow them to get their questions on the floor, and that introduced them to names and writing center buzzwords they would hear all week. This was followed by an evening reception and dinner for the entire group. During the week, plenary and breakout sessions focused on the following:

- missions and models for writing centers
- the theory and practice of tutor training
- strategic planning
- the theory–practice–research dynamic
- OWL design, tutor training, and research
- conducting and publishing writing center research
- curricular-based tutoring programs
- WAC and writing centers
- web design
- school-college collaborations
- assessment
- funding
- creative writing, art, and music in the writing center
- ESL
- writing center workshops
- community in the writing center
- and mistakes we've made as directors.

As a special feature, Deborah Brandt, a renowned composition scholar at University of Wisconsin-Madison, spoke at the institute about her current literacy research.

We agreed that we needed to provide plenty of snacks and good lunches. Breakfasts were included in the hotel rates. Long breaks, long lunches, and dinner hours on our own left ample time for participants to initiate special interest groups and one-to-one discussions and mentoring time with leaders or others. Some of these conversations took place on the student union terrace, overlooking beautiful Lake Mendota.

We included a writing project. We thought that rather than make people worry about the writing in advance, we would ask them to begin a new piece, a letter, a memo, a mission statement, an article, a syllabus, a proposal, anything they could use back home. We surprised them with this assignment, not wanting them to worry about it prior to the institute. We asked them to write at night; at scheduled times during the institute, we divided them into groups and had them read aloud and offer feedback. One main function, aside from letting them leave with a useful document, was to allow participants to get into the shoes of student writers, who have just been given an assignment they don't like or want to do, don't have time to do, and are im-

---

[1]The full schedule for the 2003 Institute can be found at <http://www.wisc.edu/writing/institute/schedule.html>; the schedule for 2004 is at <http://www.clarku.edu/resources/writing/iwca/schedule.shtml>.

patient with. We also wanted them to get into the role of tutor, to remember that tutoring has its vulnerability, too. On Friday, the final day of the institute, we divided the participants and leaders who had taken part in the process and had them read aloud to a new group of listeners. The writing impressed all of us! Although reaction was generally positive to this daily exercise, participants urged us to allow next year's members to bring works in progress. We did.

We also included student voices. We invited tutors from Marquette and the University of Wisconsin-Madison, graduates and undergraduates, and some writing center users as well. These students sat in the center of our room, talked briefly, and then took questions from the leaders and participants. This was one of the most popular sessions.

The popular poster session, "Trading Spaces," invited participants and leaders to bring images and text about their centers to share with others. A discussion afterward invited everyone to think creatively about ways their spaces reflected their function and about changes they might want to make.

Graduate student volunteers from Madison's composition and rhetoric program served on the local planning committee and took turns attending one morning or afternoon session, participating in sessions and serving as the point person, answering questions about local concerns and troubleshooting as needed. This was a professionalizing and networking experience for them.

We included two planned outings, a cruise on Lake Mendota and a bus trip to see a Shakespeare play at an outdoor theater in Spring Green, Wisconsin. These outings provided a welcome relief from the intensity of the week's sessions. We were able to give everyone a Summer Institute tote bag, and although the participants clamored for T-shirts, we never got to those.

As the institute closed on Friday, participants completed written evaluations, offering valuable suggestions for improving future institutes and reflecting on the week. Some of their comments confirmed that we'd achieved at least some of our lofty goals: "I truly loved the sharing, the intellectual conversations, the 'packed' program with a few open spaces for cooling down and debriefing. This is a wonderful group of people, and I'm grateful to be part of it." "No number of conferences could supply the great experience of getting to meet and talk with other WC professionals." "The leaders all modeled the warm, inviting pedagogical approach that constitutes writing center work. I respect their willingness to both give so much of themselves and learn from us."

The week ended with a farewell luncheon; the leaders honored each participant with a few words and a certificate, and they adorned Paula and Brad with bejeweled gold plastic crowns. The energy of the institute was electric: One by one and at different times during the week, participants had caught fire, suggested special interest groups, initiated networks of their own, and one group even composed a song they performed after claiming, "This *is* our Institute." (Grady et al.)

SUMMER INSTITUTE II—JULY 2004

In early fall 2003, Neal Lerner and Paula Gillespie asked Anne Geller to be a co-chair of the 2004 Summer Institute. In the time Neal and Anne had known one another, they had often talked about how transformative each of their National Writing Project (NWP) Summer Institute experiences had been—Neal's in San Jose, California, and Anne's in Bronx, New York.

Neal had just completed his week as a leader in the 2003 IWCA Summer Institute, and he felt the experience for participants and leaders was just as powerful as his NWP experience had been. Anne said she knew that if the Summer Institute could really provide the same experience for writing center professionals—an intensive institute that validated and utilized their experiences and knowledge even as it expanded their experiences and knowledge—she couldn't say no to being involved. We asked returning leader Jill Pennington and 2003 participant Dawn Fels as well as Howard Tinburg, Carol Haviland, Harvey Kail, and Michele Eodice to lead, and all accepted eagerly.

Anne's institution, Clark University, was chosen as the site for the 2004 Summer Institute. Clark University, an institution in central Massachusetts with approximately two thousand undergraduates and eight hundred graduate students, is very different from Madison. Clark has a real Northeastern campus feel with leafy trees, Frisbees flying on the green, and old brick buildings. But Clark also sits in the midst of a city neighborhood that is urban and poor. This local context somewhat changed the feel of the Summer Institute. Some participants stayed in dorms on the Clark campus, whereas others stayed in a hotel and rode a shuttle back and forth to campus through Worcester's cityscape and active streetlife.

Clark University is committed to partnerships with the community, both during the academic year and during the summer. From the early planning stages, we knew that the Summer Institute would share the Clark dining hall at breakfast and lunch with local high school students in residence at Clark for a month-long academic enrichment program called the Bruce Wells Scholars Upward Bound Program. At lunch on the first day of the institute, we were all reminded that we have a more authoritative presence among students than we might suspect or intend. When the Summer Institute participants arrived in the cafeteria and joined the buffet line, the highschoolers were intimidated by the adult presence and voluntarily stepped aside. For the rest of the week, we changed our schedule slightly so we would arrive later, giving the scholars time to start their lunch before the onslaught of fifty hungry writing center professionals. At the same time, the presence of the Bruce Wells Scholars meant that the program's director, Jeff Faulkerson, could join Dawn Fels and Anne Geller for their plenary presentation on secondary school/college/university writing center collaborations.

It seems important to imagine that small institutions and large institutions, public institutions and private institutions, colleges, universities, and community colleges (Perhaps, we hope, even a secondary school) can all host the Summer Institute. But there is no doubt that hosting the Summer Institute at a small institution is different from hosting it at a large one. Local context will affect the planning of the Summer Institute, and each new host institution will change the Summer Institute in an unforeseeable variety of ways, even as leaders' roles, participants' experiences, plenaries, writing time, and snacks remain similar.

To host the Summer Institute at a small institution meant the co-chairs needed to work collaboratively during the year, splitting up tasks that a larger institution's staff might be able to take on. Paula Gillespie coordinated budgets and finances and registration from Marquette. Neal Lerner coordinated much of the Summer Institute's correspondence. Anne Geller organized local arrangements, including on-campus and off-campus rooms, a Web site and a Blackboard site. To work in person, Paula flew to Boston for 4 days, and the three co-chairs worked on Summer Institute curricula, schedules and plenary planning, printed and online materials, and final local arrangements.

At a small institution, hosting an event this involved can be at once easier and more diffi-cult than at a large university. Housing was not as easy at Clark. Madison has a small confer-ence hotel at the campus, but Clark does not, so Clark Summer Institute participants had to choose between living in the Clark dorms or at a local hotel. The Clark dorms were very rea-sonably priced, and fostered a fun-loving, communal-living atmosphere, but they are not air conditioned, so in the New England summer, some participants opted for the hotel.

Small schools simply have smaller staffs, and that staff may be less likely to be on campus in the summer. Few of the Clark Writing Center's staff, graduate students from across the disci-plines, were available. Instead, the Holocaust studies and women's studies students were away at research sites in Europe, the geographers were in Miami and China, and the international development students were diving in Lake George and interning at a sustainable agriculture farm. So, although Brad Hughes had volunteer graduate students, pleased to have the oppor-tunity to attend the Summer Institute, Anne, Neal, and Paula needed to be creative. Anne hired a former work study student who had been a receptionist in the writing center as an un-dergraduate to work with the institute all week, answering questions, assisting the leaders and co-chairs, and coordinating materials and rooms.

At a small university or college, making connections with offices and services across campus is easy. One phone call or one e-mail to catering services, physical plant, public affairs or hu-man resources, and the institute had tremendous technology support, food that participants praised (including the afternoon ice cream novelties break, a tradition begun in Madison), comfortable rooms, a group picture taken by a professional photographer, and Clark tote bags.

Perhaps the most important aspect of hosting the Summer Institute at a small school, or at any variety of institutions to come in the future, is that co-chairing takes us beyond our own in-stitutions. Serving on regional writing center boards and hosting regional conferences works in much the same way—and leaders and those participants already involved in these regional meetings encouraged all present at the Summer Institute to take advantage of these accessible professional opportunities. Yet, there is something unique about co-hosting and co-chairing an IWCA Summer Institute. Many participants commented on the obvious collaboration among co-chairs and leaders and noted that this interinstitutional work inspired them to do more cross-institutional research, and to create new state and regional networks, to turn to their peers at other institutions like and unlike their own. To move the Summer Institute to dif-ferent types of institutions reminds us that writing centers do, and should, exist in all different configurations and no type of writing center or director's position makes any one writing center more central to the field.

The 2004 institute retained many of the same general topics and much of the format from the first institute, but to address the complaint that it was impossible to attend all the breakout groups, it featured a few more plenaries and fewer breakouts. We decided not to schedule out-ings to Boston or to local areas; instead, we offered participants an optional evening of live Jazz at one of the Worcester clubs. Some independently found the excellent art museum and other local interests, especially the wonderful restaurants, parks, and shops. The participants told us that they had come to work and were happy with this labor-intensive schedule.

Because the 2003 participants had told us in their evaluations that they appreciated the writing and responding but found it hard to make time to write at night, we scheduled writing times every afternoon. This was followed by five minutes of reflective writing at the end of every day, and then writers' groups took the initiative to meet either at night or right after the day concluded.

Two traditions from the 2003 institute lived on: special interest groups, including one on grant writing and another on handling complaints, suggested possible sessions for the following year's institute, and participants honored the year-old tradition and wrote and performed a song for the last session.

A grant from Prentice-Hall publishers allowed us to offer our first minority scholarship to a secondary school writing center director from a Philadelphia school serving mostly minority students with little chance to continue beyond twelfth grade.

FUTURE INSTITUTES

We hope that future institutes will follow WPA's example of choosing its chairs; that is, one chair from the current year will choose the chair for the next year, and we hope to alternate genders of chairs as well, so a male chair chooses a female co-chair for the next year and so forth. We hope the chairs can be drawn from the pool of experienced institute leaders, although that might be complex, because it would commit a leader to participating in three institutes in a row. We hope the co-chairs continue to choose the leaders, and we hope that, if possible, one of the leaders can be drawn from among previous years' participants. We hope to encourage at least one minority scholarship to be awarded to a member of an underrepresented group or an underrepresented school.

We hope to incorporate geographical accessibility: The institute, beginning in the midwest, moved east and then back to the midwest. We hope it will move west or south next, finding a good home in a new, accessible location. We have faith that with a wealth of writing center professionals of all kinds, the institute will not become associated with a small cohort of leaders, but rather that leadership will pass to the most qualified willing leaders and chairs who can bring new ideas and energy, year to year.

The goals of the twenty-first century institutes are admittedly lofty, but the first two attempts, in addition to teaching us through their assessments, show us that the institutes are serving previously unmet needs, drawing new professionals into the field, and helping them identify areas they want to continue to pursue back home, either individually or with their newfound network of new friends and colleagues. The Summer Institutes of the future now have a solid foundation on which to build, to offer spaces and places where real professional development can take place alongside fun, song, and intense creativity.

WORKS CITED

Balester, Valerie, and James C. McDonald. "A View of Status and Working Conditions: Relations between Writing Program and Writing Center Directors." *WPA: Writing Program Administration* 24.3 (Spring 2001): 59–82.

Boquet, Elizabeth H. "'Our Little Secret': A History of Writing Centers, Pre- to Post-Open Admissions." *College Composition and Communication* 50.3 (1999): 463–82.

Carino, Peter. "Early Writing Centers: Toward a History." *The Writing Center Journal* 15.2 (1995): 103–15.

Christ, Frank. "History of the [Learning Center] Institutes 1977–1999." <http://www.pvc.maricopa.edu/~lsche/wiarchives/history/index.htm>.

___. "What Is the Winter Institute Philosophy?" <http://www.pvc.maricopa.edu/~lsche/wiarchives/about_philosophy.htm>.

"Clinical Aids to Freshman English: Report of Workshop No. 14." *College Composition and Communication* 4.3 (1953): 102–03.

Goggin, Maureen Daly. *Authoring a Discipline: Scholarly Journals and the Post-World War II Emergence of Rhetoric and Composition*. Mahwah, NJ: Lawrence Erlbaum Associates, 2000.

Grady, Kelli, Carol Mattingly, Leslie Olsen, Connie Sirois, Katie Hupp Stahlnecker, and Sheryl Tschetter. "Connecting through Humor: Collaboration at the Institute." *Writing Lab Newsletter* 28.7 (March 2004): 13–15.

Kail, Harvey. E-mail correspondence. June 15, 2004.

Lerner, Neal. "Punishment and Possibility: Representing Writing Centers, 1939–1970." *Composition Studies* 31.2 (2003): 53–72.

"Organization and Use of a Writing Laboratory: Report of Workshop No. 9." *College Composition and Communication* 2.4 (1951): 17–19.

"The Organization and Use of the Writing Laboratory: The Report of Workshop No. 9A." *College Composition and Communication* 1.2 (1950): 31–32.

"Skills Laboratories for Any Student." *College Composition and Communication* 7.3 (1956): 143–44.

Steward, Joyce S., and Mary K. Croft. *The Writing Laboratory: Organization, Management, and Methods.* Glenview, IL: Scott, Foresman, 1982.

Winterowd, W. Ross, and Vincent Gillespie. "Editors' Introduction." *Composition in Context: Essays in Honor of Donald C. Stewart.* Ed. W. Ross Winterowd and Vincent Gillespie. Carbondale: Southern Illinois U P, 1994. vii–xiv.

"Writing Clinics: The Report of Workshop No. 2." *College Composition and Communication* 6.3 (1955): 125–26.

"The Writing Laboratory: The Report of Workshop No. 9." *College Composition and Communication* 3.4 (1952): 23–25.

5

Growing Our Own: Writing Centers as Historically Fertile Fields for Professional Development

Ray Wallace
Clayton College and State University

Susan Lewis Wallace
Georgia Perimeter College

Most education experts would agree that the primary purpose of the writing center (WC) has always been to help those who come to improve their own writing effectiveness. However, this chapter takes a different tack in discussing the writing center's perhaps more latent role in helping all associated with the center develop as professionals in their respective careers. Whereas such development has obvious benefits for most who avail themselves of the center's services, perhaps it is the director's professional development that has had the greatest historical effect on the writing center field. This chapter looks at ways in which writing centers themselves have developed historically, examines how the various constituents accessing the writing center (from both sides of the tutoring table if you will) have used (either actively or passively) the writing center to develop themselves professionally, and finally in what ways so many successful writing center directors have historically "moved on" (or professionally developed to the point were they are promoted) to other administrative positions within the academy. It concludes that the history of writing center development has lead both to beneficial professional development experiences on the individual level for those who work in writing centers, and has also lead to a more ambiguous development experience on the part of the writing center profession itself with regard to the professional development of the administrators who guide these very same writing centers.

IN THE BEGINNING

When introducing writing center history, there is the risk of overextending an already dreadfully long line of puns about what is done in these centers. However, in this case, puns lead to an interesting metaphor, one that perhaps speaks more to our accepted role as nurturers and developers than to our respective place in academe. As writing centers began to develop into an early "bloom" as many as thirty years ago (this chapter acknowledges from the outset that writing centers have existed well before this point, but as a movement per se, most point to the early to mid-1970s as the beginning of the WC movement), many in the "field" at that time were not entirely certain where this "garden" might spread.

In these early days, most people had no grandiose plans on *how* to change composition instruction, *how* to change English departments, and *how* to change universities. Instead, many in this early period knew *why* we needed to approach our students differently, but it did take us much longer to develop resources, strategies, position, and currency to answer the question of *how* we could go about developing these needed changes. In these early days, many writing center personnel were poorly paid, nontenure track instructors who noone in "power" listened to anyway. Writing center personnel were, however, student-centered activists. These people were hired to help the myriad of new students coming to their colleges and universities for the first time. Most of these instructional positions (they would teach and work in writing labs as part of their loads) did not exist before this time, but through the late 1960s and early 1970s, the influx of open admissions students was felt quite dramatically in many of our state universities and colleges, and something had to be done.

Several new genres of students came to our campuses who twenty years before would not have been admitted for a variety of academic and social reasons. These included women, nontraditional students (i.e., working adults), poorly prepared undergraduates, English as a second language (ESL) immigrants, recently discharged and disenfranchised military, minority pupils, and those with inadequate academic successes given the crumbling inner-city school systems, to name just a few. These students were not proficient in academic discourse, and they were "sent" to English departments to "prepare" them. English departments, in turn, had few personnel who were either interested or trained to offer these students help, and so a new breed of instructor was born, focusing on the developmental needs of these newly admitted students. Obviously, the numbers grew, and places needed to be set up to deal with them; the dreaded writing lab in the damp basement of the English department was germinated as a way to deal with these increasing numbers.

EARLY STAFFING OF LABS AND THE RISE
OF COMPOSITION AS A DISCIPLINE

Although these developmental students entered universities needing a great deal of help in writing (and other basics), university administrators certainly were pleased with the added income (no matter were it came from) they brought with them. As might be expected, long established faculty were aghast at the falling standards, the end of civilization as they knew it, and the general openness (read "laxness") of the university. However, more students meant more funds, which in turn meant more opportunities for these very same horrified faculty, and whereas they certainly did not want to teach "the great unwashed," they were only too happy to spend the profits from their inclusion (somewhat) into the university.

Writing labs certainly solved some problems for all concerned. They were staffed by personnel who cared, which was perhaps their biggest advantage. These were newly hired instructors who taught a series of classes in developmental writing and grammar drills (until we knew better) and then also worked in these labs to help students on an individual basis. These instructors worked in the dark, searching for methods that worked with a myriad of students. These were faculty building a discipline from the ground up.

As writing labs grew in size and use, the gradual professionalism of the faculty associated with them grew also. It is not a coincidence that as more of these new instructors wanted additional training in composition and other writing related areas, the rise of composition studies also grew. We began to see doctoral programs spring up to help train this first generation of writing personnel, and with ever-increasing numbers of new, still unprepared, students entering higher education, came the ever-increasing popularity of these composition programs. These were not the days of wine and roses; instead, these were the days of Shaughnessy and Emig, of early process studies, of talk about invention and revision and alternatives to grammar drills, and of the introduction of journaling (all old hat now, we know, but the stuff of revolution back then).

FROM LAB TO CENTER: FROM NO STATUS TO A SEAT AT THE TABLE

As the composition field exploded with trained personnel gaining credentials, a change in status occurred—the writing center took "root" if you will. In English departments in the early to mid-1980s, more writing instructors attained the "currency" that their literature colleagues demanded in the form of the doctorate. As already noted, many fine institutions actually offered composition studies as an option in their doctoral degree programs, and there were many people who jumped at the chance to take advantage of these opportunities.

Even more students who needed help (we would not call this a national problem yet) in English enrolled in our colleges and universities, and more positions in composition were opened in these institutions; at this point, they had become tenure track positions. Our newly minted compositionists filled these positions, and one of their primary roles was to direct writing programs (i.e., take care of the lower division writing "problems"). Savvy compositionists rightly saw this as "a foot in the door" and went to work hiring the very best people they could, including friends finishing in these very same composition doctoral programs. Most English departments left this new breed of assistant professors alone because they were taking care of a perceived problem area. Of course, there were horror stories of writing professionals not gaining tenure in the early day (talk of composition not being a "real" discipline and all that), but gradually English departments woke up to find themselves with a composition director and a writing center director, and soon a director of technical writing perhaps, and then tenure track faculty hired as compositionists. This evolution was not by chance, however; compositionists solved problems and therefore composition lines appeared to solve more problems.

During this time, the writing lab morphed into the writing center as roles and expectations for this facility broadened. Now writing centers not only dealt with first-year writing problems (still "band aid" treatments in many cases), but also assumed tutoring expectations for advanced writing courses and then writing across the curriculum projects. English departments (and university-level administrators) helped funnel staffing money to these centers as soon as they understood that the entire campus looked to them as places for real help.

Tutor training also became important as these spaces grew. More peer and graduate students were used to tutor, more information had been written on effective tutor training strategies, and more was expected from these tutors. The writing center world had become professional almost overnight, and publications and conference venues dedicated to writing center work appeared, as well as more inclusion into our other mainstream composition conferences and publications. As tenure track positions became available in composition, they also became available specifically in writing center administration, and our profession was ready to fill these positions. Yes, the early days of tenure track writing center administration were fraught with difficulties, but now we had a seat at the table, and we were being listened to.

Writing centers pushed their way to importance through the diligent work of its early pioneers (many of whom are writing in this collection) and they are now a force to be reckoned with across most campuses in the United States (and beyond today).

THE CURRENT STATE OF WRITING CENTERS

When one discusses current states, it is often easy to fall into the generalizing pit, but we can make some statements with a degree of certainty here. We have more writing centers now than ever before. They are lead now by more trained personnel that ever before. We have more trained tutors than ever before. We are respected across campus more now than ever before. Finally, we have a more fully developed professional network now than ever before. We have journals, online discussion boards, presses publishing our work, various associations dedicated to improving writing centers and tutoring in general, and international, national, and regional conferences dedicated to our field. We have arrived.

In the years from development to arrival, we have seen many movements in the writing center world—from looking for acceptance, to angst over collaboration issues, to subverting the power structure, to breaking away from English departments, to reexamining our claims, and many more. At close range we seem to be in a state of flux, but standing back a little we look like most other new fields; we are exploring our boundaries and assumptions. We are in good shape, and we have produced a few generations of writing center personnel who have learned what it is to be involved in a movement. But, perhaps most importantly, the writing center has been responsible for the professional development of many associated with these centers.

PROFESSIONAL DEVELOPMENT
OF THE WRITING CENTER COMMUNITY

As we said from the outset, the professional development of many constituents involved in writing centers has been one of our most successful by-products of the writing center experiences. Over the years we have been responsible, directly or indirectly, for the professional development of several key dramatis personae in the writing center movement: the student, the peer tutor, the graduate student, and the instructor.

The Professional Development of the Student

When students are having problems in the writing classroom, the writing center is there to help. However, most students approach their first visit to the writing center with great trepidation, and the next visit is more productive than the first. Fears have been addressed, and student and tutor together have developed a plan to best meet the student's needs. Students then come to the writing center prepared and ready to work with an understanding that they can work with impunity here because this is a place they can explore their language and rhetorical choices and to begin to grow as a writer.

In the writing center, students develop as students. They learn the importance of time management, organization of ideas, and staying on task. These are development skills that transfer to other classes and to their careers. The writing center quickly becomes more than a fix-it shop. Students prepare in an atmosphere of professionalism. They are responsible for their own choices, but they have the help they need to make these choices wisely. The writing center plants "development seeds" and provides a fertile ground to watch these seeds grow professionally.

The Professional Development of the Peer-Tutor

The writing center is also a hot house of development for the peer-tutors. Here they receive training in group management as well as working one-to-one with individuals with a myriad of different problems. Here they learn to communicate, to listen, and to act. These again are transferable skills to their future careers as teachers or in other professional arenas. The result of peer-tutors' experiences in the writing center is that it provides these young professionals with documented work experiences and enhances the possibility for a more lucrative professional career having demonstrated successful outcomes in their work environment. They are indeed ripe for the picking after peer tutoring.

The Professional Development of the Graduate Student

Writing centers offer graduate students an opportunity to take on a position of authority in the quest for professional development. Here graduate students learn the importance of communicating clearly to students individually and in small groups, of good record keeping, of interaction between colleagues, of student management skills, and of keeping different students on task. These are all professional development skills that will transfer. The writing center is indeed a fertile field in the professional development of future classroom professionals, a bounteous crop ready to harvest after the writing center experience.

The Professional Development of the Instructor

Numerous instructors of writing today got their start in writing centers, either by working in them or developing into better instructors by working closely with writing center personnel.

Working with writing center personnel, these instructors develop professionally by devising better assignments, by learning to respond more effectively to students' writing attempts, by understanding what the writing process actually entails, and by understanding that each student is an individual writer (something others who have never been in a writing center never learn). Instructors develop professionally into better instructors by knowing their writing centers.

WRITING CENTER DIRECTORSHIPS AS INCUBATORS FOR FUTURE ADMINISTRATORS

However, it is indeed ironic that, by and large, those within the writing center world look with suspicion on those who administer for a living. Writing center personnel are apt to think of chairs, associate deans, deans, and beyond in negative terms, as those who control the purse strings, those who say "no," or those who ask for and expect accountability. It often results in the same "us versus them" dichotomy that compositionists are good at getting themselves lodged in: "No one understands us." "What we do is important, but different from what others do." "We should not be held accountable to the same standards as others." These are all familiar refrains coming from the writing center. Added to this chorus is the famous "we do a lot of good work here and no one seems to see it or even care about it." Unfortunately, people who sing these songs usually are singing to the mirror or to those either too polite or too inconsequential to ever voice dissention. However, those to whom writing center directors report are usually neither overly polite nor inconsequential, and as a consequence the singing soon stops.

A famous advertisement from the 1980s had the refrain "Where's the beef?" and the comment is apt here. Writing center administrators who wish to succeed in their directorships soon learn that whining about being misunderstood won't serve them very well. Instead, successful writing center directors learn quickly to demonstrate concretely what it is they and their centers do and why anyone else should care. Ironically, successful writing center directors learn rhetoric, while unsuccessful writing center directors never graduate beyond appeals to pity.

A successful writing center director is an entry-level administrator and not a faculty member. This administrator relies on statistics, spread sheets, budgets, Request for Proposal (RFP's) attrition rates, pass rates, standardized testing norms, retention figures, graphs, and projections. A successful writing center director is a person others in administration can count on to demonstrate the real picture. A successful writing center director is not the same person as a successful tutor trainer, but, instead, this director is the person who leads both the center's offense and defense. Therefore, when writing center personnel make the argument that their centers improve writing skills, they had better be able to prove it, and prove it with real statistics that others outside the humanities can comprehend.

Writing center directors who defend their centers successfully see them grow. Upper administrators will always fund areas that improve retention and graduation figures. They will not always fund areas that teach students to use a commas correctly. (Remember, this is also the dirty little secret of the academy. We have admitted huge numbers of people who can't write or read, effectively. We don't necessarily want to tell the entire outside world that we have places for all these people to get "fixed.") Perhaps a more important secret is that writing center directors are often academic adrenaline junkies, and after awhile the thrill of defending their center is not enough and they then seek different challenges. Also, successful writing center directors are seen very quickly as cross campus administrators and thus are deemed acceptable candidates for other new campus-wide administrative jobs. Therefore, many successful writing center directors professionally develop themselves out of writing centers and on to other challenges.

CONCLUSIONS

The previous phrase is a startling phrase for many writing center personnel. Writing center directors often do not remain directors. Similarly, students usually do not remain students forever, peer-tutors move on to other jobs, graduate students graduate, instructors get promoted, and directors also get advanced. This is all part of the evolution of the writing center field, and in large part describes reactions to our conferences.

If one has been in the writing center very long, going to our conferences invokes déjà vu. Many of us react to the papers because we have heard a great deal of the information before, and to some, the field is not progressing. Many feel we are simply retelling history. This is a mistake on our part, and it points to the vibrancy that is the writing center field. It is because people leave writing centers for other positions that those who stay to train another generation of writing center personnel succeed so well. The papers and essays often sound similar to those presented and published years before them because current writing center directors are training current writing center personnel. They are explaining our history and slowly getting the next generation to add to this history.

Those who leave writing centers help writing centers. Directors promoted to chair or associate dean, dean, or provost will always have the writing center in their blood. These people know writing centers and help writing centers. Many of the old turf battles therefore do not need to be fought again if one already has an ally up the ladder.

Writing center history is a history of development. Writing center personnel develop professionally into others areas. However, they never forget their roots!

6

Designing a Strategic Plan
for a Writing Center

Pamela B. Childers
The McCallie School, Chattanooga, TN

As educators, many of us start a writing center because we like the concept, have been given the task, or see this as a higher goal for ourselves, our students, our colleagues, and even our institution. Some begin with a budget that has been given to us, and a staff we have inherited for a variety of reasons. But, what if we, as do many businesses, had an opportunity to create a strategic plan for a new writing center? While taking a doctoral course on Human Resources Development in 1991, I created the first of two three-year strategic plans for a new writing center. Why create such a strategic plan? All writing center directors, whether new or experienced, can benefit from considering their own vision for the future of their writing centers and communicating that vision to their administrators in a language that they can comprehend through a strategic plan.

Starting a writing center takes research, a plan, and a vision. In the field of human resources, managers and directors must do their research and create a plan that presents a vision for several years. In the latter part of the twentieth century, businesses moved from creating five-year to three-year plans because of rapid advancements in the information age (Groff). For example, technology advances so fast and prices of technology change so often that plans and budgets must be revised more frequently. Managers/directors want to convince those with the power and money to support the plan and agree that it is a worthy project. In the same way, writing center directors must be reminded of their audience in creating such a plan for their writing centers; they are people with a clear sense of the institution's mission and a desire to meet its budgetary constraints.

The components of a strategic plan can be quite basic (Appendix A). In order to work with goals, objectives, physical plans, and budgets, we must consider many questions. For instance, why do we need a writing center? What resources already exist? Whom will it serve? The answer to these questions will impact the goals and objectives, the location and needs of the facility, as well as what to include in the budget. Through research and visitation of other writing centers, we must plan a vision for the future of that writing center to give administrators an idea of where we are going, how the facility will fit the goals of our institution, and how much this plan will cost. One of the most valuable sources to use in helping to create this strategic plan is *The Writing Center Resource Manual*, edited by Bobbie Silk. As we design our individual plan, we will want to refer to specific sections of this manual (http://www.writingcenters.org), *Writing Lab Newsletter*, and *The Writing Center Journal* and its archives. For those who have little background in writing center theory/practice, I would strongly suggest reading Murphy and Law's *Landmark Essays on Writing Centers* as a primer, followed by *Intersections: Writing Center Theory/Practice* (Mullin and Wallace), and *The Center Will Hold* (Kinkead and Pemberton).

In my work with experienced as well as new writing center directors on the secondary and college/university level, I have discovered that not many have had a strategic plan before they started the writing center, but they want to learn how to create one. Gluck, Kaufman, and Walleck described four evolving phases of strategic management in a way that we seldom do, starting with the financial planning. But, if we have no budget, then perhaps we can redesign their phases to have the budget evolve after the forecast-based planning to predict the future, the externally oriented planning to think strategically, and the strategic management that creates the future. Creating a strategic plan is not a dry, uncreative activity. In fact, it is a unique form of creative research that allows directors to imagine and fulfill a dream through a clear plan, while being flexible enough to meet the variables impacting a particular institution. In a sense, we are focusing on how we as writing center directors go about educating our own administration, faculty, students, and possible benefactors with such a concrete plan. Also, we may consider how annual updates of that plan enable us to show the effectiveness of meeting our goals and also demonstrate the role of revisions in the original plan due to concrete reasons for changes.

PREPLANNING ACTIVITY

Let us begin with a preplanning activity to help us prioritize and envision the writing center we would like to have. First, we are aware that it makes no difference whether we have an existing facility, have inherited one, or have assumed the position of starting/recreating one. This activity (Appendix B) is best done with a team within an institution. For instance, if the writing center will function within a specific department/school/college or there will be codirectors, then those people should be part of the team. This exercise also works in a graduate course on writing program administration or writing centers, as well as with a group of current writing center directors. Once we have taken the time for this preplanning and interaction with partners, most of us are ready to move on to the actual creation of a plan.

REALITY

The following questions help us to audit the strengths and weaknesses of our own institution. This audit gives us a realistic picture of where our institution is currently and how a writing center may impact the future growth and success of the institution. If we already have a writing center, then audit it as well by listing the mission, philosophy, policies, function, and budget. We must consider how our current writing center plays into the strengths and helps to overcome the weaknesses in the institution. Now, think about answers to each of these questions:

- What institutional goals do we meet?
- Whom do we serve?
- Where is the writing center located?
- What does the facility look like physically, and what image does that project?
- What resources do we have?
- How do we function within the daily/weekly/semester/yearly schedule?
- Who directs and works in the writing center?
- How is our staff trained?
- What services do we provide?
- What are our real goals and objectives?
- To whom do we report?
- How do we function within the institutional organization?

RESEARCH/RATIONALE

This book lists a plethora of resources that discuss writing center theory and practice, gives examples of outstanding writing centers, and provides Web sites of OWLS and discussion groups for all of us to use. The main question that we must answer in our rationale that demonstrates our knowledge is: "Why does our institution need a writing center or need to reinvent our writing center?" Through workshops at our regional and international conferences, we have opportunities to learn from others who have already gone through what we are trying to create/reinvent. Another important step that business planners take is to read the research on trends in their field. These predictions help in creating innovative strategies based on research. For instance, several of the books that I used for my strategic planning discussed the United States in the global 1990s, to know where we had been before looking at predictions of the workforce and higher education in the twenty-first century (Johnston & Packer; Parnell; Tough). We do not work in isolation and neither do our administrators/benefactors. In fact, they are often the ones who send us copies of articles from the *Wall Street Journal* or business periodicals to let us know what is going on in the business world. If we want to speak a language that they clearly understand, then we need to do our homework before presenting a plan.

Consider some suggestions for research before writing a rationale:

1. Check resources on writing center theory, business trends, new educational movements/ideas for the future, advancements in technology, global concerns, and workforce predictions.
2. Visit existing writing centers, virtually or live, and talk (e-mail, phone, live) with directors of similar models.
3. Consider which models of writing centers might best work at our institution.
4. Determine what ideas/information might best work in our own vision.

VISIONS

Now we are ready to create some strategic directions with scenarios and some organizational development. Create visions of the future and a preferred scenario. Strategic thinking should produce a long-term vision of the future based on an analysis of alternative scenarios and the specifications of the preferred scenario. Include an analysis of possible demographics: social, economic, technological, and political variables (Groff). By thinking about the demographics of the community within and outside the institution, we develop a better understanding of our need for outreach, changes in functions within the community, and skills that our students may need to develop for employment opportunities beyond our institution. What if the economy falls or rises? Each scenario would have a tremendous impact on the kind of writing center we would envision for the future. No, we cannot predict the future, but by being aware of possible scenarios, we can be prepared to grow/change organically to meet those variables. For example, what would happen if security suddenly became an issue on our campus so that the writing center could not be open in the evenings? In my first strategic plan, security became an issue that might impact both enrollment and hours of operation, so I did some research. I discovered that the administration had plans to change the location of the main entrance, to purchase unoccupied houses within several blocks beyond the campus, and to add secure, attractive fencing around the perimeter. This information enabled me to eliminate one of the negative scenarios that I had contemplated.

This part of the plan is both the most creative and the most time intensive. It is also important to start bouncing ideas off colleagues as well as other writing center directors. Because we know how situations change, we also do not want to limit the possibilities for future growth in planning. Consider each of these questions in creating this overall vision:

1. What other institutional goals might the writing center meet?
2. Whom might we serve?
3. Where would we imagine it to be located?
4. What will our dream facility look like physically?
5. What resources would we want?
6. How could we function within the daily/weekly/semester/yearly schedule?
7. Who would we want to direct and work with in the writing center?
8. How might we train staff?
9. What services would we like to provide?
10. What would we imagine as our goals and objectives for the future?
11. To whom should we report?
12. How would we imagine functioning within the institutional organization?

GOALS AND OBJECTIVES

If we think of goals as long term and objectives as short term, then we can probably make a list of three to five goals for our writing center. For instance, involving faculty in writing in all disciplines is a big goal, but our objectives may start with a faculty survey to determine what writing is already occurring in different disciplines. Then we might offer a practical writing workshop the first year to involve a small percentage of the faculty across disciplines because we are hoping that the word will spread to other colleagues. This objective might be the first one we list for Year One under our large goal. Basically, we are taking our vision, imagining what impact this writing center may have on our students, faculty, and larger community, then breaking down those goals into yearly attainable objectives. The nice part about all of this planning is that we have the ability to change/revise our plan each year based on how successful we are in meeting the objectives for the previous year and in dealing with changes in any of the variables. We also get to envision future plans as well because our predicted outcomes may be quite different from those in the short and long term as we proceed. For example, I originally had as an objective for the third year to apply for an NCTE Center of Excellence Award (Appendix C). That program is no longer in existence, so a more viable objective became involving faculty in writing center use in new and innovative ways. More specific details to meet this objective changed as technology enabled us to exchange and respond to student writing through the Internet.

NUTS AND BOLTS

All of these plans may seem quite abstract until we start nailing down the specific location, physical space, lighting, furniture, technology (hardware and software), use of space to convey the mission, staff training and employment, and scheduled procedures for meeting the objectives and goals. Teams are invaluable in doing this part. Let one person play the business officer of the institution, one an administrator, and one a classroom teacher so that they can ask the questions we need answered in listing the nuts and bolts. As I was selecting the location for the writing center, I also met with the director of technology to find out what computers the institution already owned and how they were using them. This meeting enabled me to coordinate compatible systems and use the same educational source for purchase and support of technology in the writing center. Because I had already used computers in a previous writing center, read about use of technology for writing, visited several writing centers with technology, and looked at layouts; I had a good idea of what would work in the space that I had been allotted. The room had two walls of windows on opposite sides, so by adding artwork on the other sides, I could create an aesthetically appealing space that did not focus on machines but on ideas and the senses. I even suggested that one of the English teachers attend the Michigan Tech summer institute on teaching writing with technology so that he would understand how my floor plan would work.

SEQUENCE/PROGRESSION OF THE PLAN

Using the preferred scenario, we can now take each goal with objectives and create a three-year plan for meeting them. We will include personnel, technology, role within the institution, physical space, and budget. In my original plan, for example, my second goal (Appendix C) was to improve student writing through the establishment of a writing center, yet the objectives follow a sequential plan that subtly leads to the third-year objective of the writing center becoming an integral part of the curriculum. People do not change easily, so the objectives built over three years allow students, faculty, and administration to discover the importance of the writing center. This sequence also allows for the building of resources, writing samples, essay competitions, and other writing-related activities. When I revise this original plan, I may keep some of the same goals in revised form (e.g., to update rather than create a writing center), but my objectives will change because of changes in all the variables we have previously discussed as well as the knowledge and experience of current students, faculty, and administration.

EVALUATION

Now that we have worked through our progression of the plan, we must be ready to think about how we will know that we have met our objectives and goals: Will we use standardized tests, holistic writing samples, attitudinal surveys, or peer review of set standards? Will there be formative (short-term) and summative (long-term) evaluations? Will we build into our plan to have a WPA onsite evaluation of our writing center at the end of the three years? What records will we be keeping during the year to help us evaluate what we have done? For instance, we may want to keep records of writing center use the first year; whereas, by the third year we may be ready to compare scores on the SAT writing samples or an institutional standardized writing test. Depending on the institutional mission, we may select an attitudinal survey, anecdotal report, or formative/summative evaluations by faculty and students using the writing center. During our first three years, we used sign-in sheets to keep records of writing center use. When students began to use the Internet or check their mail periodically during the school day, we realized that these sheets did not give us a clue as to who actually used the writing center for writing activities. Therefore, we changed our methods to keep more accurate records on shorter forms for all students who have individual conferences, to tally the number of classes whose students come to have their format checked, and to cluster other usage according to its purpose. Now we can talk in greater detail about specific use of the writing center, and we will probably come up with some new methods of evaluation of portfolios, for instance, in our next strategic plan.

BUDGETARY CONCERNS

Finally, the area we are least comfortable talking about has to become part of our plan. At this point, we must call on our writing center colleagues, other department planners within our institution, financial officers, as well as Internet sources to work out our budgets. Operating costs, salaries, and capital expenditures are all part of the budgetary concerns. In many institutions, basic operating costs come out of a schoolwide budget, whereas salaries may fall into a variety of budgets depending on our titles and positions within the institution as well as the budget lines for part-time and graduate student staff. Once we have found a source for purchase of major expenses such as technology and furniture, our annual budget may be limited to only supplies, travel, resources, and staff. Each institution will vary; however, creating this strategic plan with a realistic, and somewhat padded, budget will make it easier to find benefactors to enable the writing center plan to become a reality. I refer to the "somewhat padded budget" as the swimming pool plan. When we were submitting a plan for an expensive new secondary school in New Jersey, we offered the voters of the community the option of passing the budget to build the school with or without a swimming pool or defeating the budget. With that swimming pool option, voters had something to defeat while still voting for the new school. If we present something with options that can later be added, then we enable those with power to approve our plan while still maintaining some control.

My original summary of estimated costs for year one (Appendix D) demonstrates how much technological advancements impact the setup of a writing center. In 1991, we did not have access to the Internet so a server connected to fifteen computers provided a means of networking. I am especially surprised at the change in cost of printers. However, my plan to include money for guest artists remained for the first three-year plan before it became the swimming pool in the second plan. Through cost efficiency, I have been able to continue to offer guest workshops or presentations with money not used in other line items. I did not include membership in professional organizations and purchase of professional books in the original plan but added these items in the second year. Because the second-year estimated budget was much lower than the initial one because of the purchase of computers, I was able to add items and still be under the budget estimate of the first year. Also, once our actual budget expenses are lower than our estimate for the first year, then we can make revisions that demonstrate our good faith to stay within the estimated range for future years.

THREE-YEAR STRATEGIC PLAN

We are now ready to write out our multiyear plan of action. Each of us works in unique ways, so we might even find ourselves plotting on a graph a plan that goes well beyond the three-year plan submitted. I find it fun to look back at these earlier plans and see how the goals and objectives have been revised or remained the same years later. We may follow the components we have previously listed or design our own clear plan. My only warnings are to be as simple, clear, and direct as possible in the actual summary of the plan. Once again, I will restate the obvious for all writing center directors: Consider our purpose and audience above all else. If we look at the strategic plan for just goal two (Appendix C) and compare it with goal two on the three-year strategic summary plan (Appendix E), we can see the parallels clearly. An administrator may quickly look at the summary to get the overview of each goal without having to read all the details at once. Providing both the detailed plan after the introduction and rationale with the summary allows readers the option of finding answers to specific questions or looking at a one-page timeline.

We all need to get feedback from internal and external evaluators. Select key people within the institution who will be involved with the writing center and outside evaluators who have had experience as directors of writing centers at similar institutions—critical eyes who have dealt with pitfalls and successes are invaluable to us.

Good luck and allow plenty of time to get feedback from internal and external evaluators before the plan is submitted.

ANNUAL REPORT

Okay, we now have our plan approved, and we have just completed our first year. What happened? What worked and didn't work? What will happen in the second year? Again, we must present a clear, concise overview that offers answers to these questions. In our annual report we will include our original goals/objectives for this first year, then demonstrate how those goals were or were not met during the year. We will also list outcomes, evaluation data, actual budget compared to projected budget, conclusions, and recommendations (revisions of next year would be reflected here). In our annual report, we will emphasize what seems most important at our own institution. For instance, if the number of students served or the departments using the writing center is most important, then we will keep records and include this information. In future years, growth in certain areas by percentage may be most important. We must remind ourselves of how our audience may actually change from year to year, too.

My report for the first year restated the original goals from the summary of the three-year strategic plan (Appendix E), then took each goal and listed the ways in which we had met those goals during the 1991–92 school year. I also included a report of writing center use by semester, broken down into drop-ins, classes, and small groups. The report ended with my revised goals for the second year. Since we have been focusing on goal two, I have included the report for that particular goal in 1991–92 (Appendix F). In rereading this section, I am amazed at what I did and did not do during that first year that would have been more important or might have improved the relationship between faculty, students, and writing center. Each year's report helps one focus on priorities and revisions. Over the years, my annual reports have turned into PowerPoint presentations plus annual letters to the family that endowed the chair that I hold. We can never underestimate the value of good publicity and public relations as part of our current and future success.

CONCLUSIONS

All of this planning is hard work, involves many people working with us on the plan, and demands a great deal of our time. However, businesses do this kind of planning without batting an eye. The secret, which we are learning from all of this work, is that once we have done one multiyear strategic plan, it is much easier to revise and improve the following years. My second three-year plan had a format, previous goals to update, and basic research that I updated from my own reading, attending conference sessions and interacting with other writing center directors online. Also, I had experience in knowing my own institution better so that updating my own audit of strengths and weaknesses, looking at new long-range plans for the entire institution, and comparing the writing center plans with these enabled me to prepare a more efficient and effective plan for the future.

I have included the summary of my first three-year strategic plan (Appendix E) to demonstrate how a brief summary can give busy administrators an overview that they can absorb quickly. The detailed strategic plan must include such a summary even though we as writing center directors know how important it is to have an introduction, rationale, goals with detailed narrative, and conclusion. My plan describes a WAC-based writing center in a secondary school; however, the plan could apply to any level writing center. We will all note the changes in variables since 1991 that make this plan obsolete based solely on advances in technology; but the goals may still be valid. In February 2004, I did a preplanning activity with a group of writing center directors at the Southeastern Writing Center Association (SWCA) conference and discovered new plans I would like to implement. On our next break I am going to try another strategic plan with a different budget and new administrators, to see what happens!

WORKS CITED

Gluck, Frederick, Stephen Kaufman, and Steven Walleck. "The Four Phases of Strategic Management." *Journal of Business Strategy* 2 (Winter 1982): 9–21.

Groff, Warren H. *Human Resources Development: A Study Guide for the Core Seminar.* Ft. Lauderdale: Nova University Programs for Higher Education, 1990.

Johnston, William B., and Arnold H. Packer. *Workforce 2000: Work and Workers for the 21st Century.* Indianapolis: Hudson Institute, 1987.

Kinkead, Joyce, and Michael Pemberton. *The Center Will Hold: Critical Perspectives on Writing Center Scholarship.* Ed. Michael A. Pemberton and Joyce Kinkead. Logan: Utah State UP, 2003.

Mullin, Joan, and Ray Wallace, eds. *Intersections: Writing Center Theory/Practice.* NCTE: Urbana, IL, 1994.

Murphy, Christina, and Joe Law, eds. *Landmark Essays on Writing Centers.* Davis, CA: Hermagoras, 1995.

Parnell, Dale. *Dateline 2000: The New Higher Education Agenda.* Alexandria, VA: American Association of Community and Junior College Books, 1990.

Silk, Bobbie Bayliss, ed. *The Writing Center Resource Manual.* 2nd ed. Emmitsburg, MD: NWCA Press, 1998.

Tough, Allen H. *Crucial Questions about the Future.* Lanham, MD: Univ. Press of America, 1991.

Appendix A: Strategic Plan Components

- Introduction
- Rationale
- Goals with Objectives
- Three-Year Implementation Plan
- Conclusion
- Bibliography
- Attached Detailed Budget Estimate for Each Year
- Appropriate Documentation/Support Materials

Appendix B: Prioritizing In The Writing Center: Visions And Reality

What happens when we design or inherit a writing center? Everyone has certain visions of what will happen in that writing center; however, once the students and faculty arrive, the director learns that priorities change with reality. The reality of the writing center is influenced by the director's vision, but also by the visions of administrators, faculty, tutors, and students. No writing center director has the luxury of unlimited resources; the director must prioritize the goals of the writing center to account for budget issues, staff, student and faculty needs, and time constraints, for instance. To accomplish these goals, the director should set long-term and short-term priorities for the writing center. This workshop will guide participants through creating a three-year strategic plan, working within a budget, imagining and role playing real-life scenarios, and adapting the realities of an organic writing center.

Step One
Take five minutes to describe your writing center. If you do not have a writing center yet, you may skip this step and spend more time with the next one.

Step Two
Now, take another five minutes to describe your dream of a perfect writing center.

Step Three
Share your two descriptions with a partner. Together, list what you need to do to create your dream center, and the list cannot include the "elimination" of an administrator!

Step Four
Now reverse roles with your partner and repeat step three through the same process.

Step Five
Now that you have your list, you can begin to create your vision for the future of your own writing center. Consider how you might meet specific goals over a period of three years. Consider the progression as part of your plan.

Step Six
Begin to create your three-year plan using the format on the following page.

First Steps to Creating a Three-Year Plan

My Vision   My Goals

Overall

Year One

Year Two

Year Three

Budget for Each Year

Year One

Year Two

Year Three

Total Budget for the Three-Year Plan

Appendix C: Goal Two

Improve student writing through the establishment of a writing center

Objectives

1. To create a writing center.
2. To encourage staff to send students to use the writing center as a low-risk environment in which to write.
3. To train peer tutors and staff to work with students in the writing center to improve writing.
4. To provide faculty with mini-lessons and classroom writing workshops to improve writing.
5. To promote attitudinal changes of staff so that students will see more importance given to writing.
6. To improve student writing by using more writing and revising all subject areas.
7. To increase student performance on writing assessments, writing competitions.
8. To encourage student publication of writing.
9. To offer a professional library of materials on writing as a resource for students.

Year One

One of the duties of an endowed chair of composition will be to design a writing center facility to provide students with a low-risk environment. Students will have a place where writing response and feedback are encouraged. Response from peers or teachers produces superior results (Braddock, 1963; Diederich, 1974). Networked computers, funded by a grant, will be available in the writing center. Through public relations, guest artists, and special programs, students will recognize the writing center as a place where there is a reverence for writing. For instance, a day devoted to careers in writing, college application essays, poetry reading, or how to get published would help create a positive atmosphere. By assessing writing problems, faculty will utilize the writing center staff to present classroom mini-lessons or writing workshops across the curriculum. Each year student scores on national tests will be monitored to note changes in writing abilities and particular problem areas.

Year Two

Through a peer tutoring course, students will be trained to function as tutors in the writing center. By working with peers, tutors will recognize and correct some of their own writing problems. The writing center environment and the classroom teacher will determine student attitudes towards writing. Through the use of a writing survey, faculty will be able to determine how effective their writing activities and use of the writing center have been. Announcements of writing competitions will be posted in the writing center. Faculty will be encouraged to have students enter writing contests in all subject areas. Through school-wide writing contests, students and staff will be given recognition for outstanding writing. Faculty will be encouraged to refer students to the writing center and also to use the facility for class writing improvement activities. The director will keep up-to-date articles and books available in the writing center library. Faculty records of writing activities will also be kept in this area.

Year Three

The writing center will become an integral part of the curriculum. Students and staff will associate the writing center with writing improvement at any stage of the writing process. Faculty will also use the facility to work on their own writing. With the addition of a complete professional library of books, periodicals, writing activities and software, faculty and students will use the writing center also as a resource to improve writing. The writing center director will conduct a complete evaluation of student progress in writing. The writing center will apply for an NCTE Center of Excellence Award.

Appendix D: Summary Of Estimated Costs For Three-Year Plan—Year One (1991–92)

Hardware

15 Classic 40 Computers (M0406LL/A)	$16,656.15
3 HP Deskwriter Printers for Macintosh	2,175.00
1 Macintosh LC 2MB Hard Disk with color system	1,925.46
1 Personal LaserWriter NT w/local talk (B0341LL/A)	2,249.00
1 Fileserver system	4,214.28
Teacher's work station, chair, vertical files	500.00
Work tables, computer & printer tables and chairs, whiteboards, bulletin board	5,000.00

Software

Communications software	$5,000.00
Paper and computer supplies	1,000.00

Faculty Development

Writing Across the Curriculum Retreats	$2,700.00
Guest writers, consultants, presenters	5,000.00
Caldwell Chair conference travel budget	3,000.00

Total	**$49,919.89**

Appendix E: Three-Year Plan

Goal	Year One	Year Two	Year Three
Implement writing to think and writing to learn activities into classrooms across the curriculum	Train staff (20%) WAC committee In-service workshops (mentors) Publication of faculty newsletter Record of lessons as resources	Train staff (40%) Community of writers Enlarged network Publications and presentations Curriculum changes Implement writing to think and learn activities	Train staff (64%) Community of writers Larger network Regional and National publications and presentations More curriculum changes Collaboration of faculty on grants and projects
Improve student writing through the establishment of a writing center	Design writing center with networked computers Create positive environment with special programs Encourage use of writing center by students and faculty	Train peer tutors Conduct student writing survey Create writing resource library Promote writing competitions and faculty referrals of students to the writing center	Implement full use of staffed writing center Encourage faculty use of writing center for their own writing Revise response to writing based on student writing survey Apply for NCE Center of Excellence
Involve alumni and community in writing across the curriculum programs	Use public relations to inform alumni and community of writing across disciplines Conduct an alumni survey to determine writing needs Offer writing work-shops on alumni weekend and even-ings throughout the year	Use public relations to make alumni and community aware of student writing performance Revise writing workshop to meet alumni needs Train parent volunteers for writing center Establish The McCallie Press	Use public relations to encourage writing across disciplines by alumni and community Adapt writing work-shops to alumni needs Volunteer to offer workshops for parents Support The McCallie Press

©1991 Farrell, Three-Year Strategic Plan

Appendix F: Goals For 1991-92—Goal Two

1. Improve student writing through the establishment of a writing center.

   a. Writing center assistants participate in voluntary writing workshops and activities to help them improve their writing.

   b. Writers club meets every week during Z period to share works in progress, try new approaches to pieces of writing, and discuss concerns about writing.

   c. Teachers have folders on the file server to use for class writing projects in Bible, Spanish, French, English, history, and biology.

   d. Teachers have met with the director throughout the year for suggestions on teaching techniques to improve writing in all subject areas.

   e. The writing center director has taught lessons on essay writing in history classes, ways to improve short stories in English classes, and techniques for writing research papers in a variety of courses.

   f. Students and staff use the writing center all day, every day. As I write, history, biology, Spanish, French, and English teachers are working in the writing center. During the first semester of 1991-92, 3,148 students and 127 classes used the writing center. In the second semester (as of April 7, 1992), 2,368 students and 95 classes have used the facility. Also, individual conferences or small-group conferences in the second semester total 53.

   g. The director has worked with the NCTE Achievement in Writing nominee on revising his writing samples and preparing for the impromptu, timed writing for entry in the competition. The director also proctored the impromptu 75-minute essay.

   h. Guest artists in the writing center help to create a positive attitude towards writing and improve writing through individual and class readings, presentations, workshops, and critiques.

   Peter Stillman, author, poet, and English editor, worked with eighth graders on use of detail and personal narratives. He read from *Gilead* and gave writing assignments from *Families Writing*. He also gave a prose reading to the creative writing class and a writing across the curriculum workshop for faculty.

   Earl Braggs, poet and UTC English professor, gave a reading from *Hats* and a lecture on "What is Poetry?" for students and faculty in the writing center.

   Tim Seibles, award-winning poet, read from his latest collections and answered student and faculty questions about writing poetry. Students eagerly purchased his books, which he autographed.

   Gary Goshgarian, novelist, editor of *Contemporary Reader* and *Exploring Language* texts, and professor of English at Northeastern University, critiqued the short stories of students in tenth grade English and creative writing. He also held individual conferences with students in other classes and critiqued their short fiction that they had mailed to him before his arrival.

Malcolm Childers, artist of etchings and poet, presented his works to creative writing and art classes to make the connections between visual and written art. Through slides and original works displayed around the writing center, he read his poems and answered student questions.

Toi Derricotte, award-winning poet and visiting artist at University of Pittsburgh, gave a devotional on finding the creativity within, lead poetry workshops with two classes and one faculty group. Her latest collection, *Captivity*, has won rave reviews.

i. McCallie published the *National Directory of Writing Centers*, edited by Pamela Farrell for the National Writing Centers Association. Since McCallie is also listed in the directory, this publication gives us national exposure in two ways—the title page and the listing.

7

"If You Fail to Plan, You Plan to Fail": Strategic Planning and Management for Writing Center Directors

Kelly Lowe
Mount Union College

*The changes in writing centers—in what they mean and how they have been used, funded, and adminis-
tered over the last decade—should tell us that fluidity is a fact we must accept.*
—Jeanne Simpson ("What Lies Ahead for Writing Centers")

Of the many predictions of where writing centers are going in the future (and there are
many), perhaps none is as eloquent, or as true, as Jeanne Simpson's 1985 piece, "What Lies
Ahead for Writing Centers." Simpson's argument is simple: Writing centers have achieved,
both locally and nationally, a modicum of success; with this success, however, has come a tremendous tendency toward complacency (57). Writing center directors and staff, both new and
old, need to resist this pull toward self-satisfaction. Simpson's "answer" to this concern is to
look at the issue of professionalism and the writing center director, arguing that directors must
think of themselves as fully integrated parts of the academic culture (and, indeed, that academic institutions need to look at directors as more than clerks).

In presenting her argument, Simpson cited the work of the National Writing Centers Association's Professional Concerns Committee, arguing, among other things, that a good center
director should have some knowledge of or training in accounting, basic business administration, personnel management, records management, and decision making (60). This chapter
expands on the idea that center directors have much to learn from management and adminis-

trative theory. It is an idea that is discussed in writing center scholarship with some frequency, and then, for a number of reasons, dropped.[1] I would like to develop the idea that writing center directors, both new and experienced, need to be strategic planners of the first order. In making this argument I would like to present a second, meta-argument—namely, that writing center directors need to resist the temptation, often presented in writing center scholarship, that academic administration is somehow part of an evil empire that is "out to get" writing centers and their directors.[2]

WHAT IS STRATEGIC PLANNING?

Strategic planning is a way of planning for the future while taking into account local variables and the increasingly competitive environment of higher education. A number of competing ideas about strategic planning are available to center directors, and what I hope to do in this chapter is look at some of these ideas and apply them to issues that are or might be of particular importance to writing center directors.

According to Robert Grant, the following "characteristics of strategy" are "conducive to success" (11): goals that are simple, consistent, and long term; profound understanding of the competitive environment; objective appraisal of resources; and effective implementation.

These four "steps" or "goals," obviously (although it must be said), are not magic. Indeed, several conflicting paradigms exist with/in the world of strategic planning/management, the two most prevalent being the "rationalist-analytical" and "crafting" (as represented by the work of Henry Mintzberg). Although crafting is probably the most immediately appealing theory for humanists (because it tends to depend on "a feeling of intimacy and harmony with the materials at hand" and an overemphasis on informal research design and qualitative data; Grant 27), it is also "susceptible to the whims and preferences of individual managers, to contemporary fads, and to wishful thinking" (27). So my goal is to provide writing center directors with specific tools to enable them to discuss their writing centers with the people who make budgetary and personnel decisions. To that end, I've tried to draw from both competing theories.

One of the predominant sayings in business is the one that goes "if we fail to plan, we plan to fail" (Holloway 2). This is, of course, a troublesome cliché for many in academe because one can never really know what to plan for. In a situation as people intensive as academics is and one that tends to ebb and flow according to a variety of unpredictable factors (e.g., the financial strength of the institution; the ability and determination of the students who are on campus at any one time; the "feeling" that the faculty and staff have for the writing center at any given moment; the campus climate for writing; the administration; and the home department), strategic planning and management can be an iffy proposition at best. According to one planning theorist, strategic planning is somewhat unpredictable even in the most stable of industries because most plans are based on "the assumption of a continuation of present trends

---

[1] In other words, you find "nods" toward discussion(s) of management paradigms (see, e.g., Hobson and Lowe); or complaints that academic programs are being asked to adopt a more businesslike set of strategies (Haviland et al.; Summerfield). Perhaps the most complex treatment of this issue, although not directly addressing it, is Murphy and Law's "The Disappearing Writing Center within the Disappearing Academy."

[2] This is certainly a concern (as I write this, the WPA listserv is burning with outrage over the changes to the University of Florida's Writing Program), but I think that the cold hard fact is that writing centers, like all other entities in a college, need to consider the college/university as a marketplace and need to be able to compete in said market.

in consumption, economic growth, employment, or other factors" (Holloway 3). Of course, as most people in the academy know, "present trends" are dicey words. The real value/necessity of strategic planning/management, then, is that it both, as Holloway wrote, "simulates and stimulates" (4).

I will take on faith the fact that many in the traditional arts and humanities are less than interested in applying business strategy/theory to their academic programs. But, as Charles Hill and Gareth Jones indicated in *Strategic Management: An Integrated Approach*, "even a small not-for-profit organization … has to make decisions about how best to generate revenues, given the environment in which it is based and the organization's own strengths and weaknesses" (4–5).

The writing center at Mount Union College has succeeded for a variety of reasons, but primarily because of careful analysis, planning, and management. The basic steps we have taken in strategic management are as follows:

- Establish a mission
- Select objectives
- Set goals
- Analyze strengths and weaknesses
- Study threats and opportunities
- Prepare planning documents
- Ensure implementability
- Review the process

Of course a writing center director, especially one who is taking over an established program, probably does not have the luxury of going through these steps in order every year. Let me give you an example of how one might use the idea of strategic planning.

I immediately faced a crisis on my arrival at Mount Union College nine years ago: a dean who was demanding that I provide him with a detailed budget request. I did some analysis before I turned this document in to him; part of this analysis was the process of creating a mission and goals statement for the writing center. According to Thompson and Strickland, "Among all the things that managers do, few affect organizational performance more lastingly than how well the management team handles the tasks of charting the organization's long-term direction, developing strategic moves and approaches, and executing the strategy in ways that produce the intended results" (3). Holloway explained that a mission statement is "a statement of what an organization is, why it exists, and the unique contribution it can make" (17). Writing a mission statement for a writing center can be difficult for a number of reasons, especially if the center is already an ongoing concern. One particular worry is that there may be founding administrators who have emotional and professional stakes in the program and who want to leave a legacy in terms of the program's administrative guiding philosophy.[3]

In creating a mission statement for the writing center, directors should do the following:

1. Define the organization's business;

---

[3]For more on this see McNamara's "Founder's Syndrome: How Founders and Their Organizations Recover."

2. State the major goals; and
3. State the organization's philosophy (Hill & Jones 31).

Center directors should confer with as many of the stakeholders on campus (the dean, the former administrator, and writing center tutors, faculty, and students) as possible.[4]

After defining the *philosophy*, it is important to define the *business* of the writing center. The rest of the mission statement should include concrete information about how the center is going to execute this philosophy. Depending on the campus situation, a director might include information about working with: faculty; the campus on the creation, assessment, and maintenance of writing intensive courses; the coordination of First Year Composition (FYC) placement; and the relation between the writing center and the writing across the curriculum program. After revising the mission statement and determining what the program is and isn't going to do, it is important to establish the program's *goals*. A writing center should have both new and ongoing goals written with the idea that there are various stakeholders in the campus community. A center director needs to make sure each of these stakeholders is kept informed about what the writing center is doing. Similarly, the director needs to understand the desires of the stakeholders and must work to meet those desires or else risk rebellion, retaliation, or worse.[5]

This early work on mission and goals is perhaps the most important work a writing center administrator will do. My work with several local, nonprofit groups in my town over the last couple of years has shown me the real value of a mission statement. It is perhaps the most important document your program can have. Not only does it spell out what you will and won't do, it can, in times of struggle, protect you from being (intentionally) misunderstood by others.

STRENGTHS, WEAKNESSES, AND THREATS

The next two steps in strategic planning involve analysis, or looking at your own strengths and weaknesses as a director, and examining any possible threats to the existence of the writing center. According to Hill and Jones, the most important factor to consider when doing an internal/strengths and weaknesses evaluation is to identify what are called *distinctive competencies* (91). Essentially, each organization has unique strengths that even its closest competitors

---

[4]After completing this process, here's what I came up with: *The College Writing Center promotes excellence in writing and written communication by helping, in a variety of situations and sites, students become better writers, readers, and critical thinkers.*

[5]During my first year as director, I presented the following goals to the dean and the writing committee:
- Increase visibility in terms of community and on campus. Make sure descriptions of the writing center are in all of the materials students have/get (catalogue, handbook, first-year orientation materials); send "talking points" to the administrator of public relations and president so they can include the writing center in their discussions of "what's new" on campus.
- Hold open house in the writing center during beginning of each semester to introduce teachers and students to the writing center, the WAC program (including WAC requirement), and the writing goals.
- Work with administrator of new faculty seminar to have the writing center included on that agenda.
- Work with administrator of student orientation about having writing center administrator address new students and their parents about placement, WAC, the writing center, and goals.

Note that these were the goals for a new center, and as we progressed toward financial stability and administrative recognition our goals changed accordingly.

can't match.[6] Management theorists have identified several key areas in which distinctive competence can be found: the experience curve, the product-process life cycle, the selection of target market segments, the design of a marketing mix, positioning, materials management, research and development, human resources, information systems, and financial resources (Hill & Jones 91–119; Thompson & Strickland 89–107).

Another way of looking at this process is to ask five simple questions about the writing center:

1. How well is its present strategy working?
2. What are the strengths, weaknesses, opportunities, and threats (often referred to as SWOT analysis) of the writing center?
3. Is the writing center competitive (for money? for institutional respect?)?
4. How strong is the writing center's competitive position (within the college? externally?)?
5. What strategic issues does the writing center face?

These five questions will go a long way toward identifying a writing center's strengths and weaknesses. Thompson and Strickland defined strength as "something a [program] is good at doing or a characteristic that gives it an important capability" while a weakness is "something the a [program] lacks or does poorly comparison to others" (91).

It is important to be honest and to remember that the various audiences for this analysis—from the dean, to the department chair, to various directors of other academic programs, as well as students, tutors, parents, and faculty may well all have a different analysis of a writing center's strengths and weaknesses than the center director does.

It is important to complete not only an internal evaluation, but also an external evaluation as well. An external evaluation is generally the most difficult aspect of any academic analysis because many people in academics wish to work in a non- or countercorporate environment and like to maintain the illusion that all departments and faculty are in it together. Be that as it may, it is true that budgets at all institutions are finite, and there is always competition for resources. It is important for writing center administrators to look at the environment in which they operate and to analyze who else is in competition for the various resources available. In other words, a center director should have a clear grasp of the institution's administrative structure in terms of where the center's budget comes from and who else is in direct competition for the same dollars.[7]

When assessing the institutional environment, it is important to pay special attention to a few key indicators. The first is the technological environment, which prompts such questions as: How are changes in technology affecting the writing center? How are changes in campus technology challenging the center's mission/goals? Is an Online Writing Lab (OWL) a good idea, or a bad one, for the institution's situation and resources? Is there external pressure to trade technology for human resources? Are people on campus talking about distance learning and, if so, what will the writing center's place in a distance learning program be?

---

[6]Areas like Academic Support and Student Placement, at times, have been competitive with the Writing Center for money, students, and publicity; for example, in 1996, Placement, Academic Support, the Library, and the Writing Center all wanted to do a workshop for students about resumes and job hunting—it became a battle when no one would back down or collaborate with another group.

[7]At our institution it was the Academic Support Center, Library, and Computer Help Desk. All were able to make compelling cases for constant budget increases.

The second environment to analyze is the social environment, which also includes social changes in the culture. Key questions here might be: Has the campus climate for writing shifted? What about the ways writing is being taught? What are others on campus doing with respect to academic support? Are instructors more or less aware of the writing center than they were five years ago?

The third environment is the demographic environment, specifically with the composition of the student body and faculty. Issues that might arise in a study of demographics could include a look at SAT/ACT scores; placement rates in first-year composition courses; breakdown of students by language ability and the possible need in the writing center for English as a second language (ESL) training and increased flexibility in placement and instruction in writing; and an assessment of the current faculty in terms of their knowledge of process versus product, writing across the curriculum, writing and technology, and so forth.

The final environment is political and legal. On our campus, the writing center has served as a very visible flash point in the ongoing war on plagiarism by many faculty. Consequently, the center has needed to take the lead in disseminating information about changes in citation styles and to educate the faculty about what might constitute plagiarism and on how faculty might work with students (or might investigate their own pedagogy) to keep plagiarism from being a factor in a course. Other legal issues involve types of information that can be given to instructors about student performance. What can we tell parents? What sort of relationship should the writing center tutors have with instructors or with students?

According to Hill and Jones, "[S]uperior performance is the product of a fit between strategy and the environment. In order to achieve such a fit, strategic managers must be able to identify environmental opportunities and threats" (86), and a true strategic manager will be able to use the opportunities and counter the threats.

PLANNING AND IMPLEMENTATION

Most writing centers are awash in documentation of some sort: tutor training manuals, writing across the curriculum (WAC) manuals, and resource collections; writing center response sheets (and/or other kinds of record keeping); a mission statement or two; goals statements; placement instruments; measurement documents; and all manner of studies. In strategic management theory, the "planning documents" stage involves what Holloway called the quantification and consolidation of the previous steps (mission, objectives, goals, strength and weakness analysis, threat analysis). The planning documents involve creating a credible paper trail of the processes to date. These documents should include models of financial, staffing, and usage projections well into the future (most strategists say five to ten years minimum). Planning documents should also include a discussion of what is to be accomplished in what time frame and by whom. These documents might include a flow chart or other organizational documentation with well-established lines of reporting relationships built in.[8]

Successful completion of the documents stage involves the writing center administrator's ability to communicate to others on campus just what it is the writing center can (and cannot)

---

[8]In other words, never take for granted the "informal" arrangements you have with other programs, departments, centers, offices, or administrative entities. Put them on paper and publish them!

do. A good relationship with admissions (to get good, realistic, and reliable admissions projections, including demographics for incoming classes), the budget office, and the academic officers on campus is crucial for the completion of this project.

The implementation stage is simply the conversion of the strategic plan "into action and then into results" (Thompson & Strickland 216). There is much discussion in management texts about implementation and the organizational structures that the new strategy might take. The two main organizational processes, according to Hill and Jones, are *differentiation* and *integration*. Differentiation involves the ways in which an organization "allocates people and resources to organizational tasks," including the distribution of decision making authority (223). Integration refers to the way in which the parts (as determined by differentiation) are combined. The operating metaphor is chemical: Differentiation would be separate atoms, whereas integration would create the bonds between the atoms that help the atoms form a unique chemical compound (223). The implementation stage, then, is about uniting the total organization behind the idea of accomplishing the strategic plan/goals (Thompson & Strickland 216).

The first, and most important, question one has to ask during the implementation stage is "who will be responsible for carrying out the strategic plan?" This consideration involves getting all members of the organization to ask, "What is required for us to implement our part of the overall plan, and how can we best get it done?" (Thompson & Strickland 217). Implementation is largely about leadership. Thus, the success or failure of a strategic plan is largely about how the administrator leads/implements the process, with one caveat: The way administrators go about the implementation process is, of course, a function of their experience and accumulated knowledge of the site/situation (218).

CONCLUSIONS

The conclusions section of this chapter is rather open-ended. One thing I love most about academics is that, despite our common purpose from institution to institution (i.e., to educate students to be better writers and thinkers and citizens), each is different, and, with demographic changes from year to year, each site has constantly evolving needs and responsibilities. I would hope that this chapter can serve as a stimulus to a larger, more systematic discussion of strategic planning and writing center administration. I would, however, like to leave you with an interesting idea. In "What Strategists Can Learn From Sartre," Stanford Research Institute analyst James Ogilvy argued that the real value of strategic planning is that it helps us to avoid having to react to "the moment of urgency" (43). And although I would argue that many writing centers do excellent work in planning for some things (I've not known of a writing center that doesn't have its tutors work through some set of scenarios for tutoring), I would also argue that, in many of the same writing centers, there is a sort of day-to-day exigency in terms of budgeting and planning that, in times of crisis, will allow only the more strategically organized academic programs to survive.

WORKS CITED

Grant, Robert. *Contemporary Strategy Analysis*. 4th ed. Masden, MA: Blackwell, 2002.

Haviland, Carol, et al. "The politics of Administrative and Physical Location." *The Politics of Writing Centers.* Ed. Jane Nelson and Kathy Evertz. Portsmouth, NH: Heinemann-Boynton/Cook, 2001. 85–98.

Hill, Charles, and Gareth Jones. *Strategic Management: An Integrated Approach.* Boston: Houghton Mifflin, 1989.

Hobson, Eric, and Kelly Lowe. "An Audit of the National Writing Centers Association's Growth." *The Politics of Writing Centers.* Ed. Jane Nelson and Kathy Evertz. Portsmouth, NH: Heinemann-Boynton/Cook, 2001. 110–20.

Holloway, Clark. *Strategic Planning.* Chicago: Nelson-Hall, 1986.

Murphy, Christina and Joe Law. "The Disappearing Writing Center within the Disappearing Academy." *The Politics of Writing Centers.* Ed. Jane Nelson and Kathy Evertz. Portsmouth, NH: Heinemann-Boynton/Cook, 2001. 133–45.

McNamara, C. "Founder's Syndrome: How Founders and Their Organizations Recover." *Nonprofit World* 16.6 (1988): 38–41.

Ogilvy, James. "What Sartre Can Teach Business Strategists." *Strategy + Business* 33 (Winter 2003): 38–47.

Simpson, Jeanne. "What Lies Ahead for Writing Centers: Position Statement on Professional Concerns." *The Writing Center Journal* 5.2/6.1 (1985): 35–39. Rpt. in *Landmark Essays on Writing Centers.* Ed. Christina Murphy and Joe Law. Davis, CA: Hermagoras Press, 1995. 57–62.

Summerfield, Judith. "Writing Centers: A Long View." *The Writing Center Journal* 8.2 (1988): 3–9. Rpt. in *Landmark Essays on Writing Centers.* Ed. Christina Murphy and Joe Law. Davis, CA: Hermagoras Press, 1995, 63–70.

Thompson, Arthur, and A.J. Strickland. *Strategic Management: Concepts and Cases.* 5th ed. Boston: BPI/Irwin, 1990.

8

A Call for Racial Diversity in the Writing Center

Margaret Weaver
Southwest Missouri State University

Because so many writing center administrators are white, because the professional organization is pre-dominantly white, most of our programmatic and professional decisions have been based on assumptions informed by white experience.

—Nancy Barron and Nancy Maloney Grimm (72)

No one is prejudiced[1] any more," announced a student in my first freshman Composition course at Southwest Missouri State University. I resisted the urge to speak. No one spoke; the majority of students simply nodded their heads in agreement.

I should not have been surprised,[2] according to Barron and Grimm, by my students' responses (or lack of responses). Eighty-eight percent of the students on our campus are identified by the Office of Institutional Research as "White, Non-Hispanic" (*Factbook* 3). "These beliefs [e.g., 'no one is prejudiced any more'] keep white Americans comfortable," contended Barron and Grimm, "and they protect white Americans from accepting responsibility for honest dialogue about racial differences" (64). "Colorblindness" is the term that Barron and

---

[1]Beverly Daniel Tatum offered a useful clarification regarding the term *prejudice* that helps to explain my own motivation for linking this White student's comment to racism:

> A distinction must be made between the negative racial attitudes held by individuals of color and White individuals, because it is only the attitudes of Whites that routinely carry with them the social power inherent in the systematic cultural reinforcement and institutionalization of those racial prejudices. To distinguish the prejudices of students of color from the racism of White students is not to say that the former is acceptable and the latter is not; both are clearly problematic. The distinction is important, however, to identify the power differential between members of dominant and subordinate groups. (3)

[2]I confess that I still, even ten years later, marvel at this student's remark. I continue to hear it whispered in subtle ways in my classes.

Grimm preferred to use when referring to this desire to pretend that racial differences do not exist. To counteract this colorblindness, they suggested that Whites follow the advice given by Helen Fox. Fox recommended that Whites start by examining their own stories about race.

KEEPING TRACK OF MINORITY STUDENTS

Writing center practitioners tell stories about race, particularly when we are making programmatic and professional decisions. I begin with one thread on WCenter. In December 1996, Michael Pemberton initiated a discussion he labeled "keeping track of minority students." His post requested that other directors share how and if they keep track of minority students who visit the writing center. Before this request, however, he offered the following about his own views regarding race: "I think the center should be perceived as a place where race doesn't matter—and it doesn't matter in conferences. But I can't escape the reality that it DOES matter to many groups with a variety of vested interests for a variety of reasons" (his emphasis).

Pemberton never acknowledged the irony in his statement (nor does anyone comment on it), but he, too, has a vested interest in the belief that race does not matter. If race does not matter in the writing center, then it can be ignored and no record need be kept on the number of minority students who seek assistance in the writing center. If race does not matter, then writing center directors do not have to assume responsibility for honest dialogue about racial differences. Another version of this was supplied by Deborah Martinson: "Diversity is a given here [at my institution]." This reply mirrors my own initial response to diversity. The historical overview I originally provided in the proposal for this chapter sounds remarkably, although not surprisingly, similar to Martinson's:

> My first position after leaving graduate school was as the Director of the Writing Center at Incarnate Word College (now the University of the Incarnate Word) in San Antonio, Texas. In this geographical area in such close proximity to Mexico and home to a plethora of military bases, *diversity was a given. Diversity was not something that needed to be addressed.* The student population at the College was quite diverse, so the tutors and clientele of the writing center were, by default, diverse. No active recruitment was required to achieve diversity either in the tutoring staff or the center's clientele. *It was a safe position for a white female writing center director; I didn't have to manage diversity.* (emphasis added)

Writing center directors have a vested interest in remaining "colorblind" and pretending that color makes no difference. "It is easier to believe that race doesn't affect what we do in writing centers" (Barron and Grimm 68).

"I'M NOT RACIST MYSELF, BUT I KNOW PEOPLE WHO ARE …"

This stance of colorblindness has been fueled by the field's adherence to noninterventionist pedagogy. Articles such as Mark Hartstein's 1984 "Objectivity in Tutoring" and Jeff Brooks's 1991 "Minimalist Tutoring: Making the Student Do All the Work" have served as a foundation for writing center pedagogy. As their titles suggest, the assumption has been that writing center tutors should remain objective/neutral, and more importantly, *can* remain objective/neutral (that differences in race do not really matter).[3] One of Pemberton's *Writing Lab Newsletter*

---

[3]This stance of objectivity/neutrality is usually readily accepted by student tutors because, as Linda Brodkey discussed, students have been taught that neutrality and objectivity are possible and that "objectivity is good and subjectivity is bad" (199).

"Ethics" columns even reminds writing center practitioners to consider "the legal, social, and ethical consequences of actually trying to influence a student's beliefs or feelings or arguments" (10). Following in this vein, Steve Sherwood warned that, if tutors intervene and voice their opinion, they could risk silencing students from more fully exploring their own ideas. He suggested that "most of us [as tutors] would sooner censor ourselves—refusing to reveal our opinions on issues for fear of being too directive—than censor a student writer" (52). This fear of censorship prohibits honest dialogue, especially about racial differences.

The earliest encounter that I recall with someone of color was my first-grade teacher. She was a large woman with an Alto II voice. One day when I was talking in class to a student behind me, she grabbed my hand and slapped it hard with a ruler. It was the first and only time I have been hit by another person; it was the first and only time that I have had a teacher of color.

The desire for "peerness" has also contributed to the field's colorblindness. Practitioners have claimed that the writing center provides an alternative learning environment that differs significantly from the traditional classroom because the writing center relies on "peer" tutors. John Trimbur's description is particularly telling: "The tutors' loyalty to their peers results from their shared status as undergraduates. Both tutors and tutees find themselves at the bottom of the academic hierarchy.... This common position in the traditional hierarchy, moreover, tends to create social bonds among students, to unionize them" (290). The assumption has been that if students realize that the tutors are also students, they will also recognize that they share the same deadline pressures and experience the same fear in regard to judgment by their professors. This, then, will create a sense of peerness or "community" (Bruffee 8).

Janet Helms's model of White racial identity development provides some understanding into why noninterventionist pedagogy and peerness have been adopted widely by writing center practitioners who, as Barron and Grimm pointed out, are predominantly White. She identified six stages of development experienced by Whites: Contact, Disintegration, Reintegration, Pseudo-Independent, Immersion/Emersion, and Autonomy. The Contact stage is characterized by a sense of naiveté in regard to racism. My student's statement would be an example of this stage in which the individual is almost oblivious to racial issues as a result of having very little interaction with people of color. When White individuals become aware of racism and how they are implicated (intentionally or unintentionally) in its continuation, the individuals enter the Disintegration stage. This stage is followed by the Reintegration stage in which the person may accept the status quo and express anger toward those people of color who have caused the discomfort. It is at this stage that Helms found many Whites remain, especially if they can avoid future interactions with people of color. The desire to find more information about people of color and racism marks the Pseudo-Independent stage, and when the individual begins to search for another, more comfortable White identity, this is the Immersion/Emersion stage. Ultimately, the Autonomy stage signals the internalization of this new self identity, and the person is then able to develop an individualized action plan for combating racism.

Like most stage models, Helm's model simplifies a complex process into a reductionist linear sequence and so has difficulty accounting for stages that are bypassed or repeated. Regardless of these limitations, however, her model provides a useful lens through which to examine our programmatic decisions. Our decision to adopt noninterventionist tutoring techniques and to hire student tutors suggests that many White writing center practitioners are enmeshed in the Disintegration stage. Beverly Daniel Tatum wrote that "at this stage, the bliss of ignorance or lack of awareness is replaced by the discomfort of guilt, shame, and sometimes anger at the recognition of one's own advantage because of being White and the acknowledgment of the role of White in the maintenance of a racist system. Attempts to reduce discomfort may include denial" (13), making statements such as "Race doesn't matter" and "Diversity is a given" and "I'm not a racist."[4] Perhaps most notable is the omission of race in the (Inter)National Writing Centers Association's *Proposed Self-Study Questionnaire for Writing Center Accreditation*. Under "Population Served," writing center directors are simply asked to indicate number of clients served according to the categories of faculty, staff, students, alumni, and community, unless the center has a "program-specific population of students" (Paoli, Silver, & Tarvers). That is, race only matters *if* it assists in funding.

Denial is simply another word for colorblindness. Denial is a way to reduce the cognitive dissonance that many White writing center directors feel. It's much safer when we do not have to take responsibility for managing diversity.

"JUST TYPE UP WHAT YOU JUST TOLD ME"

Barron labeled the following as "A Story to Begin." Indeed, she provided a description of a writing center session she had with a young African American woman (a fellow writing center consultant) in which she used traditional noninterventionist pedagogy:

> I listened as she gave a quick summary of the class readings ... I asked a few questions along the way.... Throughout her ten- to fifteen-minute explanation, she revealed her conscious attempts of placing herself among a larger community. Her earlier controlled demeanor changed to excitement as she articulated her arguments faster and without hesitation to a point where she half-jokingly made statements about student race-relations at the university.... Here was a student willing to make connections and conclusions on a topic hardly discussed openly. I commented to the writing coach, "Well. Just type up what you just told me and you're done." ... The writing coach responded quickly and sharply, "Yeah right. I'm going to write all of that for the assignment."
>
> I asked why not, and she let me know she was the only black student in the classroom.... She said that even if she submitted an anonymous entry to the class electronic discussion list, the anonymity wouldn't last very long. She asked, "How many white kids would even consider what I just said? It would be so obvious who said what." ... She added, for her to sit down and write "like a black person" in a class where she was the only black student, she smiled, looked away, and shook her head, "No." (Barron and Grimm 56)

Borrowing Diane Davis's observation about how Lyotard used the word "just," I offer the same observation about Barron's use of the word "just": "here 'just' would have the double *entendre* Jean-Francois Lyotard gave it in *Just Gaming*: it would connote both 'merely' and 'justly' ... responsible, political, and ethical" (9). Although I suspect that Barron's primary intent was to

---

[4]Tatum explained that "resistance (particularly among White students) is the initial denial of any personal connection to racism.... White students typically explain their interest in the topic with such disclaimers as, 'I'm not racist myself, but I know people who are'" (8). I found her observation accurate, especially when the words "writing center practitioners" are substituted for the word "students."

imply the simplicity (and perhaps unintentionally, the neutrality) of the student's task ("just" type it up), the double *entendre* of the word does not seem to be lost on the student. The student clearly recognizes that typing up her perspective would be interpreted as a political and/or ethical move by the White students in her class. This move might prompt these students to reexamine their own thinking, but it would most likely sever any ties that she had established with the students.

Another stage model provides some insight into this student's reaction as an African American woman. Years before Helms proposed her model of White racial identity development, psychologist William Cross offered a model of Black racial identity development (a model on which Helms built her own). His five-stage model includes Preencounter, Encounter, Immersion/Emersion, Internalization, and Internalization-Commitment.[5] Most of these stages are similar to those described by Helms, but one of the stages deserves more discussion. Tatum elaborated,

> Though the internalization of negative Black stereotypes may be outside of his or her conscious awareness, the individual seeks to assimilate and be accepted by Whites.... This de-emphasis on one's racial-group membership may allow the individual to think that race has not been or will not be a relevant factor in one's own achievement, and may contribute to the belief in a U.S. meritocracy that is often a part of a Preencounter worldview. Movement into the Encounter phase is typically precipitated by an event or series of events that forces the individual to acknowledge the impact of racism in one's life. For example, instances of social rejection by White friends or colleagues (or reading new personally relevant information about racism) may lead the individual to the conclusion that many Whites will not view him or her as an equal. (10)

This student exhibited characteristics of someone who is in the Encounter stage of Black racial identity development. She clearly was aware of how her words would be heard by White students, as words not worthy of attention. As Barron pointed out, "She knows she's an involuntary minority (a concept John Ogbu uses to distinguish between voluntary immigrants to this country and those who are here due to slavery or conquest), she knows she's black, and she's had experience being alone in academic discussions" (Barron and Grimm 57). Contrary to the impression her tutor gives by using noninterventionist pedagogy that suggests color doesn't matter in writing ("just write it up"), this student realizes that color does matter. She is not simply being resistant to Barron's suggestions.

As Barron's story illustrates, the Encounter stage in Black racial identity development is intensified when the student is paired with a tutor who uses noninterventionist strategies (and/or is in the Disintegration stage of White racial identity development). Both the student and the tutor are astutely aware that they are enmeshed in maintenance of a racist educational system, and both use a form of denial to reduce their uncomfortableness. The way this denial manifests itself differs, however. The writing consultant encourages the student to include more of her own thinking in the paper, whereas the student resists the tutor's efforts to encourage her to put more of her thinking into the paper. The tutor acts as if the student's color does not matter; the student disguises her experiences of color that do matter. Both individuals engage in literacy in the ways that they are expected to in a post-Civil Rights era, that is, in ways that deny racial differences.

---

[5]Although there are many models of racial identity development that exist, I use the Cross and Helms models as frameworks for understanding Black racial identity development and White racial identity development, respectively, because they are the most frequently cited in discussions of racial identity development.

It was no surprise when Barron and Grimm observed that "a writing coach's attempts to get such a student to say more, to develop her ideas, to include more detail are likely to be frustrated. Students like the one in the story may challenge our good intentions by clearly expecting us to comment only on their sentence structure and organization" (59). This type of frustration prompted one of the undergraduate tutors in our writing center, Amber Jeffers, to examine how well our center was meeting the needs of the African American students on our campus. By way of comparison,[6] she pointed out that 10% of our writing center's clientele were international students, representing 33% of that entire student population; conversely, only 3% of our clientele were African American students (16% of that entire student population). As her major project for my "Writing Center Theory and Practice" class in spring 2001, she examined why African American students were not choosing to use the writing center.

Jeffers conducted interviews with over a dozen African American students (most of whom had visited the Writing Center). When asked, "How can the Writing Center adapt to better meet your personal needs?," these students responded in the same way as Barron's student. They wanted tutors to restrict comments to sentence structure and grammar: "Tutors need to do more editing and spend less time on redirecting papers." Also revealing were the answers given to the question, "Have you ever had a bad writing experience?" Students said such things as: "One of my teachers tore up my business plan and said I had grammar problems," "Two years in a row, my teachers didn't like my topics or the way I wrote," "I can't write in my own voice in any of my classes," and "Having to write in Standard English is good for work, but you shouldn't have to give away your identity." The experiences of these African American students sounded remarkably similar to Barron's observation about a student: "Her experience has taught her that if she needs a writing center at all, it's to help her write 'white'" (Barron and Grimm 59).

"I THINK OF MULTICULTURALISM IN THE WRITING CENTER IN A DIFFERENT WAY"

Several writing center practitioners in the 1990s began questioning the center's stance of neutrality and "peerness." Marilyn Cooper suggested that the writing center's stance of objectivity encourages a limited understanding of authorship because it does not acknowledge "the extent to which … various institutional forces impinge on how and what they [students] write" (101). Other composition theorists such as Patricia Sullivan and James Porter took a more strident position and labeled neutrality as "quite a thorny concept" that has been used to disavow political and ethical involvement in teaching (47). Grimm, too, maintained that writing centers have used the guise of a neutral community of peers to avoid acknowledging "the price some students must pay in their attempts to join this community" (87). Most recently, Karen Kopelson proposed that neutrality is not a concept as much as it is a performance: "a deliberate, reflective, self-conscious masquerade that serves an overarching and more insurgent political agenda" (123). The writing center's performance of neutral-

---

[6]Jeffers chose this comparison because "Non-Resident Alien" make up 2.5% of the overall student population on our campus, and "Black, Non-Hispanic" make up 2.1% of the campus population (*Factbook* 3).

ity has served a definite political agenda: "to ensure that that conversation [during a tutoring session] is similar in as many ways as possible to the way we would like them eventually to write" (Bruffee 7).

Trimbur and several other writing practitioners have also emphasized that student tutors are not really "peers" (Fayer; Grimm; Harris; Lunsford; Young). There exists, as Trimbur explained, "a certain institutional authority in the tutors that their tutees have not earned" (290). The difference in institutional authority is not the only difference. As Carol Severino pointed out, writing centers are contact zones where cultures inevitably collide between the tutor and the student. It is deceptive, therefore, to act as if the tutor is a neutral peer.

As a result, not all writing center administrators approach diversity as a given that does not matter in the writing center. Some directors do openly acknowledge diversity and exhibit characteristics of what Helm referred to as the Pseudo-Independent stage of White racial identity development. In addition to training that includes information about working with students who have learning disabilities and/or exhibit different Myers–Briggs personality traits, some writing centers offer tutors training in how to work with culturally diverse students by studying cultural differences in rhetorical patterns and reexamining the appropriateness and effectiveness of traditional collaborative strategies for second language writers, upon the recommendation of Judith Powers.[7] Others, such as Anne Mullin, seek out the assistance of the Student Diversity Committee and Black Student Alliance on campus to actively recruit more tutors of color.[8] Our center even opened a satellite writing center in the Multicultural Resource Center on campus.

These attempts to take an active role in the management of diversity reflect a fairly recent commitment in higher education to multiculturalism. Jay D. Sloan shared that one of Kent State University-Stark campuswide initiatives is to "embrace diversity." He asked the important question, "Where should we [writing center directors] position the writing center in the face of institutional mandates to 'embrace diversity'?" Like Kent State-Stark, all the academic departments/areas at my university were required to incorporate specific strategies and outcomes in our five-year plans to "emphasize an appreciation and understanding of cultural diversity" after NCATE denied our university's education program accreditation in the mid-1990s.[9] I took the stance that many writing center directors such as Judith Kilborn have taken; I adopted a more inclusive definition of diversity than the university's definition in my five-year plan. As Kilborn explained,

---

[7]This is complicated, however, because few tutor training manuals discuss racial differences, including *The Writing Center Resource Manual* published by the NWCA Press. Barron and Grimm contended that racial diversity is the aspect of diversity "most shied away from in our professional literature and conferences" (61).

[8]Because African American students continue to have some of the lowest recruitment and retention rates in U.S. higher education, predominantly White institutions have become more proactive in ascertaining the needs of this particular student population. In 1992, Walter R. Allen reported the results of over 2,500 Black student questionnaires given in 1981, 1982, and 1983. The questionnaires provided a mechanism to compare and contrast African American students at predominantly White versus historically Black universities. He examined three outcome variables—academic achievement, social involvement in campus life, and occupational aspirations—and five sets of predictor variables (student educational background, student aspirations, demographic characteristics, personal factors, and environmental factors—campus racial composition). Campus racial composition was the strongest predictor of social involvement and occupational aspirations, and the second strongest predictor of academic achievement. "Students in the sample who attended historically Black universities reported better academic performance, greater social involvement, and higher occupational aspirations than black students who attended predominantly White institutions" (39).

[9]Our Education program has since been reaccredited.

Although I report to the university and state university system administrators using their specific definitions of cultural diversity, I think of multiculturalism in the writing center in a different way. For me, cultural diversity includes minority, non-western, and western—Caucasian as well as African American, Hispanic, and Native American; rural as well as urban; southern as well as northern; non-traditional as well as traditional, and so on. In other words, my definition is inclusive rather than exclusive. (392–93)

Following this inclusive definition, it has not been difficult to show that our writing center emphasizes an appreciation and understanding of cultural diversity. I understand Suzanne Swiderski's posting in which she explained that her writing center collects "ethnic identification" data about clients to verify "whether we are reaching any of the nonmajority populations" and to share with the directors of Multicultural Affairs and the International Student Office.

I overheard them in the living room. My favorite great-grandmother, Mimo, was scolding my dad. "I can't believe you allow your daughter to have a colored friend." He didn't respond and when I came into the room, I pretended as if I hadn't heard. But I had. As I've gotten older, my aunt tells me I look more and more like Mimo did when she was my age.

"BE CLEAR FOR YOURSELF ABOUT WHAT IS MOTIVATING THE FOCUS ON RACE"[10]

Historian David Hollinger cautioned that race and culture are not synonymous (37). He made reference to the officially sanctioned system of demographic classification—the ethnoracial pentagon that divides the American population into African American, Asian American, Euro American, Indigenous, and Latino segments—that was created to facilitate the enforcement of the antidiscrimination and affirmative action policies of the federal government. Statistical Directive 15 of the Federal Office of Management and Budget enables government workers to collect this information and take an active role in managing diversity. Hollinger emphasized that "the lines dividing the five parts of the pentagon are not designed to recognize coherent cultures. They are designed, instead, to correct injustices committed by white people in the name of the American nation, most but not all of which can be traced back to racial classifications on the basis of morphological traits" (36). The pentagon, in other words, represents a set of political categories rather than cultural categories (36). He drew attention to Mary C. Waters's book, *Ethnic Options: Choosing Identities in America*. Waters found that

her [White] subjects' denial of the voluntary character of their own ethnic identities rendered them, in turn, insensitive to the difference between their own situation and that of Americans with non-European ethno-racial identities. These whites see a formal "equivalence between the African-American and, say Polish-American heritages." Thus, they deny, in effect, the depth and duration of the racism that has largely constructed and persistently bedeviled the African American and rendered that heritage less voluntary than an affirmation of Polishness. (Hollinger 41)

Hollinger attributed the involuntary nature of the categories to certain physical features that differentiate these individuals from White Americans—skin color, hair, and shape of the

---

[10]Barron and Grimm, p. 67.

face. Or as Iris Marion Young worded it, "[Racial] stereotypes confine [persons of color] to a nature which often is attached in some ways to their bodies" (59). Alexs Pate provided a powerful example of this confinement in his keynote address at the 2000 Midwest Writing Centers Association Conference. In his address, he reflected on a newsflash about actor Danny Glover being unable to get a cab in midtown Manhattan:

> Every time I've been refused service by a cab driver or passed by altogether, I felt ashamed and somehow guilty. Even though I'd done nothing to deserve such treatment, I always felt as though I had. As though somehow those cabbies had seen something in me that justified their instinctive rejection. What was it they saw, I wondered?.... But the real truth is that Mr. Glover and every other black man trying to hail a taxi is anything but invisible. We are the most scrutinized population in the American consciousness. Not only are we seen, but we are "read." Like the tattered pages of a salacious novel that has been passed around too many times and talked about even by people who have not read it—negatives precede us. We appear on the street anonymous and guilty.

Pate's impassioned speech continues to resonate with me as I reread Pemberton's confession of how he was keeping track of minority students, and I, like Elizabeth H. Boquet, feel uncomfortable with the system he described. Pemberton explained in his post, "I have on a very informal basis, been asking my secretary/receptionist to keep track of writing center usage by people of color. When students of color come in, she keeps a running tally of those who fall—very loosely speaking—into one of three categories: African-American, Asian, and Latino/a ... surreptitiously." That is, Pemberton's secretary looks at the individual and then chooses in which category to place the student. Hollinger seemed quite correct in his assessment that "the multiculturalism of our own time has helped us to recognize and appreciate cultural diversity, but ... this movement has too often left the impression that culture follows the lines of shape and color" (x).

Although not quite as overt as Pemberton's method, other writing center practitioners shared how they acquired information on this list thread about tracking minority students. Instead of guessing about the category of each student on the basis of physical appearance, several directors allow the university to take responsibility for managing diversity. Molly Wingate's response was fairly typical: "I don't have to ask the folks who use the writing center what their ethnic background is; I have access to that information when I ask the database [campus mainframe] to give it to me (once a year for my annual report)." This, too, is somewhat "surreptitious" because it is done without the knowledge of the students.

Jeanne Simpson wondered in her post about having students voluntarily self-identify similar to the way that job search candidates are asked to do so—"where your purposes and procedures were clear (emphasis on the purposes) and the information provided voluntarily and with the knowledge of the subjects." Her posting reflects how our writing center collects information. Students complete a "Student Background Information" card that asks students to identify their "ethnicity" by choosing one of the categories listed. These are the categories that our university uses—alas, the ethnoracial pentagon. Although I was not collecting the data surreptitiously like Pemberton, I was guilty of conflating culture and race. Furthermore, I was guilty of not identifying the purpose(s). Nothing on the card explained why the center was requesting this information or how the information would be used. I remember overhearing a work study receptionist tell a student, "We have students fill this out for record-keeping." In his response to Pemberton's post, Steven Davis wrote, "I think it is important ... the writing center not collect and store data that no one is asking for."

"Information-seeking ... marks the onset of the Pseudo-Independent stage," Tatum explained. "At this stage, the individual is abandoning beliefs in White superiority but may still behave in ways that unintentionally perpetuate the system" (16). Why was I collecting data that no external group was asking for? What was my motive? Was I collecting data, as Swiderski said, to determine whether our writing center is "reaching the non-majority populations" on our campus? Was this an "innocent" motive (exempt from any political and ethical involvement)? Could any White writing center director claim that this was/is the sole motive for tracking minority students? Kenneth Burke would answer "no." "However 'pure' one's motives may be actually, the impurities of identification lurking about the edges of such situations introduce a typical Rhetorical wrangle" (26). Burke provided multiple examples of how even the acts of "men [and women] of good will" (or using Grimm's terminology, "good intentions") can and will be necessarily warped by other motives.

Foucault's description of information seeking complicates our good intentions. Whether we openly or surreptitiously collect information, "inquiry rests on a whole system of power; it is this system that defines what must be constituted as knowledge; how, from whom, and by whom it is extracted; in what manner it moves about and is transmitted; at what point it accumulates and gives rise to a judgment or a decision" (19). Whether or not we like it and whether or not we acknowledge it, White writing center administrators are enmeshed in the maintenance of a racist educational system. We must begin to interrogate what is at stake in managing racial diversity.

Writing center programmatic and administrative decisions, such as tracking minority students, can send "an undesirable message about what we think is important" (as per Pemberton). These decisions inevitably reflect assumptions like "minority students should use the center more than Caucasians" (as per Wingate).[11] Even if these are not our assumptions but the assumptions of our university, by tracking students and using the information we are perpetuating the assumptions.

An article in a 1994 edition of a San Francisco paper reported the results of an informal survey of San Francisco residents. These individuals were asked, "How many racial categories should the U.S. Census have?" Hollinger summarized the results in this manner: Regardless of the number answered, the residents "took for granted that the reporter's question was about the public recognition of cultures, not about facilitating entitlements for victims of racism" (Hollinger 48). Even though we tell students that our purpose in tracking students is to recognize diverse cultures, are we really just tracking to facilitate entitlements, too? But not entitlements for racially different students, entitlements for our writing center that will allow us to expand and receive more recognition. How many writing center administrators have used these numbers to get federal money set aside for minority educational initiatives? How many writing center administrators have used these numbers to get funding for hiring an ESL specialist in the writing center?

---

[11]Allen's research suggests that there are a host of barriers that ensure the perpetuation of the status quo at predominantly White universities, but none of these barriers are directly linked to poor writing skills. The barriers he identities include admissions requirements, predominantly White faculty, inadequate financial aid, and destructive pedagogical styles (42).

Let's have some honest dialogue about racial differences and what's at stake in managing diversity. Are White writing center directors imposing involuntary identities on students of color and denying the racism associated with this categorization for our own vested interest? Should we be touting the percentage of minority students we assist in our annual reports? Has the pendulum swung too far from Pemberton's 1996 statement that "Race doesn't matter" to the other extreme? If we are honest, then very few of us actually use these statistics to improve our services and better meet the needs of minority students. How could we? These are (un)just numbers.

I conclude by referring back to Tatum's model of White racial identity development:

> Because of the prejudice and racism inherent in our environments when we were children, I assume that we cannot be blamed for learning what we were taught (intentionally or unintentionally). Yet as adults, we have a responsibility to try to identify and interrupt the cycle of oppression. When we recognize that we have been misinformed, we have a responsibility to seek out more accurate information and to adjust our behavior accordingly. (4)

We do have a responsibility as White writing center practitioners to manage diversity, but we need to be honest about how and why we do it. I need to believe that Barron and Grimm were correct; maybe it is enough that the African American student shared her experiences orally with the tutor, even though they never made it into her paper because "her story begins to make its ripples" (58). Tatum observed that "as white students [and writing center directors] move through their own stages of identity development, they take their friends with them by engaging them in dialogue" (23), just as I am sharing this series of stories with all of you, my writing center friends. These kinds of changes we can implement happen one to one, a student at a time, a director at a time. By rethinking how we manage diversity, perhaps we can avoid being the White Center and just be the Write Center.

Upon graduating with my Ph.D., my sister asked me what I had learned in my program. "I'm not exactly sure, but when I began the program, I never said a word in class. In my last semester, I seemed to be doing most of the talking in class—without fear of someone hitting me with a ruler."

WORKS CITED

Allen, Walter R. "The Color of Success: African-American College Student Outcomes at Predominantly White and Historically Black Public Colleges and Universities." *Harvard Educational Review* 62.1 (1992): 26–44.

Barron, Nancy, and Nancy Maloney Grimm. "Addressing Racial Diversity in a Writing Center: Stories and Lessons from Two Beginners." *The Writing Center Journal* 22.2 (2002): 55–83.

Boquet, Elizabeth H. "Re: Keeping Track of Minority Students." Online posting. 6 Dec. 1996. WCenter. 7 May 2004. <http://www.ttu.edu//WCenter/9612/msg00099.html>.

Brodkey, Linda. *Writing Permitted in Designated Areas Only.* Minneapolis: U of Minnesota P, 1996.

Brooks, Jeff. "Minimalist Tutoring: Making the Students Do All the Work." *Writing Lab Newsletter* 15.6 (1991): 1–4.

Bruffee, Kenneth. "Peer Tutoring and the 'Conversation of Mankind.'" *Writing Centers: Theory and Administration.* Ed. Gary Olson. Urbana: NCTE, 1984. 3–15.

Burke, Kenneth. *A Rhetoric of Motives.* Berkeley: U of Calif. P, 1962.

Cooper, Marilyn M. "Really Useful Knowledge: A Cultural Studies Agenda for Writing Centers." *The Writing Center Journal* 14 (1994): 97–111.

Cross, William E., Jr. "The Negro to Black Conversion Experience: Toward a Psychology of Black Liberation." *Black World* 20.9 (1971): 13–27.

Davis, D. Diane. *Breaking Up at Totality*. Carbondale: Southern Illinois UP, 2000.

Davis, Steven. "Re: Keeping Track of Minority Students." Online posting. 9 Dec. 1996. WCenter 7 May 2004. <http://www.ttu.edu//WCenter/9612/msg00119.html>.

Factbook 2003–04. Southwest Missouri State University. 11 May 2004. <http://www.smsu.edu/oir>.

Fayer, Dina. "Tutors' Column: Orthodoxy and Effectiveness." *Writing Lab Newsletter* 18 (1994): 13.

Foucault, Michel. *Ethics: Subjectivity and Truth*. Trans. Paul Rabinow. New York: New P, 1994.

Fox, Helen. *"When Race Breaks Out": Conversations about Race and Racism in College Classrooms*. New York: Peter Lang, 2001.

Grimm, Nancy Maloney. *Good Intentions: Writing Center Work for Postmodern Times*. Portsmouth, NH: Heinemann-Boynton/Cook, 1999.

Harris, Muriel. "Collaboration Is Not Collaboration Is Not Collaboration: Writing Center Tutorials vs. Peer Response Groups." *College Composition and Communication* 43 (1992): 369–83.

Hartstein, Mark. "Tutor's Corner: Objectivity in Tutoring." *Writing Lab Newsletter* 9.2 (1984): 9–10.

Helms, Janet. *Black and White Racial Identity: Theory, Research and Practice*. Westport, CT: Greenwood, 1990.

Hollinger, David A. *Postethnic America: Beyond Multiculturalism*. New York: Basic Books, 1995.

"How Many Racial Categories Should the U.S. Census Have?" *San Francisco Chronicle* 22 (Aug. 1994): B3.

Kilborn, Judith. "Cultural Diversity in the Writing Center: Defining Ourselves and Our Challenges." *The Allyn and Bacon Guide to Writing Center Theory and Practice*. Ed. Robert W. Barnett and Jacob S. Blumner. Boston: Allyn and Bacon, 2001. 391–400.

Kopelson, Karen. "Rhetoric on the Edge of Cunning; or, the Performance of Neutrality (Re)Considered as a Composition Pedagogy for Student Resistance." *College Composition and Communication* 55.1 (2003): 115–46.

Lunsford, Andrea. "Collaboration, Control, and the Idea of a Writing Center." *The Writing Center Journal* 12.1 (1991): 3–10.

Martinson, Deborah. "Re: Keeping Track of Minority Students." Online posting. 6 Dec. 1996. WCenter 28 April 2004. <http://www.ttu.edu/WCenter/9612/msg00100.html>.

Mullin, Anne. "Re: Keeping Track of Minority Students." Online posting. 10 Dec. 1996. WCenter. 7 May 2004. <http://www.ttu.edu/WCenter/9612/msg00150.html>.

Ogbu, John U. "Minority Status, Cultural Frame of Reference, and Schooling." *Literacy: Interdisciplinary Conversations*. Ed. Deborah Keller-Cohen. Cresskill, NJ: Hampton, 1994. 361–84.

Paoli, Dennis, Marcia Silver, and Jo Koster Tarvers. *A Proposed Self-Study Questionnaire for Writing Center Accreditation*. 1997. <http://faculty.winthrop.edu/kosterj/NWCA/proposal.htm>.

Pate, Alexs. "Language and Innocence." 2000 Midwest Writing Centers Association Conference, Minneapolis, MN.

Pemberton, Michael. "Keeping Track of Minority Students." Online posting. 6 Dec. 1996. WCenter. 28 April 2004. <http://www.ttu.edu/WCenter/9612/msg00096.html>.

___. "Writing Center Ethics." *Writing Lab Newsletter* 18.4 (1993): 10.

Powers, Judith K. "Rethinking Writing Center Conferencing Strategies for the ESL Writer." *The Writing Center Journal* 13.2 (1993): 39–47.

Severino, Carol. "Writing Centers as Linguistic Contact Zones and Borderlands." *Writing Lab Newsletter* 19.4 (1994): 1–5.

Sherwood, Steve. "Censoring Students, Censoring Ourselves: Constraining Conversations in the Writing Center." *The Writing Center Journal* 20.1 (1999): 51–60.

Simpson, Jeanne H. "Re: Keeping Track of Minority Students." Online posting. 6 Dec. 1996. WCenter 7 May 2004. <http://www.ttu.edu/WCenter/9612/msg00104.html>.

Sloan, Jay D. "Collaborating in the Contact Zone: A Writing Center Struggles with Multiculturalism." *Praxis: A The Writing Center Journal* (2004). 7 May 2004. <http://uwc3.fac.utexas.edu/~praxisArchive/04_spring/04_spring_files/contact_zone.html>.

Sullivan, Patricia, and James E. Porter. *Opening Spaces: Writing Technologies and Critical Research Practices*. Greenwich, CT: Ablex, 1997.

Swiderski, Suzanne. "Re: Keeping Track of Minority Students." Online posting. 6 Dec. 1996. WCenter. 7 May 2004. <http://www.ttu.edu/WCenter/9612/msg00098.html>.

Tatum, Beverly Daniel. "Talking about Race, Learning about Racism: The Application of Racial Identity Development Theory in the Classroom." *Harvard Educational Review* 62.1 (1992): 1–24.

Trimbur, John. "Peer Tutoring: A Contradiction in Terms?" *The Allyn and Bacon Guide to Writing Center Theory and Practice.* Ed. Robert W. Barnett and Jacob S. Blumner. Boston: Allyn and Bacon, 1987. 288–95.

Waters, Mary C. *Ethnic Options: Choosing Identities in America.* Berkeley: U of Calif. P, 1990.

Wingate, Molly. "Re: Keeping Track of Minority Students." Online posting. 6 Dec. 1996. WCenter. 7 May 2004. <http://www.ttu.edu/Wcenter/9612/msg00101.html>.

Young, Iris Marion. *Justice and the Politics of Difference.* Princeton, NJ: Princeton UP, 1990.

9

Managing the Center:
The Director as Coach

Michael Mattison
Boise State University

There are no secrets with the X's and O's. We all know that. I think the coaches who are successful find a way to get the best out of each individual on their team, to help them reach their potential. That's the real challenge.

—Jerry Yeagley, University of Indiana Men's Soccer

One of the more popular bits of advice for writing center tutors and consultants is to behave like a coach (Capossela; Harris; Ryan). The writer takes on the role of player, and the consultant looks to coax, prompt, and push that player to excel, all while maintaining a respectful distance from the act of writing the paper: "In sports, coaches instruct players and direct team strategy. They do not actually do the work for the team, but rather they stand on the sidelines observing how the team functions, looking at what is going well and what needs improvement" (Ryan 23). In my experience, the player–coach analogy has been a good one, easily understood by most consultants and helpful in allowing them to consider and reflect on their work in a writing center.

Yet, this helpful analogy seems to be used solely for the *consultant–writer* relationship. What of the *consultant–director* relationship? When I began my first year as writing center director at Boise State,[1] it did not occur to me that the director could also be considered a coach. But now, the connection seems obvious: A director is also on the sidelines, watching consultants perform. A director too must coax, prompt, push, and teach, aiming to allow individual consultants to work to the best of their ability. In addition, the director must handle all these

---

[1]Boise State's Writing Center handles approximately thirteen hundred consultations each semester, and employs around twenty consultants, mostly undergraduates. We take both appointments and walk-ins, and serve a campus of over eighteen thousand students, many of whom commute to school and are nontraditional.

individual relationships while simultaneously working with the group of consultants as a whole; the writing center staff is the team—my team. The coach analogy seems even stronger for the work of a director than it does for the work of a consultant.

Because I found such a strong connection between what I do as a director and what a baseball or basketball coach would do, I decided to read up on a few well-known coaches and consider how their thoughts might influence my work. For instance, how can John Wooden's guidelines for recruiting players inform my hiring practices? How might Mike Krzyzewski's approach to practice relate to the work done in staff meetings? How can Joe Torre's ideas on communication connect to my daily conversations with consultants?[2] In short, what can the sports world teach a writing center director about creating a successful writing center team?

Certainly, mine is not the first suggestion that coaching sports is relevant to another activity. The books that inform this chapter have been popular sellers, especially for those in business.[3] They have not, however, been used much to comment on the academic world or, as far as I know, to comment at all on writing centers. Yet, just as questions of leadership, trust, and responsibility are relevant for coaches on the playing field and managers in the boardroom, they are important for writing center directors.[4] And again, as we ask our consultants to visualize themselves in different roles, we can do the same. If we consider ourselves as coaches, then we can see ourselves and our responsibilities differently, even if we don't necessarily visualize ourselves strolling the sidelines during the Final Four or walking out to the mound in Yankee Stadium on a cool evening in October (although that is perfectly acceptable, too).

One last point before considering the connections between coaching and directing a writing center: It's not about winning and losing. Yes, sports mainly focus on who wins and who loses, and we do keep score, but none of the coaches cited here aims simply to win. As Kryzewski (shuh-SHEF'-skee) said, "I believe that any team that does its best is a winner. If we're constantly looking at a win–loss record to determine whether we are doing well, we're not looking at the right barometer" (28). He had a broader definition of success than one measured by the scoreboard. So did Wooden: "Success is peace of mind which is a direct result of self-satisfaction in knowing you did your best to become the best that you are capable of becoming" (88). As writing center directors, we too strive to make our consultants successful; they strive to make writers successful. To be successful, to do your best, is the main goal.

---

[2]Wooden was coach of the UCLA men's basketball team from 1948 to 1975. In that time, he coached such notable players as Lew Alcinder (Kareem Abdul-Jabbar), Bill Walton, and Gail Goodrich. During his tenure, the Bruins won ten national championships (seven of them in a row), nineteen conference championships, and had four undefeated seasons. Krzyzewski is currently the coach of the Duke men's basketball team. Under his leadership, Duke has won three national championships, and made the Final Four ten times since 1981. And Torre is (at least as of this writing) the manager of the New York Yankees. During his tenure, the team has played in six World Series, winning the championship four times, and Torre has twice been named the AL Manager of the Year.

[3]A comment or two on these works. First, none was penned solely by the coach. All of them had second authors, and it is likely that that second author did most of the writing, relying on interviews with the coach to create the work. Second, none of the works is especially full of wonderful prose. The sentence structure is fairly simple and straightforward, the stories are often quick and lacking in detail, and aphorisms often substitute for an extended discussion of rather complicated ideas about human relationships and human beings in general. Yet, there are, I believe, kernels of insight in the works, and there is also an epideictic power to them. No doubt that is part of their intent—to inspire as much as to educate. Coaching, and directing a writing center, involves inspiring others. The coaches in these books speak often to that task, and their books attempt the same with their readers.

[4]Posey connected management theory with writing center work, and this chapter strengthens that connection as well.

RECRUITING PLAYERS AND HIRING CONSULTANTS

One of the most daunting tasks for a writing center director is to choose who will work in the center. Consulting with writers can be a challenge for even the most patient and thoughtful individuals, so how do we find those who will be up to such a challenge? Coaches face a similar dilemma, especially those at the college level. Many students have athletic talent, but how many of those will fit well with a particular team, and how many will be able to handle the demands and pressures of both school and sports?[5]

Ideally, perhaps, directors could approach hiring as Wooden usually did recruiting and let the consultants come to them: "I never wanted to talk a prospective player into coming to UCLA. It was important to me that they be truly interested in us without having any pressure put on them. I wanted them to want UCLA" (220). Of course, Wooden was coaching a PAC-10 school that managed to win ten national championships during his tenure; his team had a fairly high profile. Writing centers do not always command the same attention from students, so directors do go looking for students.

When we do search, however, we can still ask that students be "truly interested" in writing center work. We can explore their motives for applying, and we can still take some lessons from Wooden, as he did occasionally court players. He described one recruiting visit, with a player he left unnamed:

> He was an excellent prospect and a good student.... While I was chatting with his parents, his mother asked me a question. Before I could answer, the young man interrupted and said, "Mom, how can you be so ignorant? Anyone so stupid should just keep still." I was appalled, although neither parent seemed to take offense at his rudeness. Very shortly I said that we must be going, and as we left I withdrew our offer of a scholarship. This was just not the kind of young man that I wanted on our team. (222)

For Wooden, character matters. So should it with consultants. Someone can be an outstanding writer yet behave condescendingly toward other writers. Like Wooden, writing center directors should consider the way their recruits interact with others.

For instance, Rick Leahy asked other teachers to recommend students for the Boise State Writing Center and specifically asked the teachers about peer interaction: "I attempt [to recruit] writing assistants carefully, not by putting out a general call for applicants but by asking faculty to nominate students they feel are excellent writers and good at working with other students—people who strike their teachers as the 'right type'" (45). Those "types" of students excel as much at peer group work and peer feedback as they do with their own essays. As Rick's successor, I have continued this practice, asking teachers to recommend those who "offer constructive, tactful responses to their peers, seem truly interested in others' writing, and willingly listen to feedback about their own writing." Such students will probably be well suited to writing center work.

---

[5]Unfortunately, we have too many examples of schools and coaches who seem to consider the recruiting process one of simply selling the school to the best athletes, regardless of character (the school's or the athlete's). The situation with the football team at the University of Colorado is a prime example, as are others.

Also, I meet with all the students who are interested in working in our center.[6] One of the most telling responses, I believe, often comes to my opening question: "Why do you want to work in the Writing Center?" Although I don't want to overanalyze any single comment, I do hesitate when a student replies, "Because I'm an excellent writer." How different that response is from others: "Because I enjoyed the group work in my 101 class" or "Because I want to learn more about different types of writing" or even "Because I think it would be interesting." Emphasizing personal writing ability in this situation seems wrong, a focus on self rather than others—like a player who aims for a scoring title rather than a team championship. I also hesitate when a student says his primary goal is to be paid or to receive class/internship credits. He does not seem "truly interested" in our work so much as in the rewards.

From that initial question, I move to a mock consultation, with me as the student writer. Here I can gain even more of a sense of how a recruit will interact with others. When they go through my draft, do they find positive things to say? Do they ask me questions and listen to my responses? Do they look to collaborate with me rather than direct me? True, I should not necessarily expect a smooth consultation from any recruit—that is why we have courses and workshops—but it is quite possible to glimpse how quickly and willingly a person will adapt to our writing center's goals. I can tell, as did Wooden, whether or not I should extend an offer.[7]

In addition to considering how a recruit will interact with writers, it's also important to consider how a recruit will interact with the other consultants. Not only should there be writer–consultant collaboration, but also consultant–consultant collaboration. All the members of a writing center should feel comfortable going to someone else and asking advice, or offering support—they should be willing to pass the ball to one another, to back one another up on a play. Some directors even have their veteran consultants conduct interviews with recruits, and that seems an ideal method for strengthening the team and the players. As Krzyzewski explained, "Bonds have to form among *all* members of the team.... Every individual must have a trusting relationship with every other member of the team" (27). If consultants can have a say in who will join them, then they can begin to form those bonds with their future coworkers.

In the best cases, after I have interviewed recruits, decided if they would be a good addition to our center, and offered a position, I receive a note like this one: "I'm in for sure. I'd love to be a part of this." I want consultants to have the sense that they are a part of something, part of a team. The idea of teamwork is doubly important in a writing center, as consultants team up with writers during consultations, and are part of a team of consultants. Consultants need to have a strong sense of team spirit, as Wooden described it: "This is an eagerness to sacrifice personal glory for the welfare of the group as a whole. It's togetherness and consideration for others" (90). Good consultants need to be considerate of the writers they work with, and one another.

---

[6] For those students who are recommended, I send out an e-mail and invite them to come in and see me, and to bring a writing sample. When students who have not been recommended ask about the class, I conduct a quick mini-interview and determine if the student and I should move on to a more formal conversation. Also, at Boise State, in order to work at the writing center, undergraduate consultants must take English 303: Theory and Practice of Tutoring Writing. On our online registration system, the course is locked and students can only register if they have received a permission number, so all those interested in the work are routed through my office.

[7] See also Loretta Cobb and Elaine Kilgore Elledge's "Undergraduate Staffing in the Writing Center," and from their piece, Leonard Podis's "Training Peer Tutors for the Writing Lab."

COMMUNICATION

If there is one constant to the advice that all books about coaching give, it is that a coach must communicate with the players. Communication of one of the "fundamental qualities" for Krzyzewski and being a strong communicator is one of the "seven secrets" that Jeff Janssen and Greg Dale discussed in their book *The Seven Secrets of Successful Coaches*.[8] Being a strong communicator means being an effective communicator:

> The foundation of effective communication is your ability to be open and direct with your athletes. The messages you send as coach have to be clear and athletes should not have to guess if there are any hidden meanings. You should be very explicit regarding roles athletes play as well as the expectations and standards that you feel are important to the team's success. You can't assume that they know what you are thinking at any time—especially in areas that are vital to success. (166)

Writing center directors should be explicit as well, ideally writing up the expectations and standards for consultants. For instance, many writing centers have handbooks that list consultant responsibilities and center policies, and directors can consider the handbook a valuable tool. Jeanette Harris indicated that "a handbook can serve as an extension of a director, reaching tutors at times when the director is not available, communicating information in another medium, adding a new dimension to the training process" (145).[9]

Torre emphasized communication too: "Communication is the key to trust, and trust is the key to teamwork in any group endeavor, be it in sports, business, or family" (71). When communicating as a baseball manager, Torre disclosed that he relies more on individual meetings with players rather than team meetings because baseball is a fairly "autonomous sport." Players have more individual activities (i.e., pitching, batting) than in other sports. Writing center consultants are much like baseball players in this regard, having to perform as individuals in most consulting sessions, so directors can follow Torre's lead and make sure they have the opportunity to talk with all their consultants one on one: "I have to establish good communication with each team member. I therefore rely on person-to-person encounters to motivate, give players a chance to share concerns, or just shoot the breeze" (79). Through those conversations, directors, like Torre, will recognize that "every team player needs something unique" and that the "tone and style" of the message should vary based on the individual (79–80).

For instance, Torre made clear that some players might get down on themselves and need more positive feedback than others; some might require a verbal push to work harder; some more reserved players might need a daily check-in so that they have an opportunity to express a concern or idea that they wouldn't normally raise on their own. All the types of players that Torre described on his team are in the Boise State Writing Center. And, I would imagine, in

---

[8]Janssen and Dale distinguished between coercive and credible coaches and aim for the latter type. Credible coaches, they indicated, are distinguished by seven characteristics; such coaches are character-based, competent, committed, caring, confidence-builders, communicators, and consistent.

[9]At BSU, we are in the process of reviving and revising our handbook, which will include a copy of the Tutoring Ethics from the NCTA, as well as a set of guidelines for our consultants. We will also have a consultant contract, a pledge that each consultant signs, agreeing to maintain a professional, productive atmosphere for the center. The writing center is also coordinating with other tutoring services on campus, looking to make the application/hiring process for tutors a more standard one across campus.

most other centers, too. There is the consultant who often doubts his abilities and needs to be told "good job"; there is the consultant who needs a firm warning about arriving on time; there is the consultant who has a wonderful suggestion for improving our Web site, but who would never offer it unless explicitly asked. As the director, I need to be aware of the different person-alities on my staff, and the only way to do that, as Torre reminded all managers, is to take the time: "What's involved in knowing team players? To know their abilities, you get reports from scouts and coaches, and closely observe them in practice and games. To know them as individ-uals, you need to look them in the eye. And you absolutely must make time for them. Sounds like a simple rule, but too many managers in too many walks of life only pay lip service to it" (18). There are, however, many ways to make time.

For instance, a director can schedule a mini-conference with each consultant at the begin-ning of the semester, just to check in and chat. What do their class schedules look like? What are they hoping to accomplish in the center this term? How was the summer/winter break? Schedules are usually much more open at the beginning of the term and this initial conversa-tion can establish a good line of communication for the rest of the year; if there are few writers visiting in the first few weeks, then directors might even schedule themselves during the con-sultant's work hours. Then, during the semester, a director can still rely on scheduled confer-ences, but also should take advantage of more informal moments, as Leahy did: "I make a point to plunk down on the couch with a cup of coffee about once a day and engage in conversation with whoever's free to talk. These are good moments. It's at these relaxed times that the writ-ing assistants express their deeper concerns and their better ideas" (47). And it's at these re-laxed times that consultants give directors a better sense of themselves.[10]

In addition to making time to talk to his players, Torre revealed he must consider the timing of his talks. A word of praise can do little if it's immediately dismissed, and a critique can be lost if it's delivered at the wrong moment: "Once you've identified the kind of communication needed, you've got to determine the best time to have that talk. Your decision must be based on your gut sense of when he or she is receptive" (83). In general, Torre's point seems most rele-vant for moments of criticism. Yes, praise can be dismissed, but I think there are few times when it is not a good idea to offer up a compliment. When offering a critique, on the other hand, di-rectors should carefully consider when, where, and how they do so.

ROLES

When coaches know the players well, they are better able to determine what they can, and should, ask them to do in order to most help the team. Who can best handle the press? Who pitches well against right-handed batters with runners in scoring position? Who thrives in a pressure situation? Who will represent the team well with the media? Part of coaching is plac-ing players into the roles in which they will be most successful. John Wooden did not play Bill Walton at point guard, and Joe Torre never had Roger Clemens roaming the outfield. A writing

---

[10]Even finding relaxed moments can be somewhat stressful. The BSU Writing Center is open till 8 on weekday evenings, and I have felt distanced from the consultants who work the later shift. I do stop in on occasion, but those occasions feel more like a check-up than a chance for conversation. Next year I hope to stagger my schedule, starting my day later once or twice a week and then working into the evening so that I'll have the same interactions with the evening consultants as I do with those who work the day shifts.

center director should also ask questions about roles: Who has had some experience writing lab reports? Who might be most comfortable visiting a classroom and answering questions about the center? Who speaks a second language? Who has an eye for design and could revise the brochure? Who enjoys leading writing workshops?

Asking these questions helps a director keep from considering the consultants as interchangeable pieces and helps to assure that the work they do will be as rewarding as possible for each of them. Evelyn Posey offered her consultants a choice of various projects and they sign up for what interests them. She noted that often the choices are made based on experience: "Experienced tutors usually volunteer for writing and workshop projects while new tutors prefer promotion and clerical projects, possibly because these do not demand as much expertise" (327). Length of tenure in a center is certainly one consideration when matching consultants and roles. Then again, so are organizational ability, willingness to socialize, and artistic talent.

At the same time, roles should not be viewed as rigid. Krzyzewski revealed that he will "shy away from even stating that certain players have to play certain positions" (96). For Duke, players other than the point guard will bring the ball up the floor, and the standard designations of guard, forward, and center do not always apply. Consultants, too, should have the opportunity, and be encouraged, to try out as many roles as they can. A quiet consultant might blossom in front of a class; a history major might have a flair for poetry; and a poet might be an astute reader of electrical engineering reports. But again, discovering matches between personalities and responsibilities happens best when the director is knowledgeable about her consultants.

PRACTICE

For Krzyzewski, Duke basketball players must be able to respond quickly to a variety of situations that they may encounter during games. They do not run set plays so much as read and respond to whatever the other team is doing. To allow them to "adjust on the run," Krzyzewski explained that he attempts to prepare his team "for as many little things, as many nuances as possible" (94). Writing center consultants also need to be prepared for the little things; they need to be flexible enough to respond to a variety of writers and texts, to adjust to each consultation on the run. For both basketball players and writing consultants, the way to keep reflexes sharp, to be open to changing situations, is simple: practice.

Of course, many writing center directors do not have the luxury of all their consultants keeping the same schedule, and we cannot rely on a daily practice session as can a college basketball coach.[11] However, we can schedule individual or paired practice sessions rather than group meetings, and, when we do have our meetings, we can aim to use the time productively.[12] Krzyzewski emphasized that his players must not simply listen to him during practice, they

---

[11]Many writing centers now require a course in consulting, as does BSU. This *is* a set time for consultants to meet and practice. Yet, practice can and should continue beyond that introductory course, and that type of practice is the focus here.

[12]And there's also Torre's opinion that team meetings are not of great value if overused: "In my view, team meetings have their place, but they're like chili peppers—a few add zest to your dish; too many and you're asking for trouble" (98). Again, baseball is more of an individual sport than others, so the team meeting might not be relevant for all, and Torre also mentioned that a team meeting is an important event, one that forces players to pay attention. But, if meetings are held all the time, "the players won't take you or your meetings as seriously as they should" (99).

must actively use the time to learn how to respond to certain situations: "How much I speak to the players on our team is important, but they'll forget a lot of what they *hear*. It's also important to make sure they watch and observe through action and videotape. Usually, the team will remember more of what they *see*. But the most crucial aspect of our team training is what the guys actually *do* and what they *understand*" (88). Players cannot only be told what to do when they are down by one in the final seconds of a game; they have to play those seconds on the court—again and again.

Consultants can go through a similar practice regimen with mock tutorials. In a mock tutorial, the consultants are *doing,* that is, they are responding to a consulting situation. Had they only considered the situation in the abstract, had they only discussed what they might *do*, they probably would not feel as prepared. And certainly they would not feel as prepared if the director had only told them what to do in a certain situation. They need the practice. By placing consultants in the types of sessions that they might encounter, directors can better prepare their staff for working with real writers.[13]

Krzyzewski also mentioned videotape in his passage. At Boise State, we are reviving the habit of videotaping real consultations. The consultants can observe themselves interacting with writers, and can reflect on what did and did not work well.[14] As Krzyzewski said of his players, "They need to know how they *really* are, not just how they *think* they are. If they can step outside themselves and watch their performances … then they may internalize both their shortcomings and their strengths" (91). In addition to watching their own sessions, the consultants also pair up and review each other's sessions. This pairing up of consultants strengthens the consulting practices of each, and can also strengthen the consultant–consultant relationship. Encouraging conversation between teammates is another important goal for Krzyzewski, so that teammates begin to coach one another: "Whether something's going wrong or something's going right, they need to talk to each other right away—as soon as they see something" (73). Prompting conversation about taped consultations can put consultants in the habit of talking to one another about all their sessions.

Important, too, for both Krzyzewski and Wooden, is the preparation that a coach must put in before practice. No practice is run off-the-cuff, and the two talk about having detailed, to-the-minute lists of what they wish to cover in their practices.[15] Such a regimented approach might go against the thinking that writing center meetings can, and perhaps should, be places for free-flowing conversations, where consultants raise and discuss their own questions and concerns. In fact, many of the meetings that I have attended and run have been of this type.

---

[13]See chapter 6 in *The Allyn and Bacon Guide to Peer Tutoring* (Gillespie and Lerner) for a discussion of mock tutorials, and see also chapter 8 in *The Bedford Guide for Writing Tutors* (Ryan) for a sample of possible writing consultation scenarios with different types of writers.

[14]We do not videotape any session without obtaining the consent of the writer. Our consultants utilize a permission slip that has been reviewed and accepted by our Office of Research Administration.

[15]One of the more oft-repeated, and true, stories about Wooden is how he began each season with a lesson on socks: "One of the little things I watched closely was a player's socks. No basketball player is better than his feet. If they hurt, if his shoes don't fit, or if he has blisters, he can't play the game. It is amazing how few players know how to put on a pair of socks properly. I don't want blisters, so each year I gave in minute detail a step-by-step demonstration as to precisely how I wanted them to put on their socks—every time. Believe it or not, there's an art to doing it right" (105). I can't help but chuckle at the image of a sock lesson, and think of the over-attention to detail that it displays. But then, considering how much concern a writer can show for the choice of a word, or how a good greeting from a consultant can set the tone for a session, I realize that Wooden is right. It's the details that matter, and "success usually accompanies attention to little details."

Yet, rarely have I been satisfied with such meetings. No one necessarily has a chance to think through the topics raised, and there is little opportunity for *doing* in this type of meeting. Better, I think, if I collect questions and concerns prior to a meeting and then prepare a meeting that can address them. Does this mean more work for me as director? It does in that I must prepare more for a meeting, but in the long run it does not because the consultants learn more from their meetings and are thus better able to handle various situations on their own, or with help from their teammates.

At the same time, directors can look to vary their meetings, to surprise consultants every once in a while. Krzyzewski related that he invents new drills and talks to his players at different times and in different locations. He wants his players always thinking: "Too many rules and too much predictability absolutely kill creativity" (98). Once he had them simply play volleyball in order to remember what it meant to have fun with a sport. Perhaps some writing center meetings could also take time for volleyball, or basketball, or an in-depth game of Dictionary. Practice is crucial for being a successful athlete or consultant, but so is not practicing on occasion. (Don't tell my consultants, but I've a call in to reserve the bowling alley.)

FINAL SECONDS (OR NINTH INNING)

Much as I enjoy making comparisons between the sports world and writing centers, I don't want to push the analogy too far. I don't see myself donning sweats and a whistle and then having the consultants run laps outside the building, nor do I see myself interfering in a difficult tutoring session in order to bring in a relief consultant from the bullpen. Yet, by thinking about the work I do as director in terms of being a coach, and by reading works from those who coach professionally, I am reminded to focus my energy on the human relationships that are at the core of any activity, whether in sports, business, or school. I often encourage my consultants to remember the human aspects of their work with writers, but I occasionally become lost in my administrative duties when dealing with them. The coach analogy helps me come back to the team.

And it is the teamwork aspect of the writing center that I enjoy the most. There's no other collection of individuals on our campus that does what we do, that experiences what we experience. I think Krzyzewski's description of a Duke basketball team is appropriate for us in the center: "Basically, we are a group of people living together over a short period of time in our own culture. How we grow that culture—how we develop communication, how we care for our people—means everything" (52). We have our own writing center culture at Boise State, as does every center. And, every center looks to grow, individually and collectively. Growing, developing, communicating, and caring requires teamwork. And teamwork requires a good coach.

WORKS CITED

Capossela, Toni-Lee. *The Harcourt Brace Guide to Peer Tutoring.* Orlando: Harcourt Brace, 1998.

Cobb, Loretta, and Elaine Kilgore Elledge. "Undergraduate Staffing in the Writing Center." *Writing Centers: Theory and Administration.* Ed. Gary A. Olson. Urbana, IL: NCTE, 1984. 123–31.

Gillespie, Paula, and Neal Lerner. *The Allyn and Bacon Guide to Peer Tutoring.* New York: Longman, 2000.

Harris, Jeanette. "The Handbook as a Supplement to a Tutor Training Program." *Writing Centers: Theory and Administration.* Ed. Gary A. Olson. Urbana, IL: NCTE, 1984. 144–51.

Harris, Muriel. *Teaching One-to-One: The Writing Conference.* Urbana, IL: NCTE, 1986.

Janssen, Jeff, and Greg Dale. *The Seven Secrets of Successful Coaches: How to Unlock and Unleash Your Team's Full Potential.* Cary, NC: Winning the Mental Game, 2002.

Krzyzewski, Mike, and Donald T. Phillips. *Leading with the Heart: Coach K's Successful Strategies for Basketball, Business, and Life.* New York: Warner, 2000.

Leahy, Richard. "Of Writing Centers, Centeredness, and Centrism." *The Writing Center Journal* 13 (Fall 1992): 43–52.

Podis, Leonard A. "Training Peer Tutors for the Writing Lab." *College Communication and Composition* 31 (February 1980): 70–75.

Posey, Evelyn J. "An Ongoing Tutor Training Program." *The Writing Center Journal* 6.2 (1986): 29–35. Rpt. In *The Allyn and Bacon Guide to Writing Center Theory and Practice.* Ed. Robert W. Barnett and Jacob S. Blumner. 326–331.

Ryan, Leigh. *The Bedford Guide for Writing Tutors.* 3rd ed. Boston: Bedford, 2002.

Torre, Joe, and Henry Dreher. *Joe Torre's Ground Rules for Winners: 12 Keys to Managing Team Players, Tough Bosses, Setbacks, and Success.* New York: Hyperion, 1999.

Wooden, John, and Jack Tobin. *They Call Me Coach.* Chicago: Contemporary, 1988.

⚞ **10** ⚟

Documentation Strategies and the Institutional Socialization of Writing Centers

Brad Peters
Northern Illinois University

Muriel Harris challenged us to consider how local writing center research contributes substantially to a broader institutional knowledge that well exceeds keeping records and justifying the need for services. More specifically, Harris challenged writing center directors to identify and disseminate the *processes* of making institutional knowledge that go into developing "the particular place, with its particular staff, student body, institutional mission, administrative structures, and faculty needs," to help directors everywhere create critical analogues "for the administrative decisions that have to be made and problems that have to be solved" ("Writing Center Administration" 76–77). Those processes don't remain stable or transparent because upper-level administration and writing center personnel come and go. However, the documentation that accrues can teach us much about what those processes are and how they evolve over time.

Borrowing the term *narratology* from literary studies—a term that includes narratives in documentation as well as in literature—this chapter takes up Harris's challenge and urges directors to engage locally in studying the processes of writing center documentation, to understand the common elements writing center documents share, the structure of relationships those documents reveal, the kind(s) of persuasive discourse those documents use, the situational contexts in which those documents are produced, the cumulative "story" the documents tell, and the historical sense the cumulative story makes (see Prince 524–27).

Incidentally, the aim of applying narratological methods to documentary research is to recover, interpret, and preserve local writing center history, which is part of a larger historical project that has considerably illuminated our disciplinary and interdisciplinary positions in the academy.[1] But more to the main, narratological methods help writing center directors identify and understand local strategies that reflect and lead to future, rhetorically effective decision making and problem solving. Accordingly, this chapter provides a case study of how one writing across the curriculum (WAC) coordinator-cum-writing center director constructed a narratology to identify the strategic documentation processes that might facilitate change vis-à-vis the institutional role that the writing center played in a large midwestern research university. A list of documentation strategies that other directors might correlate and apply to their *in situ* concerns follows the historical account that the documents told and the changes that the narratology facilitated.

PUTTING HISTORY TOGETHER

Some of the most important processes that narratology enables writing center directors to apprehend are the "*socialization patterns* between writing centers and their institutions" (Barnett 195, emphasis added). Once these socialization patterns are clear, directors can strategize documents that embed, and educate their institutions about, "writing center philosophies, pedagogies and campus services" that move writing centers "into the mainstream of the larger university community" (195). Socialization patterns do not simply announce themselves. The intra-institutional project of narratology involves techniques such as "searching personal memories of older faculty members, storage closets, archives, faculty senate records, registration records, written departmental and institutional histories, student files, hiring records," while also engaging in a hermeneutics that "gives us permission … to do a lot with very little and … fill in many blanks with what we know from events outside the documentary materials" (Mirtz 120–21). We can best position ourselves to engage in such a hermeneutics if we archive writing center documents in an order that shows how socialization patterns have come to define the writing center's institutional position in the past, how they presently define it, and how they might help to redefine it (see Rose).

When I accepted an appointment as a WAC coordinator at my current institution, I inherited three file-folders whose contents very fragmentarily recorded the rise and fall of two previous WAC initiatives. Little evidence attested that the existent writing center had played much of a role at all in the WAC program; it was a small, badly equipped facility where a few nontenured instructors, graduate assistants (GAs), and peer-tutors had worked with a fairly consistent number of students (about three hundred) for the past ten years. One of the most experienced and dedicated writing center instructors told me, "We're the poor children of the university." Yet, she also noted that if students got in the habit of using the writing center during their first year, many of them continued to return when they went on to other classes and cross-curricular writing assignments. This tendency, along with the unusual consistency of the yearly number of students served, implied that the writing center's stasis might stem mostly from underdeveloped socialization patterns between the writing center and a host of others: upper-level administrators, cross-disciplinary departments and programs, individual faculty, students, and of course the English department and the first-year composition program. With

---

[1] For example, see Murphy on theory; Carino ("Computers" 1998) on technology; Mattingly, Grady, and Hughes on early administrative practices.

this hypothesis in mind, I put the documents from my folders into chronological order to examine what types they were, what they had been written to accomplish, who had been their intended readers, and how they fit (or didn't fit) together intertextually. The history that emerged was at once distressing and promising.

I found a document that explained a great deal—a request from the English department for a Program Improvement and Expansion (PIE) grant from the state's Board of Higher Education (BHE). The English department had wanted to fund a project to provide tutorial service for all students, computer facilities for computer-assisted instruction in writing courses, training for teachers of writing, and encouragement of writing throughout the undergraduate curriculum ("NIU Writing Project" 1). By studying this document and talking to the long-standing director of composition, I learned that the English department had envisioned: establishing a writing center for first-year composition and cross-disciplinary students, developing a program to support English as second language (ESL) and at-risk students, overseeing the remodeling and implementation of several computer classrooms, training composition and cross-disciplinary teachers in writing pedagogies (including electronic pedagogies), offering WAC workshops for high school and two-year college faculty in the region, and transforming the university's undergraduate curriculum by proposing and supervising the development of writing-intensive courses. In other words, the writing center, from the onset, was in keen competition with many other exigencies.

A series of memos among a former provost, a former dean of Liberal Arts and Sciences, and the first-year composition director informed me that a conflict had also arisen over how the vision of the writing project should be realized, once the BHE approved and the state legislature granted the funding (which amounted to only half of the original funds requested). The first WAC coordinator, who was hired to administrate the grant, had wanted immediately to set up a writing center. In his initial year, he gathered training materials, got a room for the facility, and put together a staff. For his second year, he wrote a proposal to further that goal, especially in terms of acquiring full-time staff. But the former provost wanted to see more effort concentrated on promoting WAC among cross-disciplinary faculty. This provost required the first-year composition director and the WAC coordinator to revise the writing center proposal so that the budget included funds for visiting WAC scholars to speak to cross-disciplinary faculty, funds for workshops (including a fairly costly WAC retreat for faculty), and funds for grants to support faculty who wanted to study and integrate writing into their syllabi. The WAC coordinator ended up diffusing his time and resources among the writing center (which had already achieved its benchmark of working with three hundred students annually), WAC activities, and a training course for first-year composition instructors.

Yearly reports thereafter, written by the director of composition to the provost, revealed that the WAC coordinator became very overextended. He resigned after an unfavorable annual review about his lack of scholarly publication. Only two of the documents he'd written were in my files: his proposal to the provost to develop the writing center, and a report to the director of composition, evaluating three institutional models for WAC. Of the three models of WAC that his report described, the coordinator had advocated one that emphasized cross-disciplinary faculty taking on responsibility for teaching writing in the disciplines. This small-college model excluded the role a writing center might play in giving follow-up support to the students who would be writing more or the faculty who would be assigning it. However, the report described another model of WAC as well—a large university model that theoretically placed a writing center at the very hub of WAC-related activity on every level (see Kuriloff 105). It was unclear how the provost's preference had influenced the recommendations in this report, or vice versa.

During a two-year period of inertia that followed the resignation of the first WAC coordinator, a memo from the dean to the director of composition informed me that the funds for the writing project had transferred from the Provost's Office to the College of Liberal Arts and Sciences. As an associate dean of my college informed me, this transfer freed the PIE grant from being "micromanaged" by the provost. So the first year following the first WAC coordinator's resignation, a substantial amount of funding went to writing center positions for two full-time equivalent (FTE) instructors and a staff of peer-tutors. But the second year, the English department's priorities changed, and a position was created for a coordinator of computer-assisted instruction (CAI). Substantial funds also went toward establishing computer labs for first-year composition classes.

With the advent of the second WAC coordinator, memos show that the English department released control of the WAC budget to him. Because the new WAC coordinator energetically pursued expanding the model of WAC that the former provost had favored, the yearly budgets from this period demonstrate a sudden attrition of funds for tutors in the writing center: In 1996, $21,000 were allocated for nontenured instructors, English GAs, and peer-tutors. In 1997, only $4,000 was allocated for writing center staff, and $27,000 was allocated for cross-disciplinary writing consultants (all GAs). Another $4,500 also went to an assistant WAC coordinator (a GA), who served as consultant in the College of Business; he helped compile a business writing handbook that faculty still use. Surviving documents from the second WAC coordinator's term of administration also include an extensive, nationally respected Web site, the development of which amassed a collection of faculty-oriented, rhetorically informed resources in cross-disciplinary writing instruction as well as numerous hotlinks to other WAC programs and WAC resources across the nation (see Kimball 62, 69–70). Moreover, whereas documents such as schedules and announcements showed that an annual WAC workshop for faculty and pedagogy-oriented grants continued, reports also showed that the WAC coordinator joined a university initiative to step up writing assessment and a pilot project to train local high school teachers of science, math, and English in WAC.

Despite these major efforts, I learned from one GA consultant (both in an interview and from reading his dissertation) that some of the GAs in WAC served as paper graders and grammar police for faculty in cross-disciplinary departments/colleges. Other GAs morphed into instructors of disciplinary writing courses in the departments where they were assigned. A few managed writing centers-in-exile. With regard to the latter, my files contained one GA's annual reports, WAC newsletters, and class handouts, attesting to her success in developing socialization patterns among faculty and administrators in the four departments where she served. Her talks with me made it equally clear that little communication existed between the neglected writing center and her enterprise, and that a disparity in the perceived quality of tutoring seemed especially evident, which she discovered from students who complained about going to "that other place" whenever she was too booked up.

A report later written by the senior member of the English department's rhetoric and composition faculty in English informed the current associate dean of our college that the second

WAC coordinator resigned because he'd become too discouraged trying to shoulder the main of the WAC movement with too-small gains. Despite getting tenure, he felt he'd severely compromised his professional advancement—an echo of the first coordinator's resignation. The report named a nontenured instructor as interim WAC coordinator, but her duties ended when a budget recision hit, and funds for the coordinator's position were cannibalized. A budget request shows that funding for FTE instructors and peer-tutors in the writing center resumed, but the main evidence of their largely unrecognized work toward the end of this period was a modest Web site that a nontenured instructor had designed with the help of the CAI coordinator.

In confronting the challenges of directing a writing center, archival research that yields such a history may tempt us to "consider disposal of old records an eloquent and gratifying gesture for choosing a new direction for the writing program" (Rose 116). However, it's just as true that "our archives can provide the evidence we need when we present rationales for current practices or the data we need to support proposals for change" (109). Archival research convinced me, for instance, that previous versions of WAC had significantly balkanized efforts toward establishing a strong university writing center to support writing for students and faculty alike on my campus. Yet WAC had also succeeded tremendously in setting up positive socialization patterns among administrators, departments, and cross-disciplinary faculty. I felt the most evident challenge, then, was to refocus those socialization patterns toward establishing a site where writing support could be effectively expanded and centered.

NARRATOLOGY AND ITS USES

Once a comprehensive history is constructed, writing center directors can use the hermeneutics of narratology to analyze, interpret, and attract assistance from the activity systems that constitute the institution where the center resides (see Russell). Directors can also anticipate, and learn to work with, the combination of situational factors that precipitate, or freeze, the cycles of organizational development within the institution (Vaught-Alexander). Such a hermeneutics can enable a director to head off obstacles that threaten a writing center's development. Such a hermeneutics also enables directors to generate the criteria by which we—and, more importantly, upper-level administrators—gauge our measurable and immeasurable successes.

According to Vygotsky's research, a basic activity system consists of subjects (who are involved in the activity), objectives/objects (toward which the subjects are oriented), and mediational means (by which the subjects attempt to achieve the object/objectives; see Russell 51–52). Just so, most basically, a writing center is an activity system of tutors and writers (subjects) who seek better writing practices and written products (objective/object) by means of interaction and different writing technologies (tools). All activity systems share five key features in common; they are historically developed, mediated by tools, dialectically structured, analyzed as the relations of participants and tools, and changed through zones of proximal development (Russell 52).

A narratological analysis of an activity system is complex enough within its own parameters, but clearly no system is self-contained. When significant change is needed, socialization patterns must often shift—and not merely within the system. Implementing change becomes more complex at every point where a director must work through the layers of other activity systems (e.g., a first-year writing or WAC program, a disciplinary department, a committee, a college or university-level administration, a state education board, a state legislature) to plan "for information to be filtered or distorted, for more interests to be considered in decisions, for unanticipated delays, for a 'no' that stops the process" (Simpson II.2.8–9).

Moreover, organizational development cycles in institutions profoundly influence the process of change in extremely complex ways, depending on how a director observes incidents or exigencies that presage the need for change, articulates the need for change in language and formats that other activity systems can readily apprehend, generates—and negotiates constructive resistance to—potential solutions among subjects within and groups outside the writing center, and implements change in timely increments during a period of relative stability (Vaught-Alexander 123). Organizational development cycles are directly tied to, and affect, the entire network of interlocking activity systems in an institution. What follows is a positive example of where such a development cycle might lead.

Once my university began to recover from the recision, the English department pressured the College of Liberal Arts and Sciences to reinstate the position of the WAC coordinator. Many cross-disciplinary faculty who had been keenly interested and involved in the WAC movement had now moved into upper-level administrative positions—not the least being a former English faculty member who had become the interim provost. A new dean of the college was also friendly to WAC, given his contacts with colleagues in other institutions who were involved with WAC programs and writing centers. The English department memo that called for reinstating the WAC coordinator's position carefully reviewed the failures and successes of the university's former WAC efforts and recast them in terms of opportunities. The memo addressed a new associate dean—a math professor who had taken part in many WAC activities and workshops—who became chair of the search for a new WAC coordinator and consequently became my direct supervisor. In that opportune memo, the English department cited the writing center as one of the main successes that had survived the recision.

"Building upon surviving successes in WAC" became a recurrent theme in the documents I wrote and co-wrote during the cyclical upswing that brought me to campus. When meeting with the director of composition, the English chair, the associate dean, and the dean, I asserted that establishing a university writing center had to be the first objective of my appointment. Listening to their collective advice, I generated a document in which I described the multifarious ways an expanded *university* writing center would support WAC and how it would even provide a retreat for WAC in future recisions. This document included a detailed diagram of what that center should look like, because the English department's CAI coordinator told me: "If you want others to understand your vision, *draw pictures!*" I borrowed from existent writing center floor plans in other universities (see Kinkead and Harris). The diagram also included a smart classroom where writing center staff could conduct staff meetings, the English department could schedule writing classes, I could hold WAC workshops, and interdisciplinary faculty could convene for course or program events associated with writing instruction.

My associate dean and I traveled with this document to the assistant provost for resource planning—an economics professor who had also enthusiastically participated in previous WAC activities. He set up a meeting with the dean of University Libraries who, in turn, was designing a very large smart classroom in the main library that feasibly could become the new writing center site as well. In that meeting, however, it became clear that the library vision and the writing center vision were incompatible. When I reported the disappointing results of this meeting to the director of composition, he contacted the associate director of Resident Facilities, who had earned her doctorate in English from the department. She, in turn, called a meeting with her supervisor, the executive director of Student Housing and Dining Services. In a series of fortuitous discussions that eventually involved the dean of my college and the assistant provost for Resource Planning again, we located a space in a dormitory that seemed ideal to house the kind of writing center that my document portrayed. The document's objectives dovetailed with the Living-Learning Program that had been able to develop when the English department used the PIE grant funds to remodel and equip computer classrooms in dormitories.

The assistant provost, the executive director of Student Housing, and my associate dean advised me to work with the associate director of Resident Facilities to draw up a "project order" whose purpose was to identify the background and justification for the writing center, the project's scope, and specific remodeling plans (the space contained areas for a staff office, a conference room, a room to house a server, a smart classroom, a social area, and even a kitchen and bathrooms). A new, far more detailed floor plan emerged (Fig. 10.1). This document led to a series of other documents strategically designed to draw in and commit other activity systems in the university to the project.

Having learned from the narratology of my predecessors in WAC that I needed to construct an ethos and *auctoritas* that would "translate" across activity systems, I also sent out several memos to different stakeholders on why consultant-evaluators from the National Council of Writing Program Administrators (NCWPA) should visit our campus and review our plans, in

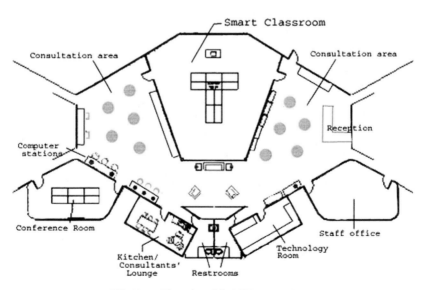

University Writing Center
Stevenson South, Tower B, Lower Level

FIG. 10.1.   Floor plan of the NIU writing center.

the context of what other institutions were doing nationally. I obtained a strong letter of support from a widely recognized writing center scholar whom my dean knew personally to reinforce my request. Because outside reviews often compel a number of university activity systems to share the responsibility of funding such a project (rather than place the burden on a single activity system), my dean approved my request.

The NCWPA's "Guidelines for Self-Study to Precede a Writing Program Evaluation" are designed to shape and help articulate the institutional research that goes into and justifies such an evaluation—in a language and format that upper-level administrations can readily appreciate (see White 304–13). I also called together a temporary WAC advisory board of cross-disciplinary faculty, consulted with my English department colleagues in rhetoric and composition, and conferred with my department chair and associate dean to help me tweak the document. I incorporated local administrative language and aims that made the self-study even more accessible. The self-study thus enlarged on my earlier narratology and placed it in a context that spoke to many activity systems on campus, giving everyone who read it not only a stronger stake in pursuing a new writing center, but also a coherent, salient understanding of how the original 1989 PIE grant had exerted significant influence on the rest of the campus by carrying forward, despite numerous obstacles, the objectives of first-year composition, WAC support, curricular change, and cross-disciplinary writing assessment (see Peters).

The ensuing visit and recommendations from NCWPA consultant-evaluators provided sound justification for writing a "Request for a New Administrative, Research, or Public Service Unit," which elaborated on the mission, objectives, priorities, organization, projected outcomes, and pedagogical resources (including a full-time core of supportive professional staff, SPS) that a well-developed university writing center would encompass. The document included an itemized budget that would adequately support such development. This document incorporated numerous elements: (a) parallels with the university's mission statement, (b) goals that matched statewide university objectives (see State of Illinois), (c) writing center research on retention (e.g., Lerner IV.6.7), (d) lists of similar institutions that had strong writing centers, (e) statistics on our own writing center usage, and (f) equitable job descriptions that the WCenter listserv had helped me formulate for our full-time core staff. The assistant provost for Academic Planning and Development invited me to present this document to the Academic Planning Council (APC)—my university's most influential committee—and after the APC approved, she helped me revise it for submission to the BHE.

We received funding. Hiring a core staff, enlarging peer-tutor staff, and remodeling the new facility began forthwith. I met countless times with carpenters, electricians, and other "craft" to go over and amend the project order as needed. The facility took shape, and we got administrators to do frequent walk-throughs, with copies of the floor plan in hand. Meanwhile, in the "old facility," a tireless associate director and an enthusiastic tutor-instructor helped me develop a peer-tutor training program and significantly expand our campus outreach. I created other crucial documents to justify our expansion and edify the campus: brochures and a Web site to inform faculty and students of ways to use an expansion of writing center services more effectively, annual reports to emphasize to administrators our rapidly growing client usage according to colleges and departments, and assessment projects to suggest to programs and departments how frequent writing center visits improved students' drafting skills.

Then the unforeseen happened. The Bush administration's spending priorities sent state education budgets into a downspin. Another recision befell us, and the entire writing center budget didn't merely freeze—along with many other new project budgets—it actually disappeared. Had our development cycle come to an end?

No. The partnerships we'd maintained across our campus's academic cultures and activity systems held sway—a necessary component of organization development cycles when they get severely tested (Vaught-Alexander 137). As the large picture came back into focus, the first question that the assistant provost for Resource Planning asked the rest of the provost's staff was: "What about the Writing Center?" Space does not permit a full recount of the answer to that question, but to sum up: Our budget reappeared, reduced by a third; the dean of my college and the provost divided responsibility for sustaining it; the assistant provost furnished the smart classroom and the tutoring area; the college provided all our technology. We moved into our new facility, and the show went on. The rationale? Our documents demonstrated how big a chunk of state funds the university had already invested in the writing center, how much we were already accomplishing, and why it was not wise to sink the project.

At this writing, we've finished a year of nearly eight thousand conferences generated by nearly three thousand students. Faculty increasingly turn to us for classroom workshops, presentations, and advice on linking their classes to writing center services. We have been designated a separate academic unit from the English department, and we hire our peer-tutors from a variety of disciplines. Yet our friendly alliance with English remains intact. I continue to use the documentation strategies I've learned to keep others abreast of our growth in tight times— most recently in a successful effort to hire a new full-time SPS tutor-instructor. My associate dean is also seeking the means to raise the salaries of all core staff and to promote the associate director to director, so I can wear fewer hats. We're also trying to figure out how to fund the replacement cycle for technology, although we've already found a way to cobble together tech support from the college. Nothing has happened right away, of course. But we are a work in progress whose exigencies are now firmly associated with meeting student demand and providing cost-effective faculty support. The evidence that we deliver what we promise has encouraged upper-level administration not to interpret our ongoing growing pains as whining.

I attribute many of the good things that have occurred in these roller-coaster times to the socialization patterns that have come about, in large part, from fifteen years of evolving documentation strategies. I've fairly consistently seen those strategies take my colleagues and me into the "zones of proximal development" so necessary for evolving a writing center into the de facto WAC program (Russell 56; Harris, "A Writing Center Without a WAC Program").

Such strategies include the following, although this list is hardly comprehensive:

- *State objectives/objects immediately* (e.g., "This draft of the FY'05 budget reallocates funds from the commodities and faculty grant lines for a new, half-time graduate assistantship because …")
- *Keep stakeholders in dialectical exchange* (e.g., "Besides you and the Dean, I'm sending this report to the Chair of English and the Director of ITS because of what our statistics reveal about the impact of tech support in relation to …")

- *Refer to previous benchmark documents and precedents* (e.g., "The goals of the 1989 PIE grant request included developing peer-tutor training, which we began in the spring of 1990, even though at present …")
- *Foreground significant data* (e.g., "To date, 4/12/04, writing center staff has conducted 7,657 conferences with 2,853 students. We turned away 521 who sought services at peak times—midterm and end of term …")
- *Follow prescribed document formats exactly* (e.g., "Attached is your requested summary of our most recent count on PSYC 555 students, a record of how many have had three tutoring sessions or more, and our observations of what some of them misunderstood about the recent assignment …")
- *Conduct all communications according to protocol* (e.g., "Before writing center staff agree to hold this workshop for Wood Industries, who besides the Office of Continuing Education should be notified?")
- *Acknowledge previous support and its effects* (e.g., "Although the College of Business can't fund a GA in the writing center this year, we thank you for your previous generosity. In 2001, we saw an overall 23% increase of business students from the departments of …")
- *Acquaint stakeholders with pertinent theory and scholarship, but wear it lightly* (e.g., "Our assessment conforms with Muriel Harris's 1997 study of ESL students at the Purdue Writing Center, where she examines assumptions …"; see "Cultural Conflicts")
- *Recognize how "failures" can represent opportunities* (e.g., "Since some of your students have been dissatisfied with their expectation of writing center services, perhaps one of our staff can visit your class to discuss …")

As these documentation strategies and examples illustrate, relationships serve as the basic unit of analysis and evaluation of the activity system we call a writing center—more so than other activity systems, I suspect (Russell 56). These relationships—among tutors and students, faculty and administration—are what we must work the hardest to develop and protect. Whether we imagine ourselves as allies of overworked colleagues, subversives of the academic hierarchy, pedagogical reformers of the classroom, and/or advocates for the underrepresented, without developing and protecting these relationships, we are nothing (see Grimm; North, (1984); Simpson and Maid).

But surely, we've always known that these relationships reside at the center of all we do.

WORKS CITED

Barnett, Robert. "Redefining Our Existence: An Argument for Short- and Long-term Goals and Objectives." *The Allyn and Bacon Guide to Writing Center Theory and Practice.* Ed. Robert W. Barnett and Jacob S. Blumner. Boston: Allyn and Bacon, 2001. 194–201

Carino, Peter. "Early Writing Centers: Toward a History." *The Writing Center Journal* 15.2 (1995): 103–15.

___. "Computers in the Writing Center: A Cautionary History." *Wiring the Writing Center.* Ed. Eric Hobson. Logan: Utah State UP, 1998. 171–93.

Grimm, Nancy Maloney. *Good Intentions: Writing Center Work for Postmodern Times.* Portsmouth, NH: Heinemann-Boynton/Cook, 1999.

Harris, Muriel. "Cultural Conflicts in the Writing Center: Expectations and Assumptions of ESL Students." *Writing in Multicultural Settings.* Ed. Carol Severino, Juan Guerra, and Johnnella Butler. New York: MLA, 1997. 220–23.

___. "A Writing Center without a WAC Program: The De Facto WAC Center/Writing Center." *Writing Centers and Writing Across the Curriculum Programs: Building Interdisciplinary Partnerships*. Ed. Robert Barnett and Jacob Blumner. Westport, CT: Greenwood Press, 1999. 89–103.

___. "Writing Center Administration: Making Local, Institutional Knowledge in Our Writing Centers." *Writing Center Research: Extending the Conversation*. Ed. Paula Gillespie, Alice Gilliam, Lady Falls Brown, and Byron Stay. Mahwah, NJ: Lawrence Erlbaum Associates, 2002. 75–89.

Kimball, Sara. "WAC on the Web: Writing Center Outreach to Teachers of Writing Intensive Courses." *Wiring the Writing Center*. Ed. Eric Hobson. Logan, UT: Utah State UP, 1998. 62–74.

Kinkead, Joyce, and Harris, Jeanette, eds. *Writing Centers in Context: Twelve Case Studies*. Urbana, IL: NCTE, 1993.

Kuriloff, Peshe. "Writing Centers as WAC Centers: An Evolving Model." *Writing Centers and Writing Across the Curriculum Programs: Building Interdisciplinary Partnerships*. Ed. Robert Barnett and Jacob Blumner. Westport, CT: Greenwood Press, 1999. 105–18.

Lerner, Neal. "Research in the Writing Center." *The Writing Center Resource Manual*. Ed. Bobbie Silk. Emmitsburg, MD: NWCA P, 1998. IV.6.1–11.

Mattingly, Carol, Kelli Grady, and Bradley Hughes. "Complicating Writing Center Narratives through Oral History." IWCA and NCPTW 2003 Joint Conference. Hershey Lodge and Convention Center, Hershey, PA. 25 Oct. 2003.

Mirtz, Ruth. "WPAs as Historians: Discovering a First-Year Writing Program by Researching Its Past." *The Writing Program Administrator as Researcher: Inquiry into Action and Reflection*. Ed. Shirley Rose and Irwin Weiser. Portsmouth, NH: Heinemann Boynton/Cook, 1999. 119–30.

Murphy, Christina. "Writing Centers in Context: Responding to Current Educational Theory." *The Writing Center: New Directions*. Ed. Ray Wallace and Jeanne Simpson. New York: Garland Publishing, 1991. 276–88.

North, M. Stephen. "The Idea of a Writing Center." *College English* 46 (1984): 433–46.

___. "Revisiting 'The Idea of a Writing Center.'" *The Writing Center Journal* 15.1 (1994): 7–19.

"NIU Writing Project: Program Improvement and Expansion Request." Unpublished English department document. Northern Illinois University, DeKalb. 1989.

Peters, Bradley. "Writing at Northern Illinois University: A Summary." November 2000. 8 May 2004. <http://www.engl.niu.edu/WAC/WritingatNIU.html>.

Prince, Gerald. "Narratology." *The John Hopkins Guide to Literary Theory and Criticism*. Ed. Michael Groden and Martin Kreiswirth. Baltimore: Johns Hopkins UP, 1994. 524–27.

Rose, Shirley. "Preserving Our Histories of Institutional Change: Enabling Research in the Writing Program Archives." *The Writing Program Administrator as Researcher: Inquiry into Action and Reflection*. Ed. Shirley Rose and Irwin Weiser. Portsmouth, NH: Heinemann Boynton/Cook, 1999. 107–18.

Russell, David. "Activity Theory and Its Implications for Writing Instruction." *Reconceiving Writing, Rethinking Writing Instruction*. Ed. Joseph Petraglia. Mahwah, NJ: Lawrence Erlbaum Associates, Publishers, 1995. 51–77.

Simpson, Jeanne. "Assessing Needs, Identifying an Institutional Home, and Developing a Proposal." *The Writing Center Resource Manual*. Ed. Bobbie Silk. Emmitsburg, MD: NWCA P, 1998. II.2.1–16.

Simpson, Jeanne, and Barry Maid. "Lining Up Ducks or Herding Cats? The Politics of Writing Center Accreditation." *The Politics of Writing Centers*. Ed. Jane Nelson and Kathy Evertz. Portsmouth, NH: Heinemann Boynton/Cook, 2001. 121–32.

State of Illinois Board of Higher Education. "The Illinois Commitment: Partnerships, Opportunities, and Excellence." 2 February 1999. 10 May 2004. <http://www.ibhe.state.il.us/Board/Agendas/1999/February/1999-02-07.pdf>.

Vaught-Alexander, Karen. "Situating Writing Centers and Writing Across the Curriculum Programs in the Academy: Creating Partnerships for Change with Organizational Development Theory." *Writing Centers and Writing Across the Curriculum Programs: Building Interdisciplinary Partnerships*. Ed. Robert Barnett and Jacob Blumner. Westport, CT: Greenwood P, 1999. 118–40.

White, Edward. *Teaching and Assessing Writing*. 2nd Ed. San Francisco: Jossey-Bass Publishers, 1994.

11

Directors at the Center: Relationships Across Campus

Lauren Fitzgerald
Yeshiva University

Denise Stephenson
Cal State University Los Angeles

Lived experience testifies to relationships that problematize conventional knowledge.

—Mahala and Swilky (363)

In short, we are the relationships we have.

—Eodice (123)

In her contribution to *The Writing Center Resource Manual*, Gail Cummins pointed out that "writing center work is highly relational" (II.6.3).[1] As others in the field have long argued, writing centers are constituted by and embedded in relationships between, for example, tutors and writers (Brooks; Bruffee); the center and other programs (Waldo); and the director, faculty, and administrators (North; Simpson "Perceptions"). In "The Politics of Collaboration," Molly Wingate related a powerful story that reminds us that we neglect any one of these relationships at our peril. Devoting her time and energy to work with tutors contributed to her not participating in the development of an academic resource center. Ultimately, the campuswide com-

---

[1] The examples come from experiences in the five different centers we've worked in. Although we would be comfortable revealing who had each experience, we hide our identities for three reasons: (a) As collaborative writers, we prefer not to diminish our coauthorship by labeling the stories individually even though they read best in first-person singular. (b) We don't see that a reader gains anything significant by knowing whose experiences they are; rather, we hope that the situations are imaginable from many-centered perspectives. (c) In a few instances, we'd rather not expose former colleagues to the scrutiny our storytelling imposes. It's not important who it was that treated us badly, for example; it's much more important to focus on the impact of that treatment on the writing center and its director.

mittee in charge called for changes in the writing center without her input. Wingate's experience is but one example of what can happen when a writing center director (WCD) focuses on one writing center relationship to the exclusion of others, leading to an undesirable situation. However, as two current WCDs who, between us, have spent over twenty years administering five centers at different kinds of institutions (big, small, public, and private) and from different positions (grad student, half-time, professional staff, tenure track), we know that being at the center of all of these different relationships can make WCDs feel pulled in many directions at once: How can we balance them all?

We believe that one key means of balancing multiple writing center relationships involves staying "writing centered." Every year, we educate tutors about how to initiate and sustain strong, workable relationships: how to prioritize, how to help without becoming overwhelmed, and how to understand and empathize with other writers, how to treat them with respect. We need to "practice what we preach," as Josephine Koster advised in an article on building effective relationships with central administration (152). Similarly, according to Jeanne Simpson, "We need to adopt the principle that we use so often in tutoring: abandon our preconceived notions and look at what is actually there" ("Perceptions" 52). Michele Eodice urged us to extend the acts of collaboration that are so central to our centers even further, to "carry on deliberate, productive conversations about writing, in writing, for writing with our technology support staff, our librarians, our student services folks, our center for teaching facilitators, our first-year-experience program designers, our faculty from anthropology to zoology" (129).

In this chapter, we recount and analyze several stories of writing center relationships from our years of directing writing centers. Although personal anecdotes may lack the appeal of quantifiable scientific data, we agree with Daniel Mahala and Jody Swilky that "writing from 'personal' experience can reveal conventionally suppressed contextual conditions that mold a discourse" (365). In other words, by examining what actually happens in writing center relationships, we hope to discover what isn't said in writing center research and to demonstrate the reflectiveness we usually expect tutors to display as they learn to navigate their own writing center relationships. Mahala and Swilky demonstrated that the role of storytelling in composition studies complicates epistemology. Through our analysis, we derive strategies and offer advice for directors learning how to grapple with the complexities of writing center relationships. But along with drawing on insights from writing center work to offer these suggestions, we also borrow strategies from a well-known business text, *Getting to Yes: Negotiating Agreement Without Giving In*, by Roger Fisher, William Ury, and Bruce Patton. The world of high stakes negotiations might seem far removed from writing centers, but central to both is how we sustain relationships with the people with which we work (i.e., colleagues, superiors, and subordinates). In writing centers, as in the worlds of business and international relations, we can ask ourselves questions to help clarify complicated scenarios involving multiple relationships:

1. Who are the participants? What do they have at stake?
2. What are the relationships among these participants? In what ways are these various relationships connected?
3. Which are the more important, valuable, or pressing of these relationships? Which can wait?
4. Are there possibilities for developing these relationships further, perhaps through collaboration? Can we make them writing centered?

We use these questions as a heuristic for thinking through relationships with four important groups of people in our centers and institutions: tutors, support staff, administrators, and faculty. In order to articulate qualities unique to relationships with each group, we section them off. However, relationships with any one of these groups usually overlap with another, often with complicated results. Writing center relationships are almost never singular: The people involved often fulfill multiple roles, and any one relationship is bound to be implicated by another.

RELATIONSHIPS WITH TUTORS

Relationships between WCDs and tutors take many different forms: We can be bosses and employees, teachers and students, mentors and apprentices, or even coworkers, collaborators, and friends. Whatever their form, these relationships are crucial to the center: Without tutors who are relatively good at and satisfied with their work, students will not be served adequately. Enthusiastic, talented tutors benefit the WC and the campus at large.

One tutor became very excited when we began using constructive toys in writing center sessions as nonverbal tools for writing and revising. The tutor and I decided that over the summer we'd write together. We collaborated and published both individual and coauthored texts, four in all. For me, her enthusiasm was contagious. For her, my organic process and use of alternative discourse challenged her lock-step method of thesis first, then paper. The pieces we coauthored were in multiple voices, contained dialogues and recipes, and were generally more collages than direct arguments. We provided the center with new expertise and the recognition that publication affords. We also developed multiple relationships beyond boss and employee; I was her teacher, her boss, her confidant, her friend, her collaborator.

Certainly not every WCD–tutor relationship can or should result in publications, but very often the bonds we form can be as rewarding for both the individuals involved and our centers. The collaboration described added to the credentials of both the WCD and the tutor and also impressed colleagues and administrators. Although some aspects of the relationship were uncomfortable (the WCD learned a bit more about the tutor's roommate problems than she would have liked), it has continued to develop: The tutor has gone on to graduate school and become a colleague. Taking the time to build strong WCD–tutor relationships can be well worth the effort. But this extra effort is no guarantee of success. Sometimes WCDs have to make the tough decision to end a tutor's relationship with the center because of all of the other relationships at stake.

Among the already bright members of the tutor training class, one tutor stuck out as exceptional. However, because he felt we were moving too slowly, he had a tendency to disrupt class, contemptuous of those who were "ignorant." I tried to draw him in, to provide theoretical perspectives that would intrigue him but not put off the other tutors. This worked to some degree. A lead tutor observed him with a group. It went well enough. He was able to keep the whole group involved and help them think outside the usual brainstorming box. But near the end of the semester, stories of disaster started pouring in. According to one of my most trusted faculty colleagues who used tutors well in her classroom, one student had refused to work with him. Then another faculty member reported that the tutor had told a student that she might as well take a match to her paper and start over. In the end-of-term evaluations of tutor performance, students wrote abundant comments about him, and few of them were good. I wasn't sure what to do. The tutor had shown progress in developing a better relationship with me, but it had required work on my part that I couldn't expect from students. When I met with him at the end of the term, he couldn't explain any of the situations or imagine why students had complained. I wish I'd intervened earlier, but at that point the best choice was to terminate his employment. Clearly, we couldn't have someone work for us whom students feared.

If, like many difficult teacher–student relationships, this situation had been limited to the classroom, then the WCD might have let the normal rhythms of the institutional calendar (and the final grade) end the relationship. But as we see from this story, with tutor training courses and with writing center work more generally, other stakeholders (other students, other classes, and other faculty) are almost always involved. As a result, we usually have to act more like bosses than teachers in these situations, to be more pro-active and provide such closure ourselves. It's good to be clear about this, both with ourselves and our tutors. It is also helpful to remind tutors that they too are implicated in various writing center relationships and have responsibilities to them. One training method that attempts to underscore these relational responsibilities is the "minimalist," nondirective model: Tutors can best help maintain the student writers' relationship with their teacher, it holds, by not helping too much. However, this minimalist model can oversimplify the tutor–writer–teacher relationship. As Nancy Maloney Grimm and Peter Carino suggested, tutors need instead an understanding of how all of these relationships fit within the institution and the "flexibility" to act accordingly (Carino 110; Grimm 113). Sometimes, as our story shows, the WCD can't even ensure that the tutor will exhibit the set of behaviors that we probably all agree are important in tutoring: respecting others and their writing. Not everyone is temperamentally suited for writing center work. Sometimes, in order for some writing center relationships to continue and thrive, others must end.

RELATIONSHIPS WITH SUPPORT STAFF

[A]s long as a writing center operates within the feudal hierarchy [of the institution], it is going to be subject to both the advantages and the constraints imposed by the hierarchy. (Simpson, Braye, & Boquet 161)

Because of an extreme budget crisis, hiring was frozen. So when our desk staff of four part-time student workers graduated or moved on to other jobs, we weren't able to replace them. Because the assistant director worried that our full-time clerical worker would bear the brunt of this labor shortage, she asked me whether we might use tutors to work at the front desk, something the center had done before I started as WCD. In theory, this seemed like a good idea: training tutors in desk-worker duties could produce a more permeable border between the two positions and lead to better relations between the two groups. It might even mean better service for students. But the practical problem was that the university paid tutors significantly more than the minimum-wage desk workers. Tutors who worked the desk would therefore get more money for doing the same job. Because of the pay discrepancy, this idea was potentially more damaging than helpful.

* * *

I was unsatisfied with the structure of the position of the writing center assistant director from my first day as WCD. It was split between two writing centers on two campuses (two days per week each); it didn't include classroom teaching; it had no departmental status or "home." So when the AD took another job, and the Center on the other campus decided not to fund its half of the position, I worked like crazy not just to hold on to the line but to change it. It became a full-time position on my campus—an English Department Lectureship (nontenure track) that included one course per term. As a result, we were able to hire someone terrific who's turned out to be not only a wonderful AD, but a friend and collaborator, both in every aspect of administering the center and in conference presentations and articles. But there have been complications that I did not foresee in my zeal to convert the position: he is a departmental colleague, but one who does clerical work (the center has no secretary or receptionist) and one I give directions to, both of which make me uncomfortable. Moreover, English department faculty now have a stake in the position, which has led to various disagreements—about what qualifies someone for the job and about the extent and nature of his responsibilities to the department (especially since it has no secretarial support either).

Perhaps more than any other writing center relationships, those involving support staff make clear the institutional hierarchies embedded in our work. In the first story, the institution imposes its valuing of tutoring staff over desk staff through pay rates. In the second, the institutional privileging of faculty lines over professional staff is expressed through the WCD's efforts to convert the AD line to faculty, even though the position contains "clerical" components. As uncomfortable as such hierarchies make some of us, they are difficult if not impossible to avoid. Clerical work is near the bottom of the institutional totem pole, but scheduling hours, completing payroll, answering the phone, addressing student questions, refilling the printers with paper, restocking handouts (and so on) are crucial to our ability to complete our missions and serve students. In fact, the usage rate of the center in the second story went up 80% following the conversion of the AD line, in no small part because the new AD had the time to do his job in ways that the two-day-a-week AD did not.

Thinking about such relationships from a "writing centered" perspective might suggest that we try to make them more egalitarian, to build desk duty into the tutor's job, for instance, or pay the desk workers better, or ensure that assistant or associate directors have the same institutional status as directors. But from the perspective of Grimm's *Good Intentions: Writing Center Work for Postmodern Times*, attempts to efface such institutional hierarchies in the name of "peerness" might actually do more harm than good, leading, in the previous stories, to relations that are even more damaged or positions that are confusing. Grimm urged us instead to recognize "that our relationships are always asymmetrical" (112): "A fair writing center practice would acknowledge the ways writing center work positions undergraduates (and the entire staff) within the culture of power. It would find ways to explicitly acknowledge that privilege as well as to call attention to ways our cultural position might blind us to other possibilities and perspectives" (113). Although these—and, as Grimm pointed out, *all*—writing center relationships are asymmetrical, that doesn't mean that they don't change or that they can't be improved: People leave, budgets fluctuate, positions can be altered. What's important is making sure that all parties can see the possibilities.

RELATIONSHIPS WITH ADMINISTRATORS

Writing center directors need to enter into collaborative relationships with other administrators, especially the writing program director. (Balester and McDonald 71)

I worked as the coordinator of a small writing center that operated within a larger writing program. Though I was in charge of running the center, there was not much room for my input: the writing program director (WPD),[2] whom I reported to, hired and trained the center's undergraduate staff, and I was to check with her even on signs advertising the center. I longed to do more, especially about the center's grim location in a student dorm, but the WPD was not interested. On a few occasions, however, I was able to speak directly to the assistant dean about my concerns. She asked for a report on usage rates. I pulled together some numbers and quoted a client who complained about the center's being "in a broom closet." The next year, we got carpeting, and a few years later the entire space was remodeled. But though the space improved, my position (half-time, no benefits) and my relationship with the WPD did not. Though I now see that I hadn't done myself any favors by going over her head to initiate changes, she never once acknowledged my contributions to the center. Frustrated by this decidedly noncollaborative relationship, I finally quit.

* * *

In my first year as WCD, an administrator from the School of Social Work asked me if I could assist students in the program. The peer-tutors of the writing center, located in an undergraduate college, were unprepared to work with these graduate students. When I asked my dean, who controls the center's budget, what I could do, he told me to agree to help only a few students a term. Initially, the AD and I ended up handling most of the appointments. As the years went by, I worked on developing the tutors' abilities and also hired experienced faculty tutors. I met with the Social Work faculty occasionally, and we defined what the center could and could not do. We added hours to accommodate their students' schedules and offered special workshops. Social Work started providing funding. MSW students lined up for assistance and became a significant part of the center's clientele. My dean liked how our work with these students showed upper administration that the college was serving the rest of the university, which improved my case for increasing the center's budget overall.

Although the ultimate outcomes are very different, the two previous stories have much in common. Each involves relationships between a WCD and two other administrators. In each story, one administrator asks for something (a report, tutoring for students) that the WCD delivers, and the WCD gets something in return she didn't initially expect (carpeting, funding). One lesson we can derive from these stories, then, is that entering into relationships with and doing a little bit of extra work for the right people can pay off, quite literally. But the stakes go beyond the physical or fiscal benefits.

---

[2]We recognize that WPA is the typical abbreviation for someone with this title. However, we find that WPA obscures the differences between directors of writing centers, first-year composition and writing across the curriculum programs. This obscuring, the kind Mahala and Swilky discussed, often leaves writing center directors as handmaidens to composition directors (see Balester and McDonald 59–60). Here we wanted to use titles and acronyms that allow us to see these various roles separately.

The connections among these primary stakeholders set up the importance of power dynamics. For example, in the first case, the WCD went against Jeanne Simpson's advice to "Never violate the chain of command" ("Assessing Needs" II.2.4). However, in the second story, it was an administrator who sought help from the WCD, rather than the other way round. Partially this may be due to the WC's being seen as a campuswide service provider, but this also highlights what happens across the institutional chart laterally. Whereas members within a unit may need to follow the hierarchical pattern, those in another unit may approach whomever seems most appropriate. This is one of the features of higher education that makes institutional relationships confusing.

Two further perspectives emerge from these cases. In the first, the "opportunity" presented itself to get carpeting by writing a report. But this opportunity carried a price tag, a high stake of violating hierarchical boundaries. In unusual situations, like an administrator's suddenly approaching us for a new report, it's important we look beyond immediate surroundings and ask ourselves about the larger implications. Although the first story didn't work out well for the WCD and the second did, both involved communicating, or not, with other stakeholders—administrators. Because the request in the first story came from the assistant dean, the WCD did not see the need to check in with the WPD before providing the report. (After all, the assistant dean was essentially the boss of the WCD's boss—and why wouldn't the WPD be interested in improving the center?) Such "opportunities" may blind us to business-as-usual, leading us to neglect full disclosure with others with which we have relationships. In the second story, the WCD did see a reason to consult with the dean; budget restrictions made it clear that his input, if not his "permission," was needed. Such stories also lead us to think about relationships as unfolding over time. We often wish for an immediate (and perfect) solution, but partial solutions that we give ourselves time to think about can develop into fuller, better solutions if the stakeholders continue to have unmet needs.

But there is another lesson, too, about what it takes to "enter into [a] collaborative relationship" with administrators, as Balester and McDonald urged us to do. The second story is filled with classic writing-centered collaboration—between Social Work and the writing center, its administrators, faculty, and students; between a WCD and dean; and finally between the dean and higher administration. In the first story, on the other hand, collaboration was impossible. With hindsight and a lot more space for story and analysis, we could ferret out some of the reasons. But what's important here is to recognize that such things do happen: People can refuse to collaborate, whether by overtly avoiding collaboration or by simply neglecting it. And when those people have higher institutional positions than we do, we need to acknowledge (to ourselves, anyway) their noncollaboration. This may mean making collaborative alliances elsewhere, or it may mean quitting. Either way, recognizing the situation allows us to be proactive rather than reactive.

RELATIONSHIPS WITH FACULTY

Are we ashamed to work for others, in service to others, in a helping profession? (Eodice 123)

1. When I offered to "help in whatever way I could," in response to a request from the medical school, I unwittingly agreed to teach the writing-intensive course being offered to all first-year med students.

2. *For several years, I led in-class writing workshops for capstone health science classes. I accepted this "duty" in my first year, only to discover that my one-hour workshop was the only in-class writing component of this writing-intensive course.*

3. *The dean asked me to hire a graduate student to grade papers for a class he wanted to be writing-intensive. Unfortunately, the professor thwarted the effort at every turn, refusing even to talk with the grader about his expectations for the assigned writing.*

4. *Both of us have been asked to edit, proofread, respond to and collaborate on (ghost-write?) articles, dissertations, and books for other faculty.*

In these short descriptions, faculty and WCDs are the primary stakeholders. The faculty's stakes range from low to high, but are usually immediate. They need help (*now*) with courses they are teaching, articles they are writing, something that affects their retention, tenure, and promotion files. The stakes for the WCD are generally low at the time of the request but may increase over time. WCDs consider the perception of themselves and their roles on campus, the long-term relationships they are making or avoiding, and the effects these interactions have on faculty perceptions of the writing center. It's worth looking closely at who is asking for help and why. In most cases, faculty ask for themselves, so there's good reason to listen carefully and problem solve with them. But in some situations, like the third scenario, chairs, deans, or provosts get involved, and their agendas may differ from those of the faculty member or the WCD. If an administrator makes a connection or suggests the need of a faculty member to a WCD, it's most appropriate to contact the faculty directly and not to work through the administrator. This allows the problem solving to fit the need as perceived by the faculty or to be abandoned if inappropriate. Getting caught between faculty and administration is not good.

Looking back at these episodes, what strikes us most is how much our time and availability has changed. In the first three instances, we took on tasks in the first year when we were uncertain about the parameters of our jobs, when our time was relatively open, and when we desperately wanted to fit into our institutions and be seen as contributors. As the semesters went by and we got busier, we recognized that there were many more faculty than we could ever have time to help in the ways they wanted us to, which made us feel overwhelmed and panicky. Because we didn't want to promise more than we could deliver, we started saying no to these requests, deciding that what we couldn't offer everyone, we wouldn't offer anyone. At that point, it felt like a simple binary: Either we fulfilled the requests or we didn't; we entered into the relationship or shut the door. We couldn't see or didn't feel empowered enough to suggest alternatives.

Now, many years later, we realize that the needs behind the many faculty requests we've gotten aren't so unreasonable. Like students, faculty need lots of different kinds of help with writing (their own and their students'), and writing centers offer many kinds of help. What can be unreasonable is *how* we're expected to fulfill some of these needs. The authors of *Getting to Yes* would say that we've finally managed to differentiate each party's "interests" from their "positions"; that is, we see faculty "needs, desires, concerns, and fears" rather than only what they explicitly state as their goals (40). There's something "writing centered" about this differentiation: Even though we help writers, we don't always do so in exactly the way they want us to. We've also learned to ask more questions in order to identify the interests. The advantage to doing so, according to Fisher, Ury, and Patton, is that it's usually easier to reconcile interests than positions, because "for every interest there usually exist several possible positions that could satisfy it." In fact, they claimed that "a close examination of the underlying interests will reveal the existence of many more interests that are shared or compatible than ones that are opposed" (42). In other words, if we keep talking, we're more likely to figure out solutions.

For instance, rather than spending years working individually with faculty, and completely draining her own energies and enthusiasm in the process, Denise started faculty writing groups. There's no question that the amount of time she spent with faculty increased, but she also served her own needs as a writer and as a director. Along with getting help on her own work, there were more discussions of teaching writing on campus, faculty altered their teaching to reflect process pedagogy, they lead workshops on teaching writing, and attended national WAC conferences, all of which led to more relationships between the writing center and faculty. When the amount of work became more than she could handle, she was able to argue for a new graduate student position (which she got) and subsequently involved the graduate student in some of this faculty work. These faculty groups haven't been a magical answer to every faculty request, but she kept asking questions to arrive at solutions. For example, a new faculty writing group was forming on campus composed entirely of humanities faculty. When a nonnative computer science faculty member wanted help with grammar, punctuation, and research methods for several publications nearing deadline, it was clear that the faculty writing group wasn't the best alternative. So Denise provided a connection to a professional editor whom the faculty could pay for services. Both the writing group and the individual faculty member were pleased with the solution.

* * *

One day a tutor showed up in my office asking if I knew why the writing center was suddenly overflowing with Psych 101 students who genuinely wanted feedback (rather than extra credit). To handle the onslaught, a number of tutors formed impromptu peer response groups, but there were still lines. The students had apparently been required to come yet they were willing to work on their assignment, an odd combination. Concerned about the large numbers waiting for service, I contacted the professor who said he'd told all 100 of his students that "prepared students" (not good or bad students) go to the writing center; if they went, their papers would not fail, unlike previous classes in which there were numerous Fs.

How do we contact faculty in tricky situations like this? E-mail might seem easiest and may lead to the quickest connection, but it can too often sound like an accusation. ("Why are 100 students from your Psych 101 class lined up outside the Writing Center?" [!]) Real-time conversation allows for easier questions and answers, give and take. Initiating contact with questions, as we would in tutoring, establishes an ethos that encourages dialog and, ultimately, collaboration. Speaking with someone also allows for the discovery of creative solutions instead of assuming business as usual. In this case, the WCD and the faculty member from psychology brainstormed ideas for how the center might assist with a class this large. And while discussing class size, the WCD took the opportunity to ask about other strategies the faculty used to deal with the writing of one hundred students, eventually persuading the professor to offer a faculty development workshop demonstrating his techniques for motivating large numbers of students to come to class ready to discuss and revise their writing assignments.

We need to explain to faculty the less than optimal results of sending all of their students to our centers without contacting us first—from the simple fact that we might not be able to serve everyone to the more complicated issue of students' taking out their resentment of this "requirement" on tutors. But we also need to try hard to understand faculty perceptions of writing centers and WCDs. Some faculty see writing centers and WCDs as service providers. And, to some extent, isn't that what we are? But the key difference might be that as WCDs, we want to collaborate *with* faculty, not do the work *for* them. It's not that we don't want to help; it's that we need to do so collaboratively. If we can recognize the gleaming hope behind one hundred students descending on the center, then we can change how we—and faculty—work within the faculty–student–tutor triangle.

CONCLUSIONS

Writing centers are inextricably bound to and influenced by our institutions, our communities, and even the state of world affairs. We're not saying anything new here. For more than a decade our writing center colleagues have called on us to think differently about our work. As Muriel Harris explained, rather than defining itself against its institutional context, "A well-functioning, effective writing center folds itself into and around the localized features, building on them" (76). This is one of the reasons we include real-life stories in this article: We learn how to develop relationships most effectively within a specific context. If we're not in conversation with those across our institutions, then how will we know that we fit the pedagogical terrain? But more than simply helping us fit in, maintaining solid ties between our centers and various stakeholders in our institutions allows for the possibility of actually having an impact on our contexts. We all dream of making a difference. Jo Koster encouraged us "to represent ourselves as effective parts of [our] institutions.... That is our best chance not only to perpetuate what we do well, but also to transform the institutions themselves" (163).

Even armed with the best advice, however, like our tutors, we can feel scared, mad, overwhelmed, even abused by our on-the-job relationships. Like our tutors, we sometimes have a lot to complain about. But unlike them, we usually don't have staff meetings at which we can vent our frustrations to peers who really understand where we're coming from. This is one reason why forming relationships with other WCDs, near and far, is so crucial. Both of us have not only participated in the national forums of WCenter and IWCA conferences, but we've formed local writing center connections within states and large urban centers. (Lauren Fitzgerald's written about the group she started in the New York City area for the *Writing Lab Newsletter*.) The relationships formed with other WCDs provides brainstorming, mentoring, and professional development opportunities. Coauthoring this chapter, for instance, helped both of us to not only cope with the losses we've experienced moving from one writing center to another, but to recognize and celebrate our many accomplishments. Only a fraction of those are represented here, but email us, talk to us at a conference or take a look at our Web sites, and you'll get a sense of why we love the work we do.

WORKS CITED

Balester, Valerie, and James C. McDonald. "A View of Status and Working Conditions: Relations between Writing Program and Writing Center Directors." *WPA* 24.3 (2001): 59–82.

Brooks, Jeff. "Minimalist Tutoring: Making the Students Do All the Work." *Writing Lab Newsletter* 15.6 (1991): 1–4.

Bruffee, Kenneth A. "Peer Tutoring and the 'Conversation of Mankind.'" *Writing Center Theory and Administration*. Ed. Gary A. Olson. Urbana, IL: NCTE, 1983. 3–15.

Carino, Peter. "Power and Authority in Peer Tutoring." *The Center Will Hold: Critical Perspectives on Writing Center Scholarship*. Ed. Michael A. Pemberton and Joyce Kinkead. Logan: Utah State UP, 2003. 96–113.

Cummins, Gail. "Standing in the Places Where We Are: What to Think about When Starting College and University Writing Centers." *The Writing Center Resource Manual*. Ed. Bobbie Silk. Emmitsburg, MD: NWCA P, 1998. II.6.1–7.

Eodice, Michele. "Breathing Lessons, or Collaboration Is" *The Center Will Hold: Critical Perspectives on Writing Center Scholarship*. Ed. Pemberton, Michael A. and Joyce Kinkead. Logan: Utah State UP, 2003. 114–29.

Fisher, Roger, William Ury, and Bruce Patton. *Getting to Yes: Negotiating Agreement Without Giving In*. 2nd ed. New York: Penguin Books, 1991.

Fitzgerald, Lauren. "Connecting Local Writing Centers: An Example from the Big Apple." *Writing Lab Newsletter* 28.5-6 (Jan./Feb. 2004): 1–5.

Grimm, Nancy Maloney. *Good Intentions: Writing Center Work for Postmodern Times*. Portsmouth, NH: Heinemann-Boynton/Cook, 1999.

Harris, Muriel. "Writing Center Administration: Making Local, Institutional Knowledge in Our Writing Centers." *Writing Center Research: Extending the Conversation* Ed. Paula Gillespie, Alice Gillam, Lady Falls Brown, and Byron Stay. Mahwah, NJ: Lawrence Erlbaum Associates, 2002. 75–90.

Koster, Josephine A. "Administration Across the Curriculum: Or Practicing What We Preach." *The Center Will Hold: Critical Perspectives on Writing Center Scholarship*. Ed. Michael A. Pemberton and Joyce Kinkead. Logan: Utah State UP, 2003. 151–65.

Mahala, Daniel, and Jody Swilky. "Telling Stories, Speaking Personally: Reconsidering the Place of Lived Experience in Composition." *Journal of Advanced Composition* 16.3 (1996): 363–88.

North, Stephen M. "The Idea of a Writing Center." *College English* 46 (1984): 433–46.

Simpson, Jeanne. "Assessing Needs, Identifying an Institutional Home, and Developing a Proposal." *The Writing Center Resource Manual*. Ed. Bobbie Silk. Emmitsburg, MD: NWCA P, 1998. II.2.1–16.

___. "Perceptions, Realities, and Possibilities: Central Administration and Writing Centers." *Writing Center Perspectives*. Ed. Byron L. Stay, Christina Murphy, and Eric H. Hobson. Emmitsburg, MD: NWCA P, 1995. 48–52.

Simpson, Jeanne, Steve Braye, and Beth Boquet. "War, Peace, and Writing Center Administration." *Landmark Essays on Writing Centers*. Ed. Christina Murphy and Joe Law. Davis, CA: Hermagoras P, 1995. 151–78.

Waldo, Mark L. "What Should the Relationship between the Writing Center and Writing Program Be?" *The Writing Center Journal* 11 Fall/Winter (1990): 73–80.

Wingate, Molly. "The Politics of Collaboration: Writing Centers within their Institutions." *Resituating Writing: Constructing and Administering Writing Programs*. Ed. Joseph Janangelo and Kristine Hansen. Boynton/Cook Heinemann, 1995. 100–07.

12

The Center Has Two Faces: Developing a Writing Center in a Multicampus University Setting

Amy Ward Martin
Pace University

In *The Politics of Writing Centers*, Carol Peterson Haviland, Carmen Fye, and Richard Colby noted that "although location is not everything, it too is important, for material spaces have political edges that are costly if ignored. Location is political because it is an organizational choice that creates visibility or invisibility, access to resources, and associations that define the meanings, uses, and users of designated spaces" (85). Whereas the politics of location are significant for writing centers in terms of their placement on campuses and within buildings, such politics become even more complicated when a university opens multiple writing centers in different geographical locations. These multiple centers technically exist at the same university and share the same mission, but the characteristics of each campus and the physical placement of each center may shape those centers in ways that may make sense for one campus but not for the other. In other words, although the "writing center" as a university-wide department presents one face to the public and to the university as a whole, the "writing center" as separate physical entities on individual campuses may present different faces to each student/faculty constituency that it serves in terms of staff, policies, and services.

The politics of multiple locations became relevant to me personally when I was asked to start and direct the writing center at Pace University in New York. Starting with the fall 2003 semester, the university was to implement a new undergraduate core curriculum, a feature of which would be a substantial focus on writing; in addition to taking two to three writing courses in the English department, students would also be required to take two writing-enhanced courses in any discipline as a requirement for graduation. Given Pace's increased focus

127

on students' writing skills, the writing center was proposed with the specific mission of support-ing students taking writing-enhanced courses and the professors who would be developing these courses. My task, when I assumed the directorship during the summer 2003, was to have the Pace University Writing Center up and running by the beginning of the fall semester. I would then become, as it were, the public "face" of the center, promoting our services to vari-ous constituencies on campus, securing grant funding, serving on university committees, and representing the Pace University Writing Center at conferences and professional meetings.

While starting a writing center is no easy task regardless of the setting, my particular charge was complicated by the fact that Pace University is housed at several geographic locations around the New York City metropolitan area, with undergraduate instruction primarily taking place on campuses in lower Manhattan and the suburban Westchester County town of Pleasantville. Therefore, a reference to the "Pace University Writing Center" describes two separate locations that serve two somewhat different student constituencies. The Pleasantville student body of over three-thousand undergraduate students is nearly 50% White. The New York campus, on the other hand, is less than 40% White and has a larger per-centage of Asian, Hispanic, and African American students than its suburban counterpart.[1] The greater ethnic diversity on the New York campus also means that more English as a second language (ESL) students take courses in the city; a representation of the disparity in numbers of ESL students between the Pleasantville and Manhattan campuses lies in the fact that the New York English department designates certain sections of core curriculum writing courses as ESL-only sections, whereas the Pleasantville English department does not. In short, although Pace University has one public face, the individual campuses have different faces in a quite lit-eral sense—the faces of their students.

I, as the "face" of the center on both campuses, struggle with adequately dividing my time between the two locations while at the same time, as a faculty member new to the university, learning about those locations and about the university as a whole. My dual status as adminis-trator and tenure track faculty member contributes to my struggle to maintain a balance in my involvement on the two campuses. Unlike other departments at Pace in which faculty teach on both campuses, the English departments are not united as one department between New York and Pleasantville.[2] Officially hired as an assistant professor in the Pleasantville English department, I teach and hold departmental committee assignments in Pleasantville and am obligated to spend more time on the Westchester campus. Travel between the two campuses within one day is certainly feasible given that the campuses are located less than an hour by car or train away from each other, but my teaching schedule frequently makes such travel prohibi-tive. As I typically teach on Mondays and Wednesdays, those days have become my designated "Pleasantville days," with Tuesdays being my "New York days." On Thursdays and Fridays I go to the campus where I have the most scheduled meetings or appointments,[3] and I take one day

---

[1] Figures are courtesy of the Pace University Fact Sheet, available at <www.pace.edu>.

[2] In fact, the Pleasantville campus technically did not have an English department until the fall 2003 semester. The Eng-lish and Communications departments were joined together as the "Literature and Communications" department, with some English course offerings being in common between the New York and Pleasantville campuses. Starting with the fall 2003 semester, the Pleasantville English and Communications departments split into two separate departments; although the New York and Pleasantville English departments are not joined as are many other departments at Pace, the two do offer many courses in common to facilitate students who may need to take courses in the two different locations.

[3] Because Pace University has multiple campus locations, many meetings are videoconferenced or teleconferenced.

(as per my contract) for my research and writing. Yet, although my schedule seems orderly enough on the surface, the fact that I cannot be everywhere at once and delegate many responsibilities to the campus writing center coordinators, who were responsible for the day-to-day operations of the centers, has left me feeling distanced from the department of which I am ostensibly the director. For example, I was unlikely to meet any tutor who worked solely on Mondays in New York or solely on Tuesdays in Pleasantville. With the coordinators responsible for arranging tutor meetings and ongoing training, I feel that I only know half of my staff on either campus. I could very well be in the cafeteria some morning, standing on line to purchase coffee, and unknowingly be right behind one of my own employees, a person whose job, salary, and training had been determined by my approval, my signatures on a form. And although this mystery employee may not care to know me (in that person's view, I am probably another one of those nameless, faceless administrators students rail against when complaining about various aspects of the university), the full-time faculty member in me, the *teacher*, wants to know that individual. But my role as a nameless, faceless administrator traveling between two campuses and dashing from meeting to meeting renders knowing this person difficult, if not impossible.

My feeling of being simultaneously faceless and two-faced—in terms of my role as an administrator on two campuses, in terms of my role as both an administrator and faculty member—was further accentuated by the physical differences between the two campuses that would impact the placement of the centers themselves. The New York campus is located primarily in a high-rise building at the foot of the Brooklyn Bridge, whereas the Pleasantville campus is located in a more traditional campus setting of multiple buildings and green space. However, what both campuses have in common is a lack of space within existing buildings for new offices, much less an entirely new department such as a writing center. The proposal for the writing center, written by the directors of writing on the respective campuses, noted the importance of a central location for the department as it would serve as a support system for writing courses in the new core curriculum. Although the campus libraries proved to be the most logical and central locations, neither library had adequate space readily available for a writing center. And as Haviland, Fye, and Colby noted through their discussion of WCenter listserv messages on location, some writing center directors feel that the library is the most sensible place for a writing center, but others, such as John Edlund, noted that "library space is often very different from writing space, particularly in tolerance of noise and disruption, and … librarians, like many other landowners, can be territorial and treat writing centers like tenants rather than neighbors." Although the library staffs on both campuses proved to be more than neighborly, even setting up a listserv through which they could keep tutors informed of new reference materials or other library news that might be relevant to their sessions with students, the spaces for the writing centers in each library emphasized the differences between "library space" and "writing center space."

In "An Ideal Writing Center: Re-Imagining Space and Design," Leslie Hadfield and her co-authors, who consist of a writing tutor along with an interior design professor and two interior design students, present (as their title suggests) a description and architectural plan for a writing center that is spatially and pedagogically ideal, a "non-threatening, comfortable environment that generates—rather than inhibits—conversation" (171). The writing center that they design has a large reception area, separate small rooms for individual tutoring, rooms for group tutoring sessions and staff meetings, easy access to a computer lab, and centrally located director's and assistant director's offices to allow for ease in observing the tutoring rooms. They also described how the center should be lit and decorated in order to foster the most comfortable atmosphere for all. Yet the center that Kinkead and her colleagues design, however ideal, is a far cry from the reality of most writing center spaces. As Jeanne Simpson noted, "Too often writing centers move into leftover, undesirable spaces or they move into spaces originally designed for other purposes" (II.2.12). Although not completely undesirable, the library spaces designated for the Pace University Writing Center were certainly originally designed for other purposes.

The space issue was resolved on the New York campus by opening an emergency exit from the library to the second floor of the high-rise building that houses most of the campus. The writing center was then essentially carved out of the leftover space of two offices and a hallway. The hallway was sealed off by installing an emergency exit (to eliminate the possibility of anyone leaving the writing center with unchecked books from the library) and the existing wall between the two offices was eliminated to allow for a larger tutoring space; a small office was also built inside this larger space. Yet, although a writing center was reconfigured out of existing space on the New York campus, no such construction took place—nor *could* take place—in Pleasantville due to the architectural constraints of the library. Housed in its own self-contained building (rather than a high rise), the library contained very little leftover space to house the writing center. Therefore, we moved into a conference room, an open study area and the former student lounge for the honors program.[4] The conference room would serve as the main tutoring area and the open area would also be a space for tutoring and a reception desk; the honors lounge would house the office to be shared by me and the writing center coordinator, who would supervise the day-to-day activities of the center. The various moves and constructions took the majority of the summer to complete (indeed, construction on the New York facility was not complete until the end of September), but the effect of the final physical spaces on both the administrative and tutoring staffs, in terms of their interactions with each other and with the wider university as a physical entity outside our doors, became evident almost immediately and manifested itself through conversation—or a lack thereof. The writing center as one department evolved into two locations with different "faces," one silent and one animated.

The story of the Pace University Writing Center in its first year is inevitably bound up in the development of its "faces" (spaces). These "faces" become even more significant as they begin to represent the writing center to not only the wider university community but to the center itself. Elizabeth H. Boquet noted in *Noise from the Writing Center*, that

> Tales of writing centers are invariably tales of location, of space. They involve a privileging of the gaze. But we have learned … that the gaze—once posited as objective, as disinterested—is actually quite partial: both limited *and* interested. The perspective of the gaze, in other words, has been called into question and we should be searching for ways of representing ourselves *to* ourselves in partial terms. Paying attention to noise might be one way of doing so. (38)

The noise coming from the respective campus writing centers, coming from the "open mouths" of our doors (and walls, as becomes evident later) has played a role in not only our

---

[4]The honors program took over a former study space outside the honors director's office for their new study lounge, a move that proved to be more palatable to them as their previous lounge had been located down the hall and away from the director's office.

interactions with the university's students and faculty but has also been a way of "representing ourselves *to* ourselves," shaping how the staff interacts with the writing center administration and each other. But, again, these interactions differ greatly in terms of the campus locations of the centers.

Although our space in a remote corner of the second floor of the library was not ideal in terms of visibility, some well-placed signs and campus promotion quickly attracted a steady stream of students to the New York campus writing center. However, too many of these students gathering at our reception desk making appointments or too many tutors congregating at our entrance for a friendly chat led to minor conflicts with students who chose to study at the library desks directly outside our front doors. In order to avoid alienating students who had come to the library for quiet study, we would (if requested) shut one of the double-doors at our entrance in order to cut down on the noise filtering out into the library. We also turned the single, isolated tutoring station just outside the director's/coordinator's office into a sort of "break room," albeit a small one. With the addition of a coffee maker and snacks, this space became an alternative to the front entrance area as a place for tutors to gather for a quiet chat away from the "action" of tutoring appointments. The adjacency of the "break area" to the office also allowed for tutor conversations to spill over into the office, giving tutors the opportunity to engage in frequent and informal discussions with the coordinator and me. These infrequent conversations made staff development much easier, because tutors felt comfortable coming into the office and closing the door or speaking in hushed tones about a difficult tutoring session.

Conversation abounded between tutors and administrative staff at the New York campus center after creating space for it, but we were unable to create such a space in Pleasantville. At the Pleasantville location, the office and the main tutoring area were not adjacent to each other, so there was no ready-made space for conversation. And it was impossible to creatively reconfigure the space to create such a gathering place; whereas the New York writing center was set off from the library in its own self-contained space, the Pleasantville writing center was, quite literally, located in the middle of the library on a third-level mezzanine. Due to fire code regulations, only so much of the third level could be "sealed off" from the second floor below. Although our main tutoring area (the former conference room) was self-contained, our reception area opened out onto a larger study room and the east wall of our office space was a half-wall, opening out onto the stacks of books and study areas of the library's second floor—the university could not build a door between the writing center and the study area or extend the wall in the office to the ceiling without violating fire codes. Whereas the issue of noise drifting into the study room never emerged because people did not congregate at the front desk, noise did become a factor in our office. Not only would any animated conversation in the office drift downward, leading to frequent complaints from library patrons on the second floor, but any private conversation about tutoring sessions was nearly impossible. For example, when the academic advisor of a student whom our coordinator had tutored called to discuss the fact that the student had expressed suicidal thoughts, the coordinator had to decline to speak about the matter over the phone due to lack of privacy. Ironically, the physical openness of the Pleasantville center closed off possibilities for conversation, whereas the closed-off structure of the New York center opened the door (so to speak) to both formal and informal conversations about tutoring.

The ability to have constant conversation in the New York center resulted in what I perceived to be a closer connection on the part of the tutors to the writing center and their work there, perceptions supported by my observations of them throughout the fall semester. Their Pleasantville counterparts would come to work and leave when they had completed their scheduled hours, but the New York staff would often linger after their scheduled tutoring sessions were finished or come to the center before their appointments in order to just "hang out," have some coffee, or grab a chat with a fellow tutor whom they may not have seen all week. Their training took on this informal, conversational tone as well; as we could not find a common time for the staff to meet as a whole, ongoing training for the undergraduate tutors assumed the guise of individual discussion sessions about sample papers between the coordinator and each tutor. By contrast, ongoing staff training in Pleasantville consisted of biweekly meetings of the entire staff, although most of the undergraduate tutors would fail to show up (even though training sessions were considered "work" and they would be paid). What I saw manifesting between the two centers were two different definitions of writing center "work"—work in the traditional, Fordist sense of being something that a low paid, unskilled worker does to earn a wage, and work in the sense of something that is an extension of one's academic and social lives, one's *self*. For example, when the writing center received some negative press in the New York campus newspaper at the end of the fall semester based mostly on inaccurate information from unnamed sources, many tutors commented to me that they felt personally violated and offered to pen letters to the editor, particularly as the article implied that the tutors were underprepared to work with students and were dissatisfied with their working conditions. The following semester, we attempted to counter any negative perception of the center by sending tutors to do classroom presentations, both within the English department and in any other courses for which professors requested our services. The promotion on the part of our tutors, both through formal means and via word of mouth, has resulted not only in an increase in the number of students coming to the center, but it has also contributed to a doubling of the enrollment in our new tutor training course from its initial run during the fall 2003 semester.

Yet, in waxing enthusiastic about the achievements of my New York tutoring staff in terms of diffusing the negativity that surrounded the writing center, I once again feel two-faced, like a mother celebrating the achievements of her intelligent, outgoing child while overlooking the accomplishments of the no-less-intelligent but considerably quieter one. Although no negative perceptions exist—at least to my knowledge—of the Pleasantville center, the enthusiasm for the tutor training course has been considerably lower, and the requests from professors to visit their courses have been few. The writing center, in other words, does not seem to have established a visible face or a vocal presence on the Pleasantville campus in terms of reaching potential tutors or interacting with faculty, although students in need of our assistance, according to our numbers, apparently have no trouble locating our Spartan quarters.

The choice of a space creates associations that define its users and shape its perceptions. Although both writing centers exist in marginalized spaces within their respective libraries, the community that has blossomed within the walls of the New York center has extended out into the wider academic community. On the contrary, no real writing center community has had the opportunity to exist within or outside the Pleasantville center mostly due to a lack of walls that kept conversation—and I would argue, the professionalization as well—to a minimum. Linda Shamoon and Deborah Burns noted that in writing center culture there has emerged a special identity that binds writing-center workers to an academic endeavor—the study of writing—that has a teaching and a research function. Unfortunately, in many instances these elements of professionalism flourish only within the cultural milieu of the center, and they are in conflict with the wider institutional and popular culture's view that helping students improve their writing is remedial work or nonacademic study-skills work. This outsider-versus-insider perception tears away at the conditions of labor in the center, holding in place a conflict that is exacerbated by the central role of standardized generalist tutoring. (68–69)

The tutors in New York, thanks to both their formal professional development and the informal professional development that takes place in their conversations, have grown to see their writing center work as an academic endeavor—and encourage others to develop an academic connection to the writing center via the new tutor training course. However, the Pleasantville staff, composed primarily of generalist tutors, have remained relatively disconnected from the center.

My own feelings of disconnect from my staffs have forced me to reexamine not only the spaces within which the writing centers exist, but also have pushed me to redefine the concepts of tutoring and tutor training on both campuses. Although the Pleasantville library staff is currently looking into ways to reconfigure building space to allow all student services housed in the building to move to a centralized location on the first floor, I cannot do anything in the immediate future about moving the centers because both campuses suffer from a lack of available space.[5] However, I have decided to capitalize on the technology available to us as a way to transcend our less-than-ideal spaces and to foster communication among our staff.

Given the fact that Pace has a multitude of campuses, in addition to substantial online and distance education offerings, the university relies on a wide spectrum of technological tools to keep its constituencies connected, including videoconferencing, teleconferencing, Blackboard, and listservs. Given that I cannot physically be at both centers at once, and given that our center space in Pleasantville precludes opportunities for animated discussion, moving a substantial portion of our training and staff development activities online in the future may be a viable solution to the disconnect I feel personally and that I perceive among my Pleasantville staff. James Inman and Donna Sewell noted the value of using electronic media to foster collegial relationships and build connections to the field of writing centers among not only writing center administrators but also staff. They defined this "electronic mentoring" as "offering responsible professional support and guidance to colleagues across institutional positions and contexts through the use of electronic media, working proactively to mediate challenging material conditions around the use of these media" (181). Through the use of videoconferencing during our fall orientation day, I hope to begin the year by establishing not only a connection among each staff—as they will be gathered together at the beginning of the school year in one conference room—but also between the two staffs, who will be able to physically see and speak with each other via the available technology. If scheduling permits, I hope to schedule subsequent videoconferences in order to maintain this connection between and among staffs.

---

[5]In addition to the writing center and the honors program, the library also houses general academic tutoring, first-year advisement, and a center for teaching with technology. The proposal for configuring the library space would involve a reconstruction of the first floor to allow all services to coexist with the library's reference services, which are already located on the first floor, in a sort of "one-stop shopping" service model for students.

However, scheduling has already proven to be an obstacle in fostering connections between the staff and the center. Through the establishment of a Blackboard site for the writing center, I hope to sidestep scheduling conflicts and build on the visual and verbal connections established between and among staffs at the fall orientation. Via Blackboard, staff members will participate in listserv discussions and journaling activities that will allow for the animated conversations that cannot easily take place in the Pleasantville center and will allow my New York staff to share their already established enthusiasm for their writing center work with their Pleasantville counterparts.

The "Pace University Writing Center" is one department with one administrative face—mine—however, after one year, I have come to accept the fact that the writing centers themselves may always have two distinct faces, based in part on the physical limitations imposed on the staffs by the spaces in which the respective centers are housed. And whereas having two different faces is not a negative in and of itself, I do find the relative silence of one face versus the animation of the other to be troubling in terms of its implications for staff development and, by extension, staff interactions with the students who come for tutoring. However, with one haphazard year behind me, I hope to use the university's available technology, coupled with the fact that unlike our first year both writing centers will be physically open and staffed at the beginning of the fall semester, to transcend the limitations of our physical spaces, both in terms of our spaces in the libraries and in terms of the geographical distance that separates our staffs on both campuses. Through technology, perhaps each writing center location can evolve by reconsidering the limitations of its own space and regarding the face of its counterpart on the other campus.

WORKS CITED

Boquet, Elizabeth H. *Noise from the Writing Center*. Logan: Utah State UP, 2002.

Edlund, John. "Re: Justifying Space for W/C to Admin. Types" Online posting. 10 Sept. 1994. WCenter Archives. <http://www.ttu.edu/wcenter/9409/msg00074.html>.

Hadfield Leslie, Joyce Kinkead, Tom Peterson, Stephanie H. Ray, and Sarah S. Preston. "An Ideal Writing Center: Re-Imagining Space and Design." *The Center Will Hold: Critical Perspectives on Writing Center Scholarship*. Ed. Michael A. Pemberton and Joyce Kinkead. Logan: Utah State UP, 2003. 166–76.

Haviland, Carol Peterson, Carmen M. Fye, and Richard Colby. "The Politics of Administrative and Physical Location." *The Politics of Writing Centers*. Ed. Jane Nelson and Kathy Evertz. Portsmouth, NH: Heinemann-Boynton/Cook 2001. 85–98.

Inman, James A., and Donna N. Sewell. "Mentoring in Electronic Spaces: Using Resources to Sustain Relationships." *The Center Will Hold: Critical Perspectives on Writing Center Scholarship*. Ed. Michael A. Pemberton and Joyce Kinkead. Logan: Utah State UP, 2003. 177–89.

Shamoon, Linda K., and Deborah H. Burns. "Labor Pains: A Political Analysis of Writing Center Tutoring." *The Politics of Writing Centers*. Ed. Jane Nelson and Kathy Evertz. Portsmouth, NH: Heinemann-Boynton/Cook, 2001. 62–73.

Silk, Bobbie Bayliss, ed. *The Writing Center Resource Manual*. Emmitsburg, MD: NWCA P, 1998.

Simpson, Jeanne. "Assessing Needs, Identifying an Institutional Home, and Developing a Proposal." *The Writing Center Resource Manual*. Ed. Bobbie Bayliss Silk. 2nd ed. Emmitsburg, MD: NWCA P, 1998. II. 2: 1–16.

⚜ **13** ⚜

Open Doors: The Community College Writing Center

Clinton Gardner
Tiffany Rousculp
Salt Lake Community College

Access, educational opportunity, center of adult education, meeting the needs of the community are goals that describe most community colleges across the country; these goals distinguish them from four-year or research institutions whose missions center mostly on their student populations. Community colleges, also known as "two-year colleges" in some locales, provide the first two years of a transfer education, associate degrees in a particular field, or certificate programs in industry. Typically, community college faculty have larger course loads than at four-year colleges or universities, although fewer (if any) requirements to research and publish. Their mission is "to teach" rather than to study or research or develop new knowledge.

Whereas community colleges have evolved from multiple educational movements, the Truman President's Commission on Higher Education (1947) codified for many the role of a comprehensive community college in response to the surging demand for postsecondary education from returning soldiers from WWII. The commission recommended creation of a network of public, community-based colleges to serve local needs. It stated:

> Whatever form the community college takes, its purpose is educational service to the entire community, and this purpose requires of it a variety of functions and programs. It will provide college education for the youth of the community certainly, so as to remove geographic and economic barriers to educational opportunity and discover and develop individual talents at low cost and easy access. But, in addition, the community college will serve as an active center of adult education. It will attempt to meet the total post-school needs of its community.

How does the multilayered mission of a community college affect its writing center? Most community colleges have writing centers, either free-standing within a department, or linked with a learning center on campus. On the face of it, most are no different in administration or function than their counterparts at other institutions of higher education. For example, according to the *Writing Center Research Project*, 62.5% of community college writing center (WC) directors are faculty members; and 37.5% are directed by full-time staff members. This ratio is not significantly different from the status of the director at other institutions. Of all respondents to the survey, 66.32% indicated they have directors who are full-time faculty and 32.64% have directors that are staff. In fact, many community college WC directors are at an advantage over their colleagues at four-year/university institutions in that they more often hold tenured or tenure track positions (50% to 37% at four-year/university institutions). Furthermore, along with other services, such as workshops, all community college writing centers offer writing tutoring/assistance/response from peer, professional, or faculty tutors. Such work, after all, is the stock and trade of what it is to be a writing center at any institution.

Ultimately, the writing center director at a community college faces a very similar situation to their four-year/university peers, with issues such as funding, obtaining space, training, and advertising. The community college (CC) context, however, does have specific challenges that a director must address. These challenges relate specifically to their two-year only status, open enrollment, and the mission to reach out into the community. The remainder of this chapter addresses the specific concerns brought up by these differentiating factors.

CHALLENGES SPECIFIC TO CC WRITING CENTERS: TWO YEARS ONLY

Staffing the Center

Because community colleges are limited to the first two years of college, students only attend lower division courses, either in academic transfer programs or in vocational training. Some WC directors may be concerned that staffing their centers exclusively with lower division undergraduate peer-tutors is problematic. Such directors may suppose that peer-tutors lack the experience to effectively respond to student writers and have not taken enough writing courses to provide useful feedback to their fellow student writers. Because of this supposition, it would be easy to conclude that professional and faculty tutors are more prevalent at community colleges. In the *Writing Centers Research Project*, however, 32% of the respondents reported that they staffed their writing centers exclusively with faculty or professional tutors. The percentage is much higher than at other institutions of higher education, with only 2% responding that they exclusively use professional or faculty tutors.

It would appear that community college writing center staffs are more complex—often including professional, faculty, and peer-tutors in the mix. Faculty tutors are either adjunct faculty paid extra to work in the writing center or full-time faculty who work in the writing center as a part of their load. Professional tutors work exclusively as tutors, often in a part-time capacity. Peer tutoring programs, of course, are made up of undergraduate students, but as stated previously, at community colleges there is less opportunity for third- and fourth-year students to work with student writers. Some might argue that this is a disadvantage because community college writing centers are forced to make use either of a staff of inexperienced peer-tutors, or professional/faculty tutors who lack a "peer connection" with the student writers.

Peer-Tutors.   The major barrier to developing and maintaining peer tutoring programs at community colleges is that at most institutions peer-tutors often stay a relatively short time (one or two years) and then transfer to four-year institutions to finish their degrees. Such a high turnover makes community college writing centers different from four-year institutions in that many such institutions keep their staff for their entire college experience, thus benefiting from veteran tutors. It would seem some feel that such inexperienced peer-tutors might not be well-equipped to respond to student writing.

Professional Tutors.   Many community college writing center directors also avail themselves of having faculty and professional work in the writing center. Faculty or professional tutors often have a great deal of experience in responding to student writers. Because of their training, as well, they can also be invaluable to the writing center director and provide feedback to peer writing tutors on their work in the center. Faculty or professional tutors often have training or a great deal of experience in developing pedagogically sound workshops with less input from the writing center director.

There can be drawbacks to using faculty and professional tutors. Although professional tutors are committed to their work in the writing center and understand its importance, unfortunately, some faculty believe that tutoring is beneath them or is something that they are too advanced to be doing.

Another fear that directors have about using faculty or professional tutors in their centers is that they will come across as "too teacherly" and will never be able to engage in a peer relationship with student writers. As one might suspect this is a complex issue, and writing center theory is split on the issue. Clark and Healy argued that there is no such thing as being too prescriptive, and Shamoon and Burns, Lundsford, and Murphy took a social constructivist approach where, it would seem, one must be careful about the way one responds to student writers and consider the power imbalance that can exist between tutor and writer, although they seem to agree that the relationship is far more relaxed from the traditionally held beliefs about the writer–tutor relationship. Because faculty play a variety of roles in the writing center, Gardner opined the problem that the power relationship between the tutor and the writer is disparate already, therefore one has to be careful not to exacerbate the situation by having highly experienced instructors responding to students who may find that problematic relationships that they have in classroom settings are being recreated in the writing center. One must necessarily always be aware of the power relationship between the tutor and the student writer, and that often the tutor has more knowledge and ability than the student writer.

Next, the workload of faculty writing center tutors can also detract from their commitment to the writing center. If a faculty member is already working with 100-plus students per semester, then writing center work could be seen as yet one more burden. Oftentimes faculty are placed in the position of either having to work in the writing center because it is a part of their contracted load, or in the case of adjunct faculty, because the writing center provides them a supplemental income. In either context, the writing center can seem to be a burden to faculty.

Another problem with faculty tutors is that some faculty who work in community college composition programs often have very little experience in teaching writing, working with student writers one-to-one, or writing center work in general. Whereas this problem has become less problematic over the past decade, it behooves a writing center director to be aware that not all people hired to teach composition are composition experts.

MEETING THE CHALLENGES OF STAFFING

The challenges of a community college writing center may seem daunting, but there are solutions.

Peer-Tutors: Turnover Can Be a Good Thing

The higher turnover rate of community college peer tutoring staffs has its beneficial side, too:

- a constant influx of peer-tutors brings in fresh ideas
- new tutors are far less likely to burn out or begin to make problematic
- assumptions about their student writers
- less experience with some types of assignments causes peer-tutors to ask more questions
- lower division students have closer connections with, and perhaps understanding of, courses they have recently taken themselves

Moreover, do not fear turnover because working in a writing center is not only a job that students hold while they work their way through college, but is in itself an educational experience—a foray into the world of writing, teaching, and learning. It is wise, therefore, to hire students who are interested in working with writers (e.g., teaching) in the future.

Overall, for peer writing tutors, be careful not to shirk on training. A course of training that lasts for as long as a semester is beneficial to both the peer tutor and the writers with whom they will meet. Tutors should be trained to be problem-solvers, that is, they should understand that their job is to rhetorically analyze complex writing situations and to come up with creative ways of addressing them.

It is also important that directors conduct regular performance reviews of tutors. Performance evaluations where the director gives direct feedback to the peer tutor on their work are essential to developing a solid tutoring program.

Finally, it is important that the director not send out the message that short tenures in the writing center are not worthwhile. Involving peer-tutors in developing, maintaining, and administering the writing center is an effective means of engaging peer-tutors in the center while increasing not only their investment in the center but also increasing their learning potential.

Faculty/Professional Tutors: All About Learning

To address the issues of faculty and professional writing tutors, the writing center director must understand the load issues and work requirements within the particular institutional context to discover methods to alleviate that burden. Of course, faculty tutors who are assigned to the writing center must have a commitment to the work of the writing center, but their personal situations should be taken into account and negotiated with the director. Although a director cannot change institutional policies alone, it would certainly be important to discuss the issue of faculty load and the effect that it has on performance in the writing center. For example, a faculty member who is expected to teach five composition courses and carry a load in the writing center is obviously overworked. The worst situation for a writing center, of course, is to have a tutor who does not wish to be there. The director should either work to help such individuals to reform their attitude or work with administration to find an alternative service that they could conduct either in or out of the writing center. There is little one can do to ameliorate such negative attitudes in faculty, and it may be necessary to remove such a person from writing center work, but an open discussion about the subject and the overall purpose and theory of writing center work is essential.

A similar situation could exist with faculty/professional tutors who are hired to work in the writing center, in that they may feel the job is just a "filler" until they find work elsewhere or move on to a "real job." It would seem that a solution for such an attitude is to impress on them the importance of writing center work, the benefits it can have, and the importance of their participation in it. A "bad attitude" that the writing center is somehow "beneath" the faculty/professional tutor could be answered in the same way.

CHALLENGES OF OPEN ENROLLMENT

As George Vaughan from the Academy for Community College Leadership and Advancement, Innovation, and Modeling (ACCLAIM) noted, the typical person who attends a community college is a "citizen-as-student," who "is concerned with paying taxes, working full time, supporting a family, paying a mortgage, and with other responsibilities associated with the everyday role of a full-time citizen" (17). It must be noted, however, that traditional college-age students also attend community colleges right alongside their nontraditional classmates. Vaughan further noted that if one wants to understand who attends a community college, all one has to do is to "stand on a busy street corner, and watch people go by. Eliminate most individuals who are under 18 … and the parade that passes will look much like the students at a typical community college" (19). Because of open enrollment, students at community colleges come from a variety of cultural and educational backgrounds.

One might draw the conclusion that because anyone can attend a community college despite poor academic performance in the past, the role of a community college writing center will be much more heavily remedial than its counterparts at other institutions of higher education. As Gardner argued previously, seeing the community college writing center as simply remedial can drag it down and prevent it from reaching a broader audience:

> I am not arguing that there is no place for remediation in a community college writing center. I do believe, however that remediation can be overemphasized to the extent that the writing center loses its place as the locus of a writing program. Instead of being a place where students come to write, such a writing center is a place where students go to be repaired. Instead of becoming a place where students come to advance their learning, it becomes a place where students go to "catch up" with other students. Such a writing center becomes adjunct to the writing program rather than central since the only role it plays in the writing program is to get students who are struggling in line with students who are not. (5.4)

Meeting the Challenge of Open Enrollment

So what approach should community college writing centers take? Ultimately, any writing center should focus on student learning and improving the writer. In this sense, there really is no such thing as remediation because students are not being "caught up" but are learning new things and developing new ideas about and through their writing. In other words, the notion of remediation itself is not problematic for a writing center. The problem lies in how we perceive and treat our clientele. If we see everyone who walks through the door as either victims or people only in need of "catching up," then the attitude is sure to carry through to how we respond to people. No one wishes to be treated like the village idiot, nor, as Shaughnessy noted, do students who have gaps in their knowledge need to be fixed. A writing center director at a community college must support the notion that it is the whole writer that is important. Making sure that the staff is aware of that and treats all equally who come into the center is essential. As we all know, writing is not easy for anyone, and there are gaps and behaviors that everyone has to contend with. A writing center should provide adequate and appropriate feedback without making sweeping assumptions about its clientele.

A further problem with a writing center that sends out the "remedial vibe" is that it will often fail to reach the middle ground of students. Ten years ago at Salt Lake Community College (SLCC), we conducted a survey of students who came to the Student Writing Center (SWC). Our findings indicated that we did a very good job of reaching students who were struggling with their writing classes as well as students who were doing very well in their courses. We were missing, however, the vast majority of students who, although not doing spectacularly well in their writing class, were doing well enough to pass with a C or better. The reverse bell curve that we observed bothered us enough to study how we were advertising or reaching students and what we could do to reach the middle ground. We then created advertisements specifically aimed at such students' needs, emphasizing that the writing center was for everyone. We focused on the idea that response was an important part of the writing process, as well as the benefits it provides. Furthermore, we strove to make it clear to faculty that they should not suggest that the SWC is a place of remediation, and to destigmatize SWC attendance.

CHALLENGE OF THE COMMUNITY

Although the majority of community colleges practice open enrollment, most have an implied obligation in their mission statements to meet the broader goals of adult education in their communities. To meet these needs, most community colleges have a continuing education department or program, which is often found under the moniker of "Personal and Individual Training," or "Custom-Fit for Industry," among others. Their goal is the same: to provide a variety of educational opportunities for the surrounding community. Further institutionalizing this role of community colleges, in 1988 the Commission on the Future of Community Colleges (American Association of Community Colleges, *Horizons*, para 6) recommended that community colleges help build a sense of community by creating partnerships and making facilities available to civic groups. They are to be one with the community, not outside of it, looking down from a hill or an ivory tower.

Along with these efforts to serve their communities, service learning has taken community colleges by storm, as it has four-year colleges and universities. According to the American Association for Community Colleges' "Horizons Service Learning Project," six hundred out of the twelve hundred community colleges already offer service learning within their curriculum, and at least 35%–40% of the rest are considering it. A 1996 study by Robert C. Serow and Diane C. Calleson for *Community College Review* found that service learning emerged from two basic community college identities: "[either] as an integral component of certain degree program [or] from part of its service commitment to the local community" (5).

Given the previous factors, one might think that writing programs and/or centers at community colleges would be leading their peers at four-year colleges and universities in regard to community outreach. From preliminary research, this does not seem to be the case.[1] According to Campus Compact, the national service learning network, only two community colleges were listed as "Model Programs" with writing-focused service learning outreach projects: Brevard Community College in Florida and Hibbing Community and Technical College in Minnesota. Three community colleges provided writing-focused service learning outreach projects.[2] On the other hand, Campus Compact noted at least thirteen four-year colleges/universities model program focusing on writing outreach.[3]

At least ten four-year colleges and university centers provide some sort of service to their communities.[4] Many of these outreach programs are linked with the National Writing Project, or with a service learning program at the institution. Several offered online writing assistance, or sponsored writing workshops and contests to their surrounding communities. A few of these institutions have developed centers out in the community, such as Carnegie-Mellon's Community Literacy Center and Weber State University's Community Writing Center in Ogden, Utah.

On the other hand, we only found four community college writing centers that provided outreach: Maple Woods Writing Center (Kansas City), Casper College (Wyoming), Johnson County Community College (Kansas), and the Collin County Community College District (Georgia).[5] Each of these centers provide writing tutoring to the community, either in-person or online.

This seeming contradiction between the community college mission and its execution in writing centers could be explained by the challenges we have noted previously in this chapter, specifically the fact that most peer-tutors at community college writing centers are freshmen or

[1]To find other community outreach projects in writing centers across the country, we submitted a survey to the Wcenter Listserve, reviewed results from the Writing Center Survey and searched the Internet with terms including *writing center, outreach, community*.

[2]Campus Compact's list of model programs does not include the large number of individual courses at community colleges and other higher education institutions across the country. However, community colleges seem to be lagging behind four-year institutions in service learning in general, including writing projects. Campus Compact recently received a grant from the Carnegie Foundation to conduct an "Indicators of Engagement Project" to collect and disseminate the best practices of service-learning. The focus of the first year is community colleges.

[3]There are also a handful of writing outreach projects initiated by K–12 institutions; especially noteworthy is the one at University City High School in St. Louis.

[4]We worked from a very open definition of "outreach" in our research. Writing centers that offered any of their services to anyone outside of the academic institution was deemed as offering "outreach." This ranged from full-blown writing centers in the community to noting on their Web sites that tutors will respond to online writing queries from the community.

[5]We believe that other community college writing centers are open to their surrounding communities, or conduct outreach projects. But, this information is not available through the research methods that we followed.

sophomores. Writing center directors may wonder if these peer-tutors could work with adults outside of the college walls. We believe this is an institutionally generated assumption. Four-year colleges, and especially universities, are considered capable of teaching beyond their walls (i.e., because these institutions train teachers in their own curriculum, it seems a natural fit that they would be able to conduct service-type training for K–12 teachers). However, community colleges do not carry the same ethos. Whereas their vocational tracks include training for industry or other fields, their academic tracks (which writing centers tend to fall under) are "only the first two years of college," not able to teach anyone but lower division students. In addition to tutor concerns, the workload of community college faculty can create a challenge for their writing center work, and inhibits many from putting in the extra hours required for starting up an outreach project. Given these constraints, reaching out to the community may seem like a fine idea for community college writing center directors, but something quite out of reach until budgets soar and workloads decrease.

However, at Salt Lake Community College, our Community Writing Center (CWC) meets the writing needs of the surrounding community in innovative ways, merging the two identities for outreach (Serow and Calleson). The CWC was developed to support the writing needs of adults in Salt Lake City; it is their way to "give back" to the community. As Dr. Helen Cox, associate academic vice president noted, the college had "a desire to serve presently un-served diverse populations." As with the Student Writing Center, the CWC staff is made up of undergraduate student part-time writing assistants with few exceptions. Also, after two years of operation, the CWC provides service internships to students and provides many opportunities for students in a variety of academic programs as we have recently started working with the college's Thayne Center for Service to incorporate service-learning scholars into CWC programs and recruit SLCC student volunteers as well. We also work with faculty who either volunteer or are compensated through reassigned time or stipends. We deal with the same challenges as the Student Writing Center does in terms of staffing and address these challenges in similar ways.

The CWC provides a physical space in the community dedicated solely to meeting the writing needs and goals of out-of-school adults. The center is located off-campus, downtown between a high-end retail complex and the city's homeless services block. In addition to the center and classroom space, the CWC offers five programs:

- Individual Assistance. This program offers the same tutoring services as those provided by student writing centers around the country. Community members work on any type of writing, from resumes to poems to grants, at the CWC and in libraries and computer centers across the city.
- Workshops. These short-term workshops, offered free or on a sliding scale, cover writing genres from short story to letters of application to radio essays. They are taught by the part-time writing assistants, volunteer faculty, and community members.
- Partners. This program offers long-term collaborative partnerships between the CWC and community organizations. The focus is to create sustainable change through writing. Past partnerships have included revamping a governmental agency's publication process, an extended grant-writing workshop, and a semester-long multigenre writing workshop in the county's jail for women.

- DiverseCity Writing Series. This program, based on the Neighborhood Writing Alliance (Chicago) and Write Around Portland (Oregon), offers several writing groups for the public and culminates in a publication and public reading event.

Challenges for WC Community Outreach: Community Perception and Funding

Opening a writing center to the community is not necessarily a smooth process. One major challenge is to explain to the general community what a writing center can do. The struggle that campus writing centers have to educate students and faculty about their benefits is multiplied exponentially with the community. The overt evaluation of writing often disappears when someone graduates from school, and the conscious need for feedback vanishes as well. Also, some have never experienced a writing center while in school, or perhaps didn't go to college. The concept of a writing center in the community is often new to many people.

In addition, a community college can experience a type of identity crisis as it tries to work with the community. If it is closely situated to four-year colleges or research universities, a community college might be identified as a "lesser" institution; local organizations may be less inclined to enter into partnerships with a writing center from a two-year institution. On the other hand, sometimes, the community college is lumped together with all "higher education" when trying to reach out to the community. Many organizations, especially those that serve underrepresented populations, have experienced being a research "subject" by a four-year college or university under the guise of "outreach" or "service." In addition, many organizations have been "provided for" by higher education outreach, as Ward and Wolf-Wendel noted, rather than working with the community. This double-bind can cause confusion for both the community partners and the writing center attempting to form community relationships.

Finally, of course, funding is always a big challenge to such an outreach project. Whereas the community tends to accept without question that Salt Lake Community College provides the Community Writing Center as a service to the community, writing center directors from around the country make it their first question at conferences and in consultation calls, "Just how do you get it funded?"

Meeting the Challenges

Unfortunately, there is no straight and simple answer for any of the previous challenges to reaching out to the community. It is a slow process to reach out into a community, but many resources, most free of charge, are typically available to writing centers. First, many local radio stations will play public service announcements, and community newspapers usually provide space for classified announcements (and newspaper staff writers are often looking for a public interest story), especially those in which higher education is crossing its borders. Also, distributing brochures in community organizations, coffee shops, libraries, and other community centers can spread the news of a writing center's community outreach quickly.

Community perception is a continual challenge, which can only be altered through quality experiences at both the individual and institutional level. Whereas the CWC has not evolved directly from service learning, we have embraced the most progressive tenets within its philosophies such as those presented by Dewey, Freire, and Rhoads and Howard. When working with community organizations, strictly following collaborative methods most familiar to writing centers, and expecting fully shared commitment and responsibility from its partners in reaching mutually determined educational goals can go a long way to undo previous experiences (Judkins and LaHurd; Peck, Flower and Higgins). In fact, one advantage that community college writing centers have in working with the community is our institutions' mission to educate, not to generate new research. When a partner organization realizes that a proposed collaboration is truly that—a collaboration conducted to reach specific writing goals—and is not a pretext to research, barriers can drop and positive experiences go a long way to spreading the word to other community organizations and individuals.

Finally, the challenge of funding is an ever-present one. The CWC has been incredibly fortunate to have Salt Lake Community College's support—a hard-funded budget—for the past several years. A claim was made at the beginning of this chapter that community college writing centers should be involved in their surrounding communities, but we do not assume that they should venture out into a fully distinct community writing center that would require such funding. However, it is infinitely possible, as demonstrated by the community colleges, to open their doors in a number of ways to the community and also limit the financial impact.

A first step is just that: offering tutoring to the members of the surrounding community. This could be accomplished either by inviting the community to come to the on-campus writing center, or by providing tutoring in local libraries or computer centers. Service learning students, or simply volunteer students or faculty, could staff these outreach sites. Just a couple of hours a week will establish a presence in the community that can grow. Also, a positive writing session can create a bridge for individuals who may not have felt able to attend college to take on that challenge. Another approach might be to offer workshops, or writing groups, to the outside community. Or, a community writing service learning course could be established by a faculty member who works in the writing center—collaborating with the writing center director, of course. The CWC started through these two methods: (a) one-credit community writing course in which students developed a biannual newsletter for a local nonprofit community developer, and (b) a writing project that established the DiverseCity Writing Series with eight-week writing workshops with community organizations focusing on self and community. These projects cost less than $500 each and we received grants for them as well.

Once small successes start, the best thing a writing center director can do is get the word out across the campus about these "outside the box" accomplishments. Doing such work raises the image of the college in the community, which is something administrators, development officers, and boards of trustees are always seeking. Especially in the current service learning climate, community outreach can bring important attention to community college writing centers, and lead to funding sources previously untapped.

CONCLUSIONS

Writing centers have become the norm in all of higher education; a community college without a writing center is becoming an anomaly. Students, faculty, and administrators expect there to be a writing center at a community college in order to support the entire college's efforts to teach writing. Even though community college writing centers serve many of the same roles that university writing centers do, as we have shown, there are some distinct differences that directors need to consider as they develop their center at their particular institution. It is important to consider the community college multifarious audience carefully, what their needs are, and how one can best reach them. These diverse needs range from the students taking classes at the college to the community in which the college is situated. Such diverse needs are a distinguishing challenge and strength for community college writing centers. Ultimately, like the ideal of community colleges in general, the community college writing center is a place of change, growth, learning, and action.

WORKS CITED

American Association for Community Colleges. "Community Colleges Past and Present." 18 May 2004 <http://www.aacc.nche.edu/Content/NavigationMenu/AboutCommunityColleges/HistoricalInformation/PasttoPresent/Past_to_Present.htm>.

American Association for Community Colleges. *Horizons Service Learning Project.* 22 June 2004 <http://www.aacc.nche.edu/Content/NavigationMenu/ResourceCenter/Projects_Partnerships/Current/HorizonsServiceLearningProject/HorizonsServiceLearningProject.htm>.

Clark, Irene L., and Dave Healy. "Are Writing Centers Ethical?" *WPA: Writing Program Administration* 20.5 (1996): 32–38.

Cox, Helen. Personal Interview. 22 May 2004.

Dewey, John. *Experience and Education.* New York: Macmillan: 1938.

Freire, Paulo. *Pedagogy of the Oppressed.* New York: Seabury Press, 1970.

___. *Education: The Practice of Freedom.* London: Writers and Readers Publishing Cooperative, 1976.

Gardner, Clinton. "Centering the Community College Writing Center." *The Writing Center Resource Manual.* Ed. Bobbie Silk. 2nd ed. Emmitsburg, MD: IWCA Press, 2002. II.5. 1–15

Judkins, B.M., and LaHurd, R.A. "Building Community from Diversity: Addressing the Changing Demographics of Academia and Society." *American Behavioral Scientist* 42 (1999): 780–93.

Lunsford, Andrea. "Collaboration, Control, and the Idea of the Writing Center." *The Writing Center Journal* 12 (1991): 3–10.

Murphy, Christina. "The Writing Center and Social Constructionist Theory." *Intersections: Theory-Practice in the Writing Center.* Ed. Joan A. Mullin and Ray Wallace. Urbana, IL: NCTE, 1994. 161–71.

Peck, Wayne, C., Linda Flower, and Lorraine Higgins. "Community Literacy." *College Composition and Communication* 46 (1995): 199–222.

President's Commission on Higher Education. (1947). Higher Education for American Democracy. Washington, DC: US Government Printing Office.

Rhoads, R. A., and P. F. Howard, eds. *Academic Service Learning; A Pedagogy of Action and Reflection.* San Francisco: Jossey-Bass, 1998.

Serow, Robert C., and Diane C. Calleson. "Service-Learning and the Institutional Mission of Community Colleges." *Community College Review* 23 (1996): 3–14.

Shamoon, Linda K., and Deborah H. Burns. "A Critique of Pure Tutoring." *The Writing Center Journal* 15 (1995): 134–51.

Shaughnessy, Mina P. *Errors and Expectations.* New York: Oxford UP, 1977.

Ward, Kelly, and Lisa Wolf-Wendel. "Community-Centered Service Learning." *American Behavioral Scientist* 43 (2000): 767–81.

"The Writing Centers Research Project Survey of Writing Centers, AY 2000–2001: Results." 2 Jul. 2004. *The Writing Centers Research Project.* U of Louisville. 20 Jul. 2004. <http://www.wcrp.louisville.edu/survey2000–2001/surveyresults.html>.

Vaughan, George B. *The Community College Story: A Tale of American Innovation.* Washington, DC: The American Association of Community Colleges, 1995.

14

Writing Centers in the Small College

Byron L. Stay
Mount St. Mary's University

Relatively little research has been done on the characteristics and unique challenges facing directors of writing centers in small colleges. Aside from Julie Neff's chapter on the University of Puget Sound writing center in *Writing Centers in Context*, the only article that addresses this issue directly is the January 2000 piece in the *Writing Lab Newsletter* by Shireen Carroll, Bruce Pegg, and Stephen Newmann. They based their findings on a survey conducted in 1999 of forty-six writing centers and concluded, among other things, that directors of small college writing centers are hampered because of problems with professional development, budget allocation, and institutional priorities. They also found that directors of small college writing centers seem to have particular obstacles with public relations.

This study provides a valuable window into small college writing centers by taking a somewhat different approach to the issue. This chapter argues that whereas writing centers at small institutions have unique limitations, the ambiance of a small institution can present the writing center director with creative opportunities as well. These writing center directors need to find innovative ways to train tutors, staff, and budget their centers. They need to be careful that new programs don't overwhelm them. However, because of the close sense of community found at most small institutions, writing center directors there might find it easier to affect the development of the academic programs profoundly.

WHAT IS A SMALL COLLEGE?

The designation "small college" was set quite arbitrarily by Carroll et al. at 3,500 full-time equivalents (FTEs). This seems quite high. Dr. Lucie Lapovsky, president of Mercy College in

Dobbs Ferry, New York, in her "Tuition Discounting Study for the National Association of College & University Business Officers (NACUBO)," used the benchmark of a freshman class of less than 850 students as a small college. Similarly, *US News & World Report* used an FTE of fewer than 2,000 as the definition of "small college" in its ranking information. So this chapter defines "small college" as fewer than 2,500 students. In fact, the average college size in the Carroll et al. survey was 1,500 students. And, by the way, although my institutional affiliation is Mount St. Mary's *University*, so designated in the summer 2004, the institution enrolls approximately 1,400 undergraduate FTEs and a freshman class of about 400 students. We have small graduate programs in business, education, and theology and a separate adult education program, but we're not quite ready to compete with UCLA.

HOW DO SMALL COLLEGE WRITING CENTERS DIFFER FROM THOSE AT OTHER INSTITUTIONS?

The Writing Centers Research Project Survey, AY 2000–2001 (WCRPS) is a particularly valuable resource for comparing writing centers at various institutions. The compilers of this survey break down their findings into those from research universities with doctoral programs, four-year comprehensive universities, four-year liberal arts colleges, two-year postsecondary colleges, secondary schools, and elementary schools. Although a four-year liberal arts college is not a perfect match for the rubric "small college" (colleges may certainly enroll more than 2,500 students), it is helpful in distinguishing the ways the liberal arts college, and by extension most small colleges, differs from larger institutions. If this survey accurately represents the writing center community, then the results are revealing. Small college writing centers are the least likely to be open during the summers, and slightly more than one half of the directors hold doctoral degrees (74.6% of directors at research universities hold a PhD). Nearly 38% of directors are tenured or tenure track, 24% are untenurable faculty, 31% are staff, and 6.9% are part-time faculty. These numbers are consistent with those in Carroll et al. Fully 70% of small college writing center directors have no other administrative staff (compared with 44.78% of research institutions).

If the designation "four-year liberal arts college" also includes some institutions with more than 2,500 students, one would expect the results of the small college to be even more dramatic than the figures here. There are a number of unique problems such writing center directors face. Because they often work as the only faculty member in the writing center, they tend to wear a number of hats. They are most likely the scheduler, administrator, tutor trainer, and tutor.

OBSTACLES FOR THE SMALL COLLEGE WRITING CENTER DIRECTOR

There are several, unique problems faced by small college writing center directors. Because they are spread so thin, out of necessity they must make careful judgments about time. Aside from record keeping and scheduling issues, perhaps one of the most important issues for small college writing centers is tutor training. I did find it pleasantly surprising that the WCRPS reported a larger percentage of writing consultants at four-year liberal arts colleges attend credit-bearing courses (43.3%) than at any other size institution, including research universities. This might suggest that writing centers at smaller institutions may be more enfranchised than Carroll et al. believed.

That still leaves 56.7% of the institutions (including Mount St. Mary's) without specific tutor-training courses. The writing center directors at these institutions need to be resourceful. Directors at small institutions should carefully read Muriel Harris's chapter on tutor training elsewhere in this book (chap. 28). Although Harris describes a credit-bearing course, her methods could easily be adapted to a workshop format. She recommends, for instance, that the training session be modeled on the stages of a tutorial, and that directors carefully consider not just the agenda of training but the interpersonal relationships as well.

There are other challenges faced by small college writing center directors. Because of their size, such writing centers can easily be overwhelmed by programs needing their services. Let me explain. The Mount St. Mary's writing center has, since its inception, handled an extensive amount of English as a second language (ESL) work. One reason for this is that the seminary attached to the college frequently attracts nonnative speakers. We have been more than happy to work with them, and the seminary has come to depend on us. However, several years ago, the Mount St. Mary's MBA program began admitting large numbers of foreign students. Many of these students needed extensive ESL work. It was assumed that the writing center would tutor these students (although we were not consulted in advance). Many brought their entire MBA theses to the writing center, oftentimes wanting multihour appointments. To make matters worse, we didn't think it ethical to ask new undergraduate tutors to take on the complicated task of graduate level ESL instruction. That meant that our faculty tutors took on most of these students. Nevertheless, it was impossible for the faculty to do all the instruction, and it was inevitable that new writing center tutors were on occasion asked to share the load. The results were not good for the writing center or for the ESL students, most of whom really wanted to have their theses edited. The problem only resolved itself when the source well of foreign students dried up and the MBA dean had to abandon recruiting them. Of course, this is not necessarily a problem faced only by directors of small college writing centers, as Judith K. Powers's example at the University of Wyoming illustrates. She found her writing center suddenly swamped by ESL instruction. However, small college writing centers, having far fewer writing consultants, are more susceptible to such overuse.

A third distinguishing characteristic of the small college writing center is its visibility. As Carroll et al. observed, this is not necessarily a good thing. "At small sites," they observed, "it is easy to acquire and hard to shake a bad reputation" (4). Because the writing center director likely has personal contact with most, if not all, faculty and administrators, it is possible for pressure to be placed on the writing center related to institutional goals and assumptions about writing. If the philosophy of the writing center is not in tune with the assumptions of the institution, then serious conflict can arise. Deborah H. Burns's experience at Merrimack College is particularly instructive. The article she co-wrote with Linda K. Shamoon detailed the problems experienced by her writing center when she attempted to make theoretical changes to move her writing center from more generalist tutors to what Burns called "expert tutors." Some faculty saw this as a threat. More importantly, Burns detailed a conflict between this new vision of the writing center and the old assumptions held by some administrators and faculty that tutoring of writing should focus on the "basics" (71).

OPPORTUNITIES FOR THE SMALL COLLEGE
WRITING CENTER DIRECTOR

However, problems faced by the small college writing center director can be turned into advantages. Writing center directors need to think carefully about the local context of their own institutions. Writing center directors can take advantage of their visibility. Directors of small college writing centers have unique opportunities to incorporate their writing centers into the academic structures of their institutions, especially freshman year (FY) and writing across the curriculum (WAC) programs. Of course, this means that the writing center staff, especially the director, needs to play a proactive role in the development of WAC and FY programs. It means getting on the right committees from the very start. If the WAC and FY programs are already in place, however, the situation becomes somewhat more complicated.

It is important to realize, for instance, that writing centers both influence and are influenced by the institutional academic programs. Even if the WAC and FY programs are functioning properly, the director must walk a fine line between, on the one hand, serving the developmental and ESL needs of the institution and, on the other hand, addressing the students' more complex cognitive needs, and then communicating these dual roles to the faculty, administration, and to the larger community.

I think that Burns's experience underscores the importance of writing center inclusion in the formation of academic programs, especially composition programs. Of course, this is not always possible, especially if the director inherits a writing center that already has established ties to a FY program. At Mount St. Mary's, for instance, the current FY program was created fifteen years ago. The person primarily in charge of the program was a faculty member who was also a writing center tutor (although never a writing center director) and a specialist in rhetoric and composition. As a result, the FY program that emerged was one informed by current trends in composition. The original director's experience as a tutor and her knowledge of composition theory helped create a program consistent with contemporary composition theories (of the late 1980s).

Students were to take a year-long freshman seminar designed to teach reading, writing, thinking, and speaking skills. Further, the seminar was not the domain of any particular department. Although the first and second directors of the program taught in the rhetoric and communications department, subsequent directors did not. The course is taught by faculty from all disciplines who undergo a month-long training workshop in the teaching of writing. The result was that the writing center could weave itself seamlessly into the freshman seminar. This is not to say the writing center had no problems, but they were not the result of competing philosophic positions.

Julie Neff described a very similar experience at the University of Puget Sound (UPS). Although Neff did not indicate that the center played a role in developing the FY and WAC programs, it is clear that the center on its creation placed itself firmly in the middle of these programs, beginning with the creation of its name: "Center for Writing Across the Curriculum." As such, the UPS writing center "helps faculty members to incorporate writing into their courses and into departmental curricula" (130).

This is not to say that creating a mission statement to position the writing center within the missions of other academic departments is the same thing as accomplishing the mission. In far too many situations, writing centers have alienated themselves from academic departments who see the inclusion of the writing center in their curricula as a threat (see Shamoon and Burns). So how did the University of Puget Sound writing center manage to establish close ties to other departments and programs? It created a series of strategic alliances. One such alliance was created with faculty by asking for their input. Some are asked to writing center meetings and some ask writing center advisors to their classes (135). Another alliance was formed with the academic computing program that allowed the writing center to move to a much larger facility (137). The center found yet another alliance with other departments through the academic advising program and with the Office of Academic Advising (135). Neff detailed other alliances as well with the honors program and with the dean of students.

The point is that such alliances can move the writing center into the mainstream of an institution in nonthreatening ways, and such alliances may be easier to attain at small institutions where committee memberships and networking may be much easier than at larger institutions. The relationships built at small institutions resemble those in a family much more than a corporation. It's much more likely that everyone knows everyone else and that the writing center and director will likely experience high visibility. Although there are limitations to this closeness, the community also presents particular opportunities for shaping not just the writing center but the academic program as well. Directors of small college writing centers need to take advantage of this informality and seek actively a central role in the decision making at their institutions.

WORKS CITED

Carroll, Shireen, Bruce Pegg, and Stephen Newmann. "Size Matters: Administering a Writing Center in a Small College Setting." *Writing Lab Newsletter* 24 (5): 1–5.

Lapovsky, Lucie. "Tuition Discounting: Results from NACUBO's Annual Survey Indicates Increases in Tuition Discounting." National Association of College and University Business Officers. <http://www.nacubo.org/documents/bom/2002_02_tuition_discounting.pdf>.

Neff, Julie. "The Writing Center at the University of Puget Sound: The Center of Academic Life." *Writing Centers in Context: Twelve Case Studies*. Ed. Joyce A. Kinkead and Jeannette G. Harris. Urbana, IL: NCTE, 1993. 127–44.

Powers, Judith K. "Rethinking Writing Center Conferencing Strategies for the ESL Writer." *The Writing Center Journal* 13.2 (1993): 39–47.

Shamoon, Linda K., and Deborah H. Burns. "Labor Pains: A Political Analysis of Writing Center Tutoring." *The Politics of Writing Centers*. Ed. Jane Nelson and Kathy Evertz. Portsmouth, NH: Heinemann-Boynton/Cook, 2001. 62–73.

U.S. News and World Report. "America's Best Colleges 2004." <http://www.usnews.com/usnews/edu/college/rankings/about/index_brief.php>.

❧ 15 ❧

Writing Centers for Graduate Students

Helen Snively
Harvard Graduate School of Education

Traci Freeman
University of Colorado-Colorado Springs

Cheryl Prentice
St. Mary's University of Minnesota

To finish their degrees and secure academic or professional jobs, many graduate students must write theses and dissertations; others must publish articles in competitive journals and compose interesting and insightful job letters, research statements, and teaching philosophies. In many disciplines, students must publish chapters of their dissertations, show that they can win research grants, and even secure book contracts before they can consider themselves competitive for academic jobs.

To support graduate students in such tasks, several schools have developed graduate writing centers (GWCs) over the past decade.[1] In this chapter, we share our experiences in developing, running, and growing programs at three very different campuses: the University of Texas at Austin, a large state-supported institution; St. Mary's University of Minnesota School of Graduate and Professional Programs, a nonresidential campus serving many immigrants and nontraditional students; and the Harvard Graduate School of Education, a private graduate school. We begin by outlining the specific needs of graduate students, which led each of us to develop services to support graduate writers. Next, following the model of Kinkead and Harris,

---

[1]We know of graduate writing centers at Pennsylvania State University, Michigan State, University of Central Florida, Claremont Graduate School in California, and Ashland University in Ohio as well as several law and divinity schools.

153

we provide case studies, describing our own institutional context, initiative, funding, and start-up, and the current status of our programs. We then suggest a few lessons from our experiences and raise questions for the future. Although the primary focus of our discussion is on GWCs that work exclusively with graduate students, many issues we present are relevant to other graduate writing models and to writing centers in general.

Although our narratives are roughly parallel, we could not have asked for three more different universities or student populations. Within each of our contexts, however, administrators, faculty, and graduate students all articulated a need for writing support that our campuses did not offer. Each of us was hired to address these needs, working from a background in undergraduate writing centers and composition studies (Texas and St. Mary's), or as a teaching assistant (TA) for a graduate writing course (Harvard).

THE UNIQUE NEEDS OF GRADUATE STUDENTS

We believe, and most writing center practitioners probably agree, that the writing needs of graduate and undergraduate students differ in a number of ways, but surprisingly little research has focused on writing centers that serve graduate students. John Farrell (3) noted the absence of such research in 1994, and his claim holds true over ten years later. Although we may not have significant research to ground our arguments, we draw from our collective experience with GWCs to define the needs of the graduate writers who frequent our centers.

We begin by acknowledging that some question the need for graduate writing support at all. Most academic departments assume that their graduate students possess basic writing competency when they are admitted and the responsibility for these students' writing generally falls to faculty supervisors. Some schools provide short writing courses to meet students' needs and expect them to seek additional support from peers or writing groups. Although many of these assumptions seem legitimate, they often do not hold true in practice.

Many graduate students are, in fact, competent writers, but the varieties of writing that their programs expect are often radically different from the writing they have done previously. Increasingly, graduate students are multilingual, nontraditional students who have been out of college for many years and often need additional support to master both the content of their subjects and the writing conventions of their disciplines.

Graduate faculty advisors are responsible for helping students with writing; however, just as students feel pressure to publish and win grants, so do faculty. With so many demands on their time, professors cannot always offer careful, thoughtful, and individualized feedback throughout their advisees' writing process. Of course, the idea that professors should take on this responsibility also rests on several assumptions: that all professors have the desire or expertise to be writing instructors, that they are native speakers of English with superior command of the language, and that students have good working relationships with their advisors. Although these are reasonable assumptions, they often do not hold in practice.

Over the past decade, academic institutions have begun to recognize the need to introduce graduate students to the conventions of academic discourse and have provided courses in research and writing. Even though such courses are ideal for familiarizing students with the genres and conventions of their disciplines, they cannot offer the kind of sustained writing support that Mullen argued graduate students need to progress in their degree programs (117–25).

Finally, peers, especially if organized in writing groups, can offer sustained feedback and crucial emotional support (Burnett 46). Valuable as they are, however, such groups often collapse under the pressure of scheduling realities: Unlike many undergraduates, graduate students are often working full-time and caring for families.

GWCs institutionalize many practices that graduate programs assume are occurring in their departments; they offer students the support of peers or professionals, without the responsibility of providing feedback to others, and they allow students to make appointments at times that suit their schedules. Consultants who have expertise in issues related to writing can also respond to the needs of nontraditional and multilingual students. GWCs can support writers throughout their years in school.

Although GWCs are not intended to replace faculty feedback, they often provide the readily available, intensive, and long-term writing support in ways that advisors often cannot. Moreover, although GWCs can never substitute for feedback from faculty over the long term, they can provide the kind of support (in the form of both mentoring and advice on writing) that advisors may not always be able to offer. Graduate students may even be more likely to bring questions they perceive as "stupid" to a consultant than to an advisor. Similarly, consultants may be better equipped than advisors to handle problems like writer's block and procrastination, which often accompany the stresses of writing at the graduate level.

Learning the specific genres and conventions of academic writing is a daunting task for many graduate students. When the assistant directors at the Undergraduate Writing Center at the University of Texas surveyed their campus' graduate students and their professors, more than 30% of the professors who responded mentioned their students lacked skills in grant writing. They also noted problems with conference abstracts and papers for publication, as well as trouble with aspects of academic literacy, such as formulating and supporting arguments, developing research questions, and explaining technical and theoretical material.

Nonnative speakers (NNS) of English and multilingual writers experience a variety of additional challenges. Along with the conventions of their specific disciplines, they must learn the conventions of standard American academic discourse, including citation strategies, and sometimes the very concept of intellectual property. They also encounter high expectations for their writing in terms of volume, complexity, quality, and "correctness." Their needs may be even more complex at the graduate level than at the undergraduate level. Although we acknowledge that such students are important clients for all of us, a discussion of their specific needs is beyond the scope of this chapter.

OUR THREE GRADUATE WRITING CENTERS

Because writing at the graduate level is highly specialized and discipline specific, graduate students often benefit from working with others who have experience writing in their disciplines. They also benefit from working with consultants who have designed and conducted research and have mastered higher levels of academic literacy in long papers. Thus, graduate students need writing centers designed for their needs and not just—or primarily—the needs of undergraduates. The Texas case that follows is an example of such a graduate writing program developed from a UWC. The centers at St. Mary's and Harvard, which follow the Texas case, exemplify different models that serve more students. St. Mary's welcomes students from all its graduate programs, whereas the Harvard center serves all students at one large graduate school.

The Graduate Writing Program at the University of Texas

I became interested in writing at the graduate level while working as a composition instructor and assistant director of the Undergraduate Writing Center (UWC) at the University of Texas. Each semester, graduate students sought help at the UWC, but were ineligible for its services because it is funded by undergraduate fees. Texas offers graduate writing courses through individual departments and through the Office of Graduate Studies (OGS), but these courses do not provide writers with sustained support.

Although the UWC administrators had plenty of anecdotal evidence that graduate students wanted our assistance with their writing, we needed empirical evidence to make a case for funding. My codirector, Chris Lecluyse, and I conducted an online survey of all 8,552 graduate students and 2,127 professors to learn their perceptions of the graduate writing support available at Texas. (The rates of response, 6% and 8% respectively, were within the norm for online surveys.) In brief, 85% of faculty and 78% of the graduate students who responded said that their departments do not offer sufficient writing support either in courses or through personal contact with faculty and peers; higher percentages responded that the university in general did not offer sufficient support. More than 85% of all respondents were interested in using writing center services or knew students who would benefit from them.

With these results, Chris and I proposed to the OGS that we extend services to graduate students in five to seven selected departments for a pilot semester. We asked the OGS for $50,000 to pay seven consultants' wages and benefits. We planned to use the UWC's physical and computer infrastructure for consultations and record keeping (although even this small use would draw on undergraduate funds) and to train advanced graduate students who were among the UWC's experienced consultants to work with writers.

The OGS was initially resistant to our proposal: We were pointing out a need they believed was addressed adequately through their writing classes. We had to argue for the complementary nature of writing classes and writing center practices, a case writing centers have been making since the beginning. Apparently, our arguments, along with our survey results, were compelling enough to win OGS support. Although OGS did not fund the pilot program outright, the deans suggested that we seek teaching assistant (TA) lines from the departments we intended to serve. In return, we would train advanced graduate students as writing consultants to work with other graduate students within their own departments, at the departments' expense. A former UWC consultant would supervise the TAs, in return for a small honorarium through the OGS. The seven hours of training I provided introduced the idea of discipline-specific writing, along with strategies for addressing grammar and syntax and working with NNS writers. I provided some readings for the tutors, simulated a consultation that we then discussed, and made myself available for follow-up consultations.

In fall 2001, the Department of Civil Engineering (CE) signed on to be a part of the pilot Graduate Writing Program (GWP). Within 24 hours after services were announced, the CE consultant was booked for the week, and she remained extremely busy throughout the semester. CE continued in the pilot through the spring semester, and we added Educational Psychology. In June 2002, Chris took over the program when I moved to another institution. In the fall 2003, another graduate student consultant, Jane Barnett, replaced Chris, and the program added the Department of Theater and Dance and developed a substantive Web site. Then the situation changed. When a new dean took over the graduate school in 2003, the GWP got lost in the shuffle. It did not operate during academic year 2003–2004, although the new dean has since expressed an interest in it.

In addition to the GWP itself, several departments (social work, law school, and nursing) have hired their own editors, most of them former UWC staff, to work with graduate students on their writing. Although the GWP's ultimate fate is still in doubt, it is clear that the need for writing support among graduate students at Texas has not diminished.

Saint Mary's University of Minnesota, Twin Cities Writing Center

Saint Mary's University is a residential liberal arts college in rural Winona, Minnesota. In 1984, it expanded its graduate offerings, opening the School of Graduate and Professional Programs at the Minneapolis campus (SMUM). SMUM, which includes a small bachelor completion program, serves 2,600 night students on a nonresidential urban campus and at outreach facilities statewide. The institution's LaSallian tradition of educating underserved populations also draws many immigrant and international students, particularly from Asia and northeast Africa. Courses are geared toward midcareer working adults, are taught mostly by adjunct professionals, emphasize practical application of skills and knowledge, and often are condensed into intense half-semester formats, allowing students more flexible scheduling and shorter degree completion times. No English program exists at SMUM, but most graduate programs require two to four professional communication credits.

Recognizing a need for graduate writing support, the SMUM faculty petitioned the administration to study the issue. A multidiscipline task force of faculty and an outside writing consultant articulated the writing center's primary charge: to address the needs of those students who are unprepared for graduate writing, have had little experience with professional styles (APA or AMA), expect instructors to "fix" their writing, fear writing, or lack resources for help outside class. A secondary part of the mission was to provide instructional support resources for teaching staff.

The task force then advertised the position, a full-time twelve-month professional staff appointment, reporting directly to the dean of students (and later, after an administrative organization, to the assistant dean of student services). After thirteen years teaching and directing an undergraduate writing center at a large state university, I was hired for the job. The university provided an office, start-up supplies, and a maintenance budget, with the understanding that I would generate offset revenue, mainly by teaching workshops. The office space was adequate at the time, but not centrally located. No allocation was made for additional staff. (Student-tutors are not feasible here, as most students are working full-time elsewhere.) A major challenge was to provide writing services to all SMUM students, including those at distant sites, with only a single staff person.

As the new director, I wanted to capitalize on the evident support from core faculty. First, I wrote and e-mailed both full-time and adjunct faculty to announce the writing center mission (as derived from task force suggestions), describe proposed services, and solicit their input through a survey on their own and their students' needs. I made one significant change to the mission recommendation, refocusing what seemed to be a remedial identity and redefining it to welcome any students seeking to develop their writing in an informal, collegial setting. Faculty and staff supported the modification. I introduced the center at student and faculty orientations, and by personal visits to classrooms both on campus and—the human connection—at outreach sites around the state. I also gave a faculty development workshop during my first year. Finally, I provided faculty with a writing center information blurb for syllabi and petitioned to make its inclusion mandatory. Creating a web page was another priority, as it was to become the main link between the center and students at remote sites. I also developed a short booklet, *Introduction to APA and Other Writing Tips*, which has sold roughly four hundred copies (for $4) at the campus bookstore.

In the second full year of operation, 166 graduate students from 11 programs requested 254 sessions totaling 482 hours. One third were nonnative speakers (NNS) of English, mostly speaking African languages. Forty percent of sessions were online or by phone, or a combination of the two. The web page had 750 hits in the first 3 months. In 2003, a survey of 300 faculty (100 responded) showed high satisfaction with our services. In April 2004, we hired a half-time writing professional as an additional consultant. Soon the center will move to a larger, more centrally located site near the library. The university is considering a proposal that, if enacted, would coordinate with the center to provide extensive language and writing support for nonnative speakers of English.

The Writing, Research, and Teaching Center (WRTC) at the Harvard Graduate School of Education (GSE)

Our center began in the context of a free noncredit course, Graduate Writing, offered since the late 1970s. Every fall, one hundred or more students attended Bruce McPherson's lectures on topics like organizing drafts, writing lively prose, and using citations correctly. The weekly sections were peer-response groups, run by TAs, to which students brought drafts of papers they were writing for other courses. I began working as a TA for the course in 1992; although my international students often stopped attending sections, they tapped me on the shoulder in the cafeteria, looking for tutoring. Curious about their needs, in summer 1994 I interviewed twenty international and U.S.-born students, as well as some staff and faculty members.

My most memorable interview was with Marisel Perez, then director of the Office of Student Affairs (OSA). Over the years, a few GSE students had gone across campus to the UWC at Harvard's Faculty of Arts and Sciences, but they were frustrated that undergraduate tutors did not know the genres and research techniques required at GSE. In response, Marisel had arranged one TA line for Anna, a GSE doctoral student, to tutor GSE students by appointment. Although Anna was very popular, students told me they wanted quicker service; one suggested a walk-in center. When I mentioned this to Marisel, she responded immediately: "We'll have an extra space in the fall. Do you want to start a writing center?" When I said, "Who, me?" she countered with, "Why not? You know we need it."

OSA let us share the visible and accessible (but hardly private) room that also housed the student government association. Marisel and Bruce arranged for the three TAs in Graduate Writing to take over Anna's TA line (conveniently, Anna was graduating). Starting in the fall 1994, three TAs from the course shared the line, offering a total of seven hours per week of drop-in office hours to any GSE student. About one half of those who came were international; most were master's students. Our supervision comprised occasional meetings with Marisel or Bruce. Thus, our center grew out of a course supported by the OSA.

In January 1997, the dean's office handled several cases of suspected plagiarism, including one writing center client, and the administration looked hard at the teaching of writing at GSE. By spring 1998, we had a new name (the Writing and Research Center, WRC) and our own tiny office, phone line, e-mail address, and three new TAs. In addition to his long-standing lecturer appointment, Bruce was appointed director to provide specific supervision of the WRC. We gave many workshops to develop credibility, and began reaching out to doctoral students. In 1998, the dean's office granted us two additional TA lines to hire TAs with specific research skills and a popular statistics professor became codirector with Bruce. When I graduated in June 1999, the school created a half-time administrative staff position for me. As we grew, the course became one offering of the center, with TAs and me on the regular school payroll, and our few expenses covered by the dean's office.

In fall 2001, "Teaching" became our second middle name as a former writing center TA launched a program to support TAs across the school. And we moved to a location specifically designed for our needs—two small but convenient rooms in the library basement—when the head librarian claimed space for us during a renovation.

In 2002–03 and again in 2003–04, we served about two hundred students in seven hundred sessions totaling about five hundred hours. This was about our limit, given our total of nine TA lines per year. Throughout our history, doctoral students (40% of the student body) have made up about a third of our clientele; bringing drafts of thesis and grant proposals and looking for models in our collection of thesis proposals. NNS students, about 25% of the student body, have traditionally made up one third to one half of our clientele. We attracted students across a wide range of needs and interests; because of the popular course and our two middle names, few people saw us as remedial.

After twenty-seven years teaching Graduate Writing and five years (co)directing the W(RT)C, Bruce resigned in fall 2003. In June 2004, as part of a major restructuring, the dean's office discontinued the course and dismantled the WRTC, handing responsibility for writing services to the library, along with a few TA lines. Dozens of students, staff, and faculty told us they will miss us.

Although all our programs started small, the one at St. Mary's began with the clearest mandate, based on faculty members' keen awareness of student needs. The other two, despite their different story lines, were the initiatives of individuals already involved in tutoring who saw student needs, conducted research, and talked to administrators. Those administrators then found a way to transfer TA lines. Although research and a formal proposal aided the start-up process at Texas, formality does not necessarily guarantee longevity: After an ad hoc beginning, the Harvard center operated for nearly ten years. The gradual development at Texas— working first with one department and then two and so on—may be another form of ad hoc development that could serve as a model for the underfunded university that wants to serve its most needy students.

ONGOING ISSUES FOR GWCS

Our cases reflect a range of issues associated with starting and maintaining a writing center for graduate students. The same policies and practices that are now established, and thus less often debated, in an undergraduate milieu, may arise again for those starting and operating GWCs. Whereas issues such as location, staffing, and funding have been discussed in great detail in writing center literature, each issue raises different questions in the context of a GWC. One reason for this difference is the greater sense of identity and autonomy that graduate departments may hold. Compared to UWCs, GWCs may be amenable to different service options and may experience different kinds of administrative concerns. We focus here on a variety of common issues as they pertain to centers that serve graduate students.

Location

Our small sample indicates that, like a UWC, a GWC can operate effectively from a variety of locations within an institution. Services at St. Mary's and Harvard are centrally located, but the Texas program was decentralized, positioned within individual departments. We see pros and cons in each situation. A centralized GWC may be able to provide a standard level of student support, regardless of the disparities among departments' resources. Operating from a central location also increases visibility, raising credibility and sustainability. On the other hand, positioning consultants within specific departments may be more convenient and attractive for graduate students who may identify more with their departments than with the university at large. It can also communicate to students a sense of departmental sanction unlike that of a campuswide center. A decentralized space may also encourage a sense of community within a department and encourage peer interaction. Of course, GWCs need not be entirely centralized or decentralized. Perhaps departmental "clusters" could use a semicentralized (or semidepartmental) model, in which departments that require writing in similar genres and formats might employ the same consultant or pool of consultants located in-house. Clearly, issues of location for GWCs deserve further discussion.

Services

All of our centers offered one-to-one consultations and web resources. St. Mary's also provides short courses on topics of interest to graduate students, as did the Harvard center, along with writing groups for doctoral students. Unlike undergraduates, who have frequent assignments for multiple classes, doctoral students work on longer term projects and can benefit greatly from the mutual feedback and camaraderie such groups provide. In fact, some studies of graduate writers, including Burnett (46), suggest that those in writing groups are often the most successful and prolific writers. Working with a group, rather than individually, is also an efficient use of consultant time. From these experiences, we suggest two directions that administrators of GWCs might develop and study: leading pilot writing across the curriculum efforts and facilitating writing groups.

Staff

Two overlapping staffing issues apply particularly to GWCs: consultants and administrators. Texas and Harvard were staffed by graduate students, whereas St. Mary's is staffed by professionals. Michael Pemberton (IV.3.1) argued that graduate students can be served by undergraduate tutors trained to respond to their special set of challenges. Our experiences, however, lead us to question this assumption. For example, few undergraduates are familiar with the genres and expectations of specific disciplines and have firsthand experience with sustained writing and research projects. Few are experts on the arcane details of citation formats that can even stump professionals on occasion. Thus, they naturally have less credibility with graduate students than do advanced graduate students, like those at Texas or Harvard, or professionals, like those at St. Mary's. Our experiences lead us to argue for graduate or professional consultants, but we leave the question open for further discussion and research.

Many of the issues related to staffing apply to both consultants and administrators. The centers at both Texas and Harvard were initiated and led by doctoral students. The director at St. Mary's is a staff member, and the administrator at Harvard was staff, with faculty as codirectors. As is true of graduate student consultants, graduate student administrators are cheap labor and can provide great energy to a new GWC; however, as the Texas case shows, graduate students are temporary employees who cannot ensure continuity, and who may lack the administrative clout needed to sustain a program. To build a reputation, a program must offer the same quality of support one semester after another. Consultants and administrators who are either staff or faculty can stay longer, providing institutional memory and consistent services, and developing long-term relationships with administration and faculty. If such relationships are strong enough, then the GWC can survive inevitable changes in the administration and eventually become part of the fabric of the school, just as many UWCs are now.

Administration

The administrators at both Texas and St. Mary's came from writing center backgrounds, unlike those at Harvard. All of us realized immediately that working with graduate students raises particular administrative issues. They may be poorly served in a campuswide center where the priority is given to undergraduate appointments. They often need longer sessions that do not fit neatly into the UWC schedule and want consultants to read drafts between meetings. Access may be a problem if a campuswide center's location or open hours are not compatible with graduate students' schedules. As at Texas, differences in funding sources for graduate and undergraduate support services may mean that UWCs risk the charge of misappropriating funds when they do serve graduate students. Finally, the staff of a UWC may not have the crucial connections to graduate faculty and advisors that facilitate and enrich support for graduate students. All these administrative issues point to the value of a writing center dedicated to graduate students. Still, we encourage discussion on whether or not graduate students can be well-served in an undergraduate center that focuses on their specific needs.

As we suggested, and the case at St. Mary's illustrates, NNS students also present special challenges to writing center administrators. At present, enrollments of international students on many U.S. campuses are holding steady or even declining because of national security issues, but immigrant student enrollments are swelling, as well as the population of multilingual students known as Generation 1.5, especially in urban areas. We have all seen how, in large numbers, their concerns can dominate a GWC. Whether universities need to offer more support than a graduate writing center can provide is an area for further concern.

Funding

At Texas, individual departments paid TAs to serve students, and the OGS gave the coordinator a small stipend. At St. Mary's, the dean provided initial funding, with the understanding that the director would try to offset costs. At Harvard, TA lines and other funding were arranged through the dean's office. Although UWCs have traditionally struggled with funding, the issue may be even more difficult for a GWC, in part because the very concept of a writing center in a graduate program may seem frivolous or inappropriate. Moreover, the usual sources of funding for UWCs may not be available for graduate centers. Federal and state grants for support services usually are reserved for undergraduates. By tradition, graduate students are not assessed general services fees and often are resistant to them, even if—as in Texas—they express a strong desire for writing support services. Fee-for-service raises serious ethical questions for tutors, directors, and referring instructors, because it presents a clear problem for financially strapped students. Clearly, funding is an issue for ongoing discussion.

Our experiences do lead us to this warning for individuals seeking funding for graduate writing support: Be prepared to find creative ways to offset costs. Our methods have included volunteer or work study tutors, workshops for which students pay fees, credit-bearing courses, allocations from academic departments, and in-house publications sold in volume. Other GWC administrators have written grants to fund specific programs and have even considered an endowment. As GWCs become more accepted, perhaps funding will come more easily. Meanwhile, the search for funding sources for GWCs deserves sustained attention.

A CALL TO ACTION

Given the enormous student demand we have all experienced, it may seem ironic that starting a GWC means convincing the administration that such a center is necessary, or even appropriate. Over time, some administrators come to appreciate the center's role on campus, especially if faculty endorse it. At the beginning, however, it may help to prepare for questions like these from the dean's office: Why don't grad students already know how to write? If they need instruction, then why don't they enroll in a writing course? What kinds of services are appropriate for a GWC? Can your GWC demonstrate its ability to improve student writing? Does the need for a GWC reflect weaknesses in curriculum, teaching, or admissions policy? The last question, if answered affirmatively, is sure to set off political sparks when the center reports its data.

In order to answer these questions in ways that will satisfy the various constituencies we serve as directors of GWCs, we need more stories, more research, and finally more communication among the members of our growing ranks.

WORKS CITED

Burnett, Paul C. "The Supervision of Doctoral Dissertations Using a Collaborative Cohort Model."*Counselor Education and Supervision* 39.1 (1999): 46–53.

Farrell, John Thomas. "Some of the Challenges to Writing Centers Posed by Graduate Students." *The Writing Lab Newsletter* (1994): 3–5.

Kinkead, Joyce A., and Jeanette G. Harris. *Writing Centers in Context: Twelve Case Studies*. Champaign, IL: NCTE, 1993.

Mullen, Carol A. "The Need for a Curricular Writing Model for Graduate Students." *Journal of Further and Higher Education* 25.1 (2001): 117–26.

Pemberton, Michael. "Working with Graduate Students." *The Writing Center Resource Manual* Ed. Bobbie Bayliss Silk. 2nd ed. Emmitsburg, MD: NWCA P, 2002. IV.3: 1–5.

❧ **16** ❦

Tutoring in a Remedial/Developmental Learning Context

Dennis Paoli
Hunter College, CUNY

It is unnecessary to problematize the role of writing centers in remedial/developmental English programs. Anyone who has run a center that serves a remedial/developmental program or tutored a student from one (and that's a lot of us) knows and understands the problems. But, simply describing the center–program relationship will unavoidably produce a list of problematic issues inherent in the effort. The bromide that problems are opportunities, ubiquitous in writing center narratives, is true here, too, in the sense that dichotomies present options (including the option to deny/transcend the dichotomy) and the hard work, every day, is making choices.

THE NOMINAL PROBLEM

What's in a name? It is a remedial program by any other name—you see where this is going? Almost from their inception, with the advent of open enrollment policies at public universities in the late 1960s and early 1970s, remedial programs were renamed by those who ran them. By 1977, there were three denominations current in public college conversations and catalogues for such courses and catch-up curricula, as noted by Mina P. Shaughnessy in *Errors and Expectations* when she planted her flag in "the territory I am calling basic writing (and that others might call remedial or developmental writing)" (4). The affective impact of that book and the authority of Shaughnessy's arguments (and, by all accounts, her personality) gave currency to "basic writing" and birth to the *Journal of Basic Writing*, published by the City University of New

York. But catalogues of CUNY's community colleges today use "remedial" and "remedial/developmental" terminology, the discourse of the last decade's debate focuses on the concept of the "developmental," and the press and the public insist on "remedial." So what's in a name?

"Remediation" implies "remedy." Beyond the patronizing medical metaphor, which characterizes students in such programs as patients, there is the more troubling suggestion of method. Diagnostic placement exams, usually in reading, writing, and mathematics, track incoming freshmen (and sometimes transfer students) by an academic triage based on skills assessment into courses in which they receive prescribed treatments for their deficiencies. Often, at the end of these courses, the students are tested again to determine whether or not they can be released into the academic community at large or need a repeat treatment. Prescriptive measures are likely to include grammar drills, requirement of the five-paragraph essay format, and plenty of exercises.

If writing centers tutor students from a program like this—and yes, they still exist, in effect or in emphasis—then the staff will be expected to know and dispense answers, to support stricture of structure, and to provide supplements (drills, exercises, information, and explanations). Instructors will send students to the center to work on their grammar (sigh) the way primary physicians send patients to specialists or to rehab. Many centers conceived as adjuncts to such programs have "skills" in their names (e.g., the Academic Skills Center) and prominent in their literature (including their Web sites) and materials.

"Developmental" writing or English programs reject the aforementioned model (if their name means anything) and design their courses in accord with a model of cognitive development, whether it is Piaget's, Bloom's, or some empirical model developed through years of practice and attention to practice. Here skills are not a separate concern from critical thinking; the code is not prior to content. They are learned together, the pressures of expression driving the acquisition of skills sufficient to adequately and accurately communicate acquired knowledge, the acquisition process itself driving cognitive development from stage to stage. Because the fundamental and systematic dynamic of the model is expressive instead of directive, the developmental model is more student-centered than are test-scorer/instructor-driven remedial programs.

The expectations of developmental program participants when they send students to, or arrive as students at, the writing center is that cognitive development will be facilitated. Tutors will engage the student writers as thinkers, ask questions and foster thought, and address grammar and mechanics when they impede or subvert meaning. As such, tutoring will complement classroom instruction more than supplement it. The student will have, upon attending class and entering the center, joined the community of academic writers, without skill-drill initiation or passing some sphinx-cum-testing-company's exclusionary exam.

The developmental model is the dominant model in contemporary writing program theory and practice. Witness CUNY's adoption of an ACT Writing Sample Test for placement, in the scoring of which an emphasis is put on the ability not just to "assert reasons" but to "develop explanations" and the scoring scale for which features specified degrees of "elaboration." This test is also used as a gatekeeper exit exam for developmental writing courses at CUNY colleges, so those courses, and the tutorial components of those programs, will necessarily focus on explanation and elaboration at least as much as "errors in mechanics, usage, or sentence structure." Placement scoring by pedagogical level, as described by Susanmarie Harrington, moves further toward the developmental model. Scored by teachers in the program into which the student will be placed, such practice displaces text features as the focus of holistic scoring and purports to assess the student directly.

But the developmental model is not unchallenged. Since the early 1990s, poststructuralist critics have claimed that the developmental model is culturally bound and discourse determined, essentially that it is a bourgeois fiction, no less a delimiting imposition on the possibilities of student development than the five-paragraph essay is on the possibilities of student expression. The narrative of instructors, and tutors, shepherding students through taxonomically determined stages of cognitive ability (or expressive method or academic adaptation) to mastery does not recognize the social construction of knowledge (including that taxonomy itself), the role of discourse in that construction, and the power of the classroom and the tutorial session to create knowledge.

The poststructuralist model is a problematic one for instruction in the academy as currently constructed. It is one thing to recognize James Joyce's *Ulysses* as an open text; it is quite another to recognize James's essay on *Ulysses* based on his tutor Joyce's ideas as an appropriate text in a class on modernism. The nagging, often deep suspicion among faculty of group work, including tutoring, hews to the remedial/developmental bias in academic culture. And although remedial/developmental students may benefit from writing assignments that require their written analysis of the academic structures that shape their academic experience, will they benefit alike from critical analysis of the discourse they are in the process of learning written in the discourse they are analyzing?

Program structures image their theoretical models. Skills acquisition programs usually separate reading and writing courses, and even separate instruction in writing courses into grammar learning and essay writing, so as to focus discrete attention on the remediation of discrete deficiencies, in conformance with (often standardized and externally imposed) exit exams that test segregated skills. Tiered programs with multiple course sequences suggest a developmental approach with students expressing their way to exposition. But sequenced programs can also accommodate code-then-mode remediation of language and rhetorical skills. The curricular pressures of coordinated freshman or general education programs have created course linkages, block programs, and "learning communities" that more or less correlate learning across a latitudinal breadth of courses and subjects, thus broadening the concept of development and suggesting a social constructivist context.

Different programs will create different assignment designs. The influence of exit exams, of atomized or integrated curricula, of programmatic or departmental factors (e.g., pass rates, class size policies, hiring policies, etc.), of text choice, what have you, will result in assignments ranging from multiple-choice quizzes, to relatively textless expressive writing, to group research projects, to you name it. Center work, then, will depend to a great deal on the nature of the program served, its theoretical foundations, and its institutional locus. Instructor, student, and tutor expectations will be shaped by knowledge of the program. Will this student's interest be likely to stop at the attainment of the right answer, at the understanding of why the answer is right, at the unearthing and examination of options? Will the English instructor appreciate the tutor's interest in the student's interpretation of the reading in her history class? Will the history teacher? The final exam is next week, so who cares about anything else? If we do create knowledge, isn't it best to have as much information as possible?

And what of "basic" writing? Is Shaughnessy's descriptor significant or merely nominal? If she herself identified it with the alternatives—"the territory I am calling basic writing (and that others might call remedial or developmental writing)"—then can't the term be taken as rhetorical, euphemistic, PR for a less pejorative connotation? Her semantic representation of the alternatives as parenthetical suggests as much. But it suggests more, as well: Parentheses enclose, include, and designate the antecedent basic writing as an umbrella term, a tent, an embrace. Not only is the term, and therefore the program it describes, meant not to exclude, not to track and trap "so-called remedial students" (293) in an "endless corridor of remedial anterooms" (on the far end of the Borgesian campus from the Library of Babel), it is also meant progressively to integrate instruction and to correlate the "prescriptive bits and pieces of instruction we once called freshman composition" in a curriculum (292).

Most basic writing (BW) programs have come to adopt this principle and, in part at least, a policy of inclusion, from the raw accrual of effective method, the coordination of dozens if not hundreds of faculty with varying experience and perspectives, the crosscurrents of politics and theory (psychological, sociological, linguistic, psycholinguistic, etc.), or the protean demographics of the student population. The BW model, then, attempts everything, starting with and from a recognition of significance, of error and trial, of the individual thinker and the accumulated learning of the academy, of the students and the enterprise. It respects meaningful difference in student writing and seeks to make one. (Historically, this model may not include but does prefigure the "context-dialectic view" of "development" of Curtis and Herrington, 70.)

Tutors who work with students from BW programs like these will be expected to have multiple methods at hand, sharp and apt analytical abilities to determine the best method for the moment, and a capacity for insight into the profundity that compels the practice. A credit-bearing course or a series of training sessions that provides tutors with broad-based theoretical foundations, and ongoing practice in the application of theory to a broad range of program-generated cases, when possible in conjunction with program instructors, is basic training for tutorial staff with these responsibilities.

Center administrators need to inform themselves of the relevant program's self-definition, its categorical imperatives, and, practically, its fundamental features, so administrators can help tutors ask the fundamental questions of students from the program, so the center can serve them—the students and the program—from knowledge:

- Is there a placement exam? What are the scoring criteria?
- Is the program tiered, sequenced, and how are the developmental levels determined?
- Is the program (at the tutored student's level) focused on grammatical skills, expressive or expository prose, academic diction and study skills, reading and research, some developmental range or combination of expectations?
- Does the program link developmental agendas (reading and writing) or link writing courses with introductory-level discipline-based courses, requiring consideration of multiple perspectives on shared content or integrated assignments?
- Is there an exit exam? What are the scoring criteria? Is it the placement exam?

THE HISTORICAL PROBLEM

Under the BW banner, programs grew in size and esteem—at least self-esteem—generating success stories, statistics, and scholarship. Ambitious curricula, like Shaughnessy's and that of Mike Rose and his colleagues (the "four-tiered plan"), made demands of and claims on the academy that shook the tower to its foundation. They adopted college-level content, offered college credit, muscled into the general curriculum, and spawned rhetoric and composition as a legitimate academic field.

And they jump-started a proliferation of writing centers. Centers were part of public higher education's remastered master plan for managing open enrollment, and, within a few years of the creation of programmatic remediation, on many urban campuses a sign was hung on a basement door, or space was made in a lounge area of the library, or an office for adjuncts in the English department was time shared, and thus a writing center started from scratch. The first impression most centers made on the academy was as a hardscrabble outpost on the newly opened "frontier" (Shaughnessy's term, 4) of freshman composition. The conceptualization of centers as supplemental services, still favored among faculty, is a product of their begetting with the program.

And from these humble but aspiring beginnings grew the bourgeois and proletarian narratives of writing center development that Peter Carino characterized as "evolutionary" and "dialectic" (31). Carino's work in opening up these story structures to broader possibility, opportunity, and operational appreciation of writing center "culture" is itself demonstrative of the history it/they trace, a chaos (in the sense of a self-actuating calculus) of appropriation/adaptation/rejection/innovation, but with an identifiable animus: to go beyond, "Beyond Remedial" (Wilson and LaBouff), "Beyond Freshman Comp" (Harris and Yancey), beyond any institution-mandated definition and mission toward self-definition and self-determination.

To go beyond, however, is not necessarily to leave behind. Many centers (like ours at Hunter) that have long since expanded their services across the curriculum and to the graduate level still serve developmental writing programs. Some centers, often in community colleges, are still attached exclusively to developmental English programs. And many faculty, from every discipline at every level, still determine that, in their professional (often personal) opinion, their students' writing is not at "college level." So, they send those students to the center to work on their "English," creating *de facto* remediation and creating frustration among writing center administrators, who labored long to go "beyond," and tutorial staffs, who eagerly adopted and polished tutoring techniques based on an "evolved" philosophy.

It was this avowed frustration that drove Stephen M. North to write "The Idea of a Writing Center," as much a watershed document and event for centers as the publication of *Errors and Expectations* was for programs. The seven-year lag between these works speaks to the fraying of North's patience. Even in BW programs, the fine qualities of which Shaughnessy described as "evolved," the classroom, as Carino pointed out (34), was privileged in part because the writing center could be underprivileged (witness the old, unfortunate, unfortunately apt "grammar ghetto" metaphor, which migrated, like the work, from composition programs; Rose 120). When Shaughnessy described the "remedial model," she wanted CUNY's program out from under because it "isolates the student and the skill from real college contexts" and "imposes a 'fix-it' station tempo and mentality" (293); she was describing the contemporary, late 1970s writing center model, and an accepted writing center philosophy of the time (Carino 36). It is a fact (not just an interpretation, a fact) of history that otherwise like-minded faculty disconnected from their philosophy in order to consign labor they considered reprehensible and unethical to tutors, who otherwise thought themselves colleagues in a communal effort. When this history repeats itself—and it does—tutor morale, followed by tutorial work, can suffer.

So history must be addressed, and its tensions investigated, so staff can consciously work through their animus and the center can refit for present duty. Carino organized his historical account into pre- and post-North periods, which is useful for study, but in the case of most centers, a trained or experienced eye can look at their breadth of services, their reach across the curriculum, or their relationships within their institutions synchronistically and recognize their history. Because to go beyond is not always to leave behind and because the lessons of local history make good training material, tutors can be prepared to anticipate challenges to their tutoring philosophy and, indeed, to test and temper that philosophy, through a study of their (or a) center's history. A historical perspective can mitigate the influence of emotional friction created by the dialectic, the affective static that can enervate a session and depress a staff.

There is another potential problem inherent in writing center history, and it lurks in the history before us, that we write for the future, in the conative quest to go beyond. It is a shock to the system when a center evolves into remediation. Say your center does a good job and is recognized for it, so when your school institutes a writing across the curriculum program, your center is given a prominent role in the initiative, a role it has earned and is ready to relish. And then that role turns out to be filled, in fact swamped, by "a dramatic increase in ESL conferencing" (Powers, 39). This causes tutors and students to be "frustrated" (40) by the ubiquity of failure, the failure of the center's "nondirective philosophy" (42) to meet the students' needs and the failure of the tutors when they indulge in directive, didactic instruction, which helps the students but leaves the staff feeling that they have "betrayed" (42) their pedagogical principles. Although not technically a remediation program, Judith K. Powers's writing center at the University of Wyoming in the early 1990s was functioning as one, and in the process what had promised to be a progressive development must have felt, not just in the struggle with failure but in the compromise with success, like devolution.

What Powers and her writing center staff faced was an ethical question: How does what we can do shape and take shape from what we think we should do? As basic writing programs matured into more principled functioning, their institutional roles became more complex, more problematic. As centers became more independent of programs, yet retained responsibility for tutoring their students, their service models became misallied, at times, with expectations. It is best to first clear the air, to understand the relationship of a remedial/developmental writing program to a writing center locally, from a historical perspective, and to ask the following:

- Has the remedial/developmental writing program changed, in population, principle, or practice? (Choose a reasonable time frame for your analysis.)
- Have the program's expectations of the center changed?
- Has the center changed, in population, principle, or practice?
- Has the center's relationship to the program changed?

If the center is a start-up, then those last three questions are not asked in terms of change but in terms of choice (How will the director decide to function? What compromises will the center make to fit the program?) revealing themselves as ethical questions. But they proceed from the historical context of the first question.

And whether centers are in start-up or maintenance mode or in a growth spurt, it is regularly a good exercise to select another center in a similar academic setting and research its history (perhaps in a mutual project in which its staff researches yours). The point of the project is not to create a narrative of evolution or a dialectic of collected dichotomies or an articulated social construction, but to find discontinuities with your own center's history (for start-up centers, with your projected history). From what points of similarity in policy and practice did (would) divergence occur? When were different choices made and why? Avoid value judgments; seek (as Carino did) complexity; come to at least a partial understanding. Then ask the ethical questions.

THE ETHICAL PROBLEM

North's "Idea" is exactly that: It enunciates an ideology. Which raises the questions: Are we ideologues? And, what if we are? Is there a generally shared writing center ethos that grounds that ideology in a moral philosophy? And when programmatic push comes to institutional shove, does anything go?

No enterprise a center undertakes stresses its principles more than remediation. And those stresses are thrown into clearest, boldest relief in the case of remedial English as a second language (ESL)-student tutoring. But before we consider the case of tutorial services for ESL-designated remedial students as indicative of the problematic nature of tutoring remedial students, we must first answer the question: Is ESL remediation exceptional or is it remedial, more unlike or like remediation for native speakers? And then we must admit that we cannot answer that question except locally, by program and center, according to local politics, fiscal "realities," international student or immigrant demographics, program and center histories and philosophies, institutional missions, and so on. At CUNY, a recent university-wide reorganization of remediation has mandated that the only remedial courses offered at the senior colleges be open to ESL students, based on an "ESL exemption" from the curricular relocation of remediation to the two-year colleges. So at Hunter, ESL is remedial, but it is also exceptional. What is persuasive for the case for identifying ESL as remedial is the identity of issues involved: (over)focus on the code, attendant academic reading and paraphrase problems, cultural variance of rhetorical forms, mainstreaming versus segregated postsecondary preparation versus parallel supplemental programs, the appropriateness of a process model or student-centered approach, and so on. Carol Severino asked these same questions and decided that the same tutorial method should be applied in the case of ESL students as is practiced with native speakers, and I expect that extends to students in remedial programs.

The challenge of effective instruction, classroom and tutorial, for ESL students is a challenge to a writing center's ideology and ethics, which in itself is ethical. Ideologies and ethical principles that become reified as rules need regular revisiting and investigation in the process of practice. There is an opportunity for research here, but not just for summative assessments (e.g., what are the outcomes on standardized exams or in curricular success of students tutored in an ideologically strict system compared with those tutored in an ethically flexible, situational ethos). Formative assessments are of serious interest, too, such as a study of the circumstances under which tutors are most likely to negotiate away their grip on principle. When do tutoring principles, of service, of process, of a center's authority over its own practice, conflict, and what then?

The answer to the "when" question, on the most basic level, occurs when tutors work with students in the tutoring session. The pressures of the program, and often of the student's own preference for directive pedagogy converge at the point at which the tutor's principles are weakest: that point in time. Remediation programs are temporal constructs; students have a determinate amount of time to master skills, or learn to elaborate thought, or acquire sufficient proficiency in enough categories of assessment to pass a gatekeeper exam, or amass enough successful efforts to pass a course. Coincident, synchronistic pressures may be piled on, in immersion methodologies or linked courses, intensifying the press of time, compelling the tutor to compromise, extorting, in the moment, abandon. Despite the research and the reminders of the wise that language acquisition, whether English or written academic English, takes time, it is for our students, as it was for Shaughnessy's, the "eleventh hour" (unpaginated Preface) and they are just "beginning" (291). Whereas Rose argued redundantly for a remedial program that progresses "slowly but steadily and systematically" (107; also see 109, 115, 121) and that teachers need to "train (themselves) to wait" (112), he admitted that "remedial writers don't have much time" (116). Shaughnessy laid the same conflict bare, advising that instructors "need to cultivate patience for the slow pace of progress in this most complex of crafts" while acknowledging a paragraph later that the BW student "must ... work harder and faster" (293). Teachers often practice patience at the expense of tutoring practice, sending students to the writing center to "catch up" (Shaughnessy 3) there, redirecting the "urgency of the students" (8) at the tutor, imposing on the tutoring session that "'fix-it' station tempo and mentality" (293) teachers want banished from the classroom and the program.

And for ESL students the reasonable time frame for learning is likely to be longer, yet the term/semester/class/session is the same length for everyone. Viewed as a supplemental service, centers offer a precious commodity, extra instructional time. And students expect that time to be filled with instruction that fits the systematic structure of the program. Studies may show and experts may argue that that system should be multitiered and carefully sequenced, include and emphasize academic reading, focus on note taking and listening skills (Hirsch), and center on/in the student. Yet, as structurally supportive as a program may be, it is likely to end in a high stakes testing event, likely to demand just as much if not more work from the student, and highly unlikely to offer more, or enough, time. And if, in a one-on-one session with a student from that program, a tutor is more likely to feel a pressing need to spend limited, fleeting time working on grammar than to feel "the need to give not simply more time but more imaginative and informed attention" (Shaughnessy 292), then the tutor is less likely to question, to express interest, to share her own peer experiences, to lift the student off the page, out of time, toward a momentary insight into how the language works to make meaning, or what Shaughnessy described as an "I see!" moment that will produce "a new plane of competence" (276) and will last for life. It is the center's work to make that moment possible, so it is the administrator's work to give tutors the wherewithal (the breadth of technique, the confidence, the knowledge, the principles, the support, i.e., the ideology and the ethos) to resist that pressure and work toward that moment of real learning.

And perhaps tutors need the freedom to watch for it and the experience to recognize it in the midst of a skill drill. It may be that it should be a principle of a center's ideology to allow practice that strays, aspires, or regresses beyond the ideological. If the philosophical context of such practice is understood by tutor and student-client to be otherwise and still in effect in the sense of being available for contextualization, if the purpose is principled (of service, e.g., in the case of a student who will not negotiate the "urgent need" for didactic instruction and otherwise not receive service), and if there is opportunity for reflection on and discussion of the incident in training, then why not? (That is not necessarily a rhetorical question.) And there is always the option of subversive supplementation, of guiding students from grammar to process, of engaging students in metacognitive activity arising from error and arriving at shared meaning making, of giving the people what they want until they want what you give them (admittedly an evolutionary narrative).

And then there is the relocation and rehabilitation of the remedial/medical metaphor. When Powers's staff came to the realization that the "instances of ineffectiveness in our typical approach became symptomatic of a broader inability to meet the needs of ESL writers" (43), the "contagion" (Shaughnessy 290) of failure spread, or rather conceptually fled from the student to the center. Powers's staff rethought their strategies, investigated and adjusted their own expectations, adopted a social constructivist model to value (in fact, privilege) ESL clients' "perspective," "reexamine(d) (their) approach as outsiders might," and reconceived their center's "best of intentions" (46) (i.e., their ethos). In short, they remediated themselves. But they did so not without a "struggle" ("Since its inception, our writing center has struggled" 46), and couldn't we all say—and haven't we all said—the same? It is a ubiquitous term in writing center and remedial program literature, often recast as a "wrestling" metaphor (Rose 105). In our less armored moments, it hurts to read these descriptions of our students and ourselves. There are moments of success in writing center work, but from inception there is suffering. When we think we have the remedy for our students' suffering, how can we withhold it? Add to the pressure on praxis the moral imperative to relieve the students' often visible distress.

A dose of ethics is strong medicine, serious stuff. The antidote to shared suffering just might be to lighten up, to play. Recast as play—playing with grammatical options and rhetorical forms, drawing visual aids for visual learners, finding humor in the cognitive dissonance of error—tutoring looks like fun, and the session is a kind of recess. What frustrated Powers's staff was the failure of their attempts "to play off" ESL writers' background writing experience the way they could with native speakers (40). Perhaps, when pedagogy becomes as "global" as the economy, tutors will be able to avoid directive instruction of international students and play off their backgrounds, too. But if that means that writing instruction, on any particular model, becomes universal, as opposed to there being more universal knowledge of diverse pedagogies, will that be a good thing? Remedial programs, and writing centers that offer programmatically attached service, have been accused almost since inception of behavior modification and socialization, of being agents of a sociopolitical ideology that deliberately limits learning by, among other means, universalizing concepts by, among other means, privileging English (a particular English at that). Counterarguments that these critics themselves use the language of the academy, which they would liberate students from learning, to espouse their criticism (Rose 108) can be extended to the argument that their freedom to "play off" and play with ideologies to gain perspective on them (i.e., reexamine them as outsiders might) allowed them to conceive of, shape, and direct—besides express—their criticism.

So a good training model for consideration and anticipation of the ethical problems likely to be confronted in tutoring remedial/developmental students would be various forms of play:

- Role play to demonstrate and investigate ethical dilemmas in tutoring practice, specifically with basic writing and ESL-designated students, and in the process, play with time (e.g., a one-minute session vs. a one-minute silence).
- Imagine circumstances in which the compromise of principle might be acceptable or even appropriate.
- Imagine circumstances in which tutors should hold fast to principle and how that can be done while addressing student expectation and instructor stipulation.
- Imagine how an outsider might view, and criticize, practice in the center (remembering Shaughnessy's description of that first generation of open admissions students as "strangers in academia" [3] and Powers's appreciation of international students' perspective).
- Research writing instruction models in local high schools or in secondary and postsecondary education in a foreign country.

Okay, that last one doesn't sound as much like play, but it could be fun or at least instructive, as could the following:

- Ask tutors to list incidents in tutorial sessions in which they were distracted from principled tutoring technique; analyze the incidents in groups to identify the pressures on the tutor to compromise principle.
- Have tutors make a list of "I see!" moments that occurred in their literacy history, or have them keep a journal of such insightful experiences in their tutorial sessions—moments for the student-client and for the tutor; have tutors share their journal entries; note and discuss the circumstances in which those moments occurred.

Now, what do we do?

THE METHODOLOGICAL PROBLEM

There are a million methods. Get on the Internet for a half hour and you'll find more heuristics, handouts, exercises, practice programs, study guides, short cuts, visual aids, prompts, and models than you'll use in a year. One of North's complaints was that too much writing center budget was spent on stuff: "drills, texts, machines, tapes, carrels, headphones—the works" (437); add computer hardware and software and digital video and the mind boggles (to say nothing of the budget). Materials aren't methods, however, unless they are. Tutors daunted by the task at hand, especially the task of tutoring basic writing students, which we have seen can be overwhelming, might resort, in exasperation and desperation, to a center's devices. Materials become de facto method.

So materials must be contextualized in technique, method in methodology. There is Socratic method, guided group work, sequential learning, dialogic analysis, Vygotskian double stimulus, program supplementation, test-structured practice, software-structured practice, scaffolding, application of the writing process model—more methodology there than you can learn in a year, much less train a staff in. To have more method than one can use does not mean the tutor has more method than is needed. Having methodological choices to make exercises the center's ethical principles and can address diversity issues that arise in tutoring a diverse population, which a remedial/developmental program is likely to provide, in terms of cultural and educational background. When there is so much method that even grammar-anchored instruction can be varied and vital, there is just enough, and just for that one instructional approach. This does not mean that a better method can't be found, and so "just enough" is not enough is never enough. Writing centers go beyond.

Let's take a test case, a student from a remedial/developmental writing course who comes to the center on a weekly basis and works with the same tutor for the term. The student is very upset that she "failed" the placement test and was tracked into the remedial program. She will not accept that you cannot fail a placement test, the purpose of which is simply to place you in a tiered skills development program so you will be at the learning level appropriate to your skills development; she "knows" she has failed her first college writing assignment, and, what's more, the "placement" test is going to be readministered at the end of the term as the remedial course exit exam. She is obviously intelligent, and even "did well in high school," but she has problems in every category of the rubric used to score the test. The tutor uses the process model and Socratic questioning to tutor the student for the first few weeks, and the student does well on her essays for class but is still unsatisfied with her progress and noticeably worried about the test. The instructor advises the student to get help on her grammar because, based on her class essays, the grammar category of the rubric is her most problematic. The tutor tries to oblige; the process model is resilient and comprehensive and can address grammar problems in a meaningful context, but undue pressures from program, through the instructor, make the hard work harder. The student insists on working on her grammar, although the tutor resists philosophically and has concluded from their sessions so far that the student's major problems are rhetorical; she does not explain her points carefully, logically, or effectively enough to the reader.

What now? The center needs to do some legwork because the best materials to apply in this case are not in the center's handout file or loaded on its OWL. Is the student's score on the test available for use in tutoring? Is the score broken down by rubric category? Studying the rubric in itself will make the student aware of the range of expressive and expository tasks to be addressed, of their equal importance in scoring, and student knowledge of the rubric will also give the student an idea of audience, turn the scorer into a reader, reading for specified qualities of argument as well as of prose. If the student did relatively well in the grammar and mechanics categories of the rubric, then the tutor has traction for his argument that they work on argumentation. If grammar is a relatively weak category for the student, then it should be addressed. And it is best addressed in context, so is the test essay itself available for the student to study? Testing company policies do not always make this option possible, but if it is, reviewing the student's test essay with the student reduces the test from a monolithic obstruction in the way of the student's college career to a set of mistakes and missteps the student made in performing the task. And in those mistakes and missteps, the tutor can find patterns to shape the application of process. And in the essay the tutor can find examples of appropriately applied grammar skills and well-expressed ideas with which to encourage the student writer.

Energized, the student wants to practice, to write a timed test essay every week. But the tutor has other plans, and after the first practice essay applies a process model, having the student reread the prompt, rethink her response, reorganize her paragraphs, and add examples and explanations as prompted by the tutor's reading (with the rubric in both their minds). The student revises the essay, maybe twice, to make, and understand what it takes to make, a full, successful response to the prompt. Then the student proofreads, after which the tutor asks about the errors that remain in relation to the patterns they saw in the original test essay. They discuss the student's voice in the practice essay, how it is different from her voice in the session, her voice in e-mails, and her voice in the original test essay. How are these voices like or unlike her voice in her writing in other classes? How are those essays like or unlike the test essay? Now the student is more likely to bring those assignments and assignments from her writing class to her tutoring sessions and to appreciate lessons learned from working on those assignments as learning that will help her pass the gatekeeper exit exam.

How much method must tutors have at their command? They need lots, and the more theory behind it and the more training in it the better. There is room in this case study for the use of every kind of material aid mentioned earlier. The determinant factor, however, is the tutor's analysis of the student's situation, the student's knowledge—some of it insecure and unfocused, some of it wrong—of the language and the subject, learning style, personal writing process, curiosity and capacity for struggle, and patience with the pressures of the program. That analysis should be fluid, regularly checked and rechecked, as part of the tutoring process. The student is the "base" in basic writing, the foundation from which "development" proceeds. Whatever the next step is, it is beyond where the student began, including behind, going back to recover lost learning, secure former progress, readdress prior problems with new knowledge. To best serve a remedial/developmental program's sequence of tiered learning, a sequence of tutorial learning might take on a more organic form; the straight line of "development," like the arrow of a product-oriented writing process, will likely be bent, broken, levitated, and lost in a student-based tutoring process. The current method of "looping" emerges as useful in this case study's case, the closing of any learning loop in a recontextualization of former learning and student recognition of the new context. Even the test, which dominated the process at the beginning of the term, has receded to a less prominent, less coercive, more amenable role, because the student is able now to place it in its institutional context and in the larger scope of her own education.

But the loop is more like a spiral, looping up, out, free, in the direction of the student's self-directed learning. The tutor will accompany the student, sometimes slightly in advance, asking leading questions, sometimes breathlessly behind, running to catch up with the student-client's concerns or new capacities. There is no substitute for experience in this effort, so we must help tutors gain as much experience as possible in:

- Applying method, as much as possible, and participating in the process of developing methods and materials.

- Analyzing student-clients' "struggles" and appreciating their "needs" situationally, respecting their academic circumstances and experiences, their foundational knowledge and operational learning, their relative readiness for various next steps.
- Looking for "loops," where/when students writers have "mastered" formerly mutable forms, clarified formerly murky concepts, transcended former entrapments, and where/when the opportunity arises for mutual recognition of achievement and reevaluation of readiness.

THE EXISTENTIAL PROBLEM

Tutoring students in a remedial/developmental program may make tutors question their methods, their ethics, their fundamental ideas of education, besides their faculty colleagues' coursework, their college's curriculum, and their writing center's ideology. It is often the hardest work they do. And, for all the political antipathy and institutional posturing, it isn't going away: Recent research declares the efficacy of "remediation" (Otheguy and O'Riordan; White), at least in terms of student retention. Still, students fail, or give up the effort and drop out. As "at-risk" students approach the exam or their wit's end, the void opens between the student and the program, the program and the curriculum, placement and no place. At this point, tutoring either rushes to remedy skills deficiencies, to fill "the academic gap" (Shaughnessy 275), or disconnects from supplementation and stays with the student, patiently serving when even the student has lost patience. At this point tutors confront the existential problem. "If we run out of time," mused Rose in a footnote, "if some of our students still have not mastered points of mechanics and usage when they leave us, they will at least be open to writing" (122). There was still room in Rose's program for these students, but most of us, and most of our tutors, have watched as students disappeared into the void. The system, even the program, may shrug such failures off, brandishing standards, but centers—nonjudgmental and ready to help everyone—have a harder time letting go, writing students off. If we are to help tutors in this Sisyphean labor, we must help them face the academy's grimmest truths, help them develop moral courage, and help them find value not in success but in the act of helping.

WORKS CITED

"A Description of the CUNY Skills Assessment Program." *CUNY.edu* 20 November 2003. <http://portal.cuny.edu/cms/id/cuny/documents/informationpage/002155.htm>.

Carino, Peter. "Open Admissions and the Construction of Writing Center History: A Tale of Three Models." *The Writing Center Journal* 17.1 (1996): 30–48.

Curtis, Marcia, and Anne Herrington. "Writing Development in the College Years: By Whose Definition?" *CCC* 55.1 (2003): 69–90.

Harrington, Susanmarie. "New Visions of Authority in Placement Test Rating." *Writing Program Administration* 22.1–2 (1998): 53–84.

Harris, Muriel, and Kathleen Blake Yancey. "Beyond Freshman Comp: Expanded Uses of the Writing Lab." *The Writing Center Journal* 1.1 (1980): 43–49.

Hirsch, Linda. "Mainstreaming ESL Students: A Counterintuitive Perspective." *College ESL* 6.2 (1996): 12–26.

North, Stephen M. "The Idea of a Writing Center." *College English* 46.5 (1984): 443–446.

Otheguy, Ricardo, and Mary O'Riordan. "The CUNY Celebration and the Disappearing Guests: The Search for ESL Students in the City University of New York." *College ESL* 9.1–2 (2000): 1–18.

Powers, Judith K. "Rethinking Writing Center Conferencing Strategies for the ESL Writer." *The Writing Center Journal* 13.2 (1993): 39–47.

Rose, Mike. "Remedial Writing Courses: A Critique and a Proposal." *A Sourcebook for Basic Writing Teachers.* Ed. Theresa Enos. New York: Random House, 1987. 104–24.

Severino, Carol. "Serving ESL Students." *The Writing Center Resource Manual.* Ed. Bobbie Bayliss Silk. 2nd ed. Emmitsburg, MD: NWCA Press, 2002. IV.2: 1–9.

Shaughnessy, Mina P. *Errors and Expectations.* New York: Oxford UP, 1977.

White, Edward M. "The Importance of Placement and Basic Studies: Helping Students Succeed Under the New Elitism." *Journal of Basic Writing* 14.2 (1995): 75–84.

Wilson, Lucy, and Olivia LaBouff. "Going Beyond Remedial: The Writing Center and the Literature Class." *The Writing Center Journal* 6.2 (1986): 19–27.

~17~

Examining Writing Center Director–Assistant Director Relationships

Kevin Dvorak
Ben Rafoth
Indiana University of Pennsylvania

It has become clear through recent WCenter listserv discussions that more attention needs to be placed on theorizing and understanding the administrative spaces writing center assistants inhabit and the professional relationships they have with writing center directors. According to Lauren Fitzgerald, the position of assistant in writing center literature is "undertheorized," meaning that "we don't seem to have language for assistants in the way that we do for other writing center workers, especially tutors but also, increasingly, writing center administrators" (Post WCenter listserv, June 4, 2004). We agree. Whereas pedagogy, tutors, administrators, and even students have historically been the main concentrations of writing center theory, it should not be surprising that assistants (i.e., codirectors, assistant directors, and graduate assistant directors), arguably the middle-management of writing center work, have been the subject of little discussion.

This chapter aims to extend these nascent conversations by examining relationships between directors and assistant directors and developing a better understanding of how collaborative administrative efforts affect writing center work. Assistants of all kinds occupy vital roles in writing center practice. Specifically, it examines what are, perhaps, the two most common assistant directorships—graduate assistant director (GAD) and professional assistant director (PAD)—and their working relationships with writing center directors.

WHAT DOES COMMUNICATION DO?

Although we realized that communication is the fundamental aspect of developing a strong director–assistant director relationship, we also recognized that stressing the idea of communication might seem rather obvious. So, rather than just discussing communication, we began asking ourselves questions regarding communication between directors and assistant directors: What does communication do? What do daily or weekly face-to-face meetings between writing center administrators accomplish? What role does communication play in running a successful writing center?

The collaborative effort of administrating a writing center is not an easy one; there are many experiences of consensus and dissensus regarding leadership and pedagogical philosophies. When collaborative-minded administrators recognize communication as a means, as something designed to work toward accomplishing goals, they can embrace these experiences and see them as achieving positive and more productive writing center work.

Whereas dialogue may be crucial to a director–assistant director relationship, dialogue and communication style between director and GAD may be considerably different from that of director and PAD. There are essential differences between these two relationships based on the hierarchical nature of each. This chapter stresses that each of these relationships requires a great deal of productive communication that addresses not only writing center work, but also the establishment and structuring of these professional relationships themselves in order to be successful.

DIRECTOR–GRADUATE ASSISTANT DIRECTOR

Institutions that provide graduate assistantships commonly designate them as temporary, one-year, and nonrenewable. This places a new GAD in that role annually, which in turn creates a new writing center dynamic every year. Therefore, the revolving door position of GAD is one that brings with it new opportunities, and sometimes hardships, for the graduate student, the director, and the writing center. As a result, a director–GAD relationship requires that both individuals get to know one another quickly, create a GAD job description, and facilitate a GAD's professional identity construction. This, in effect, should create a collaborative administrative climate; however, the relation between director and GAD remains hierarchical. A director in this circumstance may, at times, have to defer peer-ness for a moment of mentoring (e.g., guiding a GAD through a research project) or for a moment of authority (e.g., overruling a GAD's decision to establish new policies).

SETTING THE AGENDA

It is important that, when a director sits down with a new GAD for the first time prior to the graduate assistant director's term, they discuss the short- and long-term needs of the writing center, what strengths and weaknesses each person possesses, what pedagogical and leadership philosophies each subscribes to, and how they would like to define the role of the graduate assistant director. Ideally, the first conversation should establish an ongoing dialogue between directors, discuss what expectations each has of the other, establish foundations for a GAD's job description and create a GAD "identity," and promote what we call "stay-in-action," a concept that encourages and reminds both to participate as active observers of daily writing center activities, so they can best determine the writing center's strengths and weaknesses. It may also be beneficial for the director to introduce the "IWCA Graduate Student Position Statement" to the new GAD, if the latter is not already familiar with it.

Although this first conversation will probably highlight "shoptalk," it should also focus on getting to know one another personally. With a new graduate student replacing an exiting one on a regular basis, it is especially important that a director get to know the new assistant director as soon as possible, instead of regarding the new GAD as being a reincarnation of the replaced GAD. Building a personal relationship at the start is a key to developing trust.

DEFINING ROLES, CREATING EMERGENT JOB DESCRIPTIONS

One of the more challenging administrative tasks is to determine a GAD's job description. Some directors believe a formal job description is a mark of a well-established, orderly writing center, whereas others believe a graduate assistant director's role should be more of a role-in-flux with a core of responsibilities. Either way, it is important for a director and a graduate assistant director to discuss the GAD's job description, making sure both are comfortable and clearly understand it. GADs who are left wondering midsemester what their job is may easily become estranged from their assistantship.

According to the "IWCA Graduate Student Position Statement,"

> Assistant directorships should have formal, updated job descriptions written or approved by the director. Assistant directorships should be established within a clearly defined administrative structure so that assistant directors know to whom they are responsible (ideally the director), who they supervise, and exactly what their responsibilities are. If assistant directors are asked to supervise other graduate students, directors should support assistant directors' supervisory and administrative responsibilities. At the same time, graduate assistant directors remain responsible for their supervisory decisions, administrative work, and professional conduct. (61)

Formal job descriptions usually determine what the GAD's duties will be for the year, but, as Nita Danko stated, "the job description for the administrative assistant (and even more so with the aa who also tutors) is not only difficult to write but also difficult to follow" (Post WCenter listserv, June 4, 2004). The director and GAD should discuss whether the GAD would like a formal job description, as the statement suggests, or a more fluid, emergent job design.

It is because of concepts like Danko's and our experiences as administrators that we hesitate to agree with the IWCA statement's position on job descriptions entirely—based solely on the limitations a formal job description presents. On the basis of our experiences in writing center practice, we recognize that every situation is contextualized, meaning that we cannot accurately predict what will happen during the course of an academic year and must be, more often than we would like, reactive to the contexts we are presented. Therefore, we believe that an emergent job description is more conducive for a GAD position than a "formal" job description. An emergent job description, like an emergent design in qualitative research, develops on the basis of a director's and GAD's participation as active observers of writing center activities, the knowledge they gain from these situations, and the methods they employ to best meet these challenges. These methods are always evolving in response to changing environments.

To demonstrate an example of an emergent job description, we refer to a point in time from our year of working together. At the beginning of the fall semester, Ben had two additional projects on top of his regular faculty/administrative duties: chairing the 2004 IWCA-NCPTW Joint Conference in Hershey, Pennsylvania, and acting as the lead writer of IUP's Middle States Accreditation Report. Realizing Ben needed as much time as possible to focus on these tasks, Kevin offered to take on a very active role overseeing the daily administrative duties of the writing center. So, for the first two months of the semester, Kevin was in charge of running tutor training sessions, holding staff meetings, providing regular mentoring sessions for tutors, and taking care of all scheduling duties, along with spot tutoring. By the end of October, Ben had completed the conference and university accreditation report and Kevin had established an orderly writing center. With Ben's reemerging presence at the center, Kevin thought it would be beneficial if his job description emerged from "overseer" to "researcher/developer." Having spent considerable time conversing with tutors about their jobs, Kevin decided he would like to spend the rest of the semester spearheading three projects: creating a budget proposal to increase tutors' wages, creating a budget proposal for new furniture, and developing a week-long training seminar for the first week of spring semester (aspects tutors claimed they wanted more help with). After discussing this shift in job duties for a few days, Ben and Kevin decided that this emergent duty would best benefit the writing center and Kevin as well by giving him experience writing proposals and creating training sessions. For the remainder of the semester, Kevin was less involved in the front-line work of the writing center than he had been and more involved behind the scenes.

Writing centers fortunate enough to have GADs benefit from the possibilities created by someone situated as both a professional and student. GADs in this in-between position can successfully navigate each side because they are a member of both groups. And because writing centers are always changing, on student, tutor, and professional ends, GADs who can successfully negotiate the fluidity of their positions can be invaluable in helping a writing center evolve quickly to meet immediate needs and demands. An emergent job description that is always adapting to and evolving with the changing demands a writing center presents allows a GAD to best help the writing center in the way that the GAD and the director (and the GAD and the tutors and students) deem fit. This is not to say, however, that GADs should be left questioning their administrative status or that the GADs' position should never be fully defined. Both outcomes could easily lead to an uncomfortable working condition, a sentiment Danko expressed: "Maybe I'm more uneasy about the under-described position I hold" (Post WCenter listserv, June 4, 2004). We believe that a GAD should have a clearly defined position in the administrative structure, as the IWCA statement asserts. However, the duties a GAD performs may vary. Therefore, although directors, GADs, and tutors may constantly negotiate the GAD's actual job description and duties, the GAD's status within the administrative structure should be clearly defined.

A further rationale for an emergent job description is to promote the eighth statement of the "IWCA Graduate Student Position Statement": "Graduate assistant directors should be afforded opportunities for research and publication.... While directors should provide mentorship and guidance for individual and/or collaborative projects, graduate assistant directors are accountable for their own participation in research and professional development projects" (61). It is important for a director to offer a GAD flexibility because it allows the GAD to investigate what the GAD believes are the most immediate needs of the writing center and find a personal niche within that framework. As Bill Macauley explained, "As a WCD, I have a sense that it is very important that tutors feel ownership of their work, that they are not only empowered to make a lot of decisions about their own work but also about the character and environs of their shared workplace, that their WCD sees them as competent, engaged, responsible, trustworthy" (Post WCenter listserv, June 10, 2004). Whereas Macauley's direct reference is to tutors, we believe that his ideas resonate with GADs. Given the opportunity, GADs can determine what they would like to research in order to better the writing center itself and the writing center community as a whole, if possible. This fluidity grants the GADs more ownership of their work, allowing GADs to research writing center issues that matter most to GADs and to the writing center where they work. These opportunities increase a GAD's personal stake in the writing center, as well as the GAD's potential for professional growth in terms of the GAD's own researching and learning to potential conference presentations and publications. A director should be actively involved as a mentor to a GAD's research, discussing opportunities to connect the GAD's work to the larger profession. Such mentoring, personal interest, and guidance may, in turn, make everyday tasks take on added significance—for the center, for the profession, and, most importantly, for the GAD.

Finally, it should be no surprise to a director that "assistants are saturated with responsibility" (Danko, Post WCenter listserv, June 3, 2004), and may sometimes feel overworked and stressed out. To make sure that a GAD is handling all formal and emergent tasks, a director and GAD should negotiate deadlines for tasks and projects to be completed and should be in regular communication regarding them. Although a director initially may see no reason why a proposal for new writing center furniture cannot be drafted by next week, the director probably will understand that two weeks would be better upon learning that the GAD has a graduate seminar paper due next Tuesday. The practice of an ongoing dialogue on deadlines and other academic responsibilities the GAD faces is likely to help solve problems before they start. Such dialogues also should enable a director to understand a GADs workload and stress level, and vice versa.

GAD IDENTITY

To feel comfortable in the position, whether the job description is formal or emergent, the GAD will have to successfully navigate and negotiate the liminal identity the GAD occupies. As evidenced by recent WCenter listserv discussions and acknowledged by probably most everyone who has served as a GAD, numerous identity concerns seem to be a natural part of the GAD's position. For example, typical questions that may arise include the following:

- As GAD, am I an administrator or tutor?
- When I am working on administrative tasks, should I stop to tutor if necessary?
- How do tutors view me? When am I a peer or authority figure?
- Who do I turn to and ask?

Of these fairly common questions, we feel that, because all writing centers operate differently, there is only one question we can answer definitely—the last one. The answer is the director. Odds are the director has been in the GAD's position before or has had a GAD who has been in the same situation. Plus, the director is, after all, the boss and the last person in the line of accountability.

A director may not only try to provide answers to these questions, but also assist GADs in finding their way. We return, once again, to the "IWCA Graduate Student Position Statement":

> A faculty mentor, ideally the writing center director, should be directly involved with the graduate assistant director's training and development. Mentoring should adjust to the graduate student's particular professional needs and interests but may include regular meetings, joint projects, reading or research suggestions, modeling of supervision and leadership skills, conference and publication guidance, and regular evaluation and feedback. (61)

Because GADs are commonly in their positions for the first time, they do not have experience negotiating this sometimes conflicting professional/student identity. Therefore, a GAD will likely require assistance in understanding how to negotiate the complex role of professional/student. A director may suggest a few readings about this topic, such as Connie Snyder Mick's "'Little Teachers,' Big Students: Graduate Students as Tutors and the Future of Writing Center Theory"; Thomas Michael Conroy, Neal Lerner, and Pamela J. Siska's "Graduate Students as Writing Tutors: Role Conflict and the Nature of Professionalization"; and WCenter listserv archives, specifically discussions between June 3, 2004 and June 10, 2004. These articles and discussions examine the liminal framework a GAD functions within, acknowledging that there are going to be times when a GAD struggles with deciding whose side the GAD is on, faculty or student. As evidenced by these articles and discussions, if this in-between status is not openly recognized, there are chances that a GAD may become disillusioned with the position and even distant from the work, especially if the GAD is not open to speaking about it with the director. Creating a dialogue between director and GAD about this subject may guide the GAD through these difficult moments.

To help the GAD continue to create a sense of identity, a director can encourage the GAD to keep a diary/log of what the GAD does, as well as tales of "happenings" in the center in which not only the GAD but tutors can add entries (or have a separate one for tutors). A writing center journal like this creates a dialogue between a GAD and future (or past) GADs and between the GAD and the director. Journals provide informal guides for working at centers by including narratives of how situations have been solved in the past. They let GADs know that they are probably not the first to be experiencing certain difficulties. Journals also provide a creative outlet for a GAD, a way of meaning making through writing.

DIRECTOR–PROFESSIONAL ASSISTANT DIRECTOR (PAD)

For writing centers with both a director and a professional assistant director (PAD), the dynamics can be considerably different from centers with only one director or centers with one director and GAD. Along with the benefits of sharing the workload and collaborating on projects, there is the challenge of overcoming differences and defining each person's responsibilities. Communication between these directors, therefore, needs to recognize a peer professional relationship. These relationships are less hierarchical than director–GAD relationships and focus more on the construction and maintenance of solidarity. Communication between collaborative directors often emphasizes ongoing negotiations to meet ever-changing writing center dynamics and may commonly focus on three aspects: governance by external forces, personal expectations of one another, and developing an understanding of one another's communication styles.

Together, a director and PAD should understand the governance of their writing center, which is an important task that can affect the day-to-day relationship between two directors more than they realize. By recognizing and discussing these constraints, collaborative directors can choose how best to approach them or determine which person is best suited to approach individual constraints. One example of an external constraint could be a campus with a high population of nontraditional, commuting students that creates a high demand for online tutoring. Faced with this situation, one director may opt to concentrate more on establishing an efficient OWL because of the director's technological expertise, whereas the other director may focus more on training tutors for face-to-face tutorials.

Directors and PADs of writing centers that are relatively independent and free from departmental scrutiny can work together to set their own policies for hiring, tutoring, and for working with specific student populations. Such control of policies leaves collaborative directors with enough latitude to take risks and try new approaches. Directors and PADs who enjoy such freedom can more easily play to each other's strengths and compensate for most weaknesses.

Collaborative directors of writing centers that are more closely watched by deans and host departments tend to have more of their work proscribed for them, or at least that is how it may feel. The director's and PAD's roles may be more clearly delineated but also less flexible. For example, a PAD may be required to take on the instruction of an additional course one semester, leaving the PAD with less release time for the center, which may increase the director's duties. Collaborative directors should discuss such constraints to understand what limits are imposed on the writing center and on each of them and what outside forces, and not just personal idiosyncrasies, are at work at any given time.

A second topic that deserves a great deal of communication involves the expectations each director has of the other's performance. Many who work in colleges and universities are reluctant directly to clarify the expectations they have for one another. Faculty may come to regard the habit of clarifying expectations as more appropriate for their interactions with students than with each other. Jeanne Simpson observed: "We tend to form close relationships with our staff and lean toward informality of procedure. More and more, I think we need to be cautious about our informality. It is, alas, one reason we tend to be regarded with less respect than we would like" (Post WCenter listserv, June 4, 2005).

Simpson referred to the respect writing centers receive from the wider academic community, but it is important to think about the respect we accord ourselves. In all walks of life, we have expectations of one another, and for the most part we are not disappointed. This common experience is why we need to be open about expectations among all staff who work in the writing center, directors, assistant directors, GADs, and tutors. Cloaking our expectations leads only to misunderstanding and frustration, as one director expects the other to fulfill a responsibility but fails to spell out this expectation and then frets when it is not met.

Some people might rely on a job description to make expectations clear because it is a more neutral reference point for gauging each person's responsibilities. The problem, however, is that job descriptions, as Danko suggested, are only helpful to a point. It may be more beneficial (and a professional requirement) for collaborative directors to formally define their roles so that they know what their specific responsibilities include. However, not even the most specific job description can account for all situations and contexts. In the end, interpersonal communication is all that is left, and for that to succeed, directors need to be able to speak openly and honestly with one another.

How do collaborative directors communicate about things that are important to each other? Certainly, collaborative directors should meet with one another at the start of every academic year (and, perhaps, semester), and (re)create an ongoing dialogue about writing center business: immediate and future concerns and plans; each director's specific professional duties and obligations; how each plans to "stay-in-action"; and the expectations each has of the other. Communication such as this (i.e., communication that *does* something) is absolutely vital to successful collaborative administration. As busy and hectic as academic years can get, it is never a bad time for collaborative directors of any kind to pull back from their work and discuss what is important to one another professionally and what is most important for the writing center itself.

CONCLUSIONS

We have argued that productive communication can lead to successful collaborative relationships between directors and assistant directors, both graduate and professional. Because assistant directors inhabit many professional identities and are often highly influential forces in the writing centers where they work, directors and tutors must be able to communicate productively and regularly assistant directors, and assistant directors must be able to communicate back. We realize that our discussion is limited to a small but important aspect of assistant directorships, but we hope that it serves as a springboard to further the current ongoing dialogue about this undertheorized—but not underappreciated—side of writing center work.

WORKS CITED

Conroy, Thomas Michael, Neal Lerner, and Pamela J. Siska. "Graduate Students as Writing Tutors: Role Conflict and the Nature of Professionalization." *Weaving Knowledge Together: Writing Centers and Collaboration.* Ed. Carol Peterson Haviland, Maria Notarangelo, Lene Whitney-Putz, and Thia Wolf. Emmitsburg, MD: NWCA Press, 1998. 128–50.

Danko, Nita. "RE: Performance Appraisals for Tutors." Online Posting. 3 June 2004. WCenter listserv. 12 June 2004. <http://listserv.ttu.edu/cgi-in/lyris.pl?enter=wcenter&text_mode=0%E2%8C%A9=english>.

Fitzgerald, Lauren. "Administrative Assistants (Was Performance Appraisals for Tutors)." Online Posting. 4 June 2004. WCenter listserv. 12 June 2004. <http://listserv.ttu.edu/cgi-in/lyris.pl?enter=wcenter&text_mode=0%E2%8C%A9=english>.

"I WCA Graduate Student Position Statement." *The Writing Center Journal* 23 (2002): 59–61.

Macauley, William. Re: "Questions about Administrative Assistants." Online Posting. 10 June 2004. WCenter listserv. 12 June 2004. <http://listserv.ttu.edu/cgi-in/lyris.pl?enter=wcenter&text_mode=0%E2%8C%A9=english>.

Mick, Connie Snyder. "'Little Teachers,' Big Students: Graduate Students as Tutors and the Future of Writing Center Theory." *The Writing Center Journal* 20 (1999): 33–45.

Simpson, Jeanne. "Administrative Assistants (Was Performance Appraisals for Tutors)." Online Posting. 4 June 2004. WCenter listserv. 12 June 2004. <http://listserv.ttu.edu/cgi-in/lyris.pl?enter=wcenter&text_mode=0%E2%8C%A9=english>.

❧ **18** ❧

There's Something Happening Here: The Writing Center and Core Writing

Albert C. DeCiccio
Rivier College

This chapter begins by borrowing a strategy from Elizabeth H. Boquet's *Noise from the Writing Center*, in which she often used popular song lyrics to highlight a point. *For What It's Worth* has been among my favorite popular songs for more than thirty years, almost as long as I have been in higher education. I hope you can hear Stephen Stills singing the following lyrics:

> There's something happening here.
>
> What it is ain't exactly clear.
>
>   …
>
> It's time we stop, hey.…
>
> Everybody look what's going down.

It appears to me to be serendipitous to what is happening now in writing centers and in higher education. Taken together, the moves demonstrate to me that writing centers are not simply the next best thing in writing instruction, but the best next thing in education.

I have been a member of the writing center community for twenty-two years. For the last ten of those years, I have been an academic dean. In my experiences during this time, every general education—or core—curriculum I have encountered has made writing an institutional requirement (i.e., a course all students must take). Moreover, every discussion on student retention makes reference to the idea of building community and to the sense that community-based learning must inhere in the general education (or core) curriculum. One essential foundational competency of all general education (or core) curricula is writing; and, as we know, the teaching and learning of writing is naturally aligned to community-based practice. Interestingly, writing is thoroughly engaged by no less a renowned retention scholar than Harvard's Richard Light. In fact, Light put a discussion of writing in the middle of his popular book, *Making the Most of College.*

Inspired by Light and others, the Association of American Colleges and Universities' (AACU) "Greater Expectations" report (2002) on curriculum emphasizes preparing students for citizenship through mastery of public discourse (i.e., speaking and writing), and sets forth a social pedagogy, arguing that students can learn faster and better in groups than they can on their own. As a result, there are many intriguing core curricula these days (e.g., pathway models, cluster arrangements, first-year seminars, and the like), all requiring writing as a foundational competency students must develop. All of them hope that they can assist colleges and universities to attract and then retain quality students. All insist on building learning communities. As writing center scholars have maintained for some time now, this is precisely what writing center workers have practiced and researched, seemingly outside larger conversations about general education. Thus, the movements today in higher education coincide with calls writing center scholars have made to seize an opportunity to be more comprehensive. Based on his research of first-year seminars, Neal Lerner argued that writing centers "can serve as one piece of a comprehensive [educational] program—a linchpin of sorts to give coherence to the curriculum and co-curriculum" (64). Since her award-winning article in 1996, "The Regulatory Role of the Writing Center," Nancy Maloney Grimm maintained that writing centers should "redefine their mission in more global and structural ways" (15). Lerner, Grimm, and other writing center scholars have explained that such invitations are good news for those who work in the writing center. Indeed, a curriculum with writing as a core requirement allows those of us who work in the writing center to showcase the resources we have—from workshops about all the major traits of writing to those dealing with MLA, APA, Chicago, and Turabian manuscript formats. More importantly, it allows us to showcase our social pedagogy, and to talk with writers, novice and expert alike, about writing.

In the context of a core curriculum steeped in the liberal arts and sciences aimed at providing students the global perspective Lerner, Grimm, and others have called for, new university and college students are asked to take the initial steps for gaining competency in writing in their first years. Most writing teachers have practiced a social pedagogy built on conversation, collaboration, and critical consciousness. Their classes tend to be smaller than other introductory classes and usually advance an idea of a classroom in which everyone participates and to which everyone contributes. Such a pedagogical philosophy espoused by the faculty and students in writing courses should coincide nicely with writing center-inspired additional curricular refinement. In my opinion, every first-year writing class should have a writing center-sponsored writing advisor attached to it. The writing advisor should be an upper-level student-tutor; ideally, these student-tutors should be chosen from among those who have successfully completed the first-year writing course they are assigned. The writing advisor, therefore, should have disciplinary knowledge of the seminar in which they will tutor, and can help the novice student cross Cheryl Geisler's divide from disciplinary naiveté to disciplinary expertise. The writing advisor will learn about the teaching of writing through a program conducted by the college's or university's writing center director. As a result, the writing advisor can serve as an intermediary between faculty member and student, employing tested strategies for bringing about effective academic discourse. The writing advisor program, a result of evolving writing center programming, is precisely the kind of academic response demanded by higher education moves that situate writing as a literacy necessary for engaged citizenship. And, by the way, those of you knowledgeable about the rhetorical tradition will notice that the writing advisor plays a role similar to that of the rhetorician in Quintilian's *Institutes of Oratory*. This move, therefore, has roots in a classical liberal arts curriculum that should make its implementation much more readily accepted.

GENERAL CHARACTERISTICS OF WRITING FELLOWS/ASSOCIATES/ADVISORS PROGRAMS

There are many such programs emanating from the nation's writing centers (see *appendix* for a sampling). A writing fellows/associates/advisors program is based on an understanding that the mastery of writing is best accomplished through conversation and attention to a developing writer's individual needs. Writing fellows/associates/advisors reinforce the idea that writing is important; in addition, because they write, and they write well, they serve as strong role models for other students. Writing fellows/associates/advisors are trained in the pedagogy of tutoring writing as well as in how to respond to student writing through conferencing with novice writers as they draft. At all times, writing fellows/associates/advisors are supported and usually monitored by an administrator, often the writing center director. If professors request a writing fellow/associate/advisor for their class, all the students in this class must work with the advisor throughout the semester. The writing fellow/associate/advisor will intervene in initial drafts of developing papers designed to be graded. Ideally, there would be turnaround time: time for reading papers and writing comments and time for conferencing with each student individually. Writing fellows/associates/advisors should meet with the professor several times throughout the semester and, where possible, sit in on the class, especially on days papers are assigned or drafts are due. A writing fellow/associate/advisor's responsibility is to ask questions about students' drafts, considering global issues such as organization and development, thesis and evidence, analysis and logic, clarity and flow. Writing fellows/associates/advisors are not proofreaders, and they will not do the work for the student.

GENERAL COMMITMENTS OF WRITING FELLOWS/ASSOCIATES/ADVISORS PROGRAMS

Those who offer a writing fellows/associates/advisors program can make several commitments. First, writing fellows/associates/advisors should determine where students are in their writing and establish and maintain a rapport that shows interest and concern for the needs of individual writers. Second, writing fellows/associates/advisors should allow writers to do the work and resist the temptation to become rewriters. The writing fellow/associate/advisor should recognize the need for immediate, constructive responses and will suggest strategies for improvement. However, the writer should do the work and the fellow/associate/advisor should monitor and guide the process. The writing fellow/associate/advisor should allow writers time to find their own best way of working. Third, writing fellows/associates/advisors should deal with "high order" concerns before "low order" concerns. Thesis or focus, appropriate voice or tone, organization, and support and development of ideas would be examples of high order concerns. Low order concerns would include sentence structure, punctuation, usage, and spelling. We have learned well that novice writers' time is not well spent if they work with spelling and punctuation in an assignment that needs to be substantially revised and rewritten because of problems with high order concerns. Fourth, the writing fellows/associates/advisors' mission is to help writers improve each piece of writing. They should be pleased to accept small successes and should try not to expect too much. Writing fellows/associates/advisors are not miracle workers; they have limitations. Because they are confronted with writing problems students have developed after many years, writing fellows/associates/advisors cannot solve all writing problems in an hour or two—or even in a semester or two.

GENERAL CAUTIONS OF WRITING FELLOWS/ASSOCIATES/ADVISORS PROGRAMS

Writing advisors will get many requests, with proofreading probably the most common. Kelly Nagle, a University of Rochester Writing Fellow, offered the following useful caveat about proofreading: "Proofreading is not included in the Fellows' duties. The Fellow should neither write papers for students nor put ideas in their heads. The Fellow should instead help writers organize and clearly state their thoughts by asking appropriate questions."

From the University of Wisconsin's Writing Center, we learn that the fellow/associate/advisor's role is to facilitate good writing, not to serve as a judge. Fellows/associates/advisors focus on helping students write more clearly and effectively but do not grade papers. Instead, fellows/associates/advisors make suggestions for revision and talk with developing writers about how to express their ideas as effectively as possible.

Finally, consider the following caution offered by the University of Massachusetts Writing Center:

> While it is clear that manner can never be wholly separated from matter, the Writing Fellows will attempt as much as possible to limit their concerns to how material is being presented and explained rather than to the accuracy of what is being discussed: that evaluation belongs to the professor. Whenever possible, but not in all cases, then, fellows will be assigned to courses in the disciplines with which they are very familiar. The Fellows will serve as the very educated audience of works in progress.

NOTE TO FELLOWS/ADVISORS/ASSOCIATES

A writing center director should ensure clarity about goals and expectations of the writing fellows/associates/advisors program. The University of Wisconsin advances this warning to fellows/advisors/associates:

> You are responsible for doing your best to help every student you work with, but you are not responsible for ensuring every student's success. Writing is a difficult, complex skill, and as long as we continue to write, we will have more to learn about writing. As a Fellow, you are not in the business of offering miracle cures to student writers, whether they are struggling to meet the basic

requirements of an assignment or striving to earn that elusive A+. Instead, you can provide support to your peers, encourage them to challenge themselves as writers, and make a limited number of suggestions about how to improve a draft.

NOTE TO PROFESSORS

A writing center director should also communicate the expectations and goals clearly to professors. The University of Wisconsin Writing Center helps us again:

> You can expect your Writing Fellow to address writing issues (not content!) in papers. As they read, Fellows will keep in mind what you tell them about your goals for individual paper assignments as well as the general principles they learn in the seminar on tutoring writing across the curriculum…. Fellows may well engage in spirited discussions about course content during their conferences with students, but you alone must be responsible for assessing the extent to which a paper's content is "right" or "wrong."

A PEER WRITING ADVISORS PROGRAM OVERVIEW: INTRODUCTION

In "A Critique of Pure Tutoring," Linda K. Shamoon and Deborah H. Burns explained, "If writing center practices are broadened to include [for example, writing advisors], the result would be an enrichment of tutoring repertoires, stronger connections between the writing center and writers in other disciplines, and increased attention to the cognitive, social, and rhetorical needs of writers at all stages of development" (148). A peer writing advisors program will support the college or university writing initiative by providing well-prepared undergraduates who can assist participating professors in writing classes. The underlying pedagogy of such a program relies on two premises: that writing is a process involving brainstorming, drafting, writing, editing, and revising; and that individualized, constructive intervention can help others develop and improve their writing. The genius of such a program is that it benefits students in participating classes, the writing advisors themselves, and the professors. In addition, the implementation of such a program stands as evidence that the college or university values writing and is willing to help students become more proficient writers, able to engage in the civic community in all kinds of public discourse.

Advantages for students include improved writing ability, a stronger engagement with and understanding of assigned writing tasks, and the opportunity to build a collaborative relationship with peers who can provide them with strategies for becoming better writers. Advantages for the writing advisor include the chance to develop interpersonal and communication strategies, the ability to advance their own writing, and the opportunity to gain valuable experience in their chosen fields. Advantages for professors include receiving more carefully written student papers, spending less class time on clarifying and reexplaining writing assignments, and benefiting from the opportunity to mentor and collaborate with their assigned writing advisors.

PROGRAM DESCRIPTION

Each writing advisor should be assigned to a specific course. Writing advisors should be selected based on recommendations from participating departments, demonstrated writing ability and interest in helping other students, and academic performance. Where possible, writing advisors should have disciplinary knowledge of the writing course they are assigned, having had the opportunity to take that course. If not accomplished in a required course on the theory and practice of tutoring writing, training should consist of weekly seminar sessions led by the director of the writing center to discuss required readings on the theory of writing and tutoring practices, to practice and model appropriate strategies, and to share specific challenges and accomplishments as the writing advisors begin tutoring.

Based on the needs of each participating faculty member, and in coordination with the director of the writing center, writing advisors may be asked to fulfill a variety of tasks, including reading and responding to student drafts, holding individual conferences with students as they revise drafts based on faculty feedback, or running small group workshops to go over assignment criteria. If they are not tutoring for academic credit, then fellows/associates/advisors should be eligible to receive work study compensation for the hours they spend tutoring, meeting with professors and the director of the writing center, and attending weekly training seminars.

ADMINISTRATION

The director of the writing center should assume the responsibility of developing, coordinating, and overseeing all aspects of the writing advisors program. The director's responsibilities may include the following:

- Serving as an advocate for the writing advisors program on campus—promoting the program and articulating to the institution's community its principal beliefs, values, and goals.
- Working closely with the first-year (Core) writing faculty.
- Recruiting and hiring writing advisors: soliciting recommendations, reviewing applications, evaluating writing samples, and conducting interviews.
- Soliciting faculty involvement and meeting with participating professors prior to each semester to establish guidelines for working with writing advisors.
- Developing curriculum, compiling readings, and planning for weekly training seminars prior to the start of each semester.
- Running weekly training seminars—if writing advisors will not be required to take a course in the theory and practice of tutoring writing—with all participating writing advisors to discuss readings, model tutorial strategies, answer questions, address concerns, encourage positive progress, and brainstorm strategies for working effectively with participating faculty advisors.
- Closely monitoring each writing advisor's performance throughout the semester, scheduling individual meetings for additional training if necessary, and occasionally reviewing writing advisors' comments on drafts and observing tutorial sessions.
- Acting as a liaison between writing advisors and participating professors.
- Developing student and faculty evaluation forms to elicit feedback and response at the end of the term.
- Providing an assessment at the end of each term.

- Establishing a mentoring program linking experienced writing center tutors and advisors with first-time writing advisors.

TRAINING

If there will not be a required course in the theory and practice of tutoring writing, then first-time writing advisors will meet weekly throughout the semester with the director of the writing center to discuss assigned readings, participate in mock tutorial sessions, complete reflective writing assignments, and share specific challenges and successes they are having as they begin to work with students. In addition to reading numerous articles articulating pedagogy in the field of rhetoric, the process of writing, responding to writing, and one-to-one conferencing, writing advisors should read texts like the following:

Barnett, Robert W., and Jacob S. Blumner. *The Allyn and Bacon Guide to Writing Center Theory and Practice*. Boston: Allyn and Bacon, 2001.

Caposella, Toni-Lee. *The Harcourt Brace Guide to Peer Tutoring*. New York: Harcourt Brace, 1998.

Gillespie, Paula, and Neal Lerner. *The Allyn and Bacon Guide to Peer Tutoring*. 2nd ed. New York: Pearson Longman, 2003.

Murphy, Christina, and Steve Sherwood. *The St. Martin's Sourcebook for Writing Tutors*. 2nd ed. Boston: Bedford/St. Martin's, 2003.

Raforth, Ben. *A Tutor's Guide: Helping Writers One to One*. Portsmouth, NH: Heinemann-Boynton/Cook, 2000.

Continuing writing advisors will attend these weekly meetings at least twice a month; they will also be responsible for reading and responding to current literature in the field on an ongoing basis throughout the semester. In addition, they will meet, as needed, with the director of the writing center.

Writing Advisor's Responsibilities

Writing advisors will assume numerous responsibilities. These include the following:

- an assignment to one core writing class per semester.
- participation in weekly training seminars, if not required to take a course in the theory and practice of tutoring writing, designed and led by the director of the writing center, in which they will discuss assigned readings, practice appropriate tutorial strategies, raise questions, address concerns, share positive progress, and develop strategies for working effectively with participating faculty.
- meeting together with their participating professors and the director of the writing center before the start of each semester in order to establish specific guidelines for working together.
- meeting with participating professors throughout the semester as necessary.
- familiarizing themselves with course objectives, readings, writing assignments, and evaluation criteria for the specific course to which they have been assigned.

- making every effort to attend as many sessions of their assigned class as possible.
- reading and responding to student drafts and/or revisions of papers, holding individual conferences, and/or running group workshops according to the needs of participating professors.

PARTICIPATING PROFESSOR'S RESPONSIBILITIES

Participating professors will also have responsibilities. These include the following:

- meeting with the director of the writing center prior to the start of the term in order to outline, collegially, the responsibilities their writing advisors will assume.
- requiring that all students in the class participate in the program and have writing assignments assisted by a writing advisor.
- clearly specifying on their syllabi due dates for drafts, final papers, and required advising activities.
- meeting with writing advisors, and occasionally with the director of the writing center, throughout the semester to clarify assignment criteria, discuss general rhetorical and specific disciplinary concerns the student writers in their class face when approaching a particular assignment, and to facilitate ongoing conversation and collaboration.
- ensuring that writing advisors will not be employed for actual grading of papers.
- keeping the director of the writing center informed of both successes and concerns.
- participating in program evaluation.
- meeting formally at least once a term with other professors in the program.
- nominating worthy advisor candidates upon request.

If we stop and look around, we just might notice what is happening here: the alignment between writing center research and practice during the past twenty years and higher education research and study. For what it's worth, a writing advisors program to support an institution's commitment to writing is indeed the best next thing in higher education. Such a program demonstrates how

> The writing center can be a site where ongoing conversation about the rhetoric of a domain occurs in the rhetoric of the domain.... Also, the writing center can be a site where the proficient ... and the novice converse about "intersubjective knowledge," or that kind of discourse which externalizes and argues for domain-appropriate linkages to case-specific data, and which provides opportunities for reflection and critique.... Finally, the writing center can be a site where experts and novices meet often to externalize tacit information—those values, assumptions, and options that inform all texts within a discipline. (Shamoon and Burns 147–48)

ACKNOWLEDGMENTS

I want to acknowledge Leslie Van Wagner, director of the Rivier College Writing Center, for her input into this chapter. As her academic dean, I requested a proposal for a writing advisors program at the college. Leslie's work has informed many parts of this chapter.

WORKS CITED

Association of the American Colleges and Universities. "Greater Expectation: A New Vision for Learning as a Nation Goes to College." Office of Education and Quality Initiatives. Washington, D.C., 2002.

Boquet, Elizabeth H. *Noise from the Writing Center*. Logan: Utah State UP, 2002.

Geisler, Cheryl. *Academic Literacy and the Nature of Expertise: Reading, Writing, and Knowing in Academic Philosophy*. Hillsdale, NJ: Lawrence Erlbaum Associates, 1994.

Grimm, Nancy Maloney. "The Regulatory Role of the Writing Center: Coming to Terms with a Loss of Innocence." *The Writing Center Journal* 17.1 (Fall 1996): 5–29.

Lerner, Neal. "Writing Center Assessment: Searching for the 'Proof' of Our Effectiveness." *The Center Will Hold: Critical Perspectives on Writing Center Scholarship*. Ed. Michael A. Pemberton and Joyce Kinkead. Logan: Utah State UP, 2003. 58–73.

Light, Richard J. *Making the Most of College: Students Speak Their Minds*. Cambridge, MA: Harvard UP, 2001.

Nagle, Kelly. <http://www.monroeccc.edu/writing/tutoring.htm>.

Quintilian. *On the Teaching of Speaking and Writing*. Ed. James J. Murphy. Carbondale and Edwardville: Southern Illinois UP, 1987.

Shamoon, Linda K., and Deborah H. Burns. "A Critique of Pure Tutoring." *The Writing Center Journal* 15.2 (Spring 1995): 134–51.

Univ. of Massachusetts. <http://www.enl.umass.edu/InteractiveCourse/assistant/fel.html>.

Univ. of Wisconsin. <www.wisc.edu/writing/wf/handbookwf/overview.html>.

Univ. of Wisconsin. <http://www.wisc.edu/writing/wf/handbookwf/expectations.html>.

School	Writing Advisor/Fellow Profile	Training	Responsibilities	Compensation	Administration
Brown University	• Undergraduate students chosen after their first, second, or third undergraduate years • Highly competitive—over 300 students vie for 35 positions • Based on "demonstrated writing ability and interest in helping other students" • Serve 45-50 courses a year	• Complete a seminar on the theory and practice of teaching writing: ENG 195 (3 credits) • Regularly evaluated • Participate in on-going training sessions every semester	• One fellow for <u>15–20 students</u> in a course where a professor has requested assistance • Students submit a first draft of each paper to the Fellow two weeks before it is due to the professor • Fellows comment extensively on the student's writing and return the draft to the student who then have the following week to consider these suggestions, meet with his/her Fellow in a conference, and revise the paper before handing it in to the professor • Students hand in the annotated first draft as well as their final copy so the professor can consider both the process and the final product	• Stipend of $800 per semester, funded by Dean's Office	• Director of Writing Center and Writing Fellows Program (full-time) • Administrative Assistant—Writing Fellows (full-time)
University of Richmond	• Undergraduates proficient in writing who complete ENG 383 • Hired based on writing samples, letters of recommendation, personal interviews • Nearly 60 Fellows working with 25 faculty in a given semester	ENG 383: *Composition Theory and Pedagogy*	• Assigned in pairs to a course (at request of instructor); each is responsible for up to <u>15 students</u>, two-three assignments • Meet with instructor to discuss assignments, expectations, guidelines • Review first drafts two weeks prior to due date; provide written response to these drafts in keeping with the guidelines established by the instructor • Offer individual conferences about each paper one week prior to due date	• Assuming 40-50 hours of work per semester, the current stipend is $403	• Director of WAC Program and Writing Center • Writing Fellows Co-ordinator

Institution					
Brigham Young University	• Undergraduate students from a variety of disciplines who are proficient in writing, teaching, and a willingness to help others • Hired based on writing samples, recommendation letters, interviews • Interview about 60 applicants and choose 20-25 each semester • Currently have 60-70 Fellows in 22-25 different classes	• *Theory and Practice of Tutoring Writing* (3 credits)—Taken the first semester they work as fellows • *In-Service for Continuing Writing Fellows* (1 credit)— Seminar for second and third semester WF • Training Retreats—every semester all WF participate in a weekend training workshop	• One fellow for every <u>10-15 students</u>; responsible for two assignments • Meet with professor at least twice: once before reading the first assignment and once before reading the second assignment • Receive drafts from each student two weeks prior to due date • Return with marginal comments/annotations and a one-page response letter pointing out strengths and areas for revision • After the students have revised their drafts, hold an individual conference (30 minutes) to discuss strategies for further revision • Serve as resource for professor as requested (review assignment design, advise on grading criteria, give classroom presentations)	• Tried contracts, but didn't mesh with other time card jobs • Tried scholarships, but lawyers thought there might be a tax problem • Now on timecard w/ set number of hours per week—adds up to $450 a semester; each additional semester, an additional $25	• Associate Dean for University Writing heads WAC • ¼ time Administrator: ¼ working with WAC director, ¼ for Writing Fellows, and ¼ for teaching the WF training class
University of Wisconsin, Madison	• Undergraduates with "demonstrated strong writing ability and interpersonal skills" • Must submit a personal statement, transcript, two writing samples with explanations of why they chose those pieces, and a letter of recommendation from a professor • Chose 30 new fellows each year; approximately 50 Fellows working within any given year	• Honors Seminar English/L&S Interdisciplinary Programs 316: Composition and Collaboration in Theory and Practice (3 credits) • Attend staff and ongoing education meetings	• One fellow for <u>10-16 students</u> under the guidance of a course professor who has chosen to participate in the program • Meet with professor at beginning of semester, prior to paper assignments, and as needed • If schedule allows, attend a class or two • Two weeks prior to professor's due date, Fellows attend class to collect drafts • Read and provide written response to drafts • Hold individual conferences with students • Students submit revised papers along with the annotated draft to professor on due date	• Stipend of $600 for their first semester, and $700 for each subsequent semester • Paid by UW-Madison's College of Letters and Science which has committed funds specifically to the program	• Associate Director of Writing Fellows Program (Full-time) • Graduate Assistant Director (1/2 time)

Institution	Qualifications	Training	Responsibilities	Compensation
U MASS/ Dartmouth	• Undergraduates with strong writing skills • Application, writing sample, interview	• Complete ENG 279b: Peer Tutoring in Writing, the semester prior to participation in the program • Attend occasional seminars and/or workshops during the following semesters of participation	• One fellow for approximately <u>15</u> students; all students in a class are required to participate • Meet with professor to discuss expectations of each major paper assignment • Responsible for at least two, but no more than four, assignments per semester • Receive drafts from each student two weeks prior to due date • Read and provide written response to drafts • Hold individual conferences with each student • Keep records of conference attendance for instructor and Program Director • Students submit final drafts to professor along with annotated first draft	
Merrimack College	• Undergraduates with strong writing and interpersonal abilities • Hired based on writing samples, recommendation letters, interviews	• Attend required sessions during the semester on the theory and practice of tutoring writing	• One fellow for approximately <u>15-20</u> students; all students in a class are required to participate • Meet with professor to discuss expectations of each major paper assignment • Receive drafts from each student two weeks prior to due date • Read and provide written response to drafts • Hold individual conferences with each student • Keep records of conference attendance for instructor and Center Director	• Fellows paid $7.00 hourly • Writing Center Director (fulltime, faculty appointment: ¼ teaching assignment, ¾ WC/WF assignment)

198

19

Managing Encounters With Central Administration

Jeanne Simpson
Eastern Illinois University

After establishing and then directing a writing center for nine years, I entered central administration. I spent the next decade in the provost's office thinking, "I wish I had known this or that when I was directing the center!" The principles, suggestions, and examples I offer here are intended to fulfill that wish vicariously. Of course, the ideas, principles, and examples reflect my own specific experiences in central administration, as well as some of the problems. However, over the past twenty years, after attending dozens of conferences where colleagues shared war stories, and participating in WCenter discussions, I recognize that my experiences as a writing center director and then as assistant provost in central administration continue to resonate no matter the particulars of an academic setting. The more we change, the more we stay the same. The academic hierarchy remains. The dilemma of where to locate the writing center continues. Should it be under the auspices of an English department, a vice president of a particular division or school, or the provost? What are the reporting lines? Who funds the writing center? Who uses the writing center? What data do the writing center director or supervisor need to gather to obtain funding and recognition as a viable entity of the institution? Ultimately, regardless of reporting lines, all requests end up on some upper administrator's desk.

Writing center directors may have little direct contact with upper administrators, but this lack of direct interaction should not be mistaken for a lack of interest. Nor should it mean that writing center directors don't have to pay attention to central administration. They do. All the money, access to space, and approval of positions comes through the central administration. Directors' requests, plans, reports, and evaluations eventually arrive there. Writing centers are not invisible to administration.

Encounters between writing centers and central administration can be frustrating and scary, especially if the writing center director doesn't know much (anything?) about administrators except that they apparently wield great power. Adding to the terror, the writing center is frequently the director's first experience with administrative work. Nothing reduces fear and creates confidence like knowledge. This chapter is intended to give writing center directors knowledge about central administration and offer ways to make their encounters more productive and less frightening, as well as suggesting ways to be a professional and effective writing center administrator.

Writing center directors interact with central administration in several categories: budget, personnel, policy, and planning. I review each type of encounter between writing center and administration, discussing terminology, the administrative perspective, and effective writing center strategies.

UNDERSTANDING ADMINISTRATORS

Working effectively with administration requires a realistic understanding of the values, functions, and responsibilities of administrators. Writing center directors should remember the following:

- The writing center is not independent of its institution.
- Upper administration is not inherently evil, not omnipotent, not capricious.
- Although they are former faculty members, administrators generally are not well-informed about writing centers.
- Administrators face constraints imposed by laws and policies, by supervising bodies, by precedent, by public expectation, and by budgets.
- Administrators' values and expectations correspond to those of a writing center.
- Administrators are open to change, but not to subversion.
- Administrators respond negatively to whining.
- Administrators will not forgive efforts to go around the chain of command.

Writing center directors often perceive themselves as isolated on some remote academic desert island. Understandably, directors feel possessive of the center, calling it "my writing center." However, the institution's leaders have assigned space, established a budget line, defined a directorship, and otherwise supported the writing center. In reality, the writing center is a unit of the institution. The director is an employee of the institution.

Administrators must make decisions based on institutional priorities, on the requirements established by boards or legislatures or accrediting bodies. They know they will anger and alienate someone no matter what decision is made, because resources always are limited. They realize they will be labeled oppressive, uninformed, or just plain evil. Because writing center directors often are possessive about their domains, they sometimes feel personally attacked.

Administrators function much like parents in a household: They manage the money, keep the place clean and repaired, enforce the rules, and make sure everyone has what they need so that faculty and students can attend to the main matters of teaching and learning. Almost all their decisions affect more than one group.

All administrations report to boards of some kind, and many also report to a system administration. Public institutions also answer to the voting public, through legislatures and taxation bodies. Administrations interact with unions, negotiating and abiding by the terms of contracts. Civil service codes affect hiring practices. Federal laws governing affirmative action, civil rights, disabilities, access to financial aid, and grant rules also constrain administrations. To keep academic credibility, an institution must meet the standards of an accrediting agency, often more than one. Navigating the demands of all these entities occupies almost all of the time of administrators.

Every decision administrators make sets precedent. Administrators think constantly of how a choice may come back to haunt them, commonly saying, with some justification, "no good deed will go unpunished." As a result, decisions come slowly and usually with plenty of limits.

Directors must realize, however, that administrators may have limited notions of centers as grammar hospitals or proofreading shops. The tendency is to deluge them with theory and practice, while watching the listener's eyes glaze over. Administrators don't need to be experts on writing centers; they just need to know the basics. They may not realize that there is a decades-long history of writing centers, that there is a sizable body of significant scholarship devoted to writing centers, and that writing centers have professional organizations. A simple list of facts will work for this lesson.

A one-page memo is an excellent strategy for informing administrators. They can copy such items to other administrators, attach them to reports, or use them for notes in meetings. Long narratives with dense paragraphs will get filed or thrown away without being read. Administrators don't want to read essays. Directors should use bulleted lists, headings, graphs and charts, and executive summaries in documents sent to administrators.

Given the picture just described, writing center directors with problems or requests are best served by preparing carefully before visiting the administration. They should do their homework, gather convincing data, and prepare possible options to solve the problem or make the request work. They should prepare for the "no" answer, recognizing that a "no" today may become "yes" later. Whining is not an option. The quickest and surest way to hear "no" is to whine.

Circumventing the chain of command to get a more favorable hearing higher up is not an option. Directors who try to go around the chain of command make enemies and lose the trust of administrators. The world of the academy is small. Word gets around, and people who do "end runs" are remembered the same way as grade school tattle-tales and snitches.

Directing a writing center *is* administration. The principles of working with central administration equally apply to directing a center. Writing center directors too are responsible to boards, accrediting bodies, and legislatures, although more indirectly. They also need to be consistent, impartial, and aware of the perils of setting precedent. They too need to know the rules and policies that affect their operations.

Administrators value directors who are prompt with information, use their time efficiently, and work toward the institution's goals. They value directors who follow rules and procedures, without demanding exceptions or special consideration and who handle problems themselves. They appreciate flexibility and despise whiners. Being a skilled, informed, and professional writing center administrator is the most effective strategy for achieving success with central administration.

BUDGET

All decisions are budget decisions. Anything from a new building to adding a new course to buying cookies for a reception affects budget. Budgets drive all power, all decision making, and all priorities. Unfortunately, writing centers often exist at the end of the money pipeline. It takes creativity and ingenuity, as well as discipline, to make the writing center budget work.

Ideally, writing center directors should have control over establishing and managing the budget. Unfortunately, some institutions allocate writing center budget control to division or department heads. To have any real authority in the writing center or real ability to guide its direction, writing center directors must understand budget processes and schedules of their institutions, learn to manage the writing center budget, and ultimately gain control of the budget.

Knowing the fiscal calendar and meeting deadlines is critical and prevents losing money not spent within the allotted time. Although some directors do not control the budget, all directors are asked to submit requests. Submitting clear, documented requests in a timely manner demonstrates an ability to work within time frames and institutional requirements.

Institutional budgets do not generally allow for saving money. Usually, each fiscal period is a closed system. For that reason, trying to "save" money by not using all that is allocated may result in being allocated a smaller amount next time, and the money "saved" will go to someone else. Directors should spend every bit of the money allocated, within the fiscal period.

Knowing where the budget stands and keeping accounts up to date protects the center's budget and demonstrates a director's ability to manage and perhaps control the budget. Sometimes, budget windfalls happen (don't laugh—they really do), and should be recognized by keeping a "what-if" spending list on hand. Windfalls happen quickly, and funds go to those ready with needs and numbers. Directors may have only hours, at most days, to submit a request.

Controlling the Budget

In some settings, a supervisor of a division or department, not the writing center director, controls the budget. Yet the writing center director is expected to present a budget to the immediate supervisor. In other institutions, writing center directors maintain more direct control over the budget and do not have to submit to multiple levels of administration. Regardless of the hierarchy, writing center directors should exhibit knowledge and control over the monies allocated to them. The more competent the director, the more willing the administrator might be to hand over budget control.

Nothing is gained with passivity and meekness. Writing center directors must insist on seeing the budget frequently, check amounts, and question the rationale behind budget decisions. They must not be generous. If someone takes money from the budget, the director should insist on something in return. Vague promises have a way of evaporating while those put in writing do not. "Good will" cannot be had with a mere nod.

Planning the budget requires a clear grasp of the writing center's goals and priorities. A simple list of daily tutoring activities, including materials used, can be an enormous help. Does the writing center need a ready supply of pencils? Of course it does. How much do pencils cost?

How many are used and lost in a year? This example may seem to be a small item, but it is an important detail in writing center activity.

Fund-Raising

Small budgets can tempt writing center directors to engage in fund-raising. Few institutions allow independent fund-raising. Directors can forget about holding car washes, bake sales, or raffles. Before acting, directors should learn the rules for fund-raising within the institution.

The office of development may control all fund-raising. Directors should try to work with development people so that they do fund-raising on behalf of the center. The writing center represents an opportunity for the development office. If they know the needs and costs of a project, then they can look for a donor.

As is the case with any expectation to improve a writing center, directors must keep at their fingertips all the information that may be needed, such as rationale, costs, and benefits—long and short term. The more specific the plans, the more closely connected with institutional goals and priorities, the better the chances for funding.

The budget, no matter what the size of the writing center, reflects the mission and activities of the writing center. Writing center directors, whether or not they directly control the budget, must maintain active involvement in the budget matters and keep administrators at all levels aware of the importance of the writing center to the institution.

Terminology

Every institution relies on shorthand terms and assorted acronyms, especially in budgeting efforts. Writing center directors can save themselves hours of planning and designing if they learn this language and use it effectively. The following are some important terms:

Base budget—the amount designated as *permanent funding* for a unit

Budget line—a specific item listed in a budget. A budget line may be permanent or, rarely, it may be temporary, funded by a one-time infusion of money. Often, amounts in one budget line cannot be moved to another.

Development—fund-raising by means of contributions. Most institutions of higher education have a development office charged with contacting donors for contributions to foundations and scholarship funds.

Full-Time Equivalent (FTE)/Employee—full-time appointment in terms of personnel or position budgets. Personnel budgets are often funded based on FTE rather than particular positions, and how the FTE's are distributed may be negotiated with department chairs or deans.

Full-Time Equivalent (FTE)/Student—a full load of credits for the semester, quarter, or trimester. Twelve hours enrolled is considered an FTE for a semester. FTE's are used to determine enrollment level, as opposed to simple headcounts. If 6,000 credit hours are enrolled for one semester 500 FTE are generated [6,000 divided by 12 = 500]. FTE's give a more accurate picture of the teaching capacity and use of the institution than head counts, so they are often used in calculating budgets and for planning.

Fiscal year—the 12-month period for which budgets are planned and for which expenditures are tracked and reported. The *fiscal* year may or may not coincide with either the *academic* year or the *calendar* year. Frequently, fiscal years run from July to July.

Operating budget—funds used for day-to-day activities of a unit. Operating budgets cover equipment, travel, duplicating, postage, telecommunications, utilities, etc. Operating budgets differ from one-time start-up funds and from personnel budgets, which pay salaries or wages.

Personnel budget—funds used to pay salaries or wages (and possibly benefits). *Personal services* is another term used to label these funds.

Soft money—funds provided by one-time infusions. Soft money does not appear in a permanent budget line. Soft money often may be spent only on designated projects or needs.

PERSONNEL

Writing centers tend to be informal, easy-going places with lots of camaraderie among the staff members. It's easy to let personnel issues and policies slide, with most attention going to tutoring and teaching. But administrators expect the center to be consistent with the rest of the institution in its personnel procedures and policies; they will not value or reward anomaly. Writing center directors must remember that they are a part of administration. Although institution personnel manuals exist, directors should be sure a set of written personnel policies exists that conform to the institution's policies while defining duties and responsibilities within the center.

Preventing legal liability is a major administrative consideration. There are better ways to get administrative attention than with personnel problems. The center's personnel policies and procedures must be formulated before evaluations or any problems occur. Writing center staff must be provided job descriptions and be evaluated. There has to be a process for handling problems. The more professionally these issues are addressed, the better.

Reporting Lines

All institutions have categories of employees—faculty, staff, administration, civil service. Writing center directors frequently fall into more than one category. It is not usual for directors to hold 50/50 appointments. These arrangements develop gradually, without consideration of the implications. Having multiple reporting lines makes it difficult to avoid violating the chain of command.

Keeping reporting lines distinct can be challenging. It is natural to respond to an assistant vice president before responding to the English department chairperson. Yet, the evaluation conducted by the English department chair may cause more problems in the end. It is critical to the director, as well as to the writing center, that reporting lines are clear and understood by all parties involved. Any changes made should be distributed in writing to all parties concerned.

All supervisors should be aware of the constraints placed on a person who reports to more than one boss. It usually falls to the employee to remind all the bosses that they share the services of this one individual. Of course, everyone would be better served if two people were hired, each reporting 100% to one boss.

That optimal situation usually exists only in dreams, so job descriptions are necessary. It often falls to writing center directors to write their own job descriptions, which in turn must conform to institution-wide definitions.

Job Descriptions

The job description written for hiring the writing center director probably does not resemble current reality. (Go ahead and laugh.) Directors should revise and review their job description annually, consulting supervisor(s). Only the director knows what the job really involves. Having an accurate, *written* job description will help set work priorities and will encourage evaluations on the basis of what directors actually do.

Once the job description is written, annual revisions and reviews in consultation with the supervisor(s) provide opportunity to alert the administration to the realities of the job and the evolving dynamics of the position.

A job description should contain the following:

- A list of primary and secondary duties (include budget monitoring, planning, supervising and training staff, preparing materials, assessing writing center activities, gathering data, writing reports, professional development activities.)
- A statement of the percentage that each part of the job represents (e.g., 60% writing center directorship, 40% faculty)
- A statement of any released time for duties (Released time establishes the value the institution has placed on the activity, saying that this activity equals X number of classes or hours.)
- A list of the year's priorities among ongoing duties and any special projects
- A list of supervisors

Writing center directors not only are expected to write their own job descriptions, sometimes they have to do so just to survive. If they want a smooth-running operation, they must also create job descriptions for their tutoring staff. Written job descriptions reinforce the professionalism of the writing center. They explain what tutors are expected to do (and not do) and support the staff when the inevitable complaints surface about collusion and plagiarism. They may be written by the director and distributed, or they may be written in collaboration with the staff.

Writing the job descriptions in collaboration with the staff provides a teaching moment as well as the opportunity for an exchange of ideas about the duties and responsibilities of tutors. Such an occasion prepares tutors for future employment. The collaborative effort alerts directors to the needs and expectations of the tutors as well as an opportunity to explain the institutional constraints on a particular position.

Creating a clear, simple, and brief description of the position, its duties, priorities, and a requirement that staff must conform to policies of the institution and the writing center provides a more secure environment for tutors and directors.

Evaluating Writing Center Staff

Evaluation processes inspire dread and worry. So much may be at stake—retention, salary increases, promotion, or tenure. If the writing center director's position is divided between departments and institutional lines, then more than one supervisor may evaluate the director.

All parties need reminding that the writing center director wears more than one style of headgear. The director is an administrator of the writing center while teaching in the English department or some other area. Each position is evaluated according to the guidelines of the division and the department. Sometimes, the criteria applied don't match the job at all, creating terrible problems. It is crucial for all supervisory personnel to have a complete job description outlining the duties and responsibilities of each part of the position, as well as the other required supporting documents for each part.

Duties and responsibilities evolve throughout the year and from year to year. As changes occur, directors should update their personnel files accordingly. Sometimes the update is not about duties and responsibilities but involves accomplishments, publications, or activities that demonstrate advancing the cause of the writing center. Directors must keep everyone aware.

Writing center directors supervise paid staff, graduate students, undergraduate tutors, or some combination. Providing an evaluation structure becomes part of the professional training of the staff. Clearly written evaluations that include their participations will facilitate understanding and openness in the writing center workplace.

Discipline Issues

Administrators dread handling discipline problems; they see far too many. They prefer that they be handled at the lowest level possible. Writing center directors are part of the administrative team, and discipline issues are part of their portfolio of duties.

Most of the time, only minor discipline is required, easily handled with a private discussion or a single reprimand. But some issues require a formal response or the director will violate the law, as in the case of sexual harassment. A clean procedure protects the writing center director and the institution from nasty legal tangles. Keeping the handling of a serious problem localized in the writing center will demonstrate a professionalism welcomed by administrators.

Writing center directors will find it to their advantage to have a well-developed discipline policy in place, one that is fair, comprehensive, and that reflects the institution's policies.

This procedure should be part of the writing center's standard operations, established before anything happens, not in reaction to a specific issue. Although there are various processes to consider, using progressive discipline provides due process, allowing an employee more than one chance to understand and correct the problem. A staff is more comfortable knowing what the process is and knowing that cases will be handled with fairness and consistency.

Writing center directors never know which problems are temporary, one-time events. No matter what system is used for handling discipline matters, there are a few things a director absolutely must do:

- Act promptly.
- Keep detailed records.

- When an infraction occurs, provide the offender with a written follow-up memo after having discussed the matter.
- Treat each situation in accordance with established procedure (no variations).
- Withhold judgment or comment until the facts are gathered and all perspectives given consideration.
- Be prepared to defend or explain actions to the supervisor(s).

Terminology

Clearly defined job descriptions and evaluation processes for the writing center director and its employees will assist smooth operation and appropriate compensation. A consistent and fair discipline procedure will protect the center and you. The following terms should be familiar:

> *Employment category*—the type of position held; may be tenure-track faculty, temporary or nontenured faculty, administrative, civil service, part-time, staff. Compensation, benefits, and access to various services and forms of support are determined by employment category.
>
> *Evaluation*—determination of the quality of performance for the purpose of making decisions on retention or re-employment, promotion, tenure; answers the question, "How well am I doing?" Not to be confused with assessment.
>
> *Job description*—a written document describing duties, the relative importance of each duty, the percentage of each set of duties, reporting lines, and supervision responsibility.
>
> *Primary duties*—the responsibilities regarded as the largest and most important component of a job. Workload calculations may distinguish between primary and secondary duties. Assignment of released time to an activity suggests that it is a primary duty.
>
> *Progressive discipline*—responses to violations of policy or problem behaviors, increasing severity of discipline with each repetition. Includes informing the employee about the concern or violation, developing a plan for improving or changing behavior, setting a deadline for achieving improvement or change, and stating the alternative if goals are not met.

POLICY

Policies set by outside entities such as governing boards, accrediting bodies, union contracts, and legislatures constrain administrators' decisions. Writing center activities cannot violate policies imposed on the institution.

Policy Statements and Manuals

Every institution has pages and pages of policies. Being ignorant of these policies does not excuse writing center directors from abiding by them. Before developing any policies for the writing center, directors should get copies and study the institution's policies on issues relevant to the center.

Federal laws govern students' right to privacy. Writing center work inevitably includes records of student work, and some of the information may be sensitive. Writing center policies about handling student information must be developed with care; simply following the procedures of other writing centers is not sufficient. Obtaining a supervisor's opinion and expert legal advice, then preparing a clear policy understood thoroughly by the entire staff will protect both students and writing center personnel.

Because writing centers often service students with not-so-traditional backgrounds or issues, both Affirmative Actions policies and the American's with Disabilities Act (ADA) affect the policies and operations of all writing centers. Most institutions have affirmative action and ADA officers or coordinators to consult when a problem arises. What may seem to be a small problem can have legal ramifications affecting the whole institution. Always ask for clarification from a supervisor and the appropriate officer or coordinator.

Employees of the center are also employees of the institution. Writing center directors have only the flexibility allowed by the institution's rules and regulations. If clerical staff works in the center, then civil service codes possibly apply. These codes affect the definition of a position and who may be hired. The human resources office can offer valuable insights into writing job descriptions, especially for clerical staff.

A faculty handbook or possibly a union contract may apply to the writing center director's position. If so, directors need to know this document thoroughly because it affects their working conditions.

Harassment policies also need close attention. So much interaction occurs in the writing center between different cultures, languages, and attitudes, some conflicts and misunderstandings are inevitable. Harassment may be intentional or it may be a difference in perceptions. Writing center directors are responsible for doing as much as possible to prevent harassment. Supervisors are required by law to respond to harassment complaints. As with the issue of privacy, they need advice. Writing centers need a clear, strongly stated antiharassment policy. Directors must train staff so that they know the policy. Directors should consider setting aside a tutor-training session for this purpose and inviting an expert to speak or conduct the training.

Directors are not required to know and enforce all institutional policies in detail. They do need to be aware of the policies, when to apply them, and where to go for answers. Directors should always check first to determine if the institution has a policy, before attempting to formulate one of their own.

Unwritten Policies

Not all policies are written and published; the unwritten policies of the institution's culture have considerable force. The rule against circumventing the chain of command is one example. A rule against violating tradition is also common, although traditions are subject to varying perceptions. Writing center directors need to learn of unwritten policies administrators observe and be carefully selective about which ones to ignore.

Within an institution's culture, an economy usually develops around the exchange of favors. Writing center directors should observe and learn the culture of favors at their institutions. Watching *The Godfather* a couple of times provides a good lesson in the workings of favor exchange. In a strong favor-exchanging economy, every favor sets a precedent and incurs a debt. The debtor will not be allowed to select how to repay the favor. Where a favor-exchange economy exists, following *written* policies becomes even more important, protecting you from incurring favor debts unnecessarily.

Writing center directors occupy a relatively low place in the power structure of an institution. In a favor exchange economy, they should make their own private, unwritten policy to avoid incurring favor debts as much as possible. On the other hand, doing favors whenever possible increases directors' options for getting funding and support.

A working familiarity with the institution's policies will help directors develop the policies of the writing center. The writing center's policies need to conform in principle and style with institutional ones. If there is a conflict between the two, then the institutional policies will prevail.

Terminology

The following are some important terms:

Affirmative Action—federal laws regarding treatment of minority or disadvantaged groups. Affirmative Action laws cover employment procedures, particularly at public institutions. Affirmative Action also covers admission of students, access to enrollment and to financial aid. Many institutions have Affirmative Action officers charged with training employees on Affirmative Action policies and with investigating violations.

Americans with Disabilities Act—federal laws requiring accommodation for persons with disabilities who are otherwise able to perform employment duties or learning activities; qualifying disabilities include chronic diseases, physical limitations, allergies, learning disabilities, and addictions under treatment. Known as ADA.

Civil Service Codes—state or federal laws governing the hiring, employment conditions, transfer, and promotion of employees classified as civil service, usually clerical staff.

Faculty handbooks and union contracts—documents with legal force, governing the employment conditions of faculty, including workload assignments, evaluation procedures and criteria, grievances and disciplinary actions, compensation, and benefits.

Family and Medical Leave Act—federal law prohibiting employers from firing employees because of medical conditions, childbirth or adoption, or attending to ill family members. Requires up to twelve weeks of unpaid leave to be granted for these purposes. Known as FMLA.

Policy—the rules, expectations, and procedures applying to an activity. Policies are not laws, but within a campus, they have authority behind them and can be legally enforced.

PLANNING

A major function of administration is planning, including budget, personnel, enrollment management, and curriculum. Although short-term planning may be informal, long-term planning usually involves an elaborate structure of councils, task forces, committees, reports, and planning documents. The process may be called "strategic planning" or whatever name is currently fashionable; by any name, planning occurs at all institutions. The writing center director will almost certainly participate in the planning process at some level. The writing center's short- and long-term plans should be consonant with the institution's plans.

Developing a Mission Statement

Directors must know their institution's mission. For example, one school may serve traditional undergraduates, providing high quality liberal arts instruction in a rural, residential setting. Another may serve working and site-bound adults, providing job-specific training and instruction. Mission statements guide the decisions and priorities of central administration. Administrators say "yes" more easily to activities aimed at supporting the mission, so requests should be connected to the mission statement whenever possible.

The writing center's mission should assist or complement the larger mission. The center's mission statement guides planning and decisions. Directors have a much clearer concept of what a writing center is and can be than anyone else, but they should consult with the center's constituencies before creating the statement.

The mission statement contains purpose, values, and goals, stated in one to four sentences, as in this example: *"The writing center serves all students of Grimy Gulch College in a convenient, accessible, and inviting place. Tutor services supplement classroom instruction and aim to guide students to become capable of informed, appropriate decisions as they write both in and outside of academic settings. The writing center leads and supports writing-across-the-curriculum initiatives at Grimy Gulch College."*

Directors should avoid packing the sentences in a mission statement with long lists and keep the statement as simple and concise as possible so that it is easily remembered.

The mission statement should appear in brochures, reports, requests for funding, and planning documents. It will remind administrators and others of what the writing center does and aspires to be in a simple concise way.

Preparing Plans

To make progress toward goals and receive consistent funding, writing center directors must make plans and follow them. They need annual plans, containing the goals and objectives for the academic year. Additionally, they need a long-term plan covering the next three to five years, although naturally any long-term plan is subject to revision.

Planning is best done during slow times before an academic year begins. A one-day planning retreat with the writing center's staff can be time well spent, because their insights will be invaluable.

In an example, a three-year plan seeks to increase Grimy Gulch College's writing center usage from 10% to 25% of the total student population visiting the center annually. To do that, the director sets the goals of adding more tutors, expanding the center's space, and increasing the budget to pay tutors and do advertising. Objectives include getting funding for three more tutors, requesting writing center space in a new building the second year, and conducting a public relations campaign in the third.

In the first annual plan, three new tutors must be funded. This smaller plan includes visits with Grimy Gulch's athletic director and with the education department about funding tutors, plus application for a grant to pay for an ESL tutor. At the end of the year, the writing center director assesses progress toward this objective.

Selecting, Gathering, and Using Data

Next to managing the budget, data gathering is the most important task of writing center directors. They need data to plan, to determine progress, and to verify success (or failure). Administrators value quantifiable data more than anecdotal information, so most of the data should be numerical. Anecdotal information is meaningful only when it accumulates. Administrators want to discern patterns and scope—that means numbers.

Directors should begin with the data used everywhere to measure success: retention, persistence, time-to-degree. No writing center tracks these data directly, but the center can track its *effects* on them. Beginning with a record of each student who uses the center, comparisons reveal how well users of the center match with the whole student population in terms of retention, persistence, and time-to-degree.

Setting up this kind of data collection takes time, but every institution has statisticians who track its students in these basic measures, especially in the institutional research office. Their data combined with the center's records will measure the writing center's usefulness to the institution. The center's records should use the same identifiers for individual students as the institutional research office in order collate data easily by computer.

The institutional research office can help with another source of useful statistics, national and regional databases. Groups of peer institutions, defined by size, mission, curricula, and location, serve as comparison groups for all sorts of measurements. Central administrators know their peer group institutions, so using peer group data for writing center assessment and planning will make sense to them.

Inevitably, an administrator will ask how to detect if the writing center actually improves student writing. Using data that measure the effects of the center on retention, persistence, and time-to-degree helps to answer the question. Because there are so many factors that affect student writing and because grades are not a reliable indicator, directly measuring improvement in student writing and connecting it definitively to the writing center is almost impossible. On the other hand, plenty of research shows that the more time students spend writing, the more their writing improves. Writing centers offer another opportunity for writing, beyond the classroom. Writing center directors need to be direct about all these realities when responding to administrators.

Data should reveal the internal needs of the center as well as its weaknesses and strengths. These data should reveal what kinds of instruction the center needs to offer, the success of tutoring methods, the success of advertising and publicity, the appropriateness of location, the best hours to be open, peaks and valleys in use patterns, how many chemistry majors and student athletes use the center, whether the center is sufficiently staffed, and so on. Planning should address both needs and weaknesses.

Data-collecting methods should include simple counts, surveys, questionnaires, and focus groups. Directors inexperienced with these methods can go to faculty sociologists, statisticians, and marketing specialists for help, using their expertise to save time and get useful results. A well-designed survey or questionnaire can yield much useful information. A bad one is a waste of everyone's time.

Preparing Planning Documents and Reports

Many institutions have closely defined planning procedures and rigid formats for planning documents. In such cases, directors have to conform. If the planning process allows them to design their own planning documents, they should take advantage of this freedom to prepare plans that administrators find efficient and clear.

Good planning documents are simple, with no long narratives or explanations. Headings, bullet points, pie charts, graphs may present information more concisely than words. A plan should include:

- Mission statement for the writing center
- A few achievable goals (no pie-in-the-sky), including a time frame for each goal
- Two to four objectives for achieving each goal, with a time frame and the person responsible for each objective
- Expected outcomes when goals are achieved
- How the outcomes will be assessed or measured (what evidence will confirm achievement of the goal?)
- Estimated costs (round numbers, labeled as estimates, although they must be as accurate as possible; no guessing allowed)
- Sources for funding (is the money available or does the director of the center have to find it?)

Planning documents for central administration need careful attention to detail. They should be tightly edited, error free, easy to navigate, and handsomely presented. This is an excellent opportunity to demonstrate professionalism. Administrators won't read an essay; they'll ask for the executive summary that should have come in the first place.

Internal planning documents can be simpler and messier, with notes, diagrams, cross-outs, and addenda. Documents sent to administrators are as much about presentation as they are about content. Internal planning documents are the worksheets used to get things done and to measure progress.

At the end of the time frame addressed by the plan, another document reports outcomes:

- How much of the plan was realized? Changed?
- Is a continuation needed or appropriate?
- How much did the outcomes cost compared to the estimates?
- How were the outcomes measured and what did the data reveal?

Together, the plan and the outcomes report offer central administration concise and useful information about the writing center. As writing center directors prepare annual reports, they should summarize the writing center's activities for the year (again, using headings, list, charts, graphs, and bullet points), present data verifying the center's contributions to student success, and then attach their planning and outcomes reports.

These are the documents where directors make the case for the center's funding and support. Data always should be in the same format, so that longitudinal patterns are easy to discern. Directors can forget about anecdotes in written reports and save them for making points in conversation. Using internal data and comparisons with peer institutions will answer administrators' question of how the center compares to others.

Terminology

The following are useful terms o employ:

Assessment—determining if activities performed are achieving the stated goal; answers the question, "Are we actually doing what we say we want to do?" Not to be confused with evaluation. Assessment should not be used for employment decisions for individuals. It should be used to set priorities and for planning.

Enrollment management—using applicant and student demographic data to shape enrollment numbers and populations. Enrollment management matches numbers and kinds of students with the resources and mission of the institution. Institutions may try to increase enrollment, reduce enrollment, change or retain the populations they serve.

Goals statement—a brief summary of what an institution or unit wants to accomplish within a defined period

Institutional research—collection and analysis of data to determine what is happening at an institution. Data may include numbers and types of students, their progress toward degree, retention rates, graduation rates, dropout rates, transfer rates, grade averages, test scores. Data will be collected institution-wide as well as from individual units. Institutional research may also include data about employees, number of temporaries and permanent employees, proportion of faculty to administration, comparative salary data, and length of employment. Data are used internally and reported to external agencies.

Mission statement—a short expression of an institution's goals, values, and purpose. Units within an institution may also have mission statements.

Persistence—the rate at which students complete courses. A student may initially enroll for twelve semester hours but only complete six semester hours for credit, representing a 50% persistence rate.

Retention—the performance of an institution or entity in keeping students enrolled for consecutive academic periods. A high retention rate is perceived as evidence of academic success. A high retention rate is desirable financially; retaining students is less expensive than recruiting replacements for them.

Time-to-degree—at colleges and universities, the average length of time required for students to complete a degree program. Generally, undergraduate degree programs are intended to take four years provided there are no changes of major, failed courses, stops out, or scheduling problems. The closer to four years (eight semesters; sixteen quarters) the average time-to-degree is, the better the institution is perceived to be performing.

Use rate—the amount of time students actually use a service, proportionate to the time the service is available. A writing center may have one hundred hours of tutor-time available per week. If an average of seventy of those hours per week is actually devoted to tutorials, the writing center's use rate is 70%.

THE UNEXPECTED

Events such as large budget recalls, terrorist attacks, fires, and natural disasters have affected institutions and therefore writing centers. Writing centers may find themselves threatened with being closed altogether as they face a hostile administrator or department, collapsing enrollments, or a serious but more localized budget crisis. Well-designed policies and procedures can head off some problems in the event of an emergency. Writing center directors should have an evacuation plan and practice it regularly; be rigorous about back-ups for data and all major documents; develop "bench depth" by training staff in procedures; keep planning documents, data, and budget tracking up-to-date; and respond to political threats with a coherent plan and with options favorable to both the center and the threatening entity.

CONCLUSIONS

Writing center directors are professionals and administrators, even if they have only a 50% appointment. As I moved from faculty and writing center director into central administration, I gained a more global perspective. I came to understand how important it is for the writing center director to learn as much as possible about the workings of the institution and the administration.

The basic principles of effective administration apply in the writing center as much as they do in the provost's or the dean's office:

- Be informed about institution's policies and operations.
- Remember that there always is more to be learned about a situation.
- Listen before acting.
- Ask questions.
- Provide clear, simply written guidelines for the writing center personnel.
- Be fair and be consistent.
- Plan thoughtfully instead of improvising.
- Behave professionally in all situations.

Writing center directors spend a lot of time on public relations, working to improve the center's visibility on campus. Certainly fliers and Web sites and innovative programs accomplish much for centers. But directors should never overlook the one cost-free effort that will always make a good impression with central administration: administering the center with top-notch, savvy professionalism.

20

Managing Up: Philosophical and Financial Perspectives for Administrative Success

Bruce W. Speck
Austin Peay State University

So you're a new writing center director. You're an expert on writing pedagogy. You've studied the writing across the curriculum (WAC) literature. You've even been a guest lecturer at WAC seminars. You've gained a good understanding of using computers in writing instruction, even computer tutorials. You worked in a writing center as a graduate student, so you have some understanding of the ins and outs of how writing centers operate. You've had a taste of training tutors. You enjoy immensely the work associated with a writing center, and now as a writing center director you have the chance to make a difference.

In the flush of your eagerness to make a difference, I bring you congratulations and a sobering observation. Your academic preparation will both help and hinder you as a writing center director. That you have knowledge about teaching writing and training tutors will be a great advantage. That you have some understanding of the internal workings of a writing center is helpful. But, in all likelihood, you have scant knowledge, at best, of how higher education administration operates, how funding is appropriated and regulated, and how deans, provosts, and presidents arrive at decisions regarding the management of a community college, college, or university that can have a profound effect on the writing center. These deficiencies in knowledge can be amended, but the worst news is that as a member of the academic community, you likely have been influenced by a faculty perspective of administration that encourages you to see administrators as the enemy, those who erect barriers to block your aspirations to liberate students from oppressive political structures and enable them to participate fully in a critique of existing power structures. Administrators, simply because they wield power, are part of the educational problem and, as such, present a threat to the mission and goals of units like the writing center. The mission of the writing center, from the perspective of what has been called radical pedagogy, is to make students "subjects rather than the objects of historical change. Both teachers and students then will engage in critique, in a critical examination of the economic, social, and political conditions within which the signifying practices of culture take place" (Berlin and Vivion, xii). The language Berlin and Vivion employed to capture a particular attitude about pedagogy is foreign to many administrators and tends to intensify the difference between professorial and administrative perspectives, even though both perspectives are committed to student learning. In fact, although *hegemony* is commonly used in the writing center literature, I can't recall ever hearing the word *hegemony* during a budget hearing. (For a useful discussion of how the language of theory in light of shifting educational paradigms relates to the mission of the writing center, see Murphy. For a useful discussion of the language of administration, see Kinkead and Simpson.)

The mission Berlin and Vivion envisioned, which both "marginalizes" the writing center because it stands outside dominant academic structures and serves as its raison d'etre, makes positive working relationships with administration difficult. Haviland, Fye, and Colby went so far as to say that a writing center's affiliation with senior administration "may result in greater indebtedness and control, and administrative ties may create faculty and student wariness." Affiliation "may mean compromising academic collegiality and gadfly status for insider access" (88). You have just read a classic example of the "us vs. them" mentality that pits faculty and students against administrators. (Ironically, the "us vs. them" mentality may also be interpreted to mean "us wanting to be them.") Sadly, such antagonism not only does little to fulfill an organization's strategic goals but also sets up a false contest between unequal powers. Writing centers are bound to lose in such a contest because administration has both the lawful authority to manage an institution and the mandate to allocate resources to achieve administrative mandates.

Even if you are not burdened by theoretical models that "problematize" your relations with administration, you may be in the position Smith described:

> Most of us who teach writing prefer to ignore issues such as administrative efficiency. We have a higher calling. We may, in fact, boast that we never have had a course in business administration and would not take one under any circumstances. We probably have had no experience managing an office. But if we end up directing a writing center, we find ourselves faced with a rather complex task; we have the responsibility to see that a busy office runs efficiently, that services are delivered to students and faculty as effortlessly as possible. We also must keep records and worry about justifying ourselves, and our budgets, each year. (115)

Harris confirmed Smith's observation: "Writing center administration, a highly complex task as is, has an added complication in that so many new directors plunge in with an almost total lack of preparation" (63).

Still want to direct the writing center? Interested in learning how to work positively with administrators? Willing to reconsider some of your fondest theoretical positions? If so, perhaps I can help. As a senior administrator who worked his way up through the professorial ranks, ran a WAC program for six years, was selected as the founding director of a faculty development unit, moved on to positions as dean, associate vice provost, and vice president for academic affairs, I offer advice for your administrative success. I call this advice "managing up" because writing center directors can advance to higher administrative positions—if they learn how to be successful as writing center directors. The administrative skills you can learn to operate a successful writing center are necessary skills senior administrators ply daily.

In providing a primer on managing up, I address two topics. First, I spell out an administrative perspective that is critical for faculty members to adopt if they hope to take some pleasure in and find success as an academic administrator—and is interested in managing up. Second, I explain the centrality of budgetary considerations in administrative decision making.

AN ADMINISTRATIVE PERSPECTIVE

In choosing the heading for this section I deliberately use the adjective "an," not "the." I am making no claim to providing the last word about all the fine points related to a successful administrative perspective. The literature on writing centers affirms that "writing centers are institution-specific in structure and function" (Olson and Ashton-Jones 19), and the premise of institutional uniqueness holds true for any particular community college, college, or university, in part, because the people given the responsibility to administer an institution approach their charges differently. The outworking of what is commonly called an administrator's "management style" can be plotted somewhere on a spectrum with endpoints from autocratic to laissez faire. In providing advice about an administrative perspective, I am endorsing an inclusive, participatory approach that presupposes a team effort, not only among a team of administrators but also faculty and staff. Clearly, I am at risk of being charged with naiveté, a wild-eyed idealism that betrays the seemingly innate antagonism—whether relatively benign or ferociously malicious—among faculty, staff, and administrators.

This antagonism is based on two very different perspectives: the administrative perspective and the faculty perspective. The faculty perspective arises from two seemingly conflicting values: community and autonomy. Membership in a community is based on disciplinary convictions, so the concept of community endorsed by many academics is bounded by whatever theoretical paradigm dominates a discipline at any particular time. For example, evolutionists, by and large, have no patience for those within the scientific community who espouse intelligent design. In fact, those with academic credentials in the sciences who nevertheless defend intelligent design are perceived by evolutionists as propagating unscientific, even antiscientific, premises. I have cited the sciences to demonstrate that the theory wars in English departments are not atypical of the ardent, even vociferous, conflicts that help shape academic communities.

An irony of community building is its unmistakable disciplinary framework that limits membership in the community. Thus, a graduate student in English is not coached in collegiality regarding the academy as a whole, if, indeed, collegiality as the respectful acknowledgment of those with convictions in opposition to mine is in view at all. In fact, graduate students are kept busy in their disciplinary corner of the world; the immense literature for any particular discipline (and increasingly subdisciplines) helps enforce disciplinary boundaries that discourage community building beyond the discipline.

As a graduate student in English, I vividly remember my experience in a graduate course on Kenneth Burke in the speech department. My classmates, all speech majors, openly criticized me for having the audacity to invade their domain; their criticism was based merely on the ground that my home of record was the English department. At another institution, as a professor, I remember a call from the chair of the speech department to encourage me to drop the term *rhetoric* from the title of a course I had proposed because, after all, the speech department needed to preserve its sole rights to the word. That these two incidents reflect the torn history between speech and English departments was unknown to me when they happened. Nevertheless, these two incidents are grounded in the powerful reality of the primacy of the discipline in shaping a faculty member's allegiance to a particular academic community.

That primacy is only strengthened when we consider the tenure, promotion, and retention process, which relies heavily on evaluation of a candidate's research, teaching, and service from those closest to the candidate (i.e., departmental colleagues). Even at the college level, the candidate's dossier often needs to be annotated by the department representative to the college committee, a representative the candidate hopes will be a champion, not a naysayer. Thus, the department is the focal point in a professor's career, and departmental judgments can make or break candidates who seek the permanency tenure offers.

In addition to the powerful influence departmental forces have on developing faculty attitudes about their place in life, autonomy, a seemingly opposite force, helps shape faculty perceptions of themselves. This opposing force is captured in the term *independent contractor*. Fellowes said unabashedly, "For most of my academic career I had been an independent contractor" (B16), a moniker that resonates with faculty members regardless of their discipline. In fact, Fellowes was wrong. Faculty members often act as though they are independent contractors, exercising privileges of organizing their time and making critical pedagogical decisions that are in accord with the work independent contractors perform, but unlike independent contractors, faculty have the luxury of a regular paycheck, which for tenured faculty is only peripherally dependent on their performance.

The values of community and autonomy interact differently given any particular context but, in general, those values foster a limited, self-serving perspective of the academy. Thus, faculty tend to evaluate the efficacy of policies, initiatives, and changes in the status quo from both a local (departmental or disciplinary) and a personal perspective. For example, a policy that states, "Faculty will submit final grades electronically no later than 48 hours after administering a final examination," will create a great deal of resentment among faculty who are accustomed to submitting all final grades 48 hours after the last scheduled final on campus. The reasons for such a change may be cogent, but the initial outcry against such a policy change can be traced to a perceived infringement on faculty members' autonomy. Disciplinary arguments about the need for more time to grade essay exams, which faculty stress are vital in promoting writing across the campus, also will be advanced as a reason against the change. Even when the good of the university is carefully articulated as justification for the policy change, a powerful perception grounded in self-interest chafes at a change that does not seem to honor disciplinary and autonomous values.

Certainly, not every professor shares equal amounts of the professorial viewpoint described here, but my experience as a professor and as an administrator confirms to me the validity of the professorial viewpoint outlined. In fact, I have been able to articulate some of the contours of that attitude, not because I fully understood them as a professor, but because I have encountered them as an administrator. On this side of the professorial-administrator divide, I can assure you that the professorial viewpoint is inadequate in making effective administrative decisions. Why?

The administrative perspective I propose requires administrators to think globally, to consider the entire needs of the organization. An administrator with academic credentials in the sciences who favors the sciences in administrative decisions demonstrates an unwillingness to treat the whole with equal respect. A writing center director who is promoted to a senior administrative position and favors the English department when making decisions (or punishes the speech department) is making decisions based on disciplinary concerns, not the good of the whole. In both cases, equity is violated. As Hoppe noted, the ability of administrators to distance themselves from disciplinary allegiance (being allied with all but beholden to none) is critical in managing effectively in higher education:

> Unfortunately, some faculty who move into leadership roles are unable to make the right (and often tough) decisions because they are too tied to their faculty colleagues and to commonly revered privileges of the academy. For example, the role of an academic department chair requires a faculty member to balance a tightly held commitment to faculty freedom and loyalties with the need to hold a broader view of the university, its budgetary constraints, and its obligations to the whole. Many faculty cannot distance themselves enough from their faculty myopia to see the big picture and to make decisions that serve the university rather than just the faculty. As a faculty member moves through the academic pipeline, the distancing becomes increasingly critical. (5–6)

Simpson and Maid confirmed the tension between allegiance to one's disciplinary perspective and administrative goals when they say, "writing-center directors perceive themselves as being agents of change in the institution, so compliance with administrative priorities and initiatives may be at odds with their self-perception" (122). Ownership of ideas and the commitment to make those ideas a reality is part and parcel of professorial engagement with the world but, for administrators, such engagement must be tempered by "the big picture" of serving the entire university.

I have no magic formula for making the transition from the classic professorial perspective heavily informed by the conflicting forces of disciplinary paradigms and the independent contractor metaphor that celebrates autonomy, but anyone who aspires to administrative positions with increasing responsibility for the academy as a whole will be well served by recognizing that the transition from a professorial perspective to an administrative perspective is imperative. One reference that may shed light on the transition is Hoppe and Speck's edited volume on academic leadership.

FINANCIAL PERSPECTIVES

I have belabored the need to recognize the difference between a professional perspective and an administrative perspective because virtually all I will say about resource allocations assumes the validity of the administrative perspective I have described. In fact, without the administrative perspective that takes a big picture view of the academy, resource allocations can become no more than attempts to buy favors, pump-up egos, build kingdoms, and push narrow agendas. In short, a global perspective is essential in maintaining fairness in resource allocations, given an institution's strategic goals.

Fairness is particularly important in resource allocations at the executive level because the senior administrators at an institution of higher education, a group referred to here as the executive team, have the authority and responsibility to make budgetary decisions at both the macro- and microlevels. They not only have the power to make far-reaching decisions about resource allocations, they also exercise that power regularly and must do so if an institution is to function. But, in exercising that power, the executive team is accountable for the good of the organization as a whole. Power and accountability go hand in hand, and if you don't believe such is the case because you have seen abuses of power that have gone unpunished, then I recommend that you read *The Chronicle of Higher Education* regularly. You'll see a stream of articles about failed presidencies because power was unleashed from accountability for a time, but accountability caught up and made itself known. If you study those articles, a principle of accountability emerges: Leaders have to defend their decisions when those decisions are called into question. I have found that successful leaders keep foremost in their thinking a solid justification for their decisions before the decisions are made, a justification that will pass the test of public scrutiny. What I have just affirmed is counter to a common misperception that administrators often make capricious decisions.

Simpson, argued against the view that the executive team, what she called Central Administration, is often capricious in making financial decisions:

> Caprice is complicated and costly. It is very, very seldom what is behind a Central Administration decision. Rather, funding, in whatever form, is at the bottom of *most* Central Administration decisions. Period. All decisions, including tenure, are ultimately budgetary in their implications. Caprice, on the other hand, leads to lawsuits and other difficulties. It creates unusual and time-consuming problems to be solved, distracting Central Administration from the routine work that must be done. (192)

I agree with Simpson that funding is the central concern in most decisions the executive team makes, and those decisions will become increasingly data driven because financial accountability has become a watchword in higher education, especially in times of reduced funding for public higher education, which will be the case in the foreseeable future. "Increasingly," as Ede and Lunsford noted, "all academic units are required to justify their worth and funding, and to do so not just once but continuously" (36). Given this ongoing accountability requirement, Ede and Lunsford advised writing center directors, "You have to understand not only the nature and mission of your university but also the exigencies that constrain you and the opportunities that (if you can only see them) also exist" (37). In other words, writing center directors should assume the administrative perspective as they seek to justify their existence.

In short, "as senior administrators face tougher budget decisions in the face of more skilled lobbying, they look for more trustworthy data" (Bell 8; see also Blalock), and data must "convince administrations and granting agencies that the center is providing a service that will ultimately benefit them and that supporting the center financially is indeed cost effective" (Jolly 113). In giving advice about how to be a successful administrator, Kinkead and Simpson told fledging writing program administrators, "Rather than work against the institution, we need to acknowledge that we are part of the institution and can be effective change agents. Our success in writing programs can translate into success for the university at large" (72). Want resources? Explain to administrators how your unit benefits the organization as a whole. In addition, Houston gave good advice when she said that writing center directors should be proactive in their relationship with administration. I second that advice because good administrators are proactive, not wanting to be in the situation of responding to problems but initiating solutions to avert problems.

The administrative perspective also is informed by the need for flexibility, another watchword in higher education. As Simpson noted earlier, personnel decisions, such as granting tenure, have long-term implications for budget allocations. Those decisions also have long-term implications for flexibility in providing new programs and either eliminating or downsizing existing programs. Many people are not aware that approximately 80% or more of an institution of higher education's budget is tied up in salaries and benefits, and the only way to redistribute those funds is not to fill open positions or eliminate existing positions, something that is extremely difficult to do when the positions are filled by tenured faculty members, especially tenured faculty members who embrace the faculty perspective passionately, resisting change tooth and nail.

The intransigence of the academy, including both the faculty perspective and the hierarchical structures that dominate academic life, have profound economic implications. Faigley, in discussing global economic change, noted, "While corporate America merged, downsized and relocated overseas, much of higher education remained in the smoother water because it was subsidized with tax dollars. Those days are coming to an end…. There's every sign that higher education has entered a period of radical transformation of its mission and the circumstances of its existence" (8–9). Murphy and Law predicted that "the next century will find writing centers forming social alliances and finding new identities within technology and industry" (140). They based their prediction on economics:

> The "total institutional restructuring" writing centers will face in the twenty-first century will undoubtedly involve moving away from traditional and classical concepts of the academy—however cherished those concepts may be—toward the politics and policies of the entrepreneurial university. The reason for this change is dramatically simple: the traditional academy itself is disappearing and being transformed by "academic capitalism" and entrepreneurship into a complex of partnerships between academics and industry. (141)

"Ultimately, all academic issues boil down to budget decisions" (Kinkead and Simpson 74), and given the fast-paced changes in the global economy, budget decisions are inextricably intertwined with the need for flexibility to meet market demands. As members of the academic community (administrators and faculty), we live in "a climate of diminishing budgets, accountability, student retention, and sweeping curricular changes" (Barnett 125), and all of us need to figure out how to survive and thrive in that climate. As White put forth when speaking to English language teachers, "[A]lthough we may not be used to thinking in management terms, the effective running of any ELT enterprise is subject to essentially the same considerations as apply in any other industry" (211). White concluded his argument by saying, "All of us working in ELT can benefit from the experience and theories derived from the commercial sphere, with whom we may be surprised to find that we have more in common than we thought" (218).

Clearly, White is a heretic—according to the classical faculty perspective. He crossed the line and said, in essence, that higher education operates on business principles and can learn a lesson or two from the way businesses operate. Only a pariah, a stooge for administration would write (and then publish no less) such blasphemy.

Yet White's position is not substantially different from Schwalm's when Schwalm wrote positively about the development of a writing center on his campus that provided "the occasion to pull together maverick academic support initiatives into a centralized, cost effective, and efficient comprehensive learning center" (61). That's the language of business from an academic administrator—the prudent use of resources to achieve a laudable academic goal: providing students with access to the help they need to be successful writers. In fact, Schwalm provided an admirable summary of how administrators view their role as economic/academic change agents:

> The "quality" movement has left its mark on administrators, and we tend to value projects that are student centered. We like projects that encourage retention, since losing students is expensive and state legislators are on our case. We *have* to be concerned about costs. We favor solutions over problems. We like proposals that reflect an understanding of the institution at large. We also like projects that help to overcome the vertical organization of the institution, reduce duplication, and allow for recombinations of existing resources. (62)

CONCLUSIONS

I don't possess a crystal ball, and the sources I have cited that speculate about the future of the academy may be in error. However, I think their predictions are cogent, and signs of the changes they foresee are already in the making. Therefore, all of us—faculty and administrators—have a choice to make about how we are going to function in the academy as it evolves. Even in the "transformed" academy, effective administration will continue to mean "having the ability to address the often conflicting ideas and mak[ing] thoughtful decisions" (Myers-Berlin xvii). Indeed, for those who desire to manage a writing center well and aspire to other administrative positions, I recommend that you assume an administrative viewpoint that enables you to make prudent financial decisions that will promote student learning. I recommend that you prove your administrative value so that you can manage up.

WORKS CITED

Barnett, Robert W. "Refining Our Existence: An Argument for Short- and Long-Term Goals and Objectives." *The Writing Center Journal* 17.2 (1997): 123–33.

Bell, James H. "When Hard Questions Are Asked: Evaluating Writing Centers." *The Writing Center Journal* 21.1 (2000): 7–28.

Berlin, James, and Michael Vivion. "Introduction: A Provisional Definition." *Cultural Studies in the English Classroom*. Ed. James A. Berlin and Michael J. Vivion. Portsmouth, NH: Heinemann-Boynton/Cook, 1992. vii–xvi.

Blalock, Susan E. "Singing the Song of Ourselves: Projecting the Centrality of Writing Centers through Re-searching Our Records." Paper presented at the annual meeting of the Conference on College Composition and Communication. Washington, DC, 1995. ED 387 809.

Ede, Lisa, and Andrea Lunsford. "Some Millennial Thoughts about the Future of Writing Centers." *The Writing Center Journal* 20.2 (2000): 33–38.

Faigley, Lester. "Writing Centers in Times of Whitewater." *The Writing Center Journal* 19.1 (1998): 7–18.

Fellowes, Peter. "From Books to Business: The Value of a Liberal Education." *Chronicle Review* (February 28, 2003): B16.

Harris, Muriel. "Solutions and Trade-offs in Writing Center Administration." *The Writing Center Journal* 12.1 (1991): 117–25.

Haviland, Carol Peterson, Carmen M. Fye, and Richard Colby. "The Politics of Administration and Physical Location." *The Politics of Writing Centers*. Ed. Jane Nelson and Kathy Evertz. Portsmouth, NH: Heinemann-Boynton/Cook, 2001. 85–98.

Hoppe, Sherry L. "Identifying and Nurturing Potential Academic Leaders." *Identifying and Preparing Academic Leaders*. New Directions for Higher Education, Number 124. Ed. Sherry L. Hoppe and Bruce W. Speck. San Francisco, CA: Jossey-Bass, 2003. 3–12.

Hoppe, Sherry L., and Bruce W. Speck, eds. *Identifying and Preparing Academic Leaders*. New Directions for Higher Education, Number 124. San Francisco, CA: Jossey-Bass, 2003.

Houston, Linda S. "Budgeting and Politics: Keeping the Writing Center Alive." *Administrative Problem-Solving for Writing Programs and Writing Centers: Scenarios in Effective Program Management*. Ed. Linda Myers-Berlin. Urbana, IL: NCTE, 1999. 112–21.

Jolly, Peggy. "The Bottom Line: Financial Responsibility." *Writing Centers: Theory and Administration*. Ed. Gary A. Olson. Urbana, IL: NCTE, 1985. 101–14.

Kinkead, Joyce, and Jeanne Simpson. "The Administrative Audience: A Rhetorical Problem." *WPA: Writing Program Administration* 23.3 (2000): 71–84.

Murphy, Christina. "Writing Centers in Context: Responding to Current Educational Theory." *Landmark Essays on Writing Centers*. Ed. Christina Murphy and Joe Law. Davis, CA: Hermagoras Press, 1995. 117–125.

Murphy, Christina, and Joe Law. "The Disappearing Writing Center within the Disappearing Academy." *The Politics of Writing Centers*. Ed. Jane Nelson and Kathy Evertz. Portsmouth, NH: Heinemann-Boynton/Cook, 2001. 133–45.

Myers-Berlin, Linda. "Introduction." *Administrative Problem-Solving for Writing Programs and Writing Centers: Scenarios in Effective Program Management*. Ed. Linda Myers-Berlin. Urbana, IL: NCTE, 1999. xv–xxi.

Olson, Gary A., and Evelyn Ashton-Jones. "Writing Center Directors: The Search for Professional Status." *WPA: Writing Program Administration*, 12.1–2 (1988): 19–28.

Schwalm, David E. "E Pluribus Unum: An Administrator Rounds Up Mavericks and Money." *Writing Center Perspectives*. Ed. Byron L. Stay, Christina Murphy, and Eric H. Hobson. Emmitsburg, MD: NWCA Press, 1995. 53–62.

Simpson, Jeanne. "Perceptions, Realities, and Possibilities: Central Administration and Writing Centers." *The Allyn and Bacon Guide to Writing Center Theory and Practice*. Ed. Robert W. Barnett and Jacob S. Blumner. Needham Heights, MA: Allyn and Bacon, 2001. 189–93.

Simpson, Jeanne H., and Barry M. Maid. "Lining Up Ducks or Herding Cats?: The Politics of Writing Center Accreditation." *The Politics of Writing Centers*. Ed. Jane Nelson and Kathy Evertz. Portsmouth, NH: Heinemann-Boynton/Cook, 2001. 121–32.

Smith, C. Michael. "Efficiency and Insecurity: A Case Study in Form Design and Records Management." *Writing Centers: Theory and Administration*. Ed. Gary A. Olson. Urbana, IL: NCTE, 1984. 115–22.

White, Ronald V. "Managing Innovation." *ELT Journal* 41.3 (1987): 211–18.

✠ 21 ✠

Administrative (Chaos) Theory: The Politics and Practices of Writing Center Location

Joan Mullin
University of Toledo

Peter Carino
Indiana State University

Jane Nelson
University of Wyoming

Kathy Evertz
Carleton College

As directors operating within different institutional contexts, our writing centers' effectiveness depends not just on our scholarly knowledge, but also on our administrative ability to read shifting academic priorities. Yet, many of us analyze administrative decisions "without any background in organizational systems or change, … [even though] our programs hinge on our success in implementing or resisting" change (Vaught-Alexander 122). Vaught-Alexander analyzed the effects that resource and policy changes had on her own writing center by examining the subcultures of the academy, how her program got caught between them, and how she followed the organizational "rules" for creating partnerships to survive. Her tale is cautionary and her efforts did not create the desired outcome; this was not due to her administrative work or to her misunderstanding of her institution, but instead to a new administrator, another shift in priorities, and another strategic plan. The academic environment of Vaught-Alexander is familiar to us today; it is a product of budget problems, challenged by online delivery of education, and bogged in traditions that prevent it from responding to larger, complex cultural shifts: It forms an organizational context within which a writing center's reporting lines can determine its effectiveness.

The research on which Vaught-Alexander drew has played itself out in the three experienced writing center directors' narratives presented here. Each describes one of the primary units within which writing centers have traditionally been located in an English department, reporting to a chair; in a faculty development center (or larger tutorial unit) that reports to multiple supervisors—a hybrid; and in a nondepartmental academic unit (college or academic affairs office) with a reporting line to a dean or provost. These stories are meant to help writing center directors better understand why academic organizations function as they do, to encourage examination of current institutional placement within constraining organizational functions and philosophies, and to help directors effectively argue for scarce resources and institutional promotion.

ACADEMIC DECISION MAKING: INEFFECTIVE STRUCTURES

"With our English Studies or composition and rhetoric degrees in hand, WPAs often expect logic and evidence from research to create improvement or change in their programs" (Vaught-Alexander 122). The WPAs who produce pages of organized arguments about learning and ethical pedagogy for their administrators, and the directors who have carefully documented attendance and student learning outcomes that result from writing center work, may be dismayed when their program resources are nonetheless reduced. Perlman, Gueths and Weber long ago noted that decisions in higher education are less driven by result and effectiveness than by efficiency: As a leader of a service organization rather than a business, academic administrators are "prone to worry about and emphasize doing things right (efficiency) than doing the right things" (8). For a humanist/writing center director, doing things right equates less to efficiency than to effectiveness.

In addition to the academic albatross of wanting to be right (however that's defined), decision making in academe includes the tendency to focus on red tape and procedure, on process and committee, on debate and consensus (Perlman, Gueths and Weber 9). A visit to any executive leadership team or to a faculty senate meeting confirms this. Yet "evidence" within these settings often focuses on "intangible objectives" that cannot be translated into "operational and quantitative terms" (9)—although we try with our charts and learning outcomes. Ultimately, however, educational decision making centers on that which is tangible—often budgets (although success doesn't always translate to more money)—and on how to serve multiple constituents, "each important and each with different priorities. [But] [h]ow does an organization set priorities, cut non-productive programs and concentrate its efforts when it must please everyone?" (9). Consequently, organization in academe today is tied to efficiency, which is tied to money, or it is determined by how many students can be matriculated with dwindling resources. This complicates the positioning of a writing center because its "tangibles" are not easily measured in quantifiable FTEs, tuition dollars, or grant-generating overheads.

The organizational theories on which Vaught-Alexander drew recommend working one's unit into the fabric of the institution's (measurable) "tangibles," which is something that writing centers do well. They already serve multiple constituents and work across levels and disciplines to complement the curriculum. The stories that follow demonstrate the appropriateness of continuing this course of action, but there are several cautions now coming from those of us for whom this model has previously been successful. The institutions in which we now work are caught between an internal "'process culture' with a focus on bureaucracy" and an external technological culture based on speed and response (Perlman, Gueths, and Weber 44). Writing center directors, schooled to react instantly in our one-on-one situations, are what organizational theorists would call "intrapreneurs," but in a slow-moving bureaucracy, such internal agents of change face frustration, can be silenced for their innovative spirit, or burned out as they seek to be everything to everyone. As the three descriptions that follow indicate, writing center intrapreneurs are effective only in proportion to their ability to work both within and outside of the traditional university paradigm, to live in chaos and manage conflict amidst snail-like university processes, and to position themselves wisely and well within the organization, ready to change their positionality as the context demands. This may mean changing our personal allegiances to traditional organizational paradigms.

LIVING IN AN ENGLISH DEPARTMENT: PETER CARINO

The story of writing centers in English usually is an expansion narrative, a story of worlds conquered and colonies settled, beginning with a movement from merely helping with developmental skills in grammar, to dealing with an array of issues related to writing as process, to expanding into writing across the curriculum (WAC) efforts across campus. This scenario is described, in greater and lesser degrees, for five of six English-based centers in *Writing Centers in Context* (see Harris, Mohr, Clark, Kinkead, and Rodrigues and Kiefer). In each case, English provided a strong base, and as director of an English department writing center for eighteen years at Indiana State, I've concluded that an English department can be a fortress from which to launch expansion efforts or a cramped cottage built on a shaky foundation. Situated either way, the director of such a center must be constantly aware of a myriad of departmental, campus, and even national issues that can affect the direction and distance of the pathways available for expansion; the director's perception of these will determine a center's viability and budget.

Centers in English departments can be funded in many ways: an independent budget, an allotment from the department budget, grants, or a combination. A writing center housed in an English department with its own budget would enjoy both the protection of department status and budgetary freedom, but such a center is rare because to be part of a department, in the administration's eyes, is to be part of its costs. Thus, when the department faces budget cuts, the center will usually be expected to find money to replace funds for day-to-day operations that used to come from English or to cut services. In the mid-1990s, for instance, my department suffered a large cut in funding for adjunct faculty. Graduate assistants, usually available as tutors 10 hours a week (half their assistantship), began teaching two courses rather than one and no longer could work in the center. From my chair's perspective, he had to put teachers in the classroom first, a position I could not argue with as a colleague; however, as director of the center, I found myself with a depleted staff and had to work with the chair to lobby the dean to dip into her pool of "contingency funds" to hire undergraduate staff. Nevertheless, the center was underfunded and understaffed that semester, and at times students had to be turned away for lack of available appointments. Unless funded as a stable line item in a university budget, a writing center in an English department must constantly cobble together a budget from its allotment from English and any other money it can beg, borrow, or steal. For example, when our university put in a new general education program with required writing components for each class, I was able to touch the program administrator for a piece of its budget to publicize my center among general education students. Likewise, when the university started a first-year experience program, some funding was available because we work with many first-year students.

Other semesters have been happier. When flush with money, the center is well-staffed and running full speed. However, during one flush period, my center was in the process of establishing a "tutor-in-the-classroom" program, tying tutors to particular courses. This program was just becoming established when budget cuts required that fewer tutors could participate because they were needed for one-to-one work in the center. The credibility of the program suffered, and it was eventually discontinued. We experienced a similar occurrence while setting up our OWL; all went well due to state funds specified for technology development—until those funds dried up. Now if I want a computer savvy student to maintain the OWL, the money must come from elsewhere, and although I was able to get money elsewhere, sometimes more successfully than others, such efforts require a lot of energy, work, and commitment. An alternative is to remain small, as Stephen M. North recommended in his "Revisiting 'The Idea of a Writing Center,'" and to work only with writers with a strong interest in writing, who do not have to be drawn into the center through publicity campaigns or special programs with which the center is allied. In today's academic culture of productivity, such a stance is not only a luxury, but also programmatic suicide. What has worked for me best is to be an intrapreneur, and in my case, being a tenured faculty member has given me a distinct advantage.

The benefits of being a tenured faculty member are many for an English department director. First, it is more likely the faculty member will have a stronger rapport with the department chair than would an adjunct. Although chairs can be an obstacle when budgets shrink, they (as chair of the largest department on campus) are often a person of stature on campus and can be a strong ally when a director must chase funding outside the department. In such efforts, chairs are supportive because the more outside funding a center gets, the less it needs from the chair's purse. In addition, a tenured faculty member enjoys some automatic cache with faculty in other departments and often is eligible for committees and special efforts not available to an adjunct, or even an administrator of an independent center. Such assignments often provide entryways into seats of power where funding opportunities might lie. I would not have been eligible to be elected to the senate, and without tenure, I would not have been in a position to annoy the powerful about the center's needs. Such access will not solve all a center's problems, but it can go a long way toward ensuring that the center's concerns are falling on the right ears.

Locating writing centers in English is the product of a disciplinary model of organization for universities. Although this model may be changing, it has had a long shelf life and likely will persist for quite a while. Thus, centers will find themselves attached to English departments while still being expected to serve constituents beyond them, often with less than adequate funding. This need not be daunting, for all writing centers, wherever they are located, must be resilient, recognizing the advantages and disadvantages of their contexts while never forgetting that little can be done without the proper support.

HALF IN-HALF OUT: THE HYBRID WRITING CENTER:
JANE NELSON AND KATHY EVERTZ

The University of Wyoming Writing Center began in the 1970s, where it expanded from its location in Tilly Warnock's office into a reconfigured seminar room in the English department. In its first decade of growth, the department employed various ways of staffing, including faculty assignments, required graduate student hours, and credit-bearing courses, some of which worked better than others. During this time of trial and error, Tilly and John Warnock articulated their philosophy and pedagogy in "Liberatory Writing Centers: Restoring Authority to Writers," arguing that a combination of "part-time, nontenured instructors, graduate students, peer tutors, and tenured faculty" (18) is a perfect liberatory model for staffing a writing center. In the mid-1980s, the writing center changed in some significant ways as a result of a five-year legislatively funded basic writing program. The several professional lecturers hired to teach in this program were also assigned to work in the writing center, which was regarded as an essential support service for the new program. The commitment to a professionally staffed writing center has remained a hallmark of UW's writing center ever since.

The move to what we are calling a hybrid writing center occurred in the late 1980s with the creation of an all-university general education program called University Studies, which was a notable modification in undergraduate education for a land-grant institution with several professional colleges. A member of the planning committee, Tilly helped to guide the inclusion of three required writing across the curriculum courses within University Studies. With encouragement from central administration, the Department of English created a tenure track position to provide support for the significant addition of writing courses at the university. The position was defined as half-time writing center director, with administrative duties in University Studies, and half-time faculty in the Department of English, with teaching and research duties. To signal the university-wide importance of the writing center, the writing center and its director were administratively and physically housed in the newly created Center for Teaching Excellence, with space located in the university's library. Within a couple of years of acting in this position, the new writing center director realized the difficulties of two reporting lines and a review process that was required to ignore the administrative half of her job. Continuing with the creative spirit that had generated University Studies and the Center for Teaching Excellence (CTE), the university's administration, with the approval of the English department, agreed to configure the position to exist entirely outside of the departmental structure, with the director reporting 100% to Academic Affairs by way of the CTE, which has recently been renamed the Ellbogen Center for Teaching and Learning (ECTL).

Thus a hybrid writing center with two homes was created. The Department of English continues to provide professional staff by assigning faculty and lecturers every semester, and the ECTL provides the budget and support services for the director and the physical space. The arrangement has worked surprisingly well, but it is just that, an arrangement, with no official documents to describe the history, routines, or practices of the work.

This extra-departmental home for the University of Wyoming Writing Center has also helped to signify its function as a WAC support service for both students and faculty. The physical location of the writing center in prime library real estate denotes its university-wide status for both students and faculty. The positioning of the writing center director within a faculty development center has allowed the director to promote writing in a surprising variety of contexts. Faculty and staff attending events at the ECTL must walk by the writing center, and attendance at these events number more than a thousand every year.

In addition, the director, who is freed from the demands, expectations, and rhythms of a tenure track position within a department, has been able to support more fully the scholarship of teaching and learning of faculty in a variety of disciplines. For example, during her time as director, Jane Nelson coauthored articles with faculty in four different colleges (Education, Agriculture, Pharmacy, and Arts and Sciences), with the standards of journal and tenure review deriving from disciplines other than literary criticism or composition and rhetoric. The flexibility of working outside of departmental constraints has also led several writing center staff to participate in numerous grant projects, with the monies coming from a variety of internal and external sources.

Another benefit of the extra-departmental home is the writing center's support budget, which is several degrees closer to the dispenser of university funds. In an English Department housed in a massive Arts and Sciences College with competing departments, the writing center could never compete for the discretionary few dollars available to the dean. In the ECTL, whose director reports directly to the vice-president for Academic Affairs, budgets are more flexible. The writing center never has generous amounts of money to spend. However, with extra-departmental funding from the ECTL, the writing center has significantly higher budgets for copying, books and supplies, computers, travel, and summer writing center services than it would ever have from within the relatively poor budgets routinely given to humanities departments.

Nonetheless, the honors program has provided some funding every year in the last decade for undergraduate internships, but semester after semester the English department has provided the professional staff of the writing center. They have typically been lecturers, some temporary, some with extended-term (six-year) appointments. Historically, the English department has validated writing center work as invaluable professional development for teaching writing in the classroom. In turn, the writing center benefits from a professional staff that can work with graduate students on theses and dissertations, with faculty on grant proposals and publications, and with staff on university documents. The professional staff also consults with faculty about teaching, giving numerous presentations and facilitating workshops in writing classrooms across the disciplines. For several years, some of the lecturers worked in the writing center semester after semester, which professionalized the position of writing center consultant. Professional development funds, such as competitive travel grants, were available from the ECTL, and many lecturers, most with extended-term appointments, focused their professional development on writing center work.

Competing demands within the English department and the college eventually began to darken this rosy picture. A writing center appointment is considered to be a nonclassroom teaching assignment, which does not accrue to the department any of the academic currency that credit-bearing courses bear (at UW, that currency is called FTEs, or full-time equivalents). The development of a professional writing minor within the English department has further strained the resources of the department, especially the time and talents of the extended-term lecturers. Now, temporary lecturers who have no guarantee of employment from year to year increasingly staff the writing center, and they are less likely to focus on long-term professional development projects relating to writing centers.

As a result of the competing demands that naturally privilege the work that is physically and emotionally closer to the English department, writing center work—and the people who do that work—have become increasingly invisible to the English department. The writing center director has no budget to hire workers; rather, the director discovers from semester to semester, sometimes late in the process, how many lecturers the English department can assign to the center. While English and the writing center have three decades of history together, they don't necessarily agree, from year to year, or from chair to chair, what that largely oral history is and what customs that history includes. This invisibility makes it entirely possible for a chair to suddenly reduce staffing by one third with no announcement or rationale, and with little understanding of the impact on the writing center. English department lecturers who work in the writing center must also confront the issue of whether writing center work is even "teaching," a question that vexes the faculty as well as department and college administrators when lecturers go up for reappointment and promotion. Classroom teaching is something that can be assessed and evaluated by peer observations and student evaluations, both of which are difficult to conduct in a writing center context. And, thus, writing center work disappears almost completely from official university notice. It rarely gets noticed in reappointment packets, and it does not appear in the course catalogues in the kind of way that classroom teaching does.

In response to the English department's recent reduction in staffing, university administrators deflected a proposal to create a task force to study alternative ways of staffing. Instead, they requested that the English department reconsider the possibilities from within its staff. University administrators prefer to define the various academic services on campus as the responsibilities of "home" departments: The math lab belongs to the mathematics department, the oral communications lab belongs to the communications and journalism department, and the writing center belongs to the English department. Although all of these services support the infusion of quantitative reasoning, oral communication, and writing across disciplines, not just within them, administrators seem devoted to structures whose lines and responsibilities are clear and unambiguous, and are easy to count and assess. With this kind of infrastructure, we feel fortunate to have moved one step away from the silo model of management into a hybrid writing center.

LIVING WITHOUT THE ENGLISH DEPARTMENT: JOAN MULLIN

The University of Toledo's Writing Center was established nearly twenty years ago as a support for the eventual writing across the curriculum program. Located in the College of Arts and Sciences with a mandate from its faculty through Arts and Sciences Council, the center was therefore not controlled by the English department; this sent a clear signal that writing was for everyone. Besides, if the center would have been in the department, other units would have seen it as a bid for more English resources and another faculty member. As it was, the director was initially hired as professional staff. Not sure whether the individual hired or its positioning would be effective, the idea was that perhaps a tenure line would be created in the future.

Naïve about academic structure and assuming that my PhD meant something to others, I just acted like a faculty member: I taught classes in the English department, served on faculty committees as appointed, and turned in an annual report on the same format as faculty rather than professional staff and was evaluated as such. Nonetheless, being outside the department, I had no intellectual home and no real colleagues to nurture and mentor me. I learned about departmental politics by serving on the monthly dean council comprised of all the eighteen department chairs, listening to them strategize when administrative priorities changed, hearing them discuss difficult faculty cases, tenure and promotion issues, strategic planning, and budgeting. I learned to balance between thinking like a faculty member and thinking like an administrator because I was never either and could observe both. Yet, this unique position allowed me to also make contacts across levels, departments, and even colleges because I was neutral and could serve—as well as understand—their individual interests. I had no tolerance for what I perceived as the short-sightedness of the English department (and why didn't they want me as a colleague?).

Although being out of a department offered me budgetary and reporting opportunities (access to presidents, provosts, deans and that others didn't have), it also generated jealousy and suspicion. With budget control, I could hire undergraduate and graduate tutors, professional writers, part timers—whomever I chose—whereas departments were subject to hiring by committee. I could be entrepreneurial and create cross-university buy-in for grants, generating over a million dollars in external funding, whereas departmental grants, especially in the humanities, are often small, granted to individuals, and don't accrue to or supplement the unit as a whole. The departments' physical environments declined and space became scarce, but my position on college and university committees allowed me to advocate for new space and resources in the middle of campus joined prominently with the Center for Teaching and Learning with the blessings of upper administration. The writing center and the WAC program that grew out of it continually prospered within the institution, and resources, even in hard times, were not cut even when departments suffered. At one point when the center was going to have to close its doors in February because of increased student use and, therefore, an inevitable budget shortfall, the vice president of finance asked whether "tutors could just volunteer for the rest of the year, until the new budget kicks in." I replied that tutors would volunteer their talents if faculty members would volunteer to teach overtime without compensation. The point of my story is twofold: Because I could interface easily with upper administration, I knew the vice president well enough to boldly answer. Second, the vice president understood that our mission was important and that tutoring is teaching. So, the money was "found" to keep us in business until the next fiscal year kicked in.

Added to that success, however, was the fact that the English department was fighting for its continued identity as a traditional literature department, and lost its doctoral program because it hadn't changed. That and the fact that I was in that suspicious field of composition (and successful), it was no wonder that it took three times to finally convert my position to tenure. The downside of location outside a traditional academic unit is isolation, and isolation can, in times of great stress, despite partnerships, leave one standing without protection. Recently, the dean of the college has had to choose between a faculty position in a department that needs someone to teach courses so that its majors can complete their program or the assistant director of the writing center. He had no choice and, after seventeen years, that writing center position was eliminated. Seeing this inevitability years ago, I have been trying to move the writing center into the provost's office, an impossible endeavor when we had three different administrations within four years.

Recently, due to restructuring necessitated by such budgetary pressures in the state and because I am leaving my present position, I was able to articulate the problem to the president as he requested (an advantage of being a university-wide director even if I am in a college and have powerful faculty advocates). After much thought, I realized:

> The Writing Center is a unique, 21st century, interdisciplinary field, tied to writing across the curriculum, serving all members of the community; however, because of its traditions, the university has not yet accommodated or envisioned the structural placement or longitudinal planning needed for an *academic* unit that does not neatly fit into a distinct unit or department. (Mullin, April 2004)

And therein lies the heart of the organizational problem for writing centers.

LOCATION, LOCATION, LOCATION

The very nature of writing center work is to cross genres and contexts: We apply writing pedagogy to all disciplines; we work across levels, even with faculty and staff. In fact, many of us blur the line between the academy and the community in our literacy centers or through writing or poetry workshops. Some of us are "recognized" academics; that is, we are tenured or tenure track, but many others of us have long "acted" like academics, publishing, serving in national organizations and on editorial boards, and presenting at conferences. One might say that writing center work has been light-years ahead of the academy, in a sense, predicting the blurred boundaries now facing our institutions: interdisciplinarity, students from high school concurrently taking college courses, partnerships with community economic groups. In the chaotic environment of the current academy, how does one position a writing center?

The most effective metaphor through which we might examine this question and the three accompanying narratives, and every writing center, is suggested by Marc Cutright's collection on *Chaos Theory & Higher Education*. Although most people take the "chaos" part literally, the theory itself is pertinent to how writing centers have grown into campuses and for thinking about how they might continue: To ascribe to chaos theory is to recognize that the smallest acts, however random they may seem, "show complex, replicated patterns. The behavior of these systems is nonlinear, that is, behavior feeds back on itself and modifies the patterns" (4). Writing centers need to build into their structure a strong system of feedback for students, faculty, administrators, and any other stakeholders they not only serve, but also affect. Whereas such data may convince administrations of the necessity of location or budget, data should also serve as a reflection of cumulative patterns for directors, patterns that point to how effective their location and reporting lines are, at any one moment, within the institution. The "fractal" images, snapshots, tea leaves provide a mirror for future action. In organizations driven by chaos theory, "the pattern of the whole can be seen in the part" (Cutright 6).

In each of the previous narratives are threads of patterns, indicators for those who tell them as well as for other directors: The patterns that emerge include the challenging of borders, continued interdisciplinarity, wider community engagement, and intrapreneurial as well as entrepreneurial administration. Given these patterns, decisions about organizational location must consider crucial questions: Does placement in an English department limit a writing center director's ability to be intrapreneurial? Will the chair limit partnerships because energy has to be devoted to the department? Will partnerships (and/or success) be resented? Does the department consider "owning the center" and will it limit tutors to English majors? If the chair has to choose between money for tutors and a faculty member, which will it be? The same series of questions, substituting "dean" (or "faculty development or student services dean/director") should be asked with a slight addition: How does the supervisor to whom the writing center director reports define "tutors"? If they are viewed as English majors, then the disciplinarity of the center's mission may be in jeopardy at some future point. Ask: How can the organizational location of the writing center best signal to this community our intrapreneurial mission, our interdisciplinarity, and finally, our willingness to be entrepreneurial?

The strong predictive strand that runs through each of the narratives here ties to entrepreneurship in its classic sense: Writing centers need to consider intrapreneurial associations that help them generate funds. Location in a department or other office that best positions a center to generate or receive outside funding may be a necessity as public institutions become privatized and private institutions find solutions for dwindling endowments. Like it or not, writing centers need to anticipate changes in the academy by tracing patterns in organization in order to better prepare for their positions, present and future, in a chaos theorized institution. That also includes an examination of one's own paradigm. Despite our tendency to align ourselves with a "home department," chaos theory suggests getting to the heart of such assumptions on which this "silo model of management" is based—and no longer works, is what will move our writing centers, and our institutions, into the future (see Cutright 57–78).

To be an effective writing center director is often to be frustrated by the snail's pace at which institutions move. In our own centers, we can adjust according to feedback, change pedagogy within a minute, implement a new idea by calling a meeting. We already practice chaos theory, which "tells us to expect the unexpected, to have short planning cycles, and to be prepared to change in radical ways over short periods of time in specific areas of our activities." But our institutions do not move as quickly as we can; "institutions concerned with remaining relevant must continue to evolve services and curriculum in a measured and steady fashion.... In an environment that allows for, indeed protects, debate, the conflict between those eager to embrace what's new and those slower or suspicious of change is certain to be noisy if not downright acrimonious" (Kershaw and Safford 173). A writing center needs to position itself within a unit that, as in Carino's case, will fight for and nurture it in the beginning; as in Nelson and Evertz's situation, can change to accommodate change; and as in Mullin's case, needs to face the central issue in order to better prepare for the future. Besides location, the writing center director needs patience.

WORKS CITED

Clark, Irene L. "The Writing Center at the University of Southern California: Couches, Carrels, Computers, and Conversation." Kinkead and Harris. 97–113.

Cutright Marc. *Chaos Theory & Higher Education.* New York: Peter Lang, 2001.

Harris, Muriel. "A Multiservice Writing Lab in a Multiversity: The Purdue University Writing Lab." Kinkead and Harris. 1–27.

Kershaw, Adrian, and Susan Safford. "The Impact of Technology and Student Choice on Postsecondary Education: *Plus Ca Change ...*" Ed. Marc Cutright. *Chaos Theory & Higher Education.* New York: Peter Lang, 2001. 159–74.

Kinkead, Joyce. "The Land-Grant Context: Utah State University's Writing Center." Kinkead and Harris. 192–209.

Kinkead, Joyce, and Jeanette Harris, eds. *Writing Centers in Context: Twelve Case Studies.* Urbana, IL: NCTE, 1993.

Mohr, Ellen. "Establishing a Writing Center for the Community: Johnson County Community College." Kinkead and Harris. 145–65.

Mullin, Joan. Report to the President of the University of Toledo. April 2004.

North, Stephen M. "Revisiting 'The Idea of a Writing Center.'" *The Writing Center Journal* 15.1 (1994): 7–19.

Perlman, Baron, James Gueths, and Donald A. Weber. *The Academic Intrapreneur: Strategy, Innovation and Management in Higher Education.* New York: Praeger, 1988.

Rodrigues, Dawn, and Kathleen Kiefer. "The Writing Center: History, Description, and Tutorial Support." Kinkead and Harris. 216–26.

Vaught-Alexander, Karen. "Situating Writing Centers and Writing Across the Curriculum Programs in the Academy: Creating Partnerships for Change with Organizational Development Theory." Ed. Robert W. Barnett and Jacob S. Blumner. *Writing Centers and Writing Across the Curriculum Programs.* Westport, CT: Greenwood Press, 1999. 119–40.

Warnock, Tilly, and John Warnock. "Liberatory Writing Centers: Restoring Authority to Writers." *Writing Centers: Theory and Administration.* Ed. Gary A. Olson. Urbana: NCTE, 1984. 16–23.

⫷22⫸

Approaching Assessment
as if It Matters

Joan Hawthorne
University of North Dakota

About a week ago, I sat in a meeting about general education, and when someone mentioned assessment, a faculty member from English asked somewhat fretfully, "What do you mean by assessment? Are you talking about grading?" This is the sort of attitude that college faculty carried with them for years, but it is exactly the wrong attitude for today.

Program assessment doesn't have much to do with grading, and it has little to do with the performance of individual students. Instead, audiences both inside and outside our institutions are asking about institutional and programmatic effectiveness, essentially posing the question, "How do you know what you're achieving?" And it is surprising that we in higher education have had to be pushed and pulled into assessment, resisting all the way, considering that the hallmark of academics seems to be a desire to look at and describe things—microbes or poems, airplanes or patients—from a clear, dispassionate, skeptical perspective, which is exactly the perspective required for assessment.

Despite the skeptical eye that we bring to our scholarly work, we seem to have expected everyone—from colleagues and administrators to legislators, parents, and students themselves—to take the quality of our educational work on faith. When looked at through the eyes of these stakeholders, it's nothing short of a miracle that we in higher education haven't been called on to take assessment more seriously in the past.

But that is changing. If the culture of the university traditionally has been one that demands investigation and evidence, then the culture of our nation, at least as it relates to education, has increasingly followed suit. Accrediting agencies are powerful forces behind the demand for greater attention to outcomes but, in most states, legislatures and governing boards also are demanding accountability (Huba and Freed 17; Kanter, Gamson, and London 20). The automatic trust, deserved or not, that educational institutions once received no longer exists. Nowhere have I heard this more clearly articulated than in a student response to a faculty panelist last fall. In answering a student's question about what it was really important to learn, a history teacher began by saying, "Realistically, I don't expect that you're going to remember these facts a year from now." When the faculty left the room, the student crowed, "He admitted that we don't get anything out of this!" Although I differed with the student on her interpretation of the professor's remarks, I recognized that she probably spoke for many of her peers in expressing skepticism about the value of her education.

Taking assessment seriously provides us with data-driven responses that might be persuasive to this young woman, as well as to others now taking a hard look at what happens in higher education. More importantly, it allows us to be intellectually honest in our own activities and to hold our work to the same standards as we would hold that of any other professional.

TERMINOLOGY

It's logical to begin with precise definitions, but it's unfortunately possible to fill an entire chapter with them—that's how bogged down in jargon assessment is. We can distinguish between assessment and evaluation, we can identify goals or objectives, we can talk about data or information, and we can try to measure or to document. And that's just the first set of terms. For most program directors, including writing center directors, it makes sense to use terminology in ways favored by others within their own institutions, because the purpose of the specialized language is to aid communication with those people anyway.

In higher education today, assessment is mentioned more often than evaluation, and definitions of it tend to focus very heavily on student learning outcomes (e.g., see Huba and Freed 8; Walvoord 2). Taking an approach that might be welcome to those on the humanities side of campus, Palomba and Banta began with a simpler definition: "assess (v): to examine carefully" (1). By extension, assessment can be understood as the process of careful examination, which is probably a reasonable way of conceptualizing what's meant today by assessment, although it's important to note that the entire process is normally seen as beginning with a mission statement and goal-setting, continuing with a careful examination of the program in the light of those goals, and culminating with efforts to improve program effectiveness based on what was learned (Palomba and Banta 298–99).

MODELS OF ASSESSMENT

Experts describe a variety of models for assessment or program evaluation, which in one system of classification (Popham 24–25) includes goal-attainment, judgmental, decision-facilitation, and naturalistic. Essentially, models vary according to purpose, posited use of information, and general mind-set used for data collection. If the purpose of assessment is to more fully understand what is happening within a given educational program, then the evaluator could bring a naturalistic orientation to the process and simply examine the program from a variety of perspectives, eventually writing up a description of what is learned and perhaps summing up the program's value. In fact, external evaluators often use this basic approach. If the purpose is to decide whether or not a given program should be allowed to continue, or whether it should receive additional (or fewer) resources, then the evaluator could use a decision-facilitation model focused on information directly relevant to the criteria to be used for the decision. But most often in higher education, the expectation is that assessment of educational programs will be conducted in terms of the program's own goals or expected outcomes, a trend driven by and reflected in the orientation of accrediting agencies (Huba and Freed 17).

This outcome-oriented assessment should be a comfortable fit for most writing center directors, because it is consistent with other program assessment likely to be conducted on campus and leaves control of the process and plans firmly in the hands of program staff members—in this case, the writing center director and tutors. Outcome-oriented (or goal-attainment or goal-driven) assessment begins with a statement of intended outcomes (Palomba and Banta 6).

Exercising this kind of control over outcome goals for our programs is a powerful tool for maintaining control over them, a significant value of this approach. Rather than assess to find out whether our program measures up to some mythical national standard (increasingly the case for K–12 educators), we have the luxury of identifying desired outcomes in terms of our own students, contexts, and program philosophies.

However, because writing centers are academic programs, although with a student services twist, it can make sense in this context to enhance an outcomes model by adding nonoutcome data to present a fuller, more accurate picture of the program (Lerner, "Writing Center Assessment" 64). A number of components borrowed from the student services assessment model developed by Schuh and Upcraft might be pressed into service to flesh out the story told by a straightforward outcomes evaluation. Drawing from their model, assessment of the writing center could include assessment of campuswide need for the services provided, satisfaction of those who use writing center services, comparisons with similar programs nationwide, cost efficiency, and usage tracking, in addition to outcomes assessment (12–15).

ASSESSMENT AS SCHOLARLY ACTIVITY: SETTING GOALS AND FRAMING QUESTIONS

For anyone engaged in outcomes assessment of an academic program, it is important to begin by developing an appropriate list of desired outcomes (Walvoord 3). Because student learning is the presumed purpose of higher education, the expectation is that outcomes will be described primarily in terms of what students will learn or be able to do as a result of participation in a particular academic program (e.g., "Writing center users will learn to read their own work more critically."). But, also consider what can be accomplished in your own setting. Do you expect to see individual students repeatedly throughout their participation in particular courses or even their time at the university? If so, your outcome goals might be framed longitudinally (e.g., "Regular writing center users will learn strategies that can be used to focus and organize their papers in accordance with the requirements of the class."). Do you have a lot of single session users? Then maybe a goal like this makes sense: "By the end of a session, the student will have learned to use at least one new strategy."

Either of these specifies cognitive skills that writing center users might be expected to learn. But affective or attitudinal goals may also be appropriate for writing centers, because previous research over the course of many years has demonstrated the close connection between learning and feelings (e.g., see Krathwohl, Bloom, and Masia). So a list of outcomes could include affective goals: "Students who have writing center sessions will increase their confidence in their writing."

Finally, process goals might be considered for inclusion in a list of desired writing center outcomes (e.g., "Writing center users will feel comfortable and engaged during the writing center session," or "The writing center will be used by students from all colleges within the university, and by students from first-year through graduate level."). The assumption behind such process goals is that achievement of the process goal is an indicator that the program is doing the right things: That is, if the writing center succeeds in being welcoming to a broad range of students and is able to make them feel engaged and comfortable during sessions, it is reasonable to believe those students will be positioned to make progress toward goals for learning.

In some ways, writing good goals is the most rigorous part of an assessment project, which makes sense if we consider, again, the parallel with other scholarly work. Developing the premise and figuring out what to look for is the intellectual part of research. Similarly, determining what outcomes we genuinely expect from our work and deciding how to name them so we don't overstate what's possible, on the one hand, or reduce to triviality our own work, on the other, is the intellectual part of writing center assessment. (We may be confident that we can achieve positive results on assessment of trivial goals, but will those results matter to us, or to anyone else?)

In goals-driven assessment, the goals themselves can be inverted to become research questions. Thus, the outcome about learning "at least one new strategy" can be restated as a question: "At the end of a writing center session, can students make use of a new strategy?" If you've selected important goals that accurately describe what you (realistically) hope to see accomplished as a result of writing center sessions, then your research questions will be interesting and well worth the work it will take to answer them.

If you are using an assessment model that includes strategies other than outcomes assessment (e.g., needs assessment, national comparisons, usage tracking), then you will need to ask different questions of your data, but the questions should still be genuine and focus on addressing genuine interests. For example, you might ask, "Who needs the writing center and why?" or "How does the usage percentage for writing center sessions at our institution compare with the percentages at other comparable colleges or universities?" In any case, the principle of converting information needs to questions still holds; once key assessment questions are identified, it's possible to plan strategies for answering them.

ASSESSMENT AS SCHOLARLY ACTIVITY: SELECTING METHODS

It is often at the methods-selection phase of the process that writing center directors find themselves stalled. This occurs for at least two reasons. First, too often the focus is on methods or collection of data for a report rather than on goals or research questions. In such a situation, there is no reasonable basis of selecting methods other than convenience—essentially, asking the question, "What kind of information could I collect without too much work?" Although the concern about workload is reasonable, *any* work that is essentially purposeless is too much. Second, it is difficult at first to imagine ways of collecting useful information, and the challenge may feel daunting when the researcher/assessor is seeking measures that provide definitive answers to difficult questions. This is especially true in the evaluation of educational programs, where assessment and research tasks are complicated by the ethical and behavioral challenges of working with people who can't be forced to comply with rigidly controlled experiments.

The task becomes more manageable through a shift in language. Instead of "measuring" outcome, we can talk about "documenting" outcome. Instead of looking for "measurements," writing center directors can think in terms of "indicators" and "evidence." Writing center directors can document outcomes by looking for evidence or indicators, direct or indirect, of the outcome in question. A direct indicator will be one that allows the researcher/assessor to look directly at the outcome of interest. For example, we know a student has learned to use a new strategy if a person observing the session sees that the tutor models or teaches the strategy, and later (although perhaps within a single session) sees the student use it independently. In contrast, indirect indicators "suggest" rather than "demonstrate" something about the goal in question. A postsession survey in which students say they have learned new strategies is an indirect indicator: It doesn't allow us to actually observe strategy use, but it is an indication that the students believe they have achieved that learning. Students who believe they have learned useful strategies may indeed have done so. But it is also possible that they are overly optimistic at the close of the session and respond that, yes, they have learned strategies, while still being unable to use any new strategies effectively on their own.

Researchers or evaluators are often advised to triangulate when possible, which means finding two or three sources of evidence, probably including both direct and indirect indicators, for a given question (Walvoord 20–21). Each goal leads to its own research question, so the time-pressed writing center director may want to look for sources of evidence that can provide documentation relevant to more than one question. Otherwise, a simple assessment project for a writing center with a modest four or five goals could quickly balloon into a study requiring ten or fifteen different research methods. But the workload stays manageable if you limit your attention to one or two research questions (goals) per year, or one or two data sources (methods) per year. It's easier to implement this strategy if the entire project is planned in advance, even though the work may be conducted over a period of years (and even though some longer range parts of the study may be changed in response to early results, just as would be the case in any other kind of longitudinal research project).

In a recent discussion on WCenter, a wide array of types of evidence were cited as potentially useful. Among those mentioned were indirect indicators of writing center outcomes including the importance of the writing center to external audiences like admissions (Harris), surveys of faculty and student perceptions of improvement (Dowdey), participation in campus events like parent orientation (Alm), narratives from tutor journals (George-Bandy), tracking of all student contacts or usage (Lane), tracking of contact hours with student writers (Lerner, "Quantitative Measures"), and tracking of demographics of student users (Lerner, "Quantitative Measures"). Virtually all writing center directors seem to track session numbers and some characteristics of those with whom sessions are requested (e.g., grad vs. undergrad), and a great many ask students to complete end-of-session or end-of-term surveys or evaluations at least occasionally. Because these are the most readily available, least time-intensive to collect, and least intrusive data sources, it makes sense to use them to generate data relevant to as many goals as possible. For example, the survey question, "Rate your level of confidence in your ability independently to continue work that was begun in this session," would provide numerical data relevant to a goal of enabling students to work more independently. An open-ended question about writing center outcomes could be included on the same survey (e.g., "Describe what you'll do next with your paper. How, if at all, is that different from what you would have done without your writing center session?").

As sensible as it may be to collect indirect indicators and use them where possible, good researchers want to collect the best possible evidence regarding their research questions, and a similar approach should be taken to assessment. If writing center users complete pre- and post-session questionnaires during a given week, then we can find out more about any attitudinal changes than if they only do postsession surveys. If a sample of writing center sessions are taped and segments of those tapes are analyzed, or if they are observed with the observer coding for behaviors of interest, then more direct indicators of writing center outcomes can be collected. For example, if observers were to note and code various student behaviors, would they document greater numbers of independent, appropriately self-critical words and behaviors near the end of the session than near the beginning? Would there be more signs of student confidence in what to do next near the end of a session than near the beginning? If students come repeatedly from particular classes, would students in early semester sessions demonstrate knowledge of fewer strategies than those in late semester sessions? The data resulting from observations and taping of actual student "performances" can be analyzed in terms of numbers (what percentage of students used what number of strategies, complete with statistical analyses of significance), words (describing trends, behaviors, and sorts of strategies, but without doing counts and statistics), or a combination of the two.

Writing center directors, although often uncomfortable with statistical analysis (Johanek 58–59), sometimes presume that quantitative data must be collected in order for assessment to "count." That is not the case—and, if anything, audiences for assessment seem to be becoming more knowledgeable about the strengths and weaknesses of various kinds of data sources (Palomba and Banta 332). This knowledgeability, in fact, means that it is increasingly important to be careful about study design and research quality, no matter what forms of data will be collected. However, it is possible to develop useful experiments, resulting in hard numbers, as one kind of evidence of writing center outcomes (e.g., Niiler, "The Numbers Speak" 7, and Niiler, "'The Numbers Speak' Again"). Avoiding such potentially informative studies because of their statistical nature makes no sense. On the other hand, although some experiments may result in extremely useful and interesting data, it is important not to forget that the goal of assessment is to ask important questions and collect sound data that provide valid indicators in response to those questions. Thus, grade comparison studies, for example, although potentially appealing for their numerical nature, may be ultimately futile if the methodology itself is flawed and the resultant information adds little to our knowledge about the degree to which outcomes are achieved (Lerner, "Choosing Beans Wisely" 1).

Still, there are interesting possibilities for educational outcome studies, which could produce valuable and direct indicators of a writing center's effectiveness in reaching key goals, while also making significant contributions to the literature on writing centers in general. For example, Morrison and Nadeau recently conducted a largely survey-based study that documented student perceptions of session value before and after grades received, and examined those perceptions in relation to the letter grade received. Carino and Enders, also using survey data, examined the effects of variables like number of visits and student perceptions of the consultant on user satisfaction. James H. Bell, using an approach he called "small-scale evaluation" (16), looked at how user satisfaction changes across time. Not only did all of these studies clarify staff understandings of an affective outcome (student satisfaction) in their own writing centers, but they also opened the door on ways that writing center effectiveness (and student attitudes) might be improved in the future, which is the real purpose of assessment research.

ASSESSMENT AS SCHOLARLY ACTIVITY: USING WHAT WE LEARN

Ultimately, gaining information that we can use should be the purpose of assessment. It occasionally may be important for an individual writing center director to jump through hoops, however purposeless they may seem, at the behest of higher administration. But if our assessment work is nothing more than jumping through hoops and producing reports no one reads, then it is wasted effort. Assessment that answers interesting and important questions, as any research project ought, is assessment that matters for us and for our own work.

Moving from collection of data to actual use requires attention to two aspects of the research/assessment process: analysis of findings and implementation or "closing the loop." In grad school, we spend a lot of time thinking about how to analyze data to reach findings, not necessarily those we most would like to see but preferably those most consistent with the evidence itself. Afterward, analysis becomes a minor issue, a taken-for-granted kind of consideration, although apocryphal stories about writing programs with closets full of unread student portfolios serve as reminders that there is nothing automatic about analysis. Good analysis requires a systematic look at the information that's been collected, first, in search of data that shed light on our questions of interest and, second, in search of any additional information that could be unexpected but important and could possibly become the impetus for future study. When the data in question are in the form of words rather than numbers, finding a system for analysis and, if possible, a means of double-checking on the reliability of that analysis is all the more important.

Numerical data (from some surveys, usage records, demographics, some experimental studies, etc.) can be charted, summarized, or analyzed statistically. Open-ended data (e.g., from surveys, interviews, observations, taping) can be coded, categorized, or itemized. In some cases, qualitative data is even turned into numerical data through processes like coding, categorizing, and counting, although words and narratives have value and, like numbers, shouldn't be summarily dismissed. Whatever system of analysis is used, it's important to do more than browse through the data and pull out interesting but anecdotal examples. Furthermore, a mark of high quality assessment is clarity about methods of analysis. If a coding system was used to analyze data in search of evidence regarding goals, then that system should be documented for an assessment project, just as it would be for any other research. If the assessment was done collaboratively by writing center consultants, perhaps during a meeting, it is best to take notes on the discussion during that meeting so the linkage between goals, research questions, evidence, analysis, and potential actions is clear.

Documenting those linkages, at the least, makes it possible for a high quality report eventually to be produced. But many writing center directors find that thoughtfully developed assessment projects have implications for future practices, and it may be important in five years to remember why the decision was made to lengthen or shorten appointment times, or to change the way consultants begin or end sessions. Without records that allow us to review the data and analyses that led to changes, we are bound to keep reinventing the wheel. Finally, well-done assessment, as with any good research, has the potential to be publishable if any necessary Internal Review Board (IRB) forms (required for any study of human subjects that may eventually be published or presented) were completed in advance of the work. And, because obtaining IRB approval in advance is relatively simple once a study is thoroughly developed, there is every reason for a writing center director to do that paperwork and at least consider sharing findings when a question likely to be of common interest is being investigated.

So although the primary purpose of assessment should be to examine our work with a skeptical eye in order to more fully understand what the writing center actually accomplishes, and to determine whether it accomplishes what we think it ought, good projects can serve multiple needs. Those who have established clear goals and who carry out meaningful assessment projects on a regular basis will find that they have information readily at hand if they eventually want to make a case for more resources: There will be evidence of what gets accomplished with existing resources and the ability to speculate regarding possible improvements with more room, more open hours, and either more tutors or a different kind of tutors. There will be information at hand to use if and when an administrator eventually asks, "Is the writing center really worth that investment?" There will be information to refer to when tutors or students or directors themselves occasionally wonder if there's really much point to all the effort.

That kind of evidence-based approach to our work is the ideal. It is also becoming a necessity in time of greater cynicism about higher education. Those of us with responsibility for programs in higher education need to ask the hard questions of ourselves now, rather than waiting for outsiders to demand answers. If done thoughtfully, the results can be surprisingly worthwhile.

WORKS CITED

Alm, Mary. "How Do You Define a Successful Center?" Online posting. 13 Feb. 2004. WCenter listserv <http://lyris.acs.ttu.edu/cgi-bin/lyris.pl?enter=wcenter>.

Bell, James H. "When Hard Questions Are Asked: Evaluating Writing Centers." *The Writing Center Journal* 21.1 (2000): 7–28.

Carino, Peter, and Doug Enders. "Does Frequency of Visits to the Writing Center Increase Student Satisfaction? A Statistical Correlation Study—or Story." *The Writing Center Journal* 22.1 (2001): 83–103.

Dowdey, Diane. "How Do You Define a Successful Center?" Online posting. 16 Feb. 2004. WCenter listserv <http://lyris.acs.ttu.edu/cgi-bin/lyris.pl?enter=wcenter>.

George-Bandy, Rebecca. "How Do You Define a Successful Center?" Online posting. 13 Feb. 2004. WCenter listserv <http://lyris.acs.ttu.edu/cgi-bin/lyris.pl?enter=wcenter>.

Harris, Muriel. "How Do You Define a Successful Center?" Online posting. 16 Feb. 2004. WCenter listserv <http://lyris.acs.ttu.edu/cgi-bin/lyris.pl?enter=wcenter>.

Huba, Mary I., and Jann E. Freed. *Learner-Centered Assessment on College Campuses: Shifting the Focus from Teaching to Learning.* Needham Heights, MA: Allyn and Bacon, 2000.

Johanek, Cindy. *Composing Research: A Contextualist Paradigm for Rhetoric and Composition.* Logan: Utah State UP, 2000.

Kanter, Sandra L., Zelda F. Gamson, and Howard B. London. *Revitalizing General Education in a Time of Scarcity: A Navigational Chart for Administrators and Faculty.* Needham Heights, MA: Allyn and Bacon, 1997.

Krathwohl, David R., Benjamin S. Bloom, and Bertram B. Masia. *Taxonomy of Educational Objectives, Handbook II: Affective Domain.* New York: David McKay, 1964.

Lane, Carole. "Quantitative Measures for Evaluating Writing Centers." Online posting. 5 March 2004. WCenter Listserv <http://lyris.acs.ttu.edu/cgi-bin/lyris.pl?enter=wcenter>.

Lerner, Neal. "Choosing Beans Wisely." *Writing Lab Newsletter* 26.1 (2001): 1–5.

Lerner, Neal. "Quantitative Measures for Evaluating Writing Centre." Online posting. 4 March 2004. WCenter Listserv <http://lyris.acs.ttu.edu/cgi-bin/lyris.pl?enter=wcenter>.

Lerner, Neal. "Writing Center Assessment: Searching for the 'Proof' of Our Effectiveness." *The Center Will Hold: Critical Perspectives on Writing Center Scholarship.* Ed. Michael A. Pemberton and Joyce Kinkead. Logan: Utah State UP, 2003.

Morrison, Julie Bauer, and Jean-Paul Nadeau. "How Was Your Session at the Writing Center? Pre- and Post-Grade Student Evaluations." *The Writing Center Journal* 23.2 (2003): 25–42.

Niiler, Luke. "The Numbers Speak: A Pre-Test of Writing Center Outcomes Using Statistical Analysis." *Writing Lab Newsletter* 27.7 (2003): 6–9.

Niiler, Luke. "'The Numbers Speak' Again: A Continued Statistical Analysis of Writing Center Outcomes." *Writing Lab Newsletter* 29.6 (2005): 13–15.

Palomba, Catherine A. and Trudy W. Banta. *Assessment Essentials: Planning, Implementing, and Improving Assessment in Higher Education.* San Francisco: Jossey-Bass, 1999.

Popham, W. James. *Educational Evaluation.* 3rd ed. Needham Heights, MA, 1993.

Schuh, John H., and M. Lee Upcraft. *Assessment Practice in Student Affairs: An Applications Manual.* San Francisco: Jossey-Bass, 2001. NetLibrary E-Books. 17 Mar. 2004 <http://www.netlibrary.com/EbookDetails.aspx>.

Walvoord, Barbara E. *Assessment Clear and Simple: A Practical Guide for Institutions, Departments, and General Education.* San Francisco: Jossey-Bass, 2004.

Part II

Writing Centers and Praxis

23

Activist Strategies for Textual Multiplicity: Writing Center Leadership on Plagiarism and Authorship

Rebecca Moore Howard
Syracuse University

Tracy Hamler Carrick
Colby College

> *The Internet has made plagiarism easier than ever before. From elementary schools to the highest levels of academia, the ease of downloading and copying "untraceable" online information have led to a virtual epidemic of digital plagiarism.*
>
> —Turnitin.com

> *The trade in plagiarized university essays has become a multimillion-dollar industry that threatens the academic integrity of post-secondary education.*
>
> —Larry Johnsrude

Our epigraphs, from a Web site that sells plagiarism-detecting services and from the *Edmonton Journal*, a Canadian newspaper, illustrate contemporary discourse on plagiarism. That discourse is far from sparse; newspapers, magazines, and journals around the world are turning out articles and stories on plagiarism at high volume—as a quick Internet search or a Google news alert will reveal. Plagiarism is repeatedly described as an "epidemic"; a June 2004 BBC story was even titled "'Epidemic' of Student Cheating?" An academic conference paper presented in that same month attributes students' plagiarism to "disorganization," "information overload," "ethical lapses," "laziness," "ignorance," "fear," "cryptomnesia," and "thrill seeking" (Beasley 5–9)—all good reasons for teachers' revulsion and even terror.

The discourse on plagiarism functions as the academic equivalent of orange and red terrorist alerts, warning the academic populace of impending disaster unless stern precautionary measures are speedily taken. "The trade in plagiarized university essays has become a multimillion-dollar industry that threatens the academic integrity of post-secondary education," according to the *Edmonton Journal* (Johnsrude). Similarly, Lawrence M. Hinman, director of the Values Institute at the University of San Diego, believed that unchecked plagiarism could have "catastrophic" effects on society and especially the economy: "[T]rust is fundamental to the social, political and economic fabric of any successful society. 'Without trust in public and business institutions outside the family, an economy stops developing after a certain point,' he says" (qtd. in Hansen 780).

"Studies suggest 73 per cent of students use the Internet more than the library" (Johnsrude). An assumption behind this claim is that the very fact of students' use of the Internet signals an ethical peril. In Johnsrude's article, Maureen Engel, an English professor at Alberta, purported that "[t]he growing use of the Internet has produced an explosion of so-called 'paper mill' websites selling essays and term papers that students pass off as their own." The Internet itself is dangerous. It's hardly surprising, then, that teachers' precautionary measures are sometimes intemperate and misplaced: Just as nailclippers, for a time, were not allowed on airplanes, a few teachers are trying to prevent plagiarism by forbidding their students to use the Internet.

What gets lost in this discourse is the argument that curriculum needs to account for *multiplicity*, which Cameron McCarthy et al. described as "large-scale developments [that] are wholly transforming social and cultural life outside and inside schools around the globe." Multiplicity, they argued, is "brought about by globalization and rapid advances in electronic media, changing conceptions of self and other, and new explanatory discourses" (454). McCarthy et al. Indicated that postcolonial studies and cultural studies meet these challenges in a critical, measured temper, whereas in popular venues, the new challenges tend to be met with panic.

Although the analysis of McCarthy et al. may accurately describe postcolonial and cultural studies, it is certainly not the case that the textual multiplicity manifested in plagiaristic writing is reliably treated in the academy in a critical, measured manner. The public panic over textual multiplicity is widespread in the academy, as well:

> [T]he great task confronting educators as we move into the 21st century is to address the radical reconfiguration and cultural rearticulation now taking place in educational and social life. These developments are foregrounded and driven by the logics of globalization, the intensification of migration, the heightened effects of electronic media, the proliferation of images, and the everyday work of the imagination. (McCarthy et al. 462)

In this chapter, we two scholars of authorship—an experienced writing program administrator and a new writing center director—explore what we believe may be the most promising site for promoting a critical, constructive discourse on plagiarism in the academy. We believe that writing center directors are exceptionally well positioned to exert cross-curricular leadership on issues of plagiarism and authorship, guiding teachers and students alike toward productive, reasoned pedagogical and textual practices.

Given the hysteria that surrounds contemporary discourses of plagiarism, the task is not a small one. But it is one that the writing center can significantly contribute to by becoming involved in institutional plagiarism policy making and policy revising; collecting and disseminating cross-curricular materials for teaching students how to understand and write about sources; training peer-tutors to teach writing from sources; and establishing the writing center as a site for activist organizing.

BECOMING INVOLVED IN INSTITUTIONAL PLAGIARISM POLICY MAKING AND POLICY REVISING

In most college hierarchies, the writing center and its staff occupy relatively low status positions, which means, among other things, that they are accorded relatively little intellectual respect. In some colleges, they are regarded as the disposable literate, the people who perform a task that any literate person could perform just as well, the people who work in the writing center for lack of a better job. These are facts well established for all of composition studies by Sharon Crowley and Susan Miller and specifically for writing centers by, for example, Melissa Nicholas in her presentation at the 2003 meeting of the International Writing Centers Association.

Given this low status for writing centers and their workers, it may seem paradoxical for us to suggest that the writing center might become involved in institutional plagiarism policy making and policy revising. But Peter Carino pointed out that, because of their marginalization, writing centers enjoy an institutional freedom that results in a high rate of and tolerance for pedagogical innovation (91). Writing centers therefore have much to bring to institutional discussions of plagiarism, where cross-curricular faculty may, in the face of the current hysteria, be leaping to ban students' use of the Internet (as if that were possible); to subscribe to automated plagiarism-checking services (which the Council of Writing Program Administrators recommends against)[1]; or to attribute the perceived plagiarism epidemic to a general moral decline. Writing center directors can, despite their general marginalization in the academy and often their specific circumstances of being young and untenured, draw on and share their cultural capital. In Pierre Bourdieu's terms, the cultural capital of writing center workers is their close contact with, attention to, and knowledge of student learning processes. The writing center may lack the social capital conferred by academic departments and endowed chairs, but it has the embodied cultural capital conferred by its painstakingly acquired knowledge of student learners. When that embodied cultural capital participates in the making and revising of institutional policies on plagiarism, it becomes objectified cultural capital in which the institution may take pride.

Becoming involved in institutional decision making may be a slow, gradual process of inclusion. For writing center directors, some possible entry points might be volunteering for or being elected to various department and/or campus committees: library, information technologies, academic affairs, writing across the curriculum, judicial affairs. Writing center directors can do research on their campus to find out which committees are most strategic, most influential, most appropriate, beginning with the most accessible and working their way in. Their author-

---

[1]"Use plagiarism detection services cautiously. Although such services may be tempting, they are not always reliable. Furthermore, their availability should never be used to justify the avoidance of responsible teaching methods such as those described in this document" (Council 7).

ity as an expert on student learning, combined with liaisons with librarians, student life administrators, and the like can build strategic activism on the subject of plagiarism. Being able to cite authoritative national documents, such as the Council of Writing Program Administrators' plagiarism document, only adds to the WC director's capital.

Writing center directors can even establish themselves as the "go-to" person on plagiarism, academic integrity, and related pedagogical matters. Once their name is connected to the issue, faculty and administrators will expect them to be on relevant committees. This move can be made in several ways:

1. Volunteer to serve on the departmental or institutional board that hears plagiarism cases or reviews plagiarism policies.

2. Volunteer to make a brief presentation at new faculty orientations. They happen every year, and over time, those people will identify the WC director as "that person who cares about plagiarism"—which translates into membership on influential committees.

3. Volunteer to conduct a workshop on your school's plagiarism/academic honesty policy at new student orientations. This, too, happens every year, and people in the Student Affairs Office are often looking for faculty and staff who are willing to participate in their programming. This not only helps the WC director make important connections with colleagues, but also lifts some pedagogical burdens off of those who teach first-year composition and other gateway courses. Furthermore, incoming students will have an opportunity to be introduced to their college's policies and expectations from a single, informed individual to whom they have continued access at the writing center.[2]

4. Sponsor an academic integrity event connected to the writing center. The Texas A&M Writing Center, for example, conducted a 2004 weeklong event that brought a range of faculty and administrators into productive conversations that resulted in fresh perspectives on appropriate policy and pedagogy (see "Writing with Authority").

COLLECTING AND DISSEMINATING CROSS-CURRICULAR MATERIALS FOR TEACHING STUDENTS HOW TO UNDERSTAND AND WRITE ABOUT SOURCES

For writing center directors to exert campuswide leadership on textual multiplicity, they must necessarily turn the attention of faculty and administrators away from legislating against plagiarism and catching and punishing plagiarists—the remedies that contemporary hysteria naturally engenders. Instead, the WC director can guide faculty to consider proactive matters of pedagogy. This approach comports with what George Hillocks said about pedagogy in general: Instructors who are pessimistic about their students tend to enact top-down pedagogy that demands formulaic compliance from students, and when an assignment or classroom activity

---

[2]The use of the word "volunteer" in points one through three cannot be ignored because it raises concerns about just labor practices. We recognize that many writing center directors hold untenured faculty or staff positions and participation on college and university committees may not be recognized by traditional promotion and tenure structures. Yet, excluding writing center directors from such committees, by choice or institutional design, may further instantiate the marginalized status of their positions, scholarship, and expertise. Writing center directors should carefully consider their personal and local contexts before choosing to volunteer themselves in the ways we have suggested.

goes awry, these pessimistic instructors blame the students (60–62). Nowhere is Hillocks's claim about pessimistic teachers more eloquently illustrated than in academic responses to plagiarism hysteria: In these circumstances, the blame is reliably placed on the students themselves. Binaries dominate here; the only alternative, so goes the thinking, is that teachers are "to blame" for plagiarism.

What gets left out is the possibility that teachers are not the cause but the solution to plagiarism. Here the writing center director can guide faculty to optimistic attitudes toward their students. Hillocks described one such teacher, whose students did poorly on an assignment; the instructor decided that "his assignment was a bad one," and he revised it (61).

Some very pessimistic instructors do believe that teachers can be the solution to plagiarism—by preventing it in "plagiarism-proof" assignments. We would not criticize such responses, but we would suggest that they are insufficient. A much more positive approach is for instructors to figure out what students need to know in order to do the assignment well, or what Hillocks called a focus on "procedural knowledge." The rationale for this approach is that if students are well-prepared to do an assignment, only the most dedicated serial cheaters will nevertheless plagiarize. The others—those who don't understand that they are plagiarizing and those who, under pressure, succumb to temptation—will complete the assignment under their own steam. The writing center director who wants to encourage such pedagogy might pursue one or more of the following:

1. Compile and circulate materials (e.g., plagiarism statements, handouts and worksheets on working with sources, and assignment sequences that build procedural knowledge) from faculty across the disciplines. These faculty may not think of their materials in terms of plagiarism, but the writing center director may recognize the ways in which the materials prepare students to complete their work with academic integrity. Such materials may include, for example, research assignments that incorporate search strategies and a preliminary annotated bibliography.

2. Collect materials from other writing centers (often available online) or from published sources that respond to student needs and faculty expectations, and turn these into handouts that are available at the WC or its Web site. Sources such as the CBB *Plagiarism Resource Site*, the WSU *Plagiarism Information Site*, Carrick and Howard's *Authorship in Composition Studies*, or Harris's *Plagiarism Handbook* may prove useful. Better still, compose materials that respond to localized needs and make them available to both faculty and students. Whereas such materials are naturally helpful references for staff and the students who frequent the writing center, they may have an even greater impact as they circulate into the hands of faculty across campus. In many writing centers, faculty drop by and pick up handouts as often as students do. Thus, writing center materials on plagiarism are informing classroom pedagogy, if only because faculty hand them out to students in their courses.

Although creating, maintaining, and distributing this collection of materials can feel a bit burdensome, especially because so many resources are already available to colleagues, the task of collecting and producing locally inspired handouts can bring numerous rewards. First, encouraging or even requiring writing center staff to create or revise materials ensures constant and detail-oriented discussions about conventions and best practices. Whereas the expert knowledge that passes between staff and students is indeed palpable, such moments can lack the precision and thoughtfulness attached to the production of written documents that circulate beyond the time and space of a single tutorial. Second, designing handouts that reference particular writing intensive courses, draw from commonly used texts, and use local examples reflect the writing center's relationship with the campus community. And, as more members of the campus community see themselves positively reflected in writing center materials, the more they will look to the writing center as a trusted and valued resource on issues related to writing and authorship.

3. Lead workshops for faculty on teaching students how to understand and write about sources, or on designing effective writing assignments that make it less likely for students to consider plagiarism. Encourage teachers to devise nontraditional nonformulaic assignments that take advantage of local resources: They might work with the Special Collections Librarian or the local or college museum curator to identify relevant archival texts or collections of art. Or they might look elsewhere for the unexpected (e.g., lesser known works by canonical authors, texts by marginalized authors, and/or contemporary texts) as they design assignments that call for students' critical reasoning.

TRAINING PEER-TUTORS TO TEACH WRITING FROM SOURCES

Why … are writing center tutors *not* supposed to write on students' papers yet the students' teachers *are* supposed to write on them? If teachers are allowed to write on students' papers, why do we say students should "own" their papers? Why are writing centers worried about "appropriating" students' texts when assignments require "appropriate" genres, "appropriate" citation styles, and "appropriate" supporting material? Why is the "best" writing center approach considered nondirective, especially when students come to writing centers seeking explicit advice? Why is collaboration such a buzz-word and plagiarism such a serious offense? Why is it often so rewarding to work with students in the writing center and so frustrating to deal with expectations of what writing centers should do? Why is writing center pedagogy called collaborative if its purpose is individualized instruction? (Grimm 5)

To train peer-tutors to teach writing from sources is to enter the academic minefield. One should enter it only if equipped with a map that shows the mines' locations. A desire to stay out of the minefield has contributed to *nondirective tutoring*, in which the tutor acts as muse, drawing forth hidden knowledge from within the writer. Linda Shamoon and Deborah H. Burns, Irene L. Clark, Irene L. Clark and Dave Healy, and Cynthia Haynes-Burton pursued the alternative possibilities of *interventionist tutoring*, in which the tutor acts in collaboration with the writer.

Each writing center must determine the balance between nondirective and interventionist tutoring by taking local circumstances into careful consideration. One size does not fit all. Even in nondirective tutoring, peer-tutors can contribute to the writing center's campus leadership on plagiarism and authorship. For example, peer-tutors might, using the center's hardcopy or online archive of handouts and teaching materials, develop workshops for students that define plagiarism, discuss school policies, and teach students to work effectively with sources. Such discussions need to occur throughout a student's college career; they cannot begin and end in the first-year composition course. General or discipline-specific workshops (by writing center staff or co-taught with interdisciplinary faculty) can keep the conversation and learning going. The Syracuse University Writing Center has for many years led successful small and large group workshops, generalized and discipline specific, for students on a variety of topics (see "About the Writing Center"). At Colby College, the Farnham Writers' Center is working with librarians and faculty to develop a two-credit, nongraded course called "The Writing Workshop," which offers twelve one-hour workshops (students must attend at least eight for course credit) on a variety of writing issues, including plagiarism and academic honesty, working with sources, and incorporating source materials.

But pedagogical interventions such as these must be foregrounded with explicit pedagogical training for tutors. How well are tutors prepared to direct students to compose engaged research-based essays? How well are tutors prepared to teach students how to work with sources? At many institutions, WC administrators assume that peer-tutors know how to teach others to write from sources because they have demonstrated that they can do it themselves—often with considerable grace and skill. That they can produce competent research-based writing is a good indication that they know how to work with sources, but is not necessarily proof that they can effectively teach others to do the same. Tutors must be trained to teach others. At Colby College, students enrolled in the peer-tutor training course may opt to research and design a handout as part of their final writing assignment, a practice that can, incidentally, effectively build up the writing center's archive of materials. But this assignment also challenges novice tutors to critically reflect on their encounters with others (faculty, students, each other); to identify specific, recurring writing and research challenges (i.e., selecting strong passages from sources or deciding when to paraphrase or when to quote); and to create logical ways to introduce and explain concepts to others clearly and concisely. Composing handouts or minilesson plans, however useful and practical for writing centers, functions more importantly as a way for novice tutors to rehearse their pedagogical voices.

It is also important for novice and experienced tutors to learn how to approach their work with flexibility. Although reference materials are instructive and handy, they may also obscure the real challenges writers experience as their deadlines approach, especially those challenges faced by students who must adapt their writing processes for different faculty and disciplines. At Colby College, faculty members across the disciplines attend writing center staff meetings to discuss their concerns, policies, pedagogical practices, or the citation conventions of their disciplines. They might bring copies of writing assignments, guidelines for writing in their courses, or sample papers to discuss with WC staff. WC staff members might also seek out time-constrained faculty across campus, interviewing them and collecting relevant materials. Staff can report on their meetings, and notes (perhaps represented in a standardized format) on these interactions can be included in an archive of handouts and reference materials for staff and students to consult.

ESTABLISHING THE WRITING CENTER AS A SITE FOR ACTIVIST ORGANIZING

Standards of academic integrity, just as much as standards of grammatical correctness, serve as gatekeeping mechanisms for a hierarchical academy. Stephen Parks composed a history of curricular activism in English studies, which focuses on challenging and providing alternatives to grammatical instruction and testing for the purposes of academic gatekeeping. A history of curricular activism focused on encouraging pedagogy that enables students to meet textual standards (and that rewrites those textual standards so that they account for and embrace the textual multiplicity of new and more diverse media, rather than trying to contain that multiplicity within standards that were developed in a patriarchal, White supremacist, print-exclusive age) has yet to be written. The history cannot yet be written, because the curricular activism has so far been confined to individual agents (see, e.g., Haynes-Burton; Howard; and Price), and it has been met with strident resistance (see, e.g., Carlson and Goldberg).[3]

We believe that when the history of curricular activism on textual standards is written, writing centers will play a prominent role. The plagiarism statement of the Council of Writing Program Administrators provides a starting place for widespread activism, and writing centers provide potentially empowering sites for such organizing because of their institutional location and their close proximity to student and textual bodies. Plagiarism and academic honesty policies are all too often construed by students as policing structures, probably because students themselves have little to do with composing them and adjudicating them. Finding a safe space for students and faculty to work together can be problematic. But the writing center can be a remarkably neutral space, and can accordingly serve as a more welcoming meeting ground than, say, a library, an administrative conference room, or even a classroom, especially if the writing center is staffed by peer-tutors who will likely be regarded as student allies and voices of the student body.

The previous discussions have offered some strategic ways for writing centers to secure power on college and university campuses. But the sort of power described above is derived primarily through the writing center directors' ability to identify, understand, and respond to the urgently felt needs of their communities, students, and faculty who are likely reacting to the gatekeeping functions of academic integrity standards. Indeed, writing center directors should respond to these needs, and they must work to transform the reactionary, punitive language of plagiarism policies into pedagogical action through rigorous and optimistic intervention. Their most important activist role, however, may be their ability to facilitate dialogue across hierarchies of power and to organize efforts to understand the shifting politics of textual production and the changing dynamics and uses of writing. By bringing diverse members of the campus community into contact with each other and by facilitating productive encounters with others, writing center directors can help to locate current conversations about plagiarism within the broader context of textual multiplicity. Some ways to begin this process may be offering forums for students to speak out about their fears, struggles, successes, and concerns about plagiarism, authorship, and their instructional needs; for faculty and administrative staff to speak out about their own fears, struggles, successes, and concerns about writing and the teaching and policing of student writers; and that bring students, faculty, and staff together to listen to and to learn from and with each other.

Although each representative group should have opportunities to reflect on their experiences independent of each other, real ideological or institutional change will not occur if members of these groups are not communicating with each other. Writing center directors might import methods used in popular education, a plausible model that blurs distinctions between pedagogy

---

[3]The "Students' Right" document, the keystone of curricular activism on grammatical gatekeeping, also met with media resistance; see, for example, Sheils. There is, however, an important difference: Whereas the media resistance to curricular activism on grammatical gatekeeping was directed at NCTE, the *organization* endorsing that activism, the media resistance to the nascent curricular activism on textual standards is directed at isolated individuals, who become fetishized stand-ins for an entire discipline.

and social change and promotes critical thinking and empowerment (see Bernard). The learning circle technique, developed by the Highlander Research and Education Center (see Carrick, chap. 4), might be especially useful. Implicit to its design is the patient and unfolding process of listening (rather than speaking) and storytelling (rather than claims or platitudes), and participants are challenged to consider what is rendered visible and invisible within current institutional policies and practices. Writing center directors who facilitate these structured encounters might direct participants to focus on diversity: the multiple ways in which students are prepared for college-level and/or discipline-specific writing; the multiple ways that different communities work (across time and space) with the words and ideas of others; or the multiple ways that faculty and students have experienced changes in textual production because of technology. Such conversations can take remarkably candid, interesting, productive, and encouraging turns, especially when they become opportunities for coalition building.

In our age of new media and textual multiplicity, the ways in which writers work with sources are constantly changing. Thus, it is empowering for students to know that faculty and staff share or have shared in some of their struggles, and that they can participate in evolving conversations and perhaps even in college policy making (see Price). Similarly, faculty and staff can discover unexpected things about students (e.g., their histories of authorship, or what they experience as they research and compose papers) and are moved to use their institutional power to work with students for change.

We hope that writing center directors will help their institutions come to more nuanced understandings of writing from sources, plagiarism, patchwriting, and the limitations of plagiarism-checking software. At a time when pessimistic stances toward students are being adopted in response to media-fueled plagiarism hysteria, countermeasures must be taken to protect pedagogy. The leadership that we advocate for writing center workers is leadership in what we are calling *textual multiplicity*—the transformations and proliferations of text in the age of new media. Leadership in textual multiplicity will sponsor conversations of the sort that Shamoon and Burns described, conversations "that may start by being about plagiarism but will end up being about authorship, about the sources of ideas, about disciplinary life (and lives) (192)." We would like to conclude our chapter by appropriating Shamoon and Burns's optimistic concluding sentence: "From such conversations come the potential to move the writing center off the margins of the university and into the center of academic life" (192).

WORKS CITED

"About the Writing Center." *The Writing Center*. Syracuse University, 9 January 2004. 6 August 2004 <http://wrt.syr.edu/wc/wcintro.html>.

Beasley, James D. "The Impact of Technology on Plagiarism Prevention and Detection: Research Process Automation, a New Approach for Prevention." Plagiarism: Prevention, Practice and Policies conference. Northumbria University. Newcastle Upon Tyne, UK. 29 June 2004. 6 August 2004 <http://ww.powerresearcher.com/download/plagiarism _tech_ impact .pdf>.

Bernard, Elaine. "Popular Education: Training Rebels with a Cause." *Teaching for Change: Popular Education and the Labor Movement*. Ed. Linda Delp, Miranda Outman-Kramer, Susan J. Schurman, and Kent Wong. Los Angeles, CA: UCLA Center for Labor Research and Education, 2002. 6–8.

Bourdieu, Pierre. "The Forms of Capital." *Soziale Ungleichheiten*. Ed. Reinhard Kreckel. Goettingen: Otto Schartz, 1983. 183–98. Rpt. *Handbook of Theory and Research for the Sociology of Education*. Ed. John G. Richardson. Trans. Richard Nice. New York: Greenwood P, 1986. 241–60.

Carlson, Tucker. "That's Outrageous: Reading, Cheating, and 'Rithmetic.'" *Reader's Digest* 161.963 (July 2002): 39–42.

Carrick, Tracy Hamler. "(A) Just Literacy." Diss. Syracuse University, 2003.

Carrick, Tracy Hamler, and Rebecca Moore Howard. *Authorship in Composition Studies*. Boston: Wadsworth, 2006.

Carino, Peter. "Reading Our Own Words: Rhetorical Analysis and the Institutional Discourse of Writing Centers." *Writing Center Research: Extending the Conversation*. Ed. Paula Gillespie, Alice Gillam, Lady Falls Brown, and Byron Stay. Mahwah, NJ: Lawrence Erlbaum Associates, 2002. 91–110.

CBB Plagiarism Resource Site. Colby, Bates, and Bowdoin Colleges, n.d. 6 August 2004 <http://leeds.bates.edu/cbb/>.

Clark, Irene Lurkis. "Collaboration and Ethics in Writing Center Pedagogy." *The Writing Center Journal* 9.1 (Fall/Winter 1988): 3–12.

Clark, Irene L., and Dave Healy. "Are Writing Centers Ethical?" *WPA: Writing Program Administration* 20.1–2 (Fall/Winter 1996): 32–48.

Council of Writing Program Administrators. "Defining and Avoiding Plagiarism: WPA Statement on Best Policies." Council of Writing Program Administrators, January 2003. <http://www.ilstu.edu/~ddhesse/wpa/>.

Crowley, Sharon. *Composition in the University: Historical and Polemical Essays*. Pittsburgh: U Pittsburgh P, 1998.

"'Epidemic' of Student Cheating?" *BBC News* 30 June 2004. 30 June 2004 <http://news.bbc.co.uk/2/hi/uk_news/education/3854465.stm>.

Goldberg, Jonah. "Plagiarism Is Rape?" *National Review Online*. 15 March 2000. 13 March 2003 <http://www.nationalreview.com/goldberg/goldberg031500.html>.

Grimm, Nancy Maloney. *Good Intentions: Writing Center Work for Postmodern Times*. Portsmouth, NH: Heinemann-Boynton/Cook, 1999.

Hansen, Brian. "Combating Plagiarism: The Issues." *CQ Researcher* 13.32 (19 September 2003): 775–96.

Harris, Robert A. *The Plagiarism Handbook: Strategies for Preventing, Detecting, and Dealing with Plagiarism*. Los Angeles: Pyrczak, 2001.

Haynes-Burton, Cynthia. "Intellectual (Proper)ty in Writing Centers: Retro Texts and Positive Plagiarism." *Writing Center Perspectives*. Ed. Byron L. Stay, Christina Murphy, and Eric H. Hobson. NWCA P, 1995. 84–93.

Hillocks, George, Jr. *Ways of Thinking, Ways of Teaching*. New York: Teacher's College P, 1999.

Howard, Rebecca Moore. "Forget about Policing Plagiarism; Just *Teach*." *The Chronicle of Higher Education* (16 November 2001): B24. Available online. <http://leeds.bates.edu/cbb/events/docs/Howard_ForgeT.pdf >.

Johnsrude, Larry. "Paper Trail Leads Profs to Internet." *Edmonton (Canada) Journal* 30 January 2004. <http://www.canada.com/edmonton/edmontonjournal/story.asp?id=642F6226-0726-40B0-A367-0A35C7DA9AA7 >.

McCarthy, Cameron, Michael D. Giardina, Susan Juanita Harewood, and Jin-Kyung Park. "Contesting Culture: Identity and Curriculum Dilemmas in the Age of Globalization, Postcolonialism, and Multiplicity." *Harvard Educational Review* 73.3 (Fall 2003): 449–65.

Miller, Susan. *Textual Carnivals: The Politics of Composition*. Carbondale: Southern Illinois UP, 1991.

Nicholas, Melissa. "Does Composition Studies Need Writing Centers for Legitimization?" International Writing Centers Association. Hershey, Pennsylvania, 24 Oct. 2003.

Parks, Stephen. *Class Politics: The Movement for the Students' Right to Their Own Language*. Urbana, IL: National Council of Teachers of English, 2000.

Price, Margaret. "Beyond 'Gotcha!': Situating Plagiarism in Policy and Pedagogy." *College Composition and Communication* 54.1 (September 2002): 88–115.

Shamoon, Linda, and Deborah H. Burns. "Plagiarism, Rhetorical Theory, and the Writing Center: New Approaches, New Locations." *Perspectives on Plagiarism and Intellectual Property in a Postmodern World*. Ed. Alice Roy and Lise Buranen. Albany, NY: SUNY P, 1999. 183–94.

Sheils, Merrill. "Why Johnny Can't Write." *Newsweek* (8 December 1975): 58–65.

"Students' Right to Their Own Language." *College Composition and Communication* 25.3 (1974): 1–32. <http://www.ncte.org/about/over/positions/category/lang/107502.htm>.

Turnitin.com. "Plagiarism Prevention." n.d. 7 February 2004 <http://www.turnitin.com/static/products_services/plagiarism_prevention.html>.

"Writing with Authority: Academic and Professional Integrity Week, 2004." University Writing Center, Texas A&M University, [2004]. 6 August 2004 <http://uwc.tamu.edu/Events/Integrity/index.html>.

WSU Plagiarism Information Site. Washington State University, 16 January 2004. 6 August 2004 <http://www.wsulibs.wsu.edu/electric/trainingmods/plagiarism_test/main.html>.

Critique or Conformity?:
Ethics and Advocacy
in the Writing Center

Michael A. Pemberton
Georgia Southern University

The title of this chapter, "Critique or Conformity?," highlights a curious binary opposition that is sometimes used to describe the politics of writing center conferencing. Should we, as tutors or writing center directors, buy into the academic system and support its goals or should we be doing our best to critique that system in conferences and teach students the strategies they need to be effective social, political, and institutional critics as well?

Yes, the question is reductive; yes, it presupposes that these are the only choices available and thus presents a false dilemma, but it also frames an interesting debate that has been taking place for some time in some parts of our field. Although the question is simple, and some might say simplistic, the ideas and principles behind it are anything but simple. To answer this question for ourselves—even if we choose to reject its either/or structure and navigate some middle course—we must interrogate our personal politics, our theoretical beliefs, our systems of value, and our philosophies of teaching. The question touches on issues of power and authority, language use, and social goals. The issues involved are extremely complex and, ultimately, deeply rooted in our sense of who we are and what we think teaching (and tutoring) is all about. In many ways, I believe this question touches at the heart of the ethics of what we do in writing centers.

What do we think we're doing in writing conferences? Are we just helping students with their papers so they'll learn to be better writers? Or are we also doing something else—modeling and thereby implicitly teaching students to respect a vast collection of academic, institutional, and social values that may, in fact, be oppressive in a variety of ways? What are our politics? How do we project our values and our politics to others, either explicitly or implicitly, in conferences? Is it possible for us to treat the writing center as a politically neutral space? And if it is not, then what are the consequences for our tutoring?

STUCK IN THE MIDDLE WITH ME

These questions may sound pretty far removed from the day-to-day practical and sometimes grueling work of sitting down with a student to figure out where the heck a paper's thesis statement is or giving a two-minute, impromptu lesson on comma splices. But these are not tangential questions only peripherally related to our work in the writing center; they are, I believe, at the core of what we do, both as tutors and as writing center directors. In both of these roles, we work closely with students, helping them, as best we can, to become better writers and presumably better thinkers by sharing with them our perspectives, our modes of analysis, and our experience with the business of writing academic papers. We do this based on what has worked for us in the past—our processes, our strategies, our rhetorical techniques, our analyses of assignments, and our understanding of the expectations held by academic audiences. We give brief lessons in "proper" and "effective" ways to analyze writing tasks and similarly proper and effective ways to produce and present written texts. Our assessments of what is "proper" and "effective," of course, are shaped in large measure by what we think academia, or a discipline, or our institution will see as proper and effective, and in that way—among others—we support and advance its goals.

We are part of the system, and students see us that way. We are employed by our institutions in support of curricular and institutional goals. We give our tacit approval to those goals when we help students fulfill them. For many of us, this may not be a problem; we generally accept social and cultural assumptions about the value of education and the utility of conforming to certain norms in order to participate fully in a profession, a perspective that Molly Wingate articulated (albeit with some reservations) in her article on "Writing Centers as Sites of Academic Culture." For many others, however, this tacit support may be an ethical problem. Perhaps there are some aspects of academic writing and its embedded assumptions of value of which we don't approve. Perhaps we see academic language as artificial and exclusionary; perhaps we believe it reproduces cultural stereotypes of race, class, and gender; perhaps we react against the meaningless or formulaic assignments students are asked to complete in their pursuit of a degree. Perhaps we think it is more important to use our tutorials to promote the social and cognitive goals we do believe in, despite the pressures we may feel from the academy (and quite possibly the students we see) to do otherwise. Nancy Maloney Grimm expressed this point of view quite cogently in *Good Intentions: Writing Center Work for Postmodern Times.*

I have to admit that my own position in this regard is seriously conflicted. On the one hand, I'm a confirmed, die-hard, yellow-dog Democrat, leaning strongly to the left on most social issues. I enjoy vilifying right-wing troglodytes and am morally outraged by the simple-minded use of the term *political correctness* to characterize genuinely well-meaning, philosophically sound, and sincerely believed efforts to make our society, our institutions, our teaching, and our language more inclusive. On the other hand, I have to admit that I really do cringe at the thought of transforming these beliefs into explicit action and advocacy in the writing center or in a classroom environment; I can't help but feel that doing so presents a potential ethical *problem* rather than an ethical *responsibility*.

John Ruszkiewicz, a self-avowed conservative at the University of Texas, expressed a similar sense of unease:

> [W]hat then stopped me then cold was a question I realized I'd never bothered to ask myself, though I remember Stephen M. North wrestling with something like it in 1991: Why don't I want to teach politics in my writing classes? Surrounded by colleagues from graduate students to senior faculty energized by their progressive pedagogies and committed to a profession that has invented rationales for classroom advocacy for more than a decade, why don't I feel the same tug my colleagues do to use writing courses to change the world? (24)

I suspect that part of the problem, for me, can be traced to a fundamental distrust of "true believers," to borrow Eric Hoffer's term, on both sides of the political spectrum—people who are just a little too prone to believe that the abstract ends (be they "social justice," "family values," or "a democratic society") justify the means. When I read statements like the following, for example, my hackles begin to rise almost involuntarily:

> [E]quality and democracy are not transcendent values that inevitably emerge when one learns to seek the truth through critical thinking. Rather, if those are the desired values, the teacher must recognize that he or she must influence (perhaps manipulate is the more accurate word) students' values through charisma or power—he or she must accept the role as manipulator. Therefore it is of course reasonable to try to inculcate into our students the conviction that the dominant order is repressive. (Paine 564)

> We must help our students ... to engage in a rhetorical process that can collectively generate ... knowledge and beliefs to displace the repressive ideologies an unjust social order would prescribe.... I suggest that we must be forthright in avowing the ideologies that motivate our teaching and research. For instance, James Berlin ... and his colleagues might openly exert their authority as teachers to try to persuade students to agree with their values instead of pretending that they are merely investigating the nature of sexism and capitalism and leaving students to draw their own conclusions. (Bizzell 670)

I don't particularly care to affiliate myself with either of these positions. Manipulating students through the exercise of charisma, power, or authority is hardly in keeping with my goal of making them active critical thinkers. Still, it must be admitted that in some measure, none of us—myself included—can avoid testifying to our politics every time we respond to student papers, whether in the classroom or in a writing center conference. In cases where students bring in papers about controversial or other political issues, for example, we must, as good readers, engage the content as we frame the questions we plan to ask. But even with papers that are not so clearly immersed in political issues, our complicity in teaching academic and disciplinary norms, as I said before, might be considered a kind of political statement. But is teaching students about disciplinary norms and how to use them the same thing as promoting or advocating them?

TWO MODELS FOR CULTURAL CRITIQUE

I don't believe it is, and this realization helped me to understand my own position as tutor and director a bit better. Part of my dilemma, I discovered, was that I was having a hard time clarifying the central ethical issues of tutorial politics, not just because these issues are inherently complex, but because there are at least two distinctly different rationales for critical teaching—that is, teaching that works to discern and critique the sociocultural assumptions embedded in language and institutions. One of these rationales is explicitly political, grounded in the work of social critics such as Marx, Freire, Foucault, and others, advocating the development of "critical consciousness" among those who have been oppressed by a hierarchical social order and encouraging them to resist that order in the name of a presumably more equitable social system. This is sometimes referred to as the "critical liberatory" or "social justice" position. The other rationale for critical teaching is equally invested in critique as tool for writing and learning, but it is distinctly less political in its aims and more explicitly grounded in postmodernist perspectives and recent work in discourse studies. It investigates the way our interpretations of "texts" (be they written products or visual images) are affected by socially generated assumptions of value and utility, and it calls into question the rationalist belief in a stable, coherent self that exists apart from these social assumptions and influences. This is the "cultural studies" approach, and it uses critical inquiry as an investigative tool that leads people to reflect on social influences and social ends, but does not necessarily direct them to a predetermined result. I think the social and political implications of cultural studies—as they have interpreted by a variety of authors—are what often cause them to be confused with critical liberatory approaches, but I do not believe the two are equivalent or that one necessarily implies the other.

And this, I think, forms the crux of my own stance toward social and cultural critique in the writing center and political advocacy issues in general. I align myself more closely with postmodernist views, which presume that the construction of self and social identity is an ongoing process with a diverse assortment of possible and even desirable ends. I recognize the presence of conflicting voices in my own discourse, I perceive many of the ways in which social and cultural relations of power impact my daily life in both obvious and subtle ways, and I can appreciate the efforts of cultural studies to analyze many of the social and cultural assumptions that are constructed by institutions and artifacts of our popular culture. I do not, however, believe that there is a single framework for engaging in cultural critique or interpreting the results of cultural critique, and I do not believe that such critiques necessarily lead to a particular kind of enlightenment or a particular vision of resistance. It is my very awareness of the presence of multiple voices and multiple discourses that prevents me from being too quick to dismiss voices that do not conform to my own comfortable worldview. I feel an ethical responsibility to give the students I see in the writing center the same opportunity for critique and the same freedom to interpret that I enjoy, even if the results of that critique are at variance with my own.

Let me make one point explicitly clear here. I am not arguing that teachers or tutors who adopt critical liberatory approaches are unethical or do not have the best interests of their students at heart. Quite the contrary, they are doing their best to make their teaching conform as closely as possible to their personal values and they do so in pursuit of social goals that are noble and laudable. They may engage in this sort of teaching at great risk, realizing that their students, their colleagues, and their institutions may not share their values and may actually see their goals as a kind of threat. (Which, in fact, they are in many ways.) The more moderate position I'm expressing here is that my ethics and my goals for writing instruction reflect a different vision of desirable outcomes and student empowerment.

CULTURAL CRITIQUE, DISCIPLINARY NORMS, AND TIME MANAGEMENT

So, if we put aside liberatory pedagogies for the moment and look at writing center tutoring from a cultural studies perspective, what exactly does that mean for us and our ethics? What exactly does it mean to have a "cultural studies" writing center? What should we be doing in conferences? How might it change the way we work with students in tutorials? And how might a cultural studies approach work with or against other agendas for the writing center, agendas constructed by students, by institutions, or even by theories of the writing process?

There are no easy or simple answers to these questions, and most published work is either couched in abstractions about "what we should be doing" without any clear guidelines for change or devoted to single case studies that are not, in my experience, typical of most conferences. Nancy Welch, for example, in "From Silence to Noise: The Writing Center as Critical Exile," talked about her work with a student named Margie who, in Welch's words, "sought to write about her experience with workplace sexual harassment but who also struggled as she wrote with competing off-stage voices" (5). Welch discussed the nature of these voices at some length, invoking the work of Bakhtin and Julia Kristeva to make a case for the writing center as a place where tutors can "become strangers to, rather than representatives of, the social conversations and conventions students are struggling to locate themselves within" (5). Margie, the student being written about, had many writing tasks ahead of her related to an Equal Employment Opportunity Commission (EEOC) harassment suit and an appearance on a conference panel, but there was apparently an extensive amount of time available for exploring ideas, resolving the conflicting voices, keeping a writer's log, working with the same tutor in multiple meetings, and ultimately producing these texts.

This is laudable, important work, but it seems quite far removed from the realities of writing center work as I and most other writing center directors experience them. In most writing centers, I suspect, tutors typically see students once, not many times, during the course of the semester. They generally see students a few days, not several weeks or months, before their writing is due. They usually see students with first or second drafts already completed, not when they're primed to explore ideas. The students' goals are frequently tied to getting a good grade, figuring out convenient ways to get finished with one paper before moving on to the next one, and learning how to frame their arguments in ways their professors will accept, not discovering how their "subject positions" are constructed from the interplay of multiple voices in a social context.

I don't think we can ignore these realities. Time is short in writing center conferences, and our encounters with students are often fleeting. Students, for better or worse, have their own reasons for coming to the writing center, and as naïve or culturally determined or institutionally driven as those reasons might be, I think we have an ethical responsibility to respect them and work with them. That does not mean automatically acquiescing to what students want from us in a writing conference—or what a faculty member or an institution wants, for that matter—but it does mean that we cannot discount or ignore the goals that the students value merely because they do not mesh fully with some of our own.

For instance, I have no problem with teaching writers about disciplinary norms—so far as I know them and can explain them—even though I know that those norms are malleable and fluctuating, because I believe that a familiarity with those norms empowers writers as writers and as future professionals. That's an ethical goal I support, but I try not to lapse into absolutes. I'm honest about the organic nature of these norms; I've read enough Thomas Kuhn to know how paradigms shift and enough Bakhtin and Bazerman and Bartholomae to know about the transient nature of discourse communities, but very little of that makes any difference to the uncertain and concerned political science major sitting at my desk in the writing center, trying to figure out how to keep from bombing on another lit paper. He wants to know how to sound like an English major. He wants to know what he calls "the stuff lit professors are looking for in papers" and what we would call socially constructed knowledge structures that are reproduced in written texts through the replication of disciplinary norms. I would feel unethical myself if I were to withhold what I know about discipline-specific conventions and instead turned the conference to a discourse critique.

But this is not to say that there isn't an important time and place for such critical inquiry. Anis Bawarshi and Stephanie Pelkowski made a strong case for the importance of discourse critique with basic writers, many of whom may not understand how or why they are expected to abandon their home discourses for academic prose.[1] Consider, also, the tutorial conference described by Alice Gillam in "Writing Center Ecology: A Bakhtinian Perspective." Gillam described the dilemma faced by the tutor who "feels pulled between [a student's] mesmerizing narrative voice and the teacher's expectation for focus and unity of theme" (5). Although wanting to help the student explore her narrative voice in her essay, the tutor nevertheless feels bound by the pressure to "normalize" the student's discourse in a way that will render it acceptable to the academy. Because one of the student's goals is to succeed academically, the tutor feels she has no choice but to give in to the normalizing impulse. Gillam characterized this result as unfortunate, and to a certain extent I agree with her.

She described the encounter as an example of two destabilizing influences on writing center conferences: *centripetal* (or inwardly directed) directed forces that promote the authoritative discourse of the academy through the influence of grammatical rules, discourse conventions, and textbook prescriptions, and *centrifugal* forces that "destabilize language through multiple meanings, varying contexts and the free play of dialects" (4). She did not see this tension as necessarily counterproductive, however. In fact, she found it to be a useful stimulus for engaging in a kind of Bakhtinian dialogue that can help to clarify meaning for the student. It seems to me that early in the writing process there is every reason to destabilize meaning, to allow for the free play of narrative voice, and to question the limitations of the "normalizing impulse." This is exactly the point at which we should be challenging students and helping both them and their writing to go beyond the merely conventional. But, later in the process, we should be working with students to manage meaning and expression, to help them decide on appropriate and useful forms—possibly within the boundaries of disciplinary norms, possibly not.

ALREADY USEFUL KNOWLEDGE

One of the most interesting and provocative pieces about writing centers in recent years is Marilyn Cooper's "Really Useful Knowledge: A Cultural Studies Agenda for Writing Centers."

---

[1]Bawarshi and Pelkowski described the effort to impose academic discourse conventions without critique or explanation as "colonialist," "imperialist," and "hegemonic" (45–46).

She described, from a cultural studies perspective, her vision of what a writing center should really be about and what it should be doing with students in conferences. Borrowing from Lester Faigley and Andrea Lunsford, Cooper began by critiquing the "rationalist" and the expressivist (or Romantic) positions on language and the self. She characterized them as traditions that postulate a "coherent and rational self" that achieve agency by "subduing the text to the self by achieving personal control over it" (101). In contrast to this position, Cooper offered a more clearly postmodern view that maintains that we can only use language to construct brief snapshots of our "selves," imperfectly captured. Our selves are in a constant process of construction, and language use is one of the most prominent activities in enabling that construction. According to this perspective, then, "[a]gency in writing depends not on owning or taking responsibility for a text but on understanding how to construct subject positions in texts" (101).

She recommended that writing center tutors become "organic intellectuals," a term she borrowed from Antonio Gramsci, or agents of change who are perfectly positioned to engage in critique because of their marginal status within the university. Because they are removed from the traditional writing classroom, which, Cooper claimed cannot help but reinforce the institutional structures of the dominant White, middle-class social group, writing center tutors are better able to connect theory with practice and "develop really useful knowledge of writing practices and of ways of teaching writing that help students achieve agency" (106).

I have to admit, the first time I read this article, I found Cooper's dismissal of expressive and rationalist perspectives too facile and her conclusions about what constitutes "useful knowledge" and effective writing center tutoring strategies impractical and seemingly unaware of the day-to-day exigencies of tutoring in most writing centers. In some ways, I saw Cooper engaging in exactly the kind of traditional intellectualism she decried in her article, proclaiming the values of the dominant paradigm in composition studies (cultural studies/social construction) without making any significant attempt to connect theory to actual practice in the writing center.

As I've read and reread this article, however, I think I've come to a new understanding. Although I continue to have problems with Cooper's depiction of "agency" and her assertion that writers have no theoretical basis for claiming ownership of their texts, I find now that much of what she recommended—once you make your way through the rhetoric—is actually pretty good advice. In fact, I would say it is such good advice that writing center tutors have been putting it into practice for years without even knowing that they were fulfilling a cultural studies agenda by doing so.

Consider the following quote from her article:

> [I]f tutors need to help students—and themselves—realize that what they know about institutional constraints is true and important, they also need to help students understand that if they are to achieve agency in writing, they must learn how to challenge these constraints productively in the service of their own goals and needs. Agency in writing is not a matter of simply taking up the subject positions offered by assignments but of actively constructing subject positions that negotiate between institutional demands and individual needs. (102)

In essence, Cooper seemed to be saying that writing centers should help students find ways to write their papers that draw from their own knowledge and interests and goals, and still satisfy the requirements of the assignment. And, of course, this is what writing centers have always done.

Although it's fair to say that some features of a subject position may indeed be inscribed by assignments, I do not automatically see this as an expression of cultural hegemony, nor do I see a tutor's willingness to work with such constraints as a kind of slavish subservience to the power of the assignment and the institutional and cultural assumptions enacted in it. Assignments are always only starting places, and as researchers like Linda Flower and Peter Elbow pointed out repeatedly—although using distinctly different types of language to do so—writers routinely construct the rhetorical problems they want to solve, and they construct those problems and their texts in wildly divergent ways. Whether agency is the result of a unique collocation of institutional, cultural, social, and personal forces impinging on a socially constructed and constituted self at a particular moment in time, or whether it is the result of a rational self constructing meaning in a particular context with the tools of language seems immaterial. The significant point is that all writing tasks operate under constraints, and the best tutors will help students to understand what those constraints are and how they can be bent and molded and shaped to the students' interests and still be fulfilled.

A tutor's responsibilities have always gone far beyond merely helping someone to get a better grade on a paper, although that may be the underlying circumstance that occasions the conference in the first place. The tutor is there to explain and elaborate the nature of the writing problem at hand, to ask questions about audience and the writer's purpose, to discover dissonances between the writer's stated goals and her written text, to be an informed reader who has sensitivity to the student's most urgent needs at varying stages of the writing process. Sometimes that means dissecting the assignment and problematizing it, sometimes that means helping students construct a subject position, and sometimes that means hunkering down and putting social goals aside and grinding through a paragraph or two of assorted run-ons and misused semicolons. That is the best and, to me, the most ethical kind of tutoring. The best tutors show a thoughtful awareness of the many constraints, assumptions, and expectations inherent in any writing task, and they help student writers not only to understand what those implicit features are, but also to find a balance, a comfortable discursive position that will allow them to meet their own needs as well as those of the institution. If this is what it means to use critique in a writing center, to identify multiple and sometimes conflicting voices and demands and help students navigate their way through them, then I would argue that most of us have been doing that all along. I would also say that, for the most part, that is exactly the sort of teaching and respect for critical inquiry that our institutions want us to engage in with students.

Let me conclude, then with another quote from Cooper's article:

> I want to align myself with [the position] that writing centers are in a good position to serve as a site of critique of the institutionalized structure of writing instruction in college, and that, as a consequence of this, the role of the tutor should be to create useful knowledge about writing in college and to empower students as writers who also understand what writing involves and who act as agents in their writing—these two goals being closely intertwined. (98)

I want to align myself with that position too, and I think I always have. I think that nearly all of us have. Thoughtful critique and carefully constructed points of resistance to institutional and disciplinary norms are part of what we do, and it's part of good writing instruction. We don't do it all the time, certainly, because there are some points in the writing process where students don't need to have their texts further problematized, but we know how important such strategies are. And I think tutors—the best tutors—will be able to employ these critical strategies in ethical ways that let them feel they are helping their students to become better writers and at the same time are remaining true to themselves.

ACKNOWLEDGMENT

An earlier version of this chapter appeared as "Toe the Party Line or Subvert from Within?" in *Travels with the Midwest Writing Centers Association: 1996 & 1997 Conference Proceedings*. Shireen Carroll, ed. Davidson, NC: MWCA, 1998. 47–66.

WORKS CITED

Bawarshi, Anis, and Stephanie Pelkowski. "Postcolonialism and the Idea of a Writing Center." *The Writing Center Journal* 19.2 (Spring/Summer 1999): 41–58.

Bizzell, Patricia. "Beyond Anti-Foundationalism to Rhetorical Authority: Problems in Defining 'Cultural Literacy.'" *College English* 52.6 (October 1990): 661–75.

Cooper, Marilyn. "Really Useful Knowledge: A Cultural Studies Agenda for Writing Centers." *The Writing Center Journal* 14.2 (Spring 1994): 97–111.

Faigley, Lester. *Fragments of Rationality: Postmodernity and the Subject of Composition*. Pittsburgh: U of Pittsburgh P, 1992.

Gillam, Alice. "Writing Center Ecology: A Bakhtinian Perspective." *The Writing Center Journal* 11.2 (Spring/Summer 1991): 3–11.

Gramsci, Antonio. *Selections from the Prison Notebooks*. Ed. and Trans. Quintin Hoare and Geoffrey Nowell Smith. New York: International, 1971.

Grimm, Nancy Maloney. *Good Intentions: Writing Center Work for Postmodern Times*. Portsmouth, NH: Heinemann, 1999.

Lunsford, Andrea. "Collaboration, Control, and the Idea of a Writing Center." *The Writing Center Journal* 12.1 (Fall 1991): 3–10.

Paine, Charles. "Relativism, Radical Pedagogy, and the Ideology of Paralysis." *College English* 51.6 (October 1989): 557–70.

Ruszkiewicz, John. "Advocacy and Control in the Writing Class." *The Ethics of Writing Instruction: Issues in Theory and Practice*. Ed. Michael A. Pemberton. Stamford, CT: Ablex, 2000. 23–34.

Welch, Nancy. "From Silence to Noise: The Writing Center as Critical Exile." *The Writing Center Journal* 14.1 (Fall 1993): 3–15.

Wingate, Molly. "Writing Centers as Sites of Academic Culture." *The Writing Center Journal* 21.2 (Spring/Summer 2001): 7–20.

25

On Not "Bowling Alone" in the Writing Center, or Why Peer Tutoring Is an Essential Community for Writers and for Higher Education

Christina Murphy
Marshall University

In 2000, political scientist and public policy theorist Robert D. Putnam published *Bowling Alone: The Collapse and Revival of American Community,* a philosophical treatise many critics regard as the single most important study of the reasons for the disintegration of social structures in post-World War II America. Putnam used the disappearance of bowling leagues, once common entities in small-town and big-city America alike, as his metaphor for a civic crisis in which Americans no longer feel the bonds that once connected them to their communities and to their civic responsibilities. As a result, we bowl alone, and the aloneness of the average citizen points to a type of civic decline that has numerous ramifications for all social institutions, including the American higher education system.

In the broadest sense, the impact on American life of "bowling alone" has been to reduce the value of social networks and thus of social capital. As Putnam stated,

> Social capital refers to connections among individuals—social networks and the norms of reciprocity and trustworthiness that arise from them. In that sense social capital is closely related to what some have called "civic virtue." The difference is that "social capital" calls attention to the fact that civic virtue is most powerful when embedded in a dense network of reciprocal so-

cial relations. A society of many virtuous but isolated individuals is not necessarily rich in so-cial capital. (19)

Putnam considered the loss of social ties and the ensuing isolation and alienation of the individual as one of the most dramatic changes of twentieth-century America. The consequences of this shift have been great, including the weakening of family and community ties, a general indifference to social issues, and a lack of participation in the political process by upward of 50% of the populace.

For American higher education, as for all of America, the implications largely follow the insight that you don't know what you've got until you lose it. There is no question that, in the last few decades, American higher education has responded to social critics and political pressures in a far-ranging attempt to restore what has been lost, even though the losses themselves were more often prompted by dramatic and pandemic changes in society than initiated by the higher education system itself. The emergence of service learning as a major component of academic life and curricula is but one example of efforts to reconnect students with their communities and with the higher ideals of public service in order to restore a sense of civic engagement in social and political issues (Stanton, Giles, and Cruz). A focus on character education is another political mandate that higher education has pursued in an effort to rebuild the bonds between the individual and the community. The Character Education Partnership in Washington, DC, highlights this emphasis in primary and secondary education through a partnership with educators and through a series of publications and workshops, whereas institutional sites like the Center for the Advancement of Ethics and Character at Boston University seek to "stimulate a national dialogue on issues of moral education, thus helping scholars to become more competent in the study of ethics and character in our nation's schools" (CAEC Web site). The establishment of the national Campus Compact in 1985 has now grown to a coalition of more than nine hundred college and university presidents "committed to the civic purposes of higher education." As the Campus Compact stated,

> Our presidents believe that by creating a supportive campus environment for the engagement in community service, colleges and universities can best prepare their students to be active, committed, and informed citizens and leaders of their communities. Member campuses bond together as a coalition to actively engage presidents, faculty, staff, and students to promote a renewed vision for higher education—one that supports not only the civic development of students, but the campus as an active and engaged member of its community. (Campus Compact Web site)

The "renewed vision" described in the Campus Compact reflects numerous changes in the political and philosophical landscape of higher education. The renewed attention to the issue of community in political thought generated by such social theorists as Peter Lawler, Alisdair MacIntyre, Michael Sandel, and Philip Selznick has carried over into debates about the purpose and value of education in American society. The debate has recast the traditional dichotomy of conservative versus liberal values into a newly framed call for communitarianism as the principal philosophical framework for American higher education. Simply put, communitarianism is rooted in broader understandings of the concepts of community and social contexts while emphasizing the balance between individual rights and social responsibilities in educating citizens for collective self-government (Barber). There is no question that communitarianism has redefined much of the debate concerning both the role and the future responsibilities of higher education in contemporary society (Colby et al.).

Such a radical shift of paradigms and priorities invites a critique of the role of the writing center within the matrix of new ideas and commitments in higher education. Specifically, does the writing center sustain communitarian principles, or is the writing center more appropriately positioned within either liberal or conservative values and practices? Can a case be made for viewing the writing center and its primary practice of peer tutoring as a community, or is the writing center best understood as a nonhegemonic anticommunity in the best interpretation and sense of this concept as presented by Nancy Maloney Grimm in *Good Intentions: Writing Center Work for Postmodern Times?*

I would like to begin examining these questions and their implications for writing center work by positioning the discussion within the changes in philosophy and outlook that the move from modern to postmodern points of view has created. I begin with the premise that the writing center has largely always been a postmodern construct, despite the current perception fostered by Grimm and others that this is a new (or new wave) approach to writing center work. The history of the writing center is such that its precarious relationship with traditional institutional structures has provided rich opportunities for challenging the wisdom of conventional approaches and traditional attitudes toward education. This similarity of calling into question what was being done at the time and thus what might be done better unites all the many philosophical permutations that the writing center has undergone in its over century-long history of innovation, exploration, and accomplishment. Whereas Grimm puzzled over exactly whose good intentions are truly good intentions, and Elizabeth H. Boquet wondered exactly what type of noise should come from the writing center, the reality of practice and theory is that the writing center functions as a superstructural institution in which human agency is the most potent force for historical, interpersonal, and intrapersonal change (Simon; Strinati).

In the truest sense, the writing center reflects the postmodern view best expressed by Antonio Gramsci that the world of society and the world of each individual are more dialectic than deterministic, and thus the function of autonomy is central to all sociopolitical acts, including those of education. Certainly, it can be argued that Gramsci, like Karl Marx, saw the hegemonic impact of dominant groups, but Gramsci moved beyond Marx in arguing that individuals and subordinate groups have reasons of their own for accepting or critiquing—and thus revolutionizing—dominant cultures and ideologies (Strinati 166). In the fullest sense, the dynamics of hegemony and counterhegemony create the potential for transformation on societal and individual levels.

In considering the ethics and the ethical impact of writing center practice, I would like to move beyond the rather easy (if not simple) polarization discussed by Grimm between modern and postmodern educational acts to a broader discussion of what value writing centers and peer-tutors in particular might serve in resolving issues of civic disengagement in contemporary times. In essence, I want to consider the ethics of not "bowling alone" in the twenty-first century and why this might be of significance to the tutoring process and to the tutors who carry out that process. To do so, I start with a complaint against the philosophical stance presented by Grimm, who argued for a critical view of hegemony without a critical assessment of the alternatives. Certainly, one cannot argue against the reality of enculturation in academics in that no tutor, no student, no writing center administrator—or anyone else, for that matter—experiences the world completely free of the values and philosophies of the culture in which they were reared (some might say, indoctrinated). That said, it is a different argument, indeed, to contend that we are all agents of that culture and function to impose our cultural values on others. And for Grimm and others, the argument is that we seek to impose hegemonic values by virtue of being within the academy and thus functioning with the "good intentions" of academicians who seek to educate/indoctrinate students into the ways of academic learning, thinking, and writing—even if this may mean a traumatic reworking of the student's cultural and personal identity. Thus, for these individuals, it is best to work as rebels within the system in order to be counterhegemonic in our interactions with students and thus to transform the academy from a monolith acting as a single unified powerful force for conformity to a—well, to what is not exactly clear. Grimm called for a "multicultural democracy" that will change the way "writing centers interact with the differences of race, class, culture, and education" (xii). Aside from the fact that what we have here is another ideology, it is not clear from Grimm's discussion how it is that such an ideology will fall no less prey to dominance than many other ideologies. Essentially, one must buy into the "differences" that will be defined by whatever ideologies emerge from the dominant group in any social system that determines what is good and right and thus productive and possible. In other words, by those with both "good intentions" and the social power to impose their "good intentions" on others, whether by persuasion or by practice.

It is important to move beyond arguing over Grimm's notion of whose intentions are good, better, or best, to the core of the significant issue that is raised whenever intentions and intentionality enter into a consideration of writing center work—specifically as that work is enacted in the realm of tutoring. The core issue is not one of good intentions but of our understanding of the individual as a subject:

> The individual is produced by nature; the subject by culture. Theories of the individual concentrate on differences between people and explain these differences as natural. Theories of the subject, on the other hand, concentrate on people's common experiences in a society as being the most productive way of explaining who (we think) we are.... The subject ... is a social construction, not a natural one. (Fiske 288)

This distinction between the individual and the subject is an essential one that is often overlooked in discussions of writing center work. Without doubt, both Grimm and Bouquet sought to focus writing center work on a nuanced sensitivity to the individual, and certainly no one can fault that intention, even if there are questions about the premises on which such an approach might rest. Grimm repeatedly pointed out that this is an emphasis that separates the modern from the postmodern in writing center theory and practice, but I contend that writing center work needs to move beyond the postmodern (or at least the postmodern as Grimm defined it) with its intense focus on the individual to the communitarian view of the subject. This move is far different from the focus on social constructionism that dominated writing center discussions in the 1980s and 1990s (Lunsford; Murphy). It is a movement toward understanding the role of the academy in the structuring of civic engagement, that is, in the structuring of community. Whereas we often have no difficulty in arguing that the world of the writing center and its practitioners is a community, we seem to have a difficult time arguing that the writing center does and should play a role in the structuring and formation of community in contemporary times.

No doubt, such a perspective may leave some people with an uneasy sense of assigning to the writing center the moralistic role of advocating for civic engagement. Certainly, it is wise to voice such concerns about agency and how the academy as a whole and the writing center in particular should express that agency. However, this debate is not new to the writing center in that even conservative, modern, and postmodern intentions must advocate and enact some sense of what community shall mean to the individual. Grimm's argument is that the academy can do a better and kinder job of involving students from disparate home communities in the community of the academy. No doubt this is a noble and worthy goal and one with which few writing center professionals would argue. However, although it is important to consider the individual, it is equally important to consider the subject and what role the writing center may play—perhaps should play—in the dual reality of each person as both an individual and a subject.

In many ways, this emphasis can be both structural (as a practice) and humanistic (as a value) and thus need not be the threat to the quality and significance of writing center work that some critics might envision. My position is that the value, if not the very future, of the writing center lies in the fact that the writing center is not only a community but is also an agent of community formation. The first step in this process would be the recognition of communities as a structural whole. It is not that the academy stands between the home community and the world in ushering new students into the academy's mores and expectations. It is, instead, that community formation is a process in which the supposed boundaries between home communities and academic communities are artificial, if not ideological, constructs. It is not enough for the peer-tutor to accept Grimm's views that writing practices and assumptions about literacy "reproduce social divisions" (30) and thus the writing center often participates in preserving "the culture of power" (36). This is an incomplete sense of cultural dynamics as they apply to tutoring and to the writing center. What is missing from the equation is the interplay of identity within the cultural systems that the academy, the writing center, the student, and the peer-tutor occupy. Simply changing the cultural dynamics of "social divisions" and redefining "the culture of power"—if these outcomes can even be accomplished by the means Grimm described—do not guarantee an understanding of the individual as a cultural subject. Nor do they guarantee that one set of priorities, assumptions, practices, and beliefs will not merely replace another in an ongoing cycle of hegemonic duels and dualities.

The writing center is itself a highly integrated academic and societal system that reflects modularity, a fundamental concept of system design in which, upon a central platform, multiple layers are built and defined. Each layer provides a distinct service that is well-defined within the integrity of the whole and without which the whole would devolve from one integrated system into only a series of separate layers or functions that would become limited in application and value and perhaps even dysfunctional (Churchman). The writing center represents a complex of service layers across a spectrum of social realities, and the design of service layers into an integrated whole is not only structurally complex, it is also socially complicated.

To support the broad range of applications a writing center must provide, the writing center's practices must reflect what services are needed and also reconcile all of these potentially conflicting needs into the design of the whole. The design of the whole reflects the theory, the rationale, the ethos, and the culture of the writing center itself. It is the spirit, if not the ethical core, of the writing center's reason for existence—not only in relation to a particular campus or community, but in relation to the social enterprise of education itself. It is the most significant assertion that the writing center itself does not "bowl alone" but reflects, through its design, the modularity of a system that is an integration of multiple layers of experience and interaction among individuals and institutions engaged in the process of community and cultural formation. Whereas its most significant impact may be on the process of how the individual becomes a subject, the overall impact of the design of the whole is on numerous communities as manifestations of the social system.

Designing the whole can be hard to do in that applications may not have been imagined yet, and the needs of the various individuals and communities may change over time. Certainly, a great challenge for writing center professionals is to respond to the question of whether we can find more effective ways to develop the writing center in such a way as to incorporate innovations and respond to new needs. I would suggest that this is the new realm of ethical responsibility that the contemporary writing center should pursue as part of its charge. In many ways, writing center theory has focused almost exclusively on the relationship of the writing center to the academy. A new understanding is needed now of the writing center as a focal point for the study of society and culture. Acknowledging this perspective as a vital component of writing center work and as a positive aspect of peer-tutor training is a significant shift in paradigmatic outlook for the contemporary writing center. It is also a necessary refocusing lest the writing center fall into the trap of being a handmaiden to the sociopolitical philosophies that are defining the contemporary educational scene.

I have in mind, for example, the current movements to service learning and character education that are at work in academic and political circles to redefine much of what education will constitute and will seek to do. The writing center becomes a natural locus for each of these movements, but often only as an ancillary and secondary component. It will come to no one's surprise that much of the instruction in service learning and in character education involves writing assignments (especially journaling) and what better site to locate writing instruction in support of these two movements than the writing center. Rather than envisioning the writing center as having a significant role in the cultural life of the student, the academy, and the community, the writing center becomes, instead, a locus for writing instruction within the forms and formats determined by other curricular requirements and instructional agents. In many disturbing ways, such a circumscribed role for the writing center represents a return to decades past in which many a writing center theorist and practitioner had to argue for a broader and more meaningful role for the writing center than just instruction/correction. In other words, arguing for "The Idea of a Writing Center," as Stephen North so eloquently wrote in 1984, as the then-seminal essay on writing center identity, purpose, and rationale.

I would prefer to see, instead, a redefinition of the writing center through an examination of its function within society and culture. This redefinition is both missing from and much needed in contemporary times. The starting point, if not the focal point, for such an analysis should be the role of the writing center in community formation and how that process is carried out via tutoring. Because a good portion of the tutoring done in writing centers is carried out by peer-tutors, the function of peer tutoring needs to be examined more fully than as a debate over "good intentions" or "noise" from the writing center. What we need to understand is the expressive totality of which Hegel wrote in considering the role of any enterprise in shaping and directing the conceptual frameworks for inquiry and action.

For writing center professionals, pursuing the expressive totality that incorporates the subject within the process of cultural definition may mean the necessity to interrogate the everyday routines and habitual ways of operating in academic environments. If in contemporary times we actually do believe that communicative practices structure social relations and institutions, then the methods by which we train tutors and promulgate the act of tutoring itself as meaningful must take on a different cast from the traditional sense of tutoring as a habitual training of students for positive academic experiences and outcomes. On that point, Grimm was correct in arguing that we need for writing center work "a keener awareness of where the writing center is in relationship to other social systems and ideas" (xi). In essence, we need to "map out" a territory that frees us to question and to create anew versus merely reenacting tired and worn models of enculturation.

In training our peer-tutors, we must begin, in my view, with conveying to them a sense of their role in community formation. Grimm and Boquet believed that a significant part of tutoring/tutor training resides in acknowledging and examining the ways in which normative structures and practices that adhere to central tenets are privileged and those that fall outside the center are marginalized. Thus, their call for a writing center that is nonhegemonic or at least counterhegemonic in theory and practice. Although many may value this stance as a positive appreciation of differences that exemplifies an appreciation of the marginalized outsider, I do not feel that such a stance can take us much further than recognizing and empathizing with the inequities produced by hegemony and its internal constructs of power and domination. I prefer, instead, to build on Kenneth Burke's sense of identification as a means to compensate for the estrangement that comes with segregation and marginalization. As Burke noted, "Identification is compensatory to division" (22). For Burke, the concept has a double meaning at the individual and social levels. At the individual level, to identify is to recognize something. At the social level, to identify is to connect with something else. Together, these acts enable us to form and sustain relationships, community, and culture. In other words, they enable us to not "bowl alone," but to see the value and the significance of the identification of the individual with the community and the culture.

Building on Burke's theories of identification, George Cheney argued that moving identification from the subjective and personal realm into actuality and practice within an organization represents a process of coalescing around a body of knowledge, finding commonalities, and pursuing similar goals. The hoped-for outcome is that such a process gives people a way of understanding themselves, enhancing their sense of personal worth, and a mechanism for establishing common ground with other groups and constituencies. In other words, it gives them a mechanism for community formation. This process links the interpersonal with the communal and creates the irreducibility of culture that Clifford Geertz emphasized. It also supports a liberatory awareness of choice as inseparable from action and meaning, which Pierre Bourdieu claimed is the central aspect of reflexive practice in education so that educational systems can encompass sociocultural acts of meaning making. This goal, in itself, builds on structuralism—specifically as that philosophy is expressed by Claude Levi-Strauss, who traced all meaning to the functioning of systems as expressions of symbolic thinking.

In many ways, the claims of Geertz, Bourdieu, and Levi-Strauss exemplify the concept of social capital that Putnam wrote about in *Bowling Alone*. In Putnam's view, social capital is found in social connections, from which emerge the most significant types of networking and interpersonal relations that are the basis of community formation. As we consider the role of the writing center in this new century and beyond, certainly social capital must be a significant component of writing center work and of how we train our peer-tutors to carry out that work. Putnam believed that social capital can produce aggregate growth within communities and produce "externalities" that broaden the scope and impact of the aggregate whole (20). As we conceptualize "The Idea of a Writing Center" for this new century, one of our greatest ethical challenges will be to define and actualize the writing center as a form of social capital that can produce aggregate growth within academic and social communities and to train our peer-tutors and all writing center professionals to understand the role they play in community formation. We need to move beyond arguments over "good intentions" and "noise" or over minimalist tutoring versus directive tutoring; we need especially to move beyond arguments of marginalization versus adaptation and return to the principles that made writing centers such an innovative educational experiment at the turn of the twentieth century. We need to envision the writing center as a true center for the revival of community and of civic engagement. The challenge we face in the twenty-first century is broadening the sphere of the writing center's influence and developing and enacting the ways in which the writing center is more than just a community unto itself or a buffer community between the home community and the academy. As we examine our "good intentions" and celebrate our "noise," we should also recognize the transformative power of writing center work and seek to envision the writing center as the locus of significant social capital for both the academy and the community.

WORKS CITED

Barber, Benjamin R. *An Aristocracy of Everyone: The Politics of Education and the Future of America*. New York: Ballantine, 1992.

Boquet, Elizabeth H. *Noise from the Writing Center*. Logan: Utah State UP, 2002.

Bourdieu, Pierre. *Reproduction in Education, Society, and Culture*. Trans. Richard Nice. Newbury Park, CA: Sage, 1994.

Burke, Kenneth. *A Rhetoric of Motives*. Berkeley: U of California P, 1950.

Campus Compact. http://www.compact.org

Center for the Advancement of Ethics and Character, Boston University. <http://www.bu.edu/education/caec/files/mission.htm>.

Character Education Partnership. <http://www.character.org>.

Cheney, George. "The Rhetoric of Identification and the Study of Organizational Communication." *Quarterly Journal of Speech* 69 (1983): 143–58.

Churchman, C. West. *The Design of Inquiring Systems: Basic Concepts of Systems and Organization*. New York: Basic Books, 1971.

Colby, Anne, Thomas Ehrlich, Elizabeth Beaumont, and Jason Stephens. *Educating Citizens: Preparing America's Undergraduates for Lives of Moral and Civic Responsibility*. San Francisco: Jossey-Bass, 2003.

Fiske, John. "British Cultural Studies and Television." *Channels of Discourse, Reconsidered*. Ed. Robert C. Allen. London: Routledge, 1992. 284–326.

Geertz, Clifford. *Interpretation of Cultures*. New York: Basic Books, 1977.

Gramsci, Antonio. *Selections from the Prison Notebooks*. Ed. and Trans. Quintin Hoare and Geoffrey Nowell Smith. London: Lawrence and Wishart, 1971.

Grimm, Nancy Maloney. *Good Intentions: Writing Center Work for Postmodern Times.* Portsmouth, NH: Heinemann-Boynton/Cook, 1999.

Hegel, Georg. *The Philosophy of Hegel.* Ed. Carl J. Friedrich. New York: Modern Library, 1954.

Lawler, Peter. A. *Aliens in America: The Strange Truth about Our Souls.* Wilmington, DE: Intercollegiate Studies Institute, 2002.

Levi-Strauss, Claude. *The Savage Mind.* Chicago: U of Chicago P, 1966.

Lunsford, Andrea. "Collaboration, Control, and the Idea of a Writing Center." *The Writing Center Journal* 12.1 (1991): 3–10.

MacIntyre, Alisdair. *After Virtue: A Study in Moral Theory.* South Bend, IN: U of Notre Dame P, 1997.

Murphy, Christina. "The Writing Center and Social Constructionist Theory." *Intersections: Theory-Practice in the Writing Center.* Ed. Joan A. Mullin and Ray Wallace. Urbana: NCTE, 1994. 25–39.

North, Stephen M. "The Idea of a Writing Center." *College English* 46 (1984): 433–46.

Putnam, Robert. D. *Bowling Alone: The Collapse and Revival of American Community.* New York: Simon & Schuster, 2000.

Sandel, Michael J. *Democracy's Discontent: America in Search of a Public Philosophy.* Cambridge: Harvard UP, 1996.

Selznick, Philip. *The Moral Commonwealth: Social Theory and the Promise of Community.* Berkeley: U of California P, 1992.

Simon, Roger. *Gramsci's Political Thought: An Introduction.* London: Lawrence and Wishart, 1991.

Stanton, Timothy K., Dwight E. Giles, Jr., and Nadinne I. Cruz. *Service-Learning: A Movement's Pioneers Reflect on Its Origins, Practice, and Future.* San Francisco: Jossey-Bass, 1999.

Strinati, Dominic. *An Introduction to Theories of Popular Culture.* London: Routledge, 1995.

26

Identifying Our
Ethical Responsibility:
A Criterion-Based Approach

David Bringhurst
Wright State University

The subject of writing center ethics touches on a broad spectrum of issues. We serve many constituencies—institutional, departmental, student, and professional—and are often explicitly or implicitly asked to defend our conduct and even our existence to one or more constituencies at any given time. Concerns about plagiarism, oppression, fair labor practices, and our role within the institution and the larger professional and social communities in which we work and live constantly challenge our pedagogy and our self-image. Most of the published attempts to come to terms with our ethical responsibilities, however, focus on our responsibility to a single constituency (e.g., clients) or individual issues (e.g., plagiarism). This situational approach to ethics can be valuable, but only if we have first grounded ourselves in a holistic ethical approach that holds us accountable to all of our constituencies. At the end of the day, we must recognize that as professionals, who are not on the margin of but inside the academic institution, we have an ethical obligation to serve all of our constituents. Any solutions we propose to ethical problems must include an ethical response to each of the constituencies affected or we risk a response that is ethical for one constituent but unethical for another. Fortunately, all of these constituencies have much in common, including the aim of doing "good" for the primary constituency: students.

The writings of Michael Pemberton reflect the range of ethical issues tutors regularly confront. From dealing with students who present essay content that tutors find morally questionable, to the ethical ways tutors might deal with what they view as poorly defined or unfair assignments from faculty, Pemberton showed an awareness of the difficult decision-making process tutors must go through. Pemberton provided useful insights for tutors, but he struggled (as so many of us do) with the broader issues that confront us as writing center administrators. He attempted to establish three laws for tutoring based on the model of Asmiov's Three Laws of Robotics, but his attempt is ultimately flawed by its bias toward collaborative and process theory and its narrow focus on tutor–client interaction ("Writing Center Ethics: Three Laws" 13).

Collaborative and process theories are problematic as foundations on which to build an ethical system of tutoring. Although collaborative and process theories are dominant formative influences in writing center pedagogy today, the question of their ethical rightness is still clearly open for debate (as we will see later); thus, any ethical system based on them must be considered suspect. Moreover, Pemberton's focus on the tutor–client relationship, although useful to that relationship, ignores his own assessment that "writing center ethics are deeply embedded in institutional and situational contexts, and, as such, they resist reduction to a simple set of principles or universal guidelines" ("Writing Center Ethics: Three Laws" 13). Pemberton, himself, cautioned that "when considering whether or not to give advice or take ethical stands with students, tutors in writing centers must be attuned to circumstances that extend far beyond the narrow confines of the writing tutorial: What are the motivations and purposes and goals of the people involved—be they students, tutors, faculty, or administrators?" ("Writing Center Ethics" 10). This caution applies to other areas of ethical inquiry within the writing center as well. In the end, any ethical system we might adopt must encompass and provide guidance for our ethical relationship with each of our constituencies.

One of the most common areas where we find ourselves challenged by the motivations, purposes, and goals of our other constituencies is over the issue of plagiarism. A great deal of the scholarship on writing center ethics deals with our alleged complicity in student plagiarism. We often answer this charge by defending our pedagogy based on one of the dominant theories that influence it, be it collaborative theory, noninterventionism, or even questioning the concept of authorship itself.

Richard Behm offered one such defense in answer to charges from an English faculty member that the help his students received at Behm's writing center was tantamount to plagiarism. The faculty member contended that "one of the most important functions a university serves is certifying students, making judgments about their abilities so that employers and others may determine fitness for jobs and so on. When a student receives assistance on a draft of a paper, or even discovering ideas for a paper that is to be graded, the work is no longer solely that of the student, and thus this certifying function is subverted" (Behm 3). Behm countered that "the certifying function of education" threatens the "traditional mission of a university as a place of teaching and learning" (4–5). Behm believed that we have become overly concerned with life in the "real world" and this concern has led to an emphasis on certification and thus poisoned our methodologies. "[E]ach day in college is 'the real world,' and we are about a very important task, one that overshadows the political mandate to certify students as accountants or restaurant managers or English teachers" (5). Behm, himself, used a similarly "real-world" defense when he "contend[ed] that collaborative learning as practiced in most writing centers is not plagiarism, that it is not only ethical but also reflective of the way people really write" (9). He went on to "argue that the truly unethical act is *not* making such collaborative learning available to students, bowing to the demand to certify them instead of acknowledging the primary imperative of educating them" (10).

Behm was right that to withhold the collaborative option is unethical, but he was wrong in the implication that this is somehow an either/or scenario. Behm's theories undercut the very "traditional mission" to which he sought to return us. Certification is merely the stamp of approval, if you will, that the university has succeeded in its mission, which Behm earlier defined as teaching and learning. Whereas it is possible that we could or have let our priorities become skewed, Behm ignored the reality that the certifying function exists along a continuum that includes teaching and learning. One might argue that we know the teaching mission has been accomplished when the learner learns. But, in order to determine if learning has taken place, we must measure or assess the student in some way. It is only after teaching occurs that assessment is employed to determine whether or not learning has taken place. Once we have determined that it has taken place, certification serves to alert others that the student has learned what was required. Not to certify would be outrageously unethical because that certification, in the form of a grade or degree, has great value to the student. In many respects, it is their reason for entering the academy or arguably, our writing centers. To ignore our primary constituency's primary motivation—a motivation, by the way, that is ethically sound—is clearly unethical.

Collaborative learning is but one theory offered as a defense against charges of complicity in student plagiarism. Both interventionist approaches to tutoring and process theory have been implemented or invoked in our defense against charges of plagiarism. Irene L. Clark and Dave Healy argued that noninterventionist policies are "a set of defensive strategies" resulting from "a concern with avoiding plagiarism, coupled with the second-class and frequently precarious status of writing centers within the university hierarchy" (245). But, as with the collaborative theory, Clark and Healy charged that there are problems with noninterventionism as an adequate solution to the problem of plagiarism. Clark and Healy believed that "a noninterventionist policy as an absolute must ultimately be judged ethically suspect, increasing the center's marginality, diminishing its influence, and compromising its ability to serve writers" (242). Like noninterventionism, invoking process theory as a defense against plagiarism has come under attack by some scholars. Shamoon and Burns posited that a defense against plagiarism based on process theory "does nothing directly to offset the charges of unethical behavior" and "has the potential to further implicate the writing center in such charges" ("Plagiarism" 185).

Both Clark and Healy and Shamoon and Burns argued that the weaknesses of these defensive approaches stem from a failure to address the assumption of validity that sole authorship has come to possess in academic circles. Not only did Clark and Healy see the noninterventionist approach to tutoring as ultimately unethical, they argued that it

> perpetuates a limited and limiting understanding of authorship in the academy. By privileging individual responsibility and accountability and by valorizing the individual writer's authentic "voice," the writing center has left unchallenged notions of intellectual property that are suspect at best. Furthermore, as Lisa Ede, Andrea Lunsford, Marilyn Cooper, and others have argued, the idea that writing is fundamentally a solitary activity and that individual writers can and should "own" their texts relegates the writing center to a limited bystander's role, even as it limits writers' understanding of their options and of their relationship to others. (Clark and Healy 247)

Shamoon and Burns also referred to Ede and Lunsford, but also enlisted the scholarship of Rebecca Moore Howard, whose "historical overview of concepts of plagiarism demonstrates that modern definitions of authorship and plagiarism are social constructs that have taken shape in the West during the last 300 years" ("Plagiarism" 187). They found process theory wanting as a defense against charges of plagiarism because it "discounts [tutoring] in terms of publicly identified authorship and ownership." Furthermore, they argued, "The effacing of the tutor's presence has the effect of leaving the concept of sole authorship in place, surely in the instructor's mind but probably also in the student's mind, too" ("Plagiarism" 186).

It seems, then, that our past theoretical responses to plagiarism, lacking in one way or another, are insufficient answers to the charge. Clark and Healy and Shamoon and Burns argued that it is because our attempts have left the idea of sole authorship unchallenged. This is an accurate and astute assessment, but only in the valid, but limited question of our alleged complicity in plagiarism. Despite the ubiquity of the charge, plagiarism is only a smaller ethical issue that exists in a larger ethical context. Like Pemberton's focus on the tutor–client relationship, a fixation on plagiarism as an ethical issue creates a kind of myopia that prevents us from seeing the larger issues.

Nancy Maloney Grimm challenged this myopic view by suggesting that it might be the academy itself that is unethical. She did not exculpate writing centers from their role in the academy's unethical behavior. She noted that "writing centers maintain the status quo, thereby oppressing the very students most dependent on writing center assistance" (xvii). Grimm believed that "as they presently operate, writing centers are more often normalizing agents, performing the institutional function of erasing differences" (xvii). This charge stems from her view that "because writing centers are places where assimilation into the discursive systems of the university is facilitated, one rarely hears stories about the erasures: the loss of motivation, the compromise of creativity, the silencing of family stories, the impediments to agency, the suppression of other literacies and worldviews" (xvi). It is clear from the tone of this assertion, that Grimm viewed our ethical standing in the broader terms of its complicity with, in her opinion, the unethical academy. She made this claim more explicitly when she challenged us "to move toward a more 'fair' writing center practice" and "rethink the ethical codes and policies that place limits on what tutors are allowed to do for students. Ethical codes in writing centers, particularly those that support minimalist 'hands-off' tutoring, often protect those who are favorably positioned within the institution from coming to terms with the realization that the institution itself is not fair" (114–15). This is a revolutionary idea that Clark and Healy later expanded on with their "new ethics for the writing center" (253–57). Grimm's attempt to reframe the issue, which in its essence is on target, flies off the mark and is thus undercut because she used some spurious logic and fell prey to a commonly held misconception.

Grimm employed some faulty logic when she conflated the personal experiences of her family history with what happens in academe. "My maternal and paternal grandparents," she related, "came from countries where they were forbidden to speak their native languages, where the culture of the conqueror, oppressor, colonizer attempted to override their own.... [I]t is that history that troubles me when I see representations of writing center work as innocent and ideologically neutral" (xvi). The connection she saw, however, is based on a false analogy. I do not think it is disrespectful to Grimm's valid feelings for her family's own lost culture to suggest that neither in scope nor in degree is what we do on a par with the experiences of her family at the hands of their "conquerors." When a people are conquered or colonized, the intention is to wipe out the conquered people's identity, including their language and history. However mis-guided our pedagogy might be, our actions cannot be reasonably compared to such atrocities. Implicit in the terms *conqueror* and *colonizer*, if not *oppressor*, are the acts of invasion, usually by force, and occupation. But academies do not invade the lands and homes of our students; in a sense, students invade the academy. For students come to the academy and, for the most part, do so of their own free will. Moreover, students may leave at any time. They are free agents, in any meaningful use of the term, who seek us out to learn what we have to teach.

Grimm's suspicion of the institution is clear in her somewhat Orwellian charge that writing centers are "normalizing agents." And she is right; that is precisely our job. But Grimm would have us believe that this is a negative role that obliterates culture rather than our ethical re-sponsibility to prepare students to participate fully in the academic discourse community. The academic discourse community is but one community to which students belong. They are not isolated within the university, but rather partake of it even as they continue to be members of their family, social, and work communities. To see students as victims or even as just students is to rob them of their agency and identity. "Student" is just one role that people play, and the academy is but one stage on which they play that or any role.

Although it is true that some of our clients come to us from different cultures, our facile view of them as somehow helpless outsiders fending off the oppression of the academic system is misguided. Their presence in our centers is surely a sign of their need or desire, if not their will-ingness, to enter the system, to be on the inside. When we bend over backward to preserve their "voices" in the name of ethics, we are actually abdicating our ethical responsibility to help them enter into the system as embodied by the institution. In so doing, we effectively ensure their isolation much in the same way as our insistence that we are on the outside tends to mar-ginalize us. This belief in our own marginalization—in our "outsider" status—not only helps to undercut Grimm's case, it keeps us from grasping the full implications of what it means to question the academy's ethics.

The psyche of writing center professionals, and thus its scholarship, is marred by our ambiv-alence about our status and role within the academy. There are tantalizing glimpses of confi-dence and an understanding of our place within the academy, but our perception of our marginality keeps us from inheriting our true place. Pemberton came close to recognizing the problem when, if you'll remember, he said "writing center ethics are deeply embedded in insti-tutional and situational contexts" ("Writing Center Ethics: Three Laws" 13). He even named our constituencies when he cautioned tutors to be aware of "the motivations and purposes and goals of the people involved—be they students, tutors, faculty, or administrators" ("Writing Center Ethics" 10). Clark and Healy also, in proposing their new ethics for the writing center, pointed out that we "should be confident of [our] own expertise and insight and should be will-ing to use [our] unique position in the academy to challenge the status quo by critiquing institutional ideology and practice" (255).

Yet, despite such evidence, writing center literature is filled with references to our marginal-ity and status as outsiders. Shamoon and Burns played the marginalization card in two separate contexts. In arguing that, as part of the academy, we help create a "Fordist approach to produc-tion," they made the point that writing center labor is "held in place—its marginal place" by that approach ("Labor Pains" 65, 67). Although arguing that we should play a significant role in the discussion and definition of plagiarism, they urged the writing center "to reposition itself away from its precarious position on the margins and toward the center of the academy" ("Plagiarism" 184). This last affirmation of marginality is repeated in their final compelling argument for moving us "into the center of academic life" ("Plagiarism" 191–92). In both cases, their insistence on our marginality is particularly discordant given its juxtaposition within such a positive message.

Clark and Healy provided an even stronger example of this strange and ambivalent disjunction. They worry that the policy of noninterventionism is "increasing the center's marginality" (242). They referred to "the second-class and frequently precarious status of writing centers within the university hierarchy" (245). Even the underlying premise for their vision of a new ethics for writing centers is built on the foundation of our supposed marginality. Their contention "that writing centers are well positioned to question the status quo" is based on "what Harvey Kail and John Trimbur have called 'semiautonomous' institutional space located 'outside the normal channels of teaching and learning'" and "what Nancy Welch calls 'critical exile'" (253). Frustratingly, they confirmed the deep-seated misapprehension that the best place from which to "challenge the status quo by critiquing institutional ideology and practice" is from the margins. (255).

Before we challenge anyone, we should first challenge our own assumptions of our place within the academy. As someone with both writing center and administrative credentials, Jeanne Simpson provided an insightful and useful place to start. Simpson debunked many of the myths we seem to have about the role of the Central Administration. Interestingly enough, she asserted that our supposed marginalization "would be a surprise to Central Administration. If a program is being funded, space provided, salaries paid, assessment and evaluation being conducted, then the assumption … is that it is part of the institution and that some part of the institution's mission is being addressed." Simpson further contended "that writing centers have more control over what Central Administration knows about them than is perceived" (190). According to Simpson, most issues such as "instructional quality" and "evaluation decisions (retention, promotion, tenure)" are assumed to occur at the departmental level, and "[d]epartmental affiliation is not seen … as a prestige issue but as a mechanical/organizational/logistical issue" (190–91).

If Simpson was right that we are not being marginalized by the administration, and I suspect she was, then perhaps the source of our marginalization occurs at the departmental level. If this is the case, we should consider why this may be so. Perhaps departments, our own as well as others in the academy, marginalize us because they only see us when there is a perceived problem, such as potential plagiarism. Perhaps it is because, when they do approach us, we respond defensively and/or approach the problem from the perspective of what they must be doing wrong to cause such a misperception. Perhaps there is an actual or perceived problem with our credentials as professionals. Perhaps we are not aligning our missions, theories, and practices with those of our department and other departments. Perhaps it is because we act marginalized because we think we're marginalized. To be honest, I really don't know.

What I do know is that we will not be able to fully and ethically engage with our constituencies—the academy, departments, students, tutors, and ourselves—until we find out. Until we view ourselves as an integral, perhaps not central, functional part of the academy, we will not be able to effectively help it or our other constituencies accomplish their mission(s). As outsiders we can rant and rave, but we cannot affect change in any meaningful way. True revolution comes from within. This is one of "the theoretical, pedagogical, and political facts of life" Clark and Healy insisted we must acknowledge (242). Another is that there will be some policies that we will just have to accept because we won't always be able to change people's minds. But even that fact of life is not so harsh. It only seems that way because we fall prey to the meta-myth, if you will, that is at the heart of our sense of marginalization. For when we feel like we are on the margins, we view those on the "inside" as our enemies. They are somehow against us, in opposition. But this is not true.

As Simpson showed us, the administration is, at worst, neutral in regard to us. Furthermore, she proposed that by educating ourselves about the needs of the administration, we can better communicate and integrate ourselves with it:

> The kind of information that writing center directors will need to gather and distribute will not be as closely related to the philosophy and daily functioning of a writing center as it will be to larger, institutional issues. Directors need to be sophisticated enough in their own administrative activities to balance the two levels of knowledge and expertise—theoretical and managerial, pedagogical and budgetary—effectively. (193)

Simpson conceded that, currently, "our professional literature and organizations" are weak in the areas of management and budget (193). Nevertheless, having identified the need, there is no reason to believe that we cannot meet the challenge.

At the departmental level, there may be frustration with us, but only to the degree that we isolate ourselves from departmental goals and missions. Directors must navigate the local terrain in their academy, but a review of some of the general codes of ethics for faculty suggest that they will find more common ground than not. According to part II of the "Statement on Professional Ethics of the American Association of University Professors":

> As teachers, professors encourage the free pursuit of learning in their students. They hold before them the best scholarly and ethical standards of their discipline. Professors demonstrate respect for students as individuals and adhere to their proper roles as intellectual guides and counselors. Professors make every reasonable effort to foster honest academic conduct and to ensure that their evaluations of students reflect each student's true merit. They respect the confidential nature of the relationship between professor and student. They avoid any exploitation, harassment, or discriminatory treatment of students. They acknowledge significant academic or scholarly assistance from them. They protect their academic freedom. (Weingartner 132)

Furthermore, part III states, "Professors acknowledge academic debt and strive to be objective in the professional judgment of colleagues" (Weingartner 132). Further confirmation of the similar beliefs and intentions we share can be found in the "Statement of Professional Ethics of the Modern Language Association of America." The Preamble states that the freedom of inquiry that scholars should enjoy "carries with it the responsibilities of professional conduct. We intend this statement to embody reasonable norms for ethical conduct in teaching, research, and related public service activities in the modern languages and literatures" (Weingartner 135). Statements 4 through 7 develop an ethic for dealing with issues of academic integrity:

> 4. Free inquiry respects the diversity of the modes and objects of investigation, whether they are traditional or innovative. We should defend scholarly practices against unfounded attacks from within or without our community.

5. Our teaching and inquiry must respect simultaneously the diversity of our own culture and that of the cultures we study.

6. Judgments of whether a line of inquiry is ultimately useful to society, colleagues, or students should not be used to limit the freedom of the scholar pursuing it.

7. As a community valuing free inquiry, we must be able to rely on the integrity and the good judgment of our members. For this reason, we should not ... plagiarize the work of others....[2] (Weingartner 135–36)

The footnote in the original explains that the definition of plagiarism used is from *The MLA Style Manual*. Points 1 and 4 in the section entitled "Ethical Conduct in Academic Relationships," subsection A entitled, "Obligations to Students" are particularly interesting and germane. Point 1 states, "Faculty members should represent to their students the values of free inquiry," and point 4 states, "Student-teacher collaboration entails the same obligation as other kinds of research: faculty members should acknowledge appropriately any intellectual indebtedness" (Weingartner 136). One assumes that students should conduct themselves in a similar manner. In any event, there seems to be little in these ethical declarations that is at odds with our own intentions.

Shamoon and Burns offered a professional approach to engaging faculty in discussions or debates about ethical and pedagogical issues.

A writing center that is driven by the social-rhetorical approach does not frame questions of plagiarism as either ethical problems or as groundless charges from the uninformed.... Practitioners in such a writing center are ready to engage other instructors in elaborate conversations about context, about disciplinary expectations, about topical frameworks and, especially, to engage them in conversations about difference—the differing and special expectations instructors have for their specific writing assignments and for what is valued by them in student writing, including writing that is imitative and elaborative of ideas and forms of disciplinary discourse.... From such conversations come the potential to move the writing center off the margins of the university and into the center of academic life. ("Plagiarism" 191–92)

Note the lack of rebellion in this approach. An approach like Shamoon and Burns proposed, one that engages us in conversation about the issues that concern us, could raise the level of writing center discourse within the institution, but we must first expunge the outsider view that keeps us from understanding institutional roles, those of others as well as our own.

When we have more closely aligned ourselves with the mission of the academy and its departments, we will find ourselves better able to ethically serve students as well. This will help us to better determine whether or not the writing center methodologies proposed by some theorists meet the needs of both the academy and students. Alice M. Gillam looked at the peer tutorial processes espoused by Kenneth Brufree and Harvey Kail and John Trimbur:

In the Brufree model, the long-range social goal seems to supercede the immediate educational goal.... [T]he goal of Kail and Trimbur's model is cast in terms which refer specifically to education, [but] this model implicitly suggests the larger social goal of a critically conscious and politically active citizenry. Notably, neither Brufree's nor Kail and Trimbur's model focuses primarily on explicit writing goals. (44–45)

The place where the goals of the academy and its students meet is a critical area where, as Clark and Healy suggested, we can provide a window, not only into the classroom, but onto the needs of our student clients (255). There is nothing wrong with trying to expand the intellectual consciousness of our students; in fact, it is implicit in our broader educational goals. But when we paint our theories with such a broad brush, we may overlook the fact that for many students, these laudable goals are years away from being attainable. Students in a developmental phase may require more emphasis on the standards of discourse, whereas those further along the continuum may be better placed to begin questioning the community and its structure.

The pervasive view of our marginalization has devastating effects on our self-image as professionals, on our ethical conduct as professionals, and ultimately on our status as professionals. But, in many ways, more importantly, our view of ourselves as outsiders is most damaging to the one constituency that is at the heart of our mission: students. The primary reason for this is that the "outsider" view has a harmful (and rather ironic) effect on how we view student autonomy or agency. The sense of marginalization that comes through in our own scholarship is painful to confront and paralyzing in its effect. As a profession, we seem extremely insecure with our place in the world and it leads to some strange paradoxes. But this is both cause and effect. When we see ourselves as outside the system, we are led into these false or, at the very least, inadequate defenses. Only when we see ourselves as a part of the system and not apart from it will we be able to create an ethical solution that will answer the needs of all of our constituencies. Ultimately, it is the act of claiming our insider status that will have the greatest and most positive long-term ethical implications for our profession and for us as professionals.

ACKNOWLEDGMENTS

The initial drafts of this chapter were written with the assistance of the writing center in which I work. I would like to specifically thank Dr. Joe Law for his invaluable aid in helping me organize my thoughts and for discussing the issues with me.

WORKS CITED

Behm, Richard. "Ethical Issues in Peer Tutoring: A Defense of Collaborative Learning." *The Writing Center Journal* 10.1 (1989): 3–12.

Clark, Irene L., and Dave Healy. "Are Writing Centers Ethical?" *WPA: Writing Program Administration* 20.1–2 (1996): 32–38. Rpt. in *The Allyn and Bacon Guide to Writing Center Theory and Practice*. Ed. Robert W. Barnett and Jacob S. Blumner. Boston: Allyn and Bacon, 2001. 242–59.

Gillam, Alice M. "Collaborative Learning Theory and Peer Tutoring Practice." *Intersections: Theory-Practice in the Writing Center*. Ed. Joan A. Mullin and Ray Wallace. Urbana, IL: NCTE, 1994. 39–53.

Grimm, Nancy Maloney. *Good Intentions: Writing Center Work for Postmodern Times*. Portsmouth, NH: Heinemann-Boynton/Cook, 1999.

Pemberton, Michael. "Writing Center Ethics." *Writing Lab Newsletter* 18.4 (1993): 10,12.

___. "Writing Center Ethics: The Three Laws of Tutoring." *Writing Lab Newsletter* 19.4 (1994): 13–14.

Shamoon, Linda K., and Deborah H. Burns. "Labor Pains: A Political Analysis of Writing Center Tutoring." *The Politics of Writing Centers*. Ed. Jane Nelson and Kathy Evertz. Portsmouth, NH: Heinemann-Boynton/Cook, 2001. 62–73.

___. "Plagiarism, Rhetorical Theory, and the Writing Center: New Approaches, New Locations." *Perspectives on Plagiarism and Intellectual Property in a Postmodern World*. Ed. Lise Buranen and Alice M. Roy. Albany: State University of New York Press, 1999. 183–92.

Simpson, Jeanne. "Perceptions, Realities, and Possibilities: Central Administration and Writing Centers." *Writing Center Perspectives*. Ed. Byron L. Stay, Christina Murphy, and Eric H. Hobson. Emmitsburg, MD: NWCA Press, 1995. 48–52. Rpt. in *The Allyn and Bacon Guide to Writing Center Theory and Practice*. Ed. Robert W. Barnett and Jacob S. Blumner. Boston: Allyn and Bacon, 2001. 189–93.

Weingartner, Rudolph H. "The Moral Dimensions of Academic Administration." Ed. Steven M. Cahn. *Issues in Academic Ethics*. Lanham, MD: Rowman & Littlefield, 1999.

❧ 27 ❧

Staffing a Writing Center with Professional Tutors

Steven Strang
Massachusetts Institute of Technology

In 1985, Jeanne H. Simpson detailed the advantage of having professionals as writing center directors: "If we demand working conditions that encourage the best from us, we must also be willing to listen and make reasonable compromises. The situation is a reciprocal one—the more professional we are, the more we can ask for; the more we ask for, the more likely it is that we will be recognized as professionals."

Presenting writing center directors as professionals is, in fact, one of the most important tasks facing the writing center movement (par. 7) Now that we are into the twenty-first century, I would take this idea further, making a case for professional tutors as well; "the more professional we are," not only in terms of directors but also in terms of tutoring staff, the more writing center work will be officially valued (e.g., in terms of appointments, salaries).

Naturally, what type of staff you choose for your center grows from your local circumstances—for example, the type of school, your vision of the center, the local restrictions (e.g., the size of your budget, the local talent pool, the needs of other departments), and the center's relation to the institution's mission. Although this chapter should in no way be seen as a negative statement about peer tutoring, I wish to make a case here that professional tutors should be at least part of the staff of any center dealing with more than just undergraduates.

BACKGROUND

This chapter grows out of my experience during the last twenty-two years: In spring 1982, I started MIT's Writing and Communication Center and have been directing it ever since. The last twenty-one of those years have included hiring, training, and supervising professional tutors. For the first semester our center was open, I employed four peer-tutors (three juniors, one senior). It became very clear, very quickly that peer-tutors were not a good fit for MIT's circumstances. By the beginning of the following semester, we were staffed by professional tutors. In the following years, we experimented by adding some peer-tutors to the mix, but by 1995 we had abandoned that idea.

MIT's circumstances are somewhat unusual. First, we do not have a sizable population of undergraduate English majors who aspire to teach, so we don't have a built-in pool of students for whom service in a writing center would be an important addition to their resumes. Second, the educational pressures at MIT are very great (tradition has it that getting an undergraduate education at MIT is like taking a drink of water from a fire hydrant). So, by midsemester, our peer-tutors disappeared into the black hole of problem sets and labs. The prestige of being selected to work in the center paled against the desire to do well in physics classes. Third, our writing center works with as many graduate students as undergraduate students, with a healthy sprinkling of staff and faculty members. Such high-level texts (e.g., dissertations, theses, articles for publication) require professional advice. Fourth, professional tutors have experience with publishing as well as with writing theses and papers for courses, which is vital with such a varied clientele. Fifth, the Cambridge/Boston area is a treasure trove of talented professional writers and teachers from which to draw our tutors.

Overall, then, having professional tutors gives us more expertise and the ability to service the whole MIT community.

DEFINITION OF A PROFESSIONAL TUTOR

Even a definition of *professional tutor* can be problematic, because anyone paid to perform a task can, in the loosest sense of the term, be a "professional." Perhaps Valerie Balester best defined the term in her response to the 1991 "A Progress Report from the CCCC Committee on Professional Standards." Noting that the report "specifies the qualifications for classroom teachers, such as 'superior writing ability,' teaching experience, or training in the teaching of composition," she asked the following rhetorical questions:

> Given that the work in writing centers requires a greater sensitivity to the needs of individual writers and to demands of their instructors, and given that writing assistants should have at least as much knowledge about the process of writing and the conventions of English as classroom teachers, should their qualifications or training be any less? And since writing centers usually serve developmental, learning-disabled, and international students, should not the level of training be of the highest? (170)

The answer is "yes." To be specific, professional tutors for our center have five major qualifications. First, they have an advanced degree (members of our current staff have MFAs, PhDs, or are ABDs). Second, they have classroom teaching experience; it's a bonus if they have also been professional technical editors and/or tutors in other writing centers. Third, they are not enrolled in a program in your college, even if they are ABDs. Over the years, our ABDs, for example, have been from Harvard, Boston University, Brown, Tufts, and Brandeis. Why this criterion? For ABDs who do not attend the target college, working in the center is a professional job, not another graduate student task or the alternative to being a TA. It is a "real" job that demands a high level of professionalism and responsibility. They are no longer in their "academic home environment," and that too makes a difference. They relate to the director and to the rest of the staff as professional equals. Fourth, they must be writers, writing on a regular basis in their field. They have not only gone through what the students are going through now, but, unlike peer-tutors, they have the wisdom and knowledge born of success and advanced writing tasks. Often professional tutors are published writers and have presented at conferences. Fifth, a professional tutor is someone who either specializes in one-on-one teaching or is interested in doing so.

ADVANTAGES OF HAVING PROFESSIONAL TUTORS

There are many advantages to having a staff of professional tutors:

1. Faculty perceptions of a center can speed its progress toward becoming a valued institution or slow that progress to a halt. John Trimbur noted that, to many traditionalists in the academy, "peer tutoring looks like a case of the 'blind leading the blind'" (22). Although this traditionalist perception is incorrect, such assumptions are still often prevalent in the academic world beyond the writing centers' walls. Having professional tutors eliminates that perception, giving an institution's instructors confidence that sending students to the center will result in their receiving good advice. At MIT, for example, our motto has always been "Be a better writer," and our advertising stresses the fact that the center is a "teaching institution." This claim goes beyond the typical "we are not a fix-it shop" and "we are not a remedial center"; we claim that we are a *teaching* institution, and having an expert staff has made that claim much more believable much more quickly for faculty members in all departments.

2. Older clients (e.g., graduate students, faculty and staff members) feel much more confident when working with professional tutors.

3. Student clients are often much more willing to heed advice given by a professional than that given by a fellow student.

4. Much more can be accomplished in a session because the professional tutor is adept at diagnosing writing problems, at working with writer's block, at helping students decipher assignments, at dealing with sophisticated compositional and rhetorical issues.

5. Hiring professionals provides a chance to hire specialists (e.g., in ESL or in technical writing), and those professionals can, in turn, deepen the knowledge of the rest of your staff.

6. Professional tutors bring to the center a plethora of teaching styles that have grown out of their own theories and experiences of teaching. This diversity fosters a fruitful interchange of ideas and styles among the staff. Further, if students find it difficult to adapt to one style, they can easily find another.

7. They create a strong continuing core of tutors from one academic year to the next, a stable and continuing workforce whose skills and knowledge of the center's clients becomes more and more sophisticated. Further, with peer-tutors there is the inevitable amount of turnover and the concomitant requirement to train new tutors every year; some directors feel like Sisyphus, pushing the rock to the top of the mountain (managing to train peers to

be good tutors) only to have the rock roll back to the bottom of the mountain (those tutors graduate and a whole new group must be trained), stuck in a cycle stretching through eternity (or at least until retirement).

Further, the quality of peer tutoring inevitably varies from one semester to the next; some students have a gift for teaching and for empathetic understanding, some don't. As Lil Brannon and Stephen M. North pointed out, "No doubt these [peer-] tutors' fresh perspective on teaching make our work exciting and productive. Yet if we are honest, we know as well that the quality of the work is often uneven, and the yearly education programs for new tutors can become exhausting" (11). Harvey Kail echoed some of these sentiments:

> Much of the daily business of writing centers takes its shape from the ongoing necessity of recruiting new tutors and training them for the complex conversations between writer and reader that constitute the main event of writing center life. The entire training process—from interviewing potential recruits to designing and teaching the training course to celebrating the graduation of yet another group of peer writing tutors—prominently shapes the way tutors and tutor trainers alike come to the literacy work that they do together in writing centers. (74)

8. In addition, professional tutors' experience with a college's particular students and the types of assignments grows with each passing semester and becomes an ever-expanding foundation on which to build techniques for tutoring individual students and to create handouts and web pages tailored to a particular college's needs and aims.

9. They exhibit a professional level of responsibility. In the past, for example, our consultants have come to work despite everything from a case of whooping cough (past its contagious stage, of course) to a broken ankle. That is dedication. When we had a recent blackout in Cambridge, I returned from a meeting to find both tutors working with clients, all four people huddled under the emergency light. When there have been fire alarms, our tutors take their clients to other spots on campus to keep working. That's professionalism.

10. They are effective translators, interpreting "teacher speak" for students. As Nancy Maloney Grimm pointed out, "[W]riting center work is defined by the curriculum in unavoidable ways because students come to us for help interpreting the curriculum" (5). Who better to translate the complexities of the curriculum than those who have taught classes and now specialize in one-on-one teaching?

11. One of the strengths of a professional staff is the high quality of insights into process and into audience. Because students are mostly writing to their professors (or the hypothetical readers teachers posit for an assignment), what could be better than having such a reader to respond to their writing—without the pressure of a grade but with the promise of enlightenment and learning?

12. Professional tutors are sounding boards for the directors' ideas, and they are sources of new ideas and approaches. They can also take on some of the creative tasks of the center, if needed (e.g., maintaining a Web site, creating handouts, giving class presentations).

13. A professional tutor affords collegial opportunities to the director as well as to the other consultants. As director, you can learn from staff members even while training them in the specific policies, theoretical foundations, and practices of a particular center. The opportunity to learn from your staff even as you train them is a huge bonus.

14. Professional tutors are also better able to pursue what Dave Healy called the center's "prophetic mission": "Both churches and writing centers can and should have a pro-

phetic mission; they are places where renewal, innovation, and boundary breaking can challenge the existing order. But both are also places that require accommodation, compromise, and an ability to test the institutional waters" (23). Balester made a similar point, noting, "The writing center should be the place in an English department where writing is not only critiqued but also discussed, produced, researched, and enjoyed. We know writing centers can do this work because many already do, even when they lack support and recognition" (166–67). Because they have knowledge of institutional ways and of educational missions, professional tutors can accomplish these tasks.

15. By far the most important advantage of having professional tutors, however, is the consistently high quality of one-on-one teaching that results from their profound knowledge about writing.

CHALLENGES OF HAVING PROFESSIONAL TUTORS

Having professional tutors does pose some potential challenges. The most troubling one is the possibility of reverting to the "classroom teacher role." According to Janice Neuleib, "Tutoring and conferencing both demonstrate decentered teaching activities, but in both cases, the instructor retains the role of expert editor to the student's role of novice contributor" (235). JoAnne Wangeci Karui added that "[w]hen conflicts of opinion arise in a conference situation, it becomes tempting for a consultant to assume the superior stance of know-all" (79). And Andrea Lunsford warned that "collaboration can also be used to reproduce the status quo; the rigid hierarchy of teacher-centered classrooms is replicated in the tutor-centered writing center in which the tutor is still the seat of all authority but is simply pretending it isn't so" (4).

Clearly, returning to the role of authority can be even more tempting for professional tutors than for peer-tutors, and students will be more likely to slip back into the role of novice writers if the person tutoring them is a highly credentialed professional. Old habits are difficult to break, particularly when we confront students who do not speak "teacher talk" or who seem clueless and desperate for help.

Yet that authority-in-sheep's clothing possibility is trumped, I think, by processes that many of us already have in place. For instance, letting clients choose the topic of the session and acceding to their wishes even against the tutor's own best advice, keeping students actively engaged throughout the session, carrying on a conversation about the students' writing instead of feeding them rules and phrasings, and refusing to suggest an approximate grade for a paper are all processes that eliminate the temptation to back slide into the authoritarian role.

Indeed, professional tutors are in an advantageous position for achieving the goal of participating in the discourse community of their clients in a way that classroom teachers are not. Freed from the responsibility of grading, tutors can "relinquish much of the authorship and ownership in" their teaching in order to "share in the learning" of their students (Neuleib 240). In fact, such sharing-in-the-learning is one of the great advantages of being a professional tutor—the chance to learn composition from the point of view of other "cultures" (student cultures as well as international cultures).

Students are more likely to ask a professional tutor than a peer-tutor for an evaluation of their texts (e.g., a grade). We have found the following to be a useful response: "We can't know all the criteria that your professor is considering when evaluating your paper. All we can say is that you now seem to have a better sense of X, but there is still the issue of Q."

Scheduling can also be a challenge. Many professional tutors are part-time, and most have jobs in addition to tutoring in the center (and the schedule of those with other teaching jobs can change significantly from semester to semester), thus it is difficult for the director to maintain the same amount of staffing for the same hours each semester. For the same reasons, arranging staff meetings with part-time professional tutors can also be a challenge. Professional tutors often have family commitments (e.g., they may need to take off public school vacations to be with their school-age children). Still, this problem of fluctuating schedules is offset by the "if you have the conference hours, clients will come" phenomenon. A compromise between the symmetry of a center's schedule and the needs of the professional tutors is a small price to pay for the high level of tutoring that results.

HIRING OF PROFESSIONAL TUTORS

As part of the hiring process, I now ask applicants to write a short "my philosophy of tutoring statement," similar in intent to a statement of teaching philosophy. In general, this statement includes the applicant's beliefs about the process of tutoring writing and about the advantages and disadvantages of one-on-one teaching, the applicant's goals as a tutor, the applicant's perceived strengths and weaknesses as a tutor and goals for developing skills. I offer the following questions as guides for their statement:

1. What is your basic philosophy of tutoring undergraduate students? At what points do you draw the line as giving too much help or too little?

2. Does your basic philosophy of tutoring graduate students differ in any way from that of tutoring undergraduates?

3. At which point(s) in the writing process do you think it is appropriate for tutors to intervene?

4. Do you think different levels of intervention apply in different situations? For instance, would you give more or less advice about a paper being written for a grade vs. an application essay for graduate school?

5. In what cases, if any, would you help phrase a sentence? Organize a paragraph or a whole essay? Give advice about content?

6. What would you do if you suspected a student client of plagiarizing?

7. What would you do if the teacher's comments on a student's paper seemed incorrect or sarcastic?

8. At MIT, we work with clients from all fields, many of which you will be unfamiliar with. What problems do you anticipate in dealing with papers or theses from scientific, engineering, or economic fields? How will you deal with them?

9. What problems do you think might arise from working with students for whom English is a second language (ESL)? How would you solve those problems?

Written tutoring statements, however, can only tell you so much. Because personality traits are so important, interviews are crucial. Dogmatic, prescriptive personalities are not good fits in the welcoming, open environment that most centers try to provide. Similarly, sensitivity to the at-times fragile self-confidence of students is necessary. Tutors need to build students' confidence as well as their skills.

During the interview (and in training as well), we discuss the similarities and differences between a teacher–student conference and a tutoring session. In the former, the teacher has the power of grades and hence speaks with a multiple authority—the grader, the person with explicit and perhaps implicit unstated expectations for the paper, the intended audience, a reader more knowledgeable about the field than the writer. A professional tutor, on the other hand, speaks only with the authority of someone more knowledgeable about the process of writing. This diminution of authority is a huge advantage; because students can be more honest about their concerns and fears, they can admit confusion about the assignment or the content more readily with someone who will not grade the paper. And, because the students are often more expert than the tutor in terms of the content, their need to explain things to the tutor helps them clarify their own ideas and beliefs. Then the tutor can say, "That sounds like an important distinction you just said. Do you think it should be included in your paper?"

TRAINING OF PROFESSIONAL TUTORS

What Kail said about peer-tutors is applicable to the experience of professionals who start tutoring for the first time: "Tutor training can and frequently does involve a powerful and transforming rite of educational passage" (76). He noted that "[b]reaking with the traditional expectations of classrooms in exchange for the perplexing and unpredictable intimacy of the conference format calls for a radical change in the teacher's orientation to learning and teaching" (80). In my experience, most professionals embrace the idea of one-on-one tutoring. They are eager to teach and eager to learn.

Because I rarely hire more than one new person every two or three years (the result of a continuing core staff), I tailor training to the individual hired. For someone with a strong background in writing center work and classroom teaching, the training may simply be a few informal conversations. For individuals with only classroom experience, I have them watch the veteran tutors for a week, then I hold two or three joint sessions with new tutors and clients. In the first session, I take the lead with the client and draw new hires into the conversation with questions and requests for opinions. After that, I cede the lead to new hires and simply respond when spoken to. Then the new hires are on their own.

As part of ongoing training, all professional tutors read and discuss articles that any of us can suggest. Together, we discuss "problem students" and frustrations. These discussions rarely occur with the full staff present for the reasons noted earlier. Instead, three or four of us have a discussion at a time, with me attending all the discussions. Continuing staff discussions of such issues also keep us alert to the danger of overhelping clients. As Steve Sherwood pointed out, "For even given with good intentions, too much help stunts a student's intellectual growth, thwarting what should be our primary goal" (66). Professional tutors are much less likely to commit this error, having already learned "detached concern" as classroom teachers. According to Sherwood, we should "balance our empathic regard for a student with careful objectivity toward his or her writing problems. This fits nicely into the 'less is more' philosophy Jeff Brooks calls minimalist tutoring" (69).

Tutors' training is augmented by their having opportunities to teach their fellow tutors when they offer sessions in their specialties. Learning from each other occurs informally all the time: Because we encourage a free-flowing exchange of ideas and requests for opinions during tutoring sessions, our tutors are a major resource for each other as well as for their clients. Thus, no tutors are left feeling that they must "know it all."

MANAGING PROFESSIONAL TUTORS

With professional tutors, managing is often a case of getting out of the way and letting them teach. The director's basic managerial tasks are to be sure that everyone is following the same guidelines and policies and that everyone is conducting successful tutoring sessions. Here are our major guidelines that surely differ little from those at many writing centers:

1. Listen to what clients tell you about their writing process, about their feelings, about their vision of the particular assignment they have brought to the center.
2. Ask to see the teacher's written assignment.
3. Let the clients set the agenda for the session (our forms ask clients to indicate the issues they would like us to deal with during the 55-minute session).
4. All other things being equal, address first the issue(s) that most obstruct the act of communication.
5. If clients want to focus on a less crucial element, advise them of the issue that most gets in the way of communication and suggest you work on that first. If the clients demur, accede to their wishes—it is their session. At the end of the session, however, remind them of the existing problems.
6. Keep clients actively involved in the tutoring process throughout (e.g., by asking questions, by having them read their papers out loud).
7. Focus on deepening the writer's understanding rather than on improving the paper.
8. Do not write on the clients' papers.
9. Do not proofread or edit their papers.
10. Do not make substantial suggestions about content.
11. Use your professional judgment to determine whether any of the previous guidelines should be violated in an individual circumstance.

A win–win managerial situation is the fact that staff members are an integral part of the decision-making process: They have the opportunity to influence the policies and environment in which they work, and I have the opportunity to draw on their expertise and experience. Among recent decisions my tutors have had a major influence on are the decision to open for evening and Sunday hours, the decision to open at 9:00 a.m. instead of 10:00 a.m., and the decision to turn our 3:00–4:00 p.m. slot into half hour slots to give all the tutors an extended break in the midafternoon.

When there are a few free moments in the center, our professional tutors look for gaps in our resources. Over the years, they have authored several of our handouts, and next semester will start writing pages for our Web site (with bylines, of course).

CONCLUSIONS

I have chosen to focus on professional tutors not only because our experience at MIT with a fully professional staff has been so successful, but also because so little has been written about professional tutors. Local situations will greatly influence each director's decision about staffing. However, for centers dealing with a wide variety of clients (undergraduate and graduate students, faculty and staff) from a wide variety of disciplines, professional tutors are a very effective staffing option. Because they are professionals, we try to pay our tutors a salary equivalent to that of adjunct faculty, with a semester-long 25% slot in the center being equivalent to teaching one course. Professional tutors cost more than student tutors, but the value given is well worth the cost.

WORKS CITED

Balester, Valerie. "Revising the 'Statement': On the Work of Writing Centers." *College Composition and Communication* 43 (May 1992): 167–71.

Brannon, Lil, and Stephen M. North "The Uses of Margins." *The Writing Center Journal* 20 (Spring/Summer 2000): 7–12.

Grimm, Nancy Maloney. "Contesting the Idea of a Writing Center: The Politics of Writing Center Research." *Writing Lab Newsletter* 17.1 (1992): 5–7.

Healy, Dave. "In the Temple of the Familiar: The Writing Center as Church." *Writing Center Perspectives*. Ed. Byron L. Stay, Christina Murphy, and Eric H. Hobson. Emmitsburg MD: NCWA P, 1995. 12–25.

Kail, Harvey. "Separation, Initiation, and Return: Tutor Training Manuals and Writing Center Lore." *The Center Will Hold: Perspectives on Writing Center Scholarship*. Ed. Michael A Pemberton and Joyce Kinkead. Logan: Utah State UP, 2003. 74–95.

Karui, JoAnne Wangeci. "Must We Always Grin and Bear It?" *Writing Center Perspectives*. Ed. Byron L. Stay, Christina Murphy, and Eric H. Hobson. Emmitsburg MD: NCWA P, 1995. 71–83

Lunsford, Andrea. "Collaboration, Control, and the Idea of a Writing Center." *Writing Lab Newsletter* 16.4–5 (1991/92): 1–5.

Neuleib, Janice. "The Friendly Stranger: Twenty-Five Years as 'Other.'" *College Composition and Communication* 43 (1992): 231–43.

Sherwood, Steve. "The Dark Side of the Helping Personality: Student Dependency and the Potential for Tutor Burnout Professional." *Writing Center Perspectives*. Ed. Byron L. Stay, Christina Murphy, and Eric H. Hobson. Emmitsburg MD: NCWA P, 1995. 63–70

Simpson, Jeanne H. "What Lies Ahead for Writing Centers: Position Statement on Professional Concerns." *The Writing Center Journal* 5.2/6.1 (1985): 35–39. 75 pars. Rpt. On the IWCA Web site 14 May 2004. <http://writingcenters.org/positionstatement.htm>.

Trimbur, John. "Peer Tutoring: A Contradiction in Terms?" *The Writing Center Journal* 7.2 (1987): 21–28.

❧28❧

Using Tutorial Principles to Train Tutors: Practicing Our Praxis

Muriel Harris
Purdue University

Training tutors is a complex undertaking with a wildly overloaded agenda. We want tutors to know basic principles of tutorial theory and practice; assess writing based on sound rhetorical concepts; have a grasp of grammatical rules (or know where and how to find them); be able to interact in a comfortable, nonhierarchical manner with writers of various skill levels, backgrounds, and cultures; be nonevaluative in their questions and comments; keep a positive tone to all interaction; ask effective questions; recognize the difference between assisting writers and doing the work for them; feel comfortable reading writing in various fields and genres; understand and be able to distinguish—and practice—directive and nondirective tutoring (and know when to use one or the other); use the Internet for online tutoring and help writers learn how to find, evaluate, and document web resources; collaborate effectively; have a responsible work ethic; and so on (And, of course, they must be able to accomplish all this in half-hour or hour sessions.) Moreover, those of us who train tutors have to help them learn all this in several orientation sessions, at staff meetings, as in-service, or in a credit-bearing course (normally lasting only one quarter or semester).

As we contemplate how we will train tutors, there are yet other overwhelming concerns to confront. One is the sheer bulk of the literature on the subject of tutor training; it's vast, requiring many hours of reading if one wants to consult a good sampling of what has been written about training tutors. Although there are many overlaps among various listings, it is apparent that there is a wealth of writing to read: *Writing Centers: An Annotated Bibliography*, a book that catalogs materials up to 1995, which lists 96 entries on training; CompPile (a database for composition entries from 1939 to 1999 and later moved to the yearly CCCC/MLA bibliography), which lists 112 entries for tutor training; and Paula Gillespie and Neal Lerner's *Allyn and Bacon Guide to Peer Tutoring* (2nd ed.), lists almost 100 recommended readings for tutors and has over 150 listings in the Works Cited. The natural tendency, then, is to lean toward offering numerous handouts, relying on tutoring manuals or home-made packets, assigning readings from the literature on tutoring, showing videos, and so on. The danger here, which Linda K. Shamoon and Deborah H. Burns warned us of, is that tutor training manuals have "served to standardize … [tutoring], making it uniform, repetitive, bounded, and inexpert, while the discourse in the scholarly literature about tutoring extends and constantly inscribes this narrowly constructed portrait of such labor" ("Labor Pains" 64). The result, argued Shamoon and Burns, is that all this written material prepares the tutor to be only a "generalist tutor" (65), not equipped to handle the constantly differing conditions of tutorials, the variety of directions into which tutorials can extend, and the occasional need to be more directive. In short, Shamoon and Burns saw the present state of tutor training as constrictive, ignoring other avenues to travel down. Elizabeth H. Boquet's exploration in *Noises from the Writing Center* echoes this search for modes of tutoring that, as she recognized in Meg Carroll's center, produces "a community of tutors who managed to keep their options open" (143).

One way to avoid the constraints lamented by Shamoon and Burns, I suggest, would be to open up the training to let in some of the muddy reality of tutoring, the exploratory discussions that may indeed lead down unexpected avenues. To do so means admitting flexibility so that training discussions drift in directions that may lead to unplanned or new territory. This is likely to mean acknowledging the need for expertise outside the trainer's realm of knowledge or the possibility of how and why a tutorial may not follow the standard agenda of how to open a tutorial. Tutor training time that doesn't have a tight syllabus or format can help tutors (or tutors-to-be) learn to be flexible; to let curiosity lead into terra incognita; to learn skills such as how to establish rapport, set the agenda, engage others as active participants in their own learning, and acknowledge at some point in the group's conversation the very real need for a more informed discussion participant to be directive by researching or contributing the knowledge that is needed. (The "informed" person isn't necessarily the tutor trainer who takes over and explains. Tutors-to-be can tell the rest of us what it's like to live with learning disabilities or try to write in English when it's their second or third language or use strategies for tutoring learned from watching experienced tutors or from other tutoring experiences, and so on.) In short, we can open up training to possibilities that our ocean of scholarly literature and training manuals are useful, but limited because reality can be quite different. And, in the process, we can make tutoring theory come alive by enacting it during training time because asking new tutors to learn theory in no way guarantees they can put it in practice. Asking ourselves to conduct the training time as a tutorial also means that we have to have thought through what tutoring is—and could be—and be able to be the tutor we want novice tutors to become.

To muddy this all even further, we aren't exactly sure what is entailed in all those "generalist" guidelines to which Shamoon and Burns referred. As Peter Carino noted, "[T]he question of tutorial power and authority … has had a long and unresolved history in the writing center community" (97). Certainly, it's not clear as to the degree with which we want tutors to be directive or nondirective. Many writing center scholars concur with Jim Bell when he noted that "[a] tutor's job is neither to tell the student what to do nor to write the paper, but to negotiate what to work on and to help the writer learn the skills she or she needs to write successfully" (79). But, as Bell acknowledged, "[s]uch a pedagogy is difficult to teach a new tutor" (79). Still, advocates of nondirective tutoring, who emphasize nondirectiveness in a training course, include in their training literature Jeff Brook's essay on the minimalist tutor, or similar articles that affirm the noninvasive pedagogy that avoids any delivery of knowledge from the tutor. Shamoon and Burns, however, were reluctant to accept the assumption that nondirective tutoring is the only model for tutors to draw on. In "A Critique of Pure Tutoring," they drew on their own leaning experiences and other models of learning to argue "that directive tutoring … is sometimes a suitable and effective mode of instruction" (223). Carino examined the question in terms of "how centers might gain by refiguring authority as a reasonable descriptor in discussing tutorial work, and how tutors might be trained differently to recognize and use their power and authority without becoming authoritarian" (97). Carino summed up his agenda for tutor training as follows: "[T]utors should be taught to recognize where the power and authority lie in any given tutorial, when and to what degree they have them, when and to what degree the student has them, and when and to what degree they are absent in any given tutorial" (109).

But whether we choose an emphasis in training on stressing nondirectiveness—at the Brooks end of the spectrum—or move away from that to align with Carino and Shamoon and Burns, who encouraged occasions when directiveness can be more effective, the reality that Jim Bell found is that most tutoring is directive. Bell's survey of research studies on tutoring affirms the pervasiveness of directive "tutor-centered practice." Such sessions are those where, as Bell described it, "the tutor controls the topics, the content, and the pace, does most of the work, and talks much more than the student does" (80). Whatever principles the trainer values, it seems that tutors engaged in tutoring become directive. This may to a large extent result from the idea that the *what* and the *how* of tutoring are very different. New tutors may fully understand and agree with the principles that underlie nondirective tutoring (to whatever extent it is encouraged), but the *how*, the strategic knowledge for accomplishing this (and for knowing when it's appropriate and, as Shamoon and Burns reminded us, when it's not) is another matter. The *compleat tutor*, then, knows theory, isn't constrained by guidelines of exactly what to do and when to do it, and has the strategic knowledge to turn theory into practice.

The full complexity of training tutors becomes more evident. Not only is there a wealth of theoretical literature on tutoring (with different voices as to what that theory should be), there are highly informative tutoring manuals with useful guidelines that list tutoring practices. The link between theory that constructs guidelines and practices that promote it (a wealth of discussion of such practices can be found in Paula Gillespie and Neal Lerner's *Allyn and Bacon Guide to Peer Tutoring*) is the strategic knowledge that tutors need to enact those practices built on theory. But strategic knowledge can't be easily "taught" merely by explaining or describing it. For example, the manuals, which Shamoon and Burns indicated are for generalist tutors, call for interpersonal skills that are often labeled "friendly, supportive, nurturing, and responsive" (66). Tutors may be selected because we recognize their strong interpersonal skills when they apply. But how do we encourage such skills, help tutors-in-training see how to make these qualities enter the tutorial? "Be friendly," we advise; "be nurturing," we counsel; "be flexible," we urge. But saying this doesn't necessarily mean the new tutor can enact such qualities any more than telling a writer she needs to write with "voice" (that mysterious quality so glibly recommended in rhetoric texts) will result in writing with voice. We have to confront this reality—that much of the strategic knowledge of tutoring cannot easily be "taught" (in the sense of "telling learners what they need to know"). For example, in the same way that we might suggest that tutors "empathize" with the students they work with or that actors are advised to "be in the moment" when on the stage or that problem solvers are told to "think outside the box," such mental activities can be described, explained, and clarified, but that doesn't mean the novice tutor really experiences such mind-sets or becomes consciously adept at internalizing and enacting them—or recognizing the kairotic moment when they are needed.

Other first principles of tutoring are similarly resistant to being internalized only by reading about them or being told what to do. What I am focusing on, finally, are those aspects of tutoring pedagogy that can't be "taught by telling." Bell considered structured reflection as a training mode for the more difficult principles of tutoring pedagogy, but having created a number of structured reflection training exercises and tried them with two different staffs of tutors, he concluded that the types of conferences his tutors conducted didn't change much after the structured reflection work. However, Bell affirmed that any training course "will want to include some kind of reflection on practice, that is, will want tutors to monitor their practice and to learn systematically from experience" (90).

Modeling behaviors is another way to encourage growth in awareness of what it feels like to collaborate or to make a quick assessment of a puzzling student paper or to stop and realize that the student's body language is telling you something is wrong with how the session is proceeding. But even more effective can be combining modeling with helping tutors-to-be actually experience during their training much of what they have to be competent to do in tutorials. Tutors-to-be come to training with huge carpet bags filled with preconceived notions of what they are expected to do: Find and correct errors, tell the student what is needed, and so on. They might initially view their role as a front-line teacher, helping the student fix the paper for the classroom teacher, and assume they must be able to demonstrate to the student that they know all they are required to know about writing. They most likely will want immediate help with all the "what should I do?" questions that lead to discussions of strategies for tutoring (e.g., "How should I help a student see that her paper has no thesis?" or "What should I do when the student isn't happy with the topic that's assigned?"). Katie Theriault faced this familiar situation and reminded us of yet another aspect of training—the need to quell the immediate quest for strategies so that we can also introduce theories of writing center tutoring that are the underpinning of practice:

> I noticed a particular dynamic emerging in the training course I was instructing. That is, our class discussions were becoming stymied by the group's tendency to consider *how* to tutor, before understanding theoretically *what* tutoring is, or *why* it happens. Students were rushing to the practical before having fully developed a theoretical context. Among tutors-to-be, this move is a common one, I think, probably driven by a combination of nervous excitement and anticipation. I understood why it was happening, but I struggled with how to side-step it. How does one argue for the value of theoretical thinking? (3)

The challenge, then, is how to change attitudes and preconceived notions of new tutors, how to help them become adept at drawing on needed skills in the tutorial setting; how to introduce theoretical concepts when they are eager to plunge in with strategies instead; how to demonstrate for them the flexibility they'll need when tutorials don't seem to head in standard directions, in standardized ways; how to be truly collaborative, and how to help students actively seek their own solutions and answers that result in real learning. And, there's that reminder of "time's winged chariot" at our backs, to pack all that into limited training time. I have no magic answers or perfect syllabus that will achieve all this, but I offer some suggestions concerning how to make tutorial theory and practice come alive by enacting it during the training time. In a nutshell, I suggest that we make our training sessions, workshops, in-services, and classes into macrotutorials. That is, when at all possible, we play out the tutor's role and the tutors-to-be are the students in our tutorial. And, of course, we need to be clear in our minds about what we identify as a tutor's role.

We can start by envisioning the training period as stages of a tutorial, and start with the initial getting acquainted time, when it is important to set the nervous student at ease, to create a space where there's comfortable interaction, to play against the hierarchy that is inherent in the situation, both in the tutorials to come and during the training time. Whether it is a first class session, the beginning of the training workshop, or the first staff meeting, what can we do to create the same comfort zone tutors want students to be in? The physical setting, of course, can assist here with comfortable couches, some food within reach, and walls that are not sterile or barren. The trainer can engage the group in a few minutes of friendly, light chatter, just as we suggest tutors can do in the opening moments of a tutorial, to set the writer at ease. Every training session can start that way, easing into getting to know each other. (A few minutes of friendly conversation about the performance of the institution's football team, the new movie in town, or the perpetually broken elevators or air conditioning in the building announce that light chatter is acceptable here. So, later on, is asking one of the tutors-to-be how that chem test was that she was so nervous about last week.) At our very first interaction with the tutors-to-be, we can safely assume that some, or most, are as nervous as some students are when coming to a writing center for the first time. What can we do to help overcome that sense of nervousness, that feeling of inadequacy? We might put it on the table for discussion, noting that we're all nervous at first, or we can have a group discussion about other settings where we have tried to cope with similar feelings of nervous tension. (That kind of discussion should provoke some "me too's" that help to break down barriers. The stories usually reveal the many disturbing ways academicians can cause stress in students' lives. Who knew there is a film course where the movie is shown one night and the students' five-page critiques are due the next morning?) Whatever skills or strategies we have to help others calm down can be put into play both as the training begins and as it continues. And just as "rapport setting time" in the tutorial can be useful in getting to know the student, those first few minutes of our group meetings can help us learn who those novice tutors hiding behind "cool" exteriors really are and help them get to know and comfortably interact with each other.

After that initial "building rapport" opening, we can work on setting an agenda, just as tutor and student will do in their meetings. Coming to training with a set syllabus announces that we are in charge and we will make all the decisions as to what is to be learned. Flexibility with the semester's agenda is crucial. And just as agenda setting in a tutorial is a mix of what the tutor thinks should be discussed and what the student has asked for help with, so too the training time can be a collaborative effort. One way to learn what novice tutors want from the course is to ask them to reflect on this by having a first writing in which they describe their goals for the course and the specifics of what they hope to learn. Ask them to consider which skills they think need improving, what they want to know about writing centers, how the course will fit into their own interests and future careers, even what—by the end of the training period or course—they want to have learned. An extended discussion is needed to convince tutors-to-be NOT to settle for a vague "I want to become a good tutor." Discuss the need for specifics in writing, for honest writing, for writing that truly reflects their motives and interests. And use what we find out. It may mean incorporating more about working with ESL students because one tutor plans a year abroad teaching English or more on speaking skills because a couple of tutors-to-be are worried about that (especially if they plan to be teachers) or much, much more about grammatical rules than we had intended to include. (Be prepared for new tutors who can be very blunt in identifying their agendas: They need to learn how not to act nervous, how to confront a student whose paper is truly hopeless; how to write better themselves.) Compiling a list of what has been asked for and presenting it to the group to concur with (no one ever really votes down anything on the list) stresses that the writers of those papers have been heard and their requests will be included. As a member of the group, we too have a list of topics that, if not already mentioned, gets folded into the list presented to the group. And offering a rationale at that time for what we want to cover helps novice tutors see why we are including our items on the semester's agenda. Midway through the semester or training period, another useful writing assignment is to do a formative or midcourse evaluation. What haven't we covered? What has been covered and can be dropped (by that time, some are likely to note that the weekly journal writing is becoming tedious and no longer as useful as it was early on)? What new topics do we need to add to future discussions? (It's likely that some are going to be begging for larger, more generalized perspectives on ESL tutoring because they begin to see the need for a more grounded base to deal with all the mysteries of ESL tutoring.)

As the semester progresses, we continue to enact all that we want our tutors to know and to be able to do. No discussion ever gets a disgusted, disinterested, or negative response from the trainer. Every contribution to the discussion is acknowledged, heard, and examined for its usefulness. (Novice tutors learn to get into this mode of speaking and enter the conversation with comments such as "yah, I can see why Emilie thinks that we need to stick with open-ended questions, and I read about open-ended questions in my communications class, but what if that takes too long?") When that happens—when speakers in the group start by affirming that they heard the previous speaker even though they foresaw a problem with what was said—tutors-to-be are already modeling each other's discussion skills. And that becomes a way to converse in a tutorial. It's much more effective than "telling" the new tutors to be positive, to listen, to acknowledge the student's comments. It's a nice abstract notion. And we too have to sit on our hands and wait after asking a question, just as we ask new tutors not to rush into answering their own questions when there is a moment of silence that hangs heavy in the air.

Because tutoring is collaborative in that the tutor and writer work together toward the goal of improving the writer's ability to write effectively, new tutors need assistance in learning how to draw a writer into thinking through a question the writer can and should answer without doing the writer's work. It's so much easier to tell novice tutors that their job is to get the student to become an active learner and to lecture new tutors that whereas they may struggle with their inclination to "tell 'em what to do," they should refrain from this. But we can't merely tell them to do this. Instead, lead them into enacting what this aspect of collaboration entails.

How *does* a tutor transfer power to the student to think through a question? "What should I do when the student wants me to proofread the paper?" asks the worried novice tutor. Instinctively, we are ready to offer six or fourteen strategies that work for us. Instead, we need to sit on our hands, just as we expect a tutor to do when asked for an answer to the kind of question the asker must learn to solve. We can turn the question back to the tutor-to-be ("Have you seen any of the experienced tutors handle this? If so, what did they do?" or "Do you have any strategies that you use to proof your own writing?"), or if we're with the group of novice tutors, we can seek help collaboratively and wait for the brainstorming discussion to begin. We are not barred from contributing to the discussion, merely from hijacking it so that we do all the talking.

When training is truly collaborative, novice tutors should continue to shape the training. Prepared materials and syllabi for training courses most likely will have to be altered, and we may need to add some new topics and explorations to the training. But collaboration is collaboration, and everyone has a voice in shaping the final product. Sometimes, it may be only for that meeting when new tutors start off asking about a tutoring problem they confronted or observed. The discussion may go on for a large portion of the time together, but if it's a real concern and the rest of the group is interested, the discussion is not cut short. Similarly, syllabi have to remain flexible because tutors-in-training need constant affirmation that their voices are respected and acted on when the group agrees that our agenda needs adjusting. New tutors, like any other students, come to tutoring having been acculturated into the academic script of waiting to be told what to read, what to write, and when to listen. For them, just as for the student sitting down to a first tutorial, they need to wean themselves away from standard modes of academic behavior and move on to a new mode of learning. When training extends over a specific time such as presemester orientation sessions, workshops, or a course, there is still more collaboration about the training agenda. Tutors-to-be can write evaluations of what they learned, how well the trainer entered into that process, and what they would recommend for the next group of trainees. (Those suggestions are then incorporated into the training of the next group. For those of us who have proceeded on this principle, our syllabi, even though tentative, just get better and better each time.)

Because tutorials proceed in a nonevaluative space where grades and/or other inhibiting factors are removed, a training course should—if at all possible—be ungraded. Sadly, however, some students will need a grade for one reason or another, and we have to respect that—if it's truly needed. When the student selects to take a training course for a pass/fail option, we are freed of making any evaluative comments on papers. At some point in the semester or quarter, however, tutors-in-training will want to know how they are progressing in terms of a grade, even if they don't need a course grade. Students are used to measuring themselves by others' evaluations of them. That's an excellent time to reflect on how frustrated a writer will be when they, as future tutors, won't respond to a question about the paper's grade. That's a difficult issue to confront, but we might be able to model for novice tutors how they might answer by noting some of their strengths that we've noticed already and what we'd suggest they work on.

In addition to these general approaches that pervade the training period (and, of course, the whole writing center atmosphere and staff meetings), there are possible assignments that can help tutors-to-be acquire (if they don't already know) the strategic knowledge that assures they will be those collaborative, attentive, affirmative, flexible, knowledgeable tutors we want them to be. One ongoing assignment is to have occasional peer response groups meet to work together to analyze a paper. They can be asked to talk about what they would do in a tutorial with the writer of that paper, and in doing so there is much to be learned. Novice tutors build confidence as they listen and learn from each other about possible responses to the paper. They hear each other suggest a variety of topics a tutorial might address, which helps to explode the premise that there is one and only one path a tutorial might take; they learn how helpful collaboration really is by collaborating with each other; and they learn to relax as they share their uncertainties about what to do. As the world of tutoring becomes more complex in their minds and they strengthen their understanding of the uniqueness of each writer and each tutorial, their frustration level rises (usually about the second or third time they meet as a group with yet another paper to assess) because they begin to notice the conclusions they cannot draw and the questions they cannot ask because the writer isn't there. If online tutoring is part of what they will do as tutors, this can open up useful discussions of how face-to-face and online tutoring differ and how a tutor might work in each environment. (A good resource here is George Cooper, Kara Bui, and Linda Riker's "Protocols and Process in Online Tutoring.")

To enrich new tutors' growing respect for the individuality of every writer and writing situation, we can ask that they try a learning styles test or take a shortened form of the Myers-Briggs Type Inventory (MBTI) to gain insights into how people differ in acquiring and processing information. (See, e.g., Harris "Working" for a discussion of the use of the MBTI in tutor training. Various short forms of the MBTI, which lack the full power of the MBTI but do serve as a quick introduction, can be found on the World Wide Web.) Other class activities to help novice tutors understand the complexities of the writing processes of different writers and the need to explore their students' effective or dysfunctional writing processes is to spend time comparing in a group discussion how each tutor-to-be writes papers—and to follow that up with a writing assignment to interview another writer and compare their writing processes with those of the person interviewed (see Harris "When Writers Write"). To extend the appreciation for collaboration at all levels, experienced tutors can be included in the interviews and selection of new tutors, can be involved in working with the training group, and act as mentors. These are certainly not new ideas, and many are easily recognizable as practices described elsewhere in the literature. The stress here is on being consistent in having the training period enact that very important strategic knowledge as part of what is offered as training, to meld it to the theoretical underpinnings of what writing center pedagogy is. Examining where and when hierarchy, primarily directive instruction, rigid guidelines, and evaluative responses are undercutting what is being taught can lead to interesting new ways to train tutors. Moreover, it can—to bring us back to Shamoon and Burns's criticism—break the bounds of constrained, inflexible generalist tutors unable to move beyond set boundaries or explore new options.

One more recommendation is to ensure that enjoyment is a part of this whole mix. However, truly enjoying being together should not appear as the last consideration for training because it is so important. The atmosphere of the training place and time together are vital to the success of creating a pleasant interaction. New tutors can feel the mood shift the first day when we include discussions of what the snacks will be and who will bring them and when training is placed in a comfortable setting of couches or whatever is available to create a nonclassroom environment. Sessions can begin with "stupid joke of the day" to humanize our interactions or whatever the group wants as session openers. (One group I worked with wanted to begin class sessions with a mini-complaint time: who had too many exams coming at once, who had an unreasonable assignment, who wondered why a professor missed so many class hours but still had the teaching assistant pass out quizzes.) Just as Thomas Newkirk affirmed that the "first five minutes" of a tutorial are crucial to the success of what comes after, the first few minutes of training sessions are important to build enjoyment with being with each other. When that mood begins to dominate, we may also see the tutor sliding into her chair in a tutorial with a smile and a "so how's it going? Need an animal cracker [at the front desk] for a sugar fix?" Learning is and should be enjoyable, and it can pave the way for a very open kind of interaction that promotes learning. To achieve this, tutor and student should find each other's company pleasant. Besides, why not enjoy? Writing and tutoring are complex, stress-inducing processes, so why add to that by being too serious in our interactions?

I end rather deliberately here after a reminder that we all need and want to find pleasure in what we do, and to be sure that others around us enjoy writing and learning as much as we do. Working with tutors-to-be or novice tutors *is* fun because it's impossible to be immune to their enthusiasm, their conversation when "hanging" in the center and not tutoring, their interest in learning how to tutor, and their successes as they progress. When that pervades the entire writing center so that the sounds that dominate are conversation and occasional laughter, with people draped comfortably around chairs and on couches (or at computers), then we can sit back and listen to that noise—and enjoy the racket, knowing that we're doing something right when we train the tutors—and that we're continually conducting a successful tutorial.

WORKS CITED

Bell, Jim. "Tutor Training and Reflection on Practice." *The Writing Center Journal* 21.2 (2001): 79–98.

Boquet, Elizabeth H. *Noise from the Writing Center*. Logan: Utah State UP, 2002.

Brooks, Jeff. "Minimalist Tutoring: Making the Student Do All the Work." *Writing Lab Newsletter* 15.6 (1991): 1–4. Rpt. in Barnett and Blumner 219–24.

Carino, Peter. "Power and Authority in Peer Tutoring." *The Center Will Hold: Critical Perspectives on Writing Center Scholarship*. Ed. Michael A. Pemberton and Joyce Kinkead. Logan: Utah State UP, 2003. 96–113.

Cooper, George, Kara Bui, and Linda Riker. "Protocols and Process in Online Tutoring." *A Tutor's Guide: Helping Writers One to One*. Ed. Ben Rafoth. Portsmouth, NH: Heinemann-Boynton/Cook, 2000. 91–101.

Gillespie, Paula, and Neal Lerner. *The Allyn and Bacon Guide to Peer Tutoring*. 2nd ed. Boston: Allyn and Bacon, 2003.

Harris, Muriel. "When Writers Write about Writing." *Teaching Writing Creatively*. Ed. David Starkey. Portsmouth, NH: Heinemann-Boynton/Cook, 1998. 58–70.

___. "Working with Individual Differences in the Writing Tutorial." *Most Excellent Differences: Essays on Using Type Theory in the English Classroom*. Ed. Thomas Thompson. Gainesville: CAPT, 1996. 90–100.

Newkirk, Thomas. "The First Five Minutes: Setting the Agenda in a Writing Conference." *Writing and Response: Theory, Practice, and Research*. Ed. Chris Anson. Urbana, IL: NCTE, 1989. 317–31. Rpt. in Barnett and Blumner 302–15.

Shamoon, Linda K., and Deborah H. Burns. "A Critique of Pure Tutoring." *The Writing Center Journal* 15.2 (1995): 134–51. Rpt. in Barnett and Blumner 228–41.

___. "Labor Pains: A Political Analysis of Writing Center Tutoring." *The Politics of Writing Centers*. Ed. Jane Nelson and Kathy Evertz. Portsmouth, NH: Heinemann-Boynton/Cook, 2001. 62–73.

Theriault, Katie. "Reflections on an International Writing Center Week: There and Back Again." *Writing Lab Newsletter* 28.10 (June 2004): 1–4.

RESOURCES

Barnett, Robert W., and Jacob Blumner, eds. *The Allyn and Bacon Guide to Writing Center Theory and Practice.* Boston: Allyn and Bacon, 2001.

Brooks, Jeff. "Minimalist tutoring: Making the Student Do All the Work." *Writing Lab Newsletter* 15.6 (1991): 1-4. Rpt. in Barnett and Blumner 219-24.

Bruce, Shanti, and Ben Rafoth, eds. *ESL Writers: A Guide for Writing Center Tutors.* Portsmouth: NH: Heinemann Boynton/Cook, 2004.

Clark, Irene. *Writing in the Center: Teaching in a Writing Center.* Dubuque: Kendall/Hunt, 1998.

CompPile database: covers entries from 1939 to 1999. The CCCC/MLA bibliography covers 2000 and thereafter.

Cooper, George, Kara Bui, and Linda Riker. "Protocols and Process in Online Tutoring." *A Tutor's Guide: Helping Writers One to One.* Ed. Ben Rafoth. Portsmouth, NH: Boynton/Cook Heinemann, 2000. 91-101.

Gillespie, Paula, and Neal Lerner. *Allyn & Bacon Guide to Peer Tutoring,* 2nd ed. New York: Pearson Longman, 2004.

Gillespie, Paula, and Jon Olson. "Tutor Training." *The Writing Center Resource Manual,* 2nd ed. Ed. Bobbie Silk. Emmitsburg, MD: NWCA Press, 2002. III.3.1-13.

Gocsik, Karen. "Responding to Problems: A Facilitative Approach." Tutor Training <http://www.dartmouth.edu/~compose/tutor/methods/respond.html#what> March 18, 2004.

International Writing Centers Association Web site: <http://writingcenters.org>.

Murphy, Christina, and Steve Sherwood, eds. *The St. Martin's Sourcebook for Writing Tutors.* New York: St. Martin's, 1995.

Posey, Evelyn. "An Ongoing Tutor-Training Program." *Writing Center Journal* 6.2 (1986): 29-35. Rpt. in Barnett and Blumner 326-31.

Rafoth, Ben, ed. *A Tutor's Guide.* Portsmouth, NH: Boynton/Cook, 2000.

Ryan, Leigh. *Bedford Guide for Writing Tutors,* 2nd ed. Boston: Bedford Books/St. Martin's, 2001.

29

Tutors Speak: "What Do We Want from Our Writing Center Directors?"

Carol Peterson Haviland
California State University, San Bernardino

Marcy Trianosky
Hollins University

Many writing center conversations center on what directors want from their tutors, asking what tutors need to know, how to prepare them to tutor, and how to evaluate them and their tutoring. In most cases, these chapters are written by directors, and they draw on data elicited chiefly from other directors and professional writing center staff, from faculty members, and from administrators. This chapter opens those inquiries to the tutors themselves, studying tutors' views of what is important in directors.

The chapter is informed by data collected from three sources: two conference sessions on the topic (IWCA 2003 and SoCalWCA 2004) and a questionnaire addressed to tutors and circulated through WCenter. Because nearly all of the respondents identified themselves as graduate or undergraduate student tutors rather than as faculty or professional tutors, the chapter speaks specifically to their perceived needs; however, at least some of those needs may be generalized to other tutor populations.

Tutors' responses range from the global, "I expect writing center directors to be fully knowledgeable of everything there is to know about the English language and methods of tutoring," to the local, "We need comfortable chairs!" However, the most commonly mentioned tutor needs are for directors to contribute to their security and their growth. Tutors describe these functions as organizers, as protectors, as evaluators, as model educators, and as mentors, each of which raises substantive and sometimes competing ethical, political, and economic concerns. For example, one tutor described needing a "tutor guardian," pointing to the organizer/protector/evaluator roles, which challenges directors to shelter tutors from harm without disallowing their learning through their own discoveries. Thus, directors who encourage tutors to take the risks that inquiry-driven, dialogic writing conferences entail and that help them stretch as emerging tutor scholars often find themselves negotiating the same "in the middle" spaces that Sunstein and others described tutors having to negotiate.

SECURITY: ORGANIZER/PROTECTOR/EVALUATOR

Tutors' answers to "What do you expect/need from your writing center director?" cluster the first three roles, organizer/protector/evaluator, in interesting ways as tutors ask for directors to create spaces in which tutors feel secure yet not constrained.

Organizer

> *"Above all, I need clear instruction; I need to know exactly what is expected of me. If those expectations are not clearly expressed, it may result in frustration felt by both parties. I've held positions in the past where this was a problem and it was extremely frustrating because I kept being told what I was doing wrong, but as it turned out, I really had no idea how to do it 'right' since that had never been defined for me."*

> *"Orderliness, to be well organized … I need someone who keeps everything going on around me calm and running well. This allows me to concentrate on being a tutor. I like to have my main focus on the writer, and not be distracted by confusion."*

> *"[I don't want her to] ride over her tutors like a cop or a slave driver."*

Tutors note that directors who provide clear organizational and structural procedures help them understand workplace parameters as well as free them to concentrate on tutoring. However, like each of tutors' concerns, this need is complicated because tutors want enough organization to feel secure yet not so much that they feel hemmed in. Of course, these levels vary among tutors as do tutors' thresholds for chaos. Most centers are staffed with a mix of new and experienced tutors, graduate and undergraduate students, and personalities, so directors need to provide enough structure for an inexperienced and insecure tutor who likes to work with very clear expectations and guidelines yet not so much that an experienced, adventurous, and independent tutor feels constrained. Exactly the "right" level of organization provides tutors with the security they need to function optimally, but it is up to the director to find or adapt that "right" level with an always diverse and changing tutor population.

This role of organizer also raises important questions about collaborative writing center management. As one tutor pointed out, "[T]he Writing Center is based on peer-based relationships…. So, I think for a writing center to achieve this, it must first start with the energy between the Director and all the tutors working there." Through tutor preparation courses, workshops, and ongoing discussions, tutors with heightened awareness of collaborative models often are attempting to enact such models within their tutorials. When they see gaps between what the tutors try to achieve in their tutorials and the ways they relate to their directors, they may become confused and resentful. One tutor commented that "creating a collaborative environment extends the values of the tutoring session to all the work [in] the center ... [while] a top-down administrative structure in a writing center creates a schizophrenic working environment for tutors." However, as Wingate pointed out, "collaboration, in itself, is neither good nor bad; collaboration's goals and contexts must be articulated carefully if good results are to follow" (Harrington et al 57). Thoughtful directors contextualize their choices, but their choices rarely are simple because contexts almost always are multiple and often quite different. This complexity challenges directors to move between the less hierarchical collaborations they and their tutors enact in their writing centers and the intensely political and hierarchical collaborations favored by many administrators—and to clarify for themselves and their tutors how they can operate within these two contexts without becoming schizophrenic themselves.

Protector

> "It is important [for directors] ... to visibly support their staff ... both publicly and privately ... someone who I know relies on me and supports my decisions."

> "I think tutors need a writing center director to help provide a support network ... letting tutors know that despite what tutees or professors may expect, it is not our duty to have all of the answers...."

> "[It gives me a sense of security] to know that as tutors, we won't be taken advantage of."

Just as the director's role of organizer provides important security for tutors, so does the more visible protector role. Tutors say that they need directors to protect them from four groups: administrators, faculty members, students, and each other. They note that although directors often describe themselves as at risk as they negotiate from their own "middle" spaces between tutors and writers or faculty and tutors, directors never are as vulnerable as tutors, who with less experience occupy even riskier positions in the middle.

Protector from Administrators. Directors who protect tutors from administrators are willing to take responsibility for their tutors' work, ideally giving tutors the credit for their successes yet fielding criticism when things go awry. This means helping administrators to understand tutoring as interested, intelligent reading rather than editing, and to understand tutors as students themselves, students who are offering valuable writing consultation even as they always are learning themselves.

It also means protecting tutors from inappropriate administrative demands and the repercussions of those demands on writing centers. In response to the question, "What does your director do that you don't like?" one tutor responded by describing how the director "[had] tutors monitor tests while also trying to tutor." Another tutor stated, "I don't want to be at an institution that forces directors to take on so many other responsibilities that they can't spend a significant amount of time in the center." Therefore, one part of protecting tutors from administrators is interacting successfully with those administrators so that writing centers' missions are not misappropriated.

A second part, however, sometimes may involve explaining to tutors why administrators might pressure directors to "multitask" or why directors might yield to those pressures and even pass them on to tutors. Wingate acknowledged that the collaborative interaction of writing center tutorials may never be perfectly mirrored in the relationships between directors and administrators and so may fail to achieve the ideal Burkean Parlor. But writing centers and their directors do have the ability to "enter … into positive and proactive forms of collaboration with [their] host institution" (Wingate 107), allowing for productive relationships to develop among the director, the administration, the center, and the tutors themselves.

Without understanding the reasons why gaps may exist between the Burkean Parlors of many writing centers and the hierarchies of many administrations, tutors may simply feel confused by directors' decisions. As one tutor confessed, "I have trouble understanding departments' arcane administrative structures." Directors who discuss institutional politics that affect writing centers can empower tutors by helping them understand the workings of their institutions, making them partners with their directors in the management of their centers rather than just naïve, passive, or even resentful participants in the system. As one tutor stated, When I understand what's going on, "I feel that I'm empowered to act on my own without needing to be 'protected' by a director." Directors who achieve this level of empowerment for their tutors, redefine the role of protector as collaborators who share power rather than wield it.

Protector from Faculty Members.   Some of these same elements are involved in protecting tutors from faculty members: defining tutors and tutoring clearly and fielding complaints rather than putting tutors on the line. Of course, this does not mean insulating tutors from taking responsibility for their work, but it does mean offering enough guidance that tutors make catastrophic errors only infrequently and then helping them respond when they are challenged. It also means translating in the middle, recognizing that, as one tutor says, "Sometimes students will rat anyone out rather than take responsibility for their own choices." So, directors may need to help both tutors and faculty members recognize that what students report about what either tutors or faculty say is always translated by students—usually to their advantage. In this way, directors can help tutors and faculty members hear and understand each other accurately, and they can protect tutors from unreasonable or contradictory faculty expectations. For example, faculty members often are concerned that students who use the writing center do their "own" writing, yet they sometimes complain when papers that have "been to the writing center" are not "A" papers. Protecting tutors from faculty members means helping tutors become competent and confident enough that their directors can trust them and then taking responsibility when occasional problems erupt.

Protector from Students.   Protecting tutors from students also entails several concerns. Tutors need to know how to set limits, to know that they can decline requests to write for students, to meet them off campus for extra tutoring, or to turn tutor relationships into dating relationships. They need to know that directors will teach them how to make and communicate these decisions and then support them when students complain. They need directors to shield them from inappropriate student complaints.

As one tutor noted, the director "came to my rescue when a student refused to listen to anything I told her and insisted on working with a more experienced tutor.… The director took over [the session] but later assured me her session with the tutee was next to impossible and the tutee's attitude was not a personal rejection of me. Knowing the director was 'on my side' was a boost to my still fragile ego." Another noted having "a tutee who came to me for assistance without a copy of her assignment; I helped her to the best of my ability, but she did poorly, and returned upset. My director was able to support me, and to go through the scenario so that I would be able to avoid such situations in the future (clearly setting expectations, what we can/cannot do)." These kinds of interactions illustrate how directors can successfully tread that fine line between protection and guidance.

Finally, directors can indirectly provide protection through other staff members. As one tutor observed, receptionists can protect tutors "from bombardment by students. Remember that while tutors can hide from the peering and sometimes penetrating eyes of anxious students, the receptionists have to face them and often be the targets of numerous leers and jeers. So, although we gave the receptionists applause in the staff meeting, it would be wonderful if each one of us tutors did so on a personal basis before the end of the quarter." To provide this protection, of course, directors need to help receptionists role play potentially uncomfortable situations and to be quick to offer support when students try to abuse them. With their help, however, directors can protect both directly and indirectly, and this tutor's observation is an important reminder that directors rarely need or are able to do everything alone.

Protector from Other Tutors.   Although tutors mention the need for protection from students only indirectly, they do indeed also need protection from each other. Much scholarship celebrates the collaborative communities that writing centers can be, and indeed this is a pleasure all participants enjoy when the centers are functioning optimally. But they don't always function optimally! Tutors are humans, usually with many lives. One tutor said, for example, "I expect my director to understand the workload under which I am already placed as a full-time student and graduate assistant." Like most student tutors, this tutor wanted the flexibility to change scheduled appointments when the carefully configured school–work–family connections threaten to crash or to call in "sick" when simply exhausted—or even if it's the first day of good snow. However, tutoring six hours without a break when fellow tutors need the same flexibility is less appealing.

Also, tutors have wonderfully different personalities and beliefs, which sometimes collide because, like directors, they often find it easier to welcome difference in writing and writers than among their closest peers. Some tutors are politically active and others are not, some like to breeze in and chat about their lives and drink together after hours and others like to leave the personal at home, some are loud and some are quiet, some wear their emotions at all times and others contain even the most grievous pain—but all need human understanding and acceptance.

Thus, an important director responsibility is to maintain community. This need not mean keeping the writing center free of conflict. This is impossible and may limit or even subvert the critical eyes and diversity that an emerging generation of tutor-scholars can offer. However, it does mean paying attention to conflict and helping tutors negotiate it and learn from it.

Protector from Themselves.   Finally, sometimes directors need to help tutors protect themselves from their increasing attractiveness and marketability. One tutor, for example, expressed particular gratitude for a director who walked her through her negotiations with a physician who wanted to hire her to edit insurance reports. The work itself was offered as a learning experience and an economic boost, but the physician kept "renegotiating" the rate of pay and working conditions, arguing that the tutor was a student who should be grateful for the opportunity to learn outside a classroom. The tutor noted that because her director helped her see herself as a paid professional, she became confident enough to resist increasingly demeaning working conditions. She also noted that discussing her situation in a tutor meeting helped her larger community of tutors think through ways to handle future negotiations with outside contractors. As tutors develop complex written and oral communication skills through their work in the writing center, they create a new identity for themselves as emerging professionals. Directors can help tutors understand and negotiate the exciting but often contradictory and confusing opportunities that arise as a result of their writing center experiences.

Evaluator

"My writing center director helps by encouraging debriefing or self-evaluation. She also gives practical suggestions for how to improve the next time."

"I need and expect to have a director that takes the time to observe my work and give me prompt feedback from time to time."

"I'd like more feedback. I know my boss is busy, and I'm busy, and I can't expect him to always be think, 'Oh, I should pat her on the back today,' [but I still need feedback]."

A third area in which directors can provide security is through thoughtful evaluation. Most tutors care deeply about their tutoring. It is an area where professional pride, ego, and intellectual ability define them, and it is important to them to do well. Thus, evaluation is complicated. It must be fair and personal; it must help them grow, which includes both affirmation and challenge. Several tutors noted that thoughtful evaluation and encouragement can meet some of the security needs and possibly reduce the need for tighter organization. Tutors' needs for directors as evaluators, however, can create conflicts when directors encourage tutors to explore new paradigms that may conflict with current assessment practices even as they contribute to tutors' growth. Directors must achieve that delicate balance required when they function both as models and mentors.

GROWTH: MODEL EDUCATOR/MENTOR

"I need my writing center director to be setting an example. One thing I really appreciate … is that she tutors students and responds to online drafts routinely. This means that she is working on how her practice can change side-by-side with the tutors…. Observing how my writing center director is actively engaged in the same work as her employees encourages me to continue seeking how my practice could be better. She's been at this tutoring stuff for much longer than I and is still growing and learning and questioning."

"If the director shares with the staff the importance of understanding scholarship in the field, we all have a better informed practice and a vocabulary to discuss our work."

Model Educator

Almost uniformly, tutors commented that directors must be model educators. They cannot be absentee landlords but must be actively engaged in their centers' work. Tutors say, for example, that often they learn the most during busy times when directors fill in for absent tutors or take walk-ins and work right alongside other tutors. They need to tutor themselves as well as supervise, to talk about it from experience, to practice what they teach, to show that they too have to work at not dominating tutoring conferences, to ask questions, to be on time, and to examine themselves against theories. They need to be people with whom tutors can discuss failures as well as successes. "Our director sends listserv emails that model tutors' positive interaction with students—emails that note particularly effective tutor-writer interchanges that she has heard that week in our center," said one tutor. The tutor noted that these posts help with self-reflection and promote learning from strengths rather than failures, saying that the posts convey useful information but also "follow the collaborative theory taught in the tutoring course."

One tutor also reported that during tutor meetings she watched her director practice and foreground the collaborative theory she had taught tutors in their tutoring course. She said that she paid attention to language and dialogic methods, noting that some of the director's interactions with the group and with individual tutors provided useful modeling for her as she considered her own work as a tutor and TA. However, tutors' perceptions of directors as teachers can create significant conflicts for directors who encourage tutors to create new knowledge rather than follow established practices or shape their new ideas into existing theoretical frames.

Very specifically, tutors most often mentioned feeling vulnerable when asked to tutor outside their comfort zones—most often with unfamiliar disciplines, with learning disabilities, and with grammar questions, particularly those of ESL or multilingual students. English major tutors, for example, comment that sometimes all of their eagerness to work on higher order concerns in an interesting array of assignments comes back to haunt them when they face physics or finance papers. One tutor revealed, "The irony is that I have a BA in English, but my last grammar class was in high school.... [T]ruthfully, I don't understand all of the complexities of the language myself.... I wish we could have some seminars with actual assignments so that we could better explain rules to the students." Another commented, "I am most vulnerable when it comes to ESL students and grammar rules." Thus, tutors' responses point to the importance of directors' anticipating anxiety-provoking areas and modeling ways of increasing competence and confidence. Again, this pushes directors into an "in-between" collaborative space. Recognizing that many tutors, even English majors, know very little about language acquisition or about grammatical structures even though they write well themselves, one choice is simply to teach it to them—quickly—yet such a model reinforces both a focus on grammar and on "little teacher" roles that directors often work to reduce. Working confidently with the unknown is an important area in which directors can model as well as mentor.

Mentor

"Good mentoring means really believing in me but not leaving me stranded. When we do class workshops, our director sets the stage so that we aren't too paralyzed to act and turns us loose, but she's always within earshot if we get stuck."

"When I started tutoring, I never expected I'd be presenting at CCC. I thought I'd vomit before we started our session, but we were good—people were interested in our ideas—and that that's what got me serious about a PhD in composition."

Directors have significant opportunities to mentor tutors, to ease them into more complex roles both on and off campus. For example, tutors can become comfortable leading writing workshops and interacting with other faculty members if directors model one workshop and then turn the next ones over to tutors. And, as they conduct these workshops, tutors build credibility with faculty members as they model thoughtful writing pedagogies. Tutors also can build credibility with faculty members if directors ask tutors to read the assignments they write for their own classes, then inviting their faculty colleagues to use tutors similarly.

Directors also can draw tutors into larger composition conversations by including them in their research and then coauthoring or copresenting with them at conferences. Both CCCC and IWCA offer welcoming venues, as do regional writing center organizations. Of course, this is not entirely altruistic, because these collaborations are reciprocally enriching. Tutors get exposure to composition scholars, but those scholars also are able to learn from these emerging scholars, those who will be shaping our fields if we support them properly and then get out of their way! However, conference presenting is more than tacking tutors onto proposals. It means taking time to engage students in research, in working out presentations and practicing them so that tutors are both confident and competent presenters.

WHAT MIGHT OUR DATA MEAN?

In collecting the data for this chapter, we read and listened to the voices of graduate and undergraduate tutors, which reveal the conflicting demands that tutors' expectations create for directors. Reflecting on these expectations and responding to them can help us grow as directors, especially if we are willing to theorize their implications. Connecting our theorizing as closely as we can to tutors' concerns, we have attempted to avoid the pitfalls that Nancy Maloney Grimm pointed out for us: "Because theory is powerful, it often overtakes practice … and subjugates the daily knowledge that might challenge it" (ix). But, as Grimm also reminded us, by "bring[ing] theoretical understandings into contact with daily writing center practice, [we can] extend decisions about practice beyond consideration of the local context" (xv). Tutor education and collaborations between writing centers and institutions are two fertile areas.

Tutors urge directors to "keep up with writing center trends" and to "share with the staff the importance of understanding scholarship in the field … [so tutors may] develop more theoretically-informed practices and a vocabulary to discuss [their] work." This is certainly not simple, given the complexity of writing center theory and practice as well as the potential for tutors to become isolated from theorists, whose "voices are cited and named [in the literature] in a way that a writing center tutor cannot be" (Carino 132). Therefore, foregrounding tutors' voices is one of the challenges that directors face in their Model Educator/Mentor roles—sharing knowledge with tutors while simultaneously allowing them to create new knowledge of their own. This is especially important during preparatory tutor education, when tutors establish their identities as tutors and their springboards for their future tutoring practices. Directors who engage tutors as researchers during orientation and throughout their tutoring experiences set the stage for tutors to become partners in theorizing, empowering them to become writing center scholars in their own rights.

Likewise, both tutors and directors can learn from theorizing the difference between internal and external collaborations. Indeed, as Wingate reminded us, "[T]he nature of collaboration between writing centers and their hosting institutions … [is] a subject most composition scholars [or writing center scholars] rarely consider" (101). The challenge for the WPA is the same as the challenge for the WC director: "to become … embedded in partnerships, networks, conversations and collaborations with the writing program and across the campus … [a role which] grows out of … the trend towards the postmodern, which urges us all to become contextual, situated, multiply defined" (Harrington et al. 52).

Writing center directors have an opportunity to extend the boundaries of current theorizing on collaborative management, using knowledge from their writing center work to solve the problem of "how such partnerships [between] administrators and writing programs come to be created in a hierarchical university environment, [and] how power (even the decentralized, facilitative kind) is acquired, and how collaboration works on a daily basis" (Harrington et al. 53–54). As Wingate warned, "In our zeal to design and create programs with pedagogies that sometimes oppose the prevailing paradigms, we may intentionally stay a bit outside of the institution" (101). The danger is isolating writing centers from institutional missions, the consequences of which can be devastating for centers, as Wingate pointed out in describing her own situation: "By staying in the margins, I was helping to create my own powerlessness" (103).

Analyses such as Harrington's and Wingate's highlight the complexities of collaboration and remind us that tutor's roles within writing centers are inevitably shaped by institutional politics. One tutor described the very real material consequences of institutional politics: "Tutors need a writing center director to … be willing to be our voice in the political end of academics, like this year, with our pay increase." A challenge for directors, then, is to increase their awareness of the types of collaboration they engage in with their institutions, to encourage the growth of their tutors as well as their centers as a whole.

CONCLUSIONS

The easy response to learning what tutors want is to try to give it to them, recognizing that directors who meet tutors' perceived needs are likely to have happier and more productive tutors. However, it's not that easy, and chiefly because in most situations, tutors' needs are conflicted: In each category, they want some but not too much, and how much varies with several contextual factors. It is also important to be aware of tutors' perceptions of the ways particular institutional contexts shape and sometimes limit the collaboration possible within writing centers and between directors and institutions. As Anson and Brown noted, "[S]uccessful WPAs [like successful writing center directors] must critically read their institutions as complex educational cultures with powerful habits of governance, disciplinarity and interpretation" (143). How directors engage tutors in theorizing their work is another important area for directors to consider.

WORKS CITED

Anson, Chris, and Robert L. Brown, Jr. "Subject to Interpretation: The Role of Research in Writing Programs and Its Relationship to the Politics of Administration in Higher Education." *The Writing Center Administrator as Researcher: Inquiry in Action and Reflection.* Ed. Shirley K. Rose and Irwin Weiser. Portsmouth, NH: Heinemann-Boynton/Cook, 1999. 141–52.

Carino, Peter. "Theorizing the Writing Center: An Uneasy Task" *Dialogue: A Journal for Writing Specialists* 2.1 (1995), 23–27. Cited in *The Allyn and Bacon Guide to Writing Center Theory.* Ed. Robert W. Barnett and Jacob S. Blumner. Allyn and Bacon, 2001. 124–38.

Grimm, Nancy Maloney. *Good Intentions: Writing Center Work for Postmodern Times.* Portsmouth, NH: Heinemann-Boynton/Cook, 1999.

Harrington, Susanmarie, Steve Fox, and Tere Molinder Hogue. "Power, Partnership, and Negotiations: The Limits of Collaboration." *WPA* 21.2/3 (Spring 1998): 52–63.

Sunstein, Bonnie S. "Moveable Feasts, Liminal Spaces: Writing Centers and the State of In-Betweenness." *The Writing Center Journal* 18.2 (1998): 7–26.

Wingate, Molly. "The Politics of Collaboration: Writing Centers Inside Institutions." *Resituating Writing: Constructing and Administrating Writing Programs.* Ed. Joseph Janangelo and Kristine Hansen. Portsmouth, NH: Heinemann-Boynton/Cook, 1995. 100–07.

❦ 30 ❧

Crossing Thresholds: Starting a Peer Tutoring Program

Paula Gillespie
Marquette University

Harvey Kail
University of Maine

Peer tutoring in writing instruction has earned a well-respected place in higher education over the last 30 years. The systematic and now widespread employment of students to help each other become better writers has achieved the status of conventional practice in many writing programs. You will find peer tutoring in community colleges and the Ivy League, in sprawling multiversities and leafy liberal arts colleges, in secondary schools, and in universities in Germany and in the Virgin Islands. If you are thinking about starting a peer tutoring program, then we hope this brief overview of some of the key strategies, arguments, and practices will be of use to you as you negotiate your way across the various institutional thresholds that you will encounter as you bring student tutors officially into your writing center.

A BRIEF HISTORY OF PEER TUTORING IN WRITING

Peer tutoring as a staple of writing center work can be traced most recently to the extraordinary changes in the student body of American higher education in the 1970s. The enactment of the Civil Rights Act in 1964, the institutionalization of open admission policies in colleges and universities, the War on Poverty, the increase in the number of "nontraditional" students turning and returning to higher education—all this interaction of educational and social policy with individual effort came into energetic collision in the new contact zone of American higher education. It is evident that there were more than enough ingredients and heat to produce the "literacy crisis" of the 1970s. Peer tutoring programs emerged out of this powerful mixture of politics, policy, theory, grassroots know-how, and a remarkable willingness to innovate.

Within this context, certain trends in composition theory and practice at the time figure into the development of peer tutoring. The first of these is the rise of the conferencing method, an approach to teaching writing that championed one-to-one interaction between teacher and student as a viable alternative to the traditional composition classroom. The work of Roger Garrison and Donald Murray to privilege the conference over the classroom had a palpable effect on establishing peer tutoring programs. Muriel Harris's *Writing One to One: The Writing Conference* helped codify this innovation for writing center work. A second trend is the adaptation of collaborative learning to writing instruction, an innovation that tapped into a powerful and renewable energy resource for learning how to write like a college student: other college students. The work of Kenneth A. Bruffee is particularly noteworthy; his text, *A Short Course in Writing,* and his many articles on collaborative learning ("The Brooklyn Plan" 1978; "Collaborative Learning: Higher Education" 1999; and "Collaborative Learning: Some Practical Models" 1973) began to shape a pedagogy by which to train students as peer writing tutors. A third trend that contributes to the growth and development of peer tutoring is the reconception of formal writing assistance from the dominant metaphors of "labs" and "clinics" into the idea of writing "centers," with their unique literacy campaign and semiautonomous space in the academy. These three influences have interacted and continue to interact to shape, adapt, and modify each other into the current context of peer tutoring.

RATIONALES AND ARGUMENTS FOR (AND AGAINST) PEER TUTORING

You probably already have good reasons to want to start a peer tutoring program. Here are some of ours:

- Peer tutoring engages both the tutor and the writer in active, institutionally sponsored learning, suggesting that students as well as faculty take writing and reading seriously.
- Peer tutoring helps writers to develop critical thought; in the process, tutors become more aware of their own processes of thinking and writing in increasingly engaged, discourse knowledgeable ways.
- Peer tutoring releases energy for mutual aid rather than mutual struggle. Mutual aid allows both the tutor and the writer to learn from one another rather than to compete, and allows students to play a reciprocal role in each other's educational experience.
- Peer tutoring taps into and improves the informal network of help that students already offer to one another; as writers take part in the more collaborative conferences, they learn more about ways to help their own friends and roommates.
- Peer-tutors develop a useful metalanguage to describe writing and its processes and the discernment to know when to use this language in writing conferences and when to demonstrate it.

- Peer-tutors usually have institutional knowledge and savvy, putting them in a position to mentor students new to campus and to model successful strategies for academic problem solving.
- Peer tutoring helps demystify the writing process by making use of the culture and discourse that students share as students. They are all in "the same boat" and speak out of the same academic needs and experiences.
- Peer tutoring demonstrates to faculty that competent writing and useful knowledge of writing have not been lost in the student body but can be identified, developed, and usefully employed.
- Peer tutoring significantly adds to the staffing potential of a writing center, extending its range and influence while tapping into the financial support of such programs as federal and state work study aid.
- Peer tutoring provides peer-tutors with significant values and skills that they can take with them from the experience into graduate school and careers.

Of course, there are arguments to be made against peer tutoring as well, and if you start a program, you will need to respond to them. Here are several such objections with our brief responses:

- *Peer tutoring is the blind leading the blind.* This metaphor assumes that students are clueless and blindly groping in the dark. We find, on the contrary, that students come to us knowing a great deal and are eager to learn more. If we can learn from our own peers, and from our peer-tutors, students can be organized to learn from and teach each other.
- *Peer-tutors do not have the requisite specialized knowledge and discourse savvy to tutor in various disciplines.* It is true that a peer-tutor who is an English major has not experienced writing for the community of knowledgeable biologists. This does not mean that biology students cannot benefit greatly from sharing their work with a capable peer in any discipline. How many writing center professionals have the requisite discourse savvy in all the disciplines on our campuses?
- *Peer-tutors are not as good as professional tutors.* We think this may be true sometimes, and sometimes we think individual peer-tutors are better than individual professional tutors. In any case, we think they do somewhat different work.
- *Peer-tutors are only available for a short time, and even then they have complicated schedules.* True. Recruiting, training, and developing peer-tutors is an ongoing task.

STRATEGIES

These rationales and arguments are only part of moving an idea into action. The best thing you can do to facilitate the successful initiation of your program is to understand your own institution. What are the goals of your school? What do faculty and administrators want to accomplish in the next few years as well as over time? How might arguments for peer tutoring fit into this context? What student populations are at risk? (Returning students? International students? Minority students? First generation college students? First-year students? Athletes?)

What services already exist to help those students succeed? How can you network with those other services to help make your own case to the people who might be able to lend a hand or make funding available?

Some of the best allies of a peer tutoring program are faculty members who have been tutors themselves. They know the power of peer collaboration firsthand and are eloquent in discussing it. They are not, by any means, all working in English departments, either. Seek them out. Current students can also argue powerfully for the establishment of a peer-tutor training program. Undergraduate English majors, education majors, writing-intensive English majors, and journalism majors, once alerted to the possibilities, will want to work as tutors and get this valuable experience. Students can and should be powerful voices for shaping their own educational opportunities. As you think about how you might want to argue your case with chairs, deans, provosts, and presidents, don't forget how powerful student voices can be in institutional decision making. Without student support from the start, it might not happen at all.

Finally, accrediting agencies pay a great deal of attention to academic student services and to retention efforts. These important self-study reports that schools write every ten or so years make much of academic support facilities of all kinds. Cross-disciplinary connections and collaborations also strengthen an institution's standing in an accrediting study, as does student-to-student collaboration. All of these elements are powerfully at play in a writing center, but a special case can be made for student success if peers are trained to offer collaborative help in writing. Those efforts that convince accrediting bodies are also very convincing to department heads, deans, and directors in universities.

FUNDING A BUDGET

As you know, initiating a peer tutoring program requires a great investment of time, but before making that investment, it's good to have a financial plan ready to offer to those who will support you. Let's look at the finances first. Writing center directors with a peer tutoring program are likely to find themselves having to generate funding for and managing a somewhat complex budget. Where might a peer tutoring budget come from if there isn't a budget already in place? Ask your writing center colleagues to let you see their budgets so you can better anticipate the unexpected.

One of the advantages of peer tutoring programs is that many student tutors can bring their financial aid package and/or status as students to bear on their own employment. Your financial aid office may well have multiple sources of funding to employ students. Indeed, stepping across the threshold of the financial aid office and getting to know the staff who work there is a very important move in funding your new program. Student tutors can be financed in part through federal and state programs such as work study or work merit. In the former program, students themselves must request financial aid from the university, a process that involves them and their parents in filling out the Free Application for Federal Student Aid (FAFSA) form. Most students do this as part of applying to college. Encourage students who are interested in becoming peer writing tutors to apply for financial aid, if they haven't already done so. If they do qualify for financial aid, then most likely they will be granted a certain number of dollars for federal work study. Peer tutoring is a perfect way for these funds to be earned by students, and you will find likely categories to fit their job descriptions in your institution's student employment office. Students will have 80% of their wages paid for by the federal government. Your writing center or department would be responsible for the remaining 20%.

Even here, however, there can be more funding coming from outside your own budget. Many schools offer departments "free match" money for some, if not all, of their student employees. "Free match" means the institution, often through state funding, will pay the remaining 20%, and the peer-tutors so designated don't cost the writing center anything. At some institutions, students with high GPA's are eligible for a sizable "work merit" grant if the work they will be doing helps develop their academic background. Peer tutoring is a perfect role for students to assume and to qualify for this type of funding. Get to know your institution's financial aid officers. In our experience, it is reasonable to plan a budget based on 50% of prospective tutors qualifying for work study or other forms of financial aid. That means that roughly 50% of the peer-tutor payroll can come from sources outside your writing center's own budget. In addition, many institutions will fund student travel to academic conferences, so that part of your budget for staff development can come from tapping into the alumni association, the college dean, or the provost's office for student academic travel.

The fact that students can often bring their own funding with them also makes it rhetorically feasible to argue for modest "seed money" to get a peer tutoring program up and running. Perhaps the English department chair or the dean or the associate provost or the president (or some joint effort among them) need only commit 50% of the peer tutoring budget. Their dollars are needed to match work study and to employ student tutors who do not qualify for work study or work merit. A small annual budget of only $5,000 or $6,000 a year can generate a payroll easily twice that amount and serve hundreds of students. Administrators like that arithmetic, and they should.

RECRUITMENT

Recruiting tutors is the next threshold to be crossed, and it is vital to the success of a new or revised program. It is important to have a recruitment plan. We have heard of tutor training courses that filled to capacity the first time they were offered, but had to be cancelled the next year because there were no takers. It is a good idea to recruit each time a new training cycle starts, whether or not you feel it is necessary. By finding the very best students you can to become peer-tutors, you ensure better work with writers and better visibility for the center. Because you want tutors to be able to analyze and work with texts, you might look for tutors who do well in composition courses, but you might not want to limit yourself to English majors if your center will work with students from all courses. Because tutors work so intensively with writers, it helps to find students who enjoy the collaborative process in their classes, who are good listeners and good communicators. Because tutors have to work so closely with others, it helps to find tutors who are outgoing. This takes some planning and contact with potential faculty sponsors.

We feel that it is more important that tutors have the qualities we have just listed than that they have a given GPA. Some directors ask for lists of names from instructors, and here we can cast a wide net, not necessarily only asking English instructors. When you ask for names of students, it is important to spell out the qualifications you want tutors to have and those you aren't looking for, or they might assume that you only want students with perfect punctuation or a high GPA. These and other improvements in every aspect of writing occur in a well-designed training course. This kind of tutor-recruiting program builds good connections with faculty and with the institution, advertising the center and giving the faculty a stake in its success and a reason to refer their own students. Finally, a recruitment process gives the peer tutoring program credibility with administrators and others in the institution.

TRAINING AND STAFF DEVELOPMENT

A tutor training program can take several forms. Some institutions train tutors on the job; others offer a summer course or program of training. Still others have a credit-bearing course offered through one of the departments on campus. We come down strongly in favor of the credit-bearing course, although summer programs can be excellent alternatives. On-the-job training, however, may well put peer-tutors at unnecessary risk, and we want to discourage putting undergraduates in positions of authority that they are untrained to exercise properly.

A strong argument for a peer tutoring course is that it can fill requirements for some majors. Some courses can be offered using existing upper division writing or other courses that are already on the books. This is a convenient way of starting a tutor training program without all the wear and tear of creating a new course. The rationale is that by teaching advanced students academic writing in a systematic, collaborative process, students can transfer the skills of tactful analysis and critique to the writing center. But if a new course is needed, then it pays to consider the way it might fit into existing majors. At some schools the peer tutor training course satisfies requirements for both the writing-intensive English major and the English education major. At others it might fulfill a senior capstone or a service learning requirement. Some students take it as an elective, of course. But investigating these options for various majors is well worth the effort; a course that counts toward a major makes it onto advisors' recommended lists and is called to students' attention in ways it would not be if it functioned solely as an elective. It is vital to know when departments are in the process of curriculum reform and to work within their time frames. Adding a course to a major or even as an elective is usually a process that takes the approval of and committees and requires discussion by an entire department.

The course approval process can put you into rugged terrain, and knowing the difficulties will help you navigate a course through some high seas, to mix a few metaphors. D'Ann George surveyed subscribers to WCenter and researched their methods of getting their courses approved, and in her article told stories, her own and others', of things they wish they'd known. She then spelled out the processes that various writing center professionals followed to create a successful course. This article is helpful not only for those who are establishing a course but for those who are inheriting one, because the stories in it make explicit important power relationships and point to allies that we might not imagine on our own.

DECIDING ON TRAINING PROGRAM CONTENT

Perhaps the most crucial issue regarding the training of peer tutors is the complex nature of the relationship of undergraduate tutors to the students and faculty they serve. Many articles have taken up the topic of the authority of the tutor in the tutorial and the nature of peer relations in a writing center, and more questions have been raised than answered. Is peer tutoring a contradiction in terms? Where do tutors get their authority? How should that authority be brought to bear in a tutorial setting? Should tutors instruct writers or work as questioners and listeners? What is the relationship of the peer-tutor to the curriculum that the writers are working within? What is the relationship of the peer-tutor to the faculty teaching that curriculum? Struggling with these questions is bound to be a fundamental part of any peer-tutor training course.

Your writing center's relationship to an academic department or departments will help you determine the emphasis and pedagogy of the training program you design. A query on WCenter can constitute a good beginning. It will yield lots of good advice and a flurry of syllabi, but it is also a good idea to make sense of different kinds of tutor training programs by visiting a school that has one, talk in person to a director of a program, interview the tutors, ask about the institutional constraints that made the instructors choose the direction they took. And ask if they would change things if they could. Is it important that your program emphasize theory, history of rhetoric, or some other content? Getting a feel for the nitty-gritty of a training course already in place will give you lots of ideas about what you want to do—and what you want to avoid. Looking at peer-tutor training manuals will also help you decide what you want the emphasis of your course or your training to be.

Two different approaches embodied by our own schools, Marquette University and the University of Maine, illustrate the enormous range of tutor training practices. Our two programs are characterized by an emphasis on either the writer as tutor or the tutor as writer. At the University of Maine, the emphasis is on the tutor as writer. The course had its start at the Brooklyn College Summer Institute in Training Peer Writing Tutors and follows the processes introduced by Kenneth Bruffee in *A Short Course in Writing*. This method of training students to become peer writing tutors takes place in an advanced writing course whose main principle is that students can improve their own writing by systematically helping their classmates in the training course improve theirs. The course consists of increasingly complex argumentative papers and increasingly complex written critiques of one another's work. As tutors become more familiar and competent with argumentation and with analyzing argument in the training course, they begin an internship phase in the writing center, tutoring two hours a week, learning how collaborative learning works with complete strangers, transferring analytical and collaborative skills and habits from the training course to giving substantive help to writers in the writing center. By the end of the course, they should know themselves as stronger writers because of the help of their peers, and they should be in a position to help students who come to the writing center for help with their writing.

At Marquette University, the course follows the method set out in *The Allyn and Bacon Guide to Peer Tutoring* (2nd ed.), a book Paula Gillespie and Neal Lerner wrote, among other things, to fit the pedagogy of her course, which we'll characterize as developing the tutor in the writer. It involves a good amount of reflection on the tutoring and writing process, observation of others, discussions of note-taking, listening skills, nonverbal skills, and other techniques of tutoring. It integrates students into the writing center from the first week, not as tutors but as observers and as writers who are tutored by the staff. They also attend weekly staff meetings. The course requires reading of theoretical and practical articles from the fields of writing centers, composition, and pedagogy. Students are more likely to tutor one another from the start than to write critiques, so they learn question-asking and listening techniques as part of the course.

At Maine the students who are selected for the course are already good writers, but they re-fine their writing ability and learn a metalanguage for writing processes and genres. At Marquette, the students will have taken two semesters of a rhetoric course and so will have a language for discussing writing processes, but will need practice at listening, at comprehension, and on-the-spot analysis of a range of texts.

We both agree that peer-tutor training has moved away from its door-slamming insistence that peer-tutors not teach. Although we as directors want to foster the peer-to-peer bond, we want tutors to accept and understand that teaching goes on. Peer-tutors teach writers by example and modeling to go to a handbook or an online source for answers to writing ques-tions. They might teach writers on the spot what an independent clause is or how a verb functions in a sentence. We'd like to make a distinction here that good collegial teaching can go on when one member of a collaborative group has some expert knowledge without that person becoming a little teacher, that is, without taking on some of the negative connota-tions of the teacher's role, a role some writers have come to fear and distrust. The insistence on the strictest interpretation of Stephen M. North's "Idea of a Writing Center" and Jeff Brooks's "Minimalist Tutoring: Making the Student Do All the Work" has led some tutors to believe that it was wrong to ever tell anyone anything: The ideas all had to come from the writer, even if it led to a frustrating and nonproductive session. Now training programs and manuals are more likely to suggest that tutors share their expert knowledge in a collegial and collaborative way rather than frustrate writers by trying to manipulate them into guessing what is in their heads.

The discussions we have had about the differences between our two courses have led us both to revise our courses somewhat, to try to integrate some features from one another's course. A good program is seldom static and should change as you continue to observe good practices in schools around your community, at conferences, and in the literature. Most of all, it needs to fit your institution.

MIXING UNDERGRADUATES WITH GRADUATES AND PROFESSIONAL TUTORS

Some programs like to keep their professionals, grads, and undergrads quite separate. Some have centers staffed by professionals and grads while undergrads figure in as writing fellows, working as part of a writing across the curriculum (WAC) program, assigned to a given course each semester. This is an interesting blend of writing centers as site and writing centers as pro-cess, using tutors who may never have reason to step inside the writing center. Some centers provide separate offices for professional tutors, and assign them to work with special popula-tions such as dissertators.

We find undergraduate peer-tutors such a likeable population that we feel privileged to mix them with graduate tutors. This is a mutually beneficial mix, because the TAs, many of whom will go on to university teaching, see how effective the upper division student can be, how re-warding to work with. The undergrads, on the other hand, get an insider's view into graduate school, watching their coworkers and friends take qualifying exams, have proposals accepted, finish dissertation chapters, earn fellowships, and publish articles. These are moments of great excitement in a writing center.

The success of their fellow tutors inspires many undergraduates to pursue graduate degrees, perhaps not immediately, but eventually. Their firsthand observation of others going through this process makes it seem more accessible and feasible for them. The graduate students contribute an insider's knowledge of writing assignments from the teaching perspective, if they teach in a comp program. The undergraduates contribute an insider's knowledge of reading and interpreting assignments, from a student's perspective.

ASSESSMENT

Because we want peer-tutors to be accomplished readers of and/or listeners to texts, because we want them to ask good questions of writers, because we expect qualities of control and flexibility in the tutorial, it is important for us to build assessment into the program from the start. This is perhaps the most demanding threshold to cross in starting a peer tutoring program, but it is essential. An assessment plan will let tutors know that their work is important and will let those who supervise our work know that we are being responsible members of our institutions.

Formally observing tutorials is one approach to assessment. Audiotaped or videotaped sessions are alternatives. These activities are most valuable for the *self-assessment* they allow tutors to do. A conference shortly after the observation or taping the session keeps the stress levels down. Prior to the observation, it is important to specify whether your goal is *evaluation* or *assessment*. Evaluation, of course, is always part of the assessment process, but an evaluation suggests that something like a grade is going to be assigned. Assessment is a process ideally aimed at improvement, at providing feedback so tutors can know where they excel and where their areas of improvement might lie. It can be helpful to give tutors a checklist such as the one that appears on page 96 of the *Allyn and Bacon Guide to Peer Tutoring* (2nd ed.) or modify it yourself to help tutors focus and review before the observation. A checklist can also guide the discussion afterward.

Another assessment process can involve the session reports writers fill out. It would be worth your time to see if writers are satisfied with the work of your peer-tutors, and it helps to follow up with a phone call to ask for specifics, either shortly after the session or a few days or weeks later.

Tutors often assess one another, too, informally, as they work alongside their peers. Listen to them carefully when they come to you with concerns about one another and about the way other tutors represent the writing center. Taking action on these assessments takes good judgment, tact, and a willingness to take on unpleasant topics, but is worthwhile for the good running of your writing center. A job description can spell out the requirements and can be very helpful when you have to confront the occasional unpleasant situation.

CONCLUSIONS

As you integrate a peer tutoring program into your institution, you will cross thresholds, one after another, literal and figurative. Across your campus, doors are open to you, and many of your colleagues are eager to say yes to an idea that benefits writers, the institution, and the tutors. Chairs, deans, and directors are likely to agree to well-researched good ideas and often to offer invaluable help in making these goals realities. And as a result of your success, you will not be the only one crossing thresholds. Students who come to the writing center for assistance with their writing will find themselves in an academic community in which their fellow students are valued for their writing, reading, and teaching capabilities. Faculty whose students use the writing center or whose students become peer-tutors, themselves, will find in a peer tutoring program a valuable new ally in their own work to improve student writing and thinking. And the peer-tutors themselves will surely cross a threshold in their own development. Research on the learning of peer-tutors shows clearly that they develop skills, values, and qualities that they carry with them into their job interviews and work situations, into their lives for years to come. They become skilled listeners, making them better on the job, as partners, and as parents. They develop their skills of writing and of analyzing texts, helping them succeed in countless areas of professional and personal life. They become confident communicators, able to engage in one-to-one conversations with interviewers, colleagues, clients—anyone who walks in the door. They meet, get to know, and come to appreciate writers from many other cultures, races, classes, and genders. But most important, perhaps, is that they invest themselves in the successes of others, taking pride when their fellow students show that they have moved to new levels of understanding of topics and new levels of writing ability.

WORKS CITED

Brooks, Jeff. "Minimalist Tutoring: Making the Student Do All the Work." *Writing Lab Newsletter* 15.6 (1991): 1–4.

Bruffee, Kenneth. *A Short Course in Writing: A Practical Rhetoric for Composition, Writing Workshops and Tutor Training.* 4th ed. New York: Harper Collins, 1993.

___. "The Brooklyn Plan: Attaining Intellectual Growth through Peer Group Tutoring." *Liberal Education* 64 (1978): 447–68.

___. *Collaborative Learning: Higher Education, Interdependence, and the Authority of Knowledge.* 2nd ed. Baltimore: Johns Hopkins UP, 1999.

___. "Collaborative Learning: Some Practical Models." *College English* 34 (1973): 634–43.

Garrison, Roger. "One to One: Tutorial Instruction in Freshman Composition." *New Directions for Community Colleges* 2 (1974): 55–84.

George, D'Ann. "Lobbying for New Courses in Writing Center Theory/Pedagogy." *Writing Lab Newsletter* 27.2 (October 2002): 1–5.

Gillespie, Paula, and Neal Lerner. *The Allyn and Bacon Guide to Peer Tutoring.* 2nd ed. Boston: Allyn and Bacon, 2003.

Harris, Muriel. *Teaching Writing One to One: The Writing Center Conference.* Urbana: NCTE, 1986.

Murray, Donald. "The Listening Eye: Reflections on the Writing Conference." *College English* 41 (September 1979): 13–18.

North, Stephen M. "The Idea of a Writing Center." *College English* 46 (1984): 433–46.

31

The Good, the Bad, the Ugly of Certifying a Tutoring Program through CRLA

Bonnie Devet
College of Charleston

Nearly forty years ago in *The Good, the Bad, and the Ugly*, Clint Eastwood played "The Man with No Name," an anti-hero who has no identity except what the other characters impose on him. Although the characters in this classic film believe they know this antihero, they ascribe to him inaccurate features and attributes.

As a writing lab director, I often think about "The Man with No Name." Despite of having face-to-face discussions with other professors and distributing to them memos about services, I cannot always disabuse faculty of their misperceptions about my lab. All too often, faculty possess their own views about what tutors do or how they are trained, thinking that consultants write clients' papers or that clients drop off papers so consultants can read the essays before working with students. Then there are the consultants themselves who need to be reminded about their roles in the lab, about how they are advancing as tutors, and about how the lab is a professional organization with high training standards. What can directors do to validate the tutoring program both to faculty and consultants?

Help is available in what is known as "certification." It should be noted that certification is not "accreditation." The latter refers to evaluating a lab's entire mission, including targeted populations, its services, its staffing, the director's status (faculty? lecturer?), its use of technology, the research conducted in the lab, its outreach, its budget, its marketing, and its means of self-evaluation ("A Proposed Self-Study"). (See Simpson and Maid, as well as Law.) Certification, however, focuses only on judging the training program for the tutors. Unfortunately, at present, no national accreditation for writing centers exists. The accreditation process has hit roadblocks, but certification is—right now—a prime way to articulate to faculty and consultants a lab's professional status.

The most readily available certification program for colleges and universities is that offered by the national College Reading and Learning Association (CRLA; www.crla.net). This organization certifies tutorial programs based on the type of training, the number of hours of training, and the amount of experience acquired by the tutors. After a program is certified, directors issue certificates to individual consultants who have completed training requirements. Pointing to the certification process, directors can show faculty the true functions of labs and demonstrate to consultants their own progress as they advance through the certification levels.

For the last twelve years, the Writing Lab at the College of Charleston (South Carolina) has participated in this national program, with eighty-five consultants having achieved certification. As a director familiar with certifying tutors, I can report that there are—as always seems to be the case—good, bad, and, even, ugly facets to certification. Each director should decide whether or not to try for certification.

So that directors can decide about pursuing certification, I believe it is helpful to give a brief history of CRLA, to describe levels of certification, to show how the CRLA differs from similar tutor-certifying organizations, and to explain the pros and cons of certification for both directors and consultants.

BACKGROUND ON THE CRLA

Founded in 1966 and originally named the "Western College Reading Association," the CRLA was begun to help reading specialists when institutions of higher learning were admitting students with inadequate reading skills. Over the years, its name has changed and its programs have expanded. In 1978, the organization added to its title, calling itself "Western College Reading and *Learning* Association," so it could bring more activities under its aegis: math, writing, developmental studies, and counseling. In the 1980s, a specific program to help writing lab directors and other types of lab directors began: the International Tutor Certification Program. By 1989, the name of the organization changed to its current "College Reading and Learning Association," with its stated goal of "help[ing] set the standards for best practices in the profession and provide a way for your institution to be recognized as having met those standards" (College Reading). The organization, endorsed by the National Association of Developmental Education, has grown considerably. In May 1990, only 150 programs were certified; today there are 705 nationally and internationally (Crockett).

CERTIFICATION LEVELS

Consultants work toward three levels of certification: Regular, Advanced, and Master, with each requiring additional training. To become certified at the first, or Regular, level, consultants receive a minimum of ten hours training covering at least eight of the following topics, specified by the CRLA:

1. definition of tutoring and [a] tutor['s] responsibilities;

2. basic tutoring guidelines;
3. techniques for successfully beginning and ending a tutor[ing] session;
4. some basic tutoring do's;
5. some basic tutoring don'ts;
6. role modeling;
7. setting goals/planning;
8. communication skills;
9. active listening and paraphrasing;
10. referral skills;
11. study skills;
12. critical thinking skills;
13. compliance with the Ethics and Philosophy of the Tutor Program [as set by each lab];
14. modeling problem solving;
15. other (please specify). (College Reading)

As can be seen, the topics are basic to training tutors, especially in writing labs.

How can labs cover so many topics? Being part of a larger system called the Center for Student Learning (CSL), the Writing Lab at the College of Charleston participates each fall in a mass training session for all labs (accounting, biology, languages, math, and writing). During this session, tutors are trained in the CRLA areas, in addition to a session on cultural diversity. Then, the writing lab staff meets for its own training sessions that focus on topics germane to writing centers, such as the nature of Black English Vernacular, helping learning disabled (LD) students, the importance of the first five minutes of a consultation, or assisting students writing papers in history, psychology, or religious studies. Holding these regularly scheduled staff meetings instead of offering course credit to consultants, directors can easily document the training. If a writing lab offers course credit, then the CRLA's criteria reflect course objectives, so certification would fit well with such labs, too.

Besides ten hours of training in the CRLA topics, the other requirement for certification is that consultants have tutored at least twenty-five hours, a number easily reached given that our writing lab—probably like so many other labs— is open a healthy fifty-one hours a week (See the appendix for descriptions of Advanced and Master certification.).

CRLA AND THE NATIONAL TUTORING ASSOCIATION

There is another certification program called the National Tutoring Association (NTA), although it differs from the CRLA. Whereas the NTA certifies at all levels from elementary through college, the CRLA focuses only on colleges or universities. Another difference is that the NTA certifies *individual* tutors, paraprofessionals, volunteers, or administrators as well as programs. The CRLA, however, certifies just *programs*. Directors of the program then evaluate individual tutors and certify them. In addition, the NTA conducts campus visits, something the CRLA does not (Ayaz). Finally, the NTA, a relatively new organization, was founded in the 1990s (Ayaz), so its track record is less supported than that of the CRLA, which has existed since 1966 and is better known.

THE GOOD, THE BAD, AND THE UGLY
OF CERTIFICATION FOR *DIRECTORS*

Certifying a lab through the CRLA poses philosophical problems. With the CRLA's certifying a wide range of fields (reading, math, learning centers), directors might wonder if its criteria are too general for the specific needs of writing labs. However, the CRLA list is flexible enough so directors may add topics applicable to writing labs.

An even more important concern arises. For years, labs, fighting their developmental image, have stressed they are not merely band-aids for the less-well-prepared writers. Directors might question whether certification by a group born out of remediation would reconfirm that labs serve only developmental students. Despite its origins, the CRLA's tutoring standards outweigh its association with remediation. The standards concentrate on tutors and their skills, placing them front and center in any writing lab. Focusing on tutors and their training supercedes any detriment inherent in being connected to a developmental group.

Do CRLA's criteria control the lab's training so that directors "teach to the test"? Even though I find myself constantly checking CRLA criteria, directors would be fulfilling these standards anyway, so this national organization's topics validate the good work of the consultants and communicate a lab's functions to the "Doubting Thomas" faculty.

Unfortunately, training generates a large volume of paperwork for each consultant. With three levels and with so many consultants, directors find themselves mired in the time-consuming process of keeping a tally sheet for each tutor. But completing this bookkeeping lets directors closely monitor a consultant's progress and encourage each to go a bit further to become an Advanced or Master certified consultant.

Besides paperwork, certification poses other demands on directors' vital time. Certification is initially good for one year, after which it can be renewed for three years. At the end of that period, directors renew it once again, this time for five years. So lab directors must be vigilant in keeping accurate records of statistics and activities. Deciding to certify a lab, like choosing to paint a brick house, requires commitment.

CRLA certification, however, is relatively prompt. Once a lab's program submits its paperwork, the review process lasts only eight to ten weeks.

Certification also requires finding novel ways to train consultants, especially those seeking Advanced and Master levels. Not wanting to bore the more experienced consultants with the same training they covered for the first level of certification, directors are inspired to devise innovative training, such as having the consultants participate on a panel where they share their "pains and gains" as tutors or encouraging them to write for publication. Upper levels of certification keep directors alive and more creative in their training.

Certification helps with the management of tutors in another way. It allows directors to gauge how well their programs satisfy the all-important Index of Work Satisfaction, a set of benchmarks set up by Paula Stamps and Eugene Piedmonte. This famous scale lists six factors to appraise how workers feel about their jobs: "pay, autonomy, task requirements, organizational policies, interaction, and professional status" (60). Working toward certification levels lets tutors achieve several of these key indicators: "pay" when tutors get a salary raise at each certification level, "autonomy" as the consultants work through the levels, "task requirements" as they learn what each level entails, "interaction" as they train other tutors, and "professional status" when they reach each certification. Consultants, then, sense their worth as workers, a seminal quality directors must establish when managing tutors.

Certification fosters good employee morale—yet another key to effective management. My college sends its photographer to shoot a certification ceremony and to write a news release that appears in the school paper or in the certified consultant's hometown newspaper. Through the certification ceremony, consultants are honored before their peers, and more importantly, the publicity generated by the ceremony keeps the consultants' training before the public served by the lab.

Directors need to consider, as well, how their administration will react to the CRLA's certification. I wondered how the deans would view certification because CRLA makes no campus visit. However, without a national group expressly for certifying writing centers, I have accepted CRLA certification as the most useful for verifying a tutor training program at the college or university level, making sure my own administration understands the value as well as the limitations of the CRLA program.

I have also found that I can impress administrators with the lab's certified status. When they ask how the writing lab contributes to recruitment and retention, I stress that the lab's nationally recognized standards assist the school in attracting students. When parents learn that our college offers assistance through a certified writing lab, they should be convinced that their little Johnny or Jane has chosen the right school. Once Johnny and Jane are in class, a certified lab becomes a retention tool, offering at-risk students another venue of help.

And then there are the costs. Directors with their pecuniarily challenged labs are always concerned with costs. The initial one-year certification runs $75, and recertification for three years and five years each costs $75 (College Reading). Given what directors pay for reference books or subscriptions to journals, none of these fees is excessive.

THE GOOD, THE BAD, AND THE UGLY FOR *CONSULTANTS*

Certification benefits consultants. Completing each level of certification means another pay raise, and being certified distinguishes tutors as job candidates, especially on their curriculum vitae. As one newly certified consultant candidly reported, "It's something else to add to my résumé."

Besides increasing their paychecks and adding to their résumés, consultants find certification shores up confidence. In their first semester or two in the lab, consultants often wonder if they are doing all they can to help clients. Certification, with its clear list of standards, shows consultants that they are, indeed, trained professionals. Feeling validated, one certified consultant stressed that certification reflects his professional status: "I am now official. I can hang the certificate on my wall. I have taken extra steps to ensure that the clients receive the best help possible."

Another value of certification is that it helps tutors with their own writing. Consultants read articles about composition theory (e.g., "pre-writing techniques and the cognitive process," or "Toulmin logic for arguments") and apply the articles to their tutoring sessions. A biology major who has been a consultant for three years described the advantages: "Certification has allowed me to stay on top of issues/problems facing writers on every level. It acts as a sort of review of rules and stylistic ideas that I might otherwise have forgotten." Because consultants themselves learn to be better writers, one tutor commented, "The requirements [for certification] enrich my education."

Consultants, however, are the first to point out the disadvantages of certification. They question certain CRLA requirements: My consultants believe that twenty-five hours of tutoring experience seems a low requisite given that most of them tutor at least eight hours a week. It is true that twenty-five hours seems minimal, but I believe the CRLA sets the requirement at this level to benefit tutors not able to handle an eight-hour-a-week workload. Consultants also found that completing ten hours of training was, at least initially, daunting. As students carrying fifteen to eighteen hours of course credit and working in the lab as well as at another job, the ten-hour requirement appeared imposing; however, as one certified consultant remarked, "Doing it bit by bit meant it did not seem like a lot." Finally, consultants pointed out that expecting them to review the previous levels in order to achieve both Advanced and Master certification was unnecessary. After all, working eight hours a week means tutors review daily how to be tutors. I believe the consultants have a valid objection here.

CONCLUSIONS

Despite the good, the bad, and the ugly, certifying a tutorial program through the CRLA shows faculty and consultants that a lab complies with national tutoring standards. Being able to point to the certification criteria, I am now, as a director, no longer perceived as Eastwood's "Man with No Name." The lab is validated.

This desire for validation raises another issue. Why, given the long history of writing labs (a history perhaps going back fifty to one hundred years, depending on the historians consulted), must labs keep justifying themselves to others and to themselves? Even though the excellent work of labs and their consultants should be certification enough, history teaches directors that doing good work is not sufficient. Directors must be able to get out the word about the professional nature of labs, especially because administrators advocate assessment and faculty continue to possess false perceptions about labs. With no national group exclusively designed for validating writing labs, it would seem, then, that certification through the CRLA is a sound, useful way to reaffirm to ourselves and to doubting faculty the fine work of consultants and their directors.

WORKS CITED

Ayaz, Sandi. "Small Inquiry [about NTA]." E-mail to author. 17 Dec. 2003.

College Reading and Learning Association (CRLA). Home page. No yr. 23 Nov. 2003. <http:// www.crla.net>.

Crockett, Ann. "Inquiry about CRLA." E-mail to author. 17 Dec. 2003.

The Good, the Bad, and the Ugly. Dir. Sergio Leone. CBS Fox Home Video, 1966.

Law, Joe. "Accreditation and the Writing Center: A Proposal for Action." *Writing Center Perspectives.* Ed. Byron L. Stay, Christina Murphy, and Eric H. Hobson. Emmitsburg, MD: NWCA P, 1995. 155–61.

National Tutoring Association (NTA). Home page. No yr. 16 Dec. 2003. <http://ntatutor.org>.

Simpson, Jeanne H., and Barry M. Maid. "Lining Up Ducks or Herding Cats? The Politics of Writing Center Accreditation." *The Politics of Writing Centers.* Ed. Jane Nelson and Kathy Evertz. Portsmouth, NH: Heinemann-Boynton/Cook, 2001. 121–32.

Stamps, Paula, and Eugene B. Piedmonte. *Nurses and Work Satisfaction: An Index of Measurement.* Ann Arbor, MI: Health Administration Press Perspectives, 1986. "A Proposed Self-Study Questionnaire for Writing Centers Seeking Accreditation through the National Centers Association." 22 Nov. 1997. 24 Nov. 2003. <http://faculty.winthrop.edu/kosterj/nwca/ nwcadraft.htm>.

Appendix

Advanced

In addition to the review of the previous level, consultants should:

—help to train new consultants each fall.

—read and summarize two articles on composition theory, showing how consultants would apply the concepts to their work as consultants.

—attend five staff meetings.

—complete twenty-five additional hours of actual tutoring experience.

(Often at the Advance level, in lieu of reading one of the two required articles, consultants also create new handouts, such as "Writing Papers for Religious Studies" or "Literature Review.")

Master

—review level 2 (advanced) certification topics by writing a summary of four of the five topics consultants heard about in staff meetings, explaining how they would apply them to their work in the WL (about one to two typed pages).

—serve on Pains and Gains Panel during fall orientation (experienced consultants explain what they have learned from working in the writing lab).

—read and summarize two articles in notebook marked "Master Certification" on desk in WL, and then explain how they would apply the concepts to their work as consultants.

—attend five staff meetings since advanced certification.

—complete an additional twenty-five hours of tutoring beyond the Advanced level of certification.

(Often at the Master level, in lieu of reading one of the two required articles, consultants also write for publication and/or deliver papers at conferences.)

FIG. 31.1   How the College of Charleston's Writing Lab handles Advanced and Master Certification

32

Words, Images, Sounds: Writing Centers as Multiliteracy Centers

David M. Sheridan
Michigan State University

If schools are to equip students adequately for the new semiotic order ... then the old boundaries between 'writing' on the one hand, traditionally the form of literacy without which people cannot adequately function as citizens, and, on the other hand, the 'visual arts,' a marginal subject for the especially gifted ... should be redrawn. This will have to involve modern computer technology, central as it is to the new semiotic landscape.

—Kress and van Leeuwen 32–33

Nowhere is there greater potential for achieving a degree of success in this exceedingly complex venture [of fostering computer-mediated literacy] than there is in the numerous computer-supported writing centers that have been set up in schools and institutions across the country.   —Selfe 3

Imagine that Jane, a first-year writing student, comes to the writing center seeking help. When her peer consultant asks about the nature of her project, she says that her class is taking a "service learning" approach. The class has been divided into small groups, each of which has been assigned a different community partner. Jane's community partner, a nonprofit organization serving homeless people, has asked the student writers to produce a Web site. The proposed site will educate readers about the organization and about homelessness in general. The community partner envisions a visually rich site that integrates brief chunks of text with photographs and design elements to achieve a professional but emotionally engaging experience for readers.

As conversation continues, it becomes clear that Jane, although interested in the written components of her evolving Web site, is more concerned about design issues: color scheme, layout, typography, photographs. She is worried that she does not have the technical or visual skills to integrate design elements effectively.

What is the appropriate response of a writing center to a student with this set of needs? Should peer consultants offer support for the rhetorical use of visual materials and design elements? Should they guide clients through the use of web-authoring applications like Dreamweaver and photo-editing applications like Photoshop? Or should consultants limit themselves to a discussion of writing, narrowly conceived?

Gunther Kress (echoing a host of other literacy theorists) observed: "[T]he landscape of communication is changing fundamentally" (67). As the New London Group put it, in order to "participate fully in public, community, and economic life," we are all increasingly asked to employ "multiliteracies" (9). The electronic media (i.e., radio, film, and TV) of the twentieth century asked us to be consumers of multimodal compositions, a role requiring us to expand our notion of "literacy" to include the meaning-making practices necessary to parse "texts" that communicate through the integration of written and spoken words, music and other sounds, and an array of visual elements. The emergent technologies of the twenty-first century increasingly ask us to be *composers* of multimodal texts. We are asked to produce web pages, PowerPoint slides, desktop-published documents, and even digital videos—compositions that encourage and even necessitate attention to design, visual communication, and media in ways that the traditional academic essay, printed on 8½" X 11" paper with one-inch margins, historically has not.

John Trimbur and others suggested that writing centers will increasingly define themselves as "multiliteracy centers," in part to reflect these fundamental changes in the semiotic landscape (29). This chapter introduces basic theoretical and practical issues involved in this redefinition. I begin with four key questions that writing centers need to face as they move toward a multiliteracy approach:

1. What model for the relationship between writing and other modes of communication should writing centers embrace?
2. What model for the relationship between technology and rhetoric should writing centers embrace?
3. To what extent should writing centers lead and to what extent should they follow as their home institutions adopt multiliteracy pedagogy?
4. How should writing centers change existing practices of tutor recruitment and training?

After exploring these questions, I sketch more fully what multiliteracy consulting looks like in practice.

WHAT MODEL FOR THE RELATIONSHIP BETWEEN WRITING AND OTHER MODES SHOULD WRITING CENTERS EMBRACE?

One of the key ideas informing the notion of Multiliteracies is the increasing complexity and interrelationship of different modes of meaning. We have already identified six major areas in which functional grammars ... are required—Linguistic Design, Visual Design, Audio Design, Gestural Design, Spatial Design, and Multimodal Design. Multimodal Design, however, is of a different order to the others as it represents the patterns of interconnection among the other modes. (New London Group 25)

Fundamental to the notion of multiliteracies is the interconnectedness of different semiotic components. Web pages and other new media forms communicate their message through the integration of words, images, and sounds. Different elements "cooperate" to convey the "totality of the information," to borrow Roland Barthes's language (16). To support new media composing effectively, then, multiliteracy centers need to move away from models that see the written word as the exclusive or even the privileged mode of communication. Multiliteracy consultants need to engage composers in conversations about all media components.

Imagine, for instance, how a consulting session might look if the consultant conceives of her role narrowly, as one of engaging the client in matters related to writing. In this conversation, we can imagine Jane's disappointment as she is told that although her concerns about design and about photographs are certainly important, they fall outside the purview of the writing center. But even the conversation about writing, narrowly conceived, is likely to be plagued with dead ends and false starts: "As a reader, I don't get a very vivid picture of the conditions in this shelter," the consultant might say. To which the client might respond, "Oh, that's because alongside that text there will be a photograph that powerfully depicts the material conditions of the shelter." At another point the consultant might say, "As a reader, I find these short chunks of text tedious. This experience of your text is fragmented. It's hard to make connections." The client might respond, "Each of the chunks is the amount that will fit on a standard computer monitor. To help readers make connections, we plan to use color coding and hyperlinks."

In new media, the semiotic whole is greater than the sum of its parts. Words are inextricably linked to other media elements, making it difficult to talk about them in isolation. A multiliteracy consultant meeting with Jane would embrace the chance to explore the rhetorical dimensions of all elements, including photographs, color, layout, and navigation scheme.

WHAT MODEL FOR THE RELATIONSHIP BETWEEN TECHNOLOGY AND RHETORIC SHOULD WRITING CENTERS EMBRACE?

Those with a knowledge of literacy, its myriad manifestations and its ramifications, must become actively involved in shaping the complex of technology that, in turn, shapes our literacy, our cultures, and ourselves. (Haas and Neuwirth 330)

For some, I suspect, it is relatively easy to understand why writing centers should be willing to engage students in conversations about the rhetorical use of images and other media components in web pages and PowerPoint presentations. We have become accustomed to a broadening of the words "rhetoric" and "literacy" to include "visual rhetoric" and "visual literacy." But what about technology? Should writing consultants guide students through the process of editing their digital photographs in Photoshop or creating web pages in Dreamweaver? Isn't that a job for IT support on campus?

Literacy theorists have been exploring the link between technology and literacy for some time. As hybrid terms like *computer-mediated literacy* (Selfe), *cyberliteracy* (Gurak), and *electracy* (Ulmer) suggest, many theorists who examine the relation between rhetoric and technology come to the conclusion that the two are intimately related. Haas and Neuwirth warned against the "computers are not our job" attitude common in English studies (325), and Beebe and Bonevelle, speaking about writing centers specifically, concluded, "The more tutors know about the software programs that their tutees use, the more effectively tutors can help tutees" (50). Because technology and literacy are inextricably linked, I am arguing here that multiliteracy centers should include support for technical dimensions of the composing process.

For instance, let's imagine that Jane has expressed to her consultant that she hopes the photographs provided by her community partner will serve as visual critiques of stereotyping found in the mass media. In discussing the rhetorical goals for these photographs, the client and consultant will need to discuss possibilities for editing them. Perhaps a photograph of a woman in a shelter is dark and grey and taken from such a distance that her facial features are not discernable—realities that tend to undermine the ability of viewers to identify with her. Can the photograph be lightened? Can it be blown up? Can the color be adjusted?

Answers to these questions need to account for technological realities. Whether or not a photograph can be blown up, for instance, is a decision that needs to take into account the resolution of the original image. Deciding to lighten a photograph assumes the composer knows that photo-editing applications allow this operation, as well as how much a photo can be lightened, under what circumstances, and, of course, how to do it. A multiliteracy consultant who knows photo-editing applications can talk with her client about what kinds of revisions are possible, can guide her client through the process of making those revisions, and can talk about the rhetorical effectiveness of those revisions once they are made.

The interrelatedness of technology and rhetoric saturates almost every dimension of digital composing. Questions like "Can I superimpose words over an image?," "Can I have two columns?," and "Can I use a particular font?," all imply both an understanding of the rhetoric of design as well as technologies related to composing and to the medium of delivery.

Separating technical and rhetorical dimensions of multimodal communication artificially segments the composing process. It also ignores current realities about how students define their needs. Many students view multimodal communication as a purely technical challenge: They know what they want to say, they just need to make the computer work. Multiliteracy consultants can help students come to a more sophisticated understanding of multimodal communication by foregrounding the interrelationship of technical and rhetorical concerns. If students need to go to separate sources to get technical and rhetorical help, then many of them, for pragmatic reasons, will simply skip the rhetorical support altogether.

TO WHAT EXTENT SHOULD WRITING CENTERS LEAD AND TO WHAT EXTENT SHOULD THEY FOLLOW AS THEIR HOME INSTITUTIONS ADOPT MULTILITERACY PEDAGOGY?

At Michigan State, changes in writing center and instructional practices usually involve a recursive process. Student composers and writing instructors come to the center with various needs: Can someone here help me with this PowerPoint presentation? Can someone show me how to make a web page? The special needs of these students and instructors are occasions for re-interrogating the mission and practice of the center. They force us to ask: Are there existing resources on campus for these students? Should we offer new kinds of support? (web document A).[1]

But as we have extended our services to include support for certain kinds of composing, some instructors have adopted new classroom practices. Instructors who know that their students can receive support for web authoring at the center might feel more comfortable assigning a web essay. Increasing services, then, has created an increased demand for those services.

Writing centers can respond to demand, but can also be agents of institutional change, advocating for the kinds of composing and teaching they feel are important (Bruffee). As part of its mission to foster a culture of writing across campus, MSU's center, like many centers, works with instructors of writing-intensive courses across the curriculum who seek to integrate writing into their courses in pedagogically effective ways. Consistent with this approach is the invitation to help instructors integrate technology effectively (web document B). Instructors are invited to sit down with writing center consultants or faculty to discuss all aspects related to teaching with technology, from framing new media assignments to confronting logistical considerations about labs and equipment. Additionally, the center offers a series of whole-class presentations that explore basic issues related to digital composing (web document C). The center works with instructors to create generative composing environments for students through a combination of whole-class, small-group, and one-on-one support services. In this model, then, demand is not just a preexisting entity that writing centers react to; it is a function, in part, of the kinds of teaching and composing practices centers can enable.

HOW SHOULD WRITING CENTERS RECRUIT AND TRAIN MULTILITERACY TUTORS?

Multiliteracy consultants need to have three categories of knowledge and skills. They need to develop a sophisticated understanding of consulting pedagogy, including both traditional models for providing peer support as well as an understanding of how these models need to be adapted when consulting moves into a digital environment. They need to develop an understanding of multimodal rhetoric. And they need to understand the technical processes that are involved in composing digital media (web document D).

In order to develop a cadre of consultants who have knowledge in these three areas, a multifaceted approach to recruitment and training is necessary. At MSU, multiliteracy consultants, or digital writing consultants (DWCs), are part of the general consulting pool and go through the same training process as other consultants. This training is aimed at helping students build practical yet theoretically sophisticated models for writing centers and for peer consulting. To this end, trainees read extensively in writing center scholarship, observe consulting sessions, and reflect on and synthesize what they observe and read by engaging in a variety of forms of discussion (classroom, electronic, and paper based).

Within any given cadre of consultants, some subset are interested in becoming a DWC. Occasionally, this subset includes students who are formally trained in a field (e.g., graphic design) related to composing with new media. More often, some students have learned relevant skills

---

[1]Supplemental web resources are available at <http://www.msu.edu/~sherid16/wcdr>.

as part of a previous job or have taught themselves because of personal interest. Others have little or no experience as new media composers. DWCs go through supplemental training that varies according to the needs of the center and the backgrounds of the consultants, but usually includes some combination of specialized reading, additional observations of experienced DWCs, and opportunities to engage in multimodal projects. At various times we have provided this supplemental training through "special topics" courses, as well as through less formal self-paced programs (see appendix and web document E).

Before coming to Michigan State, I helped to develop a multiliteracy program through the University of Michigan's Sweetland Writing Center. To recruit students with the appropriate skill sets, we made a point of contacting graphic design majors. However, we discovered that the academic schedules and goals of these students were different from those of the liberal arts students who typically entered Sweetland's Peer Tutoring Program. To recruit effectively, we invited a graphic design professor to teach a version of our tutor training course that had been modified slightly to reflect the interests of the design majors. As writing centers seek effective multiliteracy consultants, they may need to consider alternative recruitment strategies like this.

As writing center administrators structure consultant training and recruitment programs, I submit that it is useful to conceive of this task as establishing a particular kind of culture. Patti Stock explained that the MSU Writing Center

> has taken upon itself the ambitious task of creating a culture of writing and continuous inquiry.... Taking advantage of the opportunities that exist when individuals with different but related goals teach and learn from one another for their mutual benefit ... the Center is developing a practice we call **consultative teaching**. A combination of collaborative learning, peer tutoring, service learning, student research, and jointly-conducted student-faculty research, the practice of consultative teaching recognizes students as knowledgeable individuals with valuable ideas and experiences to contribute to the learning situation. (12)

A multiliteracy center is at its best when it is based on a professional and intellectual community in which consultants are encouraged to reflect on their practice as both composers and consultants. As composers, DWCs at MSU embrace opportunities to engage in multimodal communication, producing in any given semester a variety of educational and publicity materials—Web sites, flyers, handouts, PowerPoints, videos, posters, brochures, logos—for the center and its collaborators. We workshop our compositions formally and informally at multiple points throughout the composing process, seeking constructive feedback about both rhetorical and technical issues. Our experiences as composers inform our consulting practices.

As consultants, DWCs are encouraged to be reflective practitioners and are provided a range of formal and informal venues to talk with others about their work. For instance, we seek out opportunities to explore our evolving understanding of multiliteracy consulting at professional conferences, viewing these presentations as occasions to articulate our ideas more fully, to establish a wider context for them through research, and to solicit constructive feedback from others in the writing center community.

DWCs are able to provide effective support for peers because they have an abiding interest in both the practice and theory of multiliteracy composing and consulting. This interest is kindled and developed, in part, by the general culture of the center. When a student walks in seeking help with a web project, the conversation that our consultants facilitate is energized by an ongoing personal and professional investment in understanding new media.

MULTILITERACY CONSULTING

As I have described it so far, a multiliteracy center is technology-rich space staffed by consultants who have sophisticated understandings of peer consulting pedagogy, multimodal rhetoric, and composing technologies. These consultants engage students in conversations about rhetorical choices they make concerning not just words, but images and other media elements as well. But what does multiliteracy consulting look like in practice? To make these ideas more concrete, let's imagine that Mark, a preservice elementary school teacher, comes to the writing center seeking help with his web-based teaching portfolio. He envisions a portfolio that contains written statements about his teaching philosophy, examples of lesson plans that he has created, and photographs of students with which he has worked.

When Tanya, Mark's multiliteracy consultant, learns that Mark will be working on a web project, she invites him to sit down at one of the consulting tables. Tanya explains that they can move to a computer workstation later if necessary The conversation begins with general discussion about the nature of the project and the rhetorical situation: Is this an assignment? Are there any guidelines? Who are the target audiences? What are the primary rhetorical purposes?

Mark explains that this is his own initiative, not an assignment. He's heard from friends who have gotten teaching jobs that a good digital portfolio is one way to stand out as a job candidate. His primary audience is an interview team. His purpose is to persuade his audience that he is a creative teacher with a thorough understanding of contemporary educational theory.

After this preliminary discussion, Tanya hands Mark an oversized sheet of paper containing the empty window of a web browser. She explains that this browser window is approximately the size of a computer monitor with a resolution of 800 × 600 pixels. Tanya asks Mark to sketch out the homepage of his portfolio as he imagines it might look. The sketch that Mark comes up with includes a banner across the top and central photograph. Superimposed across the bottom of the photo are links to the various sections of his portfolio: teaching philosophy, lesson plans, professional activities, and resume.

When Tanya asks about the photograph, Mark takes a stack of glossy prints out of his backpack and spreads them on the table. Some are of students sitting in rows, some of individual students, some of students working in small groups. "If you could only select one," Tanya asks, "which one do you think best represents your teaching philosophy?" Mark identifies one that shows five students working in a loose circle on the classroom floor. Paint, glue, scissors, and colored paper are scattered around them. Mark explains that this photo reflects his vision for collaboration and active learning. But he remarks that the photo looks dull and cluttered; the students in the circle appear too small, and other students in the background and on the periphery distract from the message he hopes to convey. Tanya promises that some of those problems can be resolved and suggests that this might be a good time to find a workstation.

Tanya has Mark sit down at a computer and positions herself slightly off to the side so that she can see the screen but does not have control over the keyboard. They begin with the photograph, Tanya guiding Mark through the process of scanning the photo and opening it in Photoshop. With Tanya's help, Mark selectively blurs elements in the photograph that are extraneous, which has the effect of making the students in the circle more prominent. After each change, Mark and Tanya discuss the rhetorical implications.

At some point, the conversation turns to matters of design and color. Repeatedly in this conversation, Mark has used "kid friendly" and "professional" to describe the overall style he hopes to employ throughout his site. He decides that he can achieve both of these goals by committing to a few warm colors and favoring clean shapes surrounded by lots of white space. And so the conversation continues.

In this imagined multiliteracy consulting session, I have tried to show how principles that have become fundamental to traditional consulting practice, such as a "minimalist" or "nondirective" approach to consulting, can be translated into a multiliteracy consulting session. Tanya does not do Mark's work for him, nor does she lecture him about what he should do; instead, she keeps him actively engaged in the composing process by asking strategic questions and by making sure he is always in control of the technology. Additionally, I have tried to show that a "rhetorical" approach that emphasizes the relationship between rhetorical decisions to key contextual elements such as audience and purpose is equally appropriate for multiliteracy consulting. A rich understanding of the rhetorical situation can inform decisions about navigation schemes, photographs, and other media elements in addition to writing. In this approach, "content" is not applied narrowly to the written components of a project; all media elements are seen as contributing to the overall rhetorical effect.

THE MULTILITERACY CENTER AND THE UNIVERSITY

Writing centers are often overtasked and underresourced. Developing a multiliteracy program can seem overwhelming. I have tried to suggest here that a multiliteracy program can grow incrementally, building on existing models and practices. In any cadre of consultants, a few will already possess some of the skills needed to consult with clients about multimodal projects. Basic web authoring, PowerPoint, and desktop publishing can be done on standard personal computers that many writing centers will have already purchased for other purposes.

As multiliteracy programs grow, writing centers will need to tap into resources and seek out forms of collaboration that might differ from conventional practice. Writing centers will need to cultivate relationships with IT support, graphic design, and computer science. They will need to seek out funds that have been earmarked for technology at the departmental, college, university, state, and federal levels.

The landscape of communication is changing, and so are the composing practices of the students that writing centers have traditionally served. English studies, composition theory, and the academy in general have been moving away from a narrow commitment to the study of "writing" toward a semiotic approach that examines signifying practices more generally. Writing centers continue to focus narrowly on the written word at the risk of increasing obsolescence. What I have tried to offer here are some first thoughts about how writing centers might respond to the composing practices of the twenty-first century.

WORKS CITED

Barthes, Roland. "The Photographic Message." *Image-Music-Text*. Trans. Stephen Heath. New York: Hill and Wang, 1977. 15–31.

Beebe, Randall L., and Mary J. Bonevelle. "The Culture of Technology in the Writing Center: Reinvigorating the Theory-Practice Debate." *Taking Flight with OWLs*. Ed. James A. Inman and Donna N. Sewell. Mahwah, NJ: Lawrence Erlbaum Associates, 2000. 41–51.

Bruffee, Kenneth. "Peer Tutors as Agents of Change." Proceedings of the Seventh Annual Conference on Peer Tutoring in Writing. Ed. Stacy Nestleroth. University Park, PA: Pennsylvania State UP, 1990. 1–6.

Gurak, Laura J. *Cyberliteracy: Navigating the Internet with Awareness*. New Haven: Yale UP, 2001.

Haas, Christina, and Christine M. Neuwirth. "Writing the Technology That Writes Us: Research on Literacy and the Shape of Technology." *Literacy and Computers: The Complications of Teaching and Learning with Technology*. Ed. Cynthia Selfe and Susan Hilligoss. New York: MLA, 1994. 319–35.

Kress, Gunther. "'English' at a Crossroads: Rethinking Curricula of Communication in the Context of the Turn to the Visual." *Passions, Pedagogies, and 21st Century Technologies*. Ed. Gail E. Hawisher and Cynthia Selfe. Logan: Utah State UP, 1999. 66–88.

Kress, Gunther, and Theo Van Leeuwen. *Reading Images: The Grammar of Visual Design*. London: Routledge, 1996.

New London Group. "A Pedagogy of Multiliteracies: Designing Social Futures." *Multiliteracies: Literacy Learning and the Design of Social Futures*. Ed. Bill Cope and Mary Kalantzis. London: Routledge, 2000.

Selfe, Cynthia. "Redefining Literacy: The Multilayered Grammars of Computers." *Critical Perspectives on Computers and Composition Instruction*. Ed. Gail E. Hawisher and Cynthia Selfe. New York: Teachers College P, 1989. 3–15.

Stock, Patricia. "Reforming Education in the Land-Gant U: Contributions from a Writing Center." *The Writing Center Journal* 18.1 (1997): 7–30.

Trimbur, John. "Multiliteracies, Social Futures, and Writing Centers." *The Writing Center Journal* 20.2 (2000): 29–32.

Ulmer, Gregory L. *Internet Invention: From Literacy to Electracy*. New York: Longman, 2003.

Appendix

READINGS FOR DIGITAL WRITING CONSULTANT TRAINING COURSE

(Full syllabus and list of relevant Web sites available at <http://www.msu.edu/~sherid16/wcdr>.)

Assigned Texts

Handa, Carolyn, ed. *Visual Rhetoric in a Digital World: A Critical Sourcebook*. Boston: Bedford, 2004.

Hawisher, Gail E., and Cynthia Selfe, eds. *Passions, Pedagogies, and 21st Century Technologies*. Logan: Utah State UP, 1999.

Hilligoss, Susan, and Tharon Howard. *Visual Communication: A Writer's Guide*. 2nd ed. Longman, 2001.

Williams, Robin. *The Non-Designer's Design Book*. Berkeley, CA : Peachpit P, 2003.

(Readings not from these texts are available in coursepack form.)

Week 1: Writing, the Teaching of Writing, and Technology

Costanzo, William. "Reading, Writing, and Thinking in an Age of Electronic Literacy." *Literacy and Computers: The Complications of Teaching and Learning with Technology*. Ed. Cynthia Selfe and Susan Hilligoss. New York: MLA, 1994.

Haas, Christina, and Christine M. Neuwirth. "Writing the Technology That Writes Us: Research on Literacy and the Shape of Technology." *Literacy and Computers: The Complications of Teaching and Learning with Technology*. Ed. Cynthia Selfe and Susan Hilligoss. New York: MLA, 1994.

Landow, George P. "Reconfiguring Literacy Education." *Hypertext 2.0: The Convergence of Contemporary Critical Theory and Technology*. Baltimore: Johns Hopkins UP, 1997.

Selfe, Cynthia. "Redefining Literacy: The Multilayered Grammars of Computers." *Critical Perspectives on Computers and Composition Instruction*. Ed. Gail E. Hawisher and Cynthia Selfe. New York: Teachers College P, 1989. 3–15.

Week 2: Writing Centers and Technology

Carino, Peter. "Computers in the Writing Center: A Cautionary History." *The Allyn and Bacon Guide to Writing Center Theory and Practice*. Ed. Robert W. Barnett and Jacob Blumner. Boston: Allyn and Bacon, 2001.

Clark, Irene L. "Information Literacy and the Writing Center." *The Allyn and Bacon Guide to Writing Center Theory and Practice*. Ed. Robert W. Barnett and Jacob Blumner. Boston: Allyn and Bacon, 2001.

DeVoss, Danielle. "Computer Literacies and the Roles of the Writing Center." *Writing Center Research: Extending the Conversation*. Mahwah, NJ: Lawrence Erlbaum Associates, 2002.

Thomas, Sharon, Danielle DeVoss, and Mark Hara. "Toward a Critical Theory of Technology and Writing." *The Writing Center Journal*. 19.1 (1998): 73–87.

Wallace, Ray. "Random Memories of the Wired Writing Center." *Wiring the Writing Center*. Ed. Eric Hobson. Logan: Utah State UP, 1998.

Weeks 3–5: Multiliteracies: Words, Links, and Media

Bolter, Jay David. "The Computer as a New Writing Space." *CyberReader*. Ed. Victor J. Vitanza. New York: Longman, 1999.

Cazden, Courtney et al. "A Pedagogy of Multiliteracies: Designing Social Futures." *Harvard Education Review.* Spring 1996.

George, Diana. "From Analysis to Design: Visual Communication in the Teaching of Writing." *College Composition and Communication.* 54.1 (2002): 11–38.

Handa, Carolyn, ed. *Visual Rhetoric in a Digital World: A Critical Sourcebook.* Boston: Bedford 2004. Part One (7–130) and Part Two (131–222).

Kress, Gunther. "'English' at a Crossroads: Rethinking Curricula of Communication in the Context of the Turn to the Visual." *Passions, Pedagogies, and 21st Century Technologies.* Ed. Gail E. Hawisher and Cynthia Selfe. Logan: Utah State UP, 1999. 66–88.

Landow, George P. "Hypertext: An Introduction" and "Reconfiguring the Text." *Hypertext 2.0: The Convergence of Contemporary Critical Theory and Technology.* Baltimore: Johns Hopkins UP, 1997.

Richardson, Glenn, Jr. "Pulp Politics: Popular Culture and Political Advertising." *Rhetoric & Public Affairs* 3.4 (2000): 603–26.

Sellnow, Deanna D., and Timothy L. Sellnow. "John Corigliano's *Symphony No. 1* as a Communicative Medium." *Communication Studies* 44.2. (1993): 87–95.

Wysocki, Anne Francis, and Johndan Johnson-Eilola. "Blinded by the Letter: Why Are We Using Literacy as a Metaphor for Everything Else." *Passions, Pedagogies, and 21st Century Technologies.* Ed. Gail E. Hawisher and Cynthia Selfe. Logan: Utah State UP, 1999. 349–68.

Weeks 6-7: Visual Culture/Cultural Approaches to the Visual

Handa, Carolyn, ed. *Visual Rhetoric in a Digital World: A Critical Sourcebook.* Boston: Bedford 2004. Part Five (375–474).

Hawisher, Gail E., and Patricia A. Sullivan. "Fleeting Images: Women Visually Writing the Web." *Passions, Pedagogies, and 21st Century Technologies.* Ed. Gail E. Hawisher and Cynthia Selfe. Logan: Utah State UP, 1999. 258–91.

Ruby, Jay. "Researching with a Camera: The Anthropologist as Picture Taker." *Picturing Culture.* U Chicago P, 2000.

Week 8-9: Graphic Design

Handa, Carolyn, ed. *Visual Rhetoric in a Digital World: A Critical Sourcebook.* Boston: Bedford 2004. Part Three (223–302).

Mundi, Andrew. "Principles of Graphic Design." 2001. 20 June 2004. <http://www.mundidesign.com/presentation/index2.html>.

Hilligoss, Susan, and Tharon Howard, *Visual Communication: A Writer's Guide,* 2nd ed. Longman, 2001.

Williams, Robin. *The Non-Designer's Design Book.* Berkeley, CA. Peachpit P, 2003.

Week 10-11: Academic Uses of Multimodal Communication

Handa, Carolyn, ed. *Visual Rhetoric in a Digital World: A Critical Sourcebook.* Boston: Bedford 2004. Part Four (303–74).

Hesse, Doug. "Saving a Place for Essayistic Literacy." *Passions, Pedagogies, and 21st Century Technologies.* Ed. Gail E. Hawisher and Cynthia Selfe. Logan: Utah State UP, 1999. 34–48.

Week 12–13: Civic Uses of Multimodal Communication

Faigley, Lester. "Material Literacy and Visual Design." *Rhetorical Bodies: Toward a Material Rhetoric.* Ed. Jack Selzer and Sharon Crowley. Madison: U of Wisconsin P, 1999. 171–201.

George, Diana. "Changing the Face of Poverty: Nonprofits and the Problem of Representation." *Popular Literacy.* Ed. John Trimbur. Pittsburgh: U of Pittsburgh P, 2001. 209–28.

Kenney, Keith. "Building Visual Communication Theory by Borrowing from Rhetoric." *Journal of Visual Literacy,* 22.1 (2002): 53–80.

Warschauer, Mark. "Cyber Service Learning." *Electronic Literacies: Language, Culture, and Power in Online Education.* Mahwah, NJ: Lawrence Erlbaum Associates, 1999.

Weeks 14–15: Creative Expression in New Media

Larsen, Deena. "A Quick Buzz Around the Universe of Electronic Poetry." *Currents in Electronic Literacy.* 20 June 2004. <http://www.cwrl.utexas.edu/currents/archives/fall01/index.html>.

Marsh, Bill. "Reading Time: For a Poetics of Hypermedia Writing." *Currents in Electronic Literacy.* Fall 2001. 20 June 2004. <http://www.cwrl.utexas.edu/currents/archives/fall01/index.html> .

Amerika, Mark. Home page. 20 June 2004. <http://www.markamerika.com/>.

Moulthrop, Stuart. Home page. 20 June 2004. <http://iat.ubalt.edu/moulthrop/>.

Poems That Go. 2004. 20 June 2004. <http://www.poemsthatgo.com/>.

33

Preserving the Rhetorical Nature of Tutoring When Going Online

Lisa Eastmond Bell
Utah Valley State College

There were thirty-seven broken links on the OWL and several e-mailed papers waiting in the in-box when I arrived as the new writing center coordinator. With only two weeks before the start of fall semester and no staff hired, the OWL was the least of my worries. None of the new staff would know enough about tutoring, let alone online tutoring, to answer OWLs, so I took it upon myself to send replies to submissions. Not wanting to ruffle feathers, I answered the OWL as previously done in the center. This meant inserting into the e-mailed text my comments in all blue caps. I was not an expert in computer communication, but I knew enough to suspect my all-caps responses were equivalent to a tutor standing on a chair with a bullhorn to address the adjacent writer. Also, because of the campus's open enrollment status, some students' papers were riddled with errors, and the many patterns of errors were part of what needed to be addressed in the tutorial. It was difficult to see how to help and still provide a learning experience without falling into the editing trap. Again, I found myself textually screaming, shouting out comma rules left and right.

The promised turnaround time of twenty-four hours made it difficult to get a weekend in without a couple hours of work tutoring online. However, I had no immediate access to the OWL to change the policy in writing. Three weeks into the semester, I opened our e-mail account to find twenty-one papers waiting for me. I spent the day responding and then made plans to shut the OWL down until a better format was in place.

The new format not only had to be practical and functional, it needed to better reflect what the tutors did in the center. The online work, as it stood, felt a very distant cousin to

351

what I had known as a tutor and administrator in face-to-face sessions. I wanted to tell jokes, confirm understanding with eye contact, and hear the student own the paper by reading it aloud. I knew that before bringing the OWL beast back online, I had to understand what structure I was dealing with and how it related to tutoring in the physical "sit down and talk" sense. I had to understand the rhetorical differences brought about by changes in tutoring mediums and environment. There was research to be done. My reviews of literature uncovered little more than lore—other people's stories with mostly not so happy endings. There were "how tos" but few "whys." I felt, as did SUNY Albany's Karen Rowan, the excitement surrounding online tutoring "is best served as an appetizer to a substantial entrée of research and scholarship" (10).

Yet online tutorials were and are taking place at an alarming rate considering the lack of research. We haven't determined how the service is being accepted by student writers and tutors or how the tutoring process itself has been altered by online mediums. As Sara Kimball suggested, "In working with student writers online, we are not merely transporting what we do in face-to-face conversation in our real-life writing center into cyberspace" (30). Clearly, we lack an understanding of what we are doing when we take writing center work online. As a writing center coordinator, I felt the need to acknowledge the rhetorical differences among face-to-face tutoring, asynchronous OWLing, and synchronous online tutoring and discover what tutoring and training methods are needed to address these issues in order to continue writer-centered tutoring and explore the future of writing center work.

Certainly, I needed answers. Returning to the theoretical foundations of writing center work, there were three guiding principles on which I decided to build our center's face-to-face and OWL work. First, as Stephen M. North observed, was "to produce better writers, not better writing" (438). Second, was to encourage writers to gain the skills and confidence that would help them improve their writing. As Mary M. Dossin asserted, "Tutoring is only valid when it is part of the learning process" (14). Finally, as Joan Hawthorne suggested, "Our rationale is to work with rather than for the writer" (qtd. in Moe 15).

The next step in the discovery process was returning to examine the familiar. Revisiting the recognizable would help me rethink the future of our OWL. Although some decisions had already been made (a note in the OWL committee folder said they had decided to disable the chat capabilities for OWL because "it [wasn't] being used"), I felt we could change the tide if proven necessary.

Looking at the familiar aspects of writing center work, I started with the basics of tutorials. Ideally, face-to-face, writing tutors work one-on-one with writers for approximately twenty minutes to an hour, depending on the assignment. They focus first on the broad issues of organization and content and second on sentence-level revision issues, keeping in focus the task of creating better writers and not simply better papers. As far as OWLing, over the past decade we have seen everything from Multi-Object Oriented (MOO)s to whiteboards to web cams. However, due to costs, time, and training, synchronous tutoring programs are the exception rather than the rule in web work. By and large, the majority of OWL tutorials are of the asynchronous e-mail variety. Essentially, writers e-mail their papers to the tutors along with answers to a short survey about their class, assignment, stage in the writing process, due date, and concerns. Tutors open these e-mail submissions and respond to each writer's work either at an appointed time or on the basis of other workloads in the center.

Online tutorials must complement rather than replace traditional tutorials. Justin Jackson was correct in writing of Purdue's OWL, "I am not arguing that online tutorials can ever replace f2f [face-to-face] tutorials; they cannot" (1). Sitting in an office responding to student papers online all day was not a familiar form of tutoring to me. It seemed, rhetorically, vastly different from f2f tutorials. Just as Mary Wislocki explained, "Like many writing center directors, I had found that developing my OWL was a complicated business, especially since it seemed to challenge rather than reinforce well-worn writing center practices and values" (71). This is possibly because "the paper doesn't communicate by itself—the person communicates" (Coogan qtd. in Capossela 245), and without the writer present in some form, the learning process, the dialectical engagement—exchange, clarification, justification, meaning making— does not seem entirely intact. My questions to all but one or two writers went unanswered. Eye contact was impossible. I began to feel as if I was not running a writing center online but a much used and abused "fix-it" center.

Tutoring is a discussion-based, dialectical exchange. Tutors and writers move through the motions of communication, written and oral, in order to clarify and hone arguments and ideas. Tutorials often get noisy because writers and tutors are busy making meaning. Tutors and writers talk through text and wade through words, looking for the best way to express ideas to certain discourse communities. They grapple with the ideas, assignment, and structure, then address sentence-level and stylistic concerns, making their way through the writing process, prewriting to proofreading. Throughout these global-to-local, process-based sessions, ideally tutors clarify the roles of writers and tutors, and they rely heavily on methods of questioning and reader response to facilitate discussion. They also redefine and clarify words, phrases, and ideas while reading the silences, facial expressions, and body movements of writers. For these reasons, the presence of the writer is vital to a tutoring session because "both the writer and the tutor are real individuals, with real writing needs; it is an ongoing dialogue that needs … direct and indirect questioning, and the writer's response" (Jackson 1–2). My attempts at tutoring through asynchronous e-mail exchange felt different because they lacked the vital presence of the writer.

Online mediums often omit a writer's presence or at least alter the connections between author, audience, and text, minimizing the importance of the writer's learning process. In online tutorials, tutors are not always able to read the student without an opening discussion or visual social cue, although many try to simulate it in a brief survey to be completed before sending a paper in for a tutorial. For me, as an online tutor, the survey did not provide enough of the writer's presence. The survey gave me about as much insight into the writer as a personal ad gives one about a prospective date. I didn't want a sound byte. I wanted information beyond the surface, motives, and methods. Kimball noted that the "lack of information about participants' attitudes and intentions makes a difference in a medium that seems like conversation" (9). One clear example of problems that occur when the writer is omitted is evident in Holly Moe's 2000 review of an online tutoring service. For her piece, Moe posed as a student and e-mailed a paper to the service that, in her absence, was forced to make assumptions about the text and author's intentions. According to Moe, the tutor "misread the prompt and offered me all the wrong solutions. Furthermore, he or she edited my sentences, changing my voice and meaning" (15). Moe's experience confirms that "the most frightening prospect of the online tutorial is that all one is left with is the writing and not the writer, the product and not the process" (Jackson 2).

This shift to editing rather than tutoring is especially easy because writing centers serve students from across the disciplines, and tutors certainly do not and cannot comprehend the content of such a wide range of texts. For this reason alone, tutors may assume that student authors "know what they are talking about" and revert to looking at formulaic concepts of structure, style, grammar, and usage. Additionally, tutors have to work a lot harder to maintain a global-to-local approach because only the text is present through e-mail, and editing is a lot easier to do when there is no writer there to remind you that writing is about communicating ideas just as much as it is about the technical transmittance of ideas.

What I have found after working both as an instructor and short-lived asynchronous tutor is that basic parts of face-to-face tutorials are altered significantly in asynchronous OWLing. Questions posed to student writers become little more than the sort of questions instructors pose in the margins of a paper. "How do you think that this relates to X?" is no longer a conversation-inducing question, but becomes "make this relate to X." "What is the main point of this paragraph?" is no longer a question to help engage writers in the revision process and the analysis of essay organization. Instead, it seems to tell writers that their paragraph is currently pointless. Also, when the question is posted via e-mail, the time factor makes an immediate reassuring tutor response such as "that's what I got out of the paragraph, too" almost impossible, disrupting the feedback that is so vital to the learning process.

Many of these shifts in tutoring practices when moving from face-to-face to online tutoring (synchronous and asynchronous) are never resolved because of a lack of shared time and space within a tutorial. David Coogan, of Illinois Institute of Technology, pointed out that e-mail tutorials

> change the meaning of tutorial work by challenging the rhetorical constraints of face-to-face conferencing. In other words, by replacing talk with asynchronous writing, email disrupts the most familiar boundaries in the writing center: shared space and limited time. As a result, email changes the conference's discipline by slowing it down (from 30 minutes to several days), and by collapsing the self into the text where it becomes a rhetorical construct, not a social given. Interpreting student text, rather than the student, becomes e-mail tutoring's centerpiece. (171)

Clearly, when time and space elements are altered online, defaulting to a text-focused tutorial is understandably common.

Consequently, another problem that comes with the rhetorical shift of putting tutorials online is the misunderstanding of both the tutor's and the writer's roles within a tutorial. Some writing center directors see the posting or e-mail submission of papers as equal to the student who comes into the center, unfamiliar with the tutoring process, and asks to drop off a paper and pick it up again in a few hours after it has been "corrected." Clearly, these students do not recognize their role in the process of revising their own papers. Likewise, I've had students admit to signing up for online synchronous tutorials so they won't miss watching their favorite sitcom during that same hour. I can imagine them pajama clad, TV blaring in the background, typing with one hand and eating popcorn with the other, only taking in tutor questions during commercial breaks. Their understanding of their own involvement as an active participant is very different than what we would except from them. If we return to the idea that we want "to work with rather than for the writer" (Hawthorne qtd. in Moe 15), then it is obvious that roles must be clarified. In face-to-face tutorials, the sharing of physical space and time encourages (but doesn't guarantee) a writer's involvement. However, this feeling of responsibility and involvement produced by the writer's environment is not always duplicated online. In either situation, fortunately, if the writer is present, then roles can be clarified by the tutor at any time during a session.

Although we may worry about shifts in roles and understanding of involvement, some writers are comfortable with the lack of conversation even if it means a lack of learning. According to Patricia Ericsson and Tim McGee, "Not only did the kind of help our OWL users wanted work against the creation of a dialogue, email technology itself may promote 'one shot' interactions." Eric Hobson illustrated this idea with the story of a student and a tutor sitting in the same computer lab, completing a tutorial. The tutor didn't realize the student was a few computers down, but the student said he or she had purposely chosen to have an online tutorial so he or she could leave when desired, just get specific questions answered, and not have to talk about themselves, the audience, or even the purpose of the text (487). Certainly, this scenario is not unique to asynchronous OWLing. Synchronous online tutoring has its own difficulties keeping dialectical discussions in place. My OWL tutors admit they are more directive in online tutorials, and if they don't admit it, I can show them transcripts of their tutorials. They justify this approach complaining that typing is so much slower than talking, and without nonverbal cues and voice inflection to guide communication, they are better off directly telling the writer what needs to be done. This justification is unsettling because it is very different from what we claim as theoretical foundations. Because online tutoring is so slow and communication is potentially so difficult, tutors often "cut to the chase" leaving out discussion, which should be the heart and soul of the tutorial. These situations say a lot about what is going on in some online tutorials and seems to point to a lack of training or at least the need to review with tutors the rhetorical nature of their work and the goal of providing learning experiences.

Certainly, just as a physical writing center is only as good as its tutors, the same is true for an OWL. As Jackson explained, "Much like the f2f [face-to-face] tutorial, each tutor must identify his other strengths as an online tutor [and] understand the limits and opportunities of the online 'dialogue'" (2). Tutor training is not the same face-to-face as online, but there is still the need to read theory and lore, to observe sessions, and to be mentored. Online tutors also need the opportunity to reflect, to review tutorial transcripts and make adjustments that bring them more in line with the theoretical foundations of their writing center's work. Whereas face-to-face tutors may have training on the importance of body language, online tutors may need a module on the use of emoticons (i.e., smiling faces) or the language of online chat. Will a tutor know how to respond when the writer types "brb" (be right back) or "lol" (laugh out loud)? Will they know that they need not shout responses through the bullhorn of capitalization?

However, whereas some techniques need to be introduced or reexamined, some methods still hold true in online tutoring. We may teach the value of questioning, but stress the wait time, acknowledging the time it takes to type. Additionally, reader response and modeling are common tutoring methods that work well when adapted for online instruction as long as writers know that models are teaching tools and not to be appropriated verbatim. Likewise, although OWL tutors may not be able to model the use of a handbook or pull handouts off the shelf, they can be trained to hyperlink to web guides and online handouts. These adaptations to tutoring are essential if our goal of strengthening and supporting writers is to remain intact, and tutors are to see the connections between their face-to-face and online tutorials. Devising and dispensing such tutor training may bear cost and time constraints, so as Muriel Harris and Michael Pemberton suggested, "directors have to see tutor preparation as part of building successful OWLs" (538).

One cannot claim that OWL work is easy. There are problems with authorial presence, understanding of roles, lack of shared time and space, and a need for additional and adapted tutor training. If online tutoring mediums and student involvement are so rhetorically different on OWLs and so difficult to preserve online, then why do we OWL at all? Although I shut down our OWL during my first semester on the job, our online tutoring was only gone for a month. When I brought the service back, I was more satisfied with the alignment of our face-to-face and online work. In the synchronous whiteboard format, both the writer and text are presenting in the tutorial. This format takes, on average, more time than e-mail tutorials, but remains closer to the rhetorical nature of our face-to-face tutoring with a discussion-based, dialectical approach. Additionally, tutoring online has helped us achieve our commitment to serving all students, including those learning via distance education courses or those with work and family commitments that keep them off campus. Moreover, our web presence gives us validity in the face of an administration concerned with keeping a growing college on the cutting edge of technology. In response to our commitment to the rhetorical nature of tutoring, they have been willing to grant us just enough funding to let us choose quality over convenience. Finally, our online synchronous work, although uncomfortable at times, has provided a way to grow and develop in both theory and practice. OWLers are the adolescents of writing center work—awkward and confused, but excited by the possibilities of the future.

Being involved with OWLs means being committed to evolution and being willing to see things and accept them in a new light. Cynthia Selfe explained this need for an open mind, saying, it is unwise to see ourselves "for or against technology—rather than to understand the complex ways in which technology has become linked with our conception of literacy and, possibly, to shape the relationship between these two phenomena in increasingly productive ways" (36–37). Undoubtedly, online work is changing writing center theory and practice in many promising ways. For example, as David Healy indicated:

> Online conferencing makes the "Your place or mine?" question obsolete. In doing so, it may fundamentally alter the way both clients and consultants perceive their relationship to the institution because the meeting place is no longer physically tied to the institution at all.... And might the conversations that take place online be less directly implicated in institutional hierarchy because the institution is less obviously present in those conversations? (544)

Additionally, directors, tutors, and students are experimenting with tutorials through the use of everyday communication methods, such as Instant Messenger and text messaging. Clearly, the possibilities with the work are fascinating.

Yet not all writing center directors have had or will have, anytime soon, the luxury of choosing how to develop and shape their online presence. While at my institution, I have been fortunate to have the flexibility of deciding how and when we will use technology in our center and how web work will help us better meet our goals, not all directors have the technical support, the programs available, and the time to reflect and explore, let alone maintain such services. They must work within the confines of overworked web support services and budgets too limited for additional training. As Hobson observed, "Not every center's clientele have access to the technology needed to make such projects expedient; not every center can determine its future and fate to the extent needed to follow suit; not every center's mission or philosophical foundation is commensurate with the assumptions contained in many online writing center projects" (481). So although my program has adapted and adopted certain boundaries and rhetorical structures for our work, it is not to say that those other different programs are off the mark. As Wislocki explained, "[A] multiplicity of voices and opinions—as well as expressions of frustration and enthusiasm—are the healthy sounds of an engaged community talking the emerging field of OWLs into existence." (74). While I consider ideal circumstances for OWL work, I recognize that they don't exist yet, although we may strive to approximate them by increasing our research, reflection, and experimentation.

The possibilities that accompany alternative mediums for tutoring are endless as new hardware and software are continually emerging, and undoubtedly, online practices will change with the ever-advancing medium. However, we cannot simply avoid research and reflection and wait for someone else to figure out how to preserve the rhetorical nature of our work. It is through experimentation that writing centers will discover the previously unknown pathways for transmitting their services online. With the presence of text messaging, web cams, and so forth, these pathways are making themselves clearer. As Michael D. McMaster, a social theorist, explained, "To make the shift in thinking [into the information age], we need the willingness to unlearn the old and the courage to grapple with the new and unfamiliar" (qtd. in Murphy and Law 190). In essence, the near future of online tutoring is full of experimentation and offers plenty of room for research in both that which is currently being done via OWLs and the many possibilities that are to come.

The links on our center's OWL all currently work, and our online tutoring numbers are steadily climbing, but I am still asking questions. After over a decade of OWL work in writing centers, we must look back. If we were building the first OWLs in this day, how would they be different? Would we be thinking outside the e-mail box? Surely, "attempting only to replicate familiar face-to-face tutorial settings in an electronic, text-oriented environment can lead to frustration and to defeat as OWL planners find themselves unable to simulate all characteristics of effective tutorials" (Harris and Pemberton 522), but now that we have more experience, what can we see for the future of this work and the preservation of our theoretical foundations? In examining the rhetorical nature of tutoring programs and working to preserve the essential aspects of the tutoring process, we are acknowledging not only what we have and what we want, but why writing center work is key to the learning process in the first place.

WORKS CITED

Capossela, Toni-Lee, ed. *The Harcourt Brace Guide to Peer Tutoring.* Orlando: Harcourt Brace, 1998.
Coogan, David. "Email Tutoring, a New Way to Do Work." *Computers and Composition* 12.2 (1995): 171–81.
Dossin, Mary M. "The ESL Quandary." *Writing Lab Newsletter* 20 (1996): 14–15.
Ericsson, Patricia, and Tim McGee. "The Online Tutor as Cross-Curricular Double Agent." 14 May 2003. <http://English.ttu.edu/kairos/2.2/features/double_agent/toc.html>.
Harris, Muriel, and Michael Pemberton. "Online Writing Labs (OWLs): A Taxonomy of Option and Issues." *The Allyn and Bacon Guide to Writing Center Theory and Practice.* Ed. Robert Barnett and Jacob Blumner. Needham Heights, MA: Allyn and Bacon, 2001. 521–40.

Healy, David. "From Place to Space: Perceptual and Administrative Issues in the Online Writing Center." *The Allyn and Bacon Guide to Writing Center Theory and Practice*. Ed. Robert W. Barnet and Jacob S. Blumner. Needham Heights, MA: Allyn and Bacon, 2001. 541–54.

Hobson, Eric, ed. *Wiring the Writing Center*. Logan: Utah State U P, 1998.

Jackson, J. A. "Interfacing the Faceless: Maximizing the Advantages of Online Tutoring." *Writing Lab Newsletter* 25.2 (2000): 1–7.

Kimball, Sara. "Cybertext/Cyberspeech: Writing Centers and Online Magic." *The Writing Center Journal* 18 (1997): 30–49.

Moe, Holly. "Web Study of Smarthinking.com." *Writing Lab Newsletter* 25 (2000): 13–16.

Murphy, Christina, and Joe Law. "Writing Center and WAC Programs as Infostructures: Relocating Practice with Futurist Theories of Social Change." *Writing Centers and Writing Across the Curriculum Programs: Building Interdisciplinary Partnerships*. Ed. Robert Barnett and Jacob S. Blumner. Westport, CT: Greenwood Press, 1999.

North, Stephen M. "The Idea of a Writing Center." *College English* 46 (1984): 433–46.

Rowan, Karen. Rev. of *Taking Flight with OWLS: Research into Technology Use in Writing Centers*. Ed. James Inman and Donna Sewell. *Writing Lab Newsletter* 25 (2000): 9–10.

Selfe, Cynthia. *Technology and Literacy in the Twenty-First Century: The Importance of Paying Attention*. Carbondale: Southern Illinois UP, 1999.

Wislocki, Mary. Rev. of *The OWL Construction and Maintenance Guide*. Ed. James Inman and Clint Gardener. *The Writing Center Journal* 24 (2003): 71–75.

34

Implementing Electronic Portfolios as Part of the Writing Center: Connections, Benefits, Cautions, and Strategies

Ben Click
Sarah Magruder
St. Mary's College of Maryland

Nearly twenty years ago, the use of print portfolios (and more recently electronic or digitized portfolios) in writing classrooms began to impact writing instruction because they are powerful tools in student learning and assessment. As such, portfolios, particularly electronic ones, are naturally connected to the work that happens in writing centers by what Danielle DeVoss called the "literacy demands and practices of new technologies" (178). To "create a different ecology in which the multiple and complex literacies students bring and are required to have may develop" (178), DeVoss offered three goals for writing centers: (1) "Supporting students as discussions extend beyond the walls of the classroom" (as in listservs or electronic discussion groups); (2) "Enabling students to do effective and appropriate research" (using both library and Internet sources); and (3) "Helping students with new possibilities for publication" (180). Regarding the last goal, she noted that instructors using a web focus in class often don't have the "time to address such key writing-related issues" as rhetorical choices involving voice, authorship, design, and more (180). However, many writing centers do.

On a large scale, some centers house entire portfolio projects similar to "the longitudinal study of the writing done by a group of students during their 4 years as undergraduates" conducted by the Michigan State University Writing Center, 1993–1996 (Thomas, Beavins, and Crawford 149). On a smaller scale, some centers try a pilot project for one semester, helping one instructor develop the basic electronic portfolio template for one first-year writing class. Whatever the scale, writing centers and good writing portfolios provide spaces for writers to talk about their writing. The purpose of this chapter is to demonstrate that writing centers are the ideal nexus wherein good assessment, good writing center work, and good portfolio practices can occur simultaneously. We will share some of our experience in developing the use of electronic portfolios as part of an augmented learning environment in our writing center.

DEFINING ELECTRONIC PORTFOLIOS AND THEIR RELATION TO WRITING CENTER PHILOSOPHY AND PRACTICE

Portfolios, whether used by an instructor to assess the learning outcomes of a student in a first-year writing class, developed by institutions to "demonstrate the universities' effectiveness to various groups of stakeholders" (*Urban Universities Portfolio Project*), or creatively designed by an art student to best showcase her work, share the following common principles: They "(1) show goals, intents, and plans; (2) display work and examples of progress toward goals; (3) provide evidence of accumulating feedback and subsequent reflection; and (4) reveal a trail of growth and improvement based on that feedback in order to elevate goals, intents, and plans" (Schechter, Testa, and Ender 8). Given these principles, clearly portfolios possess infinite value for assessing the short- and long-term progress of their users. Creating portfolios involves three basic activities: collection, selection, and reflection. And, generally, portfolios fall into three categories: student, faculty, or institutional. (For a full discussion of all three kinds of portfolios, see Barbara Cambridge's *Electronic Portfolios: Emerging Practices in Student, Faculty, and Institutional Portfolios*.) However, this chapter focuses on the student portfolio, specifically on how writing centers can help faculty who wish to include electronic portfolios as part of a course and can tutor their students who create and write them. Kathleen Blake Yancey defined student portfolios as "collections of work selected from a larger archive of work, upon which the student has reflected" ("Digitized Student Portfolios"16). She identified two basic kinds of student portfolios (which can be in either paper or digital format): classroom portfolios and program portfolios (drawn from several areas of a student's academic career, such as class work, extracurricular activities, and internships) (16, 18). Most examples in this chapter come from student-generated classroom portfolios that our center helped with, but Yancey offered several examples of the various kinds of student portfolios in the "Student Portfolio" section of *Electronic Portfolios: Emerging Practices in Student, Faculty, and Institutional Learning*. The links to these examples are located on the AAHE Web site (*Table of Contents and Featured Websites*).

The Writing Center Connection

Writing centers should be the place for students to talk about their portfolios. Teachers using portfolios, whether paper or electronic, recognize them as yet another pedagogical avenue that focuses on producing good writers because portfolios emphasize process, and help maintain the student-centeredness of a writing course. Cambridge wrote that "portfolios enable learning for the creator and the user and demonstrate learning for multiple audiences" (1). Similarly, in the center, tutors can enable (and even empower) student writers to see their learning, constantly aiding them in assessing their writing options, and encouraging, reminding, and even cajoling them into always considering audience needs and concerns. Clearly, an implicit, symbiotic relationship between assessment, portfolios, and writing center philosophy and practice exists, which is concerned simultaneously with process/product and student-centered learning. The following quote about portfolios from Wolcott and Legg's description of portfolios also describes the writing center tutorial: "[T]he concept of portfolios … implies that students' best or most representative pieces are displayed, that students have a choice in selecting what goes into the portfolio, and that their selections are based on knowledgeable reflections about their own work done over a period of time" (36).

Thus far we have been speaking of portfolios generically, as if paper portfolios and electronic ones were identical. In essence they are, with one key difference: the ability to link. Kathleen Blake Yancey emphasized that "key to this difference is the role that interactivity plays in students' digital portfolios, the interactivity both of the digital medium and of social action" ("Digitized Student Portfolios" 20). She noted that electronic portfolios are created using the same basic processes as found in creating print portfolios: collection, selection, and reflection. However, the look and use of each is quite different. In many ways, print portfolios seem static and finite, unable to move the reader beyond the document that is held in hand. Also, they can only be structured linearly. In contrast, electronic portfolios can be live, infinite, and nonlinear. For example, a student creating his electronic portfolio for an English 102 course (first-year composition) wanted to show his teacher relevant learning from his English 101 course (basic writing); he simply linked to the electronic portfolio he had created for that class. His teacher now possesses the ability to use both portfolios in varying and nonlinear ways. Linking allows for many options not available in print portfolios: a variety of new ways to effectively allow text to talk to and inform other text within the same portfolio and the use of images, animation, and audio features to augment text. Technologically speaking, producing various kinds of links is relatively easy considering that their rhetorical purpose and effectiveness is not. Writing centers involved in tutoring electronic portfolios can help with both issues.

MAKING CONNECTIONS: SHARED CONCEPTS IN GOOD TUTORIAL PRACTICE AND EFFECTIVE PORTFOLIO DEVELOPMENT

The previous section made some general comments on how writing centers seem ideal for housing tutorial help with electronic portfolios. This section identifies and explains four shared concepts that capture the essentials of both good tutorial practice and effective electronic portfolio development, recognizing that many of the concepts are overlapping.

Shared Concept 1: Good Tutorial Practice and Effective Electronic Portfolio Development Stress Collaboration, Revision, and Reflection

Common mantras heard when reading about center work include the following: "[O]ur job is to produce better writers not better writing" (North 438); the center's "core, its primary responsibility—[is to] work one-to-one with writers" (Harris 27); tutoring is "contextual," "collaborative," "interpersonal," and "individualized" (Murphy and Sherwood 1); writing centers are "places whose primary responsibility, whose only reason for being, is to talk to writers"

(North 446). Because centers offer an atmosphere where collaboration is encouraged, conversation between tutor and student writer invariably leads to reflecting on writing and options for revising. When students work with a tutor on developing their electronic portfolios, revision and reflection automatically happen because of the collaborative nature of the tutorial. Furthermore, in good portfolio practice, reflection on practice (an act of revision in itself) is already incorporated as part of the portfolio. Students come to view the portfolio as a document in process just as they view a paper draft as a document in process. They come to realize with the tutor's help the many options they may incorporate in their portfolio. These options have to do with the similar rhetorical concerns that accompany writing a paper for a class: organization of material, creating the appropriate tone, and addressing and creating audience.

Shared Concept 2: Good Tutorial Practice and Effective Electronic Portfolio Development Do Not Penalize Students for Weak Papers, Thus Putting Aside, Temporarily, the Paralyzing Effects of Grades and Emphasizing Student Improvement Instead

Muriel Harris discussed the enviable position that a writing tutor occupies: "[Sitting] below the teacher on the academic ladder, tutors can work effectively with students in ways that teachers can not." "[T]utors don't need to take attendance, make assignments, set deadlines, deliver negative comments, give tests, or issue grades.... [They] help [students] surmount hurdles others have set up for them" (28). Likewise, students receiving assistance with their portfolios view the tutor as occupying that space between them and the instructor, a space made even more comfortable when the planning of an electronic portfolio project involves instructor, the center, and its tutors.

Shared Concept 3: Good Tutorial Practice and Effective Electronic Portfolio Development Promote and Value Students' Producing Formative (Process-Oriented), as Well as Summative (Product-Oriented), Work

Although portfolios have tremendous value in terms of assessment, philosophically they stress what Catherine Lucas called "*enhancement of performance* through evaluative feedback and reflection" over the "*assessment of outcomes* [which are typically measured] through comparative rankings of achievement, such as those produced by grades, test scores, and percentile rankings" (Lucas 1, author's italics). Writing tutors and the writers they help recognize that process and learning are of importance in the creation of an electronic portfolio. At the same time, they know that the final submitted portfolio is a summative work that demonstrates and validates their learning and related processes.

Shared Concept 4: Good Tutorial Practice and Effective Electronic Portfolio Development Provide the Flexibility to Handle Differing Skill and Interest Levels of Students

Christina Murphy described tutoring as attending to "hurts," such as writer's block, fear of evaluation, and self-doubt (or self-delusion) about their abilities as writers; the one constant in tutors' jobs is that they display "interest, concern, and the desire to help another human being." (44). Thus, writing tutors must continually adjust their agendas, physical postures, and intellectual approaches as they become sensitive to writers' individual strengths and difficulties. We've discovered that students using electronic portfolios are subject to similar anxieties, hang-ups, and disparate areas of strength when using technology, in the same incredible variety as we see in the writers we tutor. For example, an electronic portfolio that accommodates a variety of writings, linked reflections, and assorted multimedia elements allows students to demonstrate their progress in the most effective way possible, no matter whether those students are visual, auditory, or tactile learners. An occasional open lab time and the availability of individual tutorials allow students who are facile with technology to move ahead on their own while less comfortable students receive more focused help in class or with tutors. Flexibility may be further extended when instructors offer a range of options for completing the electronic portfolio, each requiring differing amounts of time, effort, and technological expertise. A good electronic portfolio class models a writing center's value on communication, too: Instructional technologists can not only help the instructor maximize student learning in lab sessions, but in conjunction with the center director, can also keep tutors up-to-date on what the class is working on and instructors informed about what assignments or writings the students are having trouble with. Above all, a teacher using an electronic portfolio effectively in the classroom should be prepared to adjust the requirements of and opportunities to work on that portfolio based on the needs of each class. Similarly, centers must be flexible enough to accommodate (and possibly suggest) changing requirements.

MOVING FROM PHILOSOPHY TO PRACTICE: ACTUALLY SUPPORTING ELECTRONIC PORTFOLIOS THROUGH THE WRITING CENTER ENVIRONMENT

Our Model

In creating electronic portfolios, individuals must not only understand the principles of good portfolio construction but also possess the technical skills necessary for producing an electronic version of the portfolio. A daunting task, teaching technology often falls on the shoulders of the individual, the course instructor, or an instructional technologist. However, creating an augmented learning environment in an existing institutional structure offers a potentially powerful solution to the dilemma of how to bring together these two aspects of the electronic portfolio. In fall 2001, as part of a supplement grant to a larger PT3 (Preparing Tomorrow's Teachers to Use Technology) grant, the Writing Center at St. Mary's College of Maryland implemented a pilot program wherein the center provided a unified space for faculty and students to develop electronic portfolios. Our main goals were to help students and faculty improve their writing in general and within the electronic portfolios specifically; and to help with the technical aspects of producing those portfolios. We planned three ways to achieve those goals: (a) requiring a specifically trained assistant center director who could lead technology-based class sessions; (b) providing technology and portfolio training to undergraduate peer-tutors; and (c) encouraging instructors to support the idea of electronic portfolios as add-ins, not add-ons to classes.

Our assistant director, already a veteran writing tutor, began training to be the center's assistant instructional technologist, becoming an expert in Dreamweaver, a web-authoring software, and in other programs such as Photoshop and Quicktime. She trained some of our peer tutors in the basics of our web-authoring software and worked with them on how to conduct conferences with students who were using electronic portfolios. In the training, two things were constantly stressed: being aware of the various levels of student comfort (or discomfort) with technology, and helping students look more rhetorically at their portfolios. The peer tutors were not expected to be expert in the various technologies used in the portfolios; for technology issues they were unable to handle, they could refer students to the assistant director. Lastly, in planning and implementing portfolios we wanted to emphasize that using electronic portfolios should be considered an add-in to instruction, not an add-on. We recognized that it would certainly be legitimate for an instructor to use an electronic, classroom portfolio solely as a way of representing a collection of a student's work over the course of the semester, but that would be considered an add-on to a course.

To work as a true add-in to the class, electronic portfolios must be designed to be an integral part of learning in class. Here's an example: In one English 102 class where students were producing both formal papers and weekly freewrites, the instructor wanted students to examine the connections between their freewrites and final papers, thus realizing that their writing processes started much earlier than they may have thought. To achieve this, students were required to add links to their electronic portfolios that led from each paper to a freewrite that contributed to the writing of that paper. Then, the students were to annotate the link with a short explanation of how the linked freewrite affected the final paper. This add-in use of electronic portfolios not only accomplished the instructor's original goal but also showed her a context to the papers that she may not have otherwise been privy to. In addition, during tutorials, tutors were given opportunities to ask students what the instructor really needed to know in those annotations. Many students were able to realize that she didn't need a summary of what she would see in a minute anyway—she needed to know how freewriting about poverty led to a paper about feminism.

Before offering our new services to faculty, we wanted specific input on how we could best serve instructors and students. To find out, we met with several members of the faculty from various disciplines who had already employed electronic portfolios in their teaching. The most common concerns these early adopters had were the difficulties in supporting large classes and that many students failed to make the rhetorical choices that would give their electronic portfolios "depth." With an instructional technologist capable of supporting technology issues connected with large classes, and peer-tutors trained to help students make good rhetorical choices regarding electronic portfolios, we offered writing center support to early adopters and their students. We also enlisted these early adopters to help us recruit potential new users; and after several semesters of grass-roots expansion, we held a three-day workshop open to all faculty on using electronic portfolios and other technologies in the classroom. At the date of this publication, we have supported twenty-three classes, five disciplines, and over three hundred students.

We found that new adopters bring different expectations, abilities, and goals to their electronic portfolio project; thus, one of the best ways we can assist them is to begin a conversation, offering our experience with previous projects as a guide for the development of their own. A first meeting often consists of a very general discussion of the instructor's goals along with a "show and tell" of similar previous projects. (Electronic portfolio projects created at St. Mary's are linked from The Writing Center at St. Mary's College's Web site [*Audience's View*] and from the *ePortfolio Plus* web page [Mattia].) Instructors are interested in implementing electronic portfolios for a variety of reasons. Some feel that it will provide a showcase for student work or that technology is important for their students to learn; although they are also interested in the assessment opportunities that an electronic portfolio offers, the variety of assessment methods available to them, and the variety of ways we can help, has often not occurred to them. Other instructors already use (or appreciate the use of) paper portfolios for assessment and as a process record and merely need the center to help them adapt their existing portfolio into an electronic format.

When an instructor meets with the center's instructional technologist (sometimes in conjunction with the center director) for the initial planning of an electronic portfolio project, the meeting feels much like a tutorial with a student. We begin a conversation and set an agenda, examining the instructor's goals and requirements before designing the electronic portfolio project. In doing so, we have recognized two general ways to help instructors consider those goals and requirements: from an author's view, meaning according to the goals and process of the person putting the portfolio together, and from an audience's view, meaning according to the function the portfolio serves for end users or evaluators.

From an Author's View: Electronic Portfolios in Terms of Exigence. The greater part of this section deals with the requirement-driven portfolio because of complications that arise when there are multiple authors, and because portfolios associated with classes will generally require more support from the writing center than individual portfolios. Our designations of requirement-driven portfolios and purpose-driven portfolios are roughly equivalent to Yancey's classroom portfolios and program portfolios, respectively. However, we find it more useful to think of a portfolio in terms of what drives its given design and execution and how writing centers can help in those areas.

Requirement-driven portfolios are complicated because the "author" comprises both the instructor and the students. The instructor designs the overall form of the electronic portfolio, including what will be required of the students. The students shape it further by making choices about how to present what has been required. Because students often fail to appreciate the individual things they learn until they are able to look back at those things later in the semester, instructors must design the requirements to help students see the purposes and processes of what they are learning. Developing a requirement-driven portfolio requires careful thought about teaching and assessment methods, as it will be difficult to make changes in the templates after they have been given to the students.

Purpose-driven portfolios are developed and built by an individual with a particular goal in mind. At St. Mary's, these tend to be built by students working on senior capstone projects and may become Internet resources on specific subjects, presentation aids, or professional portfolios. Purpose-driven electronic portfolios tend to evolve throughout their construction as the individual's goals and ideas change. We start by walking the author through the initial process of conception and design, then meet with them periodically until the project is finished.

From an Audience's View: A Functional Description of Electronic Portfolios.   It is useful to be able to discuss the functions of various electronic portfolios with the instructors and students who wish to create them. Therefore, we've identified four descriptors of an electronic portfolio's end purpose:

1. process record portfolios—designed to archive and allow assessment of the learning process of an individual or group
2. instructional portfolios—designed to teach users about a specific subject or process
3. presentation portfolios—designed to present a previously developed project or argument
4. evolving portfolios—created with design and content that is periodically examined and updated

Keep in mind that these designations are not exclusive and in some ways are artificial; a portfolio could easily be used both as a process record and a presentation of an end product, and any portfolio can evolve. Nevertheless, they offer a good way to illustrate the flexibility of portfolios to potential users and a means to talk about the development of their own projects.

Once we have identified the key aspects of a particular electronic portfolio, we can decide on a navigational and link structure, what materials such as assignment descriptions and samples the instructor needs to populate ahead of time, and what parts of the portfolio the students will be in charge of populating. If the instructors are first-time users of Dreamweaver, we may complete some of the work for them, then walk them through the process of adding asset pages and filling them with text or images. If an instructor feels comfortable adapting an electronic portfolio from a previous project, then we may need to act only as a sounding board or a rhetorical proofreader of the new links in their work.

Also during this time, we help the instructor construct the electronic portfolio's position in the context of the class. Using the structure of the electronic portfolio and our estimation of the students in the class, we determine how many lab sessions or required center visits will be needed, whether some labs should be dedicated to learning any necessary multimedia elements, which sections of an electronic portfolio may be populated with group work and how that group work will be facilitated, and finally, whether the electronic portfolio files will be kept in individual server space, class space, or will be published to the Internet.

Some Descriptions and Examples.   The following descriptions and examples come from three electronic portfolio projects our writing center helped develop and support. For each, we will describe the portfolio project itself, what kind of electronic portfolio it was in terms of author and audience, and list some of the specific arrangements each class needed.

In Landscape and Literature, an upper-level English/environmental studies course, the class created a "gallery" portfolio: student groups developed "exhibits" featuring different landscape paintings and writings about relevant literature. Separately from the class "gallery," each student maintained an electronic portfolio of individual work toward the successive group projects. Thus, this project was a requirement-driven presentation portfolio (the gallery) including requirement-driven process records by individual students:

- Because this professor had never used technology in the classroom, we had many design meetings, helped her create the templates, and had a larger teaching role in lab sessions.
- Because these were upperclassmen working in collaborative groups, we had few lab sessions, instead making appointment times available for the groups.
- Because this project involved a great deal of image manipulation and was ultimately destined for the Internet, entire lab sessions were dedicated to image formatting, placement, and reference librarian-led sessions on copyright concerns.
- The gallery was on the Internet from January–June 2004 but was ultimately removed to campus-only access because of thorny copyright issues.

Students in English 102 produced portfolios containing nearly everything they wrote over the course of the semester, including all drafts, freewrites, peer responses, and reflections. Thus, it was a requirement-based process record portfolio. Because this professor edits and reuses the templates every semester, it is also an evolving portfolio:

- Because this professor is so comfortable with using technology, we met only once or twice before the semester began to discuss and proof design changes. The instructor also took a leading role in teaching lab sessions, needing the center's instructional technologist only for support.
- Because the students were all freshmen, we held weekly lab sessions in addition to offering writing center tutorials to make sure they felt comfortable getting help.
- Because this course required limited multimedia features, most lab sessions provided students the opportunity to work individually with the instructor and/or the instructional technologist.

One graduating senior employed an electronic portfolio to present her senior capstone project on Baroque music and rhetoric. Once completed, her project was then posted to the Internet for the general public. Thus, this portfolio was a purpose-driven presentation portfolio that became an instructional portfolio:

- Because it was an individual student with limited experience in the technology, she needed many meetings throughout the semester to plan and design the electronic portfolio based on the paper she was writing; later meetings were used to train her in Dreamweaver and audio and visual multimedia elements.
- The final product can be seen at <http://www.smcm.edu/users/gtdegentesh> (Degentesh).

CONCLUSIONS

At the start of this chapter a claim was made that many writing centers can be augmented spaces to address such key writing-related issues (e.g., voice, authorship, design, etc.) associated with electronic portfolios. In creating the electronic portfolios services that we offer, we have noted several positive impacts for our center, for our instructors, and for our students. Here are a few. Working closely with instructors and students in the development and design of individual or classroom portfolios leads to serious thinking and reflection about teaching and learning goals. Students gain a greater sense of rhetorical awareness, employing more modes of expression in their writing and learning how best to use those modes. Because of electronic portfolio's nonlinear capabilities, evidence of revision and reflection become more facile for teachers to witness and result in more student attention to process. Because our tutors are required to keep their own portfolios, our center has an excellent combination of record keeping and tutorial reflection, which can easily catalogue tutor concerns, student concerns, and specific writing issues.

Both the number and variety of classes and projects incorporating electronic portfolios on campus are expanding, and our center has played an integral role in promoting and supporting that expansion. However, in helping create and support electronic portfolios within a writing center, directors must seriously consider many factors. Directors must find teachers willing to commit to trying electronic portfolios and realize that experimenting with electronic portfolios can be risky for untenured faculty. In addition, as technologically savvy as many students are, there still remains a good deal of student resistance to technology in the classroom setting. Directors must understand the implications of various computer software, access, and infrastructure issues. Many centers may be constrained by budgets, physical space such as computer lab space, or issues regarding tutor training or computer software/hardware. In "Postmodernism, Palimpsest, and Portfolios: Theoretical Issues in the Representation of Student Work," Kathleen Blake Yancey suggested that as digital portfolios continue to develop, "it behooves us to be intentional, to understand that these portfolios, like their print cousins, bring with them opportunities and challenges" (754–55). She then asked a series of questions related to those opportunities and challenges, including "Does the *kind* of linking matter?" "What will students tell us about the learning in digital portfolios?" and "How/Will the digital portfolio change teaching, learning, and the academy itself?" (755, 756). In carefully growing tutorial help for electronic portfolios, writing centers can yield some answers to those questions.

WORKS CITED

Audience's View: A Functional Description of Electronic Portfolios. The Writing Center at St. Mary's College of Maryland. 14 June 2004. St. Mary's College of Maryland. <http://www.smcm.edu/writingcenter/workshop/WWW_LocalRoot/Assets/Defining/audience.htm>.

Cambridge, Barbara. Introduction. *Electronic Portfolios: Emerging Practices in Student, Faculty, and Institutional Learning.* Ed. Barbara Cambridge, Susan Kahn, Daniel P. Tompkins, and Kathleen Blake Yancey. Washington: American Association for Higher Education, 2001. 1–11.

Degentesh, Gwen. *Baroque Music and Rhetoric: Toward an Aesthetic.* 26 April 2002. St. Mary's College of Maryland. <http://www.smcm.edu/users/gtdegentesh>.

DeVoss, Danielle. "Computer Literacies and the Roles of the Writing Center." *Writing Center Research: Extending the Conversation.* Ed. Paula Gillespie, Alice Gillam, Lady Falls Brown, and Byron Stay. Mahwah: Lawrence Erlbaum Associates, 2002. 167–85.

Harris, Muriel. "Talking in the Middle: Why Writers Need Writing Tutors." *College English* 57.1 (1995): 27–42.

Landscape and Literature Gallery Project. 5 March 2004. St. Mary's College of Maryland. 1 May 2004. <http://www.smcm.edu/english/Gallery>.

Lucas, Catharine. "Introduction: Writing Portfolios—Changes and Challenges." *Portfolios in the Classroom: An Introduction.* Ed. Kathleen Blake Yancey. Urbana: NCTE, 1992. 1–11.

Mattia, Christopher. *Eportfolio +: St. Mary's College of Maryland.* 2002. St. Mary's College of Maryland. <http://www.smcm.edu/users/cmmattia>.

Murphy, Christina. "Freud in the Writing Center: The Pyschoanalytics of Tutoring Well." *The St. Martin's Sourcebook for Writing Tutors*. Christina Murphy and Steve Sherwood. Boston: Bedford/St. Martin's, 1995. 43–47.

Murphy, Christina, and Steve Sherwood. "The Tutoring Process: Exploring Paradigms and Processes." *The St. Martin's Sourcebook for Writing Tutors*. Ed. Christina Murphy and Steve Sherwood. Boston: Bedford/St. Martin's, 1995. 1–17.

North, Stephen M. "The Idea of a Writing Center." *College English* 46 (1984): 433–46.

Schechter, Ephraim, Alec Testa, and Douglas Eder. "Electronic Portfolios." *Assessment Update* 13.4 (2001): 8–9.

Table of Contents and Featured Websites: Electronic Portfolios: Emerging Practices for Students, Faculty, and Institutions. AAHE. American Association for Higher Education. 9 July 2004. <http://webcenter1.aahe.org/electronicportfolios/TOC.html>.

Thomas, Sharon, Julie Beavins, and Mary Ann Crawford. "The Portfolio Project: Sharing Our Stories." *Writing Center Research: Extending the Conversation*. Ed. Paula Gillespie, Alice Gillam, Lady Falls Brown, and Byron Stay. Mahwah: Lawrence Erlbaum Associates, 2002. 149–66.

Urban Universities Portfolio Project: Assuring Quality for Multiple Publics. American Association for Higher Education. 9 July 2004. <http://www.imir.iupui.edu/portfolio/>.

Wolcott, Willa, and Sue M. Legg. *An Overview of Writing Assessment: Theory Research and Practice*. Urbana: NCTE, 1998.

Yancey, Kathleen Blake. "Digitized Student Portfolios." *Electronic Portfolios: Emerging Practices in Student, Faculty, and Institutional Portfolios*. Ed. Barbara Cambridge, Susan Kahn, Daniel P. Tompkins, and Kathleen Blake Yancey. Washington: American Association for Higher Education, 2001. 15–30.

___. "Postmodernism, Palimssest, and Portfolios: Theoretical Issues in the Representation of Student Work." *College Composition and Communication* 55.4 (2004): 738–61.

❧ 35 ❧

When Compassion Isn't Enough: Providing Fair and Equivalent Access to Writing Help for Students with Disabilities

Lory Hawkes
DeVry University

As disabled students[1] arrive on university campuses in increasing numbers (Beilke and Yssel), they have already overcome significant physical, emotional, and academic difficulties to get this far. What they want is extra help and practical strategies to let them be better writers. They want understanding of their educational struggles, not sympathy and certainly not hovering. Having qualified for admission by taking academic courses in high school, these students have been involved in a mainstreaming initiative brought about in part by the Individuals with Disabilities Education Act of 1990 (IDEA). However, in order to understand disabled students' high expectation for help, we need to examine their exposure to adaptive education from elementary school through high school brought about by the efforts of educational institutions to conform to IDEA. Yearly, administrators, the student and parents, teachers, and counselors become part of an assessment team to create an individualized set of objectives to be reached on the basis of the learning potential of the student. These objectives are incorpo-

---

[1]A disabled student may be physically or mentally impaired, or have a history of medical problems. Students may have limitations in movement, thinking, or behavior adjustment, but they must be eligible for admission to the college or university because they have met the entrance requirements, fulfilled all the academic prerequisite education, and met any technical criteria (Thomas). Court rulings in response to litigation claiming discriminatory treatment in denying the disabled admission and in providing subsequent educational support has been mixed, sometimes denying discrimination suits and sometimes affirming discrimination has occurred. Because there is no clear trend, litigation was not discussed in this chapter.

371

rated into an Individualized Education Program (IEP) and are referred to as IEP learning goals. State and local requirements make documentation of the student's academic program and the school's success in meeting the objectives an essential recordkeeping component of the state's funding process.

According to the theory behind IDEA, each student should have a modified academic program that suits the individual's learning potential. Naturally, a variety of physical and cognitive disabilities calls for a range of modifications. For profoundly retarded students who cannot communicate and need assistance at all times, this would be a self-contained classroom with a teacher and an aide for the duration of the school day. However, for those students whose receptive and communicative skills are slightly impaired, program modification might be an aide who assists the individual in note taking and pushes the student in a wheel chair to a classroom. In some cases, speech or physical therapy may simply be an added class during the day. Stephen B. Thomas offered this definition of a disabled person:

> A person with a disability is anyone who has a physical (e.g., quadriplegia) or mental (e.g., anxiety disorder) impairment that substantially limits one or more major life activities (e.g., learning), has a record of such impairment (e.g., a record of having a specific learning disability), or is regarded as having such an impairment (e.g., a student is denied admission to medical school because he is HIV positive ...). With respect to postsecondary education, a qualified student with a disability is one who is able to meet a program's admission, academic, and technical standards (i.e., all essential nonacademic admissions criteria) with or without accommodation.

In contrast to the documented disability of physically or cognitively impaired students is another group of students who may have a "discovered" impairment of a learning disability or hyperactivity. These students may be capable of academic work but have some disconnect that makes it difficult to learn. Often labeled learning disabled (LD) or attention deficit hyperactivity disorder (ADHD), these students have an erratic pattern of academic performance because they may not perform well on tests or may have disruptive behavior even though they can demonstrate through other assignments and classroom interactions that they do have the ability to think and communicate. These students can usually be granted additional testing time, whether that is in the classroom or even during entrance exams for college. More importantly, these students can request additional modifications of their programs in postsecondary institutions (Gordon et al.).

Federal government statistics are not current and date back to 2000, but the estimate of the disabled population as accounting for 10% is a noteworthy number, particularly when compared to the 3% reported in 1973 (Carlson). With this threefold increase and with their numbers increasing as colleges and universities strive to find new populations to tap for tuition dollars, disabled students have become a targeted group for college recruiters who encourage them to enroll and to experience college life. However, although disabled students are motivated by their hopes for a better life as a result of college graduation, they are also savvy about their rights and insistent on their needs for instructional accommodation as a consequence of years of special education programs and parent–teacher–student goal setting made possible by IDEA (Day and Edwards). In other words, they have come to expect extra help and know how to pursue requests as part of a legislatively protected population.

The disabled were first recognized as a protected population thirty years ago when the Rehabilitation Act of 1973 granted them the right to physically access and take part in programs underwritten by the government. According to this law, the disabled had the right to participate in any federally funded program, and, more importantly, they also had the right to be made comfortable even if their participation meant that the program had to be changed (in its process, procedures, or hosting environment) in order to be more conducive to the disabled. As a result, the long-standing rule of thumb grew to be that accommodations had to be made to permit the disabled to fully participate. Extensions of the law called Sections allowed the members of Congress to enhance and clarify the various ways access ought to be given to the disabled. For example, Section 504 has been enlarged by additional amendments to clarify the scope of entitlement and the responsibilities of specific government agencies with regard to federal programs (Slatin and Rush 29).

The Rehabilitation Act had two important ramifications. First, it singled out disabled individuals as a class that legally mandated modifications of an environment and required necessary adaptations to be customarily made to enable these individuals to participate in federal programs. Second, this act became a historical legislative achievement of enabling a new cultural perspective for disabled citizens. Later, in 1990, the Americans with Disability Act (ADA) went beyond the federally controlled agencies and their vendors to examine the responsibilities of the corporate and public sector to offer unfettered access to disabled citizens. Simply stated, this law made it illegal for corporations, state and local governments, and telecommunication industries to refuse reasonable accommodations for disabled individuals. From paved inclines providing wheelchair access into stately public buildings, to assistive telephone devices to amplify sound to closed caption TV, these accommodations were all outgrowths of the ADA: "Title III of the act further prohibits entities that operate places of public accommodation from discriminating against persons with disabilities by denying them full and equal enjoyment of the goods, services, facilities, privileges, advantages, or accommodations they provide (42 U.S.C. Section 12182(a))" (Thomas). Title III goes beyond just the issue of being able to enter and exit a building and makes it a requirement that the disabled person can benefit from the involvement in much the same way as a nondisabled person. As another legislative achievement this time enabling a new corporate perspective for accommodating disabled users, Title III became a significant reference point because it did two things to determine the quality of the access: It tested the viability of the access, and it required an assessment of the equivalency of the environment so that the nondisabled and the disabled had similar ease of use and extent of access. The "fair and equivalent" use of information would be a significantly new approach to determine the efficacy of online public information spaces.

Two more laws made sweeping changes for the protected population of the disabled in digital environments of public institutions. In 1996, the Telecommunications Act sought to influence corporate product design and development to ensure that the equipment and the resulting service could be experienced by disabled users in a way for them to derive benefit from the product or service. Consequently, as this legislative act has broader implications for colleges or universities that are viewed as a public educational service environment, academic programs must factor in ways in which the disabled student must be able to derive benefit from the educational experience. Two years later, legislators recognized that the digital world held barriers to participation for the disabled individual. In response to a growing awareness of the limitations of the previous laws that primarily dealt with physical environments, Section 508 amended the Rehabilitation Act by providing that, because federal agencies and their vendors offer web-based or electronic archives of information to the public, they had the responsibility to offer fair and equivalent access to this public information to disabled individuals. Because "fair and equivalent" means that, as the public is able to easily access and navigate the information, the law requires accommodations must be made to ensure that the disabled individual can also obtain information without difficulty and can experience the environment.

With public and private colleges and universities administering federal funds, they are considered public institutions and therefore must provide fair and equivalent access to their physical environment and to their digital environment. Whether that access is in the form of wheelchair ramps and special handicap parking areas or adaptations of web-based document archives, fair and equivalent access is more than a mere attempt to accommodate. It must be a well-thought-out strategy to provide reasonable ways to make the environment more flexible to the needs of the disabled and to the ways of knowing that are possible to the disabled. Offering one of the best definitions of online accessibility in their book *Maximum Accessibility*, John Slatin and Sharron Rush believed that accessibility constitutes "an aspect or quality of the individual user's experience of the Web site, not a property of the document itself" (7).

Caught in the middle as an agency of a public educational institution, the writing center has the awesome responsibility to help all students perform better at academic tasks and thereby improve their experience of education. Often writing center staff are forced to supply tutoring services and online help to disabled students without understanding the complexity of their pivotal role in the educational process. Hampered in part by a personal lack of understanding of this emerging population and in part by an institutional void in which there is no coherent, articulated institutional policy on educating the disabled student, well-intentioned writing center staff may resort to tried and true methods of composition review and revision in face-to-face encounters that simply do not work for disabled students. Another point to consider is the fact that, during the tutoring session when the student appears to have problems understanding, writing center staff may not specifically inquire about whether the student has a disability or ask the nature of the disability. If the student does not have a declared disability, then the writing tutor must guess about the impairment in order not to infringe on the student's privacy. As a result, the face-to-face experience for both tutor and student may be one of frustrating suppositions.

A physical disability may be mild or severe. Because some physically disabled students may have tremors or combinations of gross motor or fine motor impairments, writing center staff should be willing to adapt the tutoring environment to make the student more comfortable by providing more space with less cluttered pathways and by providing a longer time for the problem assessment to make the tutoring session more productive. Offering a simple alternative of using a computer to make draft revisions versus requiring handwritten revisions will be an appreciated gesture. For students who may be learning disabled and reticent in admitting a disability, writing center staff ought to probe with a series of questions to determine whether students have problems in writing due to misunderstanding the assignment, in reaction to stress, or as a result of poor understanding of grammar. In all their dealings with disabled students, writing center staff should be patient to wait out the sometimes labored expressions of the student and to ask follow-up questions to find out what is really wrong. Caryl Sills pointed out that "strategies that work with unskilled writers are also effective for disabled students."

Sills also believed that any writing criticism should be printed so that the students can examine it and keep it. Frequently, disabled students may suffer from poor self-esteem, and they want to avoid harsh evaluations. They may arrive at the writing center near failure in their classes and truly frustrated. They need writing strategies that are customized to their shortcomings, not a boilerplate set of rules. They will be encouraged if they see that the writing center staff takes care to connect general criticism to specific areas in their essays. Care in giving critical evaluation gives them hope that they can salvage their ideas.

Unlike nondisabled writers, disabled students may exhibit thinking processes that are disconnected or random, causing these students to plod through their writing and not see illogical statements. They will need the extra time for explanations of word differences, organizational techniques, and suggested strategies for improvement that are few in number and simple to recall. For example, as Sills pointed out: "For surface revision, learning disabled writers must reread their writing several times, each time with a specific game plan.... The first proofing can focus on content; the next on organization, forms, sentences and links; and finally on spelling, capitalization, and punctuation" (CS 116). Similarly, peer review can be invigorating and welcomed if offered in a supportive environment. Peer-tutors should be oriented to the task of working with disabled students and should be observed and evaluated by writing center personnel responsible for training and supervision.

Human intervention can be augmented by innovative assistive technology devices, which can provide extra help to the disabled student in the writing center in two ways. First, the device provides a viable means for the disabled student to workaround a shortcoming. For example, as Sheryl Day and Barbara Edwards pointed out, a disabled student who has reading difficulty might listen to an audio version of a book in order to answer questions that test the student's comprehension of the subject matter. In this way, the student works around a visual reading problem that hampers comprehension. Second, the device provides a means to remediate a deficiency. When the student is able to focus on each of the words as the audio version plays, the student may be learning to read better by associating the visual text with the meaning conveyed by the sound. Dual possibilities of compensation and remediation coupled with more affordable technology make assistive devices an important addition to the learning center. From computers with spell checkers to screen readers and to voice synthesizers, all of these devices improve the experience of the disabled student. A few universities have substantially developed assistive education environments. The University of Missouri-Columbia has the Adaptive Computing Technology Center to study the impact of technology on the learning process of disabled students (Day and Edwards), whereas the University of Texas at Austin has the Accessibility Institute that offers online advice and tutorials about using technology to improve accessibility as well as to study the process of assistive technology.

Another form of technology that may be used to help disabled students with informative handouts, tutorials, and examples is the online writing center. However, revamping the Web site to be more conducive to a range of disabled users offers its own set of issues and challenges. Although online writing labs and centers may offer a wealth of information in a dense array of text and images, the content must be restructured to be simplified into short paragraphs and broken up with internal paragraph headings. Such adaptations are especially important if the content is passed through an assistive device that reads each line aloud.

For visually impaired users and cognitively challenged learners, a small font size, vaguely defined contrasts between foreground and background color, graphics rich pages, confusing navigation options, and poorly patched HTML scripting pose problems. According to Jakob Nielsen, a nationally recognized usability expert, "Making the Web more accessible for users with various disabilities is to a great extent a simple matter of using HTML the way it was intended: to encode *meaning* rather than *appearance*" (298). Nielsen believed that the content of the page should be paramount. He urged that design should complement what the content is trying to convey. He decried gee-whiz coding to impress users with lavish graphical user interfaces.

In addition to Nielsen and other usability experts, two organizations are lending their influence and support to transforming the Web into a more accessible information domain. The World Wide Web Consortium is an organization of information technology professionals who create standards for the design world. W3C's Web Accessibility Initiative provides clearly explained approaches to open web spaces to the visually impaired, hearing impaired, physically disabled, or cognitively impaired users. These guidelines help college and university designers transform online writing centers into accessible information spaces. One of the innovations of W3C that allows special use of scripting blocks to define the format of whole Web sites is Cascading Style Sheets. These style declarations enable designers to concentrate on the content and to control disable-friendly presentation. Special use of aural style sheets can also enable assistive devices to better interpret the content. Indeed, the W3C is working on new guidelines to further clarify standards for assistive devices of the future that use software agents to improve the aid assistive devices give the disabled user.

A second organization is the National Center for Accessible Media, which has encouraged "Web captioning and audio description that ensures accessibility of Web-based multimedia" (Paciello 67). Multimedia provides a rich experiential environment that is stimulating with images, music, sound cues, and human voice synthesis (Lewis).

A number of online writing environments now incorporate these standards and provide working models of accessible interfaces. For example, the venerable Purdue Writing Owl provides a large black sans serif font against a stark white background with a simple navigation structure and minimal graphics explained with alternative titles. Most of the format is controlled by a cascading style block that uses cross-browser friendly universal headings to inject bold headings. With the large text, a visually impaired user may be able to view the contents. If an assistive technology device like a screen reader processes each line of code, the simplicity of the HTML script will aid the device in successfully presenting the contents.

For ambitious campus-wide initiatives, the University of Arizona describes its transformation to a disabled friendly site. Starting in May 2001, UAWeb Resources Team began testing the home pages of various departments and determined that 79% did not meet minimum Web accessibility standards. Not only did the university develop a policy, it also worked to improve understanding of the accessibility initiative and to bring about change (http://uaweb.arizona.edu/enable/about.shtml). Subsequently, the university built a group of pages to give advice about testing a site against usability standards, about incorporating scripting techniques to improve accommodation, and to provide a primer of makeover examples to explain their process.

Writing centers can be instrumental in improving the quality of the educational experiences of disabled students. Writing centers are an important resource that, unfortunately, may be ill equipped to deal with the increasing demands of disabled students. In truth, the writing center should be the focal point of a concerted campuswide effort to know and understand the needs of the growing population of disabled students, who know they are entitled to extra help. Enlightenment and direction should produce clearly articulated institutional policies that recognize the institutional responsibility to provide fair and equivalent access to resources that improve the educational experience for disabled students. New technology resources of assistive devices should be available in writing centers to help compensate and remediate problems in learning and communication.

Writing center staff should receive an orientation about disability laws and about the varying nature of disabilities. They should be told about resources, both local and national, that can help them devise practical strategies to help disabled students. Writing center staff should be part of a real and sincere institutional initiative to welcome disabled students and to provide essential educational services to enrich their college experience.

WORKS CITED

"About the Accessibility Project." *University of Arizona Web Resources.* 2004. U of Arizona. 16 June 2004 <http://uaweb.arizona.edu/resources/about.shtml>.

Beilke, Jayne R., and Nina Yssel. "The Chilly Climate for Students with Disabilities in Higher Education." *College Student Journal* 33.3 (Sep 1999): 364+. *Academic Premier.* EBSCO. U of Texas at Arlington Lib. 17 June 2004 <http://continuum.uta.edu:2632>.

Carlson, Scott. "Left Out Online." *Chronicle of Higher Education* 11 June 2004. 23 June 2004. <http://chronicle.com/weekly/v50/i40/40a02301.htm>.

Day, Sheryl L., and Barbara J. Edwards. "Assistive Technology for Postsecondary Students with Learning Disabilities." *Journal of Learning Disabilities* 29.5: 486+. *Academic Search Premier.* EBSCO. U of Texas at Arlington Lib. 16 June 2004 <http://continuum.uta.edu: 2671>.

Gordon, Michael, Lawrence Lewandowski, Kevin Murphy, and Kim Dempsey. "ADA-Based Accommodations in Higher Education: A Survey of Clinicians about Documentation Requirements and Diagnostic Standards." *Journal of Learning Disabilities* 35.4 (Jul/Aug 2002): 357+. *Academic Search Premier.* EBSCO. U of Texas at Arlington Lib. 17 June 2004 <http://continuum.uta.edu:2632> .

Lewis, Rena B. "Assistive Technology and Learning Disabilities: Today's Realities and Tomorrow's Promises." *Journal of Learning Disabilities* 31.1 (Jan./Feb. 98): 16+. *Academic Search Premier.* EBSCO. U of Texas at Arlington Lib. 17 June 2004 <http://continuum.uta.edu:2632> .

Nielsen, Jakob. *Designing Web Usability: The Practice of Simplicity.* Indianapolis: New Riders, 2000.

OWL Online Writing Lab. 1995–2003. Purdue University. 14 July 2004 <http://owl.english.purdue.edu>.

Paciello, Michael G. *Web Accessibility for People with Disabilities.* Lawrence: CMP Books, 2000.

Sills, Carl K. "Success for Learning Disabled Writers Across the Curriculum." *College Teaching* 43.2 (Spring 1995): 66+. *Academic Premier.* EBSCO. U of Texas at Arlington Lib. 16 June 2004 <http://conintuum.uta.edu:2671>.

Slatin, John M., and Sharron Rush. *Maximum Accessibility: Making Your Web Site More Usable for Everyone.* Boston: Addison-Wesley, 2003.

Thomas, Stephen B. "College Students and Disability Law." *Journal of Special Education* 33.4 (Winter 2000): 248. *Academic Search Premier.* EBSCO. U of Texas at Arlington Lib. 17 June 2004 <http://continuum.uta.edu:2632>.

⚓ 36 ⚓

Bottom Up or Top Down: A Case Study of Two Secondary School Writing Centers

Pamela B. Childers
The McCallie School

Some writing centers begin because the faculty initiates the idea; others exist because the administrators have hired someone to start them. Does it make a difference how they begin, or are other factors more important in the successes and/or problems in writing centers? In 1981, I started a secondary school writing center in a public school; ten years later, I created another center in an independent school. The public school, Red Bank Regional High School in Little Silver, New Jersey, served a diverse population of approximately eleven hundred students in grades 9–12. The McCallie School in Chattanooga, Tennessee, a boys' college preparatory day/boarding institution, serves a somewhat less diverse population of approximately six hundred students in the Upper School (grades 9–12). Even though the academic levels varied more in the public school, both schools regularly have National Merit Scholars. Having designed a writing center from the bottom up at the public school, I had discovered the pros and cons of creating one that ran well on minimal funding through several departments, yet applied writing center pedagogy within an existing institutional structure. The writing center I began in 1991 in an independent school, however, was funded through an alumni endowment supported by the administration, so the ways of applying similar pedagogical ideas within the existing institution were impacted by the reaction to an administrative mandate. Although the specific institutions differ in some ways, there are similarities in the ways that a writing center administrator can deal with writing centers that start from the bottom up or the top down.

ORIGINS

In 1981, I spent a summer reading and researching the teaching of writing on Martha's Vineyard as part of a graduate writing program through Northeastern University. The living room in each house of four to eight people was a microwriting center where we asked questions to help us focus, considering purpose and audience. This experience enabled me to imagine how a writing center could function within my own institution, so I proposed a writing center at Red Bank Regional. My models were a few college/university writing centers and the theories of Murray, Graves, Britton, Elbow, Cooper and Odell, Shaughnessy, and Emig. I had already taught in the English department at the school for fifteen years, and was part of an interdisciplinary team to participate in a Rutgers University course, *Writing, Thinking and Learning Across the Curriculum*, taught by Robert Parker. We surveyed students and faculty (Appendix A) to determine the kinds and quality of writing being done by students. Based on responses, the team "recommended follow-up courses in writing across the curriculum (WAC), in-service workshops with various departments, and the establishment of a writing center" (Farrell, *Across the Curriculum* 3).

Teachers in different disciplines volunteered to staff a writing center space in the library for one year during lunch periods. As described in *The Politics of Writing Centers* (Childers and Upton), we made sure that the administrators publicly supported the idea as one not in conflict with the teachers' association contractual agreements. Because we knew teachers were using writing across the curriculum, the writing center would be an extension of that program with extra training for faculty in all departments.

In contrast to the slimly funded beginnings of the 1981 writing center in New Jersey, the Caldwell Writing Center began in 1991 because the Caldwell family made a donation to create an endowed chair of composition at McCallie. The funds for creating a WAC program and writing center, as well as the search to fill the position of director, were important to the administration. A consultant helped prepare the criteria and questions for the search committee, including heads of the history and English departments, members of the Caldwell family, and a few administrators and teachers. After the finalists completed an extensive interview process, I was offered the position.

Because I had already started one writing center, I thought I knew how to start another one. However, I did not know the politics and academic environment of an independent school. I was an outsider, someone who had not taught in the school with the other teachers. My first year as a consultant allowed me to observe classes, interview teachers, administrators, and students, team teach classes, and get to know life in an independent school. I chose a double room on the third floor of the academic building with a folding partition and windows on one side overlooking the city and the nearby mountains; this space was able to house computers on one side with tables for group work and individual conferences on the other. Using the WAC survey to discover the kinds of writing already being used by faculty, I planned a faculty WAC retreat led by Art Young of Clemson University in fall 1991–92 and formed a faculty WAC committee. When the 1991–92 school year started, we had fifteen Macintosh computers on one side of the writing center and a group of new ninth graders eager to volunteer their free time working in the writing center. Because I had no staff and had to learn the Local Area Network (LAN) program myself, I was anxious to take advantage of my new staff who had found a place to call home in their new school. (A complete description of the strategic plan may be found in chap. 6 of this book.)

PURPOSE

In my proposal to create a writing center at Red Bank Regional (Farrell, *Across the Curriculum*), I described it as "[a] place where students' writing may be read and heard. It should encourage writing in each subject area, assist students in the process of writing as thinking and learning, and improve student writing skills at all levels. The ultimate goal is ... 'to establish the student as a more independent writer and to give him or her some strategies that can be applied to the next piece of writing'" (Luban, Matsuhashi, and Reigstad 33). Personally, I valued equity of learning for all students, so I saw the center as a place where students could go no matter what their academic or economic level. We planned to have computers in the writing center from the start, and I wanted all students to have equal access to computers. Students also needed to be heard and to take risks with their writing that they could not do in classes of twenty-five to thirty students. Many of my own classes fell into this size bracket, so I understood how difficult it was to have conferences with individual students on a regular basis. A writing center could help all students, including those in my own classes, in a low risk environment where they would not receive a grade.

Based on my earlier experiences, I knew how a writing center could work effectively with the help of students and faculty. However, the purpose of the Caldwell Writing Center shifted a bit because of advancements in technology over ten years. McCallie had a computer lab, so boys were already excited about using technology. Therefore, although my proposal for this writing center focused on "creating an environment where writing is revered," it also stated that, "the success of the program depends on administrative financial commitment as well as staff and student involvement" (Farrell, *Human Resources* 2). This center clearly identified a schoolwide commitment to a WAC program to improve thinking, learning, and writing. The proposal also suggested attitudinal changes of students and staff toward writing; and we wanted technology to be used to improve the quality and quantity of writing.

My own added purposes were not far from the ones in 1981 because there were still students without access to computers. With a writing center open before and after school as well as during the school day, students could find time to use one of our fifteen computers to work on their writing, even in classes that averaged fifteen students. In order to help faculty understand how to use computers to improve writing, I gave sample lessons, team taught classes, and offered workshops after school. Clearly, my purpose was to educate both students and faculty on the use of technology as part of improving writing in a variety of ways. Also, new teachers at independent schools tend to be strong in subject area content but have little training in how to teach; therefore, I saw part of my job as one to encourage pedagogical changes to improve teaching and learning of writing and subject content.

BASIC THEORY/PRACTICE

In 1981, research in writing center theory/practice was limited. I paraphrased Peter Elbow when I created writing conference guidelines for what I called "listener/readers." For instance,

I suggested looking for "highlights (specific words, phrases, sentences or ideas that strike your fancy or imagination) and telling the writer why those highlights work for you" (Farrell, *Across the Curriculum* 12). Richard Adler's report to the NCTE SLATE Steering Committee, *Back to the Basics*, stated, "If we want better writing, we need to require more of it; if we require more of it, we need more full or part-time people to respond constructively to what is written" (5). But more than anything else, I used the ideas of Britton et al.

Composition theory and the writing process also had strong impacts on our writing center practice. Like Donald Murray, I decided that I would have to write with my students so they would see how I valued writing. As teachers and students used the writing center and its services, they became actively involved in what we did and how we did it. Therefore, their input, recommendations of readings, and research helped us develop the center to become truly *their* center; that is, the theories and practices evolved as technology improved and became available and as the creative writing program found a strong place in the writing center as well. Those who used writing in their professions visited the writing center regularly and influenced what we did.

Times had truly changed by the 1990s and so had composition theories and practices. As I was writing the proposal in 1981, books such as Elaine Maimon et al.'s *Writing in the Arts and Sciences* (1981), Muriel Harris's *Tutoring Writing* (1982), and Fulwiler and Young's *Language Connection: Writing and Reading Across the Curriculum* (1982) were in progress. Many others would follow so that I had new resources that dealt with practices of writing centers and WAC programs. Besides the writings of Elbow and Murray, Toby Fulwiler's *The Journal Book* (1987) plus articles in *The Writing Center Journal* and *Writing Lab Newsletter*, had an impact on theory in the Caldwell Writing Center. Stephen M. North's "The Idea of a Writing Center" (1984) and Gary Olson's *Writing Centers: Theory and Practice* (1984) also gave concrete support for writing center theory and practice.

From the day we opened, I had to convince teachers and students that I would not correct their papers for them. In my opening speech to the faculty in 1991, I stated: "The Caldwell Writing Center is not a remedial facility; it is here to serve the entire student body, faculty, staff, and administration. We do not perform band-aid surgery on student papers, and we are not responsible for their grades. Instead, we ask questions to help writers discover ways to improve their own papers and help them become better lifelong writers, thinkers and learners." Whether or not faculty would understand and support such a concept was still an unknown. At first, students would say, "Here, fix this and I'll pick it up later." My response was, "You cannot afford me as an editor, so when would you like to come in to sit down and talk about your paper." Michael Pemberton's Ethics column in *Writing Lab Newsletter* helped us in handling such problems. Part of a writing center's job is to retrain the entire institution to value good writing and the ownership of it.

ROLE OF THE WRITING CENTER DIRECTOR WITHIN THE INSTITUTION

At a public school with a strong teachers' association and encouragement for advanced degrees by staff, the administration and board of education must maintain a clear vision for the future. At Red Bank Regional, one of the schoolwide goals was to improve student writing across the curriculum. Therefore, a faculty-initiated proposal for a writing center fit the goal in a way that took little financial commitment or rescheduling. Because I was already carrying a full class load in the English and (later) performing arts departments, I could function in the capacity of director without any change in salary or teaching load by covering the writing center during my duty period. The administration provided a space, which changed each year for three years as larger spaces became available. Teachers were excited to talk with someone about their writing assignments and results of those assignments over lunch or during professional period. When we moved to our permanent space in the middle of the English area, I was then available all periods, even when I was teaching class. My students were used to people coming into our writing center/classroom to use computers or to sit in on what we were doing. During their free periods, students came in to read writing center materials, work with other students, or write at computers without disturbing us. There was a mutual trust and respect that we were all writing, thinking, and learning no matter what the content might be. Teachers in the English department were somewhat skeptical until we moved into their area, and they could observe what we were doing at any time. Their attitudes were positive, supportive, and critically constructive.

Things were not quite as positive in the independent school. Faculty saw me as a "special person" who had not taught with them and did not know about their curriculum and its history. Also, the administration had determined that I should not teach a class for the first years because I would be busy starting the writing center and WAC program. I was new, not teaching a single class, and was seen writing or reading in this room with computers. The writing center had large windows into the hallway, so I made sure most academic faculty and administrators could see me as they arrived and departed each day. When I did get a part-time assistant, I could then teach one class a day, something the administration has continued to limit because they want me seen in the writing center and cannot provide a full-time assistant. Slowly, over the years, more teachers have collaborated with the writing center on many projects, including some teachers who attended our first retreat.

Although I have attended English department meetings, supported their efforts, and presented materials for and with them, I have only taught a poetry elective and independent study writing courses through the English department. However, from the first year at McCallie, I have been actively involved with the science department, teaching writing activities in many classes. Also, since 1996, I have been team teaching an interdisciplinary science senior core course, *Oceans: Past and Present*, with a science teacher.

STAFFING

My staff at Red Bank Regional consisted of student and faculty volunteers because there was no money available to pay for anyone else. Each teacher who volunteered that first year would work half a lunch period one day per week, and I would fill in where needed. Students knew we were available when they saw one of us at the little round table in our corner of the library. I trained the faculty through periodic workshops and regularly checked with them on what they had done with students. When we moved to an office on the balcony of the library, I became dependent on student volunteers throughout the day by recruiting students from my junior English classes the previous year. We had done peer editing frequently, where I trained them to ask questions of each other. With a list of writing center procedures and guidelines, they could easily follow them to work with students who either dropped by or were sent to the writing center by a teacher. A teacher on library duty served as the faculty supervisor.

When we moved to the large enclosed space in the English area, computers were added, and more students volunteered during lunch and free periods. Occasionally, teachers were assigned to the writing center as their extra duty. Also, I investigated the Congressional Awards, which included volunteer service in the criteria for receiving bronze, silver, or gold awards. By documenting their hours of work, we could help students apply for medals, which they could then list on college applications.

At the Caldwell Writing Center, I was seen as the person hired to direct the writing center; therefore, I did not need a staff. I was, like many writing center directors, neither faculty nor administration, so I had to design a position that enabled me to do what I felt I should be doing. I started with a contingent of ninth-grade volunteers who remained faithfully for four years. During that time, I also designed a peer tutoring course. Through a series of successful recruiting efforts, I managed to get two or three students each year to take the course as an independent study. Also, the second year, I was able to convince the administration to include a budget line to hire a part-time assistant director. Over the years, I have managed to maintain a part-time assistant, find a few student volunteers, and continue to teach independent study courses that involve work in the writing center. My assistants have been adjuncts at the local university or part-time English teachers with advanced degrees in rhetoric and composition. Each has worked for several years, and I have mentored them for future full-time positions. We train volunteers by using their own work as a model, and we meet them as needed. One of us is always available to assist them in their training and work with peers.

PROBLEMS

As mentioned previously, money, time, and staffing can be the biggest problems in a public school environment. In my case, time was a constant problem. That is, I was teaching five classes and using my professional, lunch, and duty periods to cover the writing center. No one forced me to stay in the writing center during my free periods, but the writing center could not stay open without an authorized adult on duty. Most of the time I had to go in early and stay late in order to do any preparation, reflection, or record keeping. With adequate funding, we could have afforded to hire another person to share the responsibilities of the writing center and the teaching load, which would have given me more time to work with students in classes or in individual or small groups in the writing center.

Although my colleagues and administration supported having a writing center, I did not have a budget. Each year I would request certain equipment and supplies, as well as funds for any school-sponsored trips or journal subscriptions. The school budget determined whether my request would be approved, then I had to write a report about the use of the funds and wait months for the board of education to reimburse me. Also, as technology advanced, we were limited to older printers from offices, a computer donated by the Woodrow Wilson National Fellowship Foundation, and another computer and printer purchased from profits of cohosting an all-day conference sponsored by the New Jersey Council of Teachers of English. Because the creative writing majors in the performing arts program published an award-winning literary magazine through the writing center, we had one overused Macintosh for in-house publication.

At McCallie, problems did not focus on the financial concerns, although after fifteen years there is still no full-time assistant director. Because funding comes from several sources and different budget lines, I usually have little control over the amount allotted from my proposed budget each year. My main problems were making inroads with the English department and an occasional administrator who had no idea what we did in the writing center. Also, faculty did not understand how we used technology with writing. Eventually, those problems have been somewhat alleviated as more teachers have been trained on technology and have taken advantage of the services of our writing center, and administrative personnel have changed.

One unforeseen problem has been discipline. In the public school, a writing center was a luxury, and there were few behavioral problems. Of course, I was also teaching classes in this space, so there was a respect for learning in the area at all times, even when we were laughing or sitting in a circle in the middle of the room reading drafts aloud and responding. In the independent school, the writing center is a supervised space for boys to use for writing, thinking and learning. The students consider the space and what we have to offer as something they deserve when they need to work with us on a paper; however, sometimes they are not as respectful of each other as they should be. It is difficult to hold a conference with a student, while others are disruptive or distracting. This problem may be alleviated this year with the opening of a senior student lounge.

Yes, there are still many teachers who feel they do not need the services of the writing center, still consider us a position associated with the administration, or prefer to work with their own students. However, most of the time we have more work than we can handle, and we continue to try new and innovative activities to improve student writing, thinking, and learning.

Another problem for both public and independent school directors is financing of participation in national and regional conferences. In public school, I was lucky to get $500 toward expenses when I was presenting at a conference. At McCallie, I was given a substantial travel budget to fulfill national organizational duties; but, for several years now, that budget has been eliminated because of more financial burdens. Therefore, the money for most of my trips to conference workshops must come out of my own pocket.

INNOVATIONS

Beginning in 1981 at Red Bank Regional, each school year became a new learning experience for me. As I added books, tried new methods of teaching writing, and experimented with use of technology to teach writing, I shared what I learned with students and faculty. The best part of working with student volunteers was that they taught me more about technology as I trained them to respond to student writing. We had a collegial atmosphere of mutual trust and respect. Also, they watched me write, rewrite, revise, and edit my own work, frequently asking them for feedback on poems, articles, or books. I even included them in pieces that I wrote. They weren't used to a teacher writing along with them, and this innovation probably had the greatest impact on other activities. As I developed the multiyear creative writing course in the performing arts program, students were involved in revising it as I taught the course in the writing center. As part of that program, we began a guest artists-in-the-schools program, initiated our annual poetry reading, and attended the Geraldine R. Dodge Poetry Festival, as well as other writing workshops led by award-winning poets, playwrights, and fiction writers. We also participated in the Columbia Scholastic Press Association and National Playwriting competitions, winning top honors nationally for fiction and plays.

Outside the department, we interacted and collaborated with teachers in all disciplines and supported faculty in their teaching and writing efforts. The writing center sometimes became a noisy room with community volunteers describing the importance of writing in their careers or students debating or role playing to help one another develop a story or a poem. Language was important in this space, and we all willingly shared whatever we learned in a trusting atmosphere of intellect, wit, and risk taking.

In many ways, what happened at McCallie was quite similar. Student volunteers became an integral part of the program. Students have reminded me of their innovative ideas that we adapted or adopted in the Caldwell Writing Center. Through the years, the boys have collaborated with the writing center staff and teachers on the writing of articles and chapters, creating materials, making curricular decisions for course development, and even preparing presentations for teachers, board members, and parents. They have helped design and revise our Web site to offer support for writing and contributed their own writing for our online anthologies. We also work with the school chaplain on preparing the Advent booklet each year, which features the writing of students, faculty, staff, and administration. With several teachers, we have initiated online exchanges with students and faculty in other schools, colleges, and universities. Besides just working with faculty on WAC, we have facilitated the writing of faculty and student essays for publication in professional books and journals, and led many faculty development activities. Finally, we have become a faculty resource for career planning, resume and letter writing, as well as applications for graduate school, grants, and fellowships. These activities indicate a professional level of trust with colleagues, and this kind of interaction among faculty and students with writing sets a model of the importance of writing, which many students accept as normal. Therefore, students of all academic levels value coming to the writing center.

POSITIVE IMPACT

Over the years at Red Bank Regional, students became the backbone of the writing center; they trained new volunteers, and included students of all academic levels. For instance, one of my senior skills students became our best volunteer to train students on using word processing software, and one of our juniors presented at the Peer Tutoring Conference at Bucknell with a Monmouth College tutor. Several of my own honors students met in the writing center to discuss their papers; and creative writers in the performing arts program considered their classroom, the writing center, to be their home. It was a wonderful blend of academic and socioeconomic levels with one common goal to improve writing, both their own and that of others. Also, students made presentations on writing for the board of education and posted displays of student works. Our creative writers encouraged students of all ability levels to participate in the literary magazine. Faculty stopped by, volunteers went into their classrooms, and readings or workshops were available in the writing center for everyone.

At McCallie, technology has become a vital part of writing and research in an atmosphere where discussion is important. More people are now involved in writing for themselves as well as for others, and they are willing to share it. The Caldwell Writing Center Web site has replaced a grammar handbook and research format book as the online resource for students, faculty, and parents. With more collaborative writing among students and faculty, attitudes have changed. Successes in writing competitions, scholarship and application essays, and research writing have increased the quantity of writing and revising that writers now do. Currently, a few homesick ninth-grade boarders have made the writing center their home away from home, and we correspond regularly with their parents. We try to encourage excellence in writing from all who enter. Rather than focusing on the frustrations of failure, we try to have fun with the mistakes we make and use those as tools for success with writing, thinking, and learning.

Finally, attitudinal changes have taken place in both public and independent school facilities. Teachers who had been reluctant to refer students or ask writing center staff to conduct workshops began doing so when they saw the impact on the writing and attitudes of individuals who had used our services. At McCallie one major breakthrough with the English department took place when a teacher wanted to have writing conferences with all of his students in one day so that they could work on revisions at the same time. He, my assistant, and I were each able to have writing conferences with one third of his students in a single class period. The teacher was pleased, the students were excited about getting feedback on their drafts, we gained more regulars for the writing center, and the quality of the students' work improved.

CONCLUSIONS

Problems exist in every writing center, but if we face possible problems before they occur, then we may be able to avoid them. If we also look at what did work (Appendix B), then we can consider how to use those positives to create an effective writing center. Each writing center, whether it is initiated from the bottom up or top down, has to deal with unique problems of the institution, whether it is a public or independent school. Another variable in this comparison, of course, is the coed versus single sex school. Today there are public schools that are separating the sexes for their education, and most independent schools are coeducational; so that is just another variable in the uniqueness of each individual school. I do think, however, that attitudes toward writing centers may differ within and outside the institution depending on who initiated the idea and why they did so. My experiences at both institutions are unique because neither tied the creation of a writing center to improved test scores on statewide or national tests. Some institutions create writing centers as remedial facilities or English as a second language (ESL) facilities because of the needs of their student population; however, most realize that a writing center is a place where the quality of writing is closely tied to thinking and learning in all disciplines.

In both public and independent school writing centers, time, research, and preparation that go into creating a writing center are most important. With some faculty development, both types of institutions can create viable writing centers initiated from the bottom and encouraged from the top. Whether initiated by teachers or administrators, the support of the faculty, administration, students, parents, and the larger school community determine the success of the operation.

WORKS CITED

Adler, Richard. *Back to the Basics: Report of the SLATE Steering Committee.* Urbana, IL: NCTE, 1978.

Britton, James, Tony Burgess, Nancy Martin, Alex McLeod, and Harold Rosen. *The Development of Writing Abilities (11–18).* London: Macmillan, 1975.

Childers, Pamela B., and James Upton. "Pedagogies Inside and Outside the Secondary School Writing Center." *The Politics of Writing Centers.* Ed. Kathy Evertz and Jane Nelson. Portsmouth, NH: Heinemann-Boynton/Cook, 2001.

Cooper, Charles, and Lee Odell. *Evaluating Writing: Describing, Measuring, Judging.* Urbana, IL: NCTE, 1977.

Elbow, Peter. *Writing without Teachers.* New York: Oxford UP, 1973.

Emig, Janet. *The Composing Process of Twelfth Graders.* Urbana, IL: NCTE, 1971.

Farrell, Pamela B. *An Across the Curriculum Writing Center: A Proposal.* Unpublished document for Northeastern University. Presented to Red Bank Regional High School, Little Silver, NJ, Sept. 1981.

___. *The High School Writing Center: Establishing and Maintaining One.* Urbana, IL: NCTE, 1989.

___. *Human Resources Development Plan for Implementation of A Writing Across the Curriculum Program.* Unpublished document for Nova Southeastern University. Presented to The McCallie School, Chattanooga, TN, Feb. 1991.

Fulwiler, Toby. *The Journal Book.* Portsmouth, NH: Heinemann-Boynton/Cook, 1987.

Fulwiler, Toby, and Art Young, eds. *Language Connections: Writing and Reading Across the Curriculum.* Urbana, IL: NCTE, 1982.

Graves, Donald. *Balance the Basics: Let Them Write.* New York: Ford Foundation Papers on Research About Learning, Feb. 1978.

Harris, Muriel. *Tutoring Writing: A Sourcebook for Writing Labs.* Glenview, IL: NCTE, 1982.

Luban, Nina, Ann Matsuhashi, and Tom Reigstad. "One-to-One to Write." *English Journal* (Nov. 1978): 30–35.

Maimon, Elaine, et al. *Writing in the Arts and Sciences.* Cambridge, MA: Winthrop, 1981.

Murray, Donald M. *A Writer Teaches Writing.* Boston: Houghton Mifflin, 1968.

North, Stephen M. "The Idea of a Writing Center." *College English* 46 (1984): 433–46.

Olson, Gary, ed. *Writing Centers: Theory and Practice.* Urbana, IL: NCTE, 1984.

Pemberton, Michael. "Writing Center Ethics." *Writing Lab Newsletter.* Various. 1993–1999.

Shaughnessy, Mina. *Errors and Expectations.* New York: Oxford UP, 1977.

Appendix A: Student and Faculty Surveys

STUDENT SURVEY

Each day for the next three weeks of school, please list the kinds of writing, by subject that you have done during the last twenty-four hours. Use the attached form to fill in the information. Thank you for your assistance. A key to the kinds writing is listed below:

1A Friendly letter	2A Biography	3A Poem
1B Diary/journal entry	2B Autobiography	3B Play
1C Notes (for a class)	2C Resume	3C Short Story
	2D Summary	3D Dialogue
	2E Lab report	3E Written speech
	2F Answering in question in sentences	3F Storyboards
	2G Essay or composition	3G Script
	2H Outline	
	2I List	
	2J Filling out an application	
	2K Written report	
	2L Memorandum	
	2M Business letter	
	2N Written directions	
	2O Mathematical proofs	
	2P Definitions	
	2Q Test taking (short answers rather than sentences)	
	2R Other (Please specify)	
	2S Dictation	

Example:
Day 1
2A–English, 2F-History, 2E-Science, 3A-Crafts, 1C-Phys. Ed.

FACULTY SURVEY

Please answer the following questions so that we may ascertain the kinds of writing that are being used by various departments in our school. Thank you for your cooperation.

Writing Across the Curriculum Committee

I. What kinds of writing are students required to do in your course(s)? See attached list for suggested categories.

II. How many writing assignments per week do you assign? Anything that is listed on the attached sheet falls into the category of writing assignment.

III. What qualities do you consider important for good writing? Please check as many items as necessary.

___organization   ___logical thinking

___creative ability   ___original thinking

___neat handwriting   ___sentence variety

___correct spelling   ___depth of thinking

___accuracy of content   ___grammatical accuracy

___Other (Please list)

Appendix B: Comparison of Two Secondary School Writing Centers

Name of School	Red Bank Regional High School Little Silver, New Jersey	The McCallie School Chattanooga, Tennessee
Type of Institution	Public, 1,100 students Grades 9–12	Independent, 600 students Grades 9–12 Upper School
Date of Implementation	1981–82 school year	1991–92 school year
Origin of Program	Faculty	Administration/ Alumni Endowment
Original Purpose	To improve student writing across the curriculum (WAC)	To improve the quality of writing and the attitude towards WAC
Administrative Role	To provide a space, release period, and support of staffing	To support the success of designing and implementing the writing center and WAC program
Financial Support	Release period, purchase of basic technology, and space	Endowment to cover part of salary, original purchase of technology and furniture, ongoing budget for the running of the writing center, and professional expenses.
Location(s)	Under the stairs in the library, in an office above the library, in the middle of the English area	In a double room on the third floor of the Academic Building, near all academic classes
Role of Director	Full-time teacher of English in the regional high school and of creative writing in the performing arts program located in the writing center with director's duties during professional, lunch and extra duty periods	Full-time director located in the writing center with teaching of a poetry, then team teaching of a senior interdisciplinary science course plus independent study writing courses and classes in Upper and Middle School upon request
Staff	Volunteer/extra duty period teachers, then volunteer students during free periods	Volunteer students, part-time assistant director, and students taking independent study courses related to writing
Problems	• Too many roles, too little time • Inadequate funding for updated technology • Conflicts between English and performing arts department duties • Conflicts in role as teacher and writing center director • Inadequate staffing • Limited funding	• "Outsider" who had not taught a full load at this school • Collaboration for an effective role with English department • Little administrative support and lack of understanding of program at first • Unfamiliarity with technology • Seen as a place for "touchy/feely" writing at first

Innovations	• Became a resource for WAC • Introduced use of computers for teaching writing • Developed creative writing course in the performing arts department through the writing center • Encouraged students of all academic abilities to work together • Interacted and collaborated with teachers in all disciplines • Introduced guest artists-in-the-schools program • Initiated annual poetry reading • Involved community volunteers to describe the role of writing in their careers • Provided assistance with writing of college application and scholarship essays • Introduced the Congressional Awards as part of the volunteer program in the writing center • Advised award-winning in-house literary magazine • Modeled teacher as researcher by interviewing peer reader/listeners for article on role of computers in the interaction between tutors and peers in The Writing Center Journal (1987) • Participated in CSPA and Playwriting Competitions—Students won CSPA Gold Circle Award for short story and NPC first prize for one-act play • As a teacher/poetry consultant for the Geraldine R. Dodge Poetry Festival, offered students attended festivals and workshops with award-winning poets • Published The High School Writing Center: Establishing and Maintaining One (NCTE, 1998) • Modeled lifelong learning for faculty and students	• Became a resource for WAC • Introduced use of computers for teaching writing • Used student volunteers in grades 9–12 in the Caldwell Writing Center (CWC) • Created peer tutoring course for students of all academic levels • Initiated a student/faculty reading • Supported guest writer program • Advertised national student writing competitions (NCTE, Playwriting, and others) • Provided assistance with writing of college application and scholarship essays • Collaborated with faculty on writing essays for chapter in Programs and Practices: Writing Across the Secondary School Curriculum (1994) • Supported the work of faculty by nominating them for local, regional and national teaching awards (e.g., chemistry, physics, American history) • Created the CWC Web site to support writing, grammar, research, faculty, and parent information • Initiated and edited online anthologies written by students, faculty, parents, and alumni • Led faculty development activities through mentor and faculty development programs • Assisted in career planning, resume and letter writing, applications for graduate school, grants/fellowships • Encouraged collaborative workshops for faculty, and other teachers and administrators (WAC, IWCA, NSTA, and NAIS conferences).
Positive Impact	Students, faculty, administrators, parents, and board members became aware of the value of writing in all subjects and supported our attendance at various regional events.	Students, faculty, administrators, parents, and board became aware of the outstanding work of students and faculty in relation to writing. More faculty members have taken the initiative to try writing themselves, with students, and/or with colleagues. Technology has become a vital part of writing for students and faculty.

37

The Writing Center at the University of North Carolina at Chapel Hill: A Site and Story Under Construction

Kimberly Town Abels
University of North Carolina at Chapel Hill

The floor reverberates with the buzz of jack hammers. A distant horn blares warning of an impending explosion. We wait the long seconds of anticipation for the blast that jiggles our keyboards, then hear the final "hooonnnnnk" that signals all clear and progress on the building adjacent to us. While our building still stands, the bulldozers next door remind us that our basement home, which puddles when it rains and saunas in the summer, is a big green lawn in the university's architectural, long-term "master plan."

What will happen to the writing center? It's a question many directors ask over and over in the lifetime of a writing center. As WCenter teaches us, no one is alone in asking this question, as many directors face building and rebuilding, additions, and decisions that shape the progress, course, place, and purpose of their writing centers everyday. This recurring question, or some version of it, "What will happen to the writing center?" "What should we do in the face of … ?" "What are our options given …" are the building blocks, the depth charges, sometimes the dynamite, and sometimes the rubble that describe the development of a writing center over time.

Over the past ten years, the Writing Center at the University of North Carolina has been building and developing a program along our particular fault lines. Ours is a story of decisions, taken one by one, that has come to shape the center as it operates today. The decisions made here are those many directors consider, face, are saddled with, daydream about, avoid, or choose to make do with as they develop their writing centers. See if these questions sound familiar:

- Should the director's position be tenured or not?
- What happens if we move the writing center out of the English department?
- How do we get a better space?
- Who should tutor in our center?
- Should we have an online version of our services?
- How do I get more help?
- How do we manage with these budget cuts?
- What should we do next?

If only writing center directors had the power to decide these questions! Issues of agency map every writing center's future: Who decides? The staff? The Director? Chair? Dean? Provost? A committee? A board? Faculty? Friend? Foe? Who chooses, shapes, and makes the calls that chart the direction and development of a center?

As I scan down this particular list, my head bobbing to a jack hammer refrain, I feel fortunate to have had some say about half of the time. The rest of the time I've tried to inform someone else's decisions and have kept my fingers crossed. What happens in a writing center tells a representative anecdote in the university's larger story. With that in mind, a look back at Carolina's story—at what we've struggled with, succeeded in, laughed through, and learned from—may foreground what many directors share as water cooler talk at their center construction sites.

WHAT HAPPENS IF WE MOVE THE WRITING CENTER OUT OF THE ENGLISH DEPARTMENT? SHOULD THE DIRECTOR'S POSITION BE TENURED?

As is often the case, the story begins in the middle. Some of what I know comes from anecdotes told to me by others; some I've pieced together from old files left in drawers. Think of me as a first generation ancestor. I was not here when these questions first occurred and didn't have input in arguing for or against the decisions made. When I was hired, certain facts defined the center: The center would be moved out of the English department into a unit named "Academic Services," placing it under the oversight of the dean of the College of Arts and Sciences. Academic Services collects seven units, including the Learning Center, Learning Disabilities Services, the Math Center, Chemistry Center, and Academic Support for Student Athletes. We were deemed vaguely related in mission (i.e., providing instruction or support to students outside of courses) and in audience (serving the wide swath of the university community as our clientele). The position would be a full-time, permanent position of a quasi-faculty status—nontenure track.

The tenure question and department question traveled as a pair, but the department question came first. The composition faculty in the English department, which had developed and nurtured the writing center for years, felt that the center might receive more stable funding and more easily respond to demands for service from across campus were it situated outside of the English department, after too many years of wild swings in funding for the center (five TAs one year, twenty-one the next) and little continuity from year to year in the center. Whereas the English department shouldered the cost of the center, its services were clearly in demand from students, staff, and faculty across campus. Accordingly, a proposal went to the dean of Arts and Sciences outlining a center designed to serve the full university community and staff by a full-time permanent, quasi-faculty nontenured director. There might not have been support for another tenure line in composition, especially when the plan was to move it out of a traditional academic department. In addition, the other units in Academic Services, the writing center's proposed new home, were successfully led by directors with the same quasi-faculty status.

I step in the story here, when I read the advertisement for the job, and have to make the critical decision that many in the field of writing centers often face. Should I take a nontenure track job? How would this status affect my ability to lead and create a strong writing center on this campus? How would taking a nontenured position affect my personal career? Tough questions without universal answers. For me, the exigencies of the moment take precedence and help me make a decision. I am already comfortably settled in the area, and my partner has a job here. I want to have children without the pressure of publishing—a difficult balance I'd witnessed others struggle through. But probably equally important is a vibe I pick up on during my interview. Quasi-faculty seem to have respect on this particular campus and are treated as colleagues and contributors. I feel especially welcomed by my composition colleagues in the English department and know I can build professional and valuable relationships regardless of my technical status.

So, how does it turn out? Although the graduate student tutors and I have developed a strong and effective writing center (WC) from this position in the university, I still follow conversations on WCenter about the pros and cons of where WCs are placed within university structures and whether WC directors need tenure. I often wonder, "What if …" and try to imagine how changes along either dimension might affect our particular center. Maybe the provost's office is where we belong? Maybe tenure would help me solve this next problem. What do you think?

HOW DO WE GET A BETTER SPACE?

It's a steamy July 5, my first day on the job as the new WC director. I find my basement office flooded, the air conditioning broken, the garage sale cast-off furniture and cinder-block walls covered with mold, and an old-fashioned rotary dial phone on the reception desk that doesn't ring—it vibrates when a call comes in. What do I do? "Quit now" is my first thought. "Can I get my old job back? Have they processed the paperwork to put me on payroll here yet?" A trapped dragonfly flings itself repeatedly against the flourescent light overhead, and I decide to start with the phones. Drawing on prior experience at a big state school, I start calling everyone I can think of in the facilities department: the telecommunications folks, the physical plant to find the plumbers, housekeeping, the painters, and the dean when they ask for an account to create a work order. Her reply, "You have an account, but there's no money in it. You don't have a budget. What do you need?" I keep calling—discover that I can't call home ten miles away because such "long distance" calls had been blocked. I flip through the phone book imagining what other parts of the university I will need to stir up and over to the writing center to bring this place some long overdue attention.

My struggles for decent space for the center take new and numerous forms as time passes: memos to more deans, conversations with OSHA and university environmental experts, proposals to the library about expanding satellite space, losing bids against technology units on campus for new space, remodeling junkets. I spend more time than I ever would have imagined outlining salient points for why a space dedicated to serving thousands of students, not to mention the staff, might be in need of a bathroom. We try to "make do," fix the place up, keep the building habitable. We are given our own, permanent wet-vac to suck up the flood waters when it rains. I search Web sites to identify people on the campus space committee who might be allies, and just by luck, one day get an e-mail from a colleague in the English department who has heard that a computer lab in their building might be vacated 2 years from now. Would the Writing Center like to look at the space? YES.

Meanwhile, the deans, in sympathetic response to the writing center's plight in the wet basement, decide to give us space in a brand new building. Although, of course, we are elated at the prospect of new space, we learn that the building will be on the edge of campus, where students, if they come at all, will probably hope to see us at 8 a.m. or midnight in their pajamas. Our new blessing suddenly seems a curse, and although we meet with architects to design new writing center space, the e-mailing and letter writing begins again, anew for different, yet better space.

Who gets what space is a universal issue on any campus, and like many writing centers, relative newcomers in most university campus landscapes, we sometimes have little choice or clout. At this point, we hope to move into the English department satellite space first sometime next year, and then … we'll see. I'm keeping my memo writing quill sharp and my wet-vac at hand.

WHO SHOULD TUTOR IN OUR CENTER?

Jerry and Jane, doctoral candidates from history and philosophy, provide my first real introduction to the WC graduate students from history and philosophy, the WAC representation on staff, they've worked in the WC for a year already and will join me for my first year as director. They stop in to say hello (out of curiosity) and orient me to how things are done in the WC. They are a wealth of information, and I quickly learn that they are all that counts for stability and continuity in the center. They share with me the one page tutor training handout, tell me about WC hours and staff meetings. They try to get a faltering database up and running on an old computer. They don't know anything about the piles of dinosaur computer equipment in one of the tutoring rooms. They tell me that the rest of the staff are master's students from the English department that rotate in for a semester at a time with a half-day training in tutoring. Their stint in the WC is part of the teacher training plan for the English composition program.

Given my charge to bring the WC to serve the larger "university community," I see just how tricky this mission may be. The WC has been housed in the English department and functioned as part of its program for years. They deserve credit for growing it, nurturing it, and successfully arguing that it is important enough to the university mission that it needs a real director and guidance. My friends and intellectual colleagues in the English department rely on the WC for funding and training their graduate students and haven't imagined either of those things changing with the arrival of an independent WC director. So I have the political conundrum of answering to a dean with a WAC mission and wanting and needing the collegiality of my peers in the English department. How do I walk that line and develop a strong writing center along lines I value and that fit my knowledge of writing center theory and practice? Competing interests ground, overlay, crowd in around my job and complicate my actions. Is it up to me who tutors in the writing center? Can I even ask who should tutor in the center? Who might be best suited for the job on this campus? Undergrads? Grads? English department folks? Students from across the curriculum? Those are conversations I'm aware of in the literature, but they seem largely irrelevant. At the moment, it doesn't seem as if I get to decide. So what do I do? Wait.

The first year I observe that the English department master's students resent their WC assignments and believe such "training" is unnecessary. They want out of the writing center so they can move on to the "real" work of teaching in the classroom. Their short, one-semester stints in the center and lack of training as tutors makes it difficult to combat or redirect this reputation. However, this situation gives me my first move—an argument that the WC staff needs greater training and stability that can only happen with year-long assignments. This succeeds, in part, because the logistics of having all English master's students rotate through the center before the classroom clash with the department's needs. I ask some of them to stay on for another year and they do.

Next, I suggest to the WPA that we ask for volunteers from the English department who might *want* to work in the WC (rather than be assigned) and am cautioned that I'll only get dissertation writers who want easy jobs. I ask to interview them to see if that's true. Luckily, along with the returning tutors, I find some new English department graduate students who seem genuinely interested in WC work. I form a staff that has more continuity and dedication and invite them to join me in reshaping the center's policies, procedures, and mission. I also add another WAC teaching assistant from another department moving that number up to three.

After that—again helped along by natural developments and shifts in TA staffing needs in the English departments—I find in the coming years that I'm able successfully to argue that the center needs more representation from departments across campus to fulfill its WAC mission. At one point, I'm asked to guarantee a certain number of slots for the English department, and with some careful negotiation I do, but the number is now only six. However, I also succeed in sending the message that the needs of the WC's service to the university community outweigh those of an individual department.

Such slow, careful, shifts continue, and a few years later, I control all hiring. The center has gained the reputation as a terrific place to work with a supportive, fun community of teachers and has become highly prized as a graduate student teaching assistantship. Now, each February, we send out an e-mail across campus inviting applications and receive a large response. We attract some of the best graduate students on campus—often teaching award winners. Our goal is to create a diverse staff in age, race, gender, departmental representation, personality, and expertise in ESL, technology, and learning differences. Given that we are a large school and that the WC serves students writing in departments from all over the university, the staff now hails from departments across campus. In the coming year, we'll have graduate students from education, history, social work, biology, anthropology, and sociology. We're also happy to have English department folks in the mix as they often have valuable training in the teaching of writing and classroom experience. We're still hiring only graduate students, mostly due to the inertia of tradition. With the possibility of more space developing for the WC, I may have the opportunity to really ask the question: Who should tutor in our WC? Maybe undergraduates next?

SHOULD WE HAVE AN ONLINE VERSION OF OUR SERVICES?

I'm crowded in the doorway of a 4Cs conference room, standing by a fellow writing center type who carries a baby sleeping soundly in a sling. We're standing, but I take this discomfort as a good sign that we've selected a worthwhile panel from the myriad sessions swimming in the program. The topic is online writing centers and the panelists are eager to share their initial forays into this new territory. Mickey Harris and an enthusiastic techie talk about their project at Purdue, another person talks about her project in South Dakota that serves her geographically disparate students, and others share stories of their attempts, deemed successful but qualified by practical and theoretical limitations. I'm captivated by the experiment of delivering writing center services in a new way to new groups of students. I'm surprised at the baby sleeping soundly through the buzz of possibility growing in side conversations, how-to questions, and excitement. Looks like fun, I think. I wonder if we could do this at Carolina.

I come home, read up, and decide the current reservations about online services might be removed if someone could do something beyond an e-mail paper exchange. I imagine an online service that collects the context that a piece of writing grows out of—details about the writer, the assignment, the writer's concerns, history, expectations—and sends it along with the draft of an assignment. I read about people doing something like this in a Multi-Object Oriented (MOO) or Multi-User Shared Habitat (MUSH), but those environments seem complex and beyond my current techiness. Besides, I want something that uses technology to do something new, not replicate what happens in our face-to-face sessions. Asyncronicity, a newly acquired word in my vocabulary, sounds promising.

As far as I can tell, the kind of online service I imagine doesn't yet exist and a haphazard survey of existing software suggests that what we'd want, we'd need to build from scratch. Too expensive. Out of reach, I assume. Then, a casual conversation with a techie grad student alerts me to software that we might twist into what we need—a system in which students can submit their drafts and descriptions of their writing context over the web to a database that archives the exchange. The next day, the student stops by to share our chancellor's call for proposals for "technology grants." I stop work on the "nonpersonnel request" for the dean in which I eloquently, and with great futility, argue that a center that serves thousands of students each year ought to have a *bathroom*, and instead, concentrate on cranking out a technology proposal. The deadline is in seven days. Because the center has only ever had bare minimum funding for everything, I am shocked to receive the grant.

Next comes a two-year tech odyssey, blessed with tutors who catch fire as writing center theorists, techies, and site architects. We adopt the slogans "pedagogy drives our technology" and "It's an experiment" and hire a programmer to help us make it so. Together, we plot, imagine, struggle with designs and code, as well as learn html, server limitations, sys admin, who to call, and who we shouldn't. We write tutor training modules, documentation, and policies. We pilot test and revise. We find ourselves in the middle of a political tangle among the computer support people; we lose campus support for our software, find another rogue group to partner with, and most importantly, begin helping students online.

It works! (http://www.unc.edu/depts/wcweb) Students learn in our environment. They, unexpectedly, submit drafts well in advance of due dates, and often revise and resubmit for further feedback. We draw *new* clientele, students who never use the face-to-face service, and as we learn later in focus groups, probably never would have sought help otherwise. Tutors learn new ways to respond to drafts as they learn to compose as tutors rather than as conversationalists. We're excited that we've created a version of writing center work with new dimensions—one that honors reflection, independent decision making, introverts, and the stretch of time that often produces strong writing.

As this new avenue of service develops, a strange fact confronts us: We shouldn't tell anyone what we've done. Our face-to-face, appointment-governed services are already maxed out. We're turning people away. If we invite people to submit online, then we'll have more business than we can already handle. So we lay low. The English department knows about us. Then students in the history department find out through word of mouth, as do students in women's studies. The trickle of submissions becomes a steady stream, and we wonder what we've wrought. My pleas to the dean change from begging for a bathroom to the critical need for more tutors. Of course, a budget crunch comes. The pro-technology chancellor dies. We've doubled our daily workload in the writing center. Now what?

HOW DO I GET MORE HELP?

It didn't happen right off. In the beginning, I feel the luxury of having a whole job devoted to running a writing center. I recognize the value of that setup, know of many others who don't have that opportunity, and get to work building a strong center. It's soon clear that although I can devote my full attention to the WC, I'm alone. No support or clerical staff answer the phone, file, or buy more Kleenex when we run out. Tutors quickly come and go and have a supportive, but temporary, interest in the development of the center. Higher administration is glad I'm doing a good job and assume all is well because they don't hear about problems. That summer we don't have money to hire tutors. I'm it and find myself tutoring 8 hours a day in a hot basement and about to lose my mind. I have grand plans and begin to launch some of them, but I have few stakeholders, few sounding boards, but most important, little time to do more than answer the ringing phone, greet students, troubleshoot tutoring sessions, and problem solve adminstrivia.

Nevertheless, we see increasing numbers of students. Stabilizing our hours and training our staff pays off. In a couple years, demand for appointments exceeds the capacity of our staff. I've made documenting how many students we see a priority, so I have the statistics to prove our success and mounting need for more service. My annual report becomes a recurring gong tolling our need for more permanent staff to support the growing demand for writing assistance, workshops, collaborative projects, and administration of our growing center. I document ideas for a high school writing project in the community, an undergraduate peer tutoring program, English as a second language (ESL) programs, campus workshops, writing group support—you name it.

Meanwhile, the wonderful and capable graduate student staff begins to hang around from year to year. They team with me to manage and develop projects in the center. I invite them to participate in the running of the center and give them latitude and opportunities to fill in the obvious and not-so-obvious needs. Everyone takes turns sitting at the desk, and we hire some work study students to join in with clerical support. One graduate student creates a database to track our stats; another one organizes the library. One designs our Web site and others join in the larger project of building our OWL. Another one starts writing handouts and gets others to join in that project. Somebody formats them. We work together to design a training week for the incoming tutors. One of them suggests we add a session at the ropes course to our week. We do. I go on maternity leave. The tutors keep things running beautifully and only call when the mysteries of the office seem crucial. We mop when it rains, and we all learn who to call when the air conditioning breaks or there are housekeeping needs. We all tutor. We all lead workshops. We have weekly staff meetings. We figure out what to do next. We work as a collaborative community of teachers and together decide what the WC should be.

Through requests for workshops from faculty and collaborations with the Center for Teaching and Learning and technology folks on campus, I get wind of internal monies available for various projects. I write proposals requesting funding for an assistant director. I get turned down. I look into raising private funds through the development office that seems uninterested in funding salaried positions. I write more proposals and get turned down again. I become increasingly concerned that the institutional knowledge of this great place the graduate students and I have built rests squarely with me. The university increasingly relies on the WC, especially after we launch our OWL. Then one day, five years after my initial drafting of a proposal for more help, I hear from a friend about some monies through the provost's office that might be construed to be related to our WC work. I dredge up the file from my hard drive, rework it a bit, and send off another proposal. This one takes! I have approval to hire a full-time assistant director! I'm stunned.

HOW DO WE MANAGE WITH THESE BUDGET CUTS?

Laura Merrill, the last candidate in our search for an assistant director is in my office chatting, midway in her day-long interview. The phone rings and my colleague upstairs in the learning center quips, "Read your e-mail?" I explain I'm midinterview. She repeats, "Read your e-mail." Risking rudeness, I quickly do and see a message from the dean instructing us, essentially, that all monies have been frozen and all access to all accounts has been cut off. The legislature has recalled any monies in any state accounts to support the state budget crisis. We can't buy a pencil if we want to from now (May 7) until July 1. The status of funding at that point will be reviewed, but significant permanent cuts should be expected. I quickly shuffle through the ethics of filling in Laura, waiting in confusion in the chair across from me. I brief her, and she asks, "Is this interview over? Does this job still exist?" "Yes," I reply with no certainty that it does, but with full determination that we must make this hire or we might not have the opportunity for years to come.

Through a bit of luck and good timing, we can hire Laura, but we can't do much else. Our tutoring budget is cut so our staffing levels drop to what they were six years prior when we had half as many students. A 10% permanent cut comes, which is a lot of money when our existing operating budget is tiny to begin. The next year another 5% cut comes and we eliminate tutors in the summer. State employees are on their fourth year without any raise. We get bonus vacation days instead. This year we sustain a 2% cut. Our statistic tracker counted one thousand students turned away last fall due to limits in appointments. Given what I read on WCenter, I feel grateful to be open and wonder what lies ahead.

WHAT SHOULD WE DO NEXT?

Whereas budget woes color all of our thinking these days, they don't prevent us from thinking about the shape and potential of the WC of the future. New ideas keep me going, keep me reading writing center literature, attending conferences, and trying out new projects on our campus and in our community. So I put my budget blinders on and think first: "What do we want to do? What do we need to do? What could we try to do at this point in time?" For us here, that means we have lots of projects in the works. We want to revamp our online system—this time building something scalable that we might share with other North Carolina state schools. We're going to have to move to new spaces and problem solve all that will come from those challenges and opportunities. A local high school has asked us to help them start a writing center, and we'd like to help them. We may propose an undergraduate peer tutoring project to help us meet the ever-expanding demand for tutoring. I've joined several campus committees to learn more about the administration surrounding problem areas such as ESL support in the Writing Center and studies are growing from that work. We may explore funding from the graduate school. The development office has placed us on their top ten student wish list for support. The Executive Service Corp, a nonprofit group has offered to help us design a "strategic plan" to assist us in long-term planning. We're considering forming a faculty advisory board. There's lots to do ... where should we start?

These anecdotes don't have endings; these questions don't have firm conclusions. For me directing a writing center is a building process. Each director has different pieces and half-finished pictures, the process of finding the pieces, making them fit together, and figuring out what the building is going to look like is ongoing, challenging, and often uncertain. But structures emerge that fit into the landscape and support student writers in all kinds of ways.

❧ 38 ❧

Working with Faculty Consultants in the Writing Center: Three Guidelines and a Case History

Michael A. Pemberton
Georgia Southern University

It is probably safe to say that most writing centers in the United States, particularly at the college level, are staffed by undergraduate peer-tutors. Because these tutors are usually teaching novices, directors will spend significant amounts of time introducing them to the basics of writing instruction in a writing center setting. This means showing them how to identify textual problems in a variety of genres, how to explain those problems to students in nonthreatening and nondirective ways, and how to prioritize writing problems and manage time effectively during half-hour or hour-long conferences. Tutors' teaching skills will often improve dramatically over time, and directors—through regular staff meetings, assigned readings, short writing tasks, direct and indirect supervision—can shape these students into effective writing center tutors and perhaps even future teachers.

Directors seeking advice about how to create a tutoring course for undergraduates set up a writing fellows program, run regular staff meetings, or interview prospective tutors for writing center positions, will find a host of material readily available. The literature of undergraduate tutor training is well established, and there are any number of models and published guides from which directors can draw. A representative sampling would include *The Writing Center Resource Manual* (Silk), *Writing Centers in Context* (Kinkead and Harris), *Tutoring Writing* (McAndrew and Reigstad), *A Tutor's Guide* (Rafoth), *The Allyn and Bacon Guide to Peer Tutoring* (Gillespie and Lerner), and "Undergraduate Staffing in the Writing Center" (Cobb and Elledge).

There is somewhat less information available about how to train and supervise faculty members who work in writing centers, whether they happen to be volunteering their time or are assigned there as a part of their teaching duties. A handful of articles discuss the writing center's contribution to faculty training as part of a WAC program (e.g., Law; Johnston and Speck; Haviland et al.), some others describe "faculty fellow" programs in the center (Leahy), and a few more offer short accounts by faculty members who have volunteered their services for short periods of time (Chin-Shong). None of these pieces, unfortunately, address the administrative issues that pertain to working with faculty in any depth, even though faculty tutors can often present unique administrative challenges for writing center directors. Whereas it is likely that undergraduate peer-tutors will continue to dominate the ranks of writing center staffs for the foreseeable future, it is certainly possible—perhaps even probable—that directors will eventually find themselves in charge of faculty as one component of their administrative duties.

For this reason, I would like to offer a brief set of guidelines for directors who work with faculty consultants presently or who may be looking to add faculty consultants in the future. These guidelines are drawn largely from my own experiences at Georgia Southern University (GSU; where faculty members from the department of Writing and Linguistics make up the bulk of the writing center staff), and these experiences, I hope, will provide some useful illustrations of what can happen if the guidelines either are—or in my case, are not—followed. As I came to discover quickly at Georgia Southern, faculty consultants are very different from student tutors; they approach writing center work with quite different histories and from strikingly different perspectives. If writing center directors wish to work productively and effectively with faculty, then they will need to shape their administrative approaches in ways that attend to, and respect, these differences.

GUIDELINE 1: LEARN ABOUT AND BE SENSITIVE TO INSTITUTIONAL HISTORIES—*CONTEXT IS EVERYTHING*

All writing centers are different, and the circumstances under which faculty come to writing centers will likely reflect a wide range of variables:

- Some faculty might be assigned to writing centers by their department chairs as part of their normal teaching load
- Some faculty might have full-time writing center appointments in nontenure line positions
- Some faculty might be "freeway fliers" for whom a writing center gig is just one stop on a regular route of part-time work
- Some faculty might merely volunteer their services for an hour or two a week
- Some faculty might be from disciplines other than English
- Some faculty might be assigned to the writing center as a sign of "favor" or "disfavor" by departmental administrators

Whichever set of circumstances happens to be true for a particular institution, directors must learn the specific context and the idiosyncratic history leading to that configuration. If faculty are assigned to the writing center in place of teaching a course, then directors must ask how and why that arrangement came about. The answers to those questions can affect how directors delegate job responsibilities and evaluate personnel, and they can also help prevent misunderstandings about exactly what a writing center assignment entails. If the faculty are part-timers who teach a few hours a day in the writing center and then drive to two or three other local colleges each day to pick up an extra couple of courses, directors need to figure out whose decision it was to staff the center that way and how faculty tutors view that employment policy. They shouldn't automatically assume the situation is worrisome (or beneficial) without getting the full picture.[1] If the writing center faculty are volunteers, then directors must learn what caused them to volunteer: altruism? WAC initiatives? professional development? departmental encouragement? upcoming tenure reviews? Only by understanding the "rewards" that these faculty members hope to achieve through their efforts will it be possible to work with them productively, in ways that are perceived by both the faculty member and the director as beneficial. My own experiences at Georgia Southern have taught me these lessons quite clearly.

Case Study: Institutional History and the GSU Writing Center

Given what I have learned about my department and its faculty over the five years I've been director of the writing center, I now realize that several of the administrative decisions I made early on were misguided. Had I understood then what I know now about our departmental history, my initial years as writing center director might have been a bit less rocky. Unfortunately, although perhaps unavoidably, I learned this history in a piecemeal fashion over the course of several years, through brief snippets of conversation in people's offices or over lunch. If I had an inkling of how important that history was to the writing center and my place within it, I might have been a bit more assiduous in seeking out the critical details.

Although it would take far too long to detail the complete history of the GSU writing and linguistics department, a free-standing writing program that emerged from a hostile "divorce" from a literature-centered English and philosophy department in the fall 1997,[2] four aspects of this history are important to an understanding of why faculty were assigned to the writing center in the first place and how, despite my ignorance of this history, I managed—to put it quite bluntly—to piss them off:

> 1. *The split from English was unequal.* Although internal friction caused the GSU English department to split into two separate departments, "Literature and Philosophy" and "Writing and Linguistics," the division was anything but even. Literature and Philosophy (with about twenty faculty) kept the English major; Writing and Linguistics (with more than sixty faculty) had no major—only a minor—and was therefore viewed, by many, as essentially a

---

[1] A case in point: A number of years ago I interviewed to become the director of a writing center at an institution with about eight to ten part-time staffers, several of whom taught at other colleges to cobble together a reasonable living. During my meeting with these staffers, I asked, "Don't you all feel rather exploited?" They looked uneasily at one another, a couple of them muttered, "Yes, a little," and that was apparently the end of the discussion. I said something about how, if I were hired, I would try to turn some of these part-time positions into full-time ones. I didn't get the job. I learned later that several of the part-timers, notably those who had been in their positions for ten years or more, only wanted part-time work and saw my plans to change the *status quo* as a threat.

[2] For a detailed history of this split and its aftermath, see Eleanor Agnew and Phyllis Surrency Dallas's "Internal Friction in a New Independent Department of Writing and What the External Conflict Resolution Consultants Recommended."

service department (Agnew and Dallas 42).[3] This perception was exacerbated by the single criterion that was used to reallocate faculty during the split: Only those with PhDs in English literature in tenure track lines were "allowed" to remain in Literature/Philosophy. PhDs with an interest in composition (*very* few in number) and those with only master's degrees, regardless of background, training, or interest, were moved into the new Writing/Linguistics (W&L) department. This shuffling, as might be expected, caused significant tension and resentment among members of the new department. Faculty with only master's degrees felt abused and devalued, the lack of a major undermined the department's credibility, and the heavy burden of first-year composition courses (taught almost entirely by W&L faculty) not only sapped everyone's energy, but also reinforced the department's essential service function.

2. *First-year composition (FYC) was guaranteed to all students.* Until very recently, Georgia Southern had a long-standing policy in place guaranteeing that all students who *wanted* a first-year composition (FYC) course would be able to *take* one, regardless of when they registered. In effect, this meant that W&L was almost completely at the mercy of unpredictable student enrollment patterns and last minute requests for FYC courses. If an FYC section was needed and an upper division writing course (one of the few) was marginally enrolled, then a new FYC section would bump the other from the schedule. Faculty soon began to realize that their teaching schedules were probably going to be filled with nothing but first-year writing courses for the foreseeable future.

3. *Quarter to semester conversion increased teaching loads.* At more or less the same time that the departmental division was taking place, the university as a whole was undergoing a major curricular shift from a ten-week quarters to fifteen-week semesters. The impetus for this change was a desire to align GSU's schedule with other campuses in the state university system and achieve more uniform transfer equivalence, but the result was a dramatic reconfiguration of course loads and contact hours campus wide, nowhere more strongly felt than in W&L. Under the quarter system, the two required FYC courses had met five days a week, and three courses per term comprised a full teaching load for faculty. Under the semester system, however, English 1101 and English 1102 courses were to be three-hour courses (in order to align with similar courses elsewhere in the university system), and the standard teaching load for W&L faculty was to be four courses per term. Administrators, by and large, saw the increase in course load as inconsequential because the total number of contact hours with students would remain the same over the length of the entire semester. They were resistant (or oblivious) to the fact that adding one more FYC course to people's schedules meant twenty-four additional students each term who would be writing four to five additional papers apiece, with all the conferences, reading, reviewing, advising, and grading that would entail. Departmental minutes from this period reflect a great deal of anger and frustration about the increased workload.

4. *The writing center became a way to provide some relief to overburdened faculty.* In order to relieve some of the overwhelming demands on faculty who were being asked to teach a 4-4 load, nearly all of which was FYC, department chair Dr. Larry Burton and then-dean Dr.

---

[3]In February 2004, the Board of Regents of the State University System of Georgia officially approved the undergraduate major in Writing and Linguistics.

Roosevelt Newson decided that the writing center would be a kind of safety valve. In one semester each year, faculty could receive "reassigned time" in the writing center in place of a three-hour course. In effect, this would reduce faculty members' teaching loads to 4–3 or 3–4, with three hours in the writing center each week during the "off" semester. This wasn't an ideal solution by any means, but it helped a little.

Now enter a new director of the writing center (me) who was completely unaware of this background and institutional history.

What I saw was a departmental arrangement that assigned faculty to the writing center for the equivalent of a three-hour course. Well, I thought, because "three-hour" lecture/discussion courses typically included an expectation that faculty members would spend many more actual work hours preparing lectures, doing readings, grading papers, holding conferences, and so on, then it was reasonable for me to expect faculty to do more than just put in three hours of work physically meeting with students in the writing center. In fact, I rationalized, if a four course load was the equivalent of a forty-hour work week, then I could expect ten hours of work per week per faculty member in the writing center. I envisioned any number of projects they could work on, mostly in the area of materials development and publicity, and because these projects would only require an additional hour or two of effort from faculty each week, I felt I would be seen as quite generous in terms of what I *could* be asking of them.

Needless to say, my first efforts to assign additional work—asking each faculty member to provide a rhetorical handout for inclusion in the writing center's files—was met with some reluctance. Most of them acquiesced grudgingly, but about one third of those who signed up to provide a handout that first term never followed through. One longtime member of the department (who has since retired) even complained to the chair about my "arrogance" in asking senior faculty to perform such duties. Sometime later, the chair asked me for copies of every e-mail message I'd sent to writing center faculty during the course of the year so he could see for himself what sort of tone I had been adopting.[4]

It bears repeating, I think, to note that many of the rough spots I experienced during my first couple of years as writing center director at GSU were due primarily to my lack of knowledge about the larger context in which I was working. Had I been more aware of the underlying resentment about the split from English, the stultifying drudgery endured by faculty with nothing but FYC to teach all year long, the burden of a 4-4 load under those conditions, and the role of the writing center as a poultice for these ills, I wouldn't have been so quick to lay on extra tasks. Context was, indeed, everything.

GUIDELINE 2: CLARIFY LINES OF AUTHORITY— *EXPLICITNESS IS EVERYTHING*

The issue of authority becomes particularly tricky when writing center directors are asked to supervise faculty. Not only is overseeing faculty difficult in and of itself, a task frequently compared to "herding cats" (Lohmann 3), but directors may find that the sometimes precarious nature of their administrative positions will make the job even more difficult to navigate:

---

[4]The tone was, of course, completely professional and innocuous, which the chair had expected would be the case.

- The director's position may be classified as "administrative staff" rather than faculty.
- Directors may be untenured, and therefore their continued employment may hinge on maintaining the good will of faculty (some of whom may work in the center) as well as administrators (who may be influenced by those faculty).
- Directors may be junior to faculty they are asked to supervise.
- Directors may have no authority to decide which faculty are assigned to the writing center.
- Directors may have no authority to discipline or terminate faculty whose work is substandard.
- The director's supervisory obligations regarding the faculty who work there (including how faculty are evaluated and how those evaluations are used) may be unclear.
- Reporting lines may be muddled or conflicted.

Although directors' administrative authority over undergraduate tutors is usually pretty clear—they will almost always be empowered to hire, train, evaluate, and terminate tutors when necessary—the situation may be far less clear with faculty consultants. Faculty will not typically have their entire teaching load in the writing center; more often, the center will be only one component of their academic lives, and they will be prone, accordingly, to see department heads or division chairs as their immediate supervisors, not writing center directors. Directors who hold "administrative staff" rather than academic positions (approximately 33% according to a survey conducted by the Writing Centers Research Project)[5] may find their ability to exert authority over faculty even more difficult, particularly if some faculty are resolved to be uncooperative and foresee no consequences for their recalcitrance.

Writing center directors must also contend with a long history of job vulnerability, a history borne out by personal anecdotes, experiences, narratives on WCenter, and occasional journal articles. Much of this vulnerability is due to the budgetary troubles endemic to educational institutions and the misguided perception among some administrators that writing centers are ancillary to the institution's central mission (see, e.g., Amato; Sherwood), but part may also be due to interpersonal and intradepartmental frictions that arise when a director's vision for the writing center and its pedagogical goals conflict with those held by others.[6] When such conflicts are isolated and specific, such as when a classroom instructor is disturbed by the presence of comma splices in a student's paper even after a visit to the writing center, they can usually be handled amicably. But when the conflicts are deeply rooted in contending teaching philosophies, such as when a faculty member persists in focusing on grammar and nothing but grammar in writing center conferences, then directors will have to decide not only how to use the authority of their position but what the consequences will be for doing so. This decision can be especially troublesome for directors who are untenured assistant professors (about 13% of the

---

[5]This finding is little different from a similar survey conducted by Dave Healy in 1994 and reported in the spring 1995 issue of *Writing Program Administration*. Thirty-one percent of the directors who responded to Healy's survey said they were in nonfaculty lines (30).

[6]Examples of these conflicts—epistemological as well as pedagogical—can sometimes emerge in the context of a writing center with a strong WAC component. Faculty from disciplines other than Composition can hold varying and quite divergent views about what the writing center should be doing with their students, and those differences can emerge even more strongly if one of those faculty members is volunteering time in the center.

total in 2000–2001 according to the WCRP) with a strong interest in demonstrating collegiality and not making waves.

The only way for directors to head off potential problems in this regard is to clarify lines of authority as quickly as possible. *Explicitness is everything.* Directors should meet with their administrative superior (who may be a department head, dean, or Vice President for Academic Affairs [VPAA]) or their advisory boards and craft a written document that spells out exactly what authority they have over the faculty they supervise and under what circumstances that authority can and should be employed. Reporting lines for faculty should be described carefully and criteria for evaluation procedures regarding their work in the writing center should be specified in detail. Faculty who tutor in the center should be made aware of these policies well in advance, and whenever possible, they should be given an opportunity to participate actively in their own evaluation process.

As with Guideline 1, it will pay for directors to be politically savvy as they reflect on the means by which they choose to exercise their authority, particularly when it comes to assigning duties and making evaluations. I have found in my own experience, for instance, that it's better to use a light hand when asking for extra work or evaluating my colleagues' performance in the writing center. Others may find this a useful and survival-enhancing strategy as well.

Case History: Supervising Faculty in the GSU Writing Center

When I asked faculty members to create handouts for the writing center as a part of their assignment there, I was surprised by their disgruntled reactions. Although I knew (from my own students) that additional work assignments are never greeted with enthusiasm, I couldn't help feeling a certain degree of annoyance over some people's unwillingness to participate in the writing center's mission even to that small extent. I had even told them that they could take a handout they had already created for their own students and adapt it for the writing center's use. Surely that couldn't be considered an oppressive amount of work!

For some, apparently, it was. Although most of the faculty provided me with the handouts I asked for fairly quickly and in generally good spirits, as I noted earlier, about one third neglected to produce the handout they had promised, and a few chose neither to sign up for a handout topic nor discuss an alternative project with me. My first semester on the job, and already a challenge to my authority!

At the time, because I was unaware of the department's history and the writing center's role in a larger institutional context, I could not fathom why such a small request was met with such negativity. Whatever the reason, however, I knew I had to do something about it. Several options presented themselves: (a) I could be an administrative harridan and nag the slackers incessantly, (b) I could send gentle reminders with reasonable deadlines for completing the work, (c) I could ignore the problem and just be grateful for the people who did the work without complaint, or (d) I could just wait to see what happened and then tell the department chair at the end of the semester which faculty had completed their assignments and which had failed to do so.

None of these options were particularly attractive. As an untenured faculty member, I didn't want to breed a lot of animosity by pursuing the first option, but simply ignoring the problem didn't seem like the best approach either. I didn't want the good, supportive souls to feel they were shouldering an unfair proportion of writing center work when others were just refusing to do what was asked of them without any apparent consequences. Option four, reporting to my department head at the end of the semester, was a possibility, but it was not one that was likely to earn me many friends in the department. I didn't want to be seen as a tattletale or professional assassin by my colleagues, and I didn't want the chair to get the perception that I couldn't handle minor administrative difficulties on my own. Eventually, I settled on the third option—gentle, generic reminders sent periodically to the entire writing center staff via e-mail, letting them know I expected everyone to contribute a handout or complete some other project by the semester's end. This strategy garnered a few more submissions, but distressingly, several faculty still chose to ignore both my original request and my reminders.

This forced the question. What, if anything, should I do about these obstinate faculty? I must admit, I was reluctant to pursue the most obvious route and talk to each of them individually. Because I was new to the department and didn't know many of them well, I had some misgivings about confronting them directly. It hardly seemed a politic way to open what, for some, would be my first extended conversation with them.

But I had to do something that would confirm my authority over these faculty in relation to their writing center assignment. I was their supervisor, wasn't I?

Well, strictly speaking, I was, but no document in any file anywhere actually described how that "authority" was constituted. The more I investigated and the more people I talked to, including my department chair, the more I came to realize that no one had ever bothered to delineate exactly what a "writing center assignment" would consist of other than "one to three hours of reassigned time." No description of specific job duties or responsibilities for faculty had ever been written; no reporting lines had ever been specified; no specifics for supervision or evaluation of faculty in the center had ever been decided on. In the absence of explicit guidelines, then, people felt free to create their own interpretation of the job, the duties, the time obligation, and my place in the administrative scheme of things. In other words, I had no explicit, documented authority, only implicit authority by virtue of my administrative title. Once I discovered this, I knew immediately what my next step had to be.

Over the course of the next year, with the advice and guidance of the department's writing center committee, I crafted a "job description" for faculty assignments to the writing center. Included in this description was the following statement:

> An assignment to the writing center is a teaching assignment with an expectation that faculty members will participate in some writing center activities beyond the literal number of hours (1 to 4) they are expected to consult with students in the UWC itself. The time devoted to such activities will relate to the consultant's assigned time to the UWC. Faculty with appointments of three hours a week are expected to do more than faculty with one hour a week assignments. The exact nature and number of these activities will be decided upon in collaboration with the director and may include such things as outreach, mentoring, materials development, web design and/or attendance at writing center workshops.

This statement served multiple political purposes. For one thing, it reassured other administrators—department chairs, the deans of GSU's seven colleges, and the provost—that a writing center assignment given to Writing and Linguistics faculty was not a "freebie" course but a significant part of their teaching loads. Second, it made explicit my authority to assign work to faculty beyond the literal number of contact hours they had with students in the center. Third, in conjunction with the general list of writing center duties specified earlier in the same document (consulting with students, sharing routine office duties, etc.), it provided me with a clear set of criteria I could use to measure and evaluate faculty performance.

To date, however, I have chosen not to pursue formal faculty evaluations. As one faculty member put it, "I've never worked at an institution that evaluated faculty more often and in so many different ways than this one." I can't help but be sympathetic, and when it comes right down to it, I think that the students who visit the center and work directly with faculty on a daily basis are far better situated to evaluate them than I am. Therefore, we use student evaluation forms, routinely collected at the end of each conference session, as our evaluative instruments. Because students' comments on the evaluation forms tend to be strongly positive, faculty are generally pleased to receive them and quite comfortable having them sent to their department chair. I can always take a more direct evaluative role, if necessary, but for now the system seems to work pretty well.

GUIDELINE 3: THINK CAREFULLY ABOUT HOW FACULTY SHOULD BE TRAINED—*ATTITUDE IS EVERYTHING*

Lastly, writing center directors should exercise some care when thinking about how to train faculty for work in the writing center. Unlike undergraduates, faculty will often have many years of teaching experience under their belts, and some faculty members may, in fact, have spent a significant portion of their academic careers teaching writing. Some of them may even have made a habit of conferencing with their students regularly about assigned papers and be familiar with some of the basics of working one-on-one. Such being the case, many faculty may not feel they need additional training to work with students in the writing center, and they may resent a director who insists that they receive it.

This resistance is completely understandable and directors should be prepared when it appears. Just remember, attitude is everything. Faculty members have worked long and hard to get to where they are. They've developed professional expertise, earned the respect of their peers, and become—many of them—excellent classroom teachers. Directors should treat these faculty as valuable resources with important things to say and contributions to make. In other words, directors should stay true to their principles, provide the training they think is necessary, but don't be arrogant, don't be condescending, and don't be dictatorial. They should be willing to negotiate, and be patient. Change doesn't happen overnight. Writing across the curriculum (WAC) programs have long been aware that single-minded zealotry, "preaching the gospel of WAC," is one of the quickest ways to foment revolt in faculty workshops. The same lesson holds true for writing centers.

Different faculty will require different levels and types of training, of course. A mathematician might need to learn the vocabulary of basic sentence grammar; a sociologist might be a skilled editor but need help learning how to discuss texts rhetorically. Some of these matters can be addressed in large-scale orientation meetings, and others might best be handled on an individual, case-by-case basis. All faculty, however, will need training to help them recognize the critical ways in which the writing center is different from the classroom. These include what I call the "3-D's" of writing center work:

- *Directivity*: Although instructors may be textually directive in office hour conferences with their own students (making changes, rewriting passages, telling students exactly how to proceed), that pedagogical approach is almost always inappropriate in the writing center.

- *Discourse Knowledge*: Faculty will be working with students in disciplines outside their own areas of expertise. They should familiarize themselves with the rhetorical conventions of other fields and not automatically apply their own disciplinary conventions to unfamiliar genres or texts.

- *Development*: Faculty may see a particular student only once in the writing center. They will not usually have the opportunity to work with the student over an extended period of time or trace the student's progress. Their goals for each conference, then, will need to be modest and focused on the paper in front of them.

Individual directors will need to decide, based on institutional needs and faculty schedules, whether these issues would be better addressed in a series of regular, full-scale meetings or somewhat less frequent specialized workshops. But, whatever the case, ongoing faculty training and development will be critically important to the writing center's success. Besides preparing faculty for the demands of writing center work, it will provide them with a sense of community and unique opportunities to talk about teaching practices with their colleagues. Ideally, faculty will grow to enjoy these training sessions and see them as beneficial both personally and professionally.

For a long time, however, I wondered whether such a lofty goal could ever be achieved at Georgia Southern.

Case History: Training Faculty in the GSU Writing Center

The faculty who staffed the writing center at GSU were—and are—a bit of a mixed bag. At the time I stepped into the director's position, a few faculty in Writing and Linguistics had PhDs, but most faculty were teaching with master's degrees, and nearly everyone's degree was in literature.[7] Some faculty were full-time tenure track, some were permanent full-time nontenure track, some were full-time temporary, and some, as I mentioned earlier, had appointments that were split between two separate departments. A number of the faculty with master's degrees were also tenured, not unusual at the time (although GSU is now no longer tenuring faculty with nonterminal degrees).

I scheduled a full-day orientation meeting for the faculty and graduate students assigned to work in the center on the Thursday before the first week of classes. Everyone attended, and no one complained (other than a little grumbling about having to be there for a full day when they hadn't finished writing their syllabi yet). I went over policies and procedures, talked about my philosophy for the writing center, ran through some mock tutorials, and discussed some specialized discourse issues like English as a second language (ESL) and African American Vernacular English (AAVE). Overall, it was a successful meeting, and I felt that I had gotten off on

---

[7]The situation has changed rather dramatically since that time. Two rhetoric/composition PhDs were hired the year before I came, three (including myself) were hired the following year, and several more have joined the department subsequently. Nearly all of the MAs have now either completed or are in the process of completing doctoral degrees.

the right foot. They were smart, interested, experienced, and friendly. Things looked good for the future training sessions I had planned.

When I e-mailed a schedule of future "professional development meetings" to the faculty a few weeks later, I discovered that my honeymoon was apparently over. A few people wrote back quickly and said they planned to attend every session, but the rest of the responses—if they came at all—tended to be relatively terse notes saying which one of the several sessions I'd scheduled happened to fit in their calendars. It wasn't exactly the enthusiastic response I'd hoped for, but being new, I figured I'd go with the flow until I got a better sense of how things were eventually going to turn out.

The first two meetings, which included discussion of journal articles I'd selected and distributed in advance, went pretty well, I thought. The faculty members who attended seemed to enjoy talking about their work with students in the writing center, and judging by the highlighted passages and marginal notes I saw on their article copies, they'd read the pieces carefully and critically. I was impressed. But I was also disappointed by the low attendance, about ten or twelve people out of the thirty or so assigned to the writing center that semester. Intellectually, I knew that some people found it difficult to come to meetings on weekday afternoons; several were teaching classes at that time and others had family obligations that conflicted. But still, I couldn't help thinking there was something else, something brewing beneath the surface that was affecting the turnout: There was. It was a little thing, but it had an impact nonetheless.

While chatting informally with several faculty at the end of the semester, I learned that more than a few people had truly resented being asked to attend "professional development" meetings. They felt they were already professionals and had been "developing" for years. Who was I to tell them they had to go to my meetings in order to become better developed teachers? To them, the term *professional development* meant "retraining" at best, "remediation" at worst. It rankled, and it rankled all the more coming from someone with a PhD in rhetoric/composition who supervised, for the most part, people with master's in literature. Preexisting insecurities about departmental status, job security, and professional expertise were all exacerbated (albeit inadvertently) by my unfortunate choice of words to describe these gatherings.

In retrospect, this response was probably not something I could have anticipated. The self-evaluation form we complete every year for our department chair asks us to detail our "professional development activities" during the previous twelve months, and in that venue the term is not perceived to be pejorative or insulting. When I adopted the term to describe ongoing training sessions for the writing center, however, it was.

Once again, I turned to the departmental writing center committee and asked for their advice. I was determined to continue the workshops, and armed with the new description of a "writing center assignment" (from Guideline 2), I knew I could compel attendance if I had to. However, I didn't want to be too demanding of faculty time and goodwill (from Guideline 1), and I didn't want them to think I was being insulting or demeaning when I asked them to attend (from Guideline 3). Together, the committee and I crafted a new approach that we hoped would solve many of the problems and salve some of the hurt feelings as well:

- We modified the terminology: "Professional development sessions" became "writing center workshops."

- We set clear, but reasonable, requirements for attendance: Faculty assigned to the writing center had to attend at least one of the three workshops offered each semester, more if possible. Grad students had to attend a minimum of two.
- We opened the workshops to all: Instead of holding the workshops for just those faculty who were assigned to the writing center each term, I invited the entire department to participate. This approach, we hoped, would both increase attendance and change the perception that the workshops were merely an extra job duty.

I think that these changes, overall, have had a transformative effect on the faculty's perceptions of writing center training and on my perceptions of these sessions as well. In fact, it's difficult for me to think of these meetings as "training" in any conventional sense. They are, quite literally, collaborative workshops that remind me of my very best experiences in graduate school. We come together as colleagues after having read several current articles on topics of mutual interest, and we talk about theory, teaching practices, personal experiences in the writing center, and research on writing behaviors. We critique the essays we read, and we compare the findings of different investigators in different sites. We grow as teachers and academics, partly because of our intellectual engagement with scholarly texts, but more importantly, because of our ability to learn from each other in a nonthreatening environment where all voices are respected and all points of view can be expressed.

Working with faculty in the writing center has been, for me, a profoundly enriching experience. I've learned, and continue to learn, a great deal from them every day. They have stimulated my thinking and challenged me intellectually. They have broadened my academic horizons and taught me about new discourse forms and new approaches for working with students. Warm, appreciative encomiums from students fill our conference evaluation forms, and the center is so highly regarded that professors from every department on campus regularly invite us to give presentations about the center and its resources in their classrooms.

Even more gratifying, however, is my sense that faculty really enjoy working in the writing center, and not just because it gives them an occasional break from having to teach a fourth class once a year. Like those of us who have been doing this kind of work for much of our professional lives, they love the opportunity to sit down and work closely with a single student for an extended period of time and see some real progress. They like the variety of topics and texts that come into the center, often quite unlike the papers they assign or read in their own classes. And, best of all, I think, they are coming to see the writing center as a place where they, too, can learn and grow as scholars and as teachers.

It's a very nice space for me to be in now as a director, but it hasn't come easily, and I have certainly made my share of mistakes along the way. Thankfully, my faculty colleagues have been generous and forgiving, something for which I am profoundly grateful. I hope that others of you find yourselves in similar circumstances, but I also hope that the guidelines I've offered here will smooth the path a bit should you consider bringing faculty members into your writing centers for the first time. It's definitely worth the effort.

WORKS CITED

Agnew, Eleanor, and Phyllis Surrency Dallas. "Internal Friction in a New Independent Department of Writing and What the External Conflict Resolution Consultants Recommended." *A Field of Dreams: Independent Writing Programs and the Future of Composition Studies.* Ed. Peggy O'Neill, Angela Crow, and Larry W. Burton. Logan: Utah State UP, 2002. 38–49.

Amato, Katya. "Making Bricks without Straw: The Fate of One Writing Center." *Writing Lab Newsletter* 17.10 (1993): 4–7.

Chin-Shong, Edwin. "How Self-Definition Affects Tutoring: A Teacher Becomes a Tutor." *When Tutor Meets Student.* Ed. Martha Maxwel. 2nd ed. Ann Arbor: U of Michigan P, 2000. 27–29.

Cobb, Loretta, and Elaine Kilgore Elledge. "Undergraduate Staffing in the Writing Center." *Writing Centers: Theory and Administration.* Ed. Gary A. Olson. Urbana: NCTE, 1984. 123–31.

Gillespie, Paula, and Neal Lerner. *The Allyn and Bacon Guide to Peer Tutoring.* 2nd ed. Boston: Allyn and Bacon, 2004.

Haviland, Carol Peterson, Sherry Green, Barbara Kime Shields, and M. Todd Harper. "Neither Missionaries nor Colonists nor Handmaidens: What Writing Tutors Can Teach WAC Faculty about Inquiry." *Writing Centers and Writing Across the Curriculum Programs: Building Interdisciplinary Partnerships.* Eds. Robert W. Barnett and Jacob S Blumner. Westport, CT: Greenwood P, 1999. 45–57.

Healy, Dave. "Writing Center Directors: An Emerging Portrait of the Profession." *WPA: Writing Program Administration* 18.3 (1995): 26–43.

Johnston, Scott, and Bruce W. Speck. "The Writing Center as Ambassador Plenipotentiary in a Developing WAC Program." *Writing Centers and Writing Across the Curriculum Programs: Building Interdisciplinary Partnerships.* Ed. Robert W. Barnett and Jacob S Blumner. Westport, CT: Greenwood P, 1999. 13–31.

Kinkead, Joyce A., and Jeanette G. Harris, eds. *Writing Centers in Context: Twelve Case Studies.* Urbana: NCTE, 1993.

Law, Joe. "Serving Faculty and Writing Across the Curriculum." *The Writing Center Resource Manual.* Ed. Bobbie Bayliss Silk. 2nd ed. Emmitsburg, MD: NWCA Press, 2002. IV.4.1–4.10.

Leahy, Richard. "When a Writing Center Undertakes a Writing Fellows Program." *Writing Centers and Writing Across the Curriculum Programs: Building Interdisciplinary Partnerships.* Ed. Robert W. Barnett and Jacob S Blumner. Westport, CT: Greenwood P, 1999. 71–88.

Lohmann, Susanne. "Herding Cats, Moving Cemeteries, and Hauling Academic Trunks: Why Change Comes Hard to the University." *Annual Meeting of the Association of the Study of Higher Education*, Sacramento, CA, 2002. 9 June 2004 <http://www.usc.edu/dept/chepa/pdf/ASHE_lohmann.pdf>.

McAndrew, Donald A., and Thomas J. Reigstad. *Tutoring Writing: A Practical Guide for Conferences.* Portsmouth, NH: Heinemann-Boynton/Cook, 2001.

Rafoth, Ben, ed. *A Tutor's Guide: Helping Writers One to One.* Portsmouth, NH: Heinemann-Boynton/Cook, 2000.

Sherwood, Steve. "How to Survive the Hard Times." *Writing Lab Newsletter* 17.10 (1993): 4–8.

Silk, Bobbie Bayliss, ed. *The Writing Center Resource Manual.* 2nd ed. Emmitsburg, MD: NWCA Press, 2002.

Writing Centers Research Project. "Writing Centers Research Project Survey of Writing Centers, AY 2000–2001: Results" 9 June 2004 <http://www.wcrp.louisville.edu/survey2000-2001/surveyresults.html>.

❧ 39 ❦

Funding the Center Through a University Line

Evelyn Schreiber
George Washington University

T his chapter discusses a path to adequate funding of a writing center, based on experiences that led to stable funding for the center at George Washington University. I became director of an up-and-running writing center, funded by the English department and the dean of the College of Arts and Sciences. Every year my chair informed me that I had gone over budget, and we had to go begging to the dean for more funds. We called it the "rice bowl" method of funding. When the bowl was empty, we got in line for another handout. Thus, one of the first things I realized as director was that, in order for the writing center to attain proper status, prestige, excellence, and autonomy, an adequate funding structure needed to be in place. Because the writing center was underfunded by one third and we could not even cover the minimal salaries of tutors for the hours we were open, I concluded that in order for the writing center to serve the university in the best possible way, it must have stable funding as a line item in the university budget. Such permanent funding would prevent reliance on soft money (e.g., departmental funds, fellowships, grants, discretionary funds, faculty "loans" and external sources) and allow us to focus on our mission rather than our financial woes.[1] The following suggestions grow out of our successful efforts and hopefully can serve as guidelines to the funding process.

---

[1] In "What's Next for Writing Centers?" Joyce Kinkead and Jeanette Harris discussed the benefits of broad-based funding for the writing center but conclude that such funding is unstable. A line-item budget provides the most secure form of funding.

KNOWING HOW MUCH YOU NEED

Before approaching anyone about their budgets, writing center directors must know what the bottom line will be both for the optimal and minimal scenarios. By taking stock of the particular situation, directors will be able to judge and calculate their needs. It is important to take time with this first step as future needs have to be anticipated in addition to current ones. Consider the writing center's current mission and position; then anticipate program changes that might affect the budget. Be as all-inclusive as possible and think big rather than small.

It is fairly easy to calculate the amount it will take to run the writing center (and thus the inadequacy of current funding) if a writing center already exists. A bare-bones minimum budget has to fund tutor, assistant director, and director salaries plus overhead expenses. Salaries must be sufficient to cover an adequate number of tutors working a set number of hours at a given wage. For example, our writing center is open fifty-two hours per week, with a minimum of two tutors (and a maximum of six) working in any time slot (we offer fifty-minute sessions on the hour). Our numbers reflect our philosophy that no one should ever work alone. Thus, two tutors and a receptionist comprise our minimum coverage requirements. In addition, our primary space restricts us to six tables, resulting in a maximum of six tutors working at any one time. I also must factor in our wage structure, which pays different rates for new tutors, returning tutors, and graduate tutors. In addition to tutor salaries, I calculate the salaries for two assistant directors (graduate students) working a set number of hours per week, starting several weeks before our semester begins and working for several weeks after we close for the year.

To allow the tutors to focus on tutoring, a receptionist is needed to answer phones, make and confirm appointments, greet students, and be a presence so that no one ever works alone in the center. In lieu of a full-time staff position, we hire approximately five work study students in set shifts because work study funds for the receptionist duties provide an ideal way to cover this cost. In addition to salaries, overhead items include furniture, telephones, a copy machine, brochure and stationery printing, computers, paper, pencils, candy for open houses, staff meeting pizza, and other office supplies. Further, training costs (tape recorders, tapes, and travel to conferences) must go into a line-item budget. It is crucial to think of all the items needed before the budget is created because, once the budget is set, it will be difficult to go back and ask for more funds. (See Appendix A for a sample list of line items.) Finally, writing center directors should be familiar with the spending policy at their institutions. For example, I cannot transfer salary funds to cover other expenses, but my supply budget can be used to cover salaries if need be. Thus, I put the bulk of my budget into salaries. If lines are nontransferable, then salaries should be covered first and then revised each year according to spending trends.

Directors of new writing centers also need to take into consideration the hours the center will be open, how many tutors will be trained, whether or not credit or noncredit courses will be offered, and when the maximum number of tutors will be on board. If the number will increase incrementally as you get up and running, then project the budget outward. Also, design the center space to account for such items as furniture, computers, copier, and phones to avoid scrounging for desks and ending up with the "poor orphan" look. (Prior to our stable funding, we furnished the center with cast-off items we found around campus. A simple trip down the hall to the bathroom might result in a "new" front desk.) Our experiences with one abusive student taught us the necessity of having a proper check-in counter; it is best to operate like an office or department from the start. Funds that you earmark for start-up items can later be transferred to the salary column.[2]

GATHERING STATISTICS: AN IMPORTANT FIRST STEP

Compelling arguments for funding the writing center can be made only with persuasive statistics. Thus, firm documentation as to the central role of the writing center in both undergraduate and graduate education is crucial to the funding enterprise. We used several forms of data collection to argue for stable funding for the center, starting with a data sheet for every tutoring session. After our tutors work with students, they ask them to complete a data sheet (see Appendix B) that contains the information we use to create our annual report. To assess our population, we require students to list their year, school, professor, course number, first language, and topics covered in the session. We supplement this information with optional surveys (see Appendix C). Although completing the data sheet is mandatory, filling out the survey is not because we want to avoid as much onerous paperwork as possible in order to yield significant vital statistics. Therefore, crucial questions are included on the data sheet, and useful information goes on the survey. We alter the survey every other semester to generate new interest in student participation and to widen or alter our emphasis. The surveys reinforce the teaching and research component of our writing center. Also, we began to keep track of the numbers of students who could not get appointments during our peak times so as to underscore student need.[3]

Before composing data sheets or surveys, it is important to consider the audience. One question to ask, according to Neal Lerner, is "How do our writing centers contribute to the teaching and learning goals that our institutions hold dear?" (64). In other words, what are the issues that the central administration deems the most important? At George Washington University, the vice president for Academic Affairs and the board of directors put the level of student engagement and academic excellence at the forefront of university-wide concern. Our new writing program, which includes Writing in the Disciplines in addition to the First-year Writing Program, emerged from this concern. The fact that our writing center assists both mainstream and at-risk students with critical thinking and writing skills that engage them in academic pursuits and enable them to succeed outside of the university created a central role of the writing center in this campus initiative. Retention issues are also paramount, and the writing center research of Barnett, Wingate, Lerner, Simpson, Harris, Fischer, and Jolly attest to the role of the writing center with this concern. Specifically, retention results from student connectedness, intellectual stimulation, mastery of academic discourse, research interests, and professional development. Arguments for writing center funding contributed to these key issues. Perhaps Simpson summed it up best: "The kind of information that writing center directors will need to gather and distribute will not be as closely related to the philosophy and daily functioning of a writing center as it will be to larger, institutional issues" (52). Considering the

---

[2]Schwalm discussed scouting spaces/places on campus where services similar to those of the writing center occur (e.g., the honors program, the counseling center, disability support services) in order to merge resources for start-up purposes. Fischer also advocated a canvassing of departments and other campus initiatives to pool and assess resources and budgets.

[3]The executive director of Academic Planning and Assessment, in the office of the vice president for Academic Affairs, was happy to assist me in designing both our data sheet and our current survey.

big picture of university goals, and thus the university budget, solidifies the writing center's place in the greater whole. "Understanding and using appropriate budgeting language in the appropriate rhetorical situations" (Koster 156) facilitates communication with central administrators. Recruitment, faculty development, and issues of accountability also represent administrative concerns.

The data sheet and the surveys assist us in validating the need for a strong writing center for both graduate and undergraduate programs, and our annual report, complete with charts, graphs, and an interpretation of data, serves as a marketing piece. The statistics change very little from year to year, and this consistency forms the basis of our budget argument because the populations we serve are confirmed in each yearly report. The report itself runs approximately 25 pages, with an appendix of statistics adding another fifty or so, and my one-page executive summary uses bullet-points to highlight statistics of universal importance.[4] I send this summary to the executive vice president for Academic Affairs and the deans in advance of the report so that my message gets delivered. I don't expect a busy administrator to plow through my report (although the colorful charts and graphs are eye catching). With one third of our students enrolled in graduate programs, it is clear that we are not an undergraduate "remedial service" but rather a vibrant part of the educational experience at our university. Whereas two thirds of the students we work with are undergraduates, the majority come for help with courses outside of the first-year writing courses (only 20% of our visits) and the English department (only 6% of our visits). Thus, 74% of our visits are associated with classes in a variety of departments outside of the English department and the first-year writing courses. The fact that we work with students from sixty-seven to seventy-five departments (depending on the year) speaks to the universal need for the writing center. In addition, more than one half of our students come from programs outside of the College of Arts and Sciences, a fact that reinforces our argument for widespread funding of the center. Almost half of our visits are with nonnative speakers of English. Further, 13% come for help with writing projects unrelated to their courses, such as job applications and graduate school essays. As a result, the writing center assists with student career placement and academic advancement, a benefit to our students and the alumni network. Finally, the number of visits is up each year, which reinforces the trend of increasing usage. As the pie chart for AY 2002–03 in Appendix D indicates, after the College of Arts and Sciences (usage at 44%), the Elliott School of International Affairs (22%) and the School of Business and Public Management (15%) make up the bulk of our visits (other schools accounted for the remainder of visits with a range of 1% to 5% usage per school).

I began this section by stating that data collection was a necessary first step because without this data, we would be at a loss to argue the pivotal role that the writing center plays in the lives of students across the university.[5] Establishing the integral relationship between the writing center and all schools (both undergraduate and graduate) at the university sets up the foundation for funding the writing center via a line item in the university budget.

---

[4]The long appendix of our annual report catalogues our over three thousand visits by each student's year, school, instructor, course, first language, tutor, and focus of the session (e.g., analysis, audience, diction, discourse, documentation, drafting, evidence, grammar, organization, outlining, paragraphing, prewriting, punctuation, revising, spelling, structure, style, syntax, thesis, and tone).

[5]*Writing Center Research*, edited by Gillespie, Gillam, Brown, and Stay, serves as a wonderful resource for positioning the writing center as a site for academic and intellectual development as well as research. See in particular the selection by Harris, pp. 75–90.

BUILDING ALLIES

Getting funding from the academic vice president solved a funding problem that had plagued my chair and dean. Proper funding was not just my problem; it was our problem. By offering to be a problem solver, rather than a reminder of the problem itself, I became part of a vital administrative team. Working in cooperation with my dean and chair, I was able to become a colleague with agency to act. Thus, my first allies in my funding quest were my chair and my dean. Because our goal was to have all schools contribute to our funding, my next step was to address the concerns of the other deans. To this end, I introduced myself to them, met with faculty in various departments about their writing issues, and sent out letters to all faculty regarding our services. Through this networking, the attention of the top budget decision makers will be gained. I found committee work to be my most effective and personally rewarding form of networking. For example, I served for several years on our University Teaching Center Committee, where I met every month with colleagues from different schools to discuss pedagogical issues and plan brown bag and other presentation events for faculty. This collegial group led to friendships with department heads, deans, and an associate vice president, and these friendships helped me interact as a professional colleague. Subsequently, I was asked to join a faculty senate committee on admissions, recruitment, and retention, thereby gaining access to a wider circle of administrative contact and support. Granted, committee work is time consuming, but the rewards both personally and departmentally are well worth the commitment. Finally, I reinforced my status as a faculty colleague by publishing regularly (both on literary theory and writing center issues) and by receiving my promotion to associate professor.

CREATING A FUNDING SOURCE

The next step is to open lines of communication and negotiation to create the line-item funding, which has to come from funding already allocated to other departments or enterprises. In other words, someone has to give up funding in order for the writing center to receive it, and the value of doing so must be perceived as a priority. The popular saying, "follow the money," aptly describes the channels for creating writing center funding. Faculty report to department chairs, who report to deans, who report to vice presidents, who report to boards of directors. The impetus for the funding, which will be allocated from the top, must percolate through all interested parties. Thus, the funding discussion needs to include departmental and administrative segments. Statistics from reports and surveys, testimonials from faculty and students, and focus group reports equip the writing center director to address numerous venues, including faculty meetings, departmental and school retreats, council of deans meetings, and faculty senates. In short, all of the stakeholders must be part of the funding conversation. Spreading the funding among all interested constituents solidifies the financial commitment.[6]

To prepare for these various presentations, which ranged from flyers on how the writing center meets departmental needs to PowerPoint presentations on multiple issues, I began with data from my annual report. Next, I contacted all of our "market basket" schools to chart where we

---

[6]See Barnett's discussion regarding collaborating with faculty across the curriculum (199).

lagged, equaled, or excelled, with the goal of creating a writing center that would make George Washington University more attractive to prospective students. Building our writing center into a national model of excellence would bring prestige to our institution as well.

In addition to specific presentations, I built bridges with constituents around campus. I sent my annual report not only to all of the deans and my chair but to other interested parties as well, such as the chair of English as a Foreign Language (EFL). I worked for several years with the law center, first to accommodate the needs of its students and then to help set up a law center writing center. I also met with a committee of faculty members of the School of Business and Public Management who were charged with improving the writing of their students. After meeting with the chair of the Engineering department, the pre-law advisor, and the pre-med advisor, we conducted several workshops: one for graduate engineering students on writing a thesis, one for pre-law students regarding the law school application essay, and one for pre-medical students for medical school essays. At freshman orientation, I connected with parents by staffing an information table and having our brochures in orientation packets. Further, by speaking at graduate teaching assistantship (GTA) orientation, I informed the GTAs how the writing center could serve as a resource both for their own studies and for their students. The dean of Arts and Sciences asked me to participate in a seminar for new faculty, where we worked on assignment design and development of grading rubrics. Creating awareness of the pedagogical and research function of the writing center will position the director as an administrator of a vital organization for students and faculty. Those departments and schools that clearly benefit from writing center work will ultimately appreciate the need to contribute to its financial support.

CONCLUSIONS

As a result of these efforts, we not only restructured our budget and funding sources but the reporting line of the director as well. Our funding now comes from each school, according to usage (See Appendix D with pie chart). Also, as director, I have several reporting lines. I still report to the English department, as I have a faculty appointment, and I teach one course each semester. In addition, I now report to the vice president for Academic Affairs, with a marginal reporting line to the director of the Undergraduate Writing Program. These reporting lines keep the avenues of communication open and emphasize the pivotal role of the writing center in the university. The reporting line to the vice president for Academic Affairs allows me to discuss changes in our budgetary needs. For example, GWU has just instituted a new undergraduate writing program, with a new first-year writing course and two Writing in the Disciplines (WID) courses required for graduation. The faculty involved with this initiative, anticipating the addition of discipline-specific tutors and assistants to work with faculty, have expressed the need for increasing the writing center budget. Specifically, our new WID program will require discipline-specific tutors, ESL assistance, and staff to help with grammar issues. As a result, the writing center budget, interconnected with the university-wide program, will grow to meet the needs of this new program while maintaining its commitment to graduate and undergraduate students. We anticipate needing more tutors in addition to permanent administrative assistance to support this new program because our mission to serve graduate students and students outside of writing-intensive courses will remain the same.

Each institution will have different growth concerns to consider, including online writing centers, satellite writing centers, and EFL needs that may affect writing center staffing. The important thing is to anticipate these scenarios and to create channels for budget alterations. Although it may take several years to alter an existing budget or to create a new one because the paths of reallocation and approval require significant lead time, the end result is worth waiting for. As Molly Wingate noted, "Writing centers are terribly important places on campuses because they enhance and advance a culture of academic seriousness. Writing centers support the present academic culture; at their best, they model elements of what academic culture could be" (8). Knowing the worth of the writing center in the institution's big picture and articulating it in the right format to the right people provide the key to permanent funding.

WORKS CITED

Barnett, Robert. "Redefining Our Existence: An Argument for Short- and Long-Term Goals and Objectives." *The Allyn and Bacon Guide to Writing Center Theory and Practice*. Ed. Robert W. Barnett and Jacob S. Blumner. Boston: Allyn and Bacon, 2001. 194–201.

Fischer, Katherine M. "I'll Take Boardwalk for $400: The Bottom Line in Writing Center Budgets." *Writing Center Resource Manual*. Ed. Bobbie Bayliss Silk. 2nd ed. Emmitsburg, MD: NWCA Press, 2002. III.5.1–7.

Gillespie, Paula, Alice Gillam, Lady Falls Brown, and Byron Stay, eds. *Writing Center Research: Extending the Conversation*. Mahwah, NJ: Lawrence Erlbaum Associates, 2002.

Harris, Muriel. "Solutions and Trade-Offs in Writing Center Administration." *The Allyn and Bacon Guide to Writing Center Theory and Practice*. Ed. Robert W. Barnett and Jacob S. Blumner. Boston: Allyn and Bacon, 2001. 155–67.

___. "Writing Center Administration: Making Local, Institutional Knowledge in Our Writing Centers." *Writing Center Research*. Gillespie, Gillam, Brown, and Stay. 75–90.

Jolly, Peggy. "The Bottom-line." *Writing Center Theory and Administration*. Ed. Gary A. Olson. Urbana, IL: NCTE, 1984. 101–14.

Kinkead, Joyce and Harris, Jeanette. "What's Next for Writing Centers?" *The Writing Center Journal* 20.2 (Spring/Summer 2000): 23–24.

Koster, Josephine A. "Administration Across the Curriculum: Or Practicing What We Preach." *The Center Will Hold*. Ed. Michael A. Pemberton and Joyce Kinkead. Logan: Utah State UP, 2003. 151–65.

Lerner, Neal. "Writing Center Assessment: Searching for the 'Proof' of Our Effectiveness." *The Center Will Hold*. Ed. Michael A. Pemberton and Joyce Kinkead. Logan: Utah State UP, 2003. 58–73.

Schwalm, David E. "*E Pluribus Unum*: An Administrator Rounds Up Mavericks and Money." *Writing Center Perspectives*. Eds. Byron L. Stay, Christina Murphy, and Eric H. Hobson. Emmitsburg, MD: NWCA Press, 1995. 53–62.

Simpson, Jeanne. "Perceptions, Realities, and Possibilities: Central Administration and Writing Centers." *Writing Center Perspectives*. Eds. Byron L. Stay, Christina Murphy, and Eric H. Hobson. Emmitsburg, MD: NWCA Press, 1995. 48–52.

Wingate, Molly. "Writing Centers as Sites of Academic Culture." *The Writing Center Journal* 21.2 (Spring/Summer 2001): 7–20.

Appendix A: Sample Budget Line Items

Salary Faculty Regular Full Time (Director)

Federal Work Study Wages (Receptionists)
Student Wage Nonfederal Work Study (Assistant Directors, Graduate Tutors, and Undergraduate Tutors)

Fringe Benefits Allocation

Total Compensation (Sum of the Above)

Noncapitalized computing equipment
Noncapitalized Office Furniture
Special Events/Business Relations
Employee Special Activity
Miscellaneous Office Expense
U.S. Airfare Expense
U.S. Business Meals
U.S. Local Transportation
U.S. Other Travel and Related Expense
Conference/Seminar/Research/Training Expense
Office Supplies
Miscellaneous Supplies
Advertising
Alterations/Improvement Expense
Miscellaneous Services
Printing and Graphics
Phones
Copier

Total Other Operating Expenses (Sum of the Above)

Appendix B: Sample Data Sheet

The Writing Center
Rome Hall 550
801 22nd Street, NW
Washington, DC
202-994-3765

Student Name:_____ Date:____/____/____
          (First)   (Last)

First Language:_____ Time: (In)____ (Out)____ (Total)____

___Fro ___Sop ___Jun ___Sen ___Gra ___All

School (Circle One): CCAS SBPM ESIA SMPA SEHD SEAS
                    SMHS GSPM NLC DCE SPHHS

Instructor Name:_____

Department and Course #:_____

Work Completed (please choose from the following: analysis, audience, diction, discourse, documentation, drafting, evidence, grammar, organization, outlining, paragraphing, prewriting, punctuation, revision, spelling, structure, style, syntax, thesis, and tone):

White copy: Writing Center   Tutor Name:_____
Yellow copy: Student   (First)   (Last)

Appendix C

Writing Center Survey III (current survey)

___Male ___Female   ___Non-native speaker
___Graduate   ___Undergraduate   ___School

1. Is this your first visit to the Writing Center?   ___yes ___no

2. For what reasons do you use the Writing Center?

3. How confident are you about your academic writing abilities?
    (On a scale of 1 to 5, with 1 = not confident and 5 = very confident)
    ___1 ___2 ___3 ___4 ___5

4. Why did you choose the Writing Center for assistance? Check all that apply.
    ___teacher sent me ___did poorly on my first assignment ___wanted a better grade
    ___wanted to improve my writing___wanted another opinion/someone to look over my
    work ___proofreading/editing ___grammar___English is not my first language ___other

5. What are your primary concerns with your writing?
    ___grammar ___structure/organization ___thesis development ___flow ___support
    ___brainstorming ___outlining ___that it makes sense ___other ___none

6. Were your concerns addressed?
    ___yes ___no If not, why not?

7. Would you prefer a tutor to:
    be in your field of study   ___yes ___no ___no preference
    be your gender   ___yes ___no ___no preference
    be undergrad/grad   ___yes ___no ___no preference
    make corrections   ___yes ___no ___no preference
    actively change paper   ___yes ___no ___no preference
    work collaboratively   ___yes ___no ___no preference
    ask open questions   ___yes ___no ___no preference
    other _____

8. Did your session start on time?   ___yes ___no

9. Did you ask for a specific tutor?   ___yes ___no

10. Did you need more time?   ___yes ___no

11. Were your goals met?   ___yes ___no

12. Was your session a positive experience?   ___yes ___no

13. Would you recommend the Writing Center to your friends?   ___yes ___no

14. If anything, what would you change about your tutoring session or the Writing Center?

Writing Center Survey I

1. What are you here to work on today?
    __research paper__dissertation __essay __resume __personal statement
    __other __group project

2. Please identify your current state in the writing process:
    __brainstorming __outlining __rough draft __ revising __addressing teacher comments

3. Why did you choose the Writing Center for Assistance?
    __teacher sent me __did poorly on my first assignment __wanted a better grade
    __wanted to improve my writing
    __wanted another opinion/someone to look over my work
    __proofreading/editing __grammar __English is not my first language __other

4. When is the assignment due?
    __today __tomorrow __this week __next week __this month __other

5. Is this your first visit to the Writing Center? If not, how often do you come?
    __more than once a week __once a week __once a month __once a semester __other

6. What, in your opinion, is the purpose of the Writing Center?

Writing Center Survey II

1. Was this assignment in your major field of study?   ___yes ___no

2. Did you meet with your professor before coming?   ___yes ___no
    If not, why? __no time __no office hours __too shy__rather get peer input

3. Did you expect your tutor to be: __undergraduate student __graduate student
    __instructor?

4. Did you expect your tutor to:__listen to questions __help you make changes
    __actively change the paper __point out mistakes

5. Would you have preferred a more (circle one) active or passive role of your tutor?

6. Do you view the tutor as a: ___peer ___second opinion ___authority

7. Do you plan on turning in your yellow slip? Why or why not?
   If not, will you inform your teacher?   ___yes ___no

8. Did your session start on time?   ___yes ___no

9. Did you ask for a specific tutor?   ___yes ___no

10. Did you need more time?   ___yes ___no

11. Were your goals met?   ___yes ___no

12. Was your session a positive experience?   ___yes ___no
    Why?

13. Would you recommend the Writing Center to your friends?   ___yes ___no

14. How did you find out about the Writing Center?

Appendix D

Pie Chart of usage by school

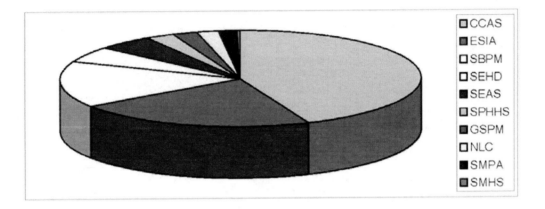

Contributor Bios

Kimberly Town Abels has served as the director of the Writing Center at the University of North Carolina at Chapel Hill for nine years. She first caught wind of the writing center spirit at Ohio State University, where she received her PhD in English in 1994. Her research interests include writing across the curriculum, writing styles, and writing center pedagogy.

Lisa Bell teaches writing, directs the writing center at Utah Valley State College. Although her background is in the broad field of rhetoric and composition, her work focuses on online tutoring, writing center administration, and the rhetorical power of landscape and story within environmental writing. Her recent work includes a chapter in *Surveying the Literary Landscapes of Terry Tempest Williams: New Critical Essays*, serving on the web editing board for the IWCA, and hosting the next Rocky Mountain Peer Tutoring Conference. Lisa received both a BA and MA in English, rhetoric emphasis and ESL minor, from Brigham Young University. Originally from upstate New York, she now feels equally as at home in the brave deserts of Utah where she lives with her husband Jason.

David Bringhurst received his BA in history and his MA in English from Wright State University. A former writing center tutor, he spent ten years as a technical writer, web coordinator, and marketing communications manager. He also taught composition for several years as an adjunct instructor. He has since returned to his alma mater to become the assistant director of the writing center. He intends to stay there until they force him out or until the Oakland Raiders call to ask him to quarterback their team to the Super Bowl, whichever comes first.

Peter Carino is professor of English and former director of the writing center at Indiana State University, where he teaches technical writing and American literature. He has published several articles on writing centers in *The Writing Center Journal* and various anthologies. He is also the author of two textbooks, editor of two collections of essays on baseball literature, and a two-time winner of the NWCA Scholarship Award for best article.

Tracy Hamler Carrick completed her graduate work at Syracuse University in the Composition and Cultural Rhetoric and Women's Studies programs. She has taught writing and worked in writing centers in both academia and the community since 1993. She is now an assistant professor of English, director of the Farnham Writers' Center, and co-coordinator of writing across the curriculum at Colby College. She coedited, with Rebecca Moore Howard, *Authorship in Composition Studies* (Wadsworth, in press) and coauthored "Ruptura: Acknowledging the Lost Subjects of the Service Learning Story" (*Language and Learning Across the Disciplines*, 1999). She is currently at work on a book that explores the relationships between popular literacy education and social change movements.

Pamela B. Childers holds the Caldwell Chair of Composition at the McCallie School in Chattanooga, Tennessee, where she directs the writing center and writing across the curriculum programs and team teaches *Oceans*, an interdisciplinary senior science seminar. She also teaches a graduate course in the Teaching of Writing for Lesley University. Former president of IWCA (1990–91), treasurer of the Assembly on Computers in English (1986–present), visiting professor at Utah State University (1997), and recipient of two NEH grants (1996, 2002), Pam has created both public and independent secondary school writing centers. Recipient of the 2003 IWCA Muriel Harris Outstanding Service Award, she has written *ARTiculating: Teaching Writing in a Visual World* (with Hobson and Mullin), *Programs and Practices: Writing Across the Secondary School Curriculum* (with Gere and Young), and *The High School Writing Center: Establishing and Maintaining One*, as well as over fifty essays, chapters, and articles in professional publications on writing and faculty development. She also writes the "CAC/WAC in Secondary Schools" column for *Across the Disciplines* (formerly *academic.writing* at http:// wac.colostate.edu). Pam has given workshops and presentations at NCTE, MLA, CCCC, IFTE, IWCA, NAIS, and WAC conferences and conventions for more than twenty years.

Ben Click is an associate professor of English at St. Mary's College of Maryland, and director of the college writing center. He began teaching (and learning from) students in 1981. Since that time he has taught a variety courses in writing, rhetoric, literature, and humor. He has published articles on collaborative learning and writing assessment, and book chapters on electronic portfolios and the teaching of writing.

Albert DeCiccio is in his fifth year at Rivier College, currently in the position as academic dean of the college. Before he began his tenure at Rivier, he worked for twenty years at Merrimack College, as a professor of English, teaching courses in the English Department's Rhetoric and Composition program; serving as a director of Merrimack's writing center; and as dean of the faculty of Liberal Arts. In 1998, he was asked to accept a position as dean of the Graduate School at Wheelock College in Boston. While at Wheelock, he worked to ensure distinguished and effective professional programs in education, social work, child life, and early intervention. In academic year 1997–98, DeCiccio completed a term as president of the IWCA; in academic year 2002–03, DeCiccio ended a five-year term as coeditor of *The Writing Center Journal*. He still regularly contributes articles and presentations about collaborative learning, writing, and writing center theory and practice. He has twice presented for the International Conference on the First-Year Experience: in York, England, and in St. Andrews, Scotland.

Bonnie Devet is a professor of English at the College of Charleston (South Carolina), where she has directed the writing lab since 1989; she also teaches graduate and undergraduate courses in grammar, technical writing, and freshman composition, the theory and practice of writing labs, and the teaching of composition. She has delivered numerous conference presentations and published widely on the training of writing lab consultants as well as on teaching grammar, business communication, and freshman composition.

Kevin Dvorak is a PhD candidate in composition and TESOL at Indiana University of Pennsylvania where he was a graduate assistant director of the writing center. He also served as graduate assistant director at Sonoma State University where he completed his MA.

Kathy Evertz directs The Write Place and the Academic Support Center at Carleton College in Northfield, Minnesota. She worked in the University of Wyoming Writing Center for sixteen years. At Wyoming, she taught in the English department and later directed the University Studies First-Year Program. She directed the Wyoming Conference on English from 1993–97. With Jane Nelson, she coedited *The Politics of Writing Centers* (Heinemann-Boynton/Cook, 2001).

Steve Ferruci is an assistant professor of English at Eastern Connecticut State University where he teaches courses in composition, rhetorical theory, writing tutor training, and Holocaust literature. **Susan DeRosa** is an assistant professor of English at Eastern Connecticut State University where she teaches courses in composition, composition and rhetorical theories, writing tutor training, and creative nonfiction. Steve and Susan have been collaborating on writing center research and scholarship for the past two years, which they anticipate will culminate in the development of a writing center at ECSU.

Lauren Fitzgerald and **Denise Stephenson** like to take turns listing their names first: see entry under Stephenson.

Traci Freeman recently received her PhD in English from the University of Texas at Austin, where she served as an assistant director in the undergraduate writing center and led an initiative to extend writing center services to graduate students. Traci taught College Writing at the University of California, Berkeley for two years, before joining the faculty of the University of Colorado at Colorado Springs in 2004 as a writing program assistant and instructor in the Department of English.

Clint Gardner is director of the Salt Lake Community College Student Writing Center. He received a MA in English from the College of William and Mary in Virginia.

Anne Ellen Geller has been director of the writing center and writing program at Clark University in Worcester, Massachusetts since 1999, where she also teaches writing classes, including a literacy class that incorporates community engagement. As part of a Carnegie Corporation funded initiative, she has, for the past two years, worked with high school literacy coaches in the Worcester Public Schools. Anne has been the chair of the Northeast Writing Centers Association, and she hosted the 2001 NEWCA Conference and the 2004 IWCA Summer Institute at Clark University. She received an IWCA Dissertation Research Grant in 1999, and she is currently writing about how we experience time in the writing center.

Paula Gillespie directs the Ott Memorial Writing Center and teaches in the English department at Marquette University in Milwaukee, Wisconsin. She is the immediate past president of IWCA, the coauthor with Neal Lerner of *The Allyn and Bacon Guide to Peer Tutoring* (2nd ed.) and coeditor with Alice Gillam, Byron Stay, and Lady Falls Brown of *Writing Center Research: Extending the Conversation.* She has co-chaired the first two annual Writing Center Summer Institutes for writing center directors and professionals. She has been involved in training peer tutors since 1991 and is engaged in a project with Harvey Kail and Brad Hughes to research the short- and long-term effects of tutoring on peer-tutors.

Carl Glover makes ends meet by teaching in the rhetoric and communications department and directing the writing center at Mount Saint Mary's University in Emmitsburg, Maryland. His real job is singing lead for the Fire City Jazz Band.

Muriel Harris has recently retired as writing lab director and professor of English at Purdue University but continues to edit *The Writing Lab Newsletter.* She plans to keep active in the world of writing centers, which is too much fun to ever completely retire from. She currently completed revisions for the 6th edition of the *Prentice-Hall Reference Guide to Grammar and Usage* (which may appear with a slightly revised title) and continues to research the complex question of how and where writing center pedagogy fits into—and is an integral part of—composition theory and pedagogy.

Carol Peterson Haviland is professor of English, writing center director, and WAC/upper-division writing coordinator at California State University, San Bernardino. She teaches undergraduate and graduate composition courses and is particularly interested in feminist theories, intellectual property, feminist theories, collaboration, writing centers, WAC, and writing program administration. She is coeditor of *Teaching/Writing in the Late Age of Print* and *Weaving Knowledge Together: Writing Centers and Collaboration*, as well as articles in writing center and composition journals and is the Pacific Coast IWCA representative. Her current research is in two areas: concepts of intellectual property and ownership across disciplines and the shared spaces that writing centers, writing programs, and WAC are shaping.

Lory Hawkes received her PhD from Texas Christian University. As a senior professor at DeVry University in Dallas, Texas, she teaches in the General Education and in the Computer Information Systems curricula. She has authored two books on the Internet: *Hyperspatial Travel into the Internet: A Guidebook* (Prentice Hall, 1996) and *The Guide to the World Web* (Prentice Hall, 1998). With coauthors Christina Murphy and Joe Law, she has published a Greenwood bibliography on virtual texts, several essays, and frequently presents at CCCC conferences. She holds the rank of Fellow in the Society of Technical Communication.

Joan Hawthorne currently serves as coordinator for the writing center and writing across the curriculum (WAC) at the University of North Dakota, a position she has held since 1997. Prior to that, she taught writing and began the WAC program at UND, using grant funding from the Bush Foundation. She teaches courses in education (Assessment in Higher Education, Foundations of Education) and English. Her PhD in Teaching and Learning is from the University of North Dakota, her MA is from the University of Colorado, and her BS is from South Dakota State University.

Rebecca Moore Howard earned her PhD in English at West Virginia University. She is now associate professor of writing and rhetoric at Syracuse University and the former writing program administrator at Syracuse, Texas Christian, and Colgate Universities. She is coauthor of the 1995 *Bedford Guide to Teaching Writing in the Disciplines*; author of *Standing in the Shadow of Giants* (1999), a book about the cultural work of plagiarism; coeditor of *Coming of Age: The Advanced Writing Curriculum*, which won the 2000–01 WPA Book Award; coeditor of *Authorship in Composition Studies*, forthcoming from Wadsworth; and author of a writers' handbook in progress for McGraw-Hill.

Brad Hughes is director of the writing center and director of writing across the curriculum at the University of Wisconsin-Madison, where he has taught for the past twenty-one years. Brad was a cofounder of the National College Learning Center Association and former chair of the Midwest Writing Centers Association. He is the author of articles about writing centers and WAC, he is a member of the editorial board of the *Writing Center Journal*, and he has led WAC workshops and been a consultant for colleges and universities around the country. In 2003, Brad cochaired, with Paula Gillespie, the inaugural IWCA summer institute, which was held at the University of Wisconsin. His current research projects focus on cross-disciplinary tutoring and on peer-tutor alumni.

Harvey Kail is associate professor of English and director of the writing center at the University of Maine. He has also directed UM's writing across the curriculum program and served as chair of its English department. He was introduced to peer tutoring and collaborative learning in the early 1980s as a Fellow of the Brooklyn College Summer Institute on Training Peer Writing Tutors directed by Kenneth A. Bruffee. He has been training peer-tutors regularly ever since and writing on collaborative learning in the *Writing Lab Newsletter* and *The Writing Center Journal*, as well as in *College English*, CCC, WPA, *Rhetoric Review*, and in various collections of essays on writing centers. His current research involves assessing the value of peer tutoring on the tutors themselves years after their work in the writing center has passed.

Neal Lerner is lecturer in writing across the curriculum at the Massachusetts Institute of Technology. He is coeditor (with Beth Boquet) of *The Writing Center Journal* and coauthor (with Paula Gillespie) of *The Allyn & Bacon Guide to Peer Tutoring* (2nd ed.). His recent publications have appeared in *The Writing Center Journal*, *The Writing Lab Newsletter*, *Composition Studies*, and several edited collections of writing center scholarship. He has twice won the IWCA Outstanding Scholarship award, and his current research focuses on the history of teaching both writing and science via "laboratory methods."

Kelly Lowe is an associate professor of English and director of writing programs at Mount Union College in Alliance, OH. Kelly was director of the college's writing center from 1995–2001 and was the founding editor of the *National Writing Centers Association Newsletter* (now *IWCA Update*). Kelly has published in the areas of program administration, institutional history, and composition theory. He is also the official archivist and historian of the Alliance (Ohio) Community Hospital.

Sarah Magruder is the assistant director of/assistant instructional technologist to the writing center at St. Mary's College of Maryland. She has recently coauthored articles in *Assessment Update* and in *Academic Exchange Quarterly*.

Amy Ward Martin is the director of the writing centers on Pace University's New York City and Pleasantville, New York campuses. In addition to her writing center-related research, her research interests include plagiarism and intellectual property, assessment, and collaborative writing.

Michael Mattison was drafted last year by Boise State University, where he is currently assistant professor of English as well as director of the writing center. He bats, throws, and writes right-handed, and has a fairly decent jump shot, especially when no one is guarding him.

Joan Mullin, professor in the Division of Rhetoric and Composition at the University of Texas, Austin, started and served as director of the WAC program and writing center at the University of Toledo for seventeen years. Over the last ten years, grants totally nearly one million dollars have supported her in-services, Summer Institutes for teachers, and the establishment of writing centers and WAC programs, contributing to the curriculum of over twenty-six high schools in the Toledo area or to faculty development in colleges and universities. Mullin publishes in writing center, WAC, and disciplinary journals across the curriculum here and abroad. Her coauthored book, *ARTiculating: Teaching Writing in a Visual Culture* (Boynton/Cook Heinemann, 1998), launched her current research interest in visual literacy across international curriculums. Past president of the National Writing Centers Association, and former coeditor of *The Writing Center Journal*, she serves on editorial boards and committees nationally and internationally, and as a consultant evaluator for the WPA.

Christina Murphy is the dean of the College of Liberal Arts and professor of English at Marshall University in Huntington, West Virginia. She has published extensively on writing centers and has authored or coauthored eight books, including *The St. Martin's Sourcebook for Writing Tutors*, *Writing Centers: An Annotated Bibliography*, *Landmark Essays on Writing Centers*, and *Writing Center Perspectives*. She has served as the president of the National Writing Centers Association (NWCA), the South Central Writing Centers Association (SCWCA), and the Texas Writing Centers Association (TWCA). She has twice received the "Outstanding Scholarship Award" from the National Writing Centers Association, and she received the "Distinguished Leadership Award" from the Texas Writing Centers Association.

Jane Nelson directed the writing center at the University of Wyoming for nearly fifteen years, where she has also taught writing, literature, and literacy courses. She is currently a project director in the Ellbogen Center for Teaching and Learning at UW. She has published numerous articles on writing and writing across the curriculum with a variety of collaborators. She and Kathy Evertz coedited *The Politics of Writing Centers* (Boynton/Cook Publishers, 2001).

Dennis Paoli is the coordinator of the reading/writing center (since 1987) and of the writing across the curriculum program (since 1999) at Hunter College. He consults with students, faculty, and administrators on the role of writing in all of Hunter's programs and professional schools, at every level, and with the City University of New York and several national testing services on writing assessment. He has served on the board of IWCA (then NWCA, 1996–2001). He also teaches academic and creative writing, literature, and humanities courses at Hunter.

Michael A. Pemberton is currently director of the university writing center and associate professor of writing and linguistics at Georgia Southern University. He has published widely on issues in writing center theory and practice, writing across the curriculum, and computers and composition. His coedited book (with Joyce Kinkead), *The Center Will Hold: Critical Perspectives on Writing Center Scholarship* recently won the 2004 Best Book Award from the Council of Writing Program Administrators. Kids, cats, cooking, and collectible comic books seem to consume most of his remaining time.

Brad Peters is associate professor at Northern Illinois University, where he coordinates writing across the curriculum and directs the university writing center. He teaches graduate courses in cultural rhetorics, theory, and pedagogy, and undergraduate courses in writing. Recent publications have appeared in Nagelhout's and Rutz's *Classroom Spaces and Writing Instruction* and Gray-Rosendale's and Harootunian's *Fractured Feminisms: Rhetoric, Context, and Contestation.*

Cheryl Prentice developed and directs the writing center at Saint Mary's University of Minnesota, School of Graduate and Special Programs. She has sixteen years of experience supervising writing centers.

Ben Rafoth directs the writing center and teaches at Indiana University of Pennsylvania. He coedited *ESL Writers: A Guide for Writing Center Tutors* (Heinemann Boynton/Cook, 2004) and edited *A Tutor's Guide* (Boynton/Cook, 2000); he is also a recipient of the Ron Maxwell Award from the National Conference on Peer Tutoring in Writing and is an executive board member of the International Writing Centers Association.

Tiffany Rousculp received her master's degree in rhetoric, linguistics and literature from the University of Southern California in 1993. She was hired by the Salt Lake Community College English department that year and is now tenured. Over the course of four years, she developed—along with Stephen Ruffus—the SLCC Community Writing Center and has directed it since its opening in October 2001.

Evelyn Jaffe Schreiber, PhD is an associate professor of English and director of the writing center at George Washington University in Washington, DC. Her scholarship includes articles on writing centers/programs, business communications, literature, collaborative writing, multicultural issues, Faulkner, Morrison, Pinter, stream-of-consciousness, psychoanalytic theory, and cultural studies. She has given presentations on writing center theory and pedagogy, as well as composition issues at CCCC, NWCA, IWCA, NPTWC, and ABC. Her publications appear in *Issues in Writing, the Journal of Business Communication, Mississippi Quarterly, The Faulkner Journal, Literature and Psychology, The Journal of the Fantastic in the Arts, Style, IEEE Transactions on Professional Communication*, and *Computers and the Humanities*. Her research applies Lacanian principles of identity/subjectivity/agency and cultural studies to literary texts and composition studies. Her book, *Subversive Voices: Eroticizing the Other in William Faulkner and Toni Morrison*, examines identity and race via the theory of Jacques Lacan and cultural studies and was awarded the Toni Morrison Society book prize for work on Morrison. She has taught at GWU since 1989. In addition, she has assisted several companies in the Washington area as a writing consultant.

David M. Sheridan is the associate director of the Michigan State University Writing Center. His interests include visual rhetoric and new media especially as these things intersect with writing and writing centers. His articles have appeared in the *Journal of Literacy and Technology* and *Michigan Quarterly Review*.

Jeanne Simpson received her BA from Texas Tech and her MA from the University of Texas at Austin before earning her doctorate from Illinois State University in 1982. From 1975 to 1990, she taught writing at Eastern Illinois University, as well as establishing and directing the writing center at Eastern for nine years. During that time, she served as a founding member of the National Writing Centers Association and was its third president. Her publications include *The Elements of Invention* and, with Ray Wallace, *New Directions for Writing Centers*, as well as articles in *Journal of Teaching Writing, Writing Lab Newsletter, and Writing Center Journal*. In 1990, she was appointed assistant vice president for Academic Affairs and director of the Summer School at Eastern. She retired in 2000 but has remained active in the writing center community. In 2001, she received the Muriel Harris award for outstanding service from the International Writing Centers Association.

Helen Snively holds an EdD from the Harvard Graduate School of Education, where she initiated, and for nearly ten years administered, the writing, research, and teaching center, possibly the nation's first graduate writing center. Her professional interests include cultural differences that affect international graduate students, the overall process of writing the dissertation, and coaching and motivational techniques that support students through that process.

Bruce W. Speck is professor of English and vice president for Academic Affairs at Austin Peay State University in Clarksville, Tennessee. He has also served as the coordinator of a WAC program, dean of a College of Arts and Sciences, and associate vice chancellor for Academic Affairs. His academic specialty is writing, and he has taught various writing classes at both the undergraduate and graduate levels. He has authored or coauthored six book-length bibliographies on various aspects of writing and publishing; authored two monographs on writing, *Grading Students' Classroom Writing* and *Facilitating Students' Collaborative Writing*; coedited eight volumes on topics such as service learning, assessment strategies for online courses, grading students' classroom performance, internationalizing higher education, and teaching nonnative English speakers; authored or coauthored articles in *English Journal, Technical Communication, Issues in Writing, Technical Communication Quarterly,* and *Journal of Business and Technical Communication*; and authored or coauthored nineteen book chapters.

Denise Stephenson and **L**auren Fitzgerald have over twenty-five years of writing center experience between them. Denise considers herself a writer of alternative discourse and enjoys writing monologs for the stage. She currently finds herself watching surfers, designing a new writing center at MiraCosta College, and generally enjoying sunny southern California. Lauren lives and works in New York City, where she directs the Yeshiva College Writing Center at Yeshiva University and likes meeting up with her NYC metro-area writing center colleagues. Both have published on writing center issues in the *Writing Lab Newsletter* and in edited collections. This is their first collaboration, but probably not their last.

Steven Strang teaches rhetoric at the Massachusetts Institute of Technology and directs its writing and communication center, which he founded in 1982. He is the author of *Writing Exploratory Essays* (Mayfield, 1995). He has published articles on Iris Murdoch and on pedagogy, as well as numerous short stories and poems. His research interests are personal essays, rhetoric, and twentieth-century British fiction. He received his PhD from Brown University and his BA from the University of Maine.

Byron L. Stay is professor of Rhetoric and Communications at Mount St. Mary's University in Emmitsburg, MD. He has edited or coedited five books, including *Writing Center Perspectives* (with Christina Murphy and Eric Hobson) and *Writing Center Research: Extending the Conversation* (with Paula Gillespie, Alice Gillam, and Lady Falls Brown). His is also the author of *A Guide to Argumentative Writing*. He is a past president of IWCA, co-chair of the first IWCA Conference, and in 1997 received the Muriel Harris award for outstanding service from IWCA. When he's not teaching, he plays trumpet with Carl Glover in the Fire City Jazz Band.

Marcy Trianosky is director of the writing center and is a member of the English faculty at Hollins University, a liberal arts institution for women. She is currently serving her second term as president of the Southeastern Writing Center Association and is also a member of the executive board of IWCA. Marcy has given conference presentations at CCCC, WPA, and regional and national writing center association meetings. Her research interests focus on tutorial discourse, collaborative writing center administration, basic writing, and writing across the curriculum.

Ray Wallace is dean of the School of Arts and Sciences at Clayton College and State University, near Atlanta. He is a past president of the IWCA, and has authored several articles and books on writing centers, composition, and English departments. He organized the first national writing centers conference in New Orleans and has served as a keynote speaker at regional, national, and international conferences. He holds the Doctor of Arts degree in composition from Illinois State University.

Susan Lewis Wallace is an instructor of English at Georgia Perimeter College in Atlanta. She has worked in writing centers for over a decade, both as a tutor and a tutor-trainer. She is the coeditor of *Reforming College Composition: Writing the Wrongs* (Garland, 2000), and writes on various composition areas. She teaches developmental English, composition, and literature. She has taught and tutored in Arkansas, Louisiana, Alabama, and Georgia, and has presented at writing center conferences for many years, including helping to organize the first national writing center conference in New Orleans.

Margaret Weaver is an associate professor of English at Southwest Missouri State University and has served as the writing center director for the past ten years. She has served on both the International Writing Centers Association board and the Midwest Writing Centers Association board. Her articles have appeared in such journals as *Journal of Advanced Composition*, *The Writing Center Journal*, *Journal of General Education*, and *Writing Lab Newsletter*.

Author Index

Subject Index